FAR EASTERN AND RUSSIAN INSTITUTE
PUBLICATIONS ON RUSSIA AND
EASTERN EUROPE

Number 2

Agrarian Policies and Problems in Communist and Non-Communist Countries

Edited by W. A. Douglas Jackson

UNIVERSITY OF WASHINGTON PRESS

Seattle and London

To the memory of
Jerzy F. Karcz

LIBRARY OF CONGRESS CATALOG CARD NUMBER 75-103292

FIRST PRINTING 1971

ALL RIGHTS RESERVED

PRINTED IN JAPAN

Preface

The present volume represents the contributions of a group of specialists who met on the campus of the University of Washington at Seattle in late August, 1967, to discuss and exchange ideas concerning agricultural development—and agrarian problems generally—in the light of Communist and non-Communist experience.

The Seattle conference was the third in a series of conferences in the United States arranged by the executive committee of a loose interdisciplinary organization named the Conference on Soviet Agricultural and Peasant Affairs. The organization was formed in September, 1962, at the University of Kansas at Lawrence, following a conference whose theme was Soviet agriculture. Subsequently, the American Association for the Advancement of Slavic Studies gave permission for the organization to be associated with it.

In August, 1965, a second conference was convened at the University of California at Santa Barbara. There the scope of the discussion was enlarged to include some aspects of agricultural development in Eastern Europe. With the successful conclusion of the Santa Barbara sessions, the Conference organization agreed that periodic meetings provided a convenient vehicle for the exchange of views on problems of agriculture within the Soviet bloc; their value had been demonstrated and they should, if possible, continue. It was decided, therefore, that there should follow within two years a third conference, the scope of which might be expanded further to encompass some of the Asian Communist countries. The opinion was expressed, too, that by comparing the agrarian experiences of the states within the bloc with selected non-Communist countries—selected primarily, though not entirely, on the basis of general physical and cultural environmental similarities (it was not the intention to seek analogues)—additional insights might be gained.

It was logical that the University of Washington should serve as host to such a conference. The Far Eastern and Russian Institute had, since the mid-forties, focused principally on that part of Eurasia which was since to fall to communism. In addition, a number of scholars and research workers at the institute had for many years been concerned with agrarian problems in China, Russia, as well as in Japan.

The broadening of the scope of the discussion led, therefore, to a more ambitious conference than that undertaken either at Lawrence or Santa Barbara. It brought together a wide array of specialists representing not only North American scholarship but also that of West Germany, the United Kingdom, France, Republic of China, Japan, and South Korea. The essays and commentaries in this volume reflect the conference's international composition.

Such a conference could not have taken place but for the cooperation and aid afforded by many people and organizations, both on campus and off. Speaking on behalf of the Conference and the participants, I should like to express my appreciation to the University's Far Eastern and Russian Institute and to the Graduate School for their generous financial support. Acknowledgement is equally due to the National Science Foundation which, together with the Graduate School, also made possible the editing and publishing of these papers.

In the months preceding the conference, as well as during the conference period, August 23–26, 1967, the Office of Short Courses and Conferences (and especially through the services of Mrs. Nadine Court, conference coordinator), was most helpful in the making of arrangements for maintaining the participants and other guests. To Mrs. Louise Martin, my secretary, I am deeply indebted. Without her efficient assistance and sustained loyalty the conference would not have functioned as smoothly as it did. Finally, I should like to thank Mrs. Margery Lang for her intelligent editorial assistance and for her courage in tackling what seemed initially a monumental task.

W. A. DOUGLAS JACKSON

Seattle
April, 1969

Contents

W. A. DOUGLAS JACKSON
Preface v

KARL AUGUST WITTFOGEL
Communist and Non-Communist Agrarian Systems, with
Special Reference to the U.S.S.R. and Communist China:
A Comparative Approach 3
    R. P. ROCHLIN, *Comment* 61
    WERNER KLATT, *Comment* 65

ALEC NOVE
The Decision to Collectivize 69
    THOMAS P. BERNSTEIN, *Comment* 98
    GEORGE L. YANEY, *Comment* 102

KARL-EUGEN WÄDEKIN
Kolkhoz, Sovkhoz, and Private Production in Soviet
Agriculture 106
    ROBERT C. STUART, *Comment* 138

EBERHARD SCHINKE
Some Peculiarities of the Employment of Factors
in Soviet Agriculture 142
    ELIZABETH CLAYTON, *Comment* 156

HENRI WRONSKI
Consumer Cooperatives in Rural Areas in the U.S.S.R. 159
    NANCY NIMITZ, *Comment* 174

JERZY F. KARCZ
Certain Aspects of New Economic Systems
in Bulgaria and Czechoslovakia 178
    CARL ZOERB, *Comment* 205

KONRAD MERKEL
The Agrarian Problem in Divided Germany 210
    EBERHARD SCHINKE, *Comment* 227

OTTO SCHILLER

The Agrarian Question: Communist Experience and Its
Implication for Developing Countries 231
    HARRY E. WALTERS, *Comment* 245

LESLIE T. C. KUO

Technical Transformation of Agriculture in
Communist China 250
    J. LOSSING BUCK, *Comment* 275
    WERNER KLATT, *Comment* 278

ANTHONY TANG

Input-Output Relations in the Agriculture of
Communist China, 1952–1965 280
    WERNER KLATT, *Comment* 302

LAWRENCE J. LAU

Peasant Consumption, Saving, and Investment in
Mainland China 305
    JERZY F. KARCZ, *Comment* 338

SHIGERU ISHIKAWA

Changes in the Structure of Agricultural Production
in Mainland China 346
    ERNST HAGEMANN, *Comment* 378

S. C. HSIEH

Taiwan's Model of Agricultural Progress: Potentials
of Small Family Farms and Their Implications for Other
Developing Asian Countries 381
    GEORGE E. TAYLOR, *Comment* 396

FUKUO UENO

Areal Specialization in Japanese Peasant Farming and
Agricultural Settlement 399
    GEORGE H. KAKIUCHI, *Comment* 432

KI HYUK PAK

A Comparative Study of the Agrarian Systems of
South and North Korea 436
    YOUNG C. ZEON, *Comment* 459

WERNER KLATT

Successes and Failures of Communist Farming: Causes
and Consequences 462

Index 479

Contributors 487

AGRARIAN POLICIES AND PROBLEMS
IN COMMUNIST AND
NON-COMMUNIST COUNTRIES

KARL A. WITTFOGEL

Communist and Non-Communist Agrarian Systems, with Special Reference to the U.S.S.R. and Communist China: A Comparative Approach

A FEW STATEMENTS CONCERNING CONCEPTS AND METHODS

The resolve to study agrarian systems and to study them comparatively is not new. But the emergence of new institutional orders has created new issues whose understanding demands new methods of investigation.

To be sure, the new always has important elements of the old. This will become evident when we contemplate three key terms used in this inquiry: *agrarian, system,* and *comparative approach.*

The "Agrarian" Context of Agriculture

The "agrarian" condition is, of course, rooted in agriculture: man's treatment of suitable plants and animals for the production of food and certain organic raw materials. Hence the study of the agrarian world presupposes familiarity with agriculture, including agronomy. But it goes further. Terminological compounds containing the word "agrarian" suggest that an agricultural core may have a complex ecological and institutional setting. We are thinking of this ecological and institutional setting when we speak of the "agrarian" context of a given agricultural situation.

Agrarian "Systems"

Like other forms of human behavior, man's agrarian activities have recognizable patterns. They contain elements that occur regularly together and that obviously are essential to the persistence of these patterns.[1] They constitute vital components of a system. Other elements do not have an equally recognizable function; or they may be clearly nonessential (their absence does not prevent the system from being a going concern).

Microanalytic[2] studies often deal with seemingly significant details without considering their place in the larger context. Macroanalytic studies, which stress this context, help us to separate essential from nonessential details. National or religious traditions may considerably color a given agrarian system without being necessary for its persistence.

For the investigation of certain ecological, agronomic, and agroeconomic details, clarity concerning the agrarian system in which they occur is irrelevant. For the investigation of others it is useful. For still others, it is vital.

The Comparative Approach

Phenomena such as agricultural intensity, water deficiency, and irrigation farming have a different significance under different agrarian systems. For this reason we must examine the various agrarian systems by means of the comparative approach.

Such an approach may enable us to distinguish analytically what otherwise would remain hazy. It may enable us to identify the peculiarities of the major types of agrarian societies that existed in preindustrial times. And it may enable us to identify the differences between the agrarian systems of modern Communist societies and modern (and older) non-Communist societies.

Agriculture has been called the Achilles' heel of Communist economy in general; and recently increasing attention has been paid to the extraordinary productivity of agricultural labor in virtually all non-Communist countries of the West (especially the United States and Canada, but also England, West Germany, and so on) and of the East (especially Japan and Taiwan).

In our endeavor to clarify these issues, we find earlier arguments worth noting. Adam Smith devoted a considerable part of his *Wealth of Nations* to the discussions of what he called "systems of political economy." Among them he distinguished, in addition to more primitive orders, two major systems: the "commercial" (including the manufac-

---

[1] See Karl A. Wittfogel, *Oriental Despotism* (New Haven: Yale University Press, 1957), p. 414 (hereafter cited as *OD*).

[2] See *OD*, paperback edition, 1963, preface, pp. 111–12.

turing industry) and the "agricultural." The agricultural systems of political economy, as he saw them, comprised (1) the systems of modern Europe, (2) those of China, ancient Egypt, and India (whose policies regarding waterworks he stressed), and (3) those of ancient Greece and Rome.[3]

There is no need to occupy ourselves here with Smith's definition of systems of political economy (he called them "a branch of the science of the statesman or legislator").[4] For our purposes it suffices to say that he undertook his very consequential comparative study of "agricultural systems" at a great historical turning point—the eve of the industrial revolution. Encouraged by his endeavors, we shall, at another great historical turning point, resort again to the comparative approach to gain new insights into some of the major agrarian systems, old and new.

Geoinstitutional Diversities

Adam Smith singled out division of labor as the crucial peculiarity of the (capitalist) industrial world that he was comparing with other economic orders. I find decisive peculiarities of the Communist agrarian system in the dimension of farming and the condition of labor. These two factors have also played a formative role in earlier agrarian orders, which are connected with recognizable ecological peculiarities. Such peculiarities appear again in the agrarian conditions of Communist China (as distinguished from those of the U.S.S.R.). What are these ecological peculiarities like, and what do they signify?

Problems of Geoinstitutional Causality

Among the modes of agriculture we can discern two major types— one oriented toward labor-intensive farming, the other toward labor-extensive farming. Globally speaking, the first type developed primarily —although not exclusively—in arid and semiarid areas or in humid areas with cultivable aquatic plants, especially rice. In these several areas, irrigation farming originated, not necessarily as the only agronomical system, but often as the dominant system—the one that separated the world of irrigation farming from that of rainfall farming.

This dichotomy has been of primary importance in the history of higher preindustrial societies. And the agricultural conditions of Communist China (as juxtaposed with those in the U.S.S.R. and Eastern

---

[3] Adam Smith, *An Inquiry into the Nature and Causes of the Wealth of Nations* (New York: Modern Library, 1937), pp. 397 ff., 627 ff.

[4] *Ibid.*, p. 397.

Europe) and of Japan (as juxtaposed with those in North America and Western Europe) show that in a few forms this dichotomy still persists.

My attempt to identify diversities in hydrological conditions as a means of distinguishing patterns of farming suggests that the ecological factor is significant. But a differentiating analysis of its effects warns us against confusing causal and deterministic relations. Causal relations between natural conditions and human responses are general; deterministic relations are not. Contrary to the claims of the geographical determinists,[5] a given natural foundation does not necessarily lead to a single type of human action.

Of course, a negative causal relation has a deterministic quality. A small wooden base cannot support a skyscraper; agriculture cannot emerge endogenously in areas lacking cultivable plants (as in aboriginal Australia); animal husbandry cannot emerge endogenously in areas lacking suitable animals (as in pre-Spanish America).[6] On the other hand, a given ecological condition is not necessarily compelling; it does not necessarily have only one institutional correlation. In most cases, the natural foundation is either permissive (offering the possibility of several types of human action) or suggestive (favoring one type of human action more than others, but without precluding them). Rarely is it compatible with only one type of human action.

Thus the deterministic variant of ecological causality is more the exception than the rule. The foundation-superstructure relation illustrates this point, and not the deterministic thesis with which it is erroneously associated. A particular architectonic foundation may be suitable for only a single type of building, but more often it will be suitable for

[5] Static concepts of environmentalism have prevailed among leading macro-analysts of society and history from the classical Greeks to Montesquieu. During the last century they have been increasingly countered with rejections that, for the most part, are equally static. Since the late twenties I have endeavored to refine the ecological thesis by stressing the "transforming" and "actualizing" impact of man's action on his environment (see Karl A. Wittfogel, "Die natürlichen Ursachen der Wirtschaftsgeschichte," *Archiv ür Sozialwissenschaft und Sozialpolitik*, LXVII, 1932, 473–84). During the last decades the geohistorical concept in its original form has found few serious defenders; but it has been implicitly accepted by a growing number of scholars who have recognized the formative role of the "hydraulic" factor in the institutional history of the "Orient." Since 1962, this trend has also gained in strength in many Communist countries and among intellectuals of non-Communist countries with Marxist-Communist leanings, such as France, Italy, Mexico, and Japan, in the form of a "great debate" on Marx' concept of the Asiatic mode of production. Having since the forties been concerned with re-evaluating the underlying ecological thesis, I consider it important to restate my new insights and conclusions in the present exposition to which the hydraulic concept is so relevant.

[6] Wittfogel, "Die natürlichen Ursachen," pp. 480–92.

more than one. And while it may be best fitted for a certain purpose, it may also be compatible with others, the final decision resulting from various considerations, among which the technical and economic may not be overriding.

The social scientist who oversimplifies the ecological foundations of labor-intensive agriculture will be unable to recognize some of the crucial complexities of the "Oriental" and non-"Oriental" agrarian systems. The social scientist who disregards them will not even reach the point at which the geoinstitutional correlations can be seriously considered.

Diversities in Irrigation - Oriented Agriculture

Systems of irrigation farming have existed for thousands of years in many parts of the world. Their natural foundation included peculiarities of climate, soil, lay of the land, available water supply, and suitable plants.

Diversities in the amount of rainfall create different degrees of need for irrigation farming. Diversities in the lay of the land explain why, in certain areas, man's handling of the available water resources necessitated special organizational arrangements: the coordination of the available (and strategically located) manpower and the emergence of a directing managerial authority. Under such conditions, an undisturbed (endogenous) development will lead to a system of "hydraulic" agriculture and society, the dominant authority being an agromanagerial and agrodespotic bureaucracy, usually headed by a supreme autocratic ruler. (European scholars, who were strongly aware that such a configuration prevailed in the Orient—but much less aware that it also existed in pre-Spanish America and on other continents—referred to it as "Asiatic" or "Oriental" despotism.)[7] In areas where irrigation farming does not involve large-scale operations, we may speak of a system of "hydroagriculture,"[8] a system compatible with various types of state and society.

Under both these systems the intensive methods employed in cultivating irrigated crops are generally also employed in cultivating nonirrigated crops, if there are any.[9] The significance of this fact for the

[7] The term "Oriental despotism," which attained wide currency in the eighteenth century, conceptualized an idea that was much older. It was used by Marx and Engels when they discussed the peculiarities of the water-control state; and it underlies Max Weber's concept of a hydraulic bureaucracy that, to him, existed mainly in the Near East, China, and India.

[8] *OD*, pp. 17–18.

[9] Karl A. Wittfogel, *Wirtschaft und Gesellschaft Chinas, Erster Teil, Produktivkräfte,*

traditional agriculture of semiarid China is obvious; its significance for the peculiar agricultural crisis in Communist China will be discussed later.

Some Agrarian Systems Geohistorically Considered

The developments outlined above occurred when a farming population endogenously "actualized"[10] the hydroagricultural or hydraulic potential of its area, or when hydroagricultural or hydraulic practices were introduced from outside, the former in a variety of ways, the latter often, but not always, through conquest.

Japan's natural conditions encouraged irrigation farming, which in all likelihood was stimulated by precedents on the Asian mainland. But Japan's broken terrain limited the dimension of its waterworks. And never having been conquered by China—and thus being spared the imposition of a Chinese agrodespotic bureaucracy—the Japanese perpetuated their endogenous system of small-scale (hydro-) agriculture dominated by a few hundred territorial overlords, who, while frequently establishing irrigation works on their domain, maintained among themselves a relatively loose, nonbureaucratic relationship.

The agrarian order in which modern Japanese rural society is rooted was headed by feudal lords. But different from their European counterparts, who often ran a manorial economy with the labor of their serfs, the Japanese *daimios* developed no such economy, preferring to have their serfs pay rent. This fact greatly weakened the ties of serfdom in Japan; and in time not a few serfs came close to enjoying a tenantlike status. Thus in Japan, hydroagricultural circumstances were a crucial factor in mitigating "feudal exploitation"; and in consequence there emerged one of the most intensive and most productive types of farming known to mankind.

A peculiar combination of geoinstitutional conditions gave Japan a special place among the agrarian systems of the feudal world. A different, but also peculiar, combination of geoinstitutional conditions gave China a special place among the agrarian systems of the hydraulic world. During the latter part of the first millenium B.C., and due to the coincidence of several changes that usually occur at different times,[11] the Chinese rulers made a decision that has few parallels in the history

Produktions-und Zirkulationsprozess (Leipzig, 1931), pp. 312 ff., 338 (hereafter cited as WGC). Karl A. Wittfogel, "Hydraulic Civilizations," *Man's Role in Changing the Face of the Earth*, ed. William L. Thomas, Jr. (Chicago: Wenner-Gren Foundation, 1956), p. 158.
   [10] "Die natürlichen Ursachen," pp. 482–83.
   [11] *OD*, pp. 289–90.

of Oriental despotism: They introduced private ownership of land. The thus-established proprietary order, which, except for an interval in the first millenium A.D., persisted until the Communists seized power, stimulated the Chinese peasants to cultivate their fields with extraordinary care and ingenuity, whether they were owners or possessors— the tenants generally retaining about one half of their main crop and the bulk of their secondary crops. Arthur Young's assertion that private property transforms sand into gold must not be taken at face value, but it goes far to explain why the private-property-based Chinese system of farming assumed a quasi-horticultural quality. It also goes far to explain why Mao Tse-tung encountered special difficulties when he replaced China's traditional peasant economy with a collective system of large-scale farming.

China enjoyed the productive advantages of hydraulic agriculture, but it was burdened with the bureaucratic despotism inherent in its agrohydraulic system. Japan enjoyed the productive advantage of hydroagriculture unhampered by a similar bureaucratic development. Muscovite and post-Muscovite Russia was burdened with the oppressive organizational and acquisitive institutions of a crude agromanagerial despotism without enjoying the productive advantage of "Oriental" irrigation farming.

Like the Western variants of extensive agriculture, the agriculture of Russia was compatible with large-scale farming, particularly in its manorial form. In pre-emancipation days, the landlords, who lived under a service-oriented autocratic regime and not under a contractual feudal order, devoted less time to farming than did the feudal lords of Western Europe.[12] And after the emancipation, which initiated the disintegration of the autocratic regime, many aristocratic estates shrank or decayed, while modern large farms slowly increased. The agrarian system of tsarist Russia included village communities in which the land was held jointly, but cultivated by the peasants individually. And while these communities were substantially modified by the emancipation, their members were still bound by many ties when the Bolshevik Revolution in the fall of 1917 inaugurated a fundamentally different development.

The Primary Comparison

The agrarian systems mentioned so far are separated from each other by important differences, but they share basic features that distinguish

[12] *Ibid.*, pp. 278–79.

all of them from the Communist system to which I am turning now. No matter whether the agricultural core is labor-extensive or labor-intensive, the non-Communist systems are not essentially based on large farms. Although large farms were significant in the medieval West and are significant in some sectors of the West today, they were (and are) imbedded in a mass of small peasant holdings. In the labor-intensive Orient and in most of the institutionally related ancient American civilizations, the small farms prevailed altogether. Furthermore, no matter whether these agricultural enterprises existed under aristocratic-democratic governments of the early Roman or pre-Hellenistic Greek type, under agromanagerial ("Oriental") despotisms, or under feudal, absolutistic, or modern representative governments, their operations were not controlled by the state but by a variety of small and large private owners or possessors. In both respects, the agrarian systems of the Communist states have no parallel among the major civilizations of history.

Did the doctrinal pioneers of Marxist-Leninist communism envisage such a singular development? The answer to this question may help us understand the theoretical foundations on which Lenin built his new order. Did the Communists' first practical experiments prove the superiority of "socialist" over "capitalist" farming? The answer to this question may help us understand the qualitative differences between the functions and aims of the Communist agrarian systems of today and those of all known Communist systems, past and present.

THE COMMUNIST AGRARIAN SYSTEM: DOCTRINAL PREPARATIONS

Marx and Engels

Key Theses

Marx and Engels were groping for a new way of organizing agriculture when Engels wrote his preparatory draft and Marx wrote the final version of the *Communist Manifesto*. In his draft Engels demanded the "creation of large palaces on the national estates [*Nationalgüter*] as communal residences for communes of citizens who engage in industry as well as agriculture and who combine the advantages of rural and urban life, without sharing the one-sidedness and disadvantages of both ways of life."[13] Both men requested the "establishment of industrial armies, especially for agriculture."[14] Fourier's influence on these ideas

[13] Karl Marx and Friedrich Engels, *Werke* (Berlin: Dietz Verlag, 1959–67), IV, 373–74 (hereafter cited as *MEW*).

[14] *Ibid.*, pp. 373, 481.

is obvious.[15] In the winter of 1847/48, Marx and Engels did not know too much about the history of agriculture; but they were very familiar with the writings and ideas of Fourier.

After the storms of 1848-49, the two friends settled down in England, where they reexamined the economic and political trends that favored —or impeded—the revolutionary changes they expected. A book review, published in April, 1850, and most likely written by Marx,[16] found the prospects of capitalist concentration in agriculture uncertain. The author was convinced that "agriculture must steadily move in a cycle [*Kreislauf*] of the concentration and fragmentation of the land as long as bourgeois conditions last at all."[17]

But Marx did not leave it at this. When, after much more research, he completed the first volume of his lifework, *Das Kapital*, he moved away from the stereotyped approach to agriculture that had characterized his early writings; at the same time he abandoned the cyclical concept presented in the 1850 review. Now he emphasized that farming had important peculiarities; in the comprehensive drafts to other volumes of *Das Kapital*, he dealt with them subtly and in detail.

But these refinements did not prevent him from asserting that there would be an advance toward large enterprise in agriculture as well as in industry, and that machinery and "big industry" would revolutionize agriculture. In a subchapter of Volume 1 entitled "Big Industry and Agriculture" he declared that "in the sphere of agriculture, big industry has the most revolutionary effect in that it annihilates the bulwark of the old society, the 'peasant,' and replaces him by the wage laborer." The capitalist large farm will overcome the irrational methods of the past by "technically applying science"; and there it will be "easier than in manufacturing industry to repress the workers' individual vitality, freedom, and independence." Why so? Because "the rural workers' dispersion over larger areas simultaneously breaks their power of resistance, while concentration increases that of the urban worker."[18]

In 1868, Engels wrote a "conspectus" of Volume 1 of *Das Kapital*, which slightly elaborated on Marx' dispersion argument (the rural workers are weakened by dispersion hence most poorly paid), and which prefaced this point by reproducing Marx' thesis concerning the replacement of the peasant by the wage laborer under the influence of ma-

[15] Charles Fourier, *Oeuvres Complets* (Paris, 1841), IV, 427, 455 ff., 458 ("palaces"), 557 ff. ("industrial armies").

[16] *MEW*, VII, 590.

[17] *Ibid.*, VII, 290.

[18] *Ibid.*, XXIII, 528–29.

chines.[19] Hence in later editions of the *Communist Manifesto*, Marx and Engels did not eliminate their request for socialized farming. And Engels, in his last articles on the peasant question, written in 1894, expressly reasserted this point. Indicating that he had discussed the problems of the agrarian revolution with Marx many times, he demanded that the landlords' estates after confiscation be immediately organized for large-scale farming and cultivated by former farmhands "under the control of the community." Eventually large farming would prevail also in the peasant sector, whose members would be led toward cooperation by example and "societal [*gesellschaftliche*] aid."[20]

Problems

Marx' and Engels' thesis of the greater rationality of large-scale farms is not, of course, the decisive reason for their predominance in the U.S.S.R., Communist China, and other Communist countries. But together with Lenin's arguments, it provides a strong doctrinal justification for the spread of such farms. This being the case, we will do well to identify the basic fallacies contained in the Marxist agrarian position.

Contrary to industrial production, which in its developed form tends to be continuous in time, concentrated in space, and monotonous in performance, agricultural production is intermittent in time, dispersed in space, and as a rule, multioperational. Marx, like virtually all serious students of the matter, was well aware of the first peculiarity.[21] But he failed to recognize a crucial aspect of the second; and he did not visualize its relation to the third.

In many of his writings, Marx pointed out that the concentration of industry affected the workers in two ways. The employers, who found it difficult to control their laborers in the period of manufacturing capitalism when work was mainly hand work, were able to establish order and discipline after machines were introduced.[22] But while machines broke the individual worker's economic resistance in the factory, they facilitated his political and professional associations in society. Conversely (I may add) the dispersion of the agricultural laborers, which for a long time prevented them from organizing professionally and politically in society, made it easier for them to resist economically on the farm. The spacial dispersion inherent in most agricultural opera-

[19] *Ibid.*, XVI, 287.
[20] *Ibid.*, XXII, 504, 499.
[21] *Ibid.*, XXIV (*Das Kapital*, II), 125–26, 238 ff., 241–49; Karl Marx, *Theorien über den Mehrwert* (Berlin: Dietz Verlag, 1956–62), III, 12 (hereafter cited as *TMW*).
[22] *MEW*, XXIII, 389 f.

tions (in most, not all) makes the effective supervision of labor very difficult and in some cases virtually impossible.

Marx was not unaware of the multioperational character of farm work. And while he did not do full justice to Adam Smith's analysis of this matter, he did comment on it approvingly.[23] Considering this, we

[23] In his history of the theory of value, which was meant to become the fourth volume of his *magnum opus*, Marx copied Smith's dispersion statement: in contrast to the townspeople (who can easily combine), the inhabitants of the country, who are "dispersed in distant places, cannot easily combine together. They have not only never been incorporated, but the corporation spirit has never prevailed among them" (*TMW*, II, 226; *Wealth of Nations*, p. 126). Here Smith is discussing rural dispersion from the standpoint of professional and political organization, whereas Marx, in the above-cited passage in the subchapter, "Big Industry and Agriculture" in *Das Kapital*, Volume 1, argues essentially in economic terms. Marx, who stressed the relation between economic and political conditions, did not, for this reason, deny the differences between the two aspects; and when, in his opinion, the argument demanded it, he did not hesitate to explain which aspect he had in mind. It seems therefore legitimate to assume that when Marx spoke without qualification, in Volume 1, of dispersion as breaking the farmhands' power of resistance, he was probably thinking of professional-political resistance. But his failure to make this clear was due in all likelihood to his failure to recognize the dispersed agricultural laborers' potential for economic resistance. If Marx had clearly understood the multiformity of most agricultural tasks—which tends to make economic resistance especially effective—he might have radically modified his thesis regarding the inevitable superiority of capitalist large farms.

In the *Theories* Marx reproduced only the first part of Smith's analysis of the superior "intelligence" of the peasants' work as juxtaposed to manufacturing work performed under the condition of the division of labor (*TMW*, II, 226). In this context he cited Smith's explanation that farming "requires much more judgement and discretion" because of changes in the weather (Marx: "of the seasons") and other accidents. But he did not cite Smith's subsequent discussion of the peculiarity of the agricultural *work targets* as necessitating special skills and experience even in seemingly inferior and simple branches of farming. Since Smith's argument (and Marx' failure to reproduce it) are essential to one of our key issues—the peculiarity of agricultural labor—I reproduce it here *in toto*:

Not only the art of the farmer, the general direction of the operations of husbandry, but many inferior branches of country labour, require much more skill and experience than the greater part of mechanic trades. The man who works upon brass and iron, works with instruments and upon materials of which the temper is always the same, or very nearly the same. But the man who ploughs the ground with a team of horses or oxen, works with instruments of which the health, strength, and temper are very different upon different occasions. The condition of the materials which he works upon too is as variable as that of the instruments which he works with, and both require to be managed with much judgement and discretion. The common ploughman, though generally regarded as the pattern of stupidity and ignorance, is seldom defective in this judgement and discretion. He is less accustomed, indeed, to social intercourse than the mechanic who lives in town. His voice and language are more uncouth and more difficult to be understood by those who are not used to them. His understanding, however, being accustomed to consider a variety of objects, is generally much

find his lack of understanding of the potential difficulties created by the dispersion of agricultural labor even more puzzling than his optimism about the to-be-expected victory of the machine and large enterprises in modern agriculture.

Marx possibly overrated the chances of large-scale farming because of the conditions in contemporary English agriculture. The rapid increase in England's urban population[24] in the early phases of England's industrial revolution, high overseas freight rates, and protective tariffs gave the English grain producers a near monopoly over prices. And this situation, which endured for several decades after the corn laws were repealed, caused even serious specialists such as Arthur Young and Albrecht Thaer to overrate the benefits of large-scale farming and underrate the difficulties presented by agricultural labor.

But while we can see why a Young and a Thaer overgeneralized from the English experience, Marx' corresponding view, which he specifically expressed in a reference to the great effectiveness of hired labor in capitalist tenant farming in England,[25] is less easily explained. Some classical economists, among them Adam Smith and John Stuart Mill, had noted the continuing possibilities of peasant farming. And this, together with Marx' awareness of the multioperational character of farming, might have warned him against making his sweeping statements about the effects of machine-based large-scale farming in *Das Kapital,* Volume 1. Marx, who accused "vulgar" economists of viewing economic conditions not as a relation between human beings, but as a relation between things (commodities and money) and thus committing the sin of mystification, came close to committing this very sin himself in his lack of concern for the conditions of man (labor) in large-scale farming and his one-sided stress on the agricultural machines.

The Old Engels

Marx' views concerning the superiority of large-scale farming may

---

superior to that of the other, whose whole attention from morning till night is commonly occupied in performing one or two very simple operations. How much the lower ranks of people in the country are really superior to those of the town, is well known to every man whom either business or curiosity has led to converse much with both. In China and Indostan accordingly both the rank and the wages of country labourers are said to be superior to those of the greater part of artificers and manufacturers. They would probably be so everywhere, if corporation laws and the corporation spirit did not prevent it.

[24] David S. Landes, "Technical Change and Development in Western Europe, 1750–1914," *The Cambridge Economic History of Europe,* eds. H. J. Habakkuk, M. Postan (2d ed.; Cambridge: Cambridge University Press, 1965), I, 279 ff.

[25] *MEW,* XXIII, 85 ff.

be explained at least in part by the privileged position English agriculture occupied when he did his research for *Das Kapital*. But by 1880 this factor had lost its validity. We will do well to remember this when we examine the attitudes of the old Engels, Kautsky, and Lenin.

The mechanization of communications revolutionized transportation. Steamships and railroads made new and cheap supplies of foreign grain accessible; and the drop in grain prices on the world market led to an agrarian crisis,[26] which in England and other similarly situated European countries was weathered more successfully by the small than by the large farmer. But although Engels knew this, he upheld the original Marxist thesis of the superiority of large-scale farming. And he continued to demand that large-scale farming be made the core of socialist agriculture.

In a passage Engels inserted in the third volume of *Das Kapital,* which was published in 1894, he dramatically described the recent changes in the global upsurge of grain production. Interestingly, he did not attribute this upsurge to the efficiency of large-scale farming abroad, but to the opening up of virgin lands (prairies, pampas, and steppes) and to the influx of Indian and Russian grain produced by peasants under the fiscal pressure imposed by a "merciless government despotism." He himself expected the resulting "agrarian misery" (*Agrarierjammer*) to bring about the ruin of all of Europe's "large landed property" and of "the small one in addition."[27]

Disregarding the fact that the new development did not challenge the small peasant farms to the degree it challenged the big farms, which were indeed in a deep crisis, Engels, in 1894, stated again that socialist agriculture should be oriented toward large-scale farming.[28] And in a lengthy postscript to *Das Kapital,* Volume 3, written shortly before his death and published in 1895/96, he reasserted the thesis Marx had propounded in *Das Kapital,* Volume 1, that "big industry," which reduced the price of all commodities, "also terminates the small production and natural economy of the self-sufficient peasant family."[29]

Why did Engels, who could be very rational, here argue so irrationally? Widening the issue, we may also ask: Why did Engels, in his *Anti-Dühring*, claim that ancient slavery had been necessary for the develop-

---

[26] Herman Levy, *Large and Small Holdings* (Cambridge: Cambridge University Press, 1911), pp. 75 ff., 202.

[27] *MEW*, XXV, 735–36.

[28] *Ibid.*, XXII, 500 ff.

[29] *Ibid.*, XXV, 916.

ment of modern Europe ("without ancient slavery no modern social-ism"), although he and Marx knew that ancient society led nowhere, and that medieval Europe had evolved institutionally, not from the slaveholding urban civilizations of Greece and Rome, but directly from primitive tribal conditions?[30] Was he so enthralled by the possibilities of power inherent in their aimed-at centralized and dictatorial regime that he recommended "socialist" large-scale state-controlled farming without proper concern for the agricultural operators (whose fate under such conditions was certainly not being realistically identified by the use of such mystifying terms as "cooperative" and "association")?

These questions come to mind when we contemplate the arguments of the old Engels, which bulwark his and Marx' earlier views about the unavoidable victory of large-scale farming. They come to mind with increasing intensity when we turn to Kautsky and Lenin.

Kautsky

In this context I shall dwell on Karl Kautsky's book, *The Agrarian Question (Die Agrarfrage)* (1899), rather than on Eduard David's *Socialism and Agriculture* (1903), although in the critical revision of the Marxist views on agriculture and agrarian policy David's study was a pioneering effort.[31] It was Kautsky's *Agrarfrage* that became the corner-stone of the orthodox Marxist attitude toward the agrarian question.

Kautsky went far beyond Marx' and Engels' discussion of modern agriculture. He explained systematically the technical improvements that were being made in agriculture;[32] and he declared frankly that this development, although benefitting essentially the large farms, did not make them the dominant type of enterprise. The peasants' capacity for "overwork" and "underconsumption," together with the difficult labor conditions existing on the large estates and the changes in the

[30] *Ibid.*, XX, 168. Marx and Engels indicated this point in 1845/46 (*MEW*, III, 24); Marx argued it clearly in the first large draft of his *magnum opus* (*Grundrisse der Kritik der Politischen Ökonomie*). And a few years after the appearance of his *Anti-Dühring*, Engels elaborated it in his *Origin of Private Property*, etc., in which he combined his and Marx' pertinent views with those of Morgan (*MEW*, XXI, 149–50).

[31] Eduard David, *Sozialismus und Landwirtschaft* (Berlin: Verlag der Sozialistischen Monatshefte, 1903), *passim*. I am glad to revise here the evaluation I gave David's book in *Wirtschaft und Gesellschaft Chinas* (see especially pp. 364 ff.). Rethinking the Marxist position on the matter, I have learned to appreciate the contribution made by David. This contribution is stimulating despite the fact that, in his endeavor to establish the advantages of the family farm, David did not fully acknowledge the significance of machine- (and capital-) intensive farming above the peasant level.

[32] Karl Kautsky, *Die Agrarfrage* (Stuttgart, 1899), pp. 33 ff., and 92 ff. (hereafter cited as *Agrarfrage*).

global grain supply, were reducing the number of large farms in favor of small ones. In fact, this situation led several prominent agricultural theoreticians at the time to announce "the approaching end of large agricultural enterprises."[33]

Kautsky did not accept this perspective. According to him, the large and small farms were mutually dependent; and oscillations in their relations led to a cyclical movement, a *Kreislauf* between the concentration and fragmentation of land "as long as bourgeois conditions exist at all."[34] But after having thus virtually abandoned the thesis of the necessary victory of capitalist large-scale farming over peasant farming, Kautsky nevertheless ended on the old Marxist note: All countertrends notwithstanding, capitalist tendencies are paving the "way for socialization of agricultural production, which must originate through the rule of the proletariat as certainly as the socialization of industry with which it will merge to form a higher unity."[35] And again: "*Societal development in agriculture is taking the same road as in industry.*"[36]

Lenin

Several years before the appearance of Kautsky's book, the young Lenin had already been propounding the superiority of capitalist large-scale farming. He had done this by a selective citing of Marx' and Engels' statements that supported this view.[37] He was even more selective when he hailed Kautsky's *Agrarfrage* as "the most important event in present-day economic literature since the third volume of *Kapital*. Until now Marxism has lacked a systematic study of capitalism in agriculture. Kautsky has filled this gap."[38]

While Lenin became aware that the development of agriculture was far more complicated than the development of industry, he wholeheartedly associated himself with Kautsky's arguments concerning the technical superiority of large-scale farming.[39] And at the center of his argument he placed Kautsky's contrived conclusion that societal development in agriculture is "taking the same direction as in industry."[40]

Large-scale capitalist farming would be the steppingstone to socialist

[33] *Ibid.*, p. 160; cf. also pp. 132 ff.
[34] *Ibid.*, p. 161.
[35] *Ibid.*, p. 298.
[36] *Ibid.*, p. 300. Italics added.
[37] V. I. Lenin, *Collected Works* (Moscow: Progress Publishers, 1963–), I, 428 ff. (1895); III, 326–27 (1899) (hereafter cited as *CW*).
[38] *Ibid.*, IV, 94 (1899).
[39] *Agrarfrage*, p. 300.
[40] *CW*, IV, 98.

farming. This was the core of Lenin's agrarian position until 1905. It remained so when, for tactical reasons, he recommended that the land-lords' land be distributed to the peasants in the "bourgeois-democratic" revolution he began propounding in 1905/6. (Once the bourgeois-democratic dictatorship of the workers and peasants was established, the continuing play of capitalist forces would again prove the superiority of large-scale agriculture.[41]) And it remained so when, in the fall of 1917, he returned to a modified version of his 1906 position, which he had abandoned after the February revolution of 1917, because this revolution was not the bourgeois-democratic revolution headed by the workers and peasants he was fighting for. (In April, 1917, he had requested that all estates be operated as model farms under Soviet control.[42])

Since the summer of 1917 Lenin had realized that the Bolsheviks could seize power only with the support of the peasants. Hence he began to associate himself with their demand to have the landlords' land transferred to the people.[43] And in the October revolution he demonstratively accepted their program for an equalitarian distribution of all land to the villagers as formulated by the Left Socialist Revolutionists. But at the same time, he clearly indicated that this was their idea of a revolutionary solution to the agrarian question, not the idea of the Bolsheviks.[44]

TWO TYPES OF MODERN AGRARIAN REVOLUTION

The Leninist Agrarian Revolution

The Appearance of Basic Peculiarities

The agrarian system that emerged in Soviet Russia and other Communist countries was the result of an agrarian revolution—a revolution that in essence was coercive (violent) and that, although it led to many changes, has not yet come to an end.

The Communists, who call their type of political and economic revolution "Leninist," are quite correct. Lenin's views and policies

---

[41] *Ibid.*, XIII, 309–10 (1908); cf. XV, 143 (1908); cf. also XXII, 65 ff. (1915).

[42] *Ibid.*, XXIV, 23 ("April Theses," published April 7). On April 10 he wrote: "In order to improve grain production techniques and increase output, and in order to develop rational cultivation, on a large scale, under public control, we must strive within the peasants' committees to secure the transformation of every confiscated landed estate into a large model farm controlled by the *Soviet Agricultural Laborers' Deputies*" (*ibid.*, XXIV, 72. Italics in original. Cf. also pp. 502–3, May 22, 1917).

[43] *Ibid.*, XXV, 173, 280–81, 316; XXVI, 64, 184, 197, 229.

[44] *Ibid.*, XXVI, 258 ff.

differ from those of Marx and Engels, which in their inconsistencies reflect the multicentered world of the mid- and late-nineteenth century (and its multicentered historical roots). And they differ still more from the operational core of the contemporary multicentered world (European, American, Japanese, and so on), which manifests itself in the peculiarities of the non-Communist agrarian revolutions.

The Leninist doctrine, too, has its inconsistencies, but in contrast to Marx' belief in the possibilities of a partnership capitalism,[45] Lenin's belief in the possibilities of popular control over the dictatorial "socialist" state he wanted did not grow out of a serious analysis of Russia's social history. He professed it despite what he knew about the "Asiatic" roots of and trends in post-emancipation Russia.

An Organizational Revolution of the Bureaucratic-Centralist (Single-Centered Despotic) Type

The modern non-Communist agrarian revolution is not dominated by a single directing center. It is the result of an interplay of a plurality of forces (agrarian and industrial, including the representatives of small-scale production, organized labor, noneconomic secular powers, churches, public opinion, and so on). The pressures of these multiple and partly antagonistic forces have brought about governments that interfere in certain areas of their citizens' economic and noneconomic affairs; and their agrarian policies tend to involve all kinds of organizational and bureaucratic measures. But while these organizational and bureaucratic trends exist and constitute serious problems for the perpetuation of our multicentered societies, they have so far been compatible with an individual and personal management of agriculture, which in a number of cases has been bolstered by public subsidies. This modern agrarian revolution is not, in its agricultural core, an organizational-bureaucratic revolution, but a revolution of means and methods aimed primarily at the improvement of the conditions and results of farming.

It is against this background that we must see the Communist agrarian revolution, which in a broad sense may be called a *Marxist-Leninist* revolution, but which, more precisely, is a *Leninist* revolution, since it was Lenin who combined certain of the distinctly totalitarian elements of orthodox Marxism with elements of a basically bureaucratic and despotic tradition.

[45] See Karl A. Wittfogel, *From Marx to Mao*, Telecourse, University of Washington, 1960, p. 6 (available at Telecourses, University of Washington, Seattle).

The social historian who asserts that the disintegration of the Orientally despotic tsarist regime permitted the growth of democratically oriented political forces is, of course, correct. But he should remember that this regime, although increasingly weakened, persisted until February, 1917. Lenin himself coined the term *Aziatchina* (1899). He spoke of Russia's "Asiatic capitalism" (1905). And in 1911 he declared that the revolution of 1905 had signalled "the beginning of the end" (not the end) of Russia's Orientally despotic order.[46]

Thus when Lenin declared that the revolutionary party he considered necessary for Russia should discipline its members by bureaucratic and centralized methods, he chose an organizational form that in Western Europe could be employed without constituting a major threat to democratic development, but that in Russia might revitalize a core principle of the very autocracy he was combating. And the opposition Lenin's proposal aroused shows that his critics were aware of this danger.

In the open historical situation[47] that evolved in Russia during the last phase of tsarism, the old agrarian (agrodespotic) order no longer exerted a compelling influence. But while the antagonistic forces gave increasing latitude to the struggle for a multicentered society, they also gave enormous encouragement to the growth of Jacobin elements that, all democratic professions notwithstanding, aimed at a new dictatorially centralized (and single-centered) order. The self-confidence of these elements (the Bolsheviks) was greatly enhanced by the personality of their supreme leader, who fully utilized the political potential created by the February revolution of 1917, which the top-ranking Social Revolutionists and Mensheviks failed to exhaust.

In the West, the perspective of a totally organized economy and society remained in suspense: Marx did not abandon it, but some of his major later writings show him doubtful about his own earlier idea, and the orthodox Kautsky finally joined the reform socialists. But in Russia, the Bolshevik believers in a "socialist" society were the heirs, not only of a selectively accepted orthodox Marxism, but also of an agrodespotic power structure whose semimanagerial functions could become totally managerial as soon as sufficient technical instrumentalities were

---

[46] For documentary evidence concerning Lenin's significant (and increasingly contradictory) views on this matter, see *OD*, pp. 377 ff.; Karl A. Wittfogel, "The Marxist View of Russian Society and Revolution," *Review of World Politics* (1960), pp. 501 ff.

[47] For this concept see *OD*, pp. 8, 15–17, 437. For its application to the Russian development of 1917 see *ibid.*, pp. 436–38.

created (Oriental despotism plus electrification, to paraphrase Lenin).

The Role of Large-Scale Production

This explains why in 1915 Lenin described the issue of "small-scale and large-scale production" as the focal point of all discussions of agricultural evolution and its laws:[48] allegedly this evolution showed that agriculture necessarily advanced to machine-based large-scale farming.[49]

This explains why Lenin on November 8 (old calendar: October 26) indicated his disagreement with the revolutionary distribution policy he had taken over from the Socialist Revolutionists, and why a few weeks after the dissolution of the Constituent Assembly he wanted to establish a *"compulsory organization of the whole population in consumer and producer communes."*[50] Although he was compelled to abandon this plan quickly, he nevertheless favored the operation of several types of "socialist" farms:[51] communes, agricultural producers' "cooperatives" ("artels," usually called collective farms), temporary producers' cooperatives serving temporary needs (TOZY),[52] and, somewhat later, state farms.

This explains why Lenin kept these collective agrarian enterprises going although he knew that, substantial government subsidies not-withstanding, most of them performed poorly,[53] and why in the summer of 1920, he directed the Communists of industrially advanced countries, once victory was theirs, to preserve as many of the big agricultural enterprises as possible, and operate them like "Soviet state farms."[54]

This explains why, even after the period of War Communism was over, Lenin continued to declare the "cooperativization" of production in industry and agriculture the aim toward which Soviet Communists must direct their supreme effort,[55] and why, under the New Economic

[48] *Ibid.*, XXIII, 65. Italics in original.

[49] *Ibid.*, XXII, 101.

[50] *Ibid.*, XXVII, 156 (March 9, 1918) (italics added), 255 (Lenin's statement concerning the abandonment of the idea of uniting the whole population of a given locality into a single cooperative society—a decision made as a concession to the older cooperative societies—was published on April 28, 1918).

[51] Robert G. Wesson, *Soviet Communes* (New Brunswick, N.J.: Rutgers University Press, 1963), p. 92.

[52] W. Ladejinsky, "Soviet State Farms," *Political Science Quarterly*, LIII (1938), 62 ff.

[53] *CW*, XXVIII, 175 ff., 338–47.

[54] *Ibid.*, XXXI, 159–60.

[55] *Ibid.*, XXXI, 214; XXX, 368, 378, 399; XXXII, 217, 323; XXXIII, 186, 467, *passim*.

Policy, when he did not want to "irritate the peasants," he did not liquidate the state farms and other forms of agricultural collectives they hated.

To be sure, he criticized them devastatingly,[56] but he preserved most of them, including the communes. Contrary to the impression given by Stalin in his article "Dizzy with Success," which was published on March 2, 1930,[57] and contrary also to the impression given by Khrushchev and Mikoyan when they criticized Mao's communes, many of the communes (and the collectives and state farms) established under Lenin continued to exist during his lifetime, and were in large part maintained by Stalin. As late as April, 1930, Stalin still held that the *good* old communes had "fully justified their existence," that they were "splendid" and deserved encouragement and support.[58]

The following figures tell some of the story: in January, 1921, there were 9,064 collective farms; in September of that year, 10,015; in 1927, 7,135; and in 1928, 11,574. In January, 1921, there were 1,829 communes; in September of that year, 1,528; in 1927, 1,335; and in 1929, 1,796.[59] In the years immediately following, the number of communes increased spectacularly, from 3,537 in 1929 to 7,564 in 1930, and to 7,600 in 1931. Then the number began to decrease. In 1932 there were 4,200, and in 1933, 4,000.[60] At this point they seem to have lost their distinctive character, becoming in effect collective farms no different from most of the large agricultural units that had been created by combining small peasant farms.[61]

ORIENTATION AND SPECIAL PROBLEMS OF THE
COMMUNIST AGRARIAN SYSTEM

When Lenin first proposed placing the entire population within a network of consumer and producer cooperatives, he did not make the implementation of this plan contingent on the existence of modern machinery. Nor did he do so when he spoke in favor of agricultural communes and other types of collective farms. Only when the difficulties of operating the large farms became painfully clear did he declare that

[56] *CW*, XXX, 197–200; XXXIII, 238 ff.

[57] J. V. Stalin, *Works* (Moscow: Foreign Languages Publishing House, 1955), pp. 202 ff.

[58] *Ibid.*, p. 229.

[59] Naum Jasny, *The Socialized Agriculture of the USSR* (Palo Alto, Calif.: Stanford University Press, 1949), pp. 300 (note), 320 (hereafter cited as *Socialized Agriculture*).

[60] *Ibid.*, pp. 320; cf. also Wesson, *Soviet Communes*, p. 202.

[61] Jasny, *Socialized Agriculture*, p. 322.

the successful collectivization of the country's agriculture could be achieved solely after certain technical preconditions had been fulfilled —especially the introduction of tractors (at least 100,000)[62] and electrification.[63] No wonder therefore that Stalin initiated the massive collectivization of agriculture when he believed that the regime possessed sufficient economic and political "strong points" in the countryside[64] (he did not, in this context, refer to tractors or electrification).

Lenin's voluntariness clause created no problem. Allegedly, by 1929 the peasants were convinced that collectivized farming was more advantageous than individual farming;[65] and although admittedly many cadres violated the principle of voluntariness, the gigantic collectivization campaign advanced under this banner. Moscow quickly provided the new collective farms with tractors and Machine Tractor Stations. These stations had over 100,000 tractors in 1932 and almost 300,000 in 1934,[66] when the newly created farms had absorbed the great majority of all peasants.

Successes and Failures of the System
Four Major Goals of the Communist Agrarian System

The Communist agrarian system was expected to fulfill at least four major goals. The units of production were to be large. They were to be government controlled. They were to operate scientifically ("rationally"), i.e., with modern equipment and advanced agronomical methods. And they were to assure the agricultural operators the superior conditions of work and life befitting a socialist society. Marx had visualized these operators as "associates" who controlled their production and/or, like the peasants, were labor-rational.[67] In such a setting labor needed no disciplining (as it did under capitalism, except for piecework, which required "almost" none).[68]

An Uneven Score

By and large the first two goals have been attained in the Communist countries that collectivized agriculture, first of all in the U.S.S.R. After collectivization we usually find two main types of large "socialist"

[62] *CW*, XXIX, 214 (March, 1919).
[63] *Ibid.*, XXX, 378, 399; XXXI, 161 (1920).
[64] Stalin, *Works*, XI, 202.
[65] *Ibid.*, XII, 135.
[66] Jasny, *Socialized Agriculture*, p. 274.
[67] *MEW*, XXV, 131 (*Das Kapital*, III).
[68] *Ibid.*, XXIII, 390; XXV, 93.

agricultural enterprises: state farms and collective farms, plus a small sector of private plots on which members of collectives and employees of the state farms, and so on, keep some animals and produce meat, milk, eggs, vegetables, and fruits. But these plots are subject to many government regulations and their existence, which the regime tolerates as temporarily expedient, does not alter the fact that the bulk of the major crops is produced on state farms and collective farms. While the farms of these two types exhibit important differences (which in the U.S.S.R. are being increasingly eradicated), they are all large and they are all under government control.

The scientific-technical part of the Communist agrarian program has not fared too well. It has often been carried out haphazardly, not because the Communists do not want their agriculture to be run scientifically—they do—but because there are obstacles over and above delays created by an investment policy that is one-sidedly oriented toward industrialization. An investment policy can be modified; and Moscow's post-Khrushchev leaders have done this. But the scientific pursuit of agriculture also depends on more than adequate machinery, fertilizers, and agronomical guidance. It depends, and at a certain point decisively so, on the condition of labor. The historical record shows that slave labor is completely incompatible with the use of refined tools and work methods, and that other types of commandeered labor tend to use tools and work methods poorly.

Obviously agriculture can be equipment-rational (and method-rational) only when it is labor-rational, i.e., when it offers the agricultural operators conditions that induce them to employ their tools effectively and perform their tasks carefully, industriously, and with initiative. It is exactly here that the Communist agrarian system flounders.

The Achilles' Heel of the Communist Agrarian System: Labor

According to Marx, the free associates of a socialist society work for their own account, and they know this. Their social relation "to their work and to the products of the work" are "transparently simple in production as well as in distribution."[69] Thus they are not alienated from their work and there is no resistance to those who organize it. Under dictatorial Communist rule, the agricultural producers are not the masters of their fate, even under a NEP; and their feelings of frustration are enormously increased when they are compelled to join a collective. Now the relations of production (which interlock with a huge

[69] *Ibid.*, XXIII, 93.

apparatus of bureaucratic planning and directing) become mysteriously complex; and the relations of distribution (which determine their remuneration) become equally so. The "immediate producers," to use another Marxist term, are fully aware that they are controlling neither production nor distribution, and they are certainly not operating "for their own account." According to criteria set by Marx himself, such conditions can lead only to the workers' alienation from, and resistance to, their work.

Psychological Facts

The archives of the Communist Party and the OGPU of the Smolensk area that were seized by the Germans and that ultimately fell into American hands give us uncensored evidence about the feelings of the Soviet peasants during the NEP and after the collectivization. They show that even during the most lenient period of the NEP, the Communists knew that the peasants were still not reconciled to their policies. The party records contained in these archives convey "something of the flavor of an army of occupation in a hostile country."[70] That the peasants hated the collectivization is not surprising. The Smolensk papers document this fact with data that cover the greater part of the thirties.[71]

After World War II, displaced Soviet nationals were interviewed by a Harvard research team. Former villagers reviled the collective-farm system for having deprived them of their "independence, autonomy, and integrity." About 75 per cent of the *kolkhozniki* interviewed "advocated violent death for the top Soviet leaders." And should there be no other way of getting rid of the hated system, "about 80 per cent of them were willing to drop an atom bomb on Moscow."[72]

The Operational Attitudes

The Harvard data are available because an unusual situation permitted the kolkhoz peasants to speak without fear of punitive sanctions. No similar situation has arisen since. But Moscow's continuing efforts to make the agricultural producers work dedicatedly in the "public" sector shows that the Communists have failed to restore the "link" between the peasants and the land, which the collectivization destroyed.

[70] Merle Fainsod, *Smolensk under Soviet Rule* (Cambridge: Harvard University Press, 1958), p. 123.

[71] *Ibid.*, pp. 265 ff., 271–72, 290, 297.

[72] Raymond A. Bauer, Alex Inkeles, Clyde Kluckhohn, *How the Soviet System Works* (Cambridge: Harvard University Press, 1956), p. 184.

Since World War II the agrarian policy of the U.S.S.R. has undergone several changes.[73] After the death of Stalin, who crassly subordinated agriculture to industrialization, the Soviet regime experimented with various devices (different patterns of payment and organization and raising prices) in order to increase the output per man-day on state farms and kolkhozy. But while the experiences of the period of 1953-57 and the attempts initiated in 1964 confirmed what no realist has doubted, that the agricultural operators' attitudes are not static, the over-all results made it equally clear that, all innovations notwithstanding, the "link" between the rural producers and their work remained "tenuous."[74]

Agricultural specialists in the U.S.S.R. and abroad have stressed the difficulty of properly evaluating the work done in the collective sector.[75] But while acknowledging the importance of this fact, we must not forget that before a collective producer's work can be evaluated it has to be performed; and it is here that the farm managers face the crucial test. In any enterprise that possesses a directing authority, the person in charge assigns the tasks he deems necessary and sees to it that they are properly carried out. This can be done with a fair chance of success when the tasks are simple and concentrated in space. But when they are dispersed and multioperational, as they are in agriculture, effective supervision and direction are very difficult to achieve. This is particularly so, when, under conditions of commandeered labor, the immediate producer is indifferent to his tasks and hostile to his masters.

To return to Soviet agriculture: What was the situation in comparable spheres of farm work before and after collectivization? What did the peasants do prior to The Great Change, and what did they do (or not do, or do poorly) afterward? Jasny has asserted that "an exact comparison of the labor input per able-bodied person before and after collectivization is unfortunately impossible."[76] Unfortunately indeed, because only by identifying the character and intensity of every operation that is undertaken on the socialist farms (or is not being done in whole

---

[73] See Harry E. Walters and Richard W. Judy, "Soviet Agricultural Output by 1970," *Soviet and East European Agriculture*, ed. by Jerzy F. Karcz (Berkeley and Los Angeles: University of California Press, 1967), pp. 314–23.

[74] *Komsomolskaya Pravda*, June 11, p. 2; cf. also *Literaturnaya Gazeta*, No. 32, August 7, 1968, p. 10.

[75] *Literaturnaya Gazeta*, No. 6, February 7, 1968, p. 10; U.S. Department of Agriculture, *Soviet Agriculture Today: Report of 1963 Agriculture Exchange Delegation* (Foreign Agricultural Economic Report No. 13 [Washington, D.C., 1963]), p. 8.

[76] Jasny, *Socialized Agriculture*, p. 418.

or in part) can we arrive at a clear understanding of the nature of the productivity problem with which the leaders have been wrestling for decades.

Approaches to Problems of Size and Labor

Earlier Sociohistorical Patterns

There are as many different ways of dealing with problematic work attitudes in agriculture as there are different agrarian systems involving the use of commandeered and noncommandeered labor. The slave, who generally has no property, and who owns no land, poses the problem in its extreme form. The ancient Greeks used little slave labor in agriculture; the peasant who used some generally worked with them in a patriarchal relationship. The Romans, who used slave labor extensively on their latifundia, assigned such labor essentially to simple tasks (vineyard culture, olive picking, and herding).[77] In the United States slave labor was used on a large scale in agriculture essentially for the production of special crops (primarily cotton) where the slaves could work in "gangs" and thus be supervised with relative ease.[78] For the cultivation of the grain crop—which requires widely dispersed operations—the American farmers used free labor. They countered the difficulties involved in grain production with slave labor by avoiding its use.

Peasants who lived in serflike subordination to feudal lords or "Oriental" officials were not so deeply frustrated as the slaves. Their masters might commandeer them for various kinds of labor; but they were per-

[77] William L. Westermann, *The Slave Systems of Greek and Roman Antiquity* (Philadelphia: The American Philosophical Society, 1955), p. 91.

[78] Kenneth M. Stamp, *The Peculiar Institution* (New York: Knopf, 1956), pp. 42, 43, 50, 54 ff. Big cotton farms employed a relatively large number of hired workers after the abolition of slavery; and this trend continued, to be sure, with decreasing strength, even when mechanization greatly reduced the need for hand labor. On the large commercial cotton farms, the operator and his family contributed only 3,200 out of a total of 25,190 work hours. On the large cotton farms of California, nonfamily labor also prevailed spectacularly.

In contrast, in wheat farming family labor contributed the greater part of all labor used: e.g., in the Southern Plains, 2,560 out of 2,880 hours; in the Northern Plains (wheat-fallow), 2,520 out of 3,740 hours; in the Pacific Northwest (wheat-fallow), 3,250 out of 3,750 work hours (*Agricultural Statistics, 1966* [Washington, D.C.: U.S. Department of Agriculture, 1966], pp. 486–87).

Today the advance of mechanized cotton farming is radically reducing the need for hand labor. In 1966, in the Mississippi Delta, "more than 90 per cent of the crop was picked by machines, and chemical fertilizer made hand weeding obsolete." Hence, between 1960 and 1965, more than 60,000 able-bodied Negroes left the state (*New York Times*, July 31, 1967).

mitted to "possess" land sufficient to maintain a small farm for their own benefit. Under feudal conditions, the peasants frequently did *corvée* labor on the lord's fields. Under agrodespotic rule, labor on "public" fields seems to have prevailed only when such special agronomical methods as the digging stick facilitated working in gangs, at least in some major operations. In the ancient higher civilizations of America, work on such fields was still being done when the Spaniards arrived. In Chou China, the emergence of plowing with oxen and the abandonment of commandeered labor on public fields occurred at about the same time; the former may well have been the major cause of the latter. In commenting on the abolition of the public fields, the *Lü-shih Ch'un-ch'iu* (chap. xvii), states that the peasants did not work so well on these fields as on their own. Thus the Chinese coped with the difficulties involved in the use of commandeered agricultural labor first by employing such labor only on a fraction of the cultivable land (theoretically, one ninth) and then by eliminating it. In imperial China, attempts to employ commandeered labor on "camp" fields (that often were under the jurisdiction of the army and mainly served defense purposes) generally ended by the tenants doing the farming.[79]

Typologically the villagers in Communist countries that have introduced collectivized farming stand between the agricultural slaves and the various types of serflike peasants. That they may till some land and breed some animals probably puts them above the slaves, who do neither. But the smallness of the "plots" (about 5 per cent of the arable land) places them far below the "Oriental" and feudal serfs. And the insecurity of these possessions separates them still more from these serfs,[80] who were usually permitted to hold their land in perpetuity.

In most modern non-Communist societies, agricultural labor is not commandeered. Among its major forms, peasant labor, all observers agree, constitutes no incentive problem, whereas hired labor does. Arthur Young and Albrecht Thaer were fully aware of this situation, and Max Weber realistically discussed the problems of East Prussian farm hands (*Landarbeiter*) in a study[81] that Kautsky cited approvingly

[79] See Karl A. Wittfogel, "Forced Labor," Part I, "Forced Labor in Traditional China," *A General Handbook on China*, MS, ed. Hellmut Wilhelm, Human Relations Area files, University of Washington, Seattle, Washington, 1957.

[80] There existed still another type of serf in Sparta and similarly conditioned countries of ancient Greece. (See Wittfogel, *OD*, pp. 417–18; for the serflike condition of the peasants in many "Oriental" countries, see *ibid.*, pp. 281 ff.)

[81] Max Weber, "Die ländliche Arbeitsverfassung," *Gesammelte Aufsätze zur Sozial- und Wirtschaftsgeschichte* (Tübingen: Verlag von J. C. B. Mohr, 1924), pp. 479 ff.

in his *Agrarfrage*.[82] In the United States, Western Europe, and elsewhere, capitalist farmers have also been faced with the problem of the productivity of hired labor; but they have met it in a way that is consonant with their institutional order, just as the Communists' way is consonant with theirs. These two ways of handling the problem tell us much about the two agrarian systems under which the problems of labor and size of agricultural enterprise occur.

The Modern Non-Communist Way

In examining the labor problem on the large farms of the U.S.S.R., Jasny declared that in collective and state farms the utilization of labor was "particularly inefficient . . . in crops needing a great deal of handwork and animal husbandry." His data, which deal essentially with prewar conditions, prove this to be true. They also show that the mechanization of farm labor (which was particularly advanced on the state farms) increased the "productivity per man."[83] But does this demonstrate the superiority of large farms using many laborers when agriculture relies more and more on mechanical aids?

The history of modern non-Communist agriculture warns us against such a conclusion. Western European farmers, like their North American counterparts, are increasingly using machines and artificial fertilizers. This has eliminated most of the "dwarf" holdings, but it has not led to the predominance of factorylike enterprises with many hired laborers ("large" enterprises in Marxist terms). In general we find that the small and middle-sized farm with both family and hired labor prevails; and that, whatever the size of the farm, the number of hired laborers has decreased greatly; and as in North America, their treatment has generally improved.[84] In West Germany, where today there are almost no large farms, one hundred hectares of cultivated land in 1960 absorbed the labor of 24.1 members of the farmers' families and of 2.4 regular hired laborers.[85] In Denmark, where middle-sized and larger peasant farms prevail, the number of regular hired laborers fell from 149,400 males and 82,100 females in 1945 to 47,800 and 11,200, respec-

[82] Kautsky, *Agrarfrage*, p. 158.
[83] Jasny, *Socialized Agriculture*, p. 437.
[84] John O. Coppock, *North Atlantic Policy, The Agricultural Gap* (New York: Twentieth Century Fund, 1963), pp. 62 ff., 68 ff.; George Blohm, *Die Neuorientierung der Landwirtschaft* (Stuttgart: Verlag Eugen Ulmen, 1963), pp. 108 ff.; cf. Gerhard Herlemann, *Grundlagen der Agrarpolitik* (Berlin and Frankfurt: Verlag Franz Vahlen, 1961), pp. 74 ff.
[85] Herlemann, *Grundlagen . . .* , p. 165.

tively, in 1964; and in this same interval, the number of day laborers fell from 17,900 males to 3,200 and from 3,600 females to 1,200.[86]

In the United States the increase in the use of capital, machinery, and fertilizer has been spectacular. As in Europe, this development has eliminated many very small farms, and different from Europe, it has favored the growth of giant enterprises. But although the average size of the American farm has increased with the increase in mechanization, and although the giant farms are economically very important,[87] they have by no means replaced the efficient family farm.[88] Without entering into the agrobusiness versus family-farm argument, we may say that in the United States as in Europe, and contrary to Marx' expectation, the number of hired laborers employed in agricultural enterprises is today very small.

According to preliminary United States' census estimates for the years 1949 to 1964, the average farm acreage increased from under 220 to about 350 acres.[89] During these fifteen years, production has increased 100 per cent and productivity per head 150 per cent.[90] These results were achieved, not by factorylike units employing many workers, but with a labor force that, in most sectors of the agricultural economy, consisted mainly of "operator and family."[91]

E. Higbee is aware of the difficulty created by the limitations of the data given in the census of agriculture on the distribution of full-time and part-time agricultural workers according to farm class and farm type. But on the basis of what is given, he found that, in the period from 1954 to 1958, "regular hired help" averaged 1.6 persons on large commercial farms that concentrated on cash grain production, and 2.4 on large farms engaged in a multi-crop business.[92]

Capitalist farming? If we use as criteria investment in money and equipment (including fertilizers), then the "first and upper middle class" farms whose production has a value of more than $10,000 an-

[86] *Report from the Danish National FAO Committee to the Food and Agriculture Organization of the United Nations* (Copenhagen, 1965), p. 55.

[87] Edward Higbee, *Farms and Farmers in an Urban Age* (New York: Twentieth Century Fund, 1963), pp. 49 ff.

[88] *The Expanding and Contracting Sectors of American Agriculture* (Washington, D.C.: U.S. Department of Agriculture, 1966), pp. 9 ff.

[89] W. B. Sundquist, *Organization and Use of Resources in Farming* (Washington, D.C.: U.S. Department of Agriculture, 1966), p. 1.

[90] *Ibid.*, p. 2.

[91] See Note 78, above.

[92] Higbee, *Farms and Farmers* . . . , p. 171. "Regularly occupied" means essentially resident hired workers.

nually must be so defined. But if we use Marx' criteria, which in a comparison between Communist and non-Communist conditions are of great interest, we arrive at very different conclusions.

According to Marx, capitalist production is distinguished from petty-bourgeois production (as pursued in towns by artisans and in villages by peasants) by the number of hired laborers occupied, the employing of a few journeymen or farm laborers not making the employer a "capitalist." Marx considered the qualitative difference between the capitalist and the petty-bourgeois use of labor so basic that, in *Das Kapital,* Vol. 1, he argued his point with specific reference to Hegel's quantity-quality concept,[93] something he had not done since the forties. In Marx' sense, the core of American farming—grain production—would not be capitalist: and his term "capitalist" would be problematic even if applied to America's large agricultural enterprises generally. For most sectors of West European (and Japanese) farming, it is completely unsuitable.

The Soviet Way

The heads of the large farms that have dominated the rural economy of the U.S.S.R. since collectivization are officials or quasi officials. Occupying the position of masters in "dominion-servitude (*Herrschaft und Knechtschaft*) relation," they have to concentrate their energies on many bureaucratic issues other than agricultural efficiency, which is the major concern of the master-farmers in modern non-Communist countries. The *kolkhozniki* and the workers on state farms stand at the opposite pole of the Communist power relation. They do not enjoy the opportunities for improving their condition that are provided by the pluralistic pressures within non-Communist societies. The result is a work attitude more negative than that of farmhands on most modern "capitalist" farms.

The Soviet leaders cope with this negative attitude in a variety of ways, among them the offering of material incentives (sporadically at first and more generally in recent days) and mechanization (which, as already noted, they have been promoting since collectivization). The mechanization of Soviet agriculture has been retarded because of the priority given to industrial investment; but, according to a report made by a group of American specialists who visited the U.S.S.R. in 1963, "the major problem of developing equipment [machines] for the prin-

[93] *MEW*, XXIII, 273, and Note 205a. Cf. *ibid.*, XXXI, 306, letter to Engels dated June 22, 1867.

cipal field crops has been solved."[94] The report particularly noted the advance made during the last decade.[95]

Hand in hand with this advance (which has not raised mechanization to the American level)[96] the Soviet regime has favored large farms —a policy that contrasts sharply with trends in modern non-Communist countries. Whereas, as shown above, a moderate increase in the average size of farms in these latter countries has been accomplished by a sharp reduction in the amount of labor used per unit, in the agricultural sector of the U.S.S.R. exactly the opposite development is taking place. The collective farms have been radically reduced numerically; and while the productivity of labor per unit of land has increased slightly, many more persons now work on these farms.

The picture is complicated by the fact that a considerable number of collective farms have been converted into state farms. Nevertheless, the figures make the trend unmistakably clear. From 1938 to 1963, the collective farms shrank in number from 240,000 to 40,000; and the individual units, which in 1938 comprised about 78 households, in 1963 comprised about 400.[97] The state farms, which are much better equipped and much larger than the collectives, increased from fewer than 4,000 in 1938 to almost 4,900 in 1953, and to 8,600 in 1963; and the average state farm cultivates several times as much land as does the average collective farm.[98]

But the Communists do not rely only on mechanization and the accumulation of many workers in large agricultural units. Since the days of The Great Change, members of collectives and state farms have been organized in "brigades,"[99] to increase discipline. This method of handling labor has outlasted the war. Said Khrushchev in 1950, "High labor discipline is the basis of collective development."[100] In 1951 he said: "The work brigade is the basic form of labor organization on the collective farm."[101] And brigades are still used today. They vary in size, some of them having more than one hundred workers.[102]

[94] *Soviet Agriculture Today*, p. 35; cf. p. 71.

[95] *Ibid.*, p. 73.

[96] *Ibid.*, p. 72.

[97] Jasny, *Socialized Agriculture*, pp. 317; *Soviet Agriculture Today*, pp. 8–9.

[98] Jasny, *Socialized Agriculture*, p. 262; *Soviet Agriculture Today*, p. 10.

[99] Jasny, *Socialized Agriculture*, pp. 51, 254.

[100] *Pravda*, April 25, 1950. For the checking of these and other Russian sources, I am indebted to Mrs. Lea Kisselgoff.

[101] *Moskovskaya Pravda*, February 8, 1951.

[102] *Soviet Agriculture Today*, p. 31.

Obviously gigantism[103] and organization have not solved the labor problem that resulted from collectivization. The American specialists cited above have concluded that Soviet agriculture is less "efficient" and less "dynamic" than American agriculture, and this because it lacks the "incentives" and "initiative" provided by the American system of individual ownership and family labor.[104]

THE CHINESE COMMUNIST APPROACH

So far I have discussed the Communist agrarian system essentially in terms of the Soviet Russian development, even though my career as an economic historian began with the study of China's geoagricultural conditions. I endeavored then and later to establish how the Chinese peasants grew their crops and what their system of farming was actually like.[105] My recent occupation with Communist China's pre- and postcollectivization agriculture is an outgrowth of my earlier research.

But in the present context, China could not be the starting point. The blueprint for the Communist agrarian policy did not originate in China; it was created—and for years solely applied and tested—in Soviet Russia. And while the Chinese Communists have significantly elaborated and modified the methods of handling agriculture and the peasants, they have accepted basic features of the Soviet model.

For various reasons, the Chinese modifications deserve careful study. Just as the East European variation of Communist agrarian policy must be analyzed against the Soviet Russian background, so must the respective policies in North Korea and North Vietnam be examined against the background of Communist China. And just as the Soviet experience gives a new (and contrasting) meaning to recent agricultural developments in Western Europe and North America, so the Chinese Communist experiences give a new (and contrasting) meaning to recent agricultural developments in Japan, Taiwan, and certain non-Communist countries on the Asian mainland.

Having in my comments on the U.S.S.R. outlined some general features of Communist agrarian policy, I shall now state briefly what I consider essential peculiarities of Communist China's agrarian system.

Special Difficulties of Chinese Collective Agriculture

Our methodological approach is again geoinstitutional. This approach enables us to identify the agrarian systems of traditional China

[103] *Ibid.*, p. 9.
[104] *Ibid.*
[105] See especially Wittfogel, *WGC*, pp. 305 ff., *passim*.

and tsarist Russia and the bureaucratic-despotic heritage reflected in Lenin's organizational concept of "socialist" power in general and "socialist" economy in particular. This approach also enables us to identify key problems in Mao Tse-tung's agrarian policy.

In extensive agriculture, the essential operations are few and relatively simple; in irrigation farming they are much more numerous, subtle, and time consuming. In an extensive agriculture there may be at times, but by no means regularly, preparatory plowings and harrowings. But once the sowing is completed, little or no work is done in the fields until the crop is harvested.

Irrigation of the Chinese type involves special operations to bring water to the crops; it also encourages other operations that are not performed in rainfall farming under which crops "can be grown satisfactorily and most economically by planting them in solid stands so that they cover all the ground equally".[106] The irrigation farmer organizes his fields in rows and furrows. This is necessary for the flow of water, and it permits intertillage and weeding. Planting is often preceded by several preparatory plowings and harrowings, and in some areas, natural fertilizers are systematically applied, particularly in China and Japan.

Since these many operations are intermittent in time, dispersed in space, and multiform, it is difficult for an outside authority to ensure their proper execution. In pre-Communist China the operations were carried out by the owner-peasants themselves, who, in the sense of Marx' concept, were labor-rational. They cultivated the fields with a work attitude that, to quote Marx again, made any superimposed discipline superfluous. Marx was aware that, in "South China and Japan" the peasants did their small-scale farming in a "horticulturelike way."[107]

After the conquest of the mainland, the Communists completed their "land reform," which radically changed the social texture of the villages, but permitted the peasants to uphold the old intensive system of farming. Could the new rulers "socialize" this agriculture? Could they counter the specific difficulties presented by the collectivization of this kind of farming?

---

[106] John S. Cole and O. R. Matthews, "Tillage," *Soil and Men: Yearbook of Agriculture*, Department of Agriculture (Washington, D.C.: U.S. Government Printing Office, 1938), p. 327.

[107] *MEW*, XXV, 111.

Devices Available for Meeting These Difficulties

Strong Organizational Footholds in the Villages

The Bolsheviks expressed their approval of the revolutionary changes that occurred in the Russian countryside in 1917–18. Essentially an urban party, they could not exert on-the-spot leadership to shape these changes and consequently were not strongly organized in the villages when they launched their collectivization in 1929.

In contrast, the Chinese Communist leaders had been controlling rural bases for almost twenty years before they initiated their final "land reform" in 1946. Communist cadres led this gigantic operation, which atomized the peasantry and provided the party with a huge *organizational* network in the countryside. In this respect, the Chinese Communists were much stronger in 1953 than the Soviet Communists had been in 1929.

The Hydraulic Potential

There was also in the Chinese countryside a potential *agronomical* strong point, which Russia's traditional rainfall agriculture could not match. I am thinking, of course, of China's agrohydraulic resources. During the last period of Manchu rule, the government's concern for these resources had lessened.[108] The countervailing trends that appeared after the fall of the monarchy[109] remained inconclusive because the effective unification of the country was held up by disruptive internal and external forces. The protracted Sino-Japanese War and the final Communist assault prevented the Nationalists from adequately utilizing the sovereignty that their allies granted them—too late.

Thus the Chinese Communist victors inherited a hydraulic opportunity that was typical for certain crisis periods of traditional "Oriental" societies—the opportunity to raise the productivity of agriculture enormously through a regenerative hydraulic revolution.[110] Any government that unified China could have done so. Historical circumstances that cannot be examined here gave this opportunity to the Communists. Soon after they had established their uncontested authority they began to initiate hydraulic works of various kinds.[111] They initiated them on

[108] See Wittfogel, *WGC*, pp. 443 ff.

[109] John Lossing Buck, *Land Utilization in China* (Chicago: University of Chicago Press, 1937), p. 188.

[110] For this concept, see *OD*, p. 171.

[111] See Y. L. Wu, *An Economic Survey of Communist China* (New York: Bookman Associates, 1956), pp. 324 ff.

the basis of a dispersed peasant economy, aware that the collectivization of agriculture would greatly increase their organizational capacity for the execution of such works.

Supplementary Agronomical Opportunities

Compared with the hydraulic opportunity, all other opportunities were of secondary importance. But two may be mentioned because, like the hydraulic opportunity, they played no role in Soviet collectivization: the chance of using improved seeds and insecticides.

Problematic Industrial Resources

The Chinese Communists were aware of the lessons provided by the Soviet experience concerning the relation between the collectivization of agriculture and industry. Changing Lenin's thesis (industrialization first, then collectivization), Stalin had argued for simultaneous action (mechanization in the course of the collectivization). During the first years of their rule, the Chinese Communists asserted that in China too, the collective farms should be mechanized.

During the last years of Stalin's life, the Chinese Communists restored their economy more or less to its prewar level. They then saw all-out collectivization as an ultimate but not an immediate goal. When Stalin died (March 5, 1953), China's industry was still far below the Soviet level, particularly with regard to heavy industry. Although the Chinese Communists, drawing heavily on the post-land-reform peasant economy, chalked up an impressive growth rate for their industry, they could not achieve a substantial mechanization of their agriculture. Would they wait until they could do so, or would they push ahead with the collectivization, whatever the risk?

Organizational Weapons

There were still other resources the Chinese Communists could tap if they decided on a new agrarian policy. In addition to the organizational potential common to all Communist-controlled regimes, the Chinese Communists had special organizational advantages. They were the heirs of China's traditional methods of mobilizing rural labor for public works and they had learned from 1928 to 1947 to use quasi-military techniques to solve many problems. If they resorted to these extraordinary weapons, they could venture upon an economic development that otherwise would have been hopeless.

The First Try: Collectivization

The Chinese Communists had been aware of their organizational strength since the forties. It was probably due in large part to this fact that they had demanded (since the days of land reform) the establishment of mutual-aid teams.[112] But while, perhaps for the same reason, they increasingly encouraged the creation of agricultural producers' cooperatives, they did not, during the first years of their regime, speak of agricultural cooperativization as a general and immediate task.

Mao's Response to an Open Historical Situation

In 1953, Mao found himself in a peculiar kind of open historical situation.[113] Under his guidance the Chinese Communists could either continue concentrating on the organization of mutual-aid associations and set up agricultural producers cooperatives only at certain advanced "key points," or they could immediately launch upon the road to collectivization, confident that their rural strong points would enable them to "socialize" their more complex peasant economy more quickly than their Soviet comrades had done. Mao stuck to the first line virtually to the end of Stalin's life, as evidenced by a resolution the party's Central Committee adopted on February 15, 1953.[114] This line was orthodox in terms of the Soviet precedent, and by upholding it, Mao continued to do what he had done for so long. Despite some serious misgivings,[115] he subordinated himself to the end of Stalin's supreme authority.

But after Stalin's death, Mao overnight became the elder statesman of world communism. He now felt free to reassess his basic economic program. He now shifted, also overnight, to a policy that was as ambitious as it was dangerous. Did he take this course, which supposedly served the glory of his party, because he was propelled by a force well-

[112] The Common Program of September 29, 1949, especially Articles 29 and 34. For the checking of these and subsequent data for which the Chinese originals are available, and for critical comments on my analysis of the Chinese agrarian policy, I am indebted to the scholarly assistance of Mr. C. S. Chao (Chinese History Project, New York).

[113] See note 47.

[114] This decision was published in *Jen-min jih-pao* (People's Daily) on March 26, 1953. On March 16, the paper had published "Directive on Spring Cultivation and Production Issued to Party Committees" that called the intensification of farm work "the central task which supersedes all other tasks," and warned against "precipitate haste . . . in the movement for agricultural productive mutual aid and cooperation." This directive was obviously formulated before the supreme leaders had visualized the new opportunities suggested by Stalin's death.

[115] See Karl A. Wittfogel, "Agrarian Problems and the Moscow-Peking Axis," *Slavic Review*, XXI, No. 4 (Dec., 1962), pp. 681, 437.

known to the student of total power—the "growing megalomania of the ageing autocrat?"[116]

However this may be, an editorial in *Jen-min jih-pao* published on March 26, 1953 (twenty-one days after Stalin's death), discussed the problem of agricultural production with "a new emphasis."[117] It declared:

> The present condition leads us to the realization that we cannot forever remain on the foundation of this economy of the small peasant. In keeping with the progress of the industrialization of our country, we must make the collectivization of agriculture the major constructional task in the rural areas.

The "new development" in the cooperativization movement became apparent first regionally,[118] then nationally. On November 12, a "new general line" toward "the socialist transformation of agriculture" and other branches of economy was announced. On December 16, 1953, the Chinese Communist leaders adopted the "Decision on the Development of Agricultural Producers Cooperatives," which requested the establishment of such organizations in all parts of China except in regions inhabited by national minorities. By the end of 1955, the majority of all Chinese peasants had joined "lower" producers' cooperatives.[119] And the big drive for the creation of "higher" cooperatives, which began early in 1956 and which was greatly intensified by the party congress in September, 1956, achieved its goal in February, 1957.

The Strategic Approach: Collectivization Combined with a Regenerative Hydraulic Revolution

The Chinese Communists launched upon their new political drive in order to promote industry, which, among other things, would provide adequate agricultural machinery *after* the collectivization was completed. Initially it was their collectivized agriculture that would serve their heavy-industry-oriented industrialization; and their collectivization went ahead without benefit of mechanical equipment such as Stalin had provided in the course of his collectivization. Teng Tsu-hui acknowledged in 1954 that the Chinese Communists had to collectivize

---

[116] See Karl A. Wittfogel, "A Stronger Oriental Despotism," *China Quarterly* (Jan.-Mar., 1960), p. 32.

[117] See Robert Carin, *Agricultural Co-operativization Movement* (Hong Kong, 1960), p. 57.

[118] *New China News Agency*, Sept. 2, 1953 (Mukden). Hereafter cited as *NCNA*.

[119] Literally, *incipient*. But the customary translation, *lower*, seems justified, since this type is generally juxtaposed to the "higher" agricultural producers' cooperatives.

before their agriculture could be mechanized.[120] Mao sloganized the point in his fateful speech "The Question of Agricultural Cooperation" on July 31, 1955: "cooperation must precede the use of big machinery." And the Eighth National Congress of the CCP restated its political resolution in September, 1956: "China will not be able in the immediate future to acquire agricultural machinery and chemical fertilizer industries on a fairly large scale."[121]

Among the above-mentioned measures that were expected to overcome this deficiency, "water-conservation projects" were paramount.[122] Stressing the success the Communists had attained in this respect until September, 1956, the Congress requested above all the expansion of "the irrigated areas."[123] The hydraulic enterprises that could be carried out at low cost by various work units (primarily labor brigades) comprised, in addition to state-financed projects,[124] many middle-sized and smaller projects for which the "agricultural producers cooperatives and the people in general should be mobilized."[125] During the years of the collectivization, these regional projects added over eight times more irrigated land to the precollectivization total than did the state projects.[126]

Peking claims that from 1953 to 1958 the irrigated land increased by 300 per cent.[127] Dawson justifiably rejects this figure; but he does not doubt that much was accomplished:[128]

[120] Cf. Teng Tzu-hui, "China's Agriculture on Way of Socialist Transformation," *For a Lasting Peace, For a People's Democracy*, Sept. 10, 1954. Teng correctly cited Stalin as having spoken of a "manufacturing period of collective farm development" in which the peasants, lacking machinery, pooled their simple tools. But Teng's presentation implies that this was Stalin's general view of the Soviet collectives, which it was not. Stalin applied Marx' concept of manufacturing industry to agriculture in December, 1929 (Stalin, *Works*, XII, 160); but he soon propounded his simultaneity thesis.

[121] *Eighth National Congress of the Communist Party of China* (Peking: Foreign Languages Press, 1965), p. 118.

[122] *Ibid.*, p. 119.

[123] *Ibid.*, p. 242.

[124] Ta-chung Liu and Kung-chia Yeh, *The Economy of the Chinese Mainland: National Income and Economic Development, 1933–1959* (Princeton: Princeton University Press, 1965), pp. 74, 171.

[125] *Eighth National Congress*, p. 243.

[126] John Lossing Buck, Owen L. Dawson, and Yuan-li Wu, *Food and Agriculture in Communist China* (New York and Washington: Praeger, 1966), p. 159 (Dawson).

[127] *Dix Grandes Années* (Peking: Foreign Languages Press, 1960), p. 130, cf. diagram: "Extension des terres."

[128] Buck, Dawson, and Wu, *Food and Agriculture in Communist China*, p. 158 (Dawson).

It is the belief of many analytical observers, both in Washington and in Hong Kong, as well as such specialists as Dr. [Yuan-li] Wu, that the tremendous effort expended on irrigation works resulted in a significant increase in the irrigated areas, at least in the early stages.

Dawson considers it possible that the acreage of irrigated land may have increased from 16, more likely 20, million hectares to 34.7 or 37.6 million hectares,[129] and that most of the expansion occurred during the collectivization period. Despite many deficiencies (a good part of the irrigated land was vulnerable to drought, and poor planning and mismanagement seriously hampered performance),[130] it still must be said that a 75 per cent increase in irrigated land did indeed represent a "tremendous effort" to improve the productivity of China's agriculture.

Supplementary Agronomical Improvements

Other measures for raising the productivity of the collectivized farms carried much less weight, but a few of them are worth noting. (1) Multiple cropping extended the sown acreage from 1953 to 1957 by 9 per cent.[131] (2) "The percentage of area sown to 'improved seeds' jumped from 5 per cent in 1952 to 63 per cent in 1957 for rice, from 5 to 69 per cent in wheat."[132] Insecticides were used increasingly: 19,000 tons in 1953, 41,000 tons in 1954, 69,000 tons in 1955, 159,000 tons in 1956, and 149,000 tons in 1957,[133] a slight decrease from the previous year.

As already noted, the Chinese use of improved seeds and insecticides, like their hydraulic effort, had no parallel in the Soviet collectivization. In the early years of Moscow's socialization, "the producers and their government were glad to have any seeds . . . . The quality of the seeds used in those years was probably worse than during the Civil War in the early twenties."[134] And effective insecticides were still unavailable anywhere when Stalin undertook his Great Change.[135]

[129] *Ibid.*, pp. 157–59.

[130] *Ibid.*

[131] Anthony M. Tang, Table 3 in "Input-Output Relations in the Agriculture of Communist China," page 289, this volume.

[132] *Ibid.*, Table 3.

[133] *Ibid.*, Table 1, p. 7; cf. *An Economic Profile of Mainland China*, Joint Economic Committee, Congress of the United States (Washington, D.C.: U.S. Government Printing Office, 1967), I, 24 (Liu).

[134] Jasny, *Socialized Agriculture*, p. 492.

[135] Insecticides became a major device for protecting crops only after World War II. See J. C. Ward, "A Dynamic Stature for Pesticides" in *The Yearbook of Agriculture,*

A Spectacular Hydraulic Input—But No Corresponding Increase in Agricultural Production

Did these various efforts cause a "spectacular increase" in agricultural production? The Chinese Communists have tried to create the impression that this was so by juxtaposing their data for the last years of the collectivization to the data of the precollectivization years.[136] But most independent analysts agree that the figures the Communists give for the early years of their regime are too low.[137] Y. L. Wu suggests that in 1958, for which the Communists claimed initially an output of 375 million tons and later of 250 million tons, the actual output was only 175 million tons.[138] The dean of Chinese agricultural studies, Dr. Buck, thinks that even this figure may be too high.[139] Wu estimates that in the years 1951–53, production was 179.8, 182.9, and 184.2 million tons, respectively, and that the production of grain (including potatoes) for 1954–58, with the exception of 1957, never again reached the 1952 level.[140] According to Liu and Yeh, the grain (plus potato) production from 1952 to 1957 showed an increase of 8 per cent, if sweet potatoes are included at their grain equivalent.[141] Since the population increase during these five years was something over 10 per cent, the increase in food output (as established by Liu and Yeh) did not (as happened in Japan and Taiwan) surpass the population increase, but fell noticeably below it.

But no matter whether the critical analysts accept Liu's and Yeh's estimates (many do) or whether their figures are higher or lower, virtually all of them conclude that the extraordinary inputs made by Peking during the time of the collectivization failed to bring about a substantial rise in production. To quote Liu and Yeh once more, "With potatoes included at their grain equivalent weight, the Communist figures of per capita food crop production in 1956 and 1957 are about

---

1966, U.S. Department of Agriculture (Washington, D.C.: U.S. Government Printing Office, 1966), p. 272. For Japan, see Takekazu Ogura, *Agricultural Development in Modern Japan* (Tokyo: Japan FAO Association, 1963), pp. 426 ff.

[136] *Economic Profile . . .* , p. 93 (Jones).

[137] Liu and Yeh, *Economy of the Chinese Mainland*, p. 45.

[138] Buck, Dawson, and Wu, *Food and Agriculture in Communist China*, p. 87 (Wu).

[139] *Ibid.*, pp. 34–35 (Buck).

[140] *Ibid.*, pp. 86 ff. (Wu).

[141] Liu and Yeh, *Economy of the Chinese Mainland*, p. 53. The grain-equivalent method, which the Communists employ, rates the potatoes at one quarter of their natural weight. Their calorie value is even smaller, namely about one fifth of the equivalent weight of rice or wheat (*ibid.*, p. 43).

6 to 8 per cent *lower* than our 1933 [prewar] estimate."[142] Y. L. Wu approaches the problem from the standpoint of a growing "shortfall" of grain (plus potatoes) below the population's "consumption requirement" as suggested by the "level of the normal prewar diet." According to him, the shortfall was about 2.2 million tons in 1954, 6.4 million tons in 1955, 12.0 million tons in 1956, and 16.7 million tons in 1957.[143] This would indicate a grain shortfall of 7 per cent and 8 per cent in 1956 and 1957, respectively—figures that are fairly close to those of Liu and Yeh.

The Basic Problem—Labor Shortage

Stalin's collectivization immediately deprived the Soviet peasants of their land and other major means of production.[144] Although his abrupt collectivization policy led to a deep crisis that was not alleviated by such aids as were available to the Chinese Communists in the fifties, the ensuing difficulties in the realm of farm labor did not necessitate a radical change in the whole of Stalin's economic program. The *kolkhozniki* were made to give more than twice as many workdays to the collectives as they had previously spent in their own fields.[145] While their performance left much to be desired, by and large they accomplished the few tasks required by the extensive system of crop raising. The ensuing agricultural situation permitted the regime to continue its over-all program, which involved the gradual reduction of the rural labor force. The urban centers with their growing industry absorbed the bulk of the rural labor surplus. (Lorimer estimates that between 1926 and 1939 at least 23 million people were transferred from the villages to the cities.)[146]

The Chinese Communists, in their collectivization, did not abruptly deprive the peasants of their private means of production; as Mikoyan said at the 1956 Congress of the CCP, they showed a praiseworthy

---

[142] *Ibid.*, p. 52. Italics in original. To be sure, if eaten in moderation, the sweet potato is a dietary asset, but the way in which Peking forced it on the people affected their nutrition adversely. It added 10 per cent bulk to food intake, and provided 20 per cent less calories than the cereal it replaced (Karl A. Wittfogel, "Food and Society in China and India," *Human Nutrition, Historic and Scientific,* Monograph III [New York: International University Press, Inc., 1963], p. 74. Cf. *Economic Profile . . . ,* pp. 94 [Jones], 254, 262–64 [Larsen]).

[143] Buck, Dawson, and Wu, *Food and Agriculture in Communist China,* p. 90 (Wu).

[144] Stalin, *Works,* XII, 202.

[145] Jasny, *Socialized Agriculture,* pp. 419–20.

[146] Frank Lorimer, *The Population of the Soviet Union, History and Prospects* (Geneva: League of Nations, 1946), p. 149.

"flexibility."[147] In the agrarian producers' cooperatives, which they set up first—and which were supposed to be set up on the basis of voluntariness—land, labor, and implements were managed collectively, i.e., under the leadership of cadres; but the peasants were still declared the owners of these means of production, and they received part of their income on the basis of the land they brought into the cooperative. The "semisocialist" farms of this type united only a limited number of households, about twenty-eight to thirty until the fall of 1955,[148] as compared to about seventy households in the Soviet collectives of 1930.[149] Unlike the larger units, these relatively small producers' cooperatives apparently still preserved something of a neighborhood quality.

Peking's "semi"-socialist collectivization policy was not always carried out on the spot. In not a few cases the local cadres forced the peasants to join the producers' cooperatives, and they disregarded the proprietary limitations set by the Communist government. In not a few cases, the perturbed peasants killed their animals and cut down their fruit trees (for quick personal use). Not infrequently they failed to manifest a "positive attitude toward agriculture" and "intensive farming."[150] While this did not immediately lead to disaster, it did seriously restrict the increase in grain production that otherwise would have accrued from the greatly increased hydraulic input.

The crisis assumed a new dimension when the regime urged the advance from "lower" to "higher" agricultural producers' cooperatives. The latter deprived the peasants of their residual rights in land and land-based income; and they comprised many more members. The advance to full collectivization was publicly recommended in November, 1955,[151] put into practice in the winter of 1955/56, and officially requested in June, 1956.[152] The average collective farm was to comprise from one hundred to two hundred households in mountains and rugged hills, and in the most important agricultural areas of China—the plains —three hundred households[153] (in 1938 the average Soviet collectives

[147] NCNA, Sept. 17, 1956.

[148] Kenneth R. Walker, Planning in Chinese Agriculture (Chicago: Aldine Publishing Company, 1965), p. 16 (hereafter cited as Planning).

[149] Jasny, Socialized Agriculture, p. 317.

[150] Jen-min jih-pao (JMJP), March 15, 1954.

[151] "Draft Model Regulations for Agricultural Producers Cooperatives," NCNA, Peking, Nov. 10, 1955.

[152] "Model Regulations for Higher Agricultural Producers Cooperatives," NCNA, Peking, June 30, 1956.

[153] Central Committee "Directives" dated Sept. 12, 1956, and published on the same day by NCNA.

comprised seventy-eight households).[154] According to the government directives, the private plots should generally occupy no more than 5 per cent of the arable land of a given locality (a party resolution of October, 1955, proposed a standard of 2 to 5 per cent).[155] The cadres kept the actual size down to 2.5 to 3 per cent.[156]

In response to the policy of full collectivization, the peasants everywhere committed overtly destructive acts: they killed their animals, felled their trees, and so on. And they greatly intensified their economic resistance. The many operations required by the public sector of China's intensive agriculture were performed so poorly that the Communist leaders began to comment on this situation—which they described in quantitative terms (too few laborers) rather than in qualitative terms (careless labor). In December, 1955, Mao, in his comments in a collection of articles published under the title, *The Socialist Upsurge in China's Countryside*, declared that "in a considerable number of localities" the new collectives "did not have enough labor." He obscured the core of the issue by claiming that the labor-deficient farms were doing their work "more skillfully" (allegedly they were having difficulties because they went into too many side lines),[157] but at least he indicated the existence of a serious labor problem in the collective farms. Many other spokesmen for the regime did likewise.

This remained the official position until 1957, when the clash between the peasants' negative work attitude and the regime's industrialization and procurement policies sharply aggravated the grain crisis. In the fall of 1957, the *People's Daily* admitted that the country's farming suffered from an inadequacy of labor.[158] And on February 23, 1958, a leading provincial daily called the labor deficiency the major stumbling block to the realization of the country's economic program. "At the present juncture, the one serious problem is: can we find a way to solve the problem of the labor shortage?"[159]

From early 1958, the Chinese Communist publications discussed the agricultural problem loudly and uniformly as a "labor shortage." This slogan was sufficiently specific to alert the cadres to the crisis in the

---

[154] Jasny, *Socialized Agriculture*, pp. 317–18.
[155] Walker, *Planning*, pp. 10–11, note 4.
[156] *Ibid.*, p. 25.
[157] *Socialist Upsurge in China's Countryside* (Preface and Notes by Mao Tse-tung) (Peking: Foreign Languages Press, 1957), pp. 285–86.
[158] *JMJP*, Sept. 22, 1957, cf. *Ta-kung pao*, Tientsin, May 18, 1955.
[159] *Fukien jih-pao*, Feb. 23, 1958.

countryside—and it was sufficiently vague to prevent the outside world from easily recognizing its true character and depth.

The Second Try: The Great Leap and the Communes
A New Variant of an Hydraulic Revolution

The regenerative hydraulic revolution in which the CCP engaged did not solve the problem of food production. It failed to do so because, unlike earlier hydraulic revolutions—which brought water to the fields, but permitted the fields to be privately cultivated by the peasants—the agrohydraulic and agropsychological elements, instead of being supplementary, were antagonistic to each other. By taking the fields away from the peasants, Mao prevented the realization of the new production potential of the added irrigated lands. In contrast to the full-fledged hydraulic revolutions of the past, he accomplished only a warped semihydraulic revolution.

Mao's Irrational Response to Another Open Historical Situation

The growing agricultural "labor shortage" again offered Mao a choice. He could appease the economically resistant peasants by making spectacular concessions, or he could use extreme measures to subdue them. Mao chose the second alternative. As we now know, the course he charted was considered starkly irrational by several leading Chinese Communists. It led to the Great Leap; it culminated in the establishment of the people's communes.

The Extreme Assault

The Chinese Communists tried to overcome the growing deficiency in labor by sending back to the villages the peasants who had run off to the cities in blind flight. In addition, they rallied for participation in farm work various groups of townspeople; first chosen were students from secondary and primary schools.[160] In 1956 they dispatched about 600,000 of them, and they sent more after the completion of collectivization. A report in August, 1957, mentioned one million,[161] another in November, 1957, three million.[162] At this time they also transferred to the villages large numbers of political cadres (about 810,000),[163]

---

[160] *JMJP*, Feb. 18, 1957.
[161] *Chiao-shih pao*, Aug. 13, 1957; *Union Research Service* (Hong Kong), IX, No. 5, 74 (hereafter cited as *URS*).
[162] *JMJP*, Nov. 11, 1957.
[163] *Kuan-ming jih-pao*, Nov. 24, 27, 1957.

intellectuals, families of government employees, and soldiers.[164] But a much vaster labor force was required for the stepped-up hydraulic activities and for cultivation proper.

The great leap. From the end of 1957 until the early spring of 1958 (the agricultural slack season in most parts of China), one hundred million able-bodied persons each spent about one hundred and thirty labor days at water-conservancy projects.[165] Allegedly this gigantic labor army increased the irrigated land by about 100 per cent.[166] It performed, in the words of its organizers, "a miracle in the world history of irrigation."[167]

But the productive potential of the hydraulic effort had to be realized through on-the-spot work in this field. In traditional China this work had been effectively carried out by the male villagers when they were released from the hydraulic *corvée*. Now their farming was inadequate, and another on-the-spot source of labor was called into service: the rural women. In December, 1955, Mao, in discussing the advancing collectivization, pointed to China's women as "a vast reserve of working power," which "should be tapped and used in the struggle to build a mighty socialist country."[168] By the fall of 1957, China's women were already earning 25 per cent of all wages in the collectives.[169]

But the rural women were still devoting most of their energies to domestic work; until then the Communists considered this entirely proper. On September, 1957: "The basic means" by which "the women can support the state in its socialist construction" is "industrious and thrifty management of the household."[170] On October, 1957: "Every able-bodied woman in the countryside should, *apart from the time spent on household work,* be able to give no less than 80 to 180 days . . . in agriculture or subsidary production (including household side occupation)."[171]

But the Peking strategists who reappraised the rural labor situation at the close of 1957 and early in 1958 arrived at a radically different

[164] *Chung-kuo ch'ing-nien pao* (China Youth Daily), Dec. 20, 1957.

[165] *JMJP*, May 3, 1958.

[166] *Ibid.*, Aug. 18, 1958.

[167] *Ibid.*, Oct. 14, 1958.

[168] *Socialist Upsurge*, p. 286 (Mao).

[169] Chang Yun, "Report to the 3rd National Congress of Chinese Women on September 9, 1957," *JMJP*, Sept. 10, 11, 1957.

[170] *Ibid.* On this occasion the Vice Chairman, Chu Teh, declared "any idea that tends to belittle domestic labor or thrifty household management [is] completely wrong" (*NCNA*, Sept. 9, 1957).

[171] *NCNA*, Oct. 28, 1957. Italics added.

conclusion. In February, 1958, a leading provincial daily asserted that the rural "labor force could be raised by 40 to 50 per cent" if public eating places and nurseries were set up.[172] The mobilization of rural females for work outside the home was to supplement the mobilization of rural males for work outside the fields, which was producing "one miracle after the other."[173] It was at this time that the term "The Great Leap" appeared.

To be sure, the thus-mobilized labor was soon also utilized in rural industry. However, we should remember that the slogan "The Great Leap" was first essentially invoked in connection with agricultural production and its hydraulic base.[174] Only after the agrohydraulic upsurge had made a promising start was the seemingly "miraculous" force applied also in industry—especially in the development of small rural furnaces for the production of pig iron and steel to support the country's heavy-industry-oriented industrialization. For a time the Communist planners obviously believed they could overcome their difficulties, not by making concessions to the villagers, but by organizing them as they had never been organized before. To accomplish this end, Peking established the people's communes. The decision to do so was made by the CCP's Central Committee on August 29. A few days later it was put into practice on a nationwide scale.

The communes. According to the commune policy, all able-bodied villagers were to concentrate their energies on work in the public sector. The private plots had absorbed much of the peasants' labor time and much of the natural manure, hence they had to be eliminated; and minor variations in the initial directives notwithstanding, they were soon eliminated. Domestic work was still consuming much of the rural female's energies. In the summer of 1958, a Communist youth leader, basing his statement on experiments made recently in Honan, asserted that the general use of the public kitchens would release "one third or even more of the labor power of all the people."[175] Calculations of this kind led to action. Article 17 of the Resolution adopted August 29 proclaimed the organization of public kitchens, nurseries, and tailoring teams "to free the women from household work."[176]

[172] *Fukien jih-pao*, Feb. 23, 1958.

[173] *JMJP*, March 3, 1958.

[174] See *Chung-kuo nung-pao* (Chinese Agricultural Bulletin), No. 5, March 8, 1958, articles on grain production; *JMJP*, May 14, 1958, re developments in Kiangsu, beginning in Nov., 1957. *Ibid.*, May 16, 1958, re developments in Shansi.

[175] *Chung-kuo ch'ing-nien pao*, Sept. 10, 1958.

[176] *JMJP*, Sept. 4, 1958.

Strict discipline would get the augmented rural labor force to work properly despite the minimum of material incentives. The peasants were to be "organized on military lines." They were to perform like the "industrial army" that the *Communist Manifesto* had demanded, "especially for agriculture."[177] Basic supplies, such as food, were to be given to everyone; and differentiated remunerations for work were to be correspondingly reduced.

The new type of villager envisaged was to be incorporated in units that would be much larger than the erstwhile collectives of two or three hundred households. All socialist farms of a "district" (*hsiang*: a cluster of villages) were to be merged into one huge unit, a commune. This supercollective would integrate all local economic, administrative, military, and educational functions that had been carried out separately in the past.

Extreme Disaster

The establishment of the people's communes during the latter part of 1958 is one of the most fascinating phenomena of our time, and deserves the most careful examination. But in the present context, we can follow this development only as it highlights the peculiarities of China's agricultural labor.

Mao and his aides tried to cope with these peculiarities by putting the peasants into the commune strait jacket, but this extreme action, instead of breaking the peasants' economic resistance, strengthened it. Half-hearted concessions that were made in late December, 1958, underlined the regime's desire to uphold the core of the commune structure. The result was a protracted agricultural disaster, which, with dramatic oscillations, lasted until the end of 1961. The Chinese Communists held bad weather responsible for the man-made calamities; and they made every effort to hide the extent of the famine and its toll in sickness and death,[178] but they did admit that the calamity at the height of the crisis was the worst China had suffered "during the last hundred years."[179]

---

[177] *Hung-ch'i* (Red Flag), 1958, No. 7, Sept. 1, 1958. Cf. *The Communist Manifesto*, Measure 5, *MEW*, IV, 373. I pointed to this request of the Manifesto as a doctrinal device for justifying extreme disciplinary controls in collective farms in my analysis of the Communist peasant policy written in 1956 (Karl A. Wittfogel, "The Peasants," *Handbook on Communism*, ed. Joseph M. Bochenski and Gerhart Niemeyer [New York: Frederick A. Praeger, 1962], pp. 369–70).

[178] I shall discuss these matters in my forthcoming book, *Russia and China*.

[179] *JMJP*, Dec. 29, 1960.

The Third Try: The Great Retreat
Extreme Efforts to Make the Peasants Produce More and Better

Although the unfeasibility of some of the commune's regulations became apparent immediately and the unfeasibility of others became apparent shortly thereafter, the regime fought hard to preserve them *in toto* or in part. Contemplating the major issues upon which the conflict was focused, we can recognize and assess the depth and complexity of the Great Retreat that followed the Great Leap and the establishment of the communes.

Domestic life. Regulations concerning the compulsory use of public eating places and nurseries were demonstratively weakened by the *Resolution on Questions Concerning People's Communes,* which the party's Central Committee adopted on December 10 and released on December 19, 1958. Gradually they were revoked altogether. That is, Peking's effort to take overnight tens of millions of rural females from their homes and put them to work in the public sector failed dismally.

Militarization and extreme economic equalization. The regime's efforts to militarize production and other aspects of commune life were also quickly abandoned, as were the attempts to lower expenses by giving free meals and reducing wages. Two other sets of measures that were carried out temporarily underwent a complex development.

The plots. In the spring of 1959 the regime restored the private plots, and in the late summer it took them away again. New concessions concerning the restoration of the plots were made in the "Twelve Rules," administrative regulations that were issued for internal use only in November, 1960; they were much more decisively set forth in the "Sixty Articles," which were issued, also for internal use,[180] in March, 1961.

In the Sixty Articles, the upper limit for the area of the plots was fixed at 5 per cent of the arable land, as had been the case during most of the early phase of the collectivization. But unlike the precommune-plot policy, which occasionally permitted a higher upper limit while being generally more restrictive,[181] the regime's new plot policy aimed at convincing the peasants that this time the Communists meant what they said.

The size of the administrative units. In the U.S.S.R. the collective farms were divided, since the thirties, into operational subunits, the bri-

[180] See Wittfogel, *Russia and China* (in manuscript).
[181] See Walker, *Planning*, pp. 25, 27.

gades,[182] and below them the squads.[183] But the staffs of the collective farms did the planning, directing, and accounting; and this remained so even when the size of the farm increased several times. In Communist China, the organization of the collectives originally followed this pattern. As already reported, the lower agricultural cooperatives, which initially handled the tasks of administering and accounting, yielded to the higher producers' cooperatives, which also handled these tasks. The latter were divided into two types of subunits: production brigades (with twenty to forty households) and teams (with seven to eight households). Then came the communes with several thousands of households and three types of subunits: large production brigades (with two-hundred and fifty households), production brigades (with thirty to forty households), and teams (with six to twenty households).[184]

The commune administration was far removed from the farm work and the compensation given the rank-and-file operators was inevitably arbitrary and offered no incentives for good production. The Peking leaders recognized this quickly. A resolution passed in March, 1959, by the party's Central Committee, which formally preserved the authority of the communes, turned over most of the actual decision making to the (large) production brigades. In the early months of 1960, the commune staffs still had some power of decision. A report from a Honan commune published in *Jen-min jih-pao* on March 14, 1960, noted that 16.4 per cent of the economy of the socialist farms was handled by the communes, and 72.7 per cent by the brigades. But the deepening crisis made it inadvisable to leave the communes even with this shadow of their previous authority. The Twelve Rules gave them operational control over only 3 per cent of their rank-and-file workers; for all practical purposes the Sixty Articles abandoned the original commune concept altogether. Article 5 directed that "the size of the various levels should not be made too large. . . . *The size of a village or a big village.*"[185] Despite terminological ambiguities (obviously to save the face of the father of the communes), it was clear by the spring of 1961 that the commune was

---

[182] Jasny, *Socialized Agriculture*, p. 335. In the thirties, slightly more than two per farm.

[183] See below.

[184] Walker, *Planning*, pp. 16–17. Throughout my presentation I have called the subunit below the production brigade the production "team." This is the customary translation of *sheng-ch'an tui*, which is linguistically not exact, but semantically defensible, and eliminates an element of confusion. (For the identification of the underlying terminological difficulties, see Walker, *Planning*, p. 19, note 1.)

[185] *URS*, XXVIII, 202.

in fact dead. The unit that was still so designated now comprised only a single village, and all managerial functions were carried out by the production brigade.

But backtracking did not stop here. On January 1, 1962, *Jen-min jih-pao* announced that from then on, the crucial functions of agricultural production and distribution would be handled by the production teams. At this time the production teams comprised from twenty to thirty households.[186] That is, the regime entrusted the basic managerial functions to units that were much smaller than the higher agricultural producers' cooperatives and that might even be smaller than the lower producers' cooperatives, which comprised twenty-eight households in the summer of 1955, thirty in the autumn, and forty at the end of that year.[187]

The size of the operational unit. The Soviet collectives resorted, at least since 1933, to the use of squads comprising five to seven persons (the squads cultivated mainly row crops, which included irrigated cotton).[188] A tendency to employ still smaller units, and in some cases only one family, appeared in the later thirties[189] and persisted in the war years; but it was reversed five years after the war ended, when Moscow set up supercollectives. According to decisions made in 1950, squads should only attend to cotton, sugar beets, and such;[190] that is, to row crops.

In China, where a restriction to row crops would have been pointless, since planting in rows was general, small operational units were favored from the early days of the Communist regime, the mutual-aid teams often comprising no more than six to eight households. After the completion of the collectivization, the government recommended operational units of seven to eight households. For the summer of 1958, an operational unit of six was again declared acceptable.[191] But at the end of the Great Retreat, still smaller units were officially recognized: work groups might then comprise as few as three households.[192]

That is, in contrast to the U.S.S.R., where the collective farms, despite their modest productivity, were tremendously expanded, Peking's socialist farms, after a mad experiment with gigantism, shrank to admi-

---

[186] *Ibid.*, XXVII (1962), 173–74 (cf. *Kung-jen jih-pao*, Sept. 26, 1961).
[187] Walker, *Planning*, p. 16.
[188] Jasny, *Socialized Agriculture*, pp. 336 (cf. p. 429).
[189] *Ibid.*, p. 337.
[190] Otto Schiller, *Das Agrarsystem der Sowjetunion* (Tübingen, 1960), p. 36.
[191] Walker, *Planning*, p. 17.
[192] *URS*, XXVII, 136–37, 141, 174.

nistrative units that were as small as or even smaller than, the mutual-aid teams of precollectivization days. Short of relinquishing their managerial control over agriculture entirely, the Peking rulers were making the most far-reaching effort to induce villagers to produce more and better.

China's Agricultural Labor Problem Remains Unsolved

The villagers were to be induced to produce better in the public sector (no prodding was needed with regard to the private sector, where the peasants worked intensively as soon as they believed that, for some time, the plots were theirs). Different from the private sector, which produced all manner of subsidiary foodstuffs[193]—and with excellent results—the public sector, which produced the bulk of the basic food-stuffs, primarily grain, did not show a similar efficiency. The official pronouncements displayed a general optimism; but not infrequently they sounded a note of caution. In the fall of 1962, i.e., at a time when the first postdisaster crop could reasonably be appraised, a report stated that the economic situation in the villages was only "slightly better" than in 1961.[194] And this trend persisted. In the summer of 1964, agricultural production admittedly "had not yet recovered"; encouraging improvements notwithstanding, agriculture still suffered from "rather abnormal conditions."[195]

Why was this so? According to official spokesmen, the peasants devoted much too much of their effort to the private sector, e.g., in Kwangtung they spent about 40 per cent of their energies on their plots (which according to regulations comprised about 5 per cent of the arable land), and only about 60 per cent on the collective fields[196] (which comprised about 95 per cent of the arable land). That is, the peasants were investing about one-third less of their labor in the public sector than the Communist managers expected (and than the crops needed). In 1964 an Aesopian commentator ascribed the perpetuation of abnormal agricultural conditions to the fact that the peasants pursued their "minor interests" (*read:* the interests of their private economy) to the disadvantage of their "major interests" (*read:* the interests of the state).[197]

---

[193] See Walker, *Planning*, p. 30.

[194] *Kuang-min jih-pao*, Oct. 31, 1962 (*URS*, XXX, 118).

[195] *Nan-fang jih-pao*, June 6, 8, 1964 (*URS*, XXXVI, 118, 122).

[196] *Nan-fang jih-pao*, Jan. 19, 1962 (*URS*, XXVII, 350–51).

[197] *Ibid.*, June 6, 8, 1964.

Persistence of the Food Problem

In the U.S.S.R. the food gap created by the collectivization crisis and its aftermath did not force the government to shift from the export to the import of grain. Russia's grain export, which before World War I had reached about 10.5 million tons annually, and which on the eve of collectivization (1927/28) had fallen to 0.4 million tons, attained a somewhat higher level after the collectivization crisis receded: for the years 1932, 1933/34-1937, and 1938, the grain export figures were 1.4, 1.3, and 1.0 million tons, respectively.[198]

It is indicative of China's peculiar agricultural conditions that the country's foreign trade in grain took a very different turn. During the first period of collective farming (1954–59), Peking had exported between 1.1 and 1.7 million tons of grain annually.[199] This policy came to an end in 1960. In 1961/62, the regime imported almost 5 million tons,[200] and it continued to make substantial grain imports in the years following. In 1962/63, 1963/64, and 1964/65, the imports reached 4.6, 5.0, and 4.5 million tons, respectively. Nor was this all. A contract Peking made with Canada in October, 1965, shows that the Chinese Communists planned to import, from that country alone, from 5 to 12.5 million tons of grain during the next three to five years.[201]

When the Chinese Communists concluded this contract, they did not foresee the political crisis that began in the winter of 1965/66 (the Proletarian Cultural Revolution) with its obvious harm to the country's economy; nor were they counting on reconciliation between Peking and Moscow (which might ease the protracted agrarian crisis). Things being what they were, R. L. Price recently stated that China may "have to continue importing grain for the foreseeable future, and probably at a gradually increasing rate of say 7 to 8 million tons per year."[202]

As already indicated, the "slight" (*read:* poor) responses to the regime's concessions show that the work incentives on the collective farms remained unsatisfactory. Hence the Chinese Communists were still faced with a protracted rural "labor shortage." Although they had been unable to dislodge tens of millions of rural women from their do-

[198] Jasny, *Socialized Agriculture*, pp. 415–16.
[199] Buck, Dawson, and Wu, *Food and Agriculture in Communist China*, pp. 86–87 (Wu).
[200] Six million tons, mainly wheat, minus an export of 1.1 million tons of rice. Over the years, the rice export amounted to about 14 per cent of the average annual grain input (*Economic Profile . . .*, II, 601 [Price]).
[201] *Ibid.*
[202] *Ibid.*

mestic chores at one fell swoop, they continued to tap this source for additional agricultural labor. They also continued to dispatch soldiers and students to the villages for longer or shorter periods.

At the same time they intensified their efforts to transfer permanently large numbers of persons from the urban and industrial centers to the countryside, openly acknowledging that for the time being the cities needed fewer workers while the countryside needed more. In April, 1962, Chou En-lai declared that the government was reducing the urban population, sending workers and cadres back "so as to strengthen the agricultural front."[203] Early in 1964, Po I-po, elaborating on this idea, declared that China's urban population must be reduced "from 130 million persons to 110 millions." For how long? According to Po, "until the mechanization of agriculture." With brutal frankness, he explained: "While our industry has been modernized, agriculture has not yet been mechanized."[204] He did not, in this context, specify the time needed. But what he had in mind was obviously not a few years, but an extended period.

Advance Toward a Different Industrialization

Po I-po's declaration was not the first of its kind. What he said was foreshadowed ideologically by an official pronouncement made on January 1, 1960, that agriculture was "the foundation of the national economy." This formulation ended the industrialization policy Peking had been pursuing since 1954, a policy that gave priority to heavy industry, and primarily to the production of iron, steel, and heavy equipment.[205] The turn to a new policy became apparent in 1960/61 when the Chinese Communists virtually suspended investment in heavy industry. When they again began promoting industry, they allocated proportionately less to industry, while giving it a different role from the one it had had in the first period of collective agriculture. As an article in the party's theoretical organ asserted in 1962, heavy industry, which was "previously developed only for the purpose of serving heavy industry," now "is developed for the sake of serving agriculture."[206]

In contrast to 1959, when Mainland China's imports of agricultural products and chemical fertilizers constituted only 4 per cent of all im-

---

[203] *NCNA*, April 16, 1962.

[204] *Ta-kung jih-pao*, Hong Kong, January 15, 1964 (interview with Anna Louise Strong).

[205] Cf. *JMJP*, Nov. 21, 1954, and especially the pronouncements made by the Party Congress in September, 1956 (Eighth National Congress, pp. 117–18, 234 ff.).

[206] *Hung-ch'i*, Nov. 1, 1962, p. 18.

ported goods, in 1965 they constituted 47 per cent. In 1965, the import of machinery and equipment had again risen above the disaster level, but it was still only one third of the 1959 figure.[207] Fixed investment in agriculture, which according to E. F. Jones, was in the neighborhood of 2 billion dollars (U.S.) in 1959, rose to about 3 billion in 1965, while the fixed investment in industrial production fell from about 4.3 to 2.2 billion dollars (U.S.).[208] As already noted, within industry itself investment was differently directed. In 1964 only a fraction of all goods produced by heavy industry (goods valued at about 2.7 billion Chinese dollars) were allocated for construction in the sector serving the production of capital goods, whereas goods valued at 23.5 billion Chinese dollars were allocated for construction in sectors serving the production of consumer's goods.[209] W. W. Hollister, who traced these developments, concludes that they do not conform to the "heavy industry push" model, which, according to him, was set up in 1953.[210] That is, in the postdisaster period of collective farming, the Chinese Communists abandoned the policy of speeding up industrialization, which they, like the Soviet Union, had made the primary objective of the collectivization of agriculture.

The Soviet Communists were able, despite serious agrarian difficulties, to maintain this policy, but the Chinese Communists were not. Whatever the more distant future may bring in terms of improvement or deterioration,[211] for the time being the Chinese Communists are maintaining their system of collective agriculture only by invoking a policy that rules out a quick industrialization.

In the Soviet Union and in Communist China, the peasants were unable to offer political resistance to their totalitarian masters (and this

[207] *Economic Profile* . . . , p. 585 (Price).

[208] *Ibid.*, p. 96 (Jones).

[209] *Ibid.*, p. 149 (Hollister).

[210] *Ibid.*

[211] Perpetuation of the present pattern is predicted by J. S. Aird, who expects a relative growth of the rural population and sees "no immediate prospect for a return to rapid urban growth" (*Economic Profile* . . . , pp. 390 ff.); by Hollister (see above); by R. L. Price, who expects as likely an increased grain import "for the foreseeable future" (*ibid.*, p. 601). The complexities and slowness of an agriculture-oriented type of industrialization are stressed by Y. L. Wu *et al.* (*Economic Survey*, pp. 233–34), and the probable extent and limitation of restored Soviet aid is discussed by the same research group (*ibid.*, pp. 386–87).

A slow upward development is considered not unlikely by another equally independent and critical economist. See Choh-ming Li, "China's Industrial Development, 1958–63," *Industrial Development in Communist China*, ed. Choh-ming Li (New York: Frederick A. Praeger, 1964), p. 38.

aspect of the matter deserves the most careful attention). In both cases, the peasants deeply resented the exploitative restrictions of a NEP or NEP-like policy; and they offered strong economic resistance to "socialist" farming. But in the case of China, the economic resistance had a qualitatively different and far more deleterious effect. This happened not because Chinese peasants love freedom more than the Russian and other East European peasants do (all peasants love freedom, as they understand it, just as all slaves, except perhaps the infirm and old, prefer freedom to enslavement), but because China's horticulturelike agriculture proved to be much more vulnerable to the peasants' economic resistance than did Russia's labor-extensive system of farming.

FURTHER PROBLEMS—WIDER VISTAS

The macroanalytic search for big structures and trends immensely benefits the microanalytic search for specific details. It draws attention to features that otherwise may be neglected. It gives them a new significance and evokes new questions.

Mass Resistance to "Socialist" Agrarian Systems
Peasant Frustrations Identified

How frustrated are the peasants under the Communist agrarian system? How did they work on their fields prior to the Communist takeover, and how have they worked on the land since?

Dr. Jasny's remarks on the forbidding difficulties of getting precise Soviet data on these points deserve serious attention. They make it all the more urgent to consult recent rural refugees from such countries as East Germany, Communist China, and North Vietnam concerning their agropolitical experiences. And they stimulate us, late though it is, to consult again some older Soviet refugees who, in addition to having participated in collective farming, still remember how agricultural work was done in pre-Communist days, during the time of War Communism, and under the NEP.

Peasant Resistance Specified

Marx' predictions regarding the behavior of agricultural operators on large farms have not been borne out. But they have led us to reevaluate and recategorize the facts. Most importantly, they have led us to distinguish between open political (and sometimes violent) resistance and (usually camouflaged) economic resistance.

Evidently this latter type of behavior expresses itself in many forms:

careless farming, sabotage, and conspicuous destructive acts. Attempts to estimate mass behavior in the back country (Herman Kahn's "B"-country) of the U.S.S.R. or other Communist areas remain unrealistic if they fail to appraise the B-country's potential for economic and political resistance.

Problems of Incentives

Equally complex and equally important is the problem of incentives under total power. Recent investigations concerned with the policy of incentives in Communist states have quite legitimately asked whether the extension of this policy is permissible from the Communist standpoint, and if so, what institutional changes may result.

The Ideological Aspect

It has been claimed that Marxist doctrine warns Communist regimes against employing incentives as extensively as the Soviet economist Lieberman and certain other economists have recommended. Supposedly such a procedure runs counter to what is considered Marx' equalitarian position. Is this indeed the case? The answer is *No*. The equalitarian thesis was propounded by the pre-Marxist Communist Babeuf whose "coarse" equalitarianism Marx rejected when he himself became a promoter of communism. And while Marx' and Engels' earliest "Marxist" work, *The German Ideology* (which during their lifetime remained unpublished), contains a passage that recommends equal pay for unequal work,[212] Marx sharply rejected such a policy for the "lower" phase of communism in his critique of the Gotha Program of the German Social Democrats in 1875. These statements of 1875—which were first circulated only among a few leaders, but which, since the end of the nineteenth century have been treated as part of Marx' political testament—postulate unequal pay for unequal work for the "lower" phase.[213]

Thus differentiations in work incentives in Communist countries, far from being anti-Marxist, actually accorded with the position of the mature Marx on this point. For the agricultural sector of a Communist-controlled country, such a policy poses serious problems, not because the differentiations in incentives contradict Marx' principles, but because large-scale farming makes it very difficult to apply them effectively.

[212] *MEW*, III, 528.
[213] *Ibid.*, XIX, 20–21.

The Sociohistorical Aspect

Obviously then, there is no doctrinal barrier to the increased employment of incentives. But is there an institutional barrier? Does the self interest of a ruling bureaucracy exclude an incentive policy that increases economic and social differentiations? Again the answer is *No*. Agromanagerial societies of the past have often made such differentiations—so often in fact, that in numerous cases, the original "simple" order was replaced by an economic and societal structure of considerable complexity.[214] And these differentiations, far from breaking up the dominant system of class and power from within, apparently contributed to its self-perpetuation.

The Sociohistorical Present

To be sure, by including in our evaluation of Communist agriculture and society the experience of the bureaucratic-despotic past, we are making only one important preparatory step. The new system is *not* a replica of the old "Asiatic society," as Plekhanov and Lenin thought in 1906 when they passionately discussed the possibility of an "Asiatic restoration" in Russia. Such a restoration, they argued, was bound to occur, if, after the victory of a Russian revolution, Lenin-style, certain protective "guarantees" failed. And after the October Revolution, these guarantees did fail.

But in this case, as in others, a simple equation of the present and the past is not enough. Both Plekhanov and Lenin underrated the institutional potential of a dictatorial bureaucratic regime equipped with the technical and organizational weapons of the twentieth century. They did not recognize that the masters of such a regime could attain far more comprehensive managerial control than did their counterparts under Oriental despotism, and that, going beyond the *semi*managerial conditions of "Asiatic society," they would develop a *total* managerial state and society. Even if and when these new dictatorial regimes tolerate private peasant farming (as happened in the U.S.S.R. under the NEP and in Communist China after the "land reform," and is happening today in Yugoslavia and Poland), they are not modernized replicas of the old order. Due to their managerial control over industry, communication, and the like, and their dictatorial regulation of peasant agriculture, they constitute incipient forms of a new (totalitarian) system of economy and society.[215]

[214] *OD*, pp. 171–72, 419–20, 422 *passim*, 427 ff., 436 ff.
[215] *Ibid.*, pp. 440–41.

The Road Ahead

The Communist order and Oriental despotism have a common denominator: under both systems a functional bureaucracy dominates a single-centered society. But the Communist ruling class exercises a qualitatively new type of power. The modern non-Communist world and its institutional predecessors also have a common denominator: under both systems, multicentered societies are based essentially on private property. But the modern representatives of these societies exhibit qualitatively new institutions. The modern private-property-based order, it appears, is moving toward a partnership capitalism, a condition that John Stuart Mill found desirable, and that Marx ambivalently recognized as an historical possibility.

Today a nihilistic revolution is being directed against the great heritage of ideas and values that is ours. But despite this attack, which is very serious, the great heritage persists. Potentially its appeal is much stronger than the attraction the West had in the nineteenth century for the Orientally despotic world.

Modern non-Communist agriculture has made an impressive record in Western Europe, the United States, Canada, Japan, and Taiwan. It has done so on the basis of private property and initiative and largely within the framework of a family-farm economy. Fully known, this record would intensify the discontent of the collectivized villagers. And this their masters know. Hence they maintain Iron and Bamboo curtains to keep the rural (and urban) toilers in an enduring communication limbo. The members of the Communist upper groups, who know more, are restrained by the very privileges they enjoy. The criticisms that some of them voice may be stimulated in part by conditions abroad, and in several instances this obviously has been the case. But like the officials and literati under Oriental despotism, they focus their complaints on selected details and carefully avoid the underlying basic causes.

Khrushchev told his Western listeners that their grandchildren would live under communism. The spokesmen for communism delight in repeating this thought, but they do not want the tables turned. They do not want us to tell their grandchildren how we see the future. They do not want their peasants to share our perspective of agrarian systems under which those who till the soil will do so under conditions of genuine political and economic responsibility and freedom.

For obvious reasons, these ideas reach the voiceless masses behind the

Iron and Bamboo curtains only with the greatest difficulty. For obvious reasons, too, no similar barriers prevent their spread among men and women in developing countries. Those most directly concerned will not fail to recognize that in the realm of extensive agriculture the American (and European) way is superior to the Soviet way, and that in the realm of intensive agriculture the Japanese (and Taiwanese) way is superior to the Chinese Communist way. It is in these zones that new opportunities unfold for scientific dialogue and practical cooperation. It is in these zones that the unexhausted potential of the non-Communist agrarian systems may, and can, be creatively realized.

R. P. ROCHLIN

Comment[1]

Professor Wittfogel in his excellently elaborated paper analyzes the various aspects of agrarian systems. He points out that Marx and his followers did not sufficiently take into account the peculiarities of farming. They considered the development of agriculture in the same way they considered the development of industry, and asserted that mechanization would revolutionize agricultural production and the future would belong to large agricultural enterprises.

Karl Kautsky admitted in 1899 that peasant farming would also profit by technical progress, but nevertheless he advocated the Marxist view that the "societal development in agriculture is taking the same road as industry."

Lenin, too, subscribed to the Marxist opinion about agriculture and the superiority of the large-scale enterprise, but he was aware that without the expropriation of the estates and their distribution among the peasants, the latter would not support the planned overthrow of the Kerensky Provisional Government in 1917. Therefore, Lenin temporarily adopted the program of the Social-Revolutionary Party that demanded the immediate surrender of the gentry's land to the peasants. In this way, the success of the revolution was secured. Lenin remained a supporter of socialist farming and drove the peasants to revolt by the class war and requisitions in the villages in 1918–20. Surely, the disorganization of the Soviet economy during the Civil War and especially during the Kronstadt uprising forced him in 1921 to announce the New Economic Policy (NEP), which granted to the peasants a relative liberty and safeguarded their property. But even at that time, some large estates were not distributed among the peasants. The government transformed them into state farms, although they could not be operated

[1] This comment treats only the part of Professor Wittfogel's paper that concerns the U.S.S.R.

without subsidies. In the same way, the state patronized the first collective farms of various types that developed after the revolution. In all these cases, the Marxist dogma gained a victory over a rational approach to agriculture. The same point of view prevailed during the brutal collectivization in the early thirties, which progressed without regard to the devastating consequences. Apart from the doctrinal standpoint, three other considerations played an important role in collectivization: agriculture had to bear the main cost of accelerated industrialization; all strata of the population were to be dominated by government, not only economically but also politically; and supplies for the towns were to be secured by the most drastic measures. Kolkhoz managers nominated by the Communist Party were obliged to carry out ruthlessly all governmental orders.

According to Professor Wittfogel, the Communist agrarian system has at least four major goals: (1) Establishment of large enterprises; (2) Government control; (3) Application of modern equipment and advanced agronomical methods; (4) Creation of superior conditions of work and life befitting a socialist society for the agricultural operators.

In the Soviet Union, only the first two goals were reached. The third is still a long way off, and the fourth belongs to the permanent wishful thinking of all Soviet leaders during the past fifty years. Only the existence of private plots enabled many peasants to outlive the dreadful misery of the first two decades of collectivization.

Professor Wittfogel calls labor the Achilles' heel of the Soviet agrarian system.[2] In fact, the productivity of labor in the agriculture of the U.S.S.R. is very low compared with that of labor in the United States, Western Europe, or Japan. No technical innovation or modern agronomical methods can replace the human factor, i.e., the personal interest of the peasant in his work. Certainly, there is no doctrinal barrier to material incentives. In 1878, Marx rejected equal pay for unequal work for the lower phase of communism, but Professor Wittfogel regards an institutional barrier as vital. It is his opinion that bureaucracy will never renounce its privileges, because the existence of this class is the core of the Oriental despotic order. Even a greater differentiation of material incentives and an increased social mobility cannot change "the Oriental agromanagerial despotism."

The assertions of Professor Wittfogel concerning Russia call for some

---

[2] Four other weak points of Soviet agriculture are: the complicated and expensive bureaucratic management; the poor rentability of numerous farms; the lowest living standard in the U.S.S.R.; and, finally, the price policy of the government.

comments. It is possible to speak about tsarist despotism, but it was an autocracy *sui generis,* a specifically Russian phenomenon, and had nothing in common with Oriental despotic rule. The Mongol conquerors (between the thirteenth and fifteenth centuries) actually occupied the country a comparatively short time, and were interested only in receiving tributes, extracted, if necessary, by punitive expeditions and pillage. They isolated Russia from western neighbors and skillfully supported the policy of *divide et impera* in their relations with the Russian feudal princes. But the habits and character of the Russian people, the language, and—what was essential at that time—the Christian faith remained untouched.

On the contrary, the influence of Western Europe was constantly growing during the last three centuries. The modernization of Muscovy that began early in the eighteenth century with the adoption of European military and educational systems continued in the Age of Enlightenment with the dissemination of French language and culture. Thus, Western civilization was brought to a great part of Russian nobility. In the nineteenth century, German philosophy found many ardent adherents among Russian intellectuals. It is very important to realize that the formation of the famous Russian intelligentsia, which aspired to independent thinking and critical, mostly passionate, judgment of all human problems, fell in the reign of the reactionary Tsar Nicholas I (1825–55). After his death, the pluralistic development of Russian society continued in spite of some setbacks. It ended in the years 1905–17 with the introduction of parliamentary rule that was, of course, very restricted, but represented great progress in comparison with the type of government existing in former times. Industrial production, too, increased quickly according to the West European technical pattern. And the successful Bolshevik Revolution signified the victory of Marxism, which also came from Europe.

Surely, the total character of the Soviet government prevented freedom of thought with more effect than Tsar Nicholas I ever had. But the most cruel period of Soviet tyranny, the Stalin era, lasted twenty-five years, historically a short space of time. The changes after Stalin's death had little to do with real liberalization, but the end of the bloody terror, easier communication with the free world, and many economic improvements created a more conciliatory atmosphere. A comeback of Stalin's rule is at present improbable, despite some attempts of the Soviet oligarchy to rehabilitate the dead dictator in some respects.

Also, the thesis of Professor Wittfogel that bureaucracy in an Oriental despotism will never abandon its privileges is not valid in Russian history. Many enemies of the ancient regime were members of the aristocracy. Nor did the internal opposition within the Communist Party against the total system ever cease in Soviet history. The public unmasking of Stalin's crimes was, among other things, the revolt against the domination of one man and his arbitrary rule. In this way, the Communist police state was discredited, although dictatorship by a single party has remained.

The Soviet agrarian system, too, experienced considerable change after Stalin's death. It is known that two opposite forces are at work in Soviet agriculture: the Leninist-Marxist ideology and the necessity to secure, in some way, efficiency in farming. Since 1953, the latter has predominated, but not without some reverses. Collectivized agriculture and large-scale farming are here to stay, but critics of the bureaucratic management find a broad place in the Soviet press and literature. Not only the low efficiency of farming, but also the rising discontent of peasants with their living standard have forced the Soviet government to make many concessions during the last fourteen years. The most important of these are: a substantial increase in state prices for compulsory deliveries of agricultural products; selling of machine tractor stations to the kolkhozy; pensions, since 1965, for kolkhoz peasants; and higher investments for agriculture. Despite its reluctance, the government is compelled to consider the demands of the peasantry, not only concerning its material situation, but also in respect of its personal rights. Self assurance and education of the peasants have now reached a much higher level than during the collectivization in the thirties. The lessening of bureaucratic pressure on the kolkhozy since 1955 remains, of course, largely nominal, but the passive resistance of peasants against intervention and abuse by official machinery has augmented in recent years. It proves that the allegedly unchanged sacrosanct privileges of the bureaucracy are in a state of flux.

These criticisms concerning Oriental despotism in Russia diminish in no way the high value of Professor Wittfogel's paper. His analysis of the Marxist-Leninist agrarian doctrine can be called classic.

In his conclusions, Professor Wittfogel envisages an agrarian system where "those who till the soil will do so under conditions of genuine political and economic responsibility and freedom." As long as the Soviet government is determined to command and to control the whole economy of the country, such a solution will be impossible.

WERNER KLATT

Comment

Professor Wittfogel has not only made a major contribution to the proceedings of this conference, but he has in fact provided the framework within which the discussion should take place. I find myself so much in agreement with the basic theses of Professor Wittfogel's paper that my contribution to the discussion will be supplementing rather than contradicting what he has said.

A great many misunderstandings about the role of agriculture in modern society are due to the misrepresentations of the Marxist school whose thoughts have to be studied critically if current Communist agricultural policies are to be understood. A critical review of Marxist agrarian thought can only be effective, however, if it avoids the pitfalls of such utopian and romantic concepts as Populism and Agrarianism, which were in vogue in some countries of Eastern Europe during the transitional period from agrarian to industrial society. They have not provided a viable alternative to Marxist agrarian thought.

As Professor Wittfogel has shown, the Marxist school never understood the position of agriculture as one of several forms of human activity. Unlike industry, agriculture is tied to the land as one of its principal factors and, unlike industry, its operation is decisively affected by natural conditions. Space, distance, and seasonality are essential elements in the process of farm production; or, as Professor Wittfogel puts it "agricultural production is intermittent in time and dispersed in space."

If one were to define in one sentence the meaning of farming as a form of human endeavor, it could be described as man's attempt to reduce, if not to abolish, the limitations set by nature to his effort to grow plants and animals to meet his needs. Excess water is removed by drainage; lack of water is made good by means of irrigation; lack of plant nutrients is made up for by the application of industrial fertilizers. Where land is abundant, man employs capital to overcome distances with the aid of tractors and other machines moving faster than man and beast. Where human labor is plentiful but land is scarce, man intensifies the use of labor and capital and exploits the soil in depth. It is the degree of intensity that matters and not the acreage, and any economies of scale have to be seen within this context.

As Professor Wittfogel rightly observes, a given natural foundation does not necessarily lead to a single type of human action. In other words, the term *agriculture* covers a multitude of different forms of human endeavor, which have often little in common except the use of land— a commodity that is not always available in unlimited quantity and which therefore fetches a price determined by its scarcity value. The absence of a rental charge in Communist-controlled countries has caused untold harm to agricultural performance.

Marxists have always tended to treat farming as if it were a single uniform mode of human occupation—notwithstanding the fact that extensive grain or wool production in Australia, for example, is completely different from intensive vegetable, meat, or dairy production in Holland or Denmark. The global theoretical treatment by Marxist dogma has had its practical counterpart in Khrushchev's nationwide blanket policies of producing maize or plowing up grassland from Wilno in Lithuania to Vladivostok in the Far East.

From Marx to Mao, the seasonal nature of farming has not been understood by the Marxist school. This lack of understanding has played them some nasty tricks. For instance, labor surplus and labor shortage have always existed side by side in the rural areas of China, both in time and space. The withdrawal of labor, which was supposedly abundant, during the harvest of 1958 was probably the most important factor that contributed to the failure of the Great Leap Forward in Chinese agriculture.

The pattern of farming is affected by many factors, of which the natural and economic aspects are merely those that have been studied longest. But cultural and institutional factors can create important variants under otherwise identical conditions. To give one example: The fact that in pre-Communist China the second crop was not subject to a rental levy has probably contributed more to the development of intensive cultivation, i.e., double cropping, than the orderly supply of irrigation water throughout the season. In any event, the two developments have been interdependent.

Where land and labor are the only resources available, the pattern of farming is largely determined by the man/land ratio. As man learns to apply capital, the function of the land changes dramatically. The metal plow turns farming from a two-dimensional into a three-dimensional operation and thus mobilizes plant nutrients formerly untapped. Eventually, as in hydroponics and on battery poultry farms, the soil changes from a major factor of production to a rather insignificant incidental, as in the erection of a factory—or it ceases to be needed altogether.

Whatever the ratio of man to land and whatever therefore the degree of intensity of farming, most of it takes place in the form of individual family businesses. The hunter's family may need to exploit several hundred hectares—seemingly a "large" estate—to eke out a modest existence. The intensive family farm on which spring onions or broiler chicken are produced can yield a comfortable income from a fraction of one hectare. The same is true of intensive double cropping by owner/occupier/cultivators in Japan or Taiwan.

Observations of this kind could have been made and were in fact made in the days of Marx and Engels. But being urban intellectuals, who knew what little they knew about farming from Britain after the era of the enclosures, they drew utterly wrong conclusions. Having rejected the peasants as economically backward and politically reactionary, they found themselves in a predicament from which their followers have been unable to extricate themselves. Hence the dichotomy of the Communist farm policy that tries, in the revolutionary phase, to gain the support of the peasants and cultivators by breaking up existing estates, only to amalgamate them in collectives and communes when the immediate need for the support of the farming community has passed.

In this connection I should have liked to have seen more in Professor Wittfogel's address about the essential aspects of the fierce controversy that raged at the end of the last century between Kautsky, who at that time stuck to the dogma, and David, who was much impressed by current census data that seemed to reveal an unexpected resilience in the farming family in face of serious agricultural difficulties.

Similarly a word of appraisal might have been paid to Otto Bauer, the Austro-Marxist, who in his little-known book on the role of forests and pastures in Austrian agrarian history came nearer to discovering the fallacy of Marxist agrarian concepts than any of his predecessors or contemporaries. Yet, in his political conclusions, which he drew from his realistic analysis, he pleaded for a favorable treatment of the peasants in the phase of the political struggle for power, but he saw the ultimate form of farming no differently from the traditionalists of the Marxist school.

The Marxist school has never understood that the size of the farm is a function of the ratio between man (and his technical tools) to land. Mistakenly they have always measured farm sizes by the acreage, instead of using the yardsticks they rightly employed when analyzing the nonagricultural activities of capitalist society. The contention of some contemporary Marxists that the concentration of land in large units was necessary in order to obtain grain and labor for the nonfarm sectors of the modernizing Soviet society amounts to a rationalization after the event. Japan industrialized while retaining small-scale farming, and Taiwan and Thailand are following this pattern.

In conclusion, one cannot but agree with Professor Wittfogel's observation that the Communist agrarian system has no parallel among the major civilizations known throughout history. In fact, while the Communist solutions of the problems of industrialization are not diametrically opposed to the way things are done in capitalist, industrial society, the Communist agrarian concept flies in the face of all historical precedent. Whether it can be abandoned at this late stage in Communist history seems doubtful. If ever it is abandoned, it will probably be the beginning of the end of communism as it has been known for the last fifty years.

ALEC NOVE

The Decision to Collectivize*

This paper deals first with the stages by which the decision to collectivize was reached, and secondly with the stages of its implementation.

It had not escaped the notice of Stalin that the ambitious industrial investment plans and the existing structure of peasant agriculture were inconsistent with one another. In his speech to the Fifteenth Party Congress (December, 1927), he spoke about the relatively slow rate of development of agriculture, advanced familiar reasons to explain this backwardness, and then said:

> What is the way out? The way out is to turn the small and scattered peasant farms into large united farms based on cultivation of the land in common, to go over to collective cultivation of the land on the basis of a new and higher technique. The way out is to unite the small and dwarf peasant farms gradually but surely, not by pressure but by example and persuasion, into large farms based on common, cooperative, collective cultivation of the land. . . . There is no other way out.[1]

In the resolution adopted by the Fifteenth Congress one finds the following words: "At the present time, the task of uniting and transforming the small individual peasant holdings into large collectives must become the principal task of the party in the village." Yet this was not understood to mean the imminence of a revolution from above. The general desirability of collective agriculture was not in dispute. If it was to be done voluntarily and by example, there was no danger of anything particularly drastic happening quickly.

Undoubtedly what brought matters to a head was the problem of

---

* The text of this paper has to a great extent been extracted from a larger work, *Economic History of the U.S.S.R.*, currently in progress.
[1] J. V. Stalin, *Works* (Moscow-London, 1952–) X, 312.

marketings and, in particular, of state procurements. Every year the leaders watched anxiously as deliveries mounted in the autumn and winter, wondering if there would be enough to feed the towns and the army and, who knows, something for export, too. Attention was particularly concentrated on grain, the key crop since bread was the staff of life in Russia.

Difficulties accumulated after 1926. The most important causes were directly related to the government's price policy, to which must be attributed a major part of the responsibility for the crisis in the relations with the peasants. Indeed, one can now see that in 1926 the government took several measures inherently inconsistent with the principles of the New Economic Policy (NEP). It is from 1926 that measures began to be taken to penalize private trade. In the same year, the policy of imposing price cuts on the products of state industry led to an increasing "goods famine," and with it a rapidly growing disparity between official and free market prices. The intention behind this price policy may have been to improve the terms of trade to the peasants, but instead the effect was quite different, since the peasants found the cheaper goods to be unobtainable. Last, but very far from least, the government in 1926 reduced state procurement prices of grain by as much as 20–25 per cent. This naturally discouraged marketings. The peasants tried to sell grain to the still surviving private traders rather than to the state procurement agencies, or to hold grain in expectation of higher prices, or to feed it to livestock. As Stalin subsequently pointed out, the better-off peasants were able to maneuver more effectively than their poorer neighbors to take advantage of any possibility of obtaining better terms. The government reacted by measures against Nepmen, by streamlining the state procurement apparatus to avoid a situation in which different procurement agencies bid against one another, and also by measures against kulaks, who were held responsible for the shortages. Thus the resolution of the Fifteenth Congress instructed the Central Committee to devise higher and more progressive taxes on the better-off peasants. The tone of party pronouncements on the kulak question became sharper. The idea of liquidating them as a class was not yet born, or at least not yet mentioned. However, they were to be limited, penalized, and generally discouraged. This was a policy hardly designed to encourage the more ambitious peasants to expand production or investment.

As already mentioned, the Fifteenth Congress advocated the spread of collectivization. Of the various kinds of agricultural producers' associations, the most promising seemed to be the loosest, the TOZ (Association for the Joint Cultivation of the Land). In these associations the members retained ownership of their tools and implements, most of their livestock, and even of their land. They simply carried out some of the farm work jointly. The more advanced forms of producers' cooperation that then existed were thought to be unattractive to the peasants, and, for instance, in the decree of March 16, 1927, it was laid down that the TOZ was to be favored. However, in 1927 all the various types of collectives and cooperatives accounted for but a tiny proportion of agricultural production and peasants, and the few and inefficient state farms made little difference to the general picture.

There were still no grounds to suppose that a storm would break over the heads of the entire peasantry. But the storm clouds were gathering; the procurement difficulties of 1927 led to the first flash of lightning. Procurements had been apparently going more or less according to plan until December of that year. Then there was trouble. It became abundantly clear that procurement would be well below the previous year's level, insufficient to meet the needs of the towns and the army. The shortfall in grain procurements may be seen from the fact that by January, 1928, the state had succeeded in purchasing only 300 million poods, as against 428 million on the same date in the previous year. The shortfall was particularly great in Siberia, the Volga, and the Urals, where the harvest was reasonably good (bad weather was the cause of difficulties in the North Caucasus).[2] The effect was not only to create acute problems in supplying the cities with bread, but also to threaten supplies of industrial crops. Thus the maintenance of the cotton acreage in Uzbekistan was threatened by grain shortage there. Archive materials show a flow of complaints about this from local party organizations to the Central Committee.[3] Some of the reasons for this critical situation have already been given: the low price of grain, shortage of manufactured goods, the gap between official and free prices.

With grain procurement prices so low, peasants concentrated on other commodities. For example, in the Urals, grain sales to the state were only 63 per cent of the previous year, but meat sales increased by 50 per cent, while sales of eggs doubled, bacon quadrupled, and eleven times as much bacon fat was delivered as in the previous year.[4] Nat-

[2] Detailed figures by regions may be found in I. A. Koniukhov, *KPSS v borbe s khlebnymi zatrudineniiami v strane*, pp. 64–65.

[3] *Ibid.*, p. 66.

[4] *Ibid.*, p. 68.

urally the peasants waited for the rise in official grain prices, the necessity for which seemed quite obvious. However, Stalin and his colleagues drew very different conclusions. Ignoring the proposals of Bukharin and others to increase grain prices, Stalin decided instead to launch a direct attack, which revived memories of the excesses of War Communism. There had been a good harvest in the Urals and West Siberia. There went Stalin with a task force of officials and police. Free markets were closed, private traders thrown out, peasants ordered to deliver grain and punished as criminals for failing to do so. Stalin made speeches, which were not published until twenty years later, denouncing laggard officials, requiring them to seize kulak grain, demanding that they invoke a hitherto unused article of the criminal code (Art. 107) against speculation, to legalize the seizures. He mocked the "prosecuting and judicial authorities [who] are not prepared for such a step." He used extreme language to the party officials, who were slow to understand that a basic change of attitude was expected of them:

Can it be that you are afraid to disturb the tranquillity of the kulak gentry? You say that enforcement of Article 107 against the kulaks would be an emergency measure, that it would not be productive of good results, that it would worsen the relations in the countryside. Suppose it would be an emergency measure. What of it? . . . As for your prosecuting and judicial officials, they should be dismissed. . . .[5]

At the same time, scarce industrial goods were directed to the grain-surplus regions.

Rumors spread that the government "will pay all foreign debts with grain and is, therefore, reinstating *prodrazverstka,* taking all grain away." Reporting this and citing contemporary archives, a Soviet writer gave the following typical instance: "In the village of Pankrushino the kulaks spread the rumor that all grain is being collected in one vast storehouse in the town of Kamensk, that the peasants will be put on a bread ration, that armed detachments are scouring the villages for bread and that they will soon arrive here."[6] The same source cites numerous reports in newspapers about alleged kulak opposition, though it seems more than probable that what was being reported was simply the strength of peasant reaction to the seizure of their produce.

The kulaks undertook large-scale agitation, asserting that Soviet power impoverishes the peasant, does not allow him to improve his income, that

[5] Stalin, *Works,* XI, 5, 6.

[6] Koniukhov, *KPSS v borbe* . . . , p. 72.

NEP is being abolished. Kulaks, priests, former white-guardists endeavored to utilize in their counterrevolutionary agitation certain cases of distortion [*sic*] of the Party line in credit and tax policy. . . . In the village of Troitsk in the Don area there was unmasked a priest who hid grain and organized in the cemetery a kulak meeting, where he made a report on "grain procurements and the international situation."[7]

The same Soviet source admits that there were indeed grounds for agitation.

Not infrequently measures were taken that hit not only the kulaks but the middle peasant. Such measures were: the confiscation of grain surpluses without the judgment of a court under Article 107, administrative pressure on the middle peasant, the use of barrier detachments, forcible issuing of bond certificates in payment for grain and as a condition for the sale of scarce commodities to the peasants, and so on.[8]

Indeed, arbitrary confiscation was a common phenomenon, and on a strict interpretation of Article 107 the authorities could choose to regard the mere possession of grain stocks as illegal hoarding with a speculative purpose and, therefore, a fit subject for confiscation without payment. Newspapers of the time were full of reports about evil kulak hoarders of grain, and also of reports concerning peasant meetings in which the delivery of grain to the state was extolled and the kulaks condemned. Such reports must be taken with a grain of salt. Thus the very same source that referred to the payments of peasants with bond certificates instead of money, and referred to it as an impermissible excess, cites approvingly an alleged spontaneous decision by peasants "to refuse to accept money and to request payment in bonds for the entire amount of delivered grain," and a resolution worded thus: "Not a single pound to the private speculator."[9]

Stalin himself concentrated on West Siberia and the Urals, and other senior officials pursued the procurement campaign in other areas: for example, Zhdanov in the Volga region, Kossior in the Ukraine and the Urals, Andreev in the North Caucasus. The chief coordinator of the entire operation was said to have been Mikoyan.[10] All the above were devoted members of the Stalin faction.

These arbitrary procedures became known—and Stalin so described them himself—as the "Urals-Siberian method." In retrospect this must

[7] *Ibid.*, p. 78.
[8] *Ibid.*, p. 128.
[9] *Ibid.*, pp. 146–47.
[10] *Ibid.*, p. 119.

be regarded as a great turning point in Russian history. It upset once and for all the delicate psychological balance upon which the relations between party and peasants rested, and it was also the first time that a major policy departure was undertaken by Stalin personally, without even the pretense of consultation with his "comrades."

Bukharin, Rykov, and Tomsky, three of the Politburo of the party, protested vehemently. In April, 1928, at the plenum of the Central Committee, Stalin beat an apparent retreat, and accepted a resolution condemning excesses, reasserting legality, and promising that nothing similar would be repeated. But events showed that Stalin's compliance was a mere maneuver. Forcible procurements were repeated in many areas in 1928–29. Stalin soon made it clear that the "Urals-Siberian method" would be used whenever necessary. Yet surely it was obvious that peasants would not increase marketed production if the state would seize the produce at whatever price it chose to pay and imprison anyone who concealed grain. The outbreak of argument among the leaders was carefully concealed from the public, and from the party membership at large. It only became known later that Bukharin, at last realizing what his erstwhile ally was up to, began to speak of Genghis Khan, of "military-feudal exploitation" of the peasantry, of "tribute" (*dan*) levied on the village. In the already suffocating political atmosphere, he was unable to voice his real fears in public. These concerned most of all the consequence of the coming clash with the peasants.

Stalin and his faction did not yet show any sign that they had decided on an all-out collectivization campaign. Indeed, there is no evidence at all that such a decision was taken until the early autumn of 1929, and the Soviet public first heard of it on November 7, 1929. Some may consider that Stalin had a secret plan all ready for the propitious moment, but this seems unlikely. What he clearly wished to do after the "Urals-Siberian" episode of February, 1928, was to free the regime from overdependence on the peasantry. This view he expressed already during his Urals-Siberian tour: "In order to put grain procurements on a satisfactory basis other measures are required. . . . I have in mind developing the formation of collective farms and state farms."[11] An immediate consequence to this was the decision in April, 1928, to set up a "grain trust" (*Zernotrest*), aiming to create new state farms covering fourteen million hectares (thirty-six million acres). However, this was still not to be regarded as a step toward more collectivization, since these farms were to be set up on unused land. No land was to be expro-

[11] Stalin, *Works*, XI, 7. Note that this was not published until 1949.

priated or no one forced. Consequently this decision was not a challenge to Bukharin and his friends, and may even have been accepted by them. It proved unworkable and insufficient.

The July, 1928, plenum of the Central Committee was still, so far as its official statements were concerned, dominated by the need to reassure the peasants (or to keep the Bukharin group quiet). True, the resolution spoke of "voluntary union of peasants into collectives on the basis of new technique," but no one could object to this, the more so as the absence of new technique was a principal argument of the "go-slow" school. The resolution admitted that low grain prices contributed to existing difficulties and resolved to increase them, but this was a case of much too little and too late. The resolution also spoke of "the further raising of the level of small and medium-size individual (peasant) economies." So *at the time* there seemed to be a return to moderation. But here again the historian faces the difficulty that some key policy statements were made only behind closed doors. If they were included in a chronological account, the surprise and shock that greeted subsequent announcements of policy changes would be incomprehensible. At the same July plenum, Stalin admitted the need for "tribute" from the peasants, admitted that the peasants do and must overpay for manufactures and are underpaid for farm produce. This follows from the need to "industrialize the country with the help of *internal* accumulations."[12] In other words, Preobrazhensky (and Trotsky) were right all along. But this speech too was published in 1949, and when it was made Trotsky was in Alma Ata under effective house arrest, while Preobrazhensky had been deported. If anyone chose to remind Stalin of the source of his ideas, this was omitted from the belatedly published record.

In a public speech after the July plenum, Stalin took up an apparently moderate position: "We need neither detractors nor eulogizers of individual peasant farming," but he did urge once again the gradual development of collective and state farms. His tone sharpened in his first *public* attack on "right wing deviationists" (naming, as yet, no names) on October 19, 1928, and at the November, 1928, plenum of the Central Committee one heard more of industry held back by a backward agriculture, of the encouragement of collective and state farms, measures to limit the kulaks. Silently, in the winter, the "Urals-Siberian method" was reapplied to the peasants, and under cover of antikulak measures the "method" once again hit the middle peasants hard, since, after all, most of the grain came from them. Stalin attacked

[12] *Ibid.*, p. 166.

Bukharin vigorously in the April, 1929, plenum of the Central Committee, but most of his words remained unpublished at the time.

Confusion over peasant policies in the public mind was heightened by the resolution of this plenum, when the word "tribute," accepted by Stalin in the previous year in an *unpublished* speech, was treated as a slanderous and lying accusation directed at Stalin by Bukharin, now openly attacked. It was admitted that peasants do overpay for some industrial goods, but this would be speedily put right.

The Sixteenth Party Congress, meeting in April, 1929, approved the "optimal" version of the Five-Year Plan. This included a section on agriculture. There was to be a marked advance in collectivization, but by the end of the Five-Year Plan it was hoped to have twenty-six million hectares cultivated by state and all kinds of collectives (including TOZY); these would provide over 15 per cent of total agricultural output. It was not at all clear by what means this expansion in agricultural collectivization was to be achieved. However, given five years and the necessary resources, it was not an unrealistic perspective. While in the years 1921–27 there had been no move by the peasants toward any type of collective farming, this could be blamed on the lack of inducement, indeed on the neglect of the few collectives that did exist. Such a program, if carried out, would have still left the vast majority of the Soviet peasantry in the private sector, producing the bulk of every crop and owning most of the livestock.

Now that Bukharin was at last openly denounced as a right-wing deviationist (he was not expelled from the Politburo until November, 1929), Stalin must have felt free to launch the campaign that was maturing in his mind. Yet by not a word or gesture did he prepare the party, the people, or the peasants for the great turn, the "revolution from above," that was to shake Russia to its foundations. In fact even so late as June 27, 1929, a decree on agricultural marketing cooperation still assumed the predominance of the private sector in agriculture for an indefinite period, and we shall see that it was not until the campaign had begun that there was an amendment of the plan to achieve a mere 15 per cent collectivization by 1933.

No document exists that can tell us exactly when Stalin made up his mind. During 1929 the strains and stresses of the investment program of the Five-Year Plan began to affect all sectors of the economy. Rationing for consumers in cities was introduced gradually during 1928 in some areas and became general early in 1929, perhaps the first and only recorded instance of the *introduction* of rationing in time of peace. The goods famine increased in intensity. The gap between free and official prices widened, as Table 1 demonstrates.

TABLE 1
FREE AND OFFICIAL PRICES, 1926—1929
(1913=100)

	Private Sector		Official Sector	
	Food	Manufactured Goods	Food	Manufactured Goods
1926 (Dec.)	198	251	181	208
1927 (Dec.)	222	240	175	188
1928 (Dec.)	293	253	184	190
1929 (Dec.)	450	279	200	192

Source: A. N. Malafeev, *Istoriia tsenoobrazovaniia v SSSR, 1917–1963* (Moscow, 1964) pp. 384, 385.

By 1930 the difference increased very rapidly.

Voices from the "right" urged slowdown, higher farm prices, a modification of the investment program. Rykov proposed a "Two-Year Plan," with emphasis on agriculture. Grain procurement prices were in fact raised, far too late, in 1929, by 14 to 19 per cent,[13] but the market situation was such that private traders were buying in that year at prices that rose by over 100 per cent. In the Ukraine, for instance, private traders were buying at prices 170 per cent above state procurement prices.[14] However, there were a number of arguments for an all-out drive forward. In the first plan, it must have already seemed impossible to continue on the basis of a combination of private agriculture and periodic coercion. Secondly, Stalin's faction wanted to prove the "right" to be wrong, and would benefit from stealing the clothes of the "left" opposition now that it had been defeated and its leader, Trotsky, exiled. Thirdly, many party activists had all along hated NEP and were willing to throw their energy and enthusiasm into the great tasks of "socialist construction."

So the decision was taken: force the tempo of industrial construction up still further, and launch the campaign to collectivize the peasantry, and this meant the majority of the peasantry, not 15 per cent, and immediately, not by 1933. The relevant data are examined in the next pages.

Why then did the "great turn" happen? Why the revolution from above, why collectivization? Much ink has been expended in discus-

[13] The lower figure is given in the Five-Year Plan document, II, 30.
[14] A. N. Malafeev, *Istoriia tsenoobrazovaniia v SSSR, 1917–1963* (Moscow, 1964), p. 119.

ing these questions. The following factors were of evident importance:

1. The desire of many party members, and notably Stalin himself, to eliminate an individual peasantry that, as Lenin had said and Stalin repeated, "produces capitalists from its midst, and cannot help producing them, constantly and continuously."[15] True, Lenin advised caution, persuasion, example. True, the brutal methods that will be described later were quite unjustified by doctrine and ideology, a fact that explains the secrecy and plain lies that were characteristic of the entire operation. But what if adherence to the voluntary principle meant the indefinite dominance of individualist agriculture?

2. The problem of industrial development, with priority of heavy industry, and the linked issues of capital accumulation and farm surpluses. Stalin did not deny that there was an alternative road, that of "making agriculture large scale by implanting capitalism in agriculture." He rejected this as he rejected the kulaks.[16] He left himself little choice thereafter (after all, even kulaks were very modest farmers by Western standards).

3. The price policies, in industry and agriculture, which developed in 1926 and were obstinately continued, would *of themselves* have destroyed NEP, even if no other complications ensued.

4. The political atmosphere, the prejudices against the market and Nepmen generally, the rise of monolithism and of Stalin, the "leap-forward" psychology. Fears of internal class enemies, and also of the hostile external environment, affected both the social policies of the regime and the degree of priority accorded to heavy industry, as the basis of military capacity.

Years later, a Menshevik wrote of Stalin's methods as "primitive Socialist accumulation by the methods of Tamerlane." He added "The financial basis of the first Five-Year Plan, until Stalin found it in levying tribute on the peasants, was extremely precarious . . . [it seemed that] everything would go to the devil. . . ."[17] All this in no way justified what actually occurred. It did occur, and it was not an accident or a consequence of private whims. To understand is not to forgive. It is simply better than the alternative, which is not to understand.

On June 11, 1929, the total number of peasant members of collectives of all kinds was barely one million, and of these 60 per cent were in the TOZ (loose) type of producers' cooperatives. By October 1 the

---

[15] Stalin, *Works*, XII, 43.
[16] *Ibid.*, p. 152.
[17] N. Valentinov, *Sotsialisticheskii vestnik* (New York), April, 1961.

number had risen to 1.9 million (62 per cent TOZ).[18] It was this increase that gave Stalin the basis for his statement, in his famous article of November 7, 1929, that "the middle peasant is joining collectives" and that the great turn was under way. That these figures were due at least in part to illegitimate pressures is now admitted by Soviet historians, who also now deny that the peasants were in process of "going collective" en masse.[19] It seems that, silently and secretly, Stalin and his friends ordered local officials in a few selected areas to try out mass collectivization by whatever means were handy. When the result showed that victory was possible, Stalin, with Molotov and Kaganovich as his closest associates in the matter, decided to launch the collectivization campaign, using for the purpose the activists already mobilized to enforce grain collection by the well-tried "Urals-Siberian method." This, at least, is the reasonable conclusion of M. Lewin, in his admirable study of these events. Readers may be confidently referred to his book for details.[20]

No doubt the final defeat of the Right opposition facilitated the opening of the offensive. This, indeed, is a point specifically made by one of the ablest recent Soviet analysts of the period, Moshkov: "The condemnation of the Rightists enabled the central committee to operate more consistently the line of the offensive against the kulaks. . . ." And not only the anti-kulak policy was affected. Moshkov refers also to instructions of the central committee to party organs in selected grain regions, issued in August, 1929, urging them to reach high collectivization percentages in that very year. "In party circles the view was hardening to the effect that only by collectivization can the problem of grain production be solved." Moshkov laid considerable stress on the effect on the peasants of the "new system of procurements," which he identifies as having been enforced by the decrees of June 28, 1929 (R.S.F.S.R.) and July 3, 1929 (Ukraine). These have not, as a rule, been noted as important by other analysts, and yet Moshkov treats them as in effect signaling the end of NEP in the village.[21]

There is much evidence to support this point of view. Until this date, the forcible collections of grain, which had begun early in 1928, were officially described and viewed as emergency measures. However, these

---

[18] N. Ivnitskii, in *Voprosy istorii KPSS*, No. 4, 1962, p. 56.

[19] For example, see M. Vyltsan *et al.*, *Voprosy istorii*, No. 3, 1965, p. 5.

[20] Moshe Lewin, *La Paysannerie et le pouvoir Sovietique* (Paris: Mouton, 1966) and English translation (London: Allen & Unwin, 1968).

[21] Iu. A. Moshkov, *Zernovaia problema v gody sploshnoi kollektivizatsii* (Moscow University, 1966), pp. 56, 59, 63–66.

decrees provided for the imposition of procurement plans on particular areas by the government, and also empowered the authorities to fine (and in some cases, imprison) recalcitrant householders who failed to deliver the quantities specified by the delivery plan as it affected them, and to sell their property if need be. This power, it is true, was to be exercised by local soviets, which were obliged to call a general meeting. However, whole villages were now receiving procurement quotas, and were encouraged to place the maximum burden on the kulak or other prosperous elements. But all were doomed indefinitely to deliver grain surpluses to the state at low prices. Moshkov very properly makes two further comments. Firstly, this decree, as applied by the government, served as the judicial foundation of the first wave of "dekulakization," which, as we shall note, had begun already in the second half of 1929, without any declaration or decree specifically to that effect. That is to say, in selected grain-growing areas the kulaks were deliberately overassessed for grain deliveries and their property was then expropriated when they failed to obey.

Secondly, and more fundamentally, further great changes were bound to follow, since "as the experience of the civil war showed, the [imposed] planned delivery of grain to the state at prices that were unfavorable to the peasants inevitably led to the reduction in production of grain to subsistence level."[22] In other words, the peasants in general (not just the kulaks) were bound to reduce sowings, once the fundamental basis of NEP was subverted. This method of procurement was successful, at least in the short run. The breakdown of the total procurement plan by regions, the mobilization of party personnel, led to a 49 per cent increase in state procurements of grain over the previous year. This could well have increased Stalin's confidence in the effectiveness of political pressure in general, and so "procurements went parallel with the process of the wholesale collectivization of whole regions . . . and was closely linked with it."[23] There is much in favor of such an interpretation of events.

Be this as it may, after Stalin's article on the "great turn," published on November 7, 1929, a plenum of the central committee was held on November 10 to 17. It decided that there existed "a move of the broadest mass of poor and middle peasant households toward collective forms of agriculture," which was described as "spontaneous" (*stikhiinaia*). Given that no such spontaneous move existed in nature, while the

[22] *Ibid.*, p. 65.
[23] *Ibid.*, p. 69.

entire campaign was conducted on the mythical supposition that it did, and given also that there was no kind of inquiry or prior warning, the events that followed were both confused and, above all, ill planned. There is not the slightest evidence that there had been a party or state subcommittee engaged in assessing how best to change the way of life of most of the population of a vast country. Since in fact it was to be decided that the loose TOZ was not "collective" enough, that the artel with its more advanced degree of collectivism was to be preferred, it is truly extraordinary that nothing was done before December to clarify what kind of artel was intended, for there were many variants: some paid members "by eaters" (*po edokam,* i.e., in relation to mouths to food), some, in a rough proportion to work done, some, in accordance with the land and implements contributed; in some farms a good deal of livestock was collectivized, in others not. Indeed the party cadres were not too clear whether the full-fledged commune, with total collectivization, was not in the minds of the leaders. We shall see that these confusions had considerable influence on events.

As a Soviet writer on this theme has pointed out, "excesses . . . were due in part to the fact that there was no clear explanation of the nature of the methods and forms of wholesale collectivization, or of the criteria for its completion. . . . Many officials interpreted it . . . as the immediate incorporation of all toiling peasants in kolkhozy." "Stalin and his closer co-workers did not consider it essential to discuss the party's new policy in the villages in a broad party forum, such as a congress or conference." If proper discussion had taken place, many mistakes would have been avoided, asserted another writer.[24]

An all-union collective-farm center (*Kolkhoztsentr*) was created, and also an all-union *Narkomzem* (People's Commissariat of Agriculture), under Iakovlev. The same Iakovlev headed a special Politburo committee set up on December 8, 1929, a month *after* Stalin announced the great turn, to discuss how to collectivize. It sprouted a whole number of subcommittees, among them one on "tempos," another on the organizational structure of collectives, yet another on kulaks, and so on. On December 16 and 17 they met to argue various proposals. On December 22 the commission presented proposals to the Politburo, which became the basis of a decree passed on January 5, 1930. It might be proper to conclude that it had no time to consider the colossally com-

[24] M. L. Bogdenko, "Kolkhoznoe stroitelstvo vesnoi i letom 1930 goda," *Istoricheskie zapiski,* No. 76, p. 20 and S. Trapeznikov, *Istoricheskii opyt KPSS* (Moscow, 1959), p. 175.

plex issues involved. Ahead of any report, orders were already going out to the localities, urging instant action. Thus a telegram from *Kolkhoztsentr* on December 10, 1929, read: "To all local organizations in the areas of total collectivization: to achieve 100 per cent collectivization of working animals and cows, 80 per cent of pigs, 60 per cent of sheep and also poultry, and 25 per cent of the collectives to be communes."[25]

Meanwhile the commission proposed the following timetable "for total (*sploshnaia*) collectivization": the lower Volga by the autumn of 1930, the Central Black Earth area and the Ukrainian steppes by the autumn of 1931, the "left bank Ukraine" by the spring of 1932, the North and Siberia by 1933.

According to evidence published in 1965,[26] Stalin and Molotov pressed for more rapid tempos. By contrast, others—such as Andreev (from the North Caucasus) and Shlikhter (Ukrainian Commissar for Agriculture) argued for delay. They were overruled. The same source, which had access to archives and quotes them, tells that the unfortunate Iakovlev's draft included the provision that collectivization should take place "with the preservation of private peasant ownership of small tools, small livestock, milch cows, etc., where they serve the needs of the peasant family," also that "any step toward communes must be cautious and must depend on persuasion." Both these limits on arbitrary excesses were crossed out by Stalin himself. It was Stalin's fault, therefore, that the decree of January 5, 1930, contained nothing to suggest to ill-prepared and confused local cadres that they were not to go ahead and collectivize all peasant property down to chickens, rabbits, hoes, and buckets. To make their confusion worse, and to ensure the wildest excesses, the head of the party's agitation and propaganda department, G. Kaminsky, declared in January, 1930: "If in some matters you commit excesses and you are arrested, remember that you have been arrested for your revolutionary deeds."[27]

Stalin and Molotov urged all possible speed. The local cadres appear to have understood their task as *full steam ahead*. It was hardly surprising that there was "unjustified forcing the pace." Iakovlev warned in vain: avoid "administrative enthusiasm, jumping ahead, excessive haste." The party cadres were to "lead the spontaneous growth"

---

[25] All this from Ivnitskii, *Voprosy istorii KPSS*, No. 4, 1962, pp. 61–65 (not published until more than thirty years after the event).

[26] Vyltsan, *Voprosy istorii*, No. 3, 1965, p. 6.

[27] *Ibid.*, p. 7.

(*vozglavliat stikhiinii rost*) of collectivization.[28] He and the recipients of his warning were victims of the myth and the lie. How could they lead a nonexistent spontaneous movement? How could they achieve voluntarily what they knew from what they saw in front of them was a coercive operation in its very essence? A Soviet researcher found a report in the archives that stated the following: "Excesses are to a considerable extent explained by the fact that regional and local organizations, fearful of right wing deviation, preferred to overdo rather than underdo [*predpochli peregnut, chem nedognut*]." Similarly, Kalinin reported that collectivization of all livestock was being undertaken by officials "not of their own free will, but owing to fear of being accused of right wing deviation."[29]

Local officials announced: "He who does not join a kolkhoz is an enemy of Soviet power." Or, in the words of a novelist, F. Abramov, recalling the position of the local officials: "Either achieve 100 per cent (*sploshnaia*) in two days, or hand in your party card." The assault was launched, regardless of lack of preparation, regardless of local conditions, of opinion, of everything except the great campaign. There was, one can see, some logic against going slow: peasants who knew what was coming would react by cutting down production, perhaps destroying their tools and livestock. Better get it over, and before the spring sowing.

But if whole regions were to be 100 per cent collectivized, what was to be done with the kulaks? During the second half of 1929, a debate on this question went on. It was at this point not yet clear what kind of collectivization campaign there would be, but already the issue of possible expulsion of the kulaks or the expropriation of their property was posed. The majority view was against such drastic solutions. In June, 1929, *Pravda* headed an article with the words: "neither terror nor dekulakization, but a Socialist offensive on NEP lines." Others believed in the existence of a grave danger to Soviet power on the part of the kulaks,[30] although one might have thought that their opposition was due in large part to the measures that were being taken against them. The debate ceased when Stalin, in his statement to the "agrarian Marxists" at the end of December, 1929, asserted and justified the principle of their "liquidation as a class." They were not allowed to enter

28 Ivnitskii, *Voprosy istorii KPSS*, No. 4, 1962, p. 64.
29 Bogdenko, "Kolkhoznoe stroitelstvo . . . ," pp. 21, 26.
30 Numerous citations may be found in M. Lewin, chap. xvii.

the collectives, presumably in case they dominated them from within, as they dominated many a village assembly (*skhod*) in the twenties.

Stalin's justification of these drastic measures showed how, once the opposition was silenced, he became contemptuous of serious argument. Millions were to be uprooted, a mountain of human misery created, because the grain produced and marketed by kulaks could now be replaced by collective and state farms. In consequence,

> . . . now we are able to carry on a determined offensive against the kulaks, eliminate them as a class. . . . Now dekulakization is being carried out by the masses of poor and middle peasants themselves. . . . Now it is an integral part of the formation and development of collective farms. Consequently it is ridiculous and foolish to discourse at length on dekulakization. When the head is off, one does not mourn for the hair. There is another question no less ridiculous: whether kulaks should be permitted to join collective farms. Of course not, for they are sworn enemies of the collective farm movement.[31]

These harsh phrases put a stop to a painful and serious discussion about the kulaks' fate. But in fact, by a mixture of local party cadres' improvisations and semispontaneous quasi looting, the process of dekulakization had begun before Stalin's words had seen the light of day. At first there was no clear line. Local officials, acting "at their own risk and peril" began deportations, these being linked at first not with collectivization but with measures to enforce grain deliveries, as mentioned above. Only about February 4, 1930, was there an instruction issued from the Center about how to treat the kulaks.[32] According to this source, over 320,000 kulak households (presumably about 1.3 million people) were "dekulakized" by July 1, 1930, i.e., their property was confiscated and, presumably, they were resettled. But the total number of kulaks seems to have numbered about a million households. What ultimately happened to this much larger number—four and one-half million people, at least—is left unclear.

What is quite clear is that collectivization went hand in hand with dekulakization, and dekulakization with half-disguised robbery. Poorer peasants seized their neighbors' goods in the name of the class struggle, or with no excuse at all, and the officials found themselves instructed to "win the support of poor peasants" and were then blamed for "allowing the distribution of kulak property among the poor and landless, in contravention of party directives."[33] In fact, Stalin intervened to prohibit

[31] Stalin, *Works*, XII, 176, 177.
[32] Vyltsan, *Voprosy istorii*, No. 3, 1965, p. 17.
[33] *Ibid.*, p. 18.

the dispersal of kulak property among poor peasants, since this would make their subsequent collectivization more difficult by giving them something to lose. His conclusion (in February, 1930) was: since dekulakization only made sense in relation to collectivization, "work harder for collectivization in areas in which it is incomplete."[34]

Details of just who was or should have been dekulakized are still inadequately documented. Even the text of the decree of February, 1930, must be reconstructed from indirect evidence. However, several sources confirm that kulaks were divided by this decree into three categories. The first, described as actively hostile, was to be handed over to the OGPU and sent to concentration camps, while "their families were subject to deportation to distant regions of the North, Siberia, and the Far East."[35] The second category was described as "the most economically potent kulak households." These were to be deported outside the region of their residence. Finally, the third group, regarded as least noxious, were to be allowed to remain in the region but were to be given land of the worst kind. The property of the first two categories was virtually all to be confiscated. Those in the third category were to be allowed to keep essential equipment, which implies partial confiscation. On their inferior land they were to grow enough crops to meet the very large demands of the state for compulsory deliveries. The same Soviet source specifically mentions extremely high procurement quotas, and taxes rising to 70 per cent of their income. Failure to deliver produce or to pay taxes was considered as anti-Soviet activity, and was often followed by deportation. It is clear from the evidence that many of these deportations took place after July 1, 1930, and so it is quite probable that in the end all the persons described as kulaks were in fact deported. Some details of the procedures used may be found in the captured archives of the Smolensk party committee. Others will be cited here.

It is also clear that persons who were not kulaks at all were arrested and deported. How else can one interpret warnings found in the Smolensk archives against continuing to deport so-called "ideological" kulaks, these, regardless of economic category, being plainly opponents of collectivization. In the archives may also be found references to kulaks being robbed of their clothes and boots, and those engaged in the process of dekulakization were known to requisition and drink any

---

[34] Stalin, *Works*, XII, 194.

[35] I. Trifonov, *Ocherki istorii klassovoi borby v SSSR v goda Nepa* (Moscow, 1960), p. 237.

vodka found in the kulak house.[36] Orders were issued to stop such behavior. But what could the government expect? There were few reliable party members in the village and they had to utilize and encourage any ragged ruffians who could be prevailed upon to chase out their better-off neighbors (in the name of the class struggle, of course), and to expropriate their land. The party and police officials found themselves vying with each other in their dekulakizing zeal. If families were separated, children left uncared for, thousands went on journeys to Siberia in railway wagons with little food and water, then this seems to have been accepted as an inevitable part of the struggle to extirpate the last exploiting class. There were far more warnings against "rotten liberalism" and sentimentality than there were against excesses. Soviet sources insist to this day that the excesses of this class struggle were due in the main to the strong anti-kulak feelings in the countryside among the ordinary people. This point is made by Trifonov, even though he does say that numerous errors of policy also occurred. One would like to see more evidence of the extent of spontaneous action. Some of the resolutions cited in Trifonov's book look suspiciously as if they were adopted by a party activist and rammed down the peasants' throats.

The great assault was launched amid indescribable confusion. It may be, as has been argued by Olga Narkiewicz,[37] that some or much of collectivization remained on paper, or was confined to reports by perplexed, confused, or overenthusiastic comrades. The fact remains that it was announced that by February 20, 1930, 50 per cent of the peasants had joined collective farms, and most of these were either artels or "communes." The TOZ was largely discarded. Half the peasants, in seven weeks!

Of course, the threat of being labeled a kulak was widely used as a means of cajoling peasants to join. Those strongly opposed could be, and were, deported as kulaks, whatever their real economic status. This was a vast exercise in coercion, and the bewildered peasants wondered what had hit them. No doubt, in the absence of adequate briefing or preparation, there were great variations in different localities. Until much more is published, we simply cannot tell. But this was indeed a "revolution from above."

Large numbers of conflicting instructions have been cited by Soviet

[36] Merle Fainsod, *Smolensk under Soviet Rule* (London: Macmillan, 1958), chap. xii.
[37] O. A. Narkiewicz, "Stalin, War Communism and Collectivisation," *Soviet Studies*, XVI (July, 1966).

analysts, which help to explain the variety of policies followed on the spot. Occasional warnings were published in the central press in January and February, 1930, particularly on the undesirability of forcing collectivization in the more backward national republics. However, the warnings were sometimes ambiguously worded, and the regional party committees issued orders equally ambiguous. Thus Bogdenko quoted from the archives some Siberian party resolutions warning severely against excesses, but demanding at the same time the completion of collectivization by that very spring. Since at the date of the "warnings" (February 2, 1930) only 12 per cent of Siberia's peasants had been collectivized, the campaign inevitably continued, or even intensified. In Georgia, Armenia, Kazakhstan, and Uzbekistan there were said to be a few areas (ill-defined) suitable for wholesale collectivization.[38] Not very surprisingly, all these measures produced a sharp reaction on the part of the peasants. Thus, in Central Asia alone in the first five days of March, 1930, the archives record 37 open demonstrations (*vystupleniia*) involving 17,400 persons.[39] Another source refers to "rebellions and agitations" (*miatezhi i volneniia*), provoked by "kulaks and anti-Soviet elements in some places."[40]

Why deport so many real or alleged kulaks? Did this not, at a blow, deprive Soviet agriculture of its most energetic and knowledgeable husbandmen? Lewin has suggested the most probable reason: to drive the middle peasants into the collectives, not only by scaring them but also by finally slamming in their faces the door to their further advance qua individual peasants; that door, it was demonstrated, led to kulak status and that was a fairly sure ticket to Siberia. As well as kulaks, the terminology of the time identified an even less definable category, *podkulachnik*, or "kulak-supporter" (or "subkulak"), to whom repressive measures were also applied as and when necessary.

A Soviet writer has stated quite frankly that "most party officials" thought that the whole point of dekulakization was its value as an "administrative measure, speeding up the tempo of collectivization,"[41] which clearly means that it had great value as a weapon of coercion in relation to the peasantry as a whole. (Kulaks were not eligible to join the collectives!)

But chaos, despair, and coercion would not get the spring sowing

---

[38] Bogdenko, "Kolkhoznoe stroitelstvo . . . ," pp. 22, 24.
[39] *Ibid.*, p. 29.
[40] Moshkov, *Zernovaia problema* . . . , pp. 82–83.
[41] Bogdenko, "Kolkhoznoe stroitelstvo . . . ," p. 20.

done. After encouraging excesses of every kind, in early March Stalin called a halt. With a rare effrontery, he blamed the local officials. They were "dizzy with success." He wrote: "the successes of our collective farm policy are due, among other things, to the fact that it rests on the *voluntary character* [his emphasis] of the collective-farm movement." He warned against ignoring regional and national differences. He admitted that there was some "bureaucratic decreeing" of collectivization, which lacked reality, and also threats, such as depriving some peasants in Turkestan of irrigation water and manufactured goods unless they joined. In the same article, Stalin advocated the artel form of collectives, and said that within the artel "small vegetable gardens, small orchards, the dwelling houses, a part of the dairy cattle, small livestock, poultry, etc., are *not socialized*." He denounced the collectivization of poultry, of dwelling houses, of all cows, the removal of church bells, the "overzealous socializers."[42]

This seemed to imply a renunciation of the coercion principle, a condemnation of what the party cadres in the villages had been so feverishly seeking to accomplish, and the renunciation was from the very highest level.

Within weeks the proportion of the peasantry collectivized fell from 55 per cent (March 1) to 23 per cent (June 1). Perplexed and demoralized officials were made into scapegoats and fools. The letter of one such to Stalin has been published. This is what Khataevich wrote on April 6, 1930:

We have to listen to many complaints (from party cadres) that we have been wrongly declared to be dunderheads [*golovotiapy*]. Really, instructions should have been given to the central press so that, in criticizing the deviations and excesses that took place, they should attack and mock not only local officials. Many directives on collectivizing all livestock, including the smallest types, came from *Kolkhoztsentr*, from the agricultural commissariat.[43]

He might have been trying to shame Stalin. (No prize is offered for guessing whether Khataevich survived the great purge.)

Others "went so far as to forbid people to read Stalin's article, removed the issues of the newspapers containing the article, and so on." Archives show that some local officials treated the new policy as a surrender to the peasants.[44] In fact, the confusion was increased because Stalin's article was ambiguous. He called, it is true, for the end of ex-

[42] Stalin, *Works*, XII, 197; published in *Pravda*, March 2, 1930.
[43] Vyltsan, *Voprosy istorii*, No. 3, 1965, p. 7.
[44] Bogdenko, "Kolkhoznoe stroitelstvo . . . ," p. 28.

cesses and of coercion. But he also called the party to "make firm" (*zakrepit*) the existing level of collectivization. It was not too clear whether, and if so on what terms, peasants could be allowed to leave the farms. It took many weeks of clarification before it finally was forced upon party officials in some regions that Stalin's directive, and the resolution of the central committee that followed it, really did mean that one could walk out. The very great regional variations are shown by Table 2, an extract from a much longer table.

TABLE 2
PER CENT OF PEASANT HOUSEHOLDS COLLECTIVIZED, 1930

	March	March 10	April 1	May 1	June 1
TOTAL, U.S.S.R.	55.0	57.6	37.3	?	23.6
North Caucasus	76.8	79.3	64.0	61.2	58.1
Middle Volga	56.4	57.2	41.0	25.2	25.2
Ukraine	62.8	64.4	46.2	41.3	38.2
Central Black Earth region	81.8	81.5	38.9	18.0	15.7
Urals	68.8	70.6	52.6	29.0	26.6
Siberia	46.8	50.8	42.1	25.4	19.8
Kazakhstan	37.1	47.9	56.6	44.4	28.5
Uzbekistan	27.9	45.5	30.8	?	27.5
Moscow province	73.0	58.1	12.3	7.5	7.2
Western region	39.4	37.4	15.0	7.7	6.7
Belorussia	57.9	55.8	44.7	?	11.5

Source: M. L. Bogdenko, "Kolkhoznoe stroitelstvo vesnoi i letom 1930 goda," *Istoricheskie zapiski*, No. 76 (citing archive and other materials), p. 31.

Several conclusions follow. One is the fantastic ups-and-downs in the lives of the large majority of the population of the Soviet Union within a few short months. Another is the variation in the extent to which the peasants could (or were allowed to, or wanted to) leave collectives. Thus a high level was retained, no doubt by appropriate pressures, in such key grain-surplus areas as the North Caucasus and Ukraine, whereas in some other areas collectivization was almost abandoned (see Table 2 for Moscow, the West, and Belorussia). Finally, the pressure to collectivize in some Asian republics started late and was continued well after "dizzy with success," as the Kazakhstan figures show—and this despite particularly emphatic warnings to go carefully and slowly in the complex circumstances of these backward areas. But by the end of April there was an outflow of peasants from the half-baked kolkhozy in all areas, though at different rates, while, in the words of a Soviet scholar, "conditions in the village, created by excesses, were strained in the highest degree." In many areas, a very large proportion even of poor peasants and landless laborers walked out.[45] It is interest-

[45] *Ibid.*, p. 30.

ing that many of them formed what were described as "cooperatives of the simplest type" and tried to work together.[46] It is one of the trage-dies of this period that this and other kinds of genuine cooperation were so quickly wiped out. Yet, amid all this chaos, the heavens chose to smile. The weather was excellent, somehow most of the sowing did get done, and the 1930 harvest was better than that of 1929, and notably better than the harvest that succeeded it.

The official Soviet explanation suffers to this day from an inbuilt defect. Thus the authoritative article published in 1965[47] takes the fol-lowing line: It asked if it was wrong to press on with collectivization, and answered: "No. Under conditions of capitalist encirclement and constant threat of intervention, it was impossible to delay for long the reconstruction of agriculture, the liquidation of counterrevolutionary kulaks." It was admitted that in November–December, 1929, Stalin exaggerated the peasants' desire to be collectivized, that he pushed officials into excessive haste and harshness; warnings that "the Leninist voluntary principle" was being disregarded were ignored by him. In discussing whether heavy losses in livestock could have been avoided, the authors declared: they were avoidable "if the Leninist principle of the voluntary entry of peasants into kolkhozy were undeviatingly observed." But this (if the authors will forgive me) is simply not a ten-able position. How can one assert the necessity of collectivization (and defend "dekulakization" too, thirty years after the event), and solemnly assert that collectivization should have been voluntary? It could not have been done without mass coercion, and they must know it per-fectly well. Privately, Soviet scholars are willing to admit this. But this whole area remains thickly strewn with myths.

The old village community organizations (*obshchiny* and such) were formally dissolved in areas subject to collectivization by decree of June 30, 1930. Their functions were taken over by the collective farms and by rural soviets.

Gradually, the peasants were forced, persuaded, cajoled, taxed, ordered back into collective farms. The growing figures for collectivi-zation in the U.S.S.R., from 1930 to 1936, are shown in Table 3.

The full story of how it was done has yet to be told. Only a part of the facts are yet visible. Peasants outside the kolkhoz were given inferior land, were loaded with extra taxes or delivery obligations, or both. There were repeated instances in 1931–32 of compulsory purchase of

[46] *Ibid.*, p. 36.
[47] Vyltsan, *Voprosy istorii*, No. 3, 1965, p. 4.

TABLE 3
PERCENTAGE OF HOUSEHOLDS AND CROPS COLLECTIVIZED, 1930–1936

	1930	1931	1932	1933	1934	1935	1936
Peasant households collectivized	23.6	52.7	61.5	64.4	71.4	83.2	89.6
Crop area collectivized	33.6	67.8	77.6	83.1	87.4	94.1	-

Source: *Sotsialisticheskoe stroitelstvo SSSR* (1936), p. 278 (state farm area and households included).

peasant livestock.[48] More areas were declared as due for *sploshnaia* collectivization. Thus a decree in 1931 (August 2) specified the "cotton-growing area of Central Asia, Kazakhstan, and Transcaucasia and beet-growing areas of the Ukraine and Central Black Earth regions" as being due for collectivization during 1932. A long and bitter struggle raged. Peasants slaughtered livestock. The new farms lacked all experience in handling the collectivized livestock. Many died of neglect. The townsmen party activists sent to supervise the peasants were ignorant of agriculture, suspicious of advice. The already-cited authoritative article admits something of a crisis in 1932, owing to bad planning, low pay, crude coercion within kolkhozy, poor organization of work, and also unfavorable weather ("subjective and objective factors"). With remarkable restraint, the authors comment: "the kolkhozy could not immediately show the superiority of socialized over individual production."[49]

Collectivization spread into primitive, pastoral Kazakhstan, with catastrophic results. Livestock losses were disastrous everywhere, but in Kazakhstan they virtually wiped out the sheep population (Table 4) (and many of the Kazakhs, too, since this nationality declined by over 20 per cent between the 1926 and 1939 censuses).

TABLE 4
DECLINE OF HERDS IN KAZAKHSTAN, 1928–1940
(In Millions)

1928	1935	1940
19.2	2.6	7.0

Source: *Narkhoz-Kazakh.-1957*, p. 141.

Shortage of fodder was a major cause of the reduction in livestock numbers in some areas, notably in the Ukraine, where the state's exactions left very little on which to feed animals. Sowing in 1931 suffered acutely from the appalling state of the hungry horses.[50]

[48] This was criticized in a Central Committee decision of March 26, 1932, but, of course, was due to centrally imposed policies.
[49] Vyltsan, *Voprosy istorii*, No. 3, 1965, p. 10.
[50] Moshkov, *Zernovaia problema . . .* , p. 112.

Among methods used to force peasants back into collectives were arbitrary exactions known as "hard obligations" (*tviordie zadaniia*) to deliver vast quantities of grain to the state. Thus, to take one example, in September–October, 1930, in the Crimea, 77 per cent of all those assessed for special obligatory deliveries failed to deliver the required amount, despite what the source called "the toughest struggle," and they were punished by sale of their property, fines, imprisonment, and so on, the exact figures being cited from the archives by the source.[51]

Similar measures were taken in other regions. Kulaks had been largely liquidated in 1930, so the attack was now on "kulak-and-better-off" peasants, and was quite clearly intended, in the winter of 1930/31, to drive the peasants back into the collectives. To cite the same source again, "this struggle grew into another wave of liquidations of kulaks as a class, which in its turn was directly linked with the new wave of collectivization in the winter and spring of 1931." This was repeated in 1931–32, and there were also many cases reported where obstinate individual peasants' privately owned horses were compulsorily used on the collective farms.[52] Some victims of these measures were deported, others evaded ever growing delivery obligations by joining collectives "voluntarily." Moshkov commented: "The [exceptional] delivery obligations affected not only kulaks but also the upper strata of the middle peasants. However, in practice, they were treated differently to kulaks, being given the chance [*sic*] to enter the kolkhozy."[53] Percentages rose, though detailed evidence shows that some peasants left the kolkhozy, many fleeing to work in town and on construction sites.

In 1932, faced with mass pillage of "socialist" property by the demoralized and often hungry peasantry, the following Draconian legislation was adopted, as an amendment to Article 58 of the Criminal Code: pilfering on the railways and of kolkhoz property (including the harvest in the fields, stocks, animals, and so on) was to be punished "by the highest means of social defense, shooting, or, in case of extenuating circumstances, deprivation of freedom [i.e., prison or camp] for not less than ten years, with confiscation of all property."[54] Even Stalin did not do such things without good reason. The fact that such laws were passed in peacetime shows that he, at least, knew he was at war. His letter to Sholokhov, which Khrushchev cited thirty years later,

[51] *Ibid.*, pp. 155–56.
[52] *Ibid.*, p. 156; also pp. 101, 176.
[53] *Ibid.*, p. 176.
[54] Quoted from *RSFSR. Ugolovnyi kodeks*, 1936, pp. 120–21.

showed what he thought. Sholokhov had protested against excesses in the area of the Don in 1933, which had included mass arrests (also of Communists), illegal seizures, excessive grain procurements; Stalin in his reply admitted that some officials, in working against "the enemy," also hit friendly persons

> and even commit sadism. . . . But . . . the honorable cultivators of your region, and not only your region, committed sabotage and were quite willing to leave the workers and the Red Army without grain. The fact that the sabotage was silent and apparently gentle (no blood was spilt) does not change the fact that the honorable cultivators in reality were making a "silent" war against Soviet power. War by starvation, my dear comrade Sholokhov.[55]

This, of course, was the point made by Stalin in his famous talk with Churchill, reported in Churchill's war memoirs. Stalin it was who compared his struggle against the peasants with the terrible experience of the war against the Germans.

The essential problem was all too simple. Harvests were poor. The peasants were demoralized. Collective farms were inefficient, the horses slaughtered or starving, tractors as yet too few and poorly maintained, transport facilities inadequate, the retail distribution system (especially in rural areas) utterly disorganized by an overprecipitate abolition of private trade. Soviet sources speak of appallingly low standards of husbandry, with 13 per cent of the crop remaining unharvested as late as mid-September in the Ukraine, and some of the sowing being delayed until after the first of June.[56] Very high exports in 1930 and 1931 depleted reserves, and the rapid growth of the urban population led to a sharp increase in food requirements in towns, while livestock products declined precipitately with the disappearance of so high a proportion of the animals. The government tried to take more out of a smaller grain crop. We now have food and fodder balances for the years 1928–32, and also per capita consumption figures (see Table 5). These figures show that urban citizens ate more bread and potatoes in 1932 than in 1928, in place of meat and butter. But the peasants ate less of everything. That was the result of deliberate policy. A Soviet scholar commented that the vast increase

in state procurements during the years of wholesale collectivization, with low levels of grain production, cannot be explained merely by errors, imper-

---

[55] *Pravda*, March 10, 1963.
[56] Moshkov, *Zernovaia problema* . . . , p. 227.

fections of planning, or . . . by the ignoring of the interests of agriculture and of the rural population, as is alleged by bourgeois writers in the west. The country was laying the foundation of a mighty industrial base.[57]

Yes, but primarily at the peasants' expense.

Procurements in 1931 left many peasants and their animals with too little to eat. The Ukraine and North Caucasus suffered particularly severely, and detailed figures to this effect are now available. Collectivized peasants relied almost exclusively on grain distribution by kolkhozy for their bread, since money was virtually useless in this period and bread was rationed in towns and unobtainable in the country save at astronomic "free" prices. These excessive procurements threatened the very existence of the peasantry in some areas. In fact, according to Moshkov, exactions were so severe that the state had to return grain that had already been collected (21.0 per cent of the total in West Siberia, for instance), so that there would be some seed, food, and fodder. There were tremendous variations between areas and between farms in the same area, owing to the almost incredible arbitrariness of the procurement organs.[58]

TABLE 5
FOOD CONSUMPTION: 1928–1932
(In Kilograms)

	Bread Grains		Potatoes		Meat and Lard		Butter	
	A	B	A	B	A	B	A	B
1928	174.4	250.4	87.6	141.1	51.7	24.8	2.97	1.55
1932	211.3	214.6	110.0	125.0	16.9	11.2	1.75	0.70
	A=Urban				B=Rural			

Source: Iu. A. Moshkov, *Zernovaia problema v gody Sploshnoi Kollectivizatsii* (Moscow University, 1966), p. 136, quoting archives.

All this led in 1932 to trouble, pilfering, undiscipline, concealment of crops. As a result, Stalin evidently decided to relax the procurements pressure somewhat, and so the procurement plan for 1932, which had been originally fixed at an impossible 29.5 million tons, was reduced to 18.1 millions, while greater freedom was offered to kolkhozy and remaining individual peasants to sell on the free market, provided the reduced delivery plan was fulfilled first.[59]

However, conditions grew chaotic. Procurement organs relaxed their pressure, and, because of the vast disparity between the low state buying prices and the very high free-market prices, grain flowed into unofficial

[57] *Ibid.*, p. 137.
[58] *Ibid.*, pp. 190–91.
[59] *Ibid.*, p. 201.

channels, and in particular into the peasants' own storehouses, since the harvest was not a good one and the food shortages of the previous winter were vividly recalled. Discipline collapsed in some areas. The reduced state procurement plan was threatened. Telegrams from Moscow had no result. In the North Caucasus the harvest was particularly poor, a mere 4.4 to 5.9 quintals per hectare, a miserable crop on the best land in the U.S.S.R. In this area, and also in the Ukraine, evil-intentioned persons

. . . succeeded in awakening private-property feelings, in directing many kolkhoz peasants from the correct path and poisoning them with individualism. Some kolkhozy in the North Caucasus and the Ukraine ceased to come under the organizing influence of the party and the state.[60]

(These are very strong words indeed for a Soviet author, indicating a kind of rebellion.)

This led to state countermeasures, which in turn led to the great tragedy: the famine of 1933. "All forces were directed to procurements." The law of April 7, 1932, which, as we have seen, provided for the death penalty for pilfering foodstuffs in kolkhozy, was used against those who

. . . with evil intent refused to deliver grain for (state) procurements. This particularly affected socially alien groups. Organizers of sabotage in kolkhozy were handed over to the courts, including degenerate Communists and kulak-supporters among the kolkhoz leadership. In accordance with the central committee directives, regions that did not satisfactorily fulfill procurement plans ceased to be supplied with commodities. . . . Illegally distributed or pilfered grain was confiscated. Several thousands of counter-revolutionaries, and saboteurs were deported. . . .[61]

The party was purged. In the North Caucasus 43 per cent of all investigated party members were expelled. There were some appalling excesses. Stalin declared, in a speech to the Politburo on November 27, 1932, that coercion was justified against "certain groups of kolkhozy and peasants," that they had to be dealt a "devastating blow." Kaganovich announced that rural Communists were guilty of being "prokulak, of bourgeois degeneration."[62] Mass arrests went beyond all bounds, half of local party secretaries in the North Caucasus were expelled on orders

[60] *Ibid.*, p. 215, quoting archive materials.
[61] *Ibid.*, p. 215.
[62] I. Zelenin, "Politotdely MTS (1933–1934 gg)" *Istoricheskie zapiski*, No. 76 (1963), p. 53.

of Kaganovich. "All grain without exception was removed, including seed and fodder, and even that already issued to peasants as an advance [payment for workdays]."[63] The result was "an extremely grave food shortage in many southern areas," and a "heavy loss of livestock," which took a long time to repair. Much of the same happened in the Ukraine. A local party secretary related: "Without administrative pressure on the peasant we will not get the grain, and so it does not matter if we overdo things a little."[64] In January, 1933, a more orderly system of compulsory procurements was decreed, based on acreage sown, replacing the purely arbitrary (though nominally voluntary) system of *Kontraktatsiia*. But the damage had already been done. The famine, part and consequence of the struggle described above, was terrible.

TABLE 6
GRAIN PROCUREMENT AND EXPORT, 1928–1933
(In Million Tons)

	1928	1929	1930	1931	1932	1933
State grain procurements	10.8	16.1	22.1	22.8	18.5	22.6
Grain exports		0.18	4.76	5.06	1.73	1.69

Source: A. N. Malafeev, *Istoriia tsenoobrazovaniia v SSSR, 1917–1963* (Moscow, 1964), pp. 175, 177; Soviet trade returns.

Grain procurements and exports did indeed increase as Table 6 demonstrates. The Soviet population in 1925 was 142 million, and for 1932 it was officially estimated at 165.7,[65] since it had been increasing at the rate of about three million a year. In 1939, seven years later, it was only 170 million. Somewhere along the way ten million people had "demographically" disappeared. Some, of course, were not born. Many died in the terrible early thirties. Eyewitnesses saw starving peasants, and I myself spoke to Ukrainians who remembered the horrors. Yet neither the local nor the national press, at the time *or since,* ever mentioned a famine, at least until 1963.

There have been, as far as can be discovered, only two references to the famine in Soviet print, even in recent years (the official histories mention only a "shortage of food," at most). One was in a novel: Stadniuk's *Liudi ne angely*. The other was in a work by Zelenin, which quoted archives concerning "mass instances of swelling from hunger, and death" as occurring in the Central Black Earth region, an area

[63] Moshkov, *Zernovaia problema* . . . , p. 217.
[64] Zelenin, "Politotdely MTS . . . ," p. 44.
[65] *Fulfillment of Second Five-Year Plan*, p. 269.

which Western observers did not regard as seriously affected by the famine.[66]

Finally, to wind up this deplorable story, the nine million peasants left outside collectives in 1934 were duly attacked. They were, it seems, cold-shouldered and treated as hostile elements, but allowed to continue to survive. This toleration was treated as a "right wing deviation." On June 2, 1934, at a conference of officials on collectivization, Stalin demanded—and this is quoted from the archives—that "in order to ensure the uninterrupted growth of collectivization, there would be a tightening of the tax screw [*nalogovii press*] on the individual peasants."[67] Yet this article ends with the still-compulsory myth: "The multi-million peasantry became even more convinced of the incontrovertible superiority of socialist agriculture, of the mighty kolkhoz system."

[66] Zelenin, "Politotdely MTS . . . ," p. 47.
[67] I. Zelenin, "Kolkhozy i selskoe khoziaistvo SSSR v 1933–1935," *Istoriia SSSR*, No. 5 (1964), pp. 3–28.

THOMAS P. BERNSTEIN

Comment

Professor Nove has presented a comprehensive and graphic account of Soviet collectivization, and he has supplied the main reasons why this "revolution from above" required so much coercion. Since I have no disagreement with his analysis, it may be helpful for an understanding of Soviet collectivization to discuss Professor Nove's paper in relation to collectivization in another Communist country, China.

In rather sharp contrast to the Soviet pattern, the Chinese succeeded in securing peasant compliance with collectivization, even though collectivization in China was also not voluntary in the Western sense of the term. Collectivization in China was achieved without eliciting a comparable degree of peasant resistance and without causing a comparable degree of economic disruption, even though the bulk of China's peasants were collectivized more rapidly than in Russia. In the period from autumn, 1955, to the spring of 1956, the CCP mobilized China's peasants to join lower-stage (semisocialist) producers' cooperatives, starting with a peasant membership of 14 per cent of households in the summer of 1955. Within the same period, two thirds of the households also made the transition to fully socialist collective farms, a process that was completed everywhere in the winter of 1956/57. Accounting for the different patterns of peasant compliance requires analysis of complex issues of history, policy, and sociopolitical structure.[1] Here I would like to take some points that emerge from Nove's paper and to compare them with the Chinese situation.

Two factors were of central importance in shaping the Soviet pattern of collectivization. The first factor was a circumstance—that of the weak Communist social and political position in the villages on the eve

[1] These comments draw on material in my article, "Leadership and Mass Mobilisation in the Soviet and Chinese Collectivisation Campaigns of 1929–30 and 1955–56: A Comparison," *China Quarterly*, No. 31 (July–Sept., 1967).

of mass collectivization. The second was a policy—the harsh and ineptly enforced grain-procurement program. These two factors interacted to produce a pattern of forced collectivization, in which peasant compliance had to be achieved by "administrative pressure" exerted on the peasants from outside the village. Both factors differed significantly in the Chinese case, and therefore led to a different pattern of collectivization.

First, with regard to the Bolsheviks' social and political position in the villages, Nove draws attention to the predominance of middle peasants. Whatever the difficulties of defining this category, it seems clear that they, as relatively successful farmers, shared common attitudes and interests with the kulaks. It is likely that kulaks provided legitimate leadership for much of the village, and it is this that made them so dangerous from the Communist viewpoint, rather than their exploitation of the poor or of the rural proletariat (*batraki*). These last two groups were the Bolsheviks' social base in the village. Mobilizing this base required organization, but despite considerable effort, the Soviet regime did not succeed in reaching many of them. In early 1929, for example, of 200,000 *batraki* in Belorussia, only 715 were party members.[2]

The contrast with China is striking. Communist-sponsored land reform had created a large group of beneficiaries. A sizable subgroup among these beneficiaries had become members and leaders of Communist organizations in the villages. After land reform, the Chinese regime retained and strengthened its organizational links with the villages, thus making it possible to mobilize village-level leaders and activists for socialist transformation, and to gain access to the peasants generally. During mass collectivization, village cadres played a major role in the drive. Because of land reform, moreover, the rich peasants were not in as strong a position in the village as they were in the Soviet Union. Indeed, in the broadest terms, Chinese *land reform* was comparable to Soviet *collectivization* in that the destruction of non-Communist village leadership was a central element of both. The relatively more vigorous prosecution of policies of socialist transformation before 1955 also helped prevent the crystallization in China of such trends as middle-rich-peasant identification and solidarity. Hence the problem of manipulating and pressuring the middle peasants into collective farms was easier for the Chinese than for the Soviets.

Given the weakness of the Soviet position in the villages, securing

[2] "Kak postavlena rabota s batrachestvom," *Izvestiia tsentralnogo komiteta rossiiskoi kommunisticheskoi partii (bolshevikov)*, No. 7 (Mar. 20, 1929).

peasant compliance with collectivization would have been a difficult undertaking under any circumstances, but the grain-procurement policy made it even more difficult. Professor Nove rightly emphasizes the role of the grain issue and he draws attention to the methods used, from Stalin's "Urals-Siberian" approach of 1928 to the one that resulted in the famine of 1932–33. The almost complete disregard of the peasants' interests in the handling of grain procurement required increasing reliance on coercion, not only against those classified as enemies (kulaks) but also against middle peasants, and ultimately against virtually all peasants. Because of the resultant peasant hostility and resistance, any manifestation of spontaneous local activity was likely to be viewed as a threat by the regime. As Nove puts it, "It is one of the tragedies of this period that [various kinds] of genuine cooperation were so quickly wiped out." Even more important, locally recruited leaders of party cells and soviets tended in many cases to identify with the peasants against the harsh claims of the regime. Probably a major cause was that they had ties of family and friendship with the peasants. There were many instances of noncooperation with and even resistance to collectivization and related policies on the part of local leaders. The most dramatic illustration of this tendency came in 1932–33. In that year the Soviet regime enforced grain procurements in such regions as the North Caucasus to the point of famine, and doing so required a sweeping purge of kolkhoz and local party leaders. In the North Caucasus, 43 per cent of investigated Communists were expelled. The driving force behind collectivization and grain procurement thus had to come from officials who did not have effective ties with the peasants, while the kolkhozy had to be subjected to tight administrative controls, as by the MTS.

If agricultural policy in Stalin's Russia was extractive, in China it has been both extractive and developmental (as Professor Tang has pointed out in his paper in this volume). The two goals have conflicted, and much of the unstable history of regime-peasant relations in China can be analyzed in terms of the shifting relationship between the two goals. From the political viewpoint, the behavior of village-level leadership can sometimes be taken as an indicator of the extent to which the extractive goal prevailed over the developmental one in particular years. In 1954/55, for example, the largest quantity of grain obtained in any one year during the period from 1953 to 1957 was procured. The result was a crisis over grain supply in the spring of 1955 that was characterized by the identification of many village cadres with the peasants against the claims of the regime.[3] Instead of responding to this situation with greatly increased coercion and purge, the Chinese responded by reducing the amount bought and by regularizing the delivery system.[4] This was a major factor in the mobilization of strong village organizations during the collectivization drive of 1955–56, and helped to account for the relative ease, compared with the Soviet pattern outlined by Professor Nove, with which the Chinese secured peasant compliance.

[3] *Jen-min jih-pao* (People's Daily), April 24, 1955, editorial, "Li-yi yi-k'ao ch'un-chung, cheng-tun nung-ts'un liang-shih t'ung-hsiao kung-tso."

[4] "Provisional Measures for Unified Purchase and Unified Sale of Grain in Rural Areas," *New China News Agency*, Aug. 25, 1955, in *Current Background* (Hong Kong, U.S. Consulate), No. 354, Sept. 7, 1955.

Comment

Professor Nove has organized his account of the forced collectivization of 1930 around one main question: was it necessary? He has not attempted to give a final answer to the question, nor should he have, but his considerations present a number of points that are very enlightening. Especially significant to a conference on comparative agrarian policies is the suggestion that the Soviet collectivization of 1930–34, from which all subsequent agricultural development in the U.S.S.R. has derived, was not at all an agrarian reform but a campaign to procure grain by force from the peasants and bring it to the cities. The kolkhozy and sovkhozy that were set up in the 1930's were not primarily systems of farm labor organization and land use but methods for compelling peasants to do something they did not wish to do. Two conclusions may be drawn from this. First, Soviet *experience* offers no useful model for an agrarian policy whose primary aim is to improve either rural political organization or agriculture. Second, the value of the kolkhozy and sovkhozy as *forms* of economic and/or political organization and instruments of agrarian policy cannot be judged by their performance in Soviet Russia. If the Soviet government has been notorious for ignoring the first of these conclusions, then Western experts have often been equally at fault for ignoring the second. Obviously, no comparison is meaningful between Soviet collective farms and other agrarian systems (such as "family farms") unless it takes both of these statements into account.

I have no quarrel at all with Professor Nove's history. Certainly, the question as to the necessity of forced collectivization is the basic one, and the elements from which he has constructed his account are quite relevant. I should like to introduce yet another element that I think deserves consideration.

It is generally assumed by both Soviet and Western scholars that

Stalin was exerting his control or imposing his will in early 1930 and that episodes in the forced collectivization can be traced upward from the excesses perpetrated in the villages direct to his headquarters and/or the machinations in the upper levels of the Communist Party. Nothing could be further from the truth. From mid-1929 on, orders went out from government and party in great abundance, but they did not reach the villages in any coherent form. Reports flooded into the central offices, but very few of them contained reliable information. In the absence of any operational legal or administrative system, the government could state nothing meaningful to the peasants but grain quotas, and it could hear nothing but grain deliveries. The government was not administering the villages; it was invading them, and its "army" lacked even so rudimentary a form of administrative organization as a chain of command. What went on in the villages in 1930 was more like a contrived social movement than the implementation of a policy.

Was it necessary to abandon the systematic processes of policy making and administrative enactment? Consideration of this question leads to a description of the organization that was available to the Bolshevik leaders in 1929 to carry out their policies in the countryside. In fact, there was none. Prior to 1917, the government of Russia had derived substantial political support in rural areas from private landholders and zemstvos. Under the stress of World War I, the government was unable to maintain the increasingly interdependent economic system it had created, and in 1917 the grain supply to the cities seemed on the verge of failing. During the course of the year, the central administration collapsed in a cloud of rhetoric; private landholders, zemstvos, and all rural institutions that had any political significance were swept away. The famine that had threatened the cities quickly became a reality; thus, the primary domestic task facing the Bolsheviks was to re-establish the cities' grain supply. In 1918–20, lacking any other means to achieve their ends, they set an urban, paramilitary mob on the peasants in order to bring the grain from country to city by force. By 1921, the central government was restored, but it had lost all roots in the countryside. Russia's new leaders had to rely entirely on the cities for support. More, they had to continue the industrialization that the tsarist government had begun without the benefit of foreign capital. The population would have to assume the whole burden of capital accumulation and since most of them were peasants, some system of legal order and agrarian policy would have to be devised to link peasants and government together.

No such system emerged in the 1920's. The Bolshevik party failed to establish any operational contact of its own with the peasants,[1] and therefore it had to rely on the cooperation of the agricultural specialists and administrators left in being after the collapse of the tsarist government and the zemstvos. These specialists—surveyors, agronomists, statisticians, *et al.*—continued the work of agrarian reform they had begun in 1906, chiefly the consolidation of the primitive peasant strips into integral fields that would lend themselves to modern farming. Through the 1920's, the older specialists set up schools to train new men to carry on their reforms,[2] and by 1929 the programs of land consolidation that had formerly been associated with the Stolypin Land Reform were going forward with greater vigor than ever before.[3] Of course, the rhetoric associated with them was altered to suit the requirements of Bolshevik ideology.

The specialists were not supporters of the Bolsheviks per se. Their cooperation hinged entirely on the continuation of Bolshevik toleration of agrarian reform. Professional agrarian reformers were no more suited to the carrying out of forced grain procurement in 1929 than they had been in 1917. Indeed, they demonstrated in 1928 that they could resist Bolshevik commands and impose their own policies on ostensibly Bolshevik projects. In December, 1927, the Fourteenth Party Congress called for the rapid formation of *large* collective farms. The specialists gave verbal support to the new party program, and in return the Bolsheviks increased their financial support for rural development in order that the specialists might intensify the collectivization campaign. What the specialists did in the field, however, was to form *small* "collectives" in which the arable land was hardly collectivized at all but was to a considerable extent consolidated.[4] This, at any rate, was their

---

[1] See Ia. A. Iakovlev, *Nasha derevnia* (Moscow, 1924), p. 109–66. A careful reading of A. Kh. Mitrofanov, *Itogi chistki partii* (Moscow, 1930), pp. 36–37, 58, indicates the continuing lack of communication between Bolshevik organs of rural government and peasant society in 1929.

[2] *Spravochnik zemleustroitelia* (Moscow, 1928), pp. 156–94, describes the development of agricultural schools in the 1920's.

[3] Ia. A. Iakovlev, *Borba za urozhai* (2nd ed.; Moscow, 1929), pp. 11–13; *Stenograficheskii otchet IV soveschaniia zemorganov 5–12 ianvaria 1929 goda* (Moscow, 1929), p. 492.

[4] The percentage of the "collectivized" sown land that was farmed collectively was somewhat under 20 per cent before 1928 (*Materialy po perspektivnomu planu razvitiia selskogo i lesnogo khoziaistva, 1928/29–1932/33*, Parts I and II [Moscow, 1929], Part I, p. 84) and this percentage decreased even further during the 1928 campaign (*Sten. otchet . . .*, p. 482). By the end of 1928, however, three fourths of the kolkhoz lands are supposed to have been consolidated (*ibid.*, p. 341).

claim in 1929, By the end of 1928, then, it had become clear that so long as the Bolsheviks wished to proceed in the countryside *within the framework of an orderly administrative system,* it would have to be a system that they could not dominate. In particular, they could not use it to procure grain by force. Given the Bolshevik program of rapid industrialization, called forth by essentially urban problems and those of the state as a whole, the problem the Soviet leaders faced in the countryside in 1929 was not only to get grain but also to create very quickly a body of men that could get it. The agricultural specialists—the only group that had any operational contact with the peasantry at all—would have to be shoved aside. In a word, Stalin had to sacrifice *control* in rural Russia in order to exercise his *power.* In early 1930, the agricultural specialists were stripped of their authority, and an urban, paramilitary mob, loyal to the regime but lacking any knowledge of agriculture or land use, was sent out to take over the villages and procure grain.[5]

The above discussion suggests two conclusions. First, we should not only avoid the use of Soviet collectivization as a model for agrarian reform; we should not even consider it as an administrative action. Second, the role that Stalin and the party leaders played in the events that took place in the countryside in 1930–34 was not so significant as Western and Soviet scholars have thought. Stalin may or may not have been brutal, depraved, and paranoic; in any case, his personal qualities had little to do with what went on in the villages. The brutal and wasteful arbitrariness of forced collectivization did not spring so much from the orders of this or that party leader as from the nature of the process itself. What the party leaders wanted done to the peasants and the land was of relatively little significance next to the simple fact that no trained men nor any organization were available to do it.

[5] Some of the orders directing the dispatch of this mob are in *Spravochnik po kolkhoznomu stroitelstvu* (Leningrad, 1931), pp. 65, 74–76, 84–86, 91, 146–47, 450–54.

KARL-EUGEN WÄDEKIN

Kolkhoz, Sovkhoz, and Private
Production in Soviet Agriculture

This study is primarily concerned with that portion of the total Soviet
agricultural output produced by each of the three sectors, and the
development that their specific importance has taken in the years since
1953 and especially since 1962. The private sector will be treated only
briefly, since the author has recently handled this topic thoroughly in
a different work.[1] In reference to the state-operated agricultural sector,
attention will be given chiefly to the sovkhozy. The other state-owned
agricultural enterprises[2] will be treated only to the extent to which
Soviet statistics combine them with sovkhozy.

   To obtain an accurate and precise picture of the relative importance
of each of the three sectors in Soviet agriculture is more difficult than
may appear at first glance. What standard should one take to measure
their comparative importance? The most obvious standard would be
the production of the kolkhozy, sovkhozy, and private producers, and
indeed *gross* agricultural production, since these Soviet figures only are
available.[3]

---

   [1] Karl-Eugen Wädekin, *Privatproduzenten in der sowjetischen Landwirtschaft* (Cologne:
Bundesinstitut für Ostwissenschaftliche und Internationale Studien, 1967).
   [2] For a summary review of these see V. G. Venzher, *Kolkhoznyi stroi na sovremennom
etape* (Moscow, 1965), pp. 41–43.
   [3] An attempt to calculate the net agricultural production has recently been made
by Roger E. Neetz, "Inside the Agricultural Index of the U.S.S.R.," *New Directions
in the Soviet Economy*, ed., Joint Economic Committee (Washington, D.C.: U.S.
Government Printing Office, 1966), pp. 485–93, and by W. Klatt, "Soviet Farm
Output and Food Supply in 1970," in *Soviet Affairs*, No. 4, ed. M. Kaser (London,
1966), p. 126; concerning this question see also Jerzy F. Karcz, "The New Soviet
Agricultural Programme, Appendix," *Soviet Studies*, XVII, No. 2 (Oct., 1965), 161.
But to divide the net production, calculated in this or another way, into that of
kolkhozy, sovkhozy, and private producers has, as far as the author knows, not yet

Even the gross production figures are extremely meager, although a recent article afforded some statistics on gross production per one hundred sovkhoz workers (workers on sovkhozy of the Ministry of Agriculture of the U.S.S.R.), from which gross production in rubles can be calculated.[4] On the other hand, E. S. Karnaukhova set for the year 1962 the proportion of all sovkhozy and other state agricultural enterprises at 25 per cent of the total gross agricultural production; and that of the kolkhozy at 41.3 per cent,[5] so that approximately 34 per cent remains for the private sector. From these figures and the total value of gross agricultural production, from the index figures of the development of gross agricultural production of the whole socialized sector, and, of these, the gross agricultural production of sovkhozy and other state enterprises, the statistics in Table 1 can be assembled.

The figures in the table give a rough over-all picture, but no more, for on the one hand they consist of approximations due to the manner of calculation; and on the other hand they suffer from the well-known Soviet deficiencies in gross production calculation.[6] For our purposes these deficiencies are even more serious than usual, because the figures for the individual sectors are based upon different price levels of sales.[7] Moreover, gross production figures indicate nothing about the differences in the direction and organization of production in the three types of producers—kolkhozy, sovkhozy, and private sector, and the interrelated economic geography of regional distribution.

In searching for other standards from data published by the Soviets, the following categories seem especially useful: *Agricultural Areas; Sown Areas; Livestock Units; Energy Available* (also as a substitute for *capital available*, because the latter is not known for the earlier years); *Labor Force*. None of these categories can of itself afford us a meaningful pic-

---

been attempted. For sovkhozy we have a Soviet figure of 9.9 billion rubles as the sum of all production sold (*realizovannyi*) by the sovkhozy of the Ministry of Agriculture in 1964—see M. D. Tumanova, *Khozraschet, Rentabelnost, Kredit* (Moscow, 1966), p. 45.

[4] L. Sineva, "O fondootdache v sovkhozakh," *Voprosy ekonomiki,* No. 12 (1966), p. 42. That author also gives, on p. 41, corresponding sets of figures per 100 rubles of production funds (*osnovnye proizvodstvennye fondy*) and 100-hectare agricultural area. But these cannot be used in the same manner, because in production funds and agricultural area the Soviet statistics do not give figures for sovkhozy only, but include all other state-owned agricultural enterprises.

[5] *Ekonomika sotsialisticheskogo selskogo khoziaistva* (Moscow, 1965), pp. 29, 34.

[6] On these cf. Wädekin, *Privatproduzenten* . . . , Appendix B.

[7] See the explanations on the derivation of these statistical data in *Narodnoe khoziaistvo SSR v 1965 g.* (Moscow, 1966), p. 812 (hereafter cited as *Narkhoz-*).

TABLE 1

GROSS PRODUCTION BY SECTORS OF SOVIET AGRICULTURE, 1958–1965

(Billion Rubles in "Comparable" Prices as of 1958)

	Total of Socialized Sector	Kolkhozy	Sovkhozy and Other State-owned Agricultural Enterprises[a]	Sovkhozy Only[a]	Private Sector
1958	30.5	*ca.* 23	7.5	6.5	18.0
1959			8.2	7.0	
1960	32.5	*ca.* 22.3	10.2	9.25	17.3
1961			12.5	10.6	
1962	34.6	*ca.* 21.3	13.3	11.3	17.3
1963	31.6	*ca.* 19		10.5	16.4
1964	38.3	*ca.* 23		13.4	16.6
1965	38.3	23–23.5	14.8–15.3	13.8	18.0

[a]Sovkhozy of the Ministry of Agriculture of the U.S.S.R. constitute by far the greater part; the production of all other sovkhozy is minimal by comparison. As to the share of other state-owned agricultural enterprises, Venzher states that of the average socialized production from 1958 to 1962, the production of sovkhozy was 31 per cent, of other state-owned agricultural enterprises, 4 per cent, and of the kolkhozy, 65 per cent. Recalculating to total production and including the private sector, these figures agree with those given in this table. (V. G. Venzher, "Osobennosti kolkhoznoi ekonomiki i problemy ee razvitiia," V. G. Venzher, I. B. Kvasha *et al.*, ed., *Proizvodstvo, nakoplenie, potreblenie* [Moscow, 1965], p. 259.) This implies a share of 85–90 per cent of the agricultural production of the state sector for the sovkhozy and fits into the figures of column 3 and 4 of the above table.

Sources: Production of sovkhozy calculated from the numbers of sovkhoz workers (for 1958–62: *Narodnoe khoziaistvo SSSR v 1962 godu*, p. 356 f. [hereafter Narkhoz-]; for 1963: *Narkhoz-1963*, p. 358; for 1964, 1965: *Narkhoz-1965*, p. 424) and from the gross production per 100 workers as given by L. Sineva, "O fondootdache v sovkhozakh," *Voprosy ekonomiki*, No. 12 (1966), p. 42.

Production of sovkhozy including other state-owned agricultural enterprises: For 1962, calculated from total gross production of Soviet agriculture (51.9 billion rubles, see *Narkhoz-1965*, p. 260) and its division by percentages as given by E. S. Karnaukhova in *Ekonomika*, pp. 29, 34; for 1965, the difference between kolkhoz production and all socialized production; for 1958–61, calculated on the basis of the figure for 1962 and the indices given in *Narkhoz-1962*, p. 358. Total of socialized production; private production: Calculated from the figure of 34.2 per cent for the private sector as given by V. Maniakin, "Preodolet otstavanie v razvitii selskogo khoziaistva," *Ekonomika selskogo khoziaistva* (hereafter *Ek. selkhoz.*), No. 2 (1965), p. 10 and the figures of total agricultural production and the indices in *Narkhoz-1964*, p. 247, and *Narkhoz-1965*, p. 260; cf. the table in Karl-Eugen Wädekin, *Privatproduzenten in der sowjetischen Landwirtschaft* (Cologne: Bundesinstitut für Ostwissenschaftliche und Internationale Studien, 1967), p. 22.

Production of kolkhozy: Except for 1962 (percentage as given by Karnaukhova, *Ekonomika*) and for 1965 (percentage as given by S. Kolesnev, "Razvitie i ukreplenie kolkhoznogo stroia," *Ek. selkhoz.*, No. 2 [1967], p. 27); all other figures calculated from the difference between all socialized production and production of sovkhozy and other state-owned agricultural enterprises.

ture but together they possess considerable significance. True, a common denominator for all of them, as in the case of gross production figures, cannot be given, but still they give the most important components of production potential. As summarized in Table 2, they contain certain problems; for example, in the comparison of the number of

TABLE 2

SELECTED DATA ON THE AGRICULTURAL PRODUCTION
POTENTIAL OF KOLKHOZY, SOVKHOZY, AND THE PRIVATE
SECTOR IN U.S.S.R., 1953—1965

	Agricultural Areas (In Thousand Hectares)	Sown Areas (In Thousand Hectares)	Livestock Units (In Thousands)	Energy Available (In Thousand Horsepower)	Households (In Thousands)	Days Worked (In Millions)
Total						
1953	481,606 (486,400[a])	157,172	56,334	87,800	21,200–21,400	11,437
1956	487,200[c]	194,750	64,157	117,100	21,600–21,700	11,589
1958	500,800	195,646	74,403	137,900	21,900–22,300	11,424
1962	527,900	215,978	89,708	189,087	21,800–22,500	12,159
1963	532,600	218,520	81,369	205,608	21,800–22,500	11,882
1964	539,500	212,802	84,408	218,568	21,700–22,400	———
1965	542,800	209,104	89,886	236,582	21,600–22,400	———
Kolkhozy						
1953	396,600[a]	132,003	29,435	63,900[d]	19,741	6,447[d]
1956	394,800[c]	152,151	30,851	85,400[d]	19,891	6,849[d]
1958	321,300	131,408	31,097	91,500[d]	18,833	5,986[d]
1962	258,900	114,420	40,859	87,961	16,255	4,787
1963	247,000	113,990	35,677	96,404	16,101	4,643
1964	236,600	110,846	36,338	101,597	15,887	———
1965	228,600	105,072	37,638	106,737	15,414	———
Sovkhozy						
1953	77,600[a] (88,700[a,b])	15,155	4,154	9,815	1,500–1,650	715
1956	91,300[b,c]	31,515	5,022	17,729	1,750–1,950	819
1958	178,000[b]	52,451	10,196	35,200	3,100–3,500	1,292
1962	266,900[b]	86,678	22,519	73,897	5,500–6,200	2,164
1963	283,100[b]	89,724	21,153	80,547	5,700–6,400	2,205
1964	300,800[b]	87,301	23,528	85,921	5,800–6,500	———
1965	311,600[b]	89,062	24,595	94,522	6,200–7,000	———
Private sector						
1953	7,910[a]	6,933	23,837	———	n.a.*	4,258
1956	7,910[a]	7,310	27,522	———	n.a.	3,893
1958	7,650	7,350	29,158	———	n.a.	4,107
1962	7,250	6,730	26,236	———	n.a.	5,155
1963	7,530	6,720	24,832	———	n.a.	4,978
1964	7,090	6,270	25,509	———	n.a.	———
1965	7,590	6,600	27,787	———	n.a.	———

*Not applicable.
a In 1954.
b Including other state-owned agricultural enterprises.
c In 1955.
d Including MTS and RTS.

Sources and explanations: Agricultural areas, as of November 1, the year following; it must be kept in mind that the privately used areas are not fully represented in Soviet statistics; in 1962, for instance (for other years this cannot be calculated), *ca.* 1.35 million hectares must be added (for details see Wädekin, *Privatproduzenten . . .*, p. 221 ff.). Sources: *Selskoe khoziaistvo SSSR, Statisticheskii sbornik* (hereafter *Selkhoz-*) (Moscow, 1960), p. 500 (for 1953, U.S.S.R. total); *Narkhoz* (1955), p. 104 f. (for 1953, i.e., Nov. 1, 1954); *Narkhoz-1956*, p. 109–11 (for 1956, i.e., Nov. 1, 1955); *Narkhoz-1958*, p. 383–85 (for 1958); *Narkhoz-1962*, p. 243–45 (for

1962); *Narkhoz-1963*, p. 238–40 (for 1963); *Narkhoz-1964*, p. 261–63 (for 1964); *Narkhoz-1965*, p. 279 (for 1965). Sown areas as at the end of spring sowing. *Sources: Selkhoz-1960*, p. 128 f. (for 1953); *Posevnye ploshchadi SSSR*, I, 172 f. (kolkhozy in 1956, 1958); *Narkhoz-1956*, p. 146 f. (sovkhozy in 1956); *Dostizheniia sovetskoi vlasti za sorok let v tsifrakh* (Moscow, 1957), p. 173 (private sector in 1956); *Narkhoz-1959*, p. 334 (U.S.S.R. total in 1959); *Narkhoz-1962*, p. 256 f. (U.S.S.R. total in 1958, 1962), p. 344 f. (kolkhozy in 1962), p. 356 f. (sovkhozy in 1958, and 1962); *Narkhoz-1963*, p. 348 f. (kolkhozy in 1963), p. 358 (sovkhozy in 1963); *Narkhoz-1964*, p. 272 (private sector in 1958, 1962), p. 402 f. (kolkhozy in 1964); *Narkhoz-1965*, p. 288 f. (private sector in 1963, 1964, 1965), p. 294 (U.S.S.R. total in 1963, 1964, 1965), p. 416 f. (kolkhozy in 1965), p. 424 (sovkhozy in 1964, 1965).

Livestock units per end of each year excluding horses, camels, reindeer, and others (i.e., in Soviet statistics for January 1 of year following). The following conversion rates were used: 1 cow=1.0 unit; all cattle other than cows=0.4 unit for U.S.S.R. on the whole, but 0.5 unit in kolkhozy and sovkhozy (because in these enterprises there are more working oxen and young cattle of more than one year of age), and 0.3 unit in the private sector (because much of the privately owned cattle is one year old or less); 1 pig=0.25 unit; 1 sheep or goat=0.1 unit. *Sources: Selkhoz-1960*, p. 266 ff. (for 1953, 1956, 1958); *Narkhoz-1964*, p. 353 f. (for 1962); *Narkhoz-1965*, p. 368 f. (for 1963, 1964, 1965).

Energy available as per end of year, including animal draft power. *Sources: Dostizheniia*, p. 163 (sovkhozy in 1953, 1956); *Narkhoz-1959*, p. 415 (U.S.S.R. total in 1956), p. 433 (kolkhozy in 1956); *Narkhoz-1960*, p. 505 (kolkhozy in 1953 and 1958), p. 516 (sovkhozy in 1958); *Narkhoz-1962*, p. 322 f. (U.S.S.R. total in 1953, 1958, 1962; sovkhozy and kolkhozy in 1962); *Narkhoz-1963*, p. 331 f. (for 1963); *Narkhoz-1964*, p. 379 (for 1964); *Narkhoz-1965*, p. 394 (for 1965).

Households: in kolkhozy, the number of households; in sovkhozy, 80 to 90 per cent of the annual average number, fully employed (for a definition of annual average see I. Paskhaver, *Balans trudovykh resursov kolkhozov* [Kiev, 1961], p. 140 f.; for the conversion rate of 80 to 90 per cent, see text of this paper). *Sources: Selkhoz-1960*, p. 46 f. (sovkhozy in 1956), p. 52 (kolkhozy in 1953, 1956, 1958); *Narkhoz-1962*, p. 344 f. (kolkhozy in 1962), p. 356 f. (sovkhozy in 1953, 1958, 1962); *Narkhoz-1963*, p. 348 f. (kolkhozy in 1963), p. 358 (sovkhozy in 1963); *Narkhoz-1964*, p. 402 f. (kolkhozy in 1964); *Narkhoz-1965*, p. 416 f. (kolkhozy in 1965), p. 424 (sovkhozy in 1964, 1965).

Days worked as given by Nancy Nimitz, *Farm Employment in the Soviet Union, 1928–1963* (Santa Monica, Calif.: The RAND Corporation, 1965), p. 7 (Table 1).

hectares of the agricultural area (counted in late fall) with those of the sown area (counted in spring), or in the equation of kolkhoz households to 80–90 per cent of the full-time workers of the sovkhozy.

The calculation of livestock units used here, especially, can cause contradiction, because cattle (except cows) have been rated lower in the private sector and higher in the social sector, (see Table 2 explanation); thus a middle value was taken for the total U.S.S.R. However, the resulting distortions can be expected to be less than those resulting from the mechanical use of a uniform key for all sectors.

On the whole, it was necessary to use the figures provided by Soviet statistics, and from this fact most of the deficiencies arise. Key years in the table are those that represent turning points and, apart from those years, each year after 1962 was included. Table 3 uses the same data converted into percentage figures.

TABLE 3

PERCENTAGE SHARE OF KOLKHOZY, SOVKHOZY, AND PRIVATE SECTOR
IN PRODUCTION POTENTIAL OF SOVIET AGRICULTURE, 1953—1965,
(Per Cent of the Corresponding U.S.S.R. Totals)

	Agricultural Areas	Sown Areas	Livestock Units	Energy Available	Households	Days Worked
Kolkhozy						
1953	81.5[a]	84	51	73[d]	92–93	56[d]
1956	81[c]	78	48	73[d]	92	59[d]
1958	64	67	42	66[d]	85–86	52[d]
1962	49	53	46	46.5	72–75	39
1963	46	52	44	47	72–74	39
1964	44	52	43	46.5	71–73	——
1965	42	50	42	45	69–71	——
Sovkhozy						
1953	16[a] (18[a,b])	10	7	11	7–8	6
1956	19[b,c]	16	8	15	8–9	7
1958	36[b]	27	14	26	14–16	11
1962	50[b]	40	25	39	25–28	18
1963	53[b]	41	26	39	25–28	19
1964	56[b]	41	28	39	26–30	——
1965	57[b]	43	27	40	28–32	——
Private sector						
1953	1.6[a]	4.4	42	n.a.	n.a.*	——
1956	1.6[c]	3.8	43	n.a.	n.a.	——
1958	1.5	3.8	39	n.a.	n.a.	——
1962	1.4	3.1	29	n.a.	n.a.	——
1963	1.4	3.1	30	n.a.	n.a.	——
1964	1.3	2.9	30	n.a.	n.a.	——
1965	1.4	3.2	31	n.a.	n.a.	——

*Not applicable.
a In 1954   b Including other state-owned agricultural enterprises.   c In 1955.
d Including MTS and RTS. *Sources*: Same as Table 2. Some small inconsistencies of the percentage figures are due to rounding (some of the absolute figures were rounded previously); differing conversion rates for the socialized and the private sectors (see explanation to Table 2) affect livestock unit figures.

The private sector plays a subordinate role in soil utilization. In animal husbandry, however, its part is still important, although its role was strongly repressed in the years between 1958 and 1962. At the same time, the importance of the sovkhoz sector increased; of the three sectors, the latter is best equipped with energy, especially energy per labor unit. However, the kolkhoz sector still has about twice the labor force of the sovkhoz sector.

Apart from these generally known facts, the following characteristics emerge from the figures:

1. The land of the kolkhozy is generally cultivated more intensively than that of the sovkhozy. The kolkhozy have a larger share of the sown

areas than of the agricultural areas. The sovkhozy have a relatively and absolutely larger share of the extensively used areas.

2. The livestock units also show a greater intensity of production in the kolkhoz sector, where there is more livestock per agricultural and per sown area.

3. Between 1953 and 1958, the sovkhoz sector showed a marked expansion, especially in its agricultural and sown areas (since 1956, at the expense of the kolkhozy) and between 1958 and 1962 the number of livestock also started to increase. Thus the difference between the sovkhozy and the kolkhozy sectors was lessened, though not eliminated.

4. The sovkhoz sector did not stop growing immediately after the fall of Khrushchev. As far as livestock units are concerned, there has been no change in its percentage share from 1964 to 1965, because the kolkhozy, too, increased their units.

5. The comparison of each sector's share of production (Table 1), with its share of the factors of production, reveals the following:

On the whole, the kolkhozy and the sovkhozy share of production is approximately the same amount less than their respective share of the factors of production. The private sector's share of production is accordingly larger (this applies also to livestock production). However, there is a difference between the kolkhozy and the sovkhozy insofar as the sovkhozy's share of the agricultural and sown areas is higher than their share of production, i.e., their productivity per hectare is lower than that of the kolkhozy. This is explained by the fact that in the sovkhozy, crop production plays a comparatively larger part, yet—apart from special uses for vegetables, fruits, industrial plants, and so on—the greater part of the soils used for the cultivation of crops are comparatively low in productivity. "The majority of the grain and fodder-producing sovkhozy have poorer soils and natural conditions than the kolkhozy."[8]

The differences between the kolkhozy and the sovkhozy cannot be simply attributed to inherent organizational differences. These differences do not say anything about efficiency of operation in the kolkhozy and the sovkhozy. In the first place, the sovkhozy play a larger part in those areas of the Soviet Union where the natural conditions dictate a more extensive utilization of the soil. In the fertile areas of black soil (Ukraine, South Russia) and in some of the southern parts of intensive utilization (cotton, fruit, and so on, in the Moldavian S.S.R., Trans-

[8] P. A. Ignatovskii, *Sotsialno-ekonomicheskie izmeneniia v sovetskoi derevne* (Moscow, 1966), p. 313.

caucasia, and Central Asia) the kolkhozy are the prevailing form of agricultural organization.

TABLE 4

DISTRIBUTION OF AREAS, ENERGY, AND LABOR FORCE OF SOVKHOZY
AND OTHER STATE-OWNED AGRICULTURAL ENTERPRISES BY REGIONS
OF THE SOVIET UNION, 1965

	All Agricultural Areas	Tilled Land	Natural Pasture	Energy Available (Thousand Horsepower, Sovkhozy Only)	Labor Force (In Thousands)
	(In Million Hectares, as of Nov. 1)				
(Figures in parentheses indicate percentage of over-all figures of each region)					
Russian S.F.S.R.	109.9	63.15	29.33	51011	4895
	(=49.5%)	(=47%)	(=52%)	(=41.5%)	
Urals, Siberia, Soviet Far East	55.3	29.55	15.69	———	———
	(=60%)	(=60%)	(=60%)	———	———
Volga, Vyatka, Central Black Earth	6.6	5.15	0.82	———	———
	(=27%)	(=27%)	(=40%)	———	———
Kazakhstan	157.3	29.15	119.81	24407	1063
	(=87%)	(=88%)	(=86%)	(=79.5%)	
Central Asia	27.3	2.18	24.44	4478	516
	(=40%)	(=35%)	(=41%)	(=28%)	
Transcaucasia	2.5	0.69	1.2	1766	333
	(=31%)	(=27%)	(=30%)	(=28%)	
Ukraine	8.6	6.64	1.2	7806	1047
	(=20%)	(=19%)	(=27%)	(=19%)	
Moldavia	0.4	0.24	0.06	332	74
	(=15%)	(=23%)	(=17%)	(=11%)	
Belorussia	3.1	2.01	0.39	2559	403
	(=31%)	(=32%)	(=30%)	(=28%)	
Baltic Republics	2.9	1.79	0.47	2163	263
	(=32%)	(=31%)	(=36%)	(=27%)	
Kaliningrad *Oblast*	0.4	0.19	0.11	———	———
	(=50%)	(=47%)	(=46%)	———	———

Sources: Agricultural area, developed area, natural pasture: *Narkhoz-1965*, pp. 279, 280, 282 f. Energy available (per end of year; includes animal draft power): *Narkhoz-1965*, p. 394. Labor force (recalculated to annual average of fully employed): *Narkhoz-1965*, p. 562 f.

This fact becomes clear after an examination of the present distribution of sovkhozy over the territory of the Soviet Union (we lack corresponding figures for the distribution of sovkhoz livestock units in recent times). Table 4 clearly indicates that in sovkhozy production the emphasis lies on the extensive cultivation and utilization of areas in Asiatic Russia, in the Urals, in Kazakhstan, and, to a lesser extent, in Central Asia; a numerically unimportant exception is Kaliningrad *oblast*. Compared to that, the sovkhozy play a subordinate part in Belorussia, in the Baltic areas, in Transcaucasia, and especially in the Moldavian

TABLE 5
PERCENTAGE SHARE OF KOLKHOZY, SOVKHOZY, AND PRIVATE SECTOR IN THE
PRODUCTION POTENTIAL OF SOVIET AGRICULTURE BY DIFFERENT
REGIONS, 1953–1965

		Agricultural Area	Sown Area	Livestock Units	Energy Available
Russian S.F.S.R.					
Kolkhozy	1953[c]	82[a]	84	49	77[d]
	1958	70	69	44	67[d]
	1962	52	53	40.5	45
	1965	49	50.5	38	43
Sovkhozy	1953[c]	14[a] (16[a,b])	11	8	14[d]
	1958	25	26	15	24[d]
	1962	42	41	30	40
	1965	44	43	31	41.5
Private	1953[c]	1.7[a]	3.4	42[f]	———
sector	1958	1.5	2.9	41[f]	———
	1962	1.5	2.3	31	———
	1965	1.4	2.4	30	———
Kazakh S.S.R.					
Kolkhozy	1953	71[a]	80	64	———
	1958	42	37	42	34
	1962	25	16	28[e]	12.5
	1965	13	13	16	10
Sovkhozy	1953	26[a] (29[a,b])	17	16	———
	1958	58[b]	60	33	58
	1962	75[b]	84	53[e]	80
	1965	87[b]	86	———	80
Private	1953	0.11[a]	1.5	20	———
sector	1958	0.14	0.7	24	———
	1962	0.07	0.5	20[e]	———
	1965	0.08	0.5	———	———
Central Asia					
Kolkhozy	1953	82[a]	89	68	———
	1958	65	71	51	63
	1962	65	67	49	62
	1965	59	62	43	60
Sovkhozy	1953	17[a] (17[a,b])	7	7	———
	1958	34[b]	25	16	20
	1962	35[b]	26	17	24
	1965	40[b]	35[b]	———	28[b]
Private	1953	0.3	0.4	25	———
sector	1958	0.3	n.a.	32	———
	1962	0.3	n.a.	———	———
	1965	0.3	0.3	———	———
Ukrainian S.S.R.					
Kolkhozy	1953	84[a]	83	54	———
	1958	81	80	56	———
	1962	77	76	63[e]	66
	1965	74	74	61	63
Sovkhozy	1953	8[a] (10[a,b])	10	5	———
	1958	13[b]	13	10[d]	———
	1962	18[b]	17	10[e]	16
	1965	20[b]	19	———	19
Private	1953	5.6[a]	7.2	43	———
sector	1958	5.6	7.3	39	———
	1962	5.2	6.4	31[e]	———
	1965	5.8	6.5	———	———

		Agricultural Area	Sown Area	Livestock Units	Energy Available
Belorussian S.S.R.					
Kolkhozy	1953	92[a]	87	35	——
	1958	82	79	38	77
	1962	64	61	38	53.5
	1965	62.5	60	39	52.5
Sovkhozy	1953	1[a] (2[a,b])	2	1	——
	1958	10 (12[b])	9	5	14
	1962	30[b]	28	19	29
	1965	30[b]	30	20	28
Private	1953	5.1[a]	9.9	65	——
sector	1958	5.1	9.7	57	——
	1962	5.3	8.7	47[e]	——
	1965	5.3	8.3	——	——

[a] In 1954.
[b] Including other state-owned agricultural enterprises.
[c] Including the then-existing Karelian S.S.R.
[d] Calculated from sown areas and energy power per 100 hectares of sown area.
[e] At the end of 1961.
[f] Excluding goats.
Sources: Calculated on the basis of the absolute figures in Tables 8a–8e.

S.S.R. and in the Ukraine. (The conditions of the Russian Black Earth Zone resemble those in the Ukraine.)

The Baltic and Transcaucasian republics of the Union, as well as the Moldavian S.S.R. and—not relatively speaking, but in the absolute order of magnitude—Kaliningrad *oblast,* include an unimportant part of all Soviet sovkhozy: providing 2 per cent of their agricultural areas, 4.5 per cent of the energy supply, and 7 to 8 per cent of their labor force. For the purpose of simplification they can thus be set aside while considering the sovkhozy in the different parts of the country. But it should be kept in mind that their sovkhoz production (as well as their agricultural production in general) is more intensive than the all-Union average, the share of their sovkhozy in energy applied more than doubling, and in labor force almost quadrupling, their share in agricultural areas.

Thus, if one takes into account not only the figures of 1965 but also the key years of development since 1953, then five large regions of importance for the sovkhozy emerge: the Russian S.F.S.R. (actually too large a region, but lacking enough statistical information to separate it into smaller sections); the Kazak S.S.R. (the Union republic that almost without exception has sovkhozy); Central Asia; the Ukraine; and Belorussia. The absolute figures for these Union republics can be seen in Tables 8a to 8e. The relative shares of the three sectors in each of these republics is shown in Table 5.

Regarding the key years of 1953, 1958, 1962, and 1965, the pattern of development shows that at first the sovkhozy played an important part only in Kazakhstan. The same could be said for the Russian S.F. S.R., in the Urals and east of it, but not in the other parts of this Union republic. In the steppes of South Siberia and Kazakhstan, the formation of and conversion into sovkhozy—the so-called *sovkhozizatsiia*—has reached its highest degree. The majority of the approximately 15,000 sovkhozy villages, as counted in 1959, existed in these areas; and here the sovkhozy population was already "prevailing on a considerable territory."[9] In fact, in some *raiony* of Kazakhstan there are no kolkhozy left except for, perhaps, a single one.[10]

In Kazakhstan and the R.S.F.S.R. the *sovkhozizatsiia* took place mainly in the years between 1954 and 1962. In the course of its second phase (1958–62), the livestock numbers of the sovkhoz sector, especially, were enlarged. In Central Asia, however, where the sovkhozy play an important part but are not yet predominant, the process came to its first conclusion as early as 1958. But in the years after 1962 it started again. In the Ukraine today the kolkhozy are by far in the majority, although the conversion into sovkhozy lasted almost continually over all three intervals of time. Here, on the whole, it took place considerably more slowly.

In Belorussia (where in 1953 there were almost no sovkhozy), it was only in 1958 that sovkhozy reached a share corresponding to the average in the Union at the end of the time of Stalin. But then, between 1958 and 1962 the *sovkhozizatsiia* made rapid progress here, too, and has now reached a level distinctly higher than that of the Ukraine. Yet such an acceleration in Belorussia resulted in considerably lessening the difference between the material and technical organization of the sovkhozy and the kolkhozy. In 1965 the Belorussian sovkhozy were equipped with a capital of 22,800 rubles per 100 hectares of agricultural land and 35,700 rubles per 100 hectares of the total area. The kolkhozy had a capital equipment of 20,300 rubles per 100 hectares of agricultural area and 32,800 rubles per 100 hectares tilled land. At the same time, the kolkhozy had a slightly higher output per area unit, i.e., 24,500 rubles per hectare of agricultural area and 12,600 rubles per 100 hectares of the tilled land (as compared to 24,200 and 12,200 rubles in the

[9] S. A. Kovalev, "Problemy sovetskoi geografii selskogo rasseleniia," *Geografiia naseleniia v SSSR* (Moscow, 1964), p. 132.

[10] O. S. Kolbasov, "Konferentsiia po teoreticheskim problemam budushchego primernogo ustava selskokhoziaistvennoi arteli," *Sovetskoe gosudarstvo i pravo*, No. 3 (1966), 94.

sovkhozy). The most important techniques for crop cultivation were only slightly more mechanized in the Belorussian sovkhozy than in the kolkhozy.[11]

To the degree to which the sovkhozy became more important, the kolkhozy sector decreased in importance. In a reciprocal sense, the kolkhoz sector shows the same regional changes that were seen in the development of the sovkhoz sector. But this does not mean that the changes in the kolkhoz sector are an exact reflection of the development in the sovkhoz. On the one hand, there has also been an expansion within the kolkhoz sector (e.g., through the breaking of new ground, through other new foundations,[12] through changes in internal organization, such as intensification of production or the incorporation of private plots and livestock). On the other hand, the kolkhoz sector has also given indications of shrinkage (e.g., through the migration of labor and the abandonment of tilled land), and in places agriculture has been given up completely.[13] Neither do the data supplied by the statistical yearbooks "for a comparable circle of kolkhozy" enable us to draw exact conclusions. First, as has just been explained, kolkhozy have not disappeared simply because of the transition to the sovkhozy sector, and second, these figures have not been reached on the basis of concrete, detailed data. The Central Administration of Soviet Statistics began with the changes in the total number of kolkhoz households, and from this number all their further calculations were derived by means of a common key.[14] This statistical procedure is also discernible from the otherwise unexplainable absolute numerical parallelism of gross income, indivisible funds, and the labor of the no longer existing kolkhozy outside the "comparable circle."[15]

The general repression of the private sector, especially in the years 1958–62, is well known, and has been dealt with in detail by the author.[16] Although, due to such factors as the increase or decrease of

[11] *Stroitelstvo kommunizma i sotsialnye izmeneniia v krestianstve Belorussii*, ed. K. P. Buslov, V. I. Stepanov *et al.* (Minsk, 1966), p. 74 (table).

[12] During 1957–63, 183 new kolkhozy came into existence; see V. G. Venzher, *Ispolzovanie zakona stoimosti v kolkhoznom proizvodstve* (Moscow, 1966), p. 113.

[13] E.g., the Skovorodinskii *raion* of the Amur *oblast*, where there is no agricultural enterprise at present, but where seven kolkhozy, one sovkhoz, and two other state-owned agricultural enterprises had existed up to 1960; see E. Glazkov, "Pustuiushchie zemli," *Partiinaia zhizn*, No. 20 (1966), 69.

[14] L. Grushetskii, "Sovershenstvovat metody ischisleniia sopostavimykh dannykh," *Ekonomika selskogo khoziaistva*, No. 3 (1965), 90.

[15] To be calculated from data in *Narkhoz-1965*, pp. 405, 406, and in *Narkhoz-RSFSR-1965*, p. 316.

[16] Wädekin, "Chruschtschows Kampagne gegen den Privatsektor," *Sowjetstudien*, No. 22 (1967).

the agrarian population, the facts do not clearly emerge at first glance, it is significant in this connection that the repression was most pronounced in those parts of the country where the *sovkhozizatsiia* was most widespread (R.S.F.S.R., Kazakhstan). Although the assurance had been made that in transforming kolkhozy into sovkhozy the size of the household plots would not be diminished, the campaign against the plots and livestock of sovkhoz workers and employees has in fact resulted in such restrictions in the new sovkhozy.[17] Both the general restriction of the private sector and the specific results of the conversions into sovkhozy have affected a shift of private agricultural production to the southern, climatically favored parts of the country, with their predominantly intensive soil utilization.[18] Thus the *sovkhozizatsiia* had a double significance and effect: not only did it shift weight from the kolkhozy to the sovkhozy sector, but also from the private to the socialized sector in general. Since Khrushchev's removal, the transformation of kolkhozy into sovkhozy has to a great extent lost this side effect. The reason is that the norms governing the use of the soil and the keeping of livestock for private purposes, introduced in 1964–65 for sovkhoz workers and employees, no longer differ in essence from the private operations existing in the kolkhoz sector.[19] Here one can see an important new development, the effects of which will be of great interest in the coming years.

In spite of its importance for our subject, the large complex of questions concerning the conversions of kolkhozy into sovkhozy (*sovkhozizatsiia*) can be treated here in only a few of its aspects.[20] Because of its complexity a more thorough investigation was called for, which the author has published elsewhere in 1969. It is worth mentioning that, as Khrushchev later revealed, near the end of his life Stalin was proceeding toward a liquidation of all sovkhozy.[21] Following Stalin's death, an opposite tendency developed and in the years 1954–59 about 10,500 kolkhozy were formed into sovkhozy or incorporated into sovkhozy.[22] An added 8,647[23] followed in the years 1960–63. Today, Soviet writers comment as follows: "The *sovkhozizatsiia* created not only nega-

[17] Cf. Wädekin, *Privatproduzenten* . . . , p. 65 f. (An especially significant example was given by S. Krutilin in *Lipiagi* [Moscow, 1961], p. 460.)

[18] Wädekin, *Privatproduzenten* . . . , appendices C and E.

[19] *Ibid.*, pp. 37 f., 40, also p. 44 (Table 11).

[20] For summary review by a Soviet author, see I. N. Kochin, *Preodolenie sotsialno-ekonomicheskikh razlichii mezhdu gorodom i derevnei* (Moscow, 1964), pp. 132–39.

[21] N. S. Khrushchev, *Stroitelstvo kommunizma v SSSR i rasvitie selskogo khoziaistva* (8 vols.: Moscow, 1962–64), VIII, 467 (speech of Feb. 28, 1964).

[22] "Sovetskoe krestianstvo," *Kommunist*, No. 4 (1966), p. 92.

[23] Venzher, *Ispolzovanie* . . . , p. 113.

tive economic results, but it also ran contrary to the theoretical principles" (of the party program).[24] But this refers more to the exaggerations
of the campaign than to the conversions as such.

In this connection, it must be pointed out that the *sovkhozizatsiia*
should not be pictured as a homogeneous process that took place over
the years 1953 to 1965. With regard to regional differences this has
already been mentioned above. Table 6 gives an indication of the pro-
ductional profiles of the new and the old sovkhozy. Although the numbers of sovkhozy do not precisely reflect the development, because of
some changes caused by the amalgamation or the division of sovkhozy,[25]
these figures roughly indicate the following:

1. In the first phase (1953–58) there was an increase in grain-producing sovkhozy on new territory (1954–55, 425 out of 581 new sovkhozy
were in the so-called virgin lands[26]), in extensive sheep-breeding sovkhozy,[27] and in dairy and dairy-and-meat sovkhozy.[28] The increase in
the latter occurs, almost without exception, in the years 1957–58.[29] It
introduces the development of the second phase, which starts with
Khrushchev's speech of February 16, 1957,[30] and the appeal of the
Central Committee of the CPSU and the Cabinet Council of the U.S.
S.R. to the people working in sovkhozy.[31] The task now was to supply

[24] I. Buzdalov, "Problemy rosta effektivnosti sovkhoznogo proizvodstva," *Voprosy
ekonomiki*, No. 3 (1965), pp. 4–5.

[25] Compare the footnotes to the tables in Tsentralnoe Statisticheskoe Upravlenie
pri Sovete Ministrov SSSR, *Selskoe khoziaistvo SSSR* (Moscow, 1960), p. 42, and
Narkhoz-1961, p. 448. For Belorussia, it was only recently explicitly mentioned that
diminution of sovkhoz operations through division (*razukrupnenie*) leads to an increase
of the number of sovkhozy (see *Stroitelstvo kommunizma*, ed. K. P. Buslov, note, p. 72);
on the other hand, mergers of sovkhozy also took place (see *ibid.*, p. 73).

[26] See Khrushchev's speech of Feb. 14, 1956, in Khrushchev, *Stroitelstvo* . . . , II,
206.

[27] Cf. *ibid.*

[28] Compare the decree of the Central Committee of the CPSU and the Council
of Ministers of the U.S.S.R. of April 15, 1954 "On further development of the
sovkhozy . . . ," excerpt published in *Sbornik reshenii po selskomu khoziaistvu* (Moscow,
1963), pp. 146–64; also decrees on the virgin lands campaign, which emphasized
the part to be played by the sovkhozy, of March 27, August 13, and December 25,
1954, in *Direktivy KPSS i sovetskogo pravitelstva po khoziaistvennym voprosam*, IV (Moscow,
1958), 193–205, 264–67, 319–28. Cf. Khrushchev's memorandum, of June 5, 1954,
to the Central Committee (Khrushchev, *Stroitelstvo* . . . , I, 298 f.) and his speech of
June 23, 1954 (p. 311).

[29] Between 1953 and 1956 their number increased by only 37; see Tsentralnoe
Statisticheskoe Upravlenie pri Sovete Ministrov SSSR, *SSSR v tsifrakh* (Moscow,
1958), p. 189.

[30] Khrushchev, *Stroitelstvo* . . . , II, 319.

[31] *Pravda*, March 27, 1957.

the large cities and industrial centers with potatoes and vegetables, and also with meat, milk, and poultry.

Even at that point the formation of new sovkhozy did not occur exclusively, not even—compared to the figures for the whole Soviet Union —mainly on virgin land, as has been assumed by many Western observers[32] and was later maintained by Khrushchev.[33]

2. The above refers primarily to the second phase (1958–62). In retrospect, referring to the controversy at that time between Otto Schiller and Rudolf Schlesinger,[34] it must be mentioned that Schlesinger underestimated the significance of the *sovkhozizatsiia* process. If sovkhozy are formed on already opened territory, or when sheep-and karakul sheep-breeding sovkhozy are formed on dry steppe that has been under similar extensive cultivation, this can only occur at the expense of the kolkhozy previously located in these same places.

After 1958, the number of grain-producing sovkhozy shows only a moderate increase and the milk and milk-and-meat sovkhozy show an enormous increase. (Even if it is true that dairy sovkhoz or milk-and-meat sovkhoz was only a name for many former kolkhozy without a real specialization, it seems significant enough that this name was given and not another, for instance, *potato sovkhoz* in Belorussia, and so on.) The extensive sheep-breeding sovkhozy continued to increase, but gradually eased off. The extension of fruit-and-wine, fruit-and-vegetable, and potato-vegetable sovkhozy, for the supply of the larger cities with their more sophisticated needs and changing eating habits, was resumed in 1958.[35] The now increasing number of poultry sovkhozy indicates

[32] Cf., e.g., Walter Meder, "Das sowjetische Wirtschaftsrecht," *Osteuropa-Handbuch: Sowjetunion—Das Wirtschaftssystem*, ed. Werner Markert (Cologne: Graz, 1965), p. 313, or Philip M. Raup, "Comment," *Soviet and East European Agriculture*, ed. Jerzy F. Karcz (Berkeley and Los Angeles: University of California Press, 1967), p. 261. One glance at the maps for 1958 in *Atlas selskogo khoziaistva SSSR* (Moscow, 1960), pp. 69–71, shows this widely held opinion to be erroneous, and it is even more so today than in 1958.

[33] Khrushchev, *Stroitelstvo* . . . , VI, 288 (speech of December 22, 1961).

[34] The discussion was in *Soviet Studies* and in *Osteuropa*; see the summary of the arguments: "Die Annäherung zwischen Kolchos und Sowchos," *Osteuropa*, No. 11/12 (1960), pp. 779–81; and Rudolf Schlesinger, "Zur Frage der Verwandlung von Kollektiv-in Sowjetwirtschaften," *Osteuropa*, No. 7/8 (1961), especially p. 514, where Schlesinger underrates the extent of *sovkhozizatsiia* for 1958–61. When Schlesinger maintained that there was no intention to transform *all* kolkhozy into sovkhozy (*Sowchosierung als Allgemeinlösung*), he was undoubtedly right, but it must be added that hardly anyone had expressed such an extreme interpretation.

[35] Decree of the Central Committee of the CPSU and the Council of Ministers of the U.S.S.R., "On the supply of potatoes and vegetables to the city of Moscow by means of their production in specialized sovkhozy in Moscow *oblast*," *Pravda*, Nov. 2,

the same tendency. The transfer of livestock production to the sovkhozy caused a rise in prices because the cost of production of the sovkhozy showed a high increase from 1957 to 1962, which more than made up for the decrease in cost of kolkhoz livestock production at the same time.[36]

3. The increase of sovkhozy figures in the production branches named above—fruit, wine, vegetables, poultry—was essentially reflected in the development between 1962 and 1964, and determined the growth of the sovkhoz sector to a great extent. The production potential of these sovkhozy is not well represented in Table 2 (poultry are not counted under livestock units, sown areas are not of great weight with regard to the figures of intensive soil utilization). But the production potential is represented in the sovkhoz share of production of vegetables, which almost doubled between 1958 and 1962, and eggs, which more than doubled in these years and have continued to increase.[37]

4. From 1964 to 1965 the expansion of the sovkhoz sector was speeded up, particularly in the milk-producing and in the milk-and-meat producing sovkhozy. Apart from that, hog raising (especially fattening[38]) was reinstituted in the sovkhozy. In the other branches of production a complete standstill or an insignificant growth is indicated. (The thirty-two new grain-producing sovkhozy seem to grow mainly rice. There are, for instance, as many as eighteen new rice-growing sovkhozy in Uzbekistan[39].) Evidently, "poultry factories," in which eggs or broilers are mass produced with modern methods, are included with the sovkhozy group but the breeding and incubator enterprises are not.[40] Yet they should be mentioned here to complete the picture.

1958; also similar decrees for other urban and industrial agglomerations, e.g., *Pravda*, December 12, 13, and 26, 1958. These decrees were preceded a few months earlier by a remark of Khrushchev pointing in this direction on June 17, 1958 (see Khrushchev, *Stroitelstvo* . . . , III, 229 f).

[36] Cf. the indices given by G. Kh. Rogozin, "Rezervy povysheniia proizvoditelnosti truda v zhivotnovodstve kolkhozov i sovkhozov," *Puti povysheniia proizvoditelnosti truda v selskom khoziaistve SSSR* (Moscow, 1964), p. 315.

[37] *Narkhoz-1962,* p. 238; *Narkhoz-1965,* p. 265.

[38] On the growing importance of such sovkhozy, especially cattle and pig-feeding enterprises, during the last five or six years, see A. Polunin, "Na industrialnoi osnove," *Selskaia zhizn,* April 6, 1967, p. 2 (but compare also the very critical account on the output and efficiency of such enterprises by F. Petrovskii, "V neravnykh usloviiakh," *Selskaia zhizn,* Oct. 29, 1966, p. 2).

[39] See speech of Sh. R. Rashidov of March 24, 1965, *Plenum Tsentralnogo Komiteta Kommunisticheskoi Partii Sovetskogo Soiuza, 24–26 marta 1965 goda* (Moscow, 1965), p. 65.

[40] For an example see V. Surovtsev, "96 millionov iaits v god," *Selskaia zhizn,* April 21, 1967, p. 2.

Thus, with reference to the development in 1964–65, the assumption can be made that the conversion of kolkhozy into sovkhozy was again making headway—contrary to statements made after the removal of Khrushchev.[41] Was the "transformation of an important part of the kolkhozy, through administrative channels," resumed and was there a continuation of "the campaign made in the last years for the reorganization of part of the kolkhozy into sovkhozy, and for the enlargement of the sovkhoz sector at the expense of the kolkhozy"?[42]

Against such an assumption, with reference to the present, the facts show that what is taking place in the sovkhoz sector is rather the emergence of an organization of specialized operations, an intensification of agrarian production as such, the numbers of livestock, the availability of labor, and available energy growing faster than those of the agricultural and sown areas (see Table 2). Thus it must rarely have pahpened that kolkhozy of the traditional kind were simply transformed into sovkhozy of the same kind.[43] It seems unlikely that recent *sovkhozizatsiia* was advanced as an end in itself, although *sovkhozizatsiia* is in retrospect condemned by Soviet writers only in cases where it took place "unjustifiably" and "prematurely."[44] On the other hand, if it had been deemed desirable, and if the necessary means and personnel had been made available (for the formation of sovkhozy the state must likewise raise "enormous funds"[45]), new specialized agricultural enterprises could also have been organized in the form of kolkhozy. There are high risks involved, it is true, in the marketing of perishable products in the Soviet Union, and through the formation of sovkhozy the state assumes responsibility for that, but it seems as though the state should be able to guarantee payment to the kolkhozy as well.

[41] For example, speeches by L. I. Brezhnev on March 24, 1965 (*Plenum-1965*, p. 27), on March 29, 1966 (*XXIII sezd Kommunisticheskoi Partii Sovetskogo Soiuza*, I [Moscow, 1966], 68). Cf. N. Karotamm, "Neterpelivye i realnost," *Sovetskaia Rossiia*, July 16, 1965.

[42] Thus, looking back at the Khrushchev era, I. Buzdalov, "Problemy rosta effektivnosti sovkhoznogo proizvodstva," *Voprosy ekonomiki*, No. 3 (1965), p. 4.

[43] It might be of significance that, although the First Party Secretary of Kazakhstan, D. A. Kunaev, announced on March 25, 1965, the impending formation of "dozens of new sheep-sovkozy" in his union republic (*Plenum-1965*, p. 103), by the end of 1965 there were only 21 more such sovkhozy in the whole Soviet Union than the year before (see Table 6).

[44] For example, V. Kornienko, "K voprosu o pererastanii sotsialisticheskikh otnoshenii sobstvennosti v kommunisticheskie," *Ekonomika Sovetskoi Ukrainy*, No. 4 (1967), p. 18.

[45] N. A. Aitov, "Izmeneniia sotsialnoi prirody i klassovykh osobennostei krestianstva," *Sotsiologiia*, I (Moscow, 1965), 380.

Toward the end of his administration, Khrushchev made the following statement: "The sovkhozy are state enterprises. They are easier to control and to administrate. They give better assurance that the investments of capital will be more rationally utilized."[46] That a similar attitude is prevalent today is apparent in that in all references to "specialization" and "location distribution" (*razmeshchenie*), which are emphasized over and over again, the sovkhozy are given obvious preference. It is in this sense that we should probably interpret the following words from a book that was admitted as a textbook at Khrushchev's time, but went into print only after his removal: "In the future perspective the sovkhozy, in continually improving their production, will play a continually growing part."[47]

Thus, although the formation of sovkhozy may at present not be considered as an end in itself, the emphasis on specialized production should in fact result in an indirect expansion of the sovkhoz sector. The accents have shifted slightly for the official interpretation reads now: "The importance of the sovkhozy as *exemplary socialist enterprises* in the countryside must be increased."[48] To a number of sovkhozy are being transferred the additional functions of agricultural academies and model plants.[49] The practical effect is similar to that during Khrushchev's administration when after 1958 there was a like tendency to transform the sovkhozy into specialized plants (Table 6).[50] Although specialization often existed on paper only and the organization and interior structure of these plants were not always economically efficient,[51] a distinction at a different level emerges from the fact that since the end of 1964 the conversion into sovkhozy is no longer automatically equivalent to a restriction of the private sector.

[46] Khrushchev, *Stroitelstvo* . . . , VIII, 225 (speech of Sept. 27, 1963).

[47] *Ekonomika*, p. 29; in the same sense the leading article "V interesach razvitiia sovkhoznogo proizvodstva," *Selskaia zhizn*, April 21, 1967.

[48] Resolution of the Party Congress of April 8, 1966, *XXIII sezd*, II, 309 (emphasis mine). This is very similar to what was already said in the party program of 1961, see *XII sezd kommunisticheskoi partii Sovetskogo Soiuza, 17–31 oktiabria 1961 goda*, III (Moscow, 1962), 285.

[49] V. Efimov, "Spetsialist srednego zvena," *Selskaia zhizn*, Sept. 14, 1966, p. 2 (Efimov speaks of 52 such sovkhozy in R.S.F.S.R., Ukraine, and Moldavian S.S.R.).

[50] Cf. Khrushchev's remarks to that effect on Feb. 1, 1961 (Khrushchev, *Stroitelstvo* . . . , IV, 424); of March 12, 1963 (*Stroitelstvo* . . . , VII, 465); and Feb. 14, 1964 (*Stroitelstvo* . . . , VIII, 430), and especially his memorandum to the Central Committee of March 16, 1963 (*Stroitelstvo* . . . , VII, 473–77).

[51] Kochin, *Preodolenie sotsialno-ekonomicheskikh* . . . , p. 139; V. Efimov, K. Karpov, "Sovkhozam—polnyi khoziaistvennyi raschet," *Kommunist*, No. 15 (1966), p. 79; *Stroitelstvo kommunizma i razvitie obshchestvennykh otnoshenii* (Moscow, 1966), p. 135; Khrushchev, *Stroitelstvo* . . . , VII, 395 f. (speech of Nov. 19, 1962).

TABLE 6

DEVELOPMENT IN NUMBERS OF SOVKHOZY OF VARIOUS
PRODUCTION PROFILES, SOVIET UNION TOTALS, 1953,
1958, 1962, 1964, AND 1965 (As OF END OF YEAR)

Production Profile	Number of Sovkhozy, 1953	Change (+ or −) in Number				Number of Sovkhozy, 1965
		1953–58	1958–62	1962–64	1964–65	
TOTAL SOVKHOZY	4857	+1145	+2568	+1508	+1603	11681
Grain crops, including seed grain	477	+ 559	+ 99	+ 94	+ 32	1261
Sugar beets	217	− 9	+ 69	+ 39	+ 4	320
Cotton	35	+ 71	+ 21	+ 6	+ 23	156
Other technical crops (volatile oils, tobacco, makhorka)	90	+ 2	− 5	+ 27	+ 5	119
Fruit-wine Fruit-vegetables, Potato-vegetables	806	+ 10	+ 406	+ 326	+ 120	1668
Dairy, meat and dairy	1284	+ 455	+1431	+ 565	+ 998	4633
Pigs	718	− 96	− 49	+ 8	+ 55	636
Sheep, including karakul	341	+ 269	+ 163	+ 115	+ 21	1008
Horses	153	− 81	− 5	− 1	+ 8	74
Reindeer	40	+ 3	+ 19	− 2	+ 1	61
Fur-bearing and other undomesticated animals	47	+ 6	+ 52	− 3	± 0	102
Poultry	177	+ 25	+ 241	+ 170	+ 102	715

Sources: *Narkhoz-1962*, p. 352 (for 1953, 1958, 1962); *Narkhoz-1965*, p. 422 (for 1964, 1965).

The Azerbaidzhan S.S.R. presents a good illustration of the continuation of this policy after the removal of Khrushchev. Here, after the expansion of the sovkhoz sector between 1958 and 1962, a standstill occurred (1962–63, as in most other parts of the U.S.S.R.). But afterwards an even more enthusiastic extension occurred in Azerbaidzhan, starting shortly before the removal of Khrushchev and continuing thereafter.

The increase of sovkhozy between 1958 and 1962 in Azerbaidzhan consisted mainly of an increase in the number of dairy plants and dairy-meat plants. These increased by 31,[52] whereas from 1963 to 1964, 118 of the 155 new sovkhozy were wine- and fruit-producing as well as

[52] *Narkhoz-1958*, pp. 516 f.; *Narkhoz-1962*, pp. 354 f.

vegetable- and vegetable-milk producing plants, and seven additional ones were devoted to sheep breeding.[53] The fact that the decisive increase in sovkhozy and in their agricultural and sown areas, and the corresponding decrease in kolkhozy and in their areas and households, occurred from the end of 1963 to the end of 1964 (whereas the sovkhoz labor force mainly increased only in 1965), indicates that the organization of the new sovkhozy started during the fall of 1964. Because the sovkhoz labor force is figured on a yearly average, the increase would have been greater in 1963–64 and less in 1964–65 than is statistically indicated had the new sovkhozy come into existence as early as spring or summer of 1964. On the other hand, the additional labor force of 1965 cannot have been added in that year, because there was not an equally strong increase in the number of sovkhozy (there were only 294 at late as 1966[54]) or of their agricultural and sown areas, nor was there an equally strong decrease in the number of kolkhoz households in 1965. Thus it is certain that the numerous new foundations of sovkhozy in Azerbaidzhan (relatively more than in any other Union republic[55]) began mainly during the fall of 1964 and ended in 1965. At the same time this involved principally a formation of specialized enterprises:

According to a government resolution the subtropical area on the Caspian Sea [i.e., the district of Lenkoran in Azerbaidzhan] is to be transformed into a basis of the cultivation of early vegetables for the whole country. For this purpose dozens of specialized sovkhozy were created.[56]

Sovkhozy, not kolkhozy, were formed for the purpose of such specialization. Thus, *sovkhozizatsiia* continued, even if it did not go by this name. The process seems to be handled more economically these days.

In conclusion, it is appropriate to consider the labor potential in the kolkhozy and the sovkhozy. Since we are dealing with the potential rather than the actual amount of work done, it will be appropriate to start from the household figures in order to have a basis of comparison

---

[53] *Narkhoz. Azerbaidzhanskoi SSR v 1963 godu* (Baku, 1965), p. 118, and *Narkhoz. Azerbaidzhanskoi SSR v 1964 godu* (Baku, 1965), p. 94.

[54] *SSSR v tsifrakh v 1966 godu* (Moscow, 1967), p. 112.

[55] In no other union republic did the number of sovkhozy more than double in 1963–64; see *Narkhoz-1965*, p. 423.

[56] A. Glazkov, "Nastoichivost khoshkadam," in *Selskaia zhizn*, Feb. 9, 1967, p. 2. See also articles by the same author in *Selskaia zhizn*, Dec. 25, 1966, p. 3, and Feb. 14, 1967, p. 2, and an article by A. Bakhyshev, party secretary of this southernmost district of Azerbaidzhan, where there are no longer any kolkhozy, in *Selskaia zhizn*, Feb. 19, 1967, p. 3.

for both sectors. For that purpose, the following preliminary remarks should be noted:

Soviet writers usually assume that the labor force (converted into the number of fully employed on an annual average basis[57]), corresponds to the number of sovkhoz households.[58] This does not, however, quite apply to the average for the country as a whole, for the annual average of labor force includes approximately 20 per cent temporary and seasonal workers.[59] A large part of these are family members of permanent workers—women, old people, and juveniles capable of working. They work periodically and average fifty work days per year on the sovkhoz.[60] In addition to these family members, many seasonal workers are brought in from outside the sovkhozy, some from neighboring kolkhozy[61] and some even from the cities.[62]

Thus, assuming that one household corresponds to each *permanently*

[57] Cf. I. Paskhaver, *Balans trudovykh resursov kolkhozov* (Kiev, 1961), p. 140 f.

[58] Cf. Venzher, *Kolkhoznyi stroi*, p. 57 (Table 9); the same relationship is applied, on the basis of empirical studies, for the Orenburg *oblast*, by V. P. Rodionov, "Sotsialnye razlichiia mezhdu selskim i gorodskim otriadami rabochego klassa," *Izmenenie sotsialnoi struktury sotsialisticheskogo obshchestva*, ed. M. N. Rutkevich (Sverdlovsk, 1965), p. 112.

[59] For 1959 we have a Soviet statement that for each 100 persons constantly employed in sovkhozy there were 25 temporarily employed; i.e., 13–14 in January and December, and 35–36 in August and September (see A. N. Goltsov, "Raspredelenie i ispolzovanie trudovykh resursov v selskom khoziaistve," *Trudovye resury SSSR*, ed. N. I. Shishkin [Moscow, 1961], p. 106). For 1960, the annual average of temporarily employed persons was given as 23 per 100 fully employed, with a peak of 33 in August–September (see I. A. Borodin, "Reshaiushchie faktory effektivnogo ispolzovaniia trudovykh resursov v selskom khoziaistve," *Ispolzovanie trudovykh resursov v selskom khoziaistve*, ed. I. A. Borodin [Moscow, 1964], p. 10). Approximately the same correlation for 1962 is implied by V. F. Mashenkov, *Ispolzovanie trudovykh resursov selskoi mestnosti* (Moscow, 1965), p. 140; cf. G. Shmelev, "Sezonnost truda i puti ee sokrashcheniia," *Voprosy ekonomiki*, No. 8 (1962), p. 80. For 1961, the indicated percentage is a little less, namely 18.9; see I. N. Popov-Cherkasov, V. S. Turbin, V. I. Buzykin, *Organizatsiia zarabotnoi platy rabochikh v sovkhozakh SSSR* (Moscow, 1964), p. 124.

[60] E. A. Panova, *Pravovoe regulirovanie truda v sovkhozakh* (Moscow, 1960), pp. 38–41; for the number of workdays per year, see I. S. Rusanov, *Zaniatost naseleniia i ispolzovanie trudovykh resursov* (Moscow, 1965), pp. 104 f.

[61] Cf. Paskhaver, *Balans trudovykh*, pp. 249 f. (Table 57), and M. S. Babadzhanian, O. Kh. Karchikian, F. P. Pososhnikova, "Ispolzovanie trudovykh resursov v selskom khoziaistve Armianskoi SSR," *Ispolzovanie . . .*, ed. Borodin, p. 256.

[62] Cf. the decree of the Central Committee of the CPSU and the Council of Ministers of the U.S.S.R. of July 12, 1962, which tried to restrict this kind of employment, but could not and had not wanted to abolish it completely; it was under the heading: "On the entreaties of several union republics concerning the employment of urban workers and employees in agricultural operations of kolkhozy and sovkhozy," in *Sbornik reshenii*, pp. 620–24.

employed sovkhoz worker, the number of sovkhoz households would only be 80 per cent of the statistically registered labor force. However, this statistically registered labor force refers only to people working in the "basic production" of the sovkhozy, not to those working in housing construction and general repairs. There are no more than 3–5 per cent in the latter group. In addition there are about 5 per cent working in subsidiary enterprises on the sovhozy.[63] To all appearances only part of the workers in these two categories are fully employed in these secondary areas. For the most part, they combine seasonal work in these branches with work in "basic production."[64] Taking this fact into account, the number of related sovkhoz households should not be more than 5 per cent the number of permanently employed. On the other hand, there surely are some cases in which more than one person per family is fully employed on the sovkhoz, e.g., the wife, apart from the husband, working in the area of animal husbandry or in sovkhoz administration. Thus the relation of households to the yearly average of fully employed drops down again to approximately 70–80 per cent.

If the author (in this paper as well as elsewhere)[65] regards a ratio of 80–90 per cent as close to reality, he does this for the reason that in sovkhoz villages and settlements there are households that have workers who are no longer able to work and be active members of the sovkhoz. The transformation of kolkhozy into sovkhozy has resulted in an increase of such households. Because of the unfavorable age- and sex-structure of the kolkhoz population,[66] there were a great many of these households in former kolkhozy. Also, part of the *kolkhozniki* capable of work withdrew during the conversion into sovkhozy.[67] Yet for the most part their households remained in the sovkhoz village, even though their place of work is now outside the village or part of the family has moved away.

For computing the average for the country as a whole, the assump-

---

[63] S. Valter: "Razvivat podsobnye promysly v sovkhozakh," *Ekonomika selskogo khoziaistva*, No. 2 (1967), p. 99.

[64] *Ibid.*, pp. 100 f.

[65] Wädekin, *Privatproduzenten* . . . , Appendix D, p. 245.

[66] Cf. Karl-Eugen Wädekin, "Landwirtschaftliche Bevölkerung und Arbeitskräfte der Sowjetunion in Zahlen," *Osteuropa-Wirtschaft*, No. 1 (1967), pp. 47–49.

[67] Goltsov, "Raspredelenie i ispolzovanie . . . ," p. 92, gives the percentage of those changed over to other branches of the economy as 5.8 per cent for 1959 and 1960 and the percentage of those who could not be provided with work in the new sovkhozy as 3.4 per cent. Goltsov adds that another 12.1 per cent of able-bodied kolkhoz members—presumably these were mostly women—from then on worked only in the household and for the private plot and livestock, i.e., they were mainly second members of families in which one person now worked full time in sovkhoz production.

tion is here made that the number of sovkhoz households comes to 80–90 per cent of the number of permanent sovkhoz workers and employees, and that this figure enables us to relate it to the number of households in the kolkhozy. Yet this assumption is not possible for certain parts of the U.S.S.R. because of high regional differences in family and household size and the differing share of seasonal workers in the yearly average of sovkhoz workers.[68] The conversion of sovkhoz labor force into sovkhoz households has thus been performed only for the Union as a whole (Tables 2 and 3), not for special regions of the country (Tables 8a–8e).

Table 2 reveals that the number of households in kolkhozy and sovkhozy together has remained nearly constant from 1953 to 1965. Contrary to this, all Soviet publications state that after a slight increase between 1953 and 1957 (also reflected in the number of households), the number of persons in farm labor in the Soviet Union decreased steadily.[69] This indicates not only the diminishing number of persons per household, but also the fact that a rising percentage of people not obligated to work in the kolkhozy or sovkhozy because they are under- or over-age, or for other reasons, are part of the household figures. It is necessary to mention that in the sovkhozy the relationship between the amount of labor days worked and the number of households is much more favorable than in the kolkhozy. This must be ascribed partly to an increased use of seasonal nonresident labor on the sovkhozy[70] that, combined with higher mechanization, results in a more constant utilization of the permanent workers during the course of the year. Another reason is the more favorable age structure of the sovkhozy population. Significantly, a comparison between the number of labor days worked and the number of households, which generally decreased between 1953 and 1963, reveals that the relationship in the sovkhozy by now has come closer to that existing in the kolkhozy: In 1953 there were 326 working days for each kolkhoz household and 430–480 per sovkhoz household, i.e., 32–47 per cent more to each sovkhoz household. Ten years later there were 288 days per kolkhoz household to 340–390 for a sovkhoz household—i.e., only 18–35 per cent more. This change can be attributed mainly to the conversion of many kolkhozy into sovkhozy, where-

[68] In the grain sovkhozy of the virgin lands areas of Kazakhstan, for example, the percentage of seasonal workers at harvest time reaches 50 per cent; see reader's letter by S. Azev, as given in *Voprosy ekonomiki*, No. 5 (1965), p. 129.

[69] Cf. the table in Wädekin, "Landwirtschaftliche Bevölkerung . . . ," p. 45.

[70] In kolkhozy the percentage of such labor is, on the whole, negligible and amounts to *ca.* 3 per cent; see Nancy Nimitz, *Farm Employment in the Soviet Union, 1928–1963* (Santa Monica, Calif.: The RAND Corporation, 1965), pp. 31, 131 f.

TABLE 7
SELECTED DATA ON THE DEVELOPMENT OF SOVKHOZY
IN THE AZERBAIDZHAN S.S.R., 1958–1965

| | | Sovkhozy | | | | Kolkhozy | | |
	Number of Enterprises	All Agricultural Areas (In Million Hectares)	Tilled Land	Livestock Units	Labor Force (In Thousands)	All Agricultural Areas (In Million Hectares)	Tilled Land	Number of Households (In Thousands)
1958	74	0.3	0.1ᵃ	36	22ᵇ	3.5	1.31ᵃ	324
1962	118	0.7	0.19	97	41ᵇ	3.2	1.22	363
1963	118	0.7	0.19	102	45ᵇ	3.2	1.17	367
1964	263	1.2	0.37	182	71ᵇ	2.6	0.95	289
1965	285	1.3	0.35	n.a.	132ᵇ	2.6	0.98	294

ᵃ At end of 1959.

ᵇ Includes other state-owned agricultural enterprises.

Explanation and sources: Number of sovkhozy (at end of year): *Narkhoz-1963,* p. 357 (for 1958, 1962, 1963); *Narkhoz-1965,* p. 423 (for 1964, 1965).

Total agricultural area and tilled land, as of November 1, each year: *Narkhoz-1958,* p. 385 (1958); *Selkhoz-1960,* p. 125 (tilled land, end of 1959); *Narkhoz-1962,* p. 245 f. (for 1962); *Narkhoz-1963,* p. 240 f. (for 1963); *Narkhoz-1964,* p. 263 f. (1964); *Narkhoz-1965,* p. 279 f. (for 1965).

Livestock units, as of end of year: *Narkhoz. Azerbaidzhanskoi SSR v 1964 godu* (Baku, 1965), p. 93.

Labor force in sovkhozy, annual average of employed: *Narkhoz-1958,* p. 662 f. (for 1958); *Narkhoz-1962,* p. 456 f. (for 1962); *Narkhoz-1963;* p. 478 f. (for 1963); *Narkhoz-1964,* p. 550 f. (for 1964); *Narkhoz-1965,* p. 562 f. (for 1965).

Number of kolkhoz households, per end of year: *Narkhoz. Azerbaidzhanskoi SSR v 1964 godu,* p. 85 (for 1958, 1963, 1964); *Narkhoz. Azerbaidzhanskoi SSR v 1963 godu* (Baku, 1965), p. 109 (for 1962); *Narkhoz-1965,* p. 280 (for 1965).

by, in part, the less favorable age- and sex-structure of the former kolkhoz population reduced the sovkhozy average.[71]

Even though, for the reasons given, calculations for separate regions cannot be made, the fact emerges that—in contrast to the country as a whole, or to Russian S.F.S.R. totals—the approximated regional totals of households did not remain constant. While in some regions (e.g., Non-Black-Earth zone, Siberia, Baltics) the totals clearly must have decreased (see Table 8a), Kazakhstan showed an increase in households that was caused by the opening of virgin soil and the immigration of many workers. In Central Asia (Table 8c), the increase was hardly less, although the immigration of farm workers to this area from other parts of the Soviet Union was insignificant. The same is true for Azerbaidzhan, at least for the period from 1958 to 1962. There the number of sovkhoz laborers increased, but considerably more than the

[71] From 1951 to 1964 the annual average labor force in sovkhozy and other state-owned agricultural enterprises increased by 5. 6 million; of these four million were former kolkhoz members. See "Sovetskoe krestianstvo," *Kommunist,* No. 4 (1966), p. 92.

TABLE 8a

SELECTED DATA ON THE AGRICULTURAL PRODUCTION POTENTIAL
OF KOLKHOZY, SOVKHOZY, AND PRIVATE SECTOR,
RUSSIAN S.F.S.R., 1953–1965

	Agricultural Area (In Thousand Hectares)	Sown Area	Livestock Units (In Thousands)	Energy Available (In Thousand Horsepower)	Labor Force (Kolkhoz Households; Sovkhoz Labor) (In Thousands)
R.S.F.S.R. totals					
1953	227,200[a,e]	97,051	29,209	49,700	———
1956	227,700[c]	114,405	32,715	64,500	———
1958	221,200	114,697	37,365	74,500	———
1962	221,200	129,691	45,795	98,448	———
1964	221,600	126,755	42,650	112,809	———
1965	221,900	123,945	45,358	122,963	———
Kolkhozy					
1953	187,000[a,e]	81,500	14,269	38,300[d,f]	9,204
1956	186,200[c]	92,400	14,678	———	9,164
1958	153,900	79,400	16,534	50,000[d,f]	8,411
1962	115,600	68,960	18,570	44,356	6,423
1964	114,700	66,958	16,974	51,325	6,260
1965	108,800	62,605	17,310	53,126	5,860
Sovkhozy					
1953	30,700[a] (36,400[a,b])	10,294	2,472	7,100[f]	1,075
1956	37,700[b,c]	16,245	2,964	———	1,028
1958	56,300 (64,000[b])	29,278	5,676	17,570[f]	2,122
1962	91,800	52,599	13,567	39,817	4,124
1064	92,500	51,379	12,510	45,095	4,078
1965	91,800	52,765	14,035	51,011	4,302
Private sector					
1953	3,810[a]	3,300	12,296[g]	———	———
1956	3,800[c]	3,300	14,757	———	———
1958	3,400	3,300	15,145[g]	———	———
1962	3,330	3,000	13,486	———	———
1964	3,040	2,800	12,776	———	———
1965	3,210	3,000	13,753	———	———

a In 1954.
b Including other state-owned agricultural enterprises.
c In 1955.
d Including MTS and RTS.
e Including the then existing Karelian S.S.R.
f Calculated from sown areas and energy power per 100 hectares of sown area.
g Excluding so-called single peasants and other minimal population groups.
Explanations as for Table 2.

Sources: Agricultural area: *Narkhoz* (1955), p. 105 (for 1953, i.e., per Nov. 1, 1954); *Narkhoz-1956*, p. 111 (for 1956, i.e., Nov. 1, 1955); *Narkhoz-1958*, p. 385 (for 1958: R.S.F.S.R. totals and sovkhozy, including other state-owned agricultural enterprises and private sector); *Narkhoz-1962*, p. 245 (for 1962, excluding sovkhozy); *Narkhoz-1964*, p. 263 (for 1964, excluding sovkhozy); *Narkhoz-1965*, p. 279 (for 1965, excluding sovkhozy); *Narkhoz-RSFSR-1964*, p. 297 f. (sovkhozy in 1962); *Narkhoz RSFSR-1965*, p. 316 f. (kolkhozy in 1958), p. 327 (sovkhozy in 1958, 1964, 1965).

Sown area: *Narkhoz-1962*, p. 184 f. (R.S.F.S.R. totals in 1962); *Narkhoz-RSFSR-1958*, p.

225 f. (kolkhozy and private sector in 1956), p. 229 f. (R.S.F.S.R. totals in 1956), p. 287 (sovkhozy in 1956); *Narkhoz-RSFSR-1962*, p. 182 f. (kolkhozy and private sector in 1953), p. 310 f. (kolkhozy in 1962), p. 327 f. (sovkhozy in 1953, 1958, 1962); *Narkhoz-RSFSR-1964*, p. 178 f. (private sector in 1962), p. 288 f. (kolkhozy in 1964), p. 300 f. (sovkhozy in 1964); *Narkhoz-RSFSR-1965*, p. 190 f. (R.S.F.S.R. totals in 1958, 1962, 1964, 1965, kolkhozy in 1965), p. 198 f. (private sector in 1958, 1964, 1965), p. 330 f. (sovkhozy in 1965).

Livestock units: *Selkhoz-1960*, p. 272-94 (for 1956); *Narkhoz-RSFSR-1961*, p. 302 f. (for 1953 and 1958, excluding sovkhozy), p. 360 f. (sovkhozy in 1953 and 1958); *Narkhoz-RSFSR-1962*, p. 328 (sovkhozy in 1962); *Narkhoz-RSFSR-1963*, p. 294 (for 1962, excluding sovkhozy), *Narkhoz-RSFSR-1965*, p. 279 (for 1964, 1965, excluding sovkhozy), p. 327 (sovkhozy in 1964, 1965).

Energy available: *Narkhoz-RSFSR-1958*, p. 314 (R.S.F.S.R. totals in 1953, 1956, 1958); *Narkhoz-RSFSR-1961*, p. 370 (sovkhozy in 1953, 1958, calculated from energy available per 100 hectares and from sown area); *Narkhoz-RSFSR-1962*, p. 323 (for 1962); *Narkhoz-RSFSR-1964*, p. 379 (for 1964); *Narkhoz-RSFSR-1965*, p. 394 (for 1965).

Kolkhoz households and sovkhoz labor: *Selkhoz-1960*, p. 52 (kolkhoz households in 1953, 1956, 1958); *Narkhoz-1962*, p. 344 f. (kolkhoz households in 1962); *Narkhoz-1964*, p. 402 f. (kolkhoz households in 1964); *Narkhoz-1965*, p. 416 f. (kolkhoz households in 1965); *Narkhoz-RSFSR-1958*, p. 287 (sovkhoz labor in 1956); *Narkhoz-RSFSR-1962*, p. 327 f. (sovkhoz labor in 1953, 1962); *Narkhoz-RSFSR-1965*, p. 327 f. (sovkhoz labor in 1958, 1964, 1965).

number of kolkhoz households decreased (Table 7). Thus, it is not the increase of sovkhoz labor as such that offsets the decrease of the kolkhoz population, but it is the regionally diverging population trends, which add up to fairly constant over-all labor resources.

No similar statements can be made about the private sector, whose workers come from the same households that furnish labor for the socialized sector. The only difference is that they work either on sovkhozy or kolkhozy territory, but in both cases outside socialized production. The private sector provides a reservoir of laborers and work opportunities that may not always be available on the kolkhoz or the sovkhoz farm. Most of these workers, however, are women, old people, invalids, and juveniles. The permanent male workers are usually *fully employed* on the sovkhoz or kolkhoz farm and work in the private sector only during their spare time.[72] The brilliant study by Nancy Nimitz[73] established that on the whole the use of labor in the private sector increased between 1953 and 1963. Since mechanization in this sector is of negligible importance, one can conclude from the total agricultural areas and from the number of livestock units that private use of labor may have decreased slightly in 1964, but that there was a considerable increase in 1965.

[72] Wädekin, *Privatproduzenten* . . . , pp. 129, 171 f.
[73] Nimitz, *Farm Employment* . . . , 155 f.

TABLE 8b
SELECTED DATA ON THE AGRICULTURAL PRODUCTION POTENTIAL
OF KOLKHOZY, SOVKHOZY, AND PRIVATE SECTOR,
KAZAKH S.S.R., 1953–1965

	Agricultural Area (In Thousand Hectares)		Sown Area	Livestock Units (In Thousands)	Energy Available (In Thousand Horsepower)	Labor Force (Kolkhoz Households; Sovkhoz Labor) (In Thousands)
Kazakhstan totals						
1953	124,700[a]		9,625	4,475	———	———
1958	144,200		28,542	6,203	18,019	———
1962	168,500		30,984	7,109[d]	26,916	———
1965	181,800		30,422	7,547	30,694	———
Kolkhozy						
1953	88,600[a]		7,654	2,878	———	545
1958	61,000		10,691	2,586	6,194[c]	418
1962	41,600		4,942	1,993[d]	3,366	268
1965	24,400		4,008	1,238	3,141	207
Sovkhozy						
1953	32,100[a]		1,637	696	———	147
	(36,000[a,b])					
1958	83,000[b]		17,136	2,065	10,500	562
1962	126,800[b]		25,899	3,748[d]	21,444	945[b]
1965	157,300[b]		26,264[b]	———	24,407	1,063[b]
Private sector						
1953	140[a]	*ca.* 140		899	———	———
1958	200	*ca.* 200		1,509	———	———
1962	120		143	1,406[d]	———	———
1965	140		150	———	———	———

[a] In 1954.
[b] Including other state-owned agricultural enterprises.
[c] Including MTS and RTS.
[d] At the end of 1961.

Explanations as for Table 2.

Sources: Agricultural area: *Narkhoz* (1955), p. 105 (for 1953, i.e., Nov. 1, 1954); *Narkhoz-1958*, p. 385 (for 1958); *Narkhoz-1962*, p. 245 (1962); *Narkhoz-1965*, p. 279 (for 1965).

Sown area: *Nar. Khoz. Kazakhskoi SSR v 1960 i 1961 gody* (Alma-Ata, 1963) (hereafter cited as *Narkhoz-Kazakh-1963*), p. 260 f. (sovkhozy in 1953, 1958), p. 263 (kolkhozy in 1953); *Narkhoz-1958*, p. 502 f. (kolkhozy in 1958); *Narkhoz-1962*, p. 254 f. (kolkhozy and sovkhozy in 1962), p. 256 f. (Kazakhstan totals in 1953, 1958, 1962); *Narkhoz-1965*, pp. 290–94 (for 1965). Private sector calculated through subtraction.

Livestock units: *Kazakhstan za 40 let* (Alma-Ata, 1960), pp. 158–61 (for 1953, 1958); *Narkhoz-Kazakh-1963*, pp. 222–27 (Kazakhstan totals in 1961), pp. 242–46 (private sector in 1961), p. 260 f. (sovkhozy in 1961), p. 263 (kolkhozy in 1961); *Narkhoz-1965*, pp. 370–73, and 416 f. (Kazakhstan totals in 1965, kolkhozy in 1965).

Energy available: *Kazakhstan za 40 let*, p. 194 f. (for 1958); *Narkhoz-1962*, p. 323 (for 1962); *Narkhoz-1965*, p. 394 (for 1965).

Kolkhoz households and sovkhoz labor: *Selkhoz-1960*, p. 52 (kolkhoz households in 1953, 1958); *Narkhoz-1962*, p. 344 f. (kolkhoz households in 1962), p. 456 f. (sovkhoz labor in 1962); *Narkhoz-1965*, p. 416 f. (kolkhoz households in 1965), p. 562 f. (sovkhoz labor in 1965); *Kazakhstan za 40 let*, p. 202 f. (sovkhoz labor in 1953, 1958).

TABLE 8c

SELECTED DATA ON THE AGRICULTURAL PRODUCTION POTENTIAL
OF KOLKHOZY, SOVKHOZY, AND PRIVATE SECTOR IN CENTRAL ASIA
(UZBEK, KIRGHIZ, TADZHIK, AND TURKMEN S.S.R.), 1953–1965

	Agricultural Area (In Thousand Hectares)	Sown Area	Livestock Units (In Thousands)	Energy Available (In Thousand Horsepower)	Labor Force (Kolkhoz Households; Sovkhoz Labor) (In Thousands)
Central Asia totals					
1953	59,800[a]	5,130	3,751	——	——
1958	63,600	5,550	4,762	8,042	——
1962	66,700	5,675	5,377	11,866	——
1965	67,500	5,899	5,416	16,138	——
Kolkhozy					
1953	49,200[a]	4,577	2,558	——	1,153
1958	41,600	3,929	2,429	5,037[c]	1,127
1962	43,400	3,817	2,648	7,326	1,246
1965	39,900	3,680	2,319	9,731	1,300
Sovkhozy					
1953	10,200[a] (10,400[a,b])	336	262	——	124
1958	21,800[b]	1,366	757	1,579	354
1962	23,100[b]	1,458	933	2,905	401
1965	27,300[b]	2,059[b]	n.a.	4,478	516[b]
Private sector					
1953	200[a]	217	954	——	——
1958	210	260	1,545	——	——
1962	190	300	—	——	——
1965	230	160	—	——	——

[a] In 1954.

[b] Including other state-owned agricultural enterprises.

[c] Including MTS and RTS.

Explanations as for Table 2.

Sources: Agricultural area: *Narkhoz* (1955) (Moscow, 1956), p. 105 (for 1953, i.e., Nov. 1, 1954); *Narkhoz-1958*, p. 385 (for 1958); *Narkhoz-1962*, p. 245 (for 1962, excluding private sector); *Narkhoz-1965*, p. 279 (1965), *Narkhoz. Srednei Azii v 1963 godu*, Tashkent, 1964, p. 132 (private sector, 1962).

Sown area: *Narkhoz. Srednei Azii v 1963 godu*, p. 134 f. (Central Asia totals in 1953, 1958, 1962), p. 197 (kolkhozy in 1953, 1958, 1962), p. 205 (sovkhozy in 1953, 1958, 1962); *Narkhoz-1965*, pp. 290–94 (for 1965). Private sector calculated through subtraction.

Livestock units: *Selkhoz-1960*, pp 272–93 (private sector in 1953, 1958, calculated through subtraction); *Narkhoz. Srednei Azii v 1963 godu*, p. 163 f. (Central Asia totals in 1953, 1958, 1962) p. 197 (kolkhozy in 1953, 1958, 1962), p. 205 (sovkhozy in 1953, 1958, 1962); *Narkhoz-1965*, pp. 370–73 (Central Asia totals in 1965), p. 416 f. (kolkhozy in 1965).

Energy available: *Narkhoz. Srednei Azii v 1963 godu*, p. 181 (for 1958, 1962), *Narkhoz-1965*, p. 394 (for 1965).

Kolkhoz households and sovkhoz labor: *Narkhoz. Srednei Azii v 1963 godu*, p. 197 (kolkhoz households in 1953, 1958, 1962), p. 205 (sovkhoz labor in 1953, 1958, 1962); *Narkhoz-1965*, p. 416 f. (kolkhoz households in 1965), p. 562 f. (sovkhoz labor in 1965).

TABLE 8d

SELECTED DATA ON THE AGRICULTURAL PRODUCTION POTENTIAL
OF KOLKHOZY, SOVKHOZY, AND PRIVATE SECTOR,
UKRAINIAN S.S.R., 1953—1965

	Agricultural Area (In Thousand Hectares)	Sown Area	Livestock Units (In Thousands)	Energy Available (In Thousand Horse-power)	Labor Force (Kolkhoz Households; Sovkhoz Labor) (In Thousands)
Ukraine totals					
1953	43,800[a]	30,970	11,087	———	———
1958	43,100	32,545	16,088	n.a.	———
1962	42,500	34,360	19,193[c]	31,446	———
1965	42,700	33,785	19,515	40,285	———
Kolkhozy					
1953	36,900[a]	25,714	6,093	———	5,482
1958	35,000	25,979	9,010	———	5,570
1962	32,700	26,222	12,051[c]	20,688	5,332
1965	31,600	25,054	11,826	25,533	5,241
Sovkhozy					
1953	3,600[a] (4,400[a,b])	3,021	527	———	358[d]
1958	5,700	4,172	1,537	n.a.	472[d]
1962	7,500[b]	5,930[b]	2,007[c]	5,022	649[d]
1965	8,600[b]	6,537[b]	———	7,806	953[d]
Private sector					
1953	2,460[a]	2,235	4,848	———	———
1958	2,440	2,394	6,351	———	———
1962	2,210	2,208	5,886[c]	———	———
1965	2,480	2,194	———	———	———

[a] In 1954.

[b] Including other state-owned agricultural enterprises.

[c] At the end of 1961.

[d] Whole labor force of sovkhozy, not only those employed in "main (i.e. agricultural) production" (*osnovnoe proizvodstvo*) of sovkhozy.

Explanations as for Table 2.

Sources: Agricultural area: *Narkhoz* (1955), p. 105 (for 1953 i.e., Nov. 1, 1954); *Narkhoz-1958*, p. 385 (for 1958); *Narkhoz-1962*, p. 245 (for 1962); *Narkhoz-1965*, p. 279 (for 1965).

Sown area: *Narkhoz-1958*, p. 503 (kolkhozy in 1958); *Narkhoz-1962*, p. 254 f. (kolkhozy and sovkhozy in 1962), p. 256 f. (Ukraine totals in 1953, 1958, 1962); *Narkhoz-1965*, p. 290 f. (kolkhozy and sovkhozy in 1965), p. 294 (Ukraine totals in 1965); *Narodne hospodarstvo Ukrainskoi RSR v 1961 rotsi* (Kiev, 1962), p. 228 f. (kolkhozy in 1953), p. 234 f. (sovkhozy in 1953, 1958). Privately sown area calculated through subtraction.

Livestock units: *Narkhoz-1965*, pp. 370–73 (Ukraine totals and kolkhozy in 1965); *Narodne hospodarstvo Ukrainskoi RSR v 1961 rotsi*, p. 324 f. (for 1953, 1958, 1961). Privately owned livestock calculated through subtraction.

Energy available: *Narkhoz-1962*, p. 323 (for 1962); *Narkhoz-1965*, p. 394 (for 1965).

Kolkhoz households and sovkhoz labor: *Selkhoz-1960*, p. 52 (kolkhoz households in 1953, 1958); *Narkhoz-1962*, 344 f. (kolkhoz households in 1962); *Narkhoz-1965*, p. 416 f. (kolkhoz households in 1965); *Ukrainska RSR v tsifrakh v 1965 rotsi* (Kiev, 1966), p. 8 (sovkhoz labor in 1958, 1962, 1965); *Narodne hospodarstvo Ukrainskoi RSR v 1961 rotsi*, p. 396 f. (sovkhoz labor in 1953).

TABLE 8e

SELECTED DATA ON THE AGRICULTURAL PRODUCTION POTENTIAL OF
KOLKHOZY, SOVKHOZY, AND PRIVATE SECTOR, BELORUSSIAN
S.S.R. 1953—1965

	Agricultural Area (In Thousand Hectares)	Sown Area	Livestock Units (In Thousands)	Energy Available (In Thousand Horsepower)	Labor Force (Kolkhoz Households; Sovkhoz Labor) (In Thousands)
Belorussia totals					
1953	10,600[a]	5,129	2,607	——	——
1958	9,800	5,449	3,349	4,895	——
1962	9,800	5,962	3,879	6,935	——
1965	9,900	6,034	4,307	9,025	——
Kolkhozy					
1953	9,900[a]	4,474	902	——	1,284
1958	8,049	4,286	1,278	3,766[c]	1,185
1962	6,300	3,649	1,473[e]	3,709	923
1965	6,190	3,609	1,682	4,734	885
Sovkhozy					
1953	100[a] (200[a,b])	90	37	——	27
1958	964 (1,200[b])	507	178	664	123
1962	3,000[b]	1,659	734[e]	2,010	374[b]
1965	2,940 (3,100[b])	1,791	843	2,559	385
Private sector					
1953	540	508	1,685	——	——
1958	500	531	1,898	——	——
1962	520	517	1,850[d]	——	——
1965	520	498	——	——	——

a In 1954.

b Including other state-owned agricultural enterprises.

c Including MTS and RTS.

d At the end of 1961.

e Excluding goats.

Explanations as for Table 2.

Sources: Agricultural area: *Narkhoz* (1955), p. 105 (for 1953, i.e., Nov. 1, 1954); *Narkhoz-1958,* p. 385 (Belorussia totals and sovkhozy, including other state-owned agricultural enterprises, and private sector in 1958); *Narkhoz-1962,* p. 245 (for 1962); *Narkhoz-1965,* p. 279 (for 1965, but not for sovkhozy without other state-owned agricultural enterprises); *Belorusskaia SSR v tsifrakh v 1965 godu* (Minsk, 1966), p. 47 (sovkhozy, excluding other state-owned agricultural enterprises, in 1958, 1965), p. 49 (kolkhozy in 1958, 1965).

Sown area: *Belorusskaia SSR v tsifrakh za 1964 god* (Minsk, 1965), p. 62 f. (Belorussian totals in 1953, 1962), p. 65 (kolkhozy and sovkhozy in 1953 and 1962, private sector in 1953, 1958, 1962); *Belorusskaia SSR v tsifrakh v 1965 godu,* p. 33 (Belorussia totals in 1958, 1965), p. 47 (sovkhozy in 1958, 1965), p. 49 (kolkhozy in 1958, 1965). Private sector in 1965 calculated through subtraction.

Livestock units: *Narkhoz. Belorusskoi SSR* (Minsk, 1963), p. 182 ff. (Belorussia totals in 1953, 1958, private sector in 1961); *Razvitie narodnogo khoziaistva Belorusskoi SSR za 20 let* (Minsk, 1964), p. 70 f. (private sector in 1953, 1958), p. 81 f. (kolkhozy in 1953), p. 86 f. (sovkhozy in 1953, 1958); *Belorusskaia SSR v tsifrakh za 1964 god,* p. 73 (Belorussia totals in 1962), p. 87 ff. (sovkhozy in 1962), p. 92 f. (kolkhozy in 1962); *Belorusskaia SSR v tsifrakh v 1965 godu,* p. 39 (Belorussia totals in 1965), p. 48 (sovkhozy in 1965), p. 50 (kolkhozy in 1965).

Energy available: *Narkhoz Belorusskoi SSR* (Minsk, 1963), p. 235–37 (for 1958); *Nakrhoz-1962*, p. 323 (for 1962); *Narkhoz-1965*, p. 394 (for 1965).

Kolkhoz households and sovkhoz labor: *Narkhoz-1962*, p. 344 f. (kolkhoz households in 1962), p. 456 ff. (sovkhoz labor in 1962); *Razvitie narodnogo khoziaistva Belorusskoi SSR za 20 let*, p. 81 ff. (kolkhoz households in 1953), p. 86 f. (sovkhoz labor in 1953); *Belorusskaia SSR v tsifrakh v 1965 godu*, p. 47 (sovkhoz labor in 1958, 1965), p. 49 (kolkhoz households in 1958, 1965).

Thus the socialized sector increased its gross production in spite of an equal or even decreased use of labor, owing to the yearly increasing energy available (see Table 1), whereas the private sector did not increase its labor productivity because—at least until 1964—it had to work under unfavorable conditions deliberately created by the regime.

The unfavorable age structure of the Soviet farm population differs in its effect in the private and in the social sector: The private sector gains more workers as more retired people become available. In consideration of the age structure of the permanent labor force, a great, perhaps even growing, increase in the percentage of retired people in the farm population can be expected over the next ten years. Yet considerable regional differences have to be taken into account: the previous statements mainly refer to the areas north of the Black Earth belt. In the west (Lithuania, Belorussia, Western Ukraine) and in the south (i.e., Moldavian S.S.R., Southeast Russia, Cis- and Trans-Caucasia, and Central Asia) there is no lack of permanent workers[74] and aging is not an urgent problem. But in these areas underemployment in the socialized sector makes the private sector draw these underemployed, even fully able-bodied workers and especially women of working age, out of the socialized sector.

With regard to the potential of labor in the private sector, there is not too much difference between conditions in the kolkhozy and the sovkhozy. Under Khrushchev, the sovkhozy were pressed to restrict private enterprises. But this did not change the number of workers available for the private sector, particularly not in sovkhozy formed out of kolkhozy. The able-bodied kolkhoz member is entitled to a number of days off to work on his private piece of land, but as a sovkhoz worker he no longer has this privilege. On the other hand, women with children, juveniles, invalids, and so on, who work in the private sector and are employed in the sovkhozy only for temporary or seasonal work, are not under legal obligation to work in the socialized sector at all. Since the restrictions on the private sector were abolished in the sovkhozy,

[74] Cf. the tables for 1959 in A. N. Goltsov, "Raspredelenie i ispolzovanie . . . ," p. 103, and for 1962 in Mashenkov, *Ispolzovanie trudovykh . . .* , p. 106.

this potential labor has considerable working opportunities and may have contributed to the new increase in private production (see Table 1) that occurred after Khrushchev's removal.

As long as the balance of labor in Soviet agriculture is not even, as long as there are acute deficiency symptoms in some parts of the country (due also to lack of mechanization and rationalization), and a surplus of labor in other parts, the development of production in the three sectors depends decisively on the availability of labor. It is not by chance that *sovkhozizatsiia* on a large scale took place mainly in parts of the country that had a more or less critical balance of labor. But to elaborate this in detail would be beyond the range of this paper, and the fact can be mentioned only.

ROBERT C. STUART

*Comment**

Dr. Wädekin has presented a most competent and provocative paper on an important aspect of Soviet agricultural development. As he himself points out, the question of kolkhoz, sovkhoz, and private production in Soviet agriculture could indeed be ". . . the topic of a whole book instead of a paper."

In narrowing his subject, Dr. Wädekin selects five basic indicators (agricultural areas, cultivated areas, livestock units, energy available, labor units), through which he analyzes certain shifts in the pattern of Soviet agricultural production. In the text and appended statistical materials Dr. Wädekin has applied both skill and effort to afford the reader important insights. Rather than dwell upon details with which I find myself in basic agreement, let us consider some questions of direction and emphasis.

To examine the changing relative importance of the kolkhoz and sovkhoz, we are necessarily led to the questions of amalgamation, conversion, and indeed the whole range of issues associated with structural change in this sector. If our aim is that of comparative analysis, we must be interested in the functional and dysfunctional features of these different organizational forms. Further, it would be desirable if we could generalize from the Soviet experience and consider its relevance for the development process under differing political, economic, and social conditions.

To be sure, Soviet agricultural development has thus far been extensive in character. Nevertheless, there is evidence that Soviet leaders

* Unfortunately Dr. Wädekin's paper did not reach me prior to the conference, and at that time appended materials were not translated. With the hope of improving the quality of this comment, I have taken the liberty of shifting my emphasis toward the question of brigade structure and accordingly have presented supporting statistical material. In so doing, I have benefitted by the comments made by Dr. Wädekin and Professor Jackson.

increasingly recognize the need to improve performance not through massive injections of any or all of the traditional inputs, but rather through the improved usage of the increasingly difficult-to-obtain input increments. Thus, as Dr. Wädekin points out, in recent times we are concerned with specialized institutions and intensive agrarian production.

Dr. Wädekin notes that "the differences between the kolkhozy and the sovkhozy cannot simply be deduced from inherent organizational differences." However, if we are to attempt the admittedly difficult task of comparative analysis, or for that matter simply describe developments in Soviet agriculture, surely we must better understand the organizational peculiarities of the kolkhoz and sovkhoz, especially in the light of present trends toward specialization.

TABLE 1
BRIGADE STRUCTURE OF KOLKHOZY
U.S.S.R., 1957—1960

	1957	1958	1959	1960
Number of kolkhozy	76,535	67,681	53,436	43,981
Public sown area				
(All crops, in thousand hectares)	132,410	131,408	130,268	123,025
Total brigades[a]	416,033	357,666	314,049	256,991
Field	213,495	183,980	139,090	105,353
Tractor	94,201	55,423	50,123	37,114
Tractor-Field	5,562	12,614	15,178	14,507
Complex	59,010	67,909	77,012	73,925
(Tractor[b])		(11,940)	(16,892)	(18,189)
Vegetable	26,043	21,870	17,329	14,370
Fruit	10,515	9,546	9,153	10,460
Others	7,207	6,324	6,164	1,262

[a] Total number of brigades is assumed to be the sum of subclassifications.
[b] Unknown for 1957.

Sources: *Selskoe khoziaistvo SSSR* (Moscow, 1960), pp. 51, 137; *Narodnoe khoziaistvo SSSR v 1960g.* (Moscow, 1961), p. 500–501; I. I. Sigov, *Razdelenie truda v selskom khoziaistve pri perekhode k kommunizmu* (Moscow: Ekonomicheskaia literatura, 1963), p. 139.

Consider some limited evidence on the brigade structure of Soviet kolkhozy (Table 1). During the period 1957–60, there were some important changes in the nature of the brigade vis-à-vis the kolkhoz. For example, there has been a tendency toward decreased specialization of inputs and outputs at this level. Where there formerly existed separate field and tractor brigades (partly due to the MTS and inadequate mechanization), the recent trend is combination to form a tractor-field brigade. Further, the expansion of complex (and tractor-complex) brigades brings together in a single administrative unit the previously separated animal breeding, plant growing (and equipment) sectors.

Undoubtedly amalgamation has been an important factor, for in many cases complex brigades were formed on the base of a single kolkhoz.[1]

The available evidence suggests considerable regional variation of brigade size. Thus in 1961, a field brigade occupied, on the average, 390.8 hectares of land *(pashnia)* in the U.S.S.R., while in the North Caucasus, the same form of brigade occupied 2742.4 hectares.[2] Thus it is necessary to introduce such explanatory variables as the type of crop, the level of mechanization, nature of the terrain, availability of labor supplies, and so on.[3] These factors have played an important role in the pattern of specialization, for example, in the creation of potato-vegetable sovkhozy in Moscow *oblast*.[4] This experience (along with many others) provides interesting material for examination of the kolkhoz versus the sovkhoz. In spite of the Soviet leaders preference for the latter, the results in this particular case have for many reasons been less than expected.[5]

But in addition to the purely structural changes, there has been the entire range of issues to which Durgin attached the name "monetization."[6] Thus, although there may not have been a single decisive reform to attract our attention, the nature of the kolkhoz as an economic enterprise has undergone significant change in the recent past. Even the party merits consideration, for it too grew along with the brigade and found new expression at that level in 1960.[7]

It is true that the political scientists have considered the problems of agricultural administration and indeed the works of Bergson, Domar, Nove, and others have taken us within the kolkhoz. Nevertheless, while

[1] K. P. Obolenskii, G. G. Katov, and G. K. Rusakov (eds.), *Voprosy ratsionalnoi organizatsii i ekonomiki selskokhoziaistvennogo proizvodstva* (Moscow: Ekonomika, 1964), p. 218.

[2] *Ibid.*, p. 230.

[3] *Ibid.*, p. 229. We here ignore internal differences of brigade organization.

[4] See my "Conversion of Collective Farms into State Farms: Further Note II," *ASTE Bulletin*, IX, No. 1 (Spring, 1967), 14–16.

[5] See, for example, V. G. Venzher, *Ispolzovanie zakona stoimosti v kolkhoznom proizvodstve* (2nd rev. ed.; Moscow: Nauka, 1965), p. 114; N. S. Khrushchev, "Ob uvelichenii proizvodstva ovoshchei i kartofelia," in Khrushchev, *Stroitelstvo kommunizma v SSSR i razvitie selskogo khoziaistva* (Moscow: Gospolitizdat, 1964), VIII, 114–24. For a more favorable view, see S. G. Kolesnev (ed.), *Spetsializatsiia i razmery selskokhoziaistvennykh predpriiatii* (Moscow: Selkhozizdat, 1963), p. 120.

[6] Frank A. Durgin, Jr., "Monetization and Policy in Soviet Agriculture Since 1952," *Soviet Studies*, XV, No. 4 (April, 1964), 354–407.

[7] "O sozdanii partiinykh komitetov v krupnykh partorganizatsiiakh kolkhozov i sovkhozov," in *Kommunisticheskaia partiia Sovetskogo Soiuza v rezoliutsiiakh i resheniiakh* (Part IV; Moscow: Gospolitizdat, 1960), p. 501.

recognizing the complexity of the task, we simply have not carried out a comprehensive examination of the internal economics of the kolkhoz or sovkhoz. We lack the sort of analysis that has been so valuable in understanding the industrial sector. In the case of potato-vegetable production in Moscow *oblast* we can with minimum difficulty relate what has occurred. As a case study for consideration of the kolkhoz versus the sovkhoz, we are in a much more difficult position.

All of this is not by way of contradiction to or disagreement with the important contribution made by Dr. Wädekin. It is, rather, an attempt to expand in some measure on one facet of his paper.

EBERHARD SCHINKE

Some Peculiarities
of the Employment of Factors
in Soviet Agriculture

The growth and development of productivity and per capita production in Soviet agriculture have fluctuated strongly in the past. They were high in some periods, stagnated in others, and occasionally declined in spite of a constantly increasing demand.[1] These changing trends were neither in harmony with the respective plans and goals of Soviet leadership nor can they be sufficiently explained by climatic influences. On examining the employment of factors and the production yield, one even occasionally comes across tendencies and relations that are contradictory to what we have come to expect from developments in other countries. Undoubtedly nature, the economic system, and the level of development in the Soviet Union create circumstances that prohibit us from applying those unseen measures that have validity and meaning in the conditions of Western Europe and North America.

However, one should not exclude the possibility that other forces, not founded in these special circumstances, also have an impeding or improving effect upon the process of development. They hardly can be covered in their entirety in a study of limited length and indeed are even difficult to quantify. In spite of this it is necessary to be aware of them in any appraisal of the development of Soviet agriculture to this point, as well as in making an assessment of future trends and rates of growth. By examining some particularities of expenditure in Soviet agriculture, we shall try to give some clarification of this question.

[1] See the works of A. S. Becker, A. Kahan, J. F. Karcz, D. G. Johnson, and others as well as the research published by the U.S. Department of Agriculture.

A quick survey of the various kinds of expenditure clearly shows that neither investments nor yield-increasing inputs related to the number of employed persons or to the unit of area have reached a high level compared to other countries. Up to the end of 1965 the capital invested in state and collective agriculture amounted to 56,100 million rubles,[2] that is, 105 rubles per hectare of agricultural area, or 260 rubles per hectare of arable land, or 2,110 rubles per employed person. Adding to this privately owned livestock valued at about 4,000 to 5,000 million rubles, and relating the total sum, including that from the private sphere, to Soviet agriculture, the invested capital per unit of area rises only negligibly (to 270 rubles per hectare of arable land), whereas the capital per employed person falls below 1,500 rubles. These figures are very low in comparison to the more than 10,000 dollars per laborer in the United States or 17,500 dollars per laborer in Western Germany (without the value of the land). A. M. Emelianov in 1965 noted:

The capital equipment in the [agriculture of the] United States is approximately seven times higher than in our country. . . . In the United States almost twice as much fixed capital falls upon one laborer in agriculture (without the value of the land) as in industry. . . , in our country, however, the capital equipment in agriculture is almost three times lower than in industry.[3]

But these figures give a wrong picture insofar as Soviet statistics show the assets at prime cost only, and do not indicate their present value. Since almost half of the given sum (in sovkhozy, 40.7 per cent, in kolkhozy, 51.7 per cent) falls upon buildings and installations and many of them are outdated and need to be renewed, present value plays a considerable role in the rating of the amount of invested capital. It is almost impossible to estimate the influence of this inadequate method in evaluating capital goods, all the more as Soviet investment plans and statistics include no division between new and replacement investments, and between those used for the farm, suprafarm, or communal purposes.

Especially low is the consumption of electricity, the characteristic variable for the development of internal farm economy. In 1965, it amounted in the sovkhozy to 423,000 kilowatt-hours per enterprise, which equals 664 kilowatt-hours per employed person. In the kolkhozy, which are generally less well equipped, the consumption of electric

[2] *Narodnoe khoziaistvo SSSR v 1965 g* (Moscow, 1966), p. 271. (Hereafter cited as *Narkhoz-1965*.)

[3] A. M. Emelianov, *Metodologicheskie problemy nakopleniia i rentabelnosti v kolkhozakh* (Moscow: Ekonomika, 1965), p. 216.

energy is even lower.[4] The expenditure on fertilizer, which only in the past several years rose to an amount worth mentioning, is still low. In 1965 it amounted to 28.5 kilograms per hectare of arable land; for wheat, the most important crop of Soviet agriculture, 12.2 kilograms per hectare were expended in 1965.[5]

TABLE 1
DEVELOPMENT OF TRACTION POWER SUPPLY IN THE
SOVIET UNION AND IN THE UNITED STATES[a]

	Soviet Union				United States		
Year	Supply per Thousand Hectares of Sown Area			Year	Supply per Thousand Hectares of Farming Area		
	Tractors	Trucks	Animal Traction		Tractors	Trucks	Animal Traction
1932	1.14	0.19	10.35	1920	1.51	0.85	10.77
1940	3.53	1.52	7.05	1930	5.47	5.35	7.62
1950	4.07	1.93	4.99	1940	9.71	6.48	5.75
1954	4.79	2.80	4.15	1945	14.83	9.13	3.49
1959	5.28	3.71	2.60	1950	21.82	13.34	3.11
1964	7.23	4.48	1.79				

[a] Tractors and trucks are quoted by the piece; animal traction is converted thus: 1 horse equals 0.075; 1 ox equals 0.05, 1 mule equals 0.05.

Sources: *Narodnoe Khoziaistvo SSSR v 1964 g.* (Moscow, 1965), pp. 378 ff.; *Narkhoz-1956*, pp. 155, 163; *Selkhoz-1960*, p. 127; *Selskoe Khoziaistvo SSSR (Moscow, 1939)*, p. 17; *U.S. Census of Agriculture, 1950*, II, 223, 226, 385, 387.

More remarkable than the present input level, however, is the fact that the level itself rises relatively slowly. In some cases, even an occasional decline in the factor input can be observed. The growth rate of input often stands in no relationship to the aspired growth rate of output. One of the most interesting examples of this is the development of the traction power supply since 1930. The sharp decline in the number of draft animals during and after collectivization in the early thirties was not compensated for by an equal increase in motor traction power, so that despite the increased use of tractors, trucks, and grain combines in the thirties, the traction power deficit did not lessen, but on the contrary continued to grow. The traction power supply sank from 202 million power units in 1929 to 137 million in 1932, and to 111 million in 1938. After the war losses of 1941–45, the level of 1928 was not surpassed until 1962.[6] This development is completely different from that

[4] *Narkhoz-1965*, p. 403.

[5] *Narkhoz-1965*, pp. 357, 362.

[6] Soviet statistics evaluate animal traction power as: 0.75 h.p.: 1 horse; 0.50 h.p.: 1 ox; they show a continual increase in traction power since 1932. My figures (excluding those in Table 1) deviate from these given in the Soviet statistics because the following key was used: 1 motor h.p. (nominal power of the engine): 1 traction power

in other countries where the exchange of animal and motor traction power was carried out not only without lowering the total capacity, but instead by increasing the total traction power supply. In Table 1, the development in the United States is compared with the Soviet Union, with a phase displacement probably corresponding approximately to the actual conditions. The traction power supply per hectare of sown area in the Soviet Union even today is on a lower level than before collectivization and before the starting point of mass production in the Soviet tractor industry (see Table 2).

TABLE 2
TRACTION POWER SUPPLY IN SOVIET AGRICULTURE

		Traction Power Supply				Traction Power Supply	
Year	Sown Area (In Million Hectares)	Total Agriculture (Million Units[a])	Units[a] (Per Hundred Hectares of Sown Area)	Year	Sown Area (In Million Hectares)	Total Agriculture (Million Units[a])	Units[a] (Per Hundred Hectares of Sown Area)
1928	113.0	202.5	179.2	1955	185.8	158.1	85.1
				1956	194.8	165.4	85.0
1933[b]	129.7	137.2	105.8	1957	193.7	177.0	91.3
				1958	195.6	176.8	90.4
1938	136.9	110.8	80.9	1959	196.3	181.5	92.5
				1960	203.0	186.4	91.8
1940	150.6	141.3	93.9	1961	204.6	191.4	93.5
				1962	216.0	209.4	97.0
1950	146.3	124.6	85.2	1963	218.5	220.7	101.0
				1964	121.8	228.2	107.2
1953	157.2	147.6	93.9	1965	209.1	242.9[c]	116.2[c]

[a] 1 motor h.p. (nominal power of the engine) equals 1 traction power unit; 1 horse equals 7.5 traction power units, 1 ox equals 5.0 traction power units.

[b] Sown area, 1933, in relation to the traction power supply at the end of 1932.

[c] Of these, 35.1 per cent in tractors, 14.6 per cent in harvesting machines, 34.8 per cent in trucks and motorcars, 15.4 per cent in traction animals. See *Narkhoz-1965*, pp. 493–94.

Source: E. Schinke, *Die Mechanisierung landwirtschaftlicher Arbeiten in der Sowjetunion* (Wiesbaden: Harrassowitz, 1967), pp. 29–31. (Calculated according to *Narkhoz-1958-1965*, *Selkhoz-1939*, and *Selkhoz-1960*.)

Another example may be found in the development of the production and supply of cotton-picking machines (Table 3). Output, which in 1950–51 amounted to approximately 4,000 machines annually, was almost completely stopped later in the fifties and then resumed in 1959 with a new design. In the meantime, the enterprises, were not able to replenish their equipment, which sank in number from about 26,000 machines in 1955 to about a third of that figure in 1959.

unit; 1 horse: 7.5 traction power units; 1 ox: 5.0 traction power units. To this question see my study *Die Mechanisierung landwirtschaftlicher Arbeiten in der Sowjetunion* (Wiesbaden: Harrassowitz, 1967), pp. 28–30.

TABLE 3
PRODUCTION AND STOCK OF COTTON-PICKING MACHINES
IN THE SOVIET UNION

Year	Production (In Thousands)	Number at End of Year (In Thousands)
1952	4.0	18.4
1953	n.a.	21.7
1954	n.a.	24.8
1955	0.7a	25.7
1956	0.9a	25
1957	n.a.	22
1958	0.0	10
1959	0.5	n.a.
1960	3.2	11
1961	4.3	12
1962	6.1	17
1963	7.1	20
1964	7.0	27
1965	7.7	33

a Delivered to agriculture.

Sources: Narkhoz-1956, pp. 158, 164; *Narkhoz-1962*, pp. 175, 325 f.; *Narkhoz-1963*, pp. 169, 355 f.; *Narkhoz-1964*, p. 188; *Narkhoz-1965*, pp. 399, 404; *Selkhoz-1960*, p. 415.

Even if the input of one factor in Soviet agriculture as a whole is about to rise, it may happen that regionally the input amount stagnates or even decreases, despite a great and unmet demand. The reasons for such phenomena are, in most cases, the political-economic decisions of the central authorities, which direct the scarce items into preferred regions. A good example of this may be found in the fertilizer expenditure in the western districts of the Ukraine in the years 1953–64 (see Fig. 1). In the same period of time (1959–62) in which the expenditure on fertilizer decreased or stagnated in this relatively well-equipped region, there was a strong increase in the fertilizer supply for the Soviet Union as a whole, both in absolute terms as well as per hectare of arable land. It rose from 2,459,000 metric tons in 1958 to 3,094,000 tons in 1962, i.e., from 11.5 kilograms per hectare of sown area to 14.0 kilograms.[7]

Such examples, which could be multiplied, show that the employment of factors in Soviet agriculture is strongly determined by external influences. When one also takes into consideration that scarce working funds are not always effectively distributed by the trading apparatus of *Selkhoztekhnika*,[8] and that management, especially of the state farms, is often impotent with regard to decisions over investments, the result

[7] *Narkhoz-1964*, p. 342.

[8] State monopoly trust that supplies all agricultural enterprises with machinery, fertilizers, herbicides, motor fuel, and other materials.

is a strong limitation of the factor employment. For the management of the sovkhoz or kolkhoz, with relatively short periods of business planning, such limitation quite often equals a fixing of available inputs.

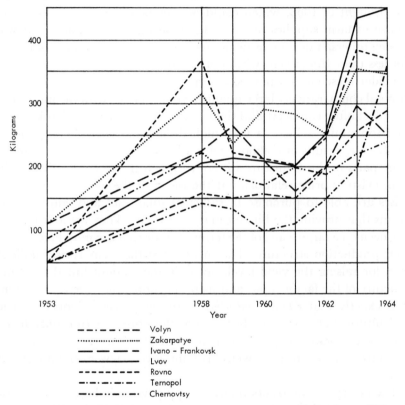

Fig. 1. Mineral fertilizer expenditure in West Ukrainian collective farms, 1953–1964 (Kilograms per hectare of arable land). *Source*: Silskogospodarskii atlas zakhidnikh raioniv URSR (Lviv: Lvivskii s-g. institut, 1965), p. 6.

However, the law of diminishing returns, strongly manifest in agriculture, is even stronger when more factors are fixed. An increase in the variable factors meets with the limiting effect of one or more of the fixed factors. This effect, which theoretically is not noticeable with free availability of all factors, becomes stronger when the input quantities are lower. Since both the low level and the fixing of numerous factors applies to Soviet agriculture as a whole, as well as to the individual enterprise, the functioning of this law provides an essential reason for the low rates of increase in agricultural production and productivity. The low reliability of yield expectation from which Soviet agriculture suffers is to a large extent based on this. Under the circumstances, the substitution possibility for many factors, and thus the buffer effect of the entire structure of factor input, is comparatively low even with the reduction of one factor only. One example is the shortage of feed after the drought of 1963, which could neither be compensated for by recourse to farm supplies nor by additional purchases. The result was, among others, a decline in swine stock on the kolkhozy and sovkhozy by not less than 48 per cent within one year.[9]

Under these circumstances, enterprises or regions that have at their disposal comparatively large quantities of the factor with the most limiting effect often can overfulfill their production plans and, thanks to this fact, sometimes achieve a very high differential rent. The extraordinarily good results of kolkhozy with a large share of specialty crops in some parts of the Caucasus are not so much the direct result of gains from existing price relations but the result of the fact that the enterprises are able to purchase in sufficient quantities and employ those means that provide the highest marginal yields. They are able to make use, even on a large scale, of the terms of trade that are most favorable to their production structure. The successes of these enterprises indicate that, for raising the yield level, not only the amount but the optimal structure of the factor input and its proportional increase is important. It is exactly that *relative proportion* of the employed factors in Soviet agriculture that is frequently far from the optimum (not only in the sense of the achieved production maximization but in the sense of a maximization of profit as well). Let me give a few examples of this, too.[10]

The growth of the traction power supply not only lagged behind the expansion of cultivated areas as a result of the absolute decrease of traction power in the thirties, but even during the new-land campaigns in the fifties there was an occasional decrease of the amount of traction power per unit of sown area (see Table 2). Since Soviet agriculture already had to fight a deficit in this sector,[11] a decline in the amount of traction power per unit of area must be compensated for by a time in-

[9] *Narkhoz-1964*, p. 353.

[10] There are new Soviet studies on this topic. See, for example, V. M. Obukhovskii, "Dinamika osnovnykh fondov spetsializirovannykh sovkhozov s raznym intensivnosti proizvodstva," *Izvestiia TSKhA*, No. 2 (1965), pp. 28–39; K. Guleichik, Ia. Blankman, G. Lych, "Vliianie struktury osnovnykh fondov na uroven proizvodstva v kolkhozakh Belorussii," *Ekonomika selskogo khoziaistva*, No. 4 (1965), pp. 66–73.

[11] In 1966 Soviet agriculture had at its disposal 8.3 tractors with 430 h.p. for 1000 hectares of sown area, *SSSR v tsifrakh-1966* (Moscow: Statistika, 1967), pp. 84, 107.

crease for various kinds of work if entire farming operations are not to be cut down. The elimination of operations in soil managment or the culture of crops, however, has a yield-diminishing effect just like surpassing the optimal deadline for sowing and harvesting, and so must at least partially consume the gains made by area expansion. A parallel example with distinctly measurable consequences was the expansion of the number of livestock in the years since 1959 that was not equalled by a respective rise in feed production (see Table 4). In the period from 1959 to 1962, cattle stock alone increased by 23 per cent, but feed production (measured in Soviet feed units) rose only by 2 per cent.[12] Therefore, a decline in the milk yield per cow from 2,067 kilograms in 1959 to 1,747 kilograms in 1962 had to be faced.[13]

TABLE 4

LIVESTOCK AND FODDER PRODUCTION ON COLLECTIVE AND STATE FARMS
1960—1965

	1960	1961	1962	1963	1964	1965
Livestock[a]	70.2	74.1	78.9	75.7	77.1	81.4
Total fodder production[b]	n.a.	191.3	190.5	170.7	167.2	193.1
Fodder production for stable feeding[b]	143.9	146.4	145.0	126.5	123.2	145.8

[a] In million Soviet livestock units.

[b] In million tons of Soviet fodder units (1 unit=1 kg. oats).

Source: A. Lutsenko, "O kormovoi baze i potreblenii kormov," *Vestnik statistiki*, No. 3 (1967), pp. 8–9.

Together with the result of a lack of harmony in factor input and—as with the exchange of animal by motor traction power—of insufficient substitution of eliminated factors are numerous other phenomena, which at first may appear incomprehensible. Despite the poor nutrient supply of many soils in the Soviet Union and the lack of mineral fertilizers, only about half of the available manure is transported to the fields,[14] primarily because there is a lack of transportation. Modern milking parlors have been erected with high cost, but they quite often remain unused because they are in enterprises whose stable buildings are equipped for completely different work.[15]

Yet only part of the blame for such faulty decisions in the propor-

[12] *Narkhoz-1964*, p. 352; A. Silin and V. Pravdin, "Nekotorye statisticheskie dannye o stoimosti kormov," *Vestnik statistiki*, No. 12 (1964), p. 15.

[13] *Narkhoz-1965*, p. 388.

[14] A. V. Romanchenko, "Rezervy i puti povysheniia proizvoditelnosti truda v zernovom khoziaistve," *Puti povysheniia proizvoditelnosti truda v selskom khoziaistve SSSR* (Moscow: Nauka, 1964), p. 133.

[15] A. M. Emelianov, *Metodologicheskie . . .* , pp. 247–48.

tions or in the chronological order of the employment of means may be placed on the kolkhoz or sovkhoz. The reason lies principally in the actions of governmental organs at a level beyond the individual enterprise; instructions from above are sometimes contradictory to the will of its management. The figures on the decrease of fertilizer supply in the western Ukraine is one example, Khrushchev's corn campaign is another.

The corn campaign points to the essential fact that Soviet agricultural enterprises in their management organization are bound by production orders. The fulfillment of these is the primary goal of any operational activity, and in certain circumstances high operational losses are accepted as necessary. It does not make a great difference whether these production orders take the form of plans for crop areas and livestock numbers or whether they are delivery schedules for certain products, the same results may ensue. According to M. Lemeshev (1966)[16] the present system has hardly improved the previous system of prescribed crop rotation and livestock breeding.

Even with the gradual slackening of planning and the granting of limited freedoms to the enterprises, there is no guarantee of an efficient use of the employed factors. It is true that, with delivery plans fixed and applicable over a period of several years, there is less danger that the investments in buildings and machinery for the fulfillment of a certain delivery program can no longer be used optimally or even, perhaps, become a burden to the enterprise. The management can now make its own decisions regarding a number of individual problems in organization and investment. The entire structure of the enterprise, however, is still determined by the planning authority, which lays down the delivery target for the most important products. Thus it is still not unusual, as the Soviet economist Kravchenko notes, that within the scope of the premises fixed by this delivery target "an optimal combination of tractors and machinery is decided for an extremely unfavorable combination of operational branches."[17]

With the close interdependence of the various production branches on agricultural enterprises, the state production orders have more far-reaching consequences in agriculture than in some other spheres of the economy. The farm is not ordinarily a single-product operation, but a

[16] M. Lemeshev, "Problemy sovershenstvovaniia planirovaniia selskogo khoziaistva na sovremennom etape," *Voprosy ekonomiki*, No. 3 (1966), p. 53.

[17] R. G. Kravchenko, *Ekonomiko-matematicheskie modeli zadach po selskomu khoziaistvu* (Moscow: Ekonomika, 1965), p. 266.

producer of a number of interdependent products that have to be combined with each other in fairly fixed order, since the same means of production are employed for all.

TABLE 5
STRUCTURE OF EXPENDITURES IN THE COLLECTIVE FARMS OF
THE UKRAINIAN S.S.R. AND OF THE KRASNODAR *KRAI*, 1962

| | Ukrainian S.S.R. | | Krasnodar *Krai* | |
	Million Rubles	Per Cent	Million Rubles	Per Cent
Capital investments	1279.1	28.2	147.2	27.1
Production expenditures	801.4	17.7	93.7	17.3
Of these:				
Mineral fertilizers	47.2	1.0	4.6	0.85
Motor fuels	164.7	3.6	18.0	3.3
Repairs	212.4	4.8	22.4	4.1
Seeds and foodstuffs				
(Additional procurements)	245.9	5.4	30.7	5.65
Labor payment	1902.2	42.1	230.6	42.4
Taxes and insurance	449.1	9.9	62.4	11.5
Other expenditures	96.3	2.1	9.2	1.7

Source: V. G. Venzher, *Ispolzovanie zakona stoimosti v kolkhoznom proizvodstve* (2nd rev. ed.; Moscow: Nauka, 1965), pp. 322–23.

These short-sighted procedures, which apply to agriculture dependent on the soil as well as to part of the livestock production, are more noticeable in the Soviet Union than in the agriculture of countries with better developed exchange relations between the spheres of the economy. Soviet kolkhozy and sovkhozy do not only have to re-use or re-employ by-products and complementary products, they are forced to produce the largest part of the feed, seed, and other means of production, all of which is ordinarily purchased by the agricultural enterprise of other countries. Illustrating this are some data of the Ukrainian S.S.R. and the Krasnodar *krai*. In 1965, all kolkhozy of these two very important agricultural districts spent less than 1.0 per cent of their total outlay for mineral fertilizers, and only about 5.5 per cent for purchases of seed and livestock feed (see Table 5). This high degree of self-supply in the Soviet enterprises draws upon the production capacities, diminishes the possibilities of operational planning, and complicates the organization of management.

With such connections in the structure of an agricultural enterprise, a quantitative production order can have a decisive influence on the entire management organization. Consider, for instance, the order to deliver a certain amount of milk: the enterprise does not only need the appropriate herd of cows but must also have feeds of a certain composition and quantity. This entails the setting up of crop rotation and so reflects in the organization of farming. Since a dairy herd produces calves as a complementary product, the most favorable use has to be found for them, and, if necessary, feed production must be raised. All of these factors limit the expansion of other plant products.

It must be extremely difficult for a central planning authority to combine the allotment of the desired total production with a sensible evaluation of the capacity of each enterprise, yet that is undoubtedly their goal. In the last analysis, however, no maximization of profit for the entire economy is possible without optimal employment of the resources in the enterprise. Considering that there is still uncertainty in the Soviet Union about the most advantageous distribution of location of agricultural production[18] and that there are still no effective planning procedures for the enterprises available,[19] it is surprising that there is such a persistent effort to plan in detail.

One may perhaps see a certain parallel to the difficulties of management and planning in the Soviet kolkhozy and sovkhozy in the farmer who, under the conditions of a market economy, is restricted by the existing price relations and has to be satisfied with a suboptimal employment of means. However, there is no parallel to another difficulty with which the Soviet kolkhoz and sovkhoz has to contend—the peculiar dualism of the operational goal that is called, simultaneously, production maximization and profit maximization. In the planning orders, the goal of the entire economy of production maximization is implied, which probably changes into the minimizing of costs as soon as the covering of the demand is achieved.[20] In addition, there is in the new system of planning in Soviet agriculture the operational goal of profit maximization. Both goals can be seemingly identical, especially in the sphere of low profits; they can be approached in the same way and in order to reach them the same means can be employed. Yet at a certain

[18] R. G. Jensen, "The Soviet Concept of Agricultural Regionalization and Its Development," *Soviet and East European Agriculture*, ed. Jerzy F. Karcz (Berkeley and Los Angeles: University of California Press, 1967), pp. 75–103; M. Rauth, *Raumgliederung, Raumordnung und Regionalplanung in der Sowjetunion aus landwirtschaftlicher Sicht* (Wiesbaden: Harrassowitz, 1967), pp. 120–217.

[19] See my report "Landwirtschaftliche Betriebsplanung in der Sowjetunion," *Osteuropa-Wirtschaft*, X (Sept., 1965), 205–10.

[20] The usual requirement, "maximum production per land unit combined with maximum saving of human and machine labor" (K. P. Obolenskii, *Opredelenie ekonomicheskoi effektivnosti selskokhoziaistvennogo proizvodstva* [Moscow: Sotsekgiz, 1963], pp. 26–27), which in this form cannot be fulfilled, is usually, in actual practice, still interpreted to mean that preference is given to the production maximation.

profit level the enterprise is faced with the decision to give preference to one or the other. Soviet farms reach this point especially early since the desired production maximization is not usually an over-all value but a specific quantity of certain products that often require other factor combinations than those needed for the achievement of a maximum profit, or even for a total product of maximum value.

Undoubtedly, this is a decisive factor for the efficiency of means input. As long as the fulfillment of specific delivery plans remains the first criterion for the planning and management of agricultural enterprises, the kolkhozy and sovkhozy, as well as the regional planning authorities, are forced to employ the available means in appropriate relations. Even when all factors are available in any amount, this limitation remains. In general terms, the fixing of product/product-relations, laid down in the delivery plans, entails fixing of the factor/factor-relations if once the limited possibilities of factor substitution are disregarded. This can possibly lead to achieving neither the optimum for the economy as a whole (maximum total product or minimum total cost), nor the operational optimum (maximum profit). Of course, this could be avoided in the ideal case of a centrally planned economy; however, in actual practice, at least within the Soviet economy, such faulty decisions are no rarity.

In the small countries of Europe and Eastern Asia, one usually attributes a key role to the factor of area for agricultural production. This is the most strongly limiting factor of all if sufficient quantities of water are available. It guides the employment of all other production means, and to it expenditure and profit are related. But with regard to the factor of area, Soviet agriculture is relatively mobile: it has at its disposal a proportionately large land area per capita, even in the most densely populated regions, as well as having a large area per each required production quantity. Thus the possibility of compensating for increasing production expenditures by farming additional land is relatively great. This circumstance should be taken into consideration at the rating of the level of intensity, i.e., the expenditure per unit of area in Soviet agriculture. In a comparison with countries in which land area is decisively limited, this is especially important.

The exchangeability of material expenditure by area, however, is limited in the Soviet Union, not only when crop farming is extended into dry areas where the yield is uncertain. The regularities formulated in the law of diminishing returns apply also when the factor of land is variable while other important factors are held on a constant but low level. There is also the additional problem of increasing transportation costs for both the means of production and for products.

In the Soviet Union the question of the optimum combination of area with other production factors is usually not discussed on an over-all basis, but only with regard to individual agricultural enterprises. The finding of the optimal size for the enterprise is considered a prerequisite for the achievement of maximum operational success, however it may be defined.

By centralization of control over the production means, the Soviet Union is able to adjust the amount of the area cultivated by one enterprise according to the size considered advantageous at any particular time. The combination or division of enterprises is also not exceptional. Soviet agricultural statistics reveal that competent authorities have been making great use of these means of achieving flexibility, but such actions are not taken with economic considerations only. It is significant that such an important factor of agricultural production as the land area of an individual enterprise has become, practically, variable to an unlimited degree. However, to judge by the successes achieved to date in Soviet agriculture, the possibilities and advantages have hardly been exploited. This is apparent in the relations in the employment of means, which, as the examples revealed, are often far from the optimum. It is apparent that a change in size of an enterprise or of an employed area in itself does not give a guarantee of approaching the national economic or operational optimum. We cannot discuss this question nor the interesting problem of the assignment of labor in Soviet agriculture in detail in this context. The very high regional and seasonal differences in utilization of farm-labor capacity are also symptoms of a suboptimum structure of factor employment and, more especially, of an unbalanced relation between the labor and the capital factor.[21]

As a result of an inappropriate combination, the means employed in Soviet agriculture, not excepting labor and land, have not always been able to create the returns expected by the absolute input quantities. From 1960 to 1965, fixed assets of the state farms of the R.S.F.S.R. rose

[21] See N. Nimitz, *Farm Employment in the Soviet Union, 1928–1963*, RM-4623-PR (Santa Monica, Calif.: The RAND Corporation, Nov., 1965), and works cited there. In addition, see *Izpolzovanie trudovykh resursov v selskom khoziaistve SSSR* (Moscow: Nauka, 1964); E. Karnaukhova, "Povyshenie proizvoditelnosti truda i snizhenie sebestoimosti produktsii — korennaia problema razvitiia selskogo khoziaistva," *Ekonomika selskogo khoziaistva*, No. 11 (1966), pp. 29–45; V. K. Merzlov, "Problemy ispolzovaniia rabochei sily pri intensifikatsii selskogo khoziaistva," *Izvestiia TSKhA*, No. 3 (1965), pp. 196–206.

by 59 per cent, but gross production rose by only 12 per cent;[22] in the state farms of the Moscow *oblast,* fixed assets rose by 41.6 per cent per hectare of agricultural area from 1960 to 1963, or by 41.0 per cent per laborer, "but gross production of these sovkhozy remained standing about on the same level."[23] Such a marked reduction in capital productivity with the present level of intensity in Soviet agriculture "cannot be considered inavoidable,"[24] yet efforts for "determination of the most effective direction of capital investments,"[25] turned out to be successful only rarely. The main reason lies not only in the bureaucratic debilities of the Soviet economy, but probably also in the absence of useful price relations. After the completion of the present price reform and with an appropriate assessment of achievement within the enterprises, it is possible that faulty decisions in factor employment with regard to time and quantities will decrease, and the efficiency of the employed means increase.

[22] A. Bochko, "Uluchshit ispolzovanie proizvodstvennykh fondov sovkhozov," *Finansy SSSR,* No. 2 (1967), p. 8.

[23] A. Pokinchereda, "Nekotorye voprosy analiza ekonomiki kolkhozov i sovkhozov po ikh godovym otchetam," *Vestnik statistiki,* No. 11 (1964), p. 56.

[24] L. Sineva, "O fondootdache v sovkhozakh," *Voprosy ekonomiki,* No. 12 (1966), p. 50.

[25] K. Eremeev, "Opredelenie napravleniia naibolee effektivnogo vlozhenia sredstv," *Ekonomika selskogo khoziaistva,* No. 11 (1966) p. 60.

ELIZABETH CLAYTON

Comment

Dr. Schinke has discussed the factors of production in Soviet agriculture and evaluated them as real and potential sources of growth in output. Dr. Schinke's first consideration is the growth in output that has been incurred through increases in the inputs of factors of production. In this context he has noted the slow growth in the quantity of such major inputs as capital, fertilizers, electricity, and traction energy. These inputs, however, grew more rapidly than output during the 1950–64 period. Output increased by about 70 per cent during this period[1] and each of these inputs (excluding horse-traction power) increased more.

Economic theory has several explanations for the failure of output to grow as fast as the aggregate of inputs. The first is an offsetting or omitted factor. Quantity of land increased less than output despite expansion into new lands. Quantity of labor has not been considered; labor input, measured by either man-days or employment, decreased, offsetting the disproportionate increase in other inputs. The second consideration is the decrease in the quality of inputs that might have occurred and lowered the rate of growth. Quality of the new lands is generally lower than the quality of land previously under cultivation and requires a higher proportion of land in fallow. Data on the quality of other inputs is not so accessible, but the embodied nature of technological change implies that the quality of new material inputs either rose or held constant; the quality of previously produced inputs may have declined over-all, due to depreciation and planning deficiencies, as in Dr. Schinke's example of cotton-picking machines. A third consideration is the sharp decline in productive efficiency that offsets the

[1] Output and labor input data are taken from D. B. Diamond, "Trends in Output, Inputs and Factor Productivity in Soviet Agriculture," *New Directions in the Soviet Economy*, ed. Joint Economic Committee (Washington, D.C.: U.S. Government Printing Office, 1966), p. 346.

increases in inputs. Dr. Schinke discusses the efficiency with which factors are utilized, and this change in intensive growth is the aspect under consideration here. Other considerations that are relevant, but beyond the scope of this paper, are the plausibility of a production function with constant returns to scale in agriculture and the problems of data comparisons.

Discussion of the relationship between inputs and outputs specifies assumptions about the nature of the functional relationship between the two, either explicitly or implicitly. For example, Dr. Schinke's discussion of extensive growth considered deviations from constant returns to scale. It is necessary to specify the functional relationship in evaluating the efficiency with which inputs are utilized. Dr. Schinke proposes that fixing outputs also fixes input relationships because the elasticity of substitution between factors of production is zero. He proposes that there is no allowance for substituting one factor of production for another, even if the supplies of factors of production were to be perfectly elastic, and that fixing output by delivery plans or quotas will immutably fix the use of factors of production so that they cannot substitute for one another. This implies that capital cannot substitute for labor, that one feed cannot substitute for another feed, that one worker cannot substitute for another. This stringent specification of the relationship between inputs is used to explain why economic inefficiency results from setting output mix. While it seems likely that setting the output mix might lead to inefficiency, this assumption of fixed input proportions does not seem likely or necessary. Further, the data used in discussing extensive growth do not support this assumption.

If the output mix and some factors of production are fixed to the producing enterprise, there still may be substitution between the remaining factors, such as the allocation of labor between field crops and machine repair. In addition, the elasticity of substitution is higher during longer time periods when labor, for example, is free to migrate. The erratic factor allocations by central planning authorities would tend to lower the range of substitutability, but it is unlikely that it would reach zero.

Inefficiency due to specification of outputs by the central planners may occur because of other reasons, however. Dr. Schinke specifies several: the erratic changes in output quotas necessitating unused structures and equipment, the excesses and deficiencies in allocation of crops between time periods or geographical areas, and lack of consideration of complementarities in multiproduct enterprises. Further consideration in discussing the efficiency of plans must include the difficulties in evaluation due to prices that do not express scarcity relationships. If prices are not rational in the Western sense of scarcity, then it is impossible to ascertain the extent of efficiency or inefficiency in planning outputs and spatial distribution of several crops without specifying the nature of price deviations.

Dr. Schinke discusses the conflict between operational goals that is experienced in Soviet agriculture. It is again useful to specify the functional relationship that obtains between the goals and constraints of both the producing unit and the central planners in order to ascertain why these multiple goals might impair the efficient combination of inputs. Both the goals and constraints must be considered; production maximization, for example, might continue to infinity if there were no constraints on the supplies of factors to the economy. In addition, each factor possesses its goals and constraints: the labor supply of the kolkhoz, for example, is shared between the collective crop and the private crop as workers maximize their income from both sources. Again, price relationships must be considered to get determinate analytical results; nonscarcity prices influence each goal differently. For example, non-scarcity prices of outputs may not affect the attainment of physical output goals directly, but through effects on the labor supply.

To summarize these comments, the analysis of data requires an underlying model of functional and behavioral relationships both in the selection of the data to be analyzed and the conclusions to be drawn from these data. Conclusions in this paper relating growth of outputs and inputs depend on the assumptions used in selecting the data; they also depend on the nature of implied relationships, such as the elasticity of substitution. In examining the conclusions drawn from this set of data, it is found that the assumptions used are not consistent nor are the implied relationships clarified sufficiently.

HENRI WRONSKI

Consumer Cooperatives
in Rural Areas in the U.S.S.R.

In the U.S.S.R. the consumer cooperative, which holds a monopoly of the commercial services in rural areas, is an economic organization complementary to the kolkhoz structure and responsible for distribution and trade. Because of its role, the structure of the consumer cooperative is fairly similar to that of the agricultural cooperative itself. The rules of its organization are based on the same principles as those for the kolkhozy.

The consumer cooperative embraces the whole rural population: kolkhoz peasants, sovkhoz workers, and other social and professional categories in small towns. In this respect, it is broader than the kolkhoz sector. On the other hand, the situation of the rural population is, in respect to consumption, essentially different from that of urban consumers. The difference between rural and urban consumers is similar to that between kolkhoz peasant and wage earner.

The consumer cooperative, which plays an integral part in the rural economy of the U.S.S.R., is still not very well known; it is useful, therefore, to include it in an analysis of Soviet collectivist experience.

THE BOLSHEVIK PARTY AND THE COOPERATIVE

The cooperative movement, which appeared among the exploited classes under the influence of the utopian socialists as a form of self-defense, created some distrust in the "Leninist" Party. This party suppressed private capitalism and identified itself with the working class, whose interests it alone claimed to defend.

According to Lenin, cooperatives in capitalist countries and in Russia before the revolution and at the beginning of the postrevolution years were not of a truly socialist nature. Calling them "capitalist collective organizations," he felt that they were a middle-class society apparatus, subject to middle-class interests.[1]

In Russia, early cooperatives were directed by Mensheviks, Revolutionary Socialists, and opportunists,[2] but since they could not remain in this form under Soviet power, a special framework was set up for them. In publications between 1918 and 1923, Lenin limited their functions and defined their role in the building of socialism.[3] These ideas, taken as a whole, have since been called "Lenin's cooperative plan."[4]

To understand its terms, we must remember that Lenin, influenced by American experience and industrial working methods, wanted to transform Russian agriculture into large-scale farming based on the most efficient use of machinery and a rational organization of work. To achieve this objective under the direction of the working class,[5] he expected the cooperative to provide the transition from small, individual peasant farms to large-scale socialist farming.[6]

The cooperatives, charged with the sale of agricultural produce and with the supply of industrial goods to the country, were designed to accustom the individual peasant (and the artisan) to a close collaboration with large productive units, and the cooperative's organization was modelled so as to make possible a smoother transition to collectivism. Lenin foresaw a period of transition lasting from ten to twenty years.

Under these conditions, consumer cooperatives and other types of agricultural cooperatives replaced the private middlemen in dealings between agriculture and industry. The cooperatives also had the other

[1] V. Lenin, "The Urgent Tasks of the Soviet Power," *Izvestiia VCIK*, No. 85 (Apr. 28, 1918); "About Cooperation," *Pravda*, No. 15 (March 26, 1923).

[2] V. Lenin, Report during the Eighth Congress of the Communist Party (b), March 19, 1919, *Sochineniia* (4th ed.; Moscow: Gospolitizdat, 1950), XXIX, 155–56.

[3] The following studies are especially pertinent:

"About Cooperation" (Jan., 1923); "The Tax in Kind" (April, 1921); "The Urgent Tasks of the Soviet Power" (April, 1918), Sochineniia (2nd ed.; Moscow: Gospolitizdat, 1930), XXVII, 391–97; XXVI, 321–52; XXII, 435–68.

"Historical Day," Editorial in *Sovetskaia potrebitelskaia kooperatsia*, No. 1 (1965), p. 29; S. Poznanski, *Lenin o spoldzielczosci* (Warsaw: C.Z.S., 1949), p. 98.

[4] A. Klimov, *Sovetskaia potrebitelskaia kooperatsia* (Moscow: Pravda, 1948), p. 4 (hereafter cited as *Sov. potr. koop*); J. Drozdowicz, *Organizacja spoldzielczosci w Polsce Ludowej* (Warsaw: C.Z.S., 1951), pp. 28–33.

[5] V. Lenin, "About the Workers' Cooperative Movement," speech on Dec. 7, 1917, *Sochineniya* (4th ed.), XXVIII, 305–13.

[6] In fact, it was the kolkhoz of the common type (*komuna*) that seemed to serve as a base of the projected organization of peasant collective agriculture.

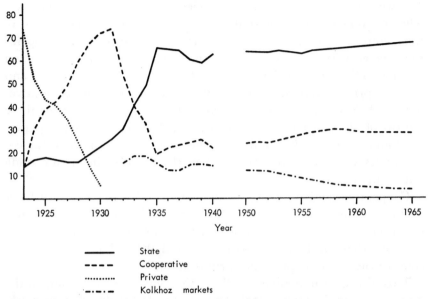

Fig. 1. Evolution of the part played by the three distribution channels in retail turnover (in percentage).

function of easing the process of transition for the peasants to the kolkhoz.[7] This concept of the role of the cooperative movement was borrowed later by Stalin who put the "cooperative plan" into practice. Naturally, this role did not correspond to the notion that the cooperatives had of their own function. Any resistance to the "cooperative plan" was quickly broken by the workers' and peasants' control commissions, which checked the character of the cooperatives[8] and purged those members not amenable to the proposed change. The societies were then reorganized according to the directives of the party. During the mass collectivization of 1929–31, the technicians of the cooperatives were sent to the kolkhozy to serve as economic technicians in the new organizations.

[7] I. Mikolenko, *Pravo kooperativnoi sobstvennosti* (Moscow: Akademiia Nauk S.S.S.R., 1961), p. 47; V. Khorin, *Tovarooborot potrebitelskoi kooperatsii* (Moscow: Tsentrosoiuz, 1959), p. 21.

[8] So, for example, in the spring of 1930, before the beginning of the Second Congress of the cooperative movement (July, 1930), 546 managers of the Tsentrozoiuz, 21.5 per cent of the employees in the urban cooperatives and 20.7 per cent of the employees in the agricultural cooperatives were eliminated. They were replaced by the workers, members of the kolkhoz, and the specialists recommended by the party. *Tri goda raboty* (Moscow: Tsentrosoiuz, 1934), p. 168. According to Y. Kistanov, *Potrebitelskaia kooperatsia S.S.S.R.* (Moscow-Tsentrosoiuz, 1951), p. 280.

If we examine Lenin's plan for cooperatives, we might ask ourselves whether cooperative trade would remain when mass collectivization of the country had been realized. The survival of the consumer cooperative seemed very uncertain as collectivization advanced in a direction parallel to the intensive development of state trade.[9] Between 1922 and 1930, as private trade was liquidated, the activities of the cooperatives increased very rapidly and, in 1931, they were responsible for three fourths of all transactions. But this trend declined immediately after 1929 and, between 1932 and 1935, the decrease in activity in the cooperatives was even more drastic than the decrease in private trade during the liquidation (Fig. 1).

Cooperative activity declined, in that period, from 74 to 19.3 per cent of the turnover of the retail trade. In 1935, the cooperatives provided only 1.1 billion rubles worth of goods for cities (less than 20 per cent of urban trade was cooperative) and 0.7 billion rubles in the country (less than 30 per cent of rural sales).[10]

Two directives of September 29, 1935, confirmed the decline of the cooperatives in the towns. At that point, they lost their urban network, and a part of their enterprises was transferred to the state trade organization.[11]

THE MAINTENANCE OF THE COOPERATIVE SECTOR

The authorities conferred on the cooperative sector a monopoly of the rural trade and charged it with the collection of agricultural products. In that way the Soviet government set up a territorial division of distribution between the two sales channels—the state and the cooperative groups. The 1936 constitution confirmed the collectivist nature of the kolkhoz ownership (Art. 5).[12] There were undoubtedly several major reasons why the cooperative and state marketing channels were allowed to survive side by side after the collectivization of agriculture.

Collectivization succeeded at the cost of heavy sacrifice, but was not complete enough to satisfy the doctrinaires of the period. The farms

[9] *Ibid.*, p. 305.

[10] A. Klimov, *Sov. potr. koop.*, p. 11. All the monetary figures in this paper are expressed in new rubles.

[11] Decisions of the Council of the People's Commissars of the U.S.S.R. and of the Central Committee of the Communist Party (b) about the activity of the consumers' cooperative movement in the countryside and about the reorganization of the Tsentrosoiuz.

[12] H. Wronski (Preface by P. Fromont and A. Piatier), *Rémunération et niveau de vie dans les kolkhoz* (Paris: S.E.D.E.S., 1957), pp. 14, 25.

were organized into artels and not into communes or sovkhozy.[13] The framework of the artel was determined on February 17, 1935.

Apart from the peasant dwelling, the artel left the breeding of livestock and the cultivation of vegetables to the *kolkhozniki*, so that the peasant remained to a certain extent an individual producer (the word "private" was prohibited). This small survival of "private" production left the socialization of agriculture unfinished, and required that the consumer cooperative continue in its role as a guide toward a more complete form of collectivization. Moreover, the consumer cooperative is better adapted than the state trade network to satisfy the particular characteristics of rural demand. As a matter of fact, peasant demand reflects regional habits depending essentially on local resources: the *kolkhozniki* are remunerated partly in kind, and they have at their disposal the crops from their individual plots. They buy agricultural goods in small quantities only, looking for those products that they do not produce themselves. In addition, peasant demand changes considerably from year to year, depending on their own crop output.[14] Such fluctuations have direct repercussions on the demand for industrial goods, both durable and semidurable.

From the planner's point of view, the existence of two separate channels of trade enables the variety of goods on sale to be more easily adapted to the structure of the demand of different consumer groups. This dual system also enables the authorities to regulate the flow of goods and to discriminate in any way they see fit. When the sharp division between trade in the towns and trade in the country occurred, the rationing of food products handled by the state trade network could be abolished and the very high commercial prices of nonrationed goods could be suppressed.[15] This duality of distribution helps to maintain the priority of the town supply[16] when there is an insufficient supply of consumer goods, and the lack is felt only in the rural cooperative network.[17]

For this reason, the existence of two separate sectors of distribution can be considered as a useful tool of Soviet economic policy. The rural sector supports the burden of socialist accumulation of capital for

[13] *Partiinoie stroitelstvo*, No. 3/4 (1932), pp. 94–95; *Ekonomicheskaia zhizn SSSR 1917–1959* (1961), p. 270.

[14] K. Boczar, *Podstawy obrotu towarowego* (Warsaw: P.W.E., 1959), p. 51.

[15] Decision of September 25, 1935, *Directyvy KPSS*, II, 476–77.

[16] L. Kozminski, "The Role of Wholesale Trade in Distribution," *Roczniki Instytutu Handlu Wewnetrznego*, No. 1 (1964), p. 21.

[17] A. Klimov, Report of July 2, 1964, *Sov. potr. koop.*, No. 8 (1964).

reinvestment. On the other hand, up to now the cooperatives have paid higher prices for the goods received from the producers. From their own resources, which are obtained from the subscriptions of their members, they must finance all the social charges that in urban trade organizations are paid for by the state. These include the formation of capital and the training of staffs.

In short, dual channels of trade and the manner in which they function allow the authorities to discriminate between consumers. This can be compared to the situation existing between kolkhoz peasants and sovkhoz workers. In fact, the future of consumer cooperatives is closely linked to kolkhoz development. Many juridical concepts applicable to cooperative property were elaborated on in connection with the rules that govern kolkhoz property.[18]

Although both the kolkhoz and the cooperative are forms of group ownership, state ownership is considered a more advanced degree of socialization, and is the ultimate objective of the Soviet authorities in their march towards communism. However, neither the time when this higher phase is to be reached nor the means by which it can be achieved has ever been defined.[19]

THE ECONOMIC ACTIVITIES OF THE COOPERATIVE

In the present economic structure of the U.S.S.R., the scope of the cooperatives is so wide that their functions enter into a number of economic branches. This is especially remarkable in the Soviet system in which the sectors are generally closely identified with a well-determined economic function. Some of these economic activities are:

1. Trade: the supplying of the rural population with consumer goods.
2. Catering establishments: the management of a chain of canteens and restaurants.
3. Direct production: industrial or artisan production of consumer goods and services.
4. Collection of agricultural products.
5. Sale of agricultural surpluses in the town markets.
6. Sale of producers' goods.
7. External commercial transactions.

---

[18] Mikolenko, *Pravo kooperativnoi* . . . , p. 7.

[19] J. Stalin, *Les Problèmes Economiques du Socialisme en U.R.S.S.* (Paris: Editions Sociales, 1953), pp. 71–75; V. Eliseev (ed.), *Ekonomika i planirovanie sovetskoi kooperativnoi torgovli* (Moscow: Tsentrosoiuz, 1965), p. 8.

Trade

With its 363,200 sales outlets, which constitute 58 per cent of such outlets in the Soviet Union, cooperative trade had in 1967 a turnover of 37 billion rubles or 29.1 per cent of the total turnover of Soviet retail trade. The cooperative commercial organizations supply 120 million people: the entire rural population and several million people in urban areas.[20]

On January 1, 1961, rural consumers (representing 705,000 households[21]) and 8,000,000 urban consumers (living in 2,000 of the smallest urban localities) received their supplies from consumers' cooperatives. In comparison to this, state trade outlets existed in 2,500 cities.

A glance at the geographical distribution of the commercial activities of the cooperative helps us to understand the importance of the services it provides better than would a study of turnover data alone. The chain of cooperatives is composed of several types of establishments. There are the kiosks and small, rural shops selling only a modest assortment of goods, those that are most frequently in demand, and there are the department and specialized stores that offer a much wider assortment of goods. By far the more common of the two extremes, however, is the small, rural, one-man shop. The trade service density in the villages is low; for example, in 1965 one sales employee served 222 inhabitants.[22] The plan for 1980 foresees one employee serving 157 to 166 inhabitants, which will equal the commercial density in the cities in 1963[23] (see Table 1).

TABLE 1
INHABITANTS SERVED BY ONE SOVIET
RETAIL ESTABLISHMENT (in 1963)

Number	Soviet Union Total	Cities	Villages
By commercial enterprise	370	385	345
By sales employee	196	159	270

Source: *Sovetskaia torgovlia. Statisticheskii sbornik* (Moscow, 1964), p. 440.

But an equal commercial density (that is to say, the number of inhabitants by sale outlet or by sales employee) does not mean that the urban and rural consumers are supplied with the same convenience. The

[20] *Ibid.*, p. 36; *Narodnoe khoziaistvo v 1967g.* (Moscow: 1968), pp. 714-45.

[21] *Vestnik statistiki*, No. 7 (1962), pp. 83, 90.

[22] *Ekonomicheskaia gazeta*, No. 46 (1966), p. 27.

[23] K. Feriukovich, *Organizatsia i tekhnika sovetskoi kooperativnoi torgovli* (Moscow: Tsentrosoiuz, 1963), p. 59.

distances between houses and shops, the state of the roads, and so on, all lessen the ease of purchase for the rural dweller.

Of the goods distributed by the cooperative chain, one third is provided from the cooperatives' own resources (the direct production and supplies of agricultural surpluses from kolkhozy and members of the cooperatives[24]) and the remainder, which is an essential point, is supplied by state wholesalers.

The ministries of commerce in the federal republics decide for their territories the division of merchandise between cooperative and state trade from the resources that are given to them by superior authorities.[25] In cases of difficulty of supply, i.e., when the volume of disposable goods does not correspond to planned consumption, the ministry gives priority to the state sector and tries to achieve the objectives of the plan in the latter. In this way tensions in supply have greater repercussions on the cooperative than on the state trade sector.[26] Also, the division of merchandise is most frequently carried out on the basis of out-of-date coefficients that do not take into consideration the increase in income of the rural population.[27]

Very often the supply of the most necessary consumer goods is insufficient, and the selection available in the cooperative shops does not correspond to demand.[28] In the cooperatives the stock of unsalable goods, those which constitute a burden on the Soviet economy, is double that in the state commercial organizations.[29]

Not so long ago, cooperative trade employed special rural prices that were higher than those obtained in the cities for the same article. These prices were applied to goods supplied by the state sector, and on their introduction into the cooperative chain, a tax averaging 7 per cent of the retail price in the cities was placed on them.[30] This tax constituted a supplementary source of centralized accumulation for the government. But its application began to disrupt the whole planned-distribution framework, and rural consumers were driven to satisfy their need for industrial products in the cities.

---

[24] Z. Bim, *Tovarnoe obrashchenie* (Moscow: Vysshaia shkola, 1960), p. 3.

[25] S. Vasilev, *Ekonomika sovetskoi torgovli* (Moscow: Gospolitizdat, 1962), p. 241.

[26] *Sov. potr. koop.*, No. 8 (1964), p. 4; *ibid.*, No. 5 (1966), p. 2.

[27] *Ibid.*, No. 8 (1964), pp. 17–18, 20; *ibid.*, No. 6 (1965), p. 8.

[28] V. Tiukov, R. Lokshin, *Sovetskaia torgovlia v period perekhoda* (Moscow: Ekonomika, 1964), pp. 28–29.

[29] B. Mochalov, *Tovarnoe obrashchenie* (Leningrad: University of Leningrad, 1965), p. 159.

[30] V. Tiukov, R. Lokshin, *Sovetskaia torgovlia . . .* , pp. 28–29.

In 1960, the government abolished this tax on some products, and on March 2, 1965, Brezhnev, answering the questions of rural workers, promised them the same prices for their supplies as those in the cities. But this was not the only peculiarity of cooperative prices. The sales outlets work under difficult conditions and at a very high cost—the low turnover increases the expense, and the high freight charges and the loss of goods owing to shipping distances add heavily to the distribution cost.

In order to take into account these different elements, the profit margin granted to the cooperatives is slightly higher than that granted to the state shops.[31] The margin on sugar is 8.5 per cent in the cooperatives and only 6 per cent in state stores; for tobacco it is 8 and 5.5 per cent, respectively, and on material goods it is 7.6 and 4 per cent.[32] By July 1, 1967, most of these margins in state stores had been noticeably increased.

When a sales outlet is more than ten kilometers from the distribution center, the railway station, or the river port, cooperatives have the option of increasing their retail price in order to allow for freight charges. The cooperatives may also take real cost prices into account in order to calculate the retail prices of goods produced from raw materials that are either bought at the kolkhoz market or produced in factories where the processing cost is at a high level.[33]

Finally, it seems that cooperative distribution will never be improved until basic structural reforms have been made and, above all, a large investment program is worked out.

Catering Establishments

Like the state sector, the cooperatives also possess a network of collective catering establishments, i.e., canteens and restaurants. At the end of 1965, they numbered 60,300 and had a staff of 246,000 employees. Their turnover amounted to 1.9 billion rubles.[34] The most important of these institutions are the sovkhoz canteens and the restaurants in the T.R.S. (Technical Repair Stations) and the Tractor Training Schools. Sometimes the kolkhoz peasants take their meals in canteens during their working hours; in other cases the canteens deliver meals to the

[31] V. Eliseev, *Ekonomika i planirovanie* . . . , p. 391; B. Gogol, *Ekonomika sovetskoi torgovli* (Moscow: Gostorgizdat, 1960), p. 390.

[32] D. Moliakov, *Finansirovanie narodnovo khoziaistva* (Moscow: Finansy, 1966), pp. 137, 632, 646, 658.

[33] B. Mochalov, *Tovarnoe obrashchenie*, p. 158;—*La coopérative de consommation* (Moscow: Tsentrosoiuz, 1962), 38.

[34] *Narodnoe khoziaistvo SSR v 1965 g.* (Moscow, 1966), pp. 632, 646, 658.

home. The canteens are near the kolkhozy, the schools, and each of the enterprises. The roles of the catering establishments show a tendency to grow in relation to the extension of peasant participation in collective tasks.

Direct Production

While the state trade organizations tend to reduce their production and relinquish it to state industry, the cooperatives continue to maintain and develop their own production. Thus, from 1955 to 1963, the number of people employed in production in cooperatives increased from 185,700 to 330,900.[35]

Direct cooperative production is carried on in approximately 46,000 centers; their total turnover in 1965 was 2.3 billion rubles.[36] Activity is carried out over a very wide area and contains important units of food production: bakeries (17,000), butcheries, and food canners. There also are branches producing clothes, durable consumption goods (plates, cutlery, domestic equipment, furniture), construction materials (bricks, tiles, slates, lumber), and equipment for retail shops and warehouses.

Many services for the rural population are provided by the cooperative sector: repairing and maintaining clothes, shoes, radios, domestic equipment, bicycles, sewing machines, and so on. Because of the extension of production, the cooperative sector even supplies towns with some food products (canned food and beverages), as well as with agricultural surpluses.

In general the cooperative industrial plants use local raw materials of secondary importance and agricultural surpluses from the kolkhozy. The limited character of those resources tends to intensify utilization, but also makes the expansion of cooperative production impossible, despite the need. The pressure of the demand is even stronger now that the production that used to come from artisan cooperatives has declined to a low level, following their nationalization in 1960.

Collection of Agricultural Products

One of the most important tasks of the cooperatives is to collect and to stock some of the agricultural products for the state, but without its intervention. Thus, the cooperatives have a monopoly in the collection of eggs and wool. Also the *Tsentrosoiuz* (the central union of consumer cooperatives) operates in any district or branch where production is low

---

[35] *Sovetskaia torgovlia* (Moscow, 1956), p. 114; *ibid.* (1964), pp. 133, 36.
[36] *Sov. potr. koop.*, No. 5 (1966), p. 5.

and where for reasons of efficiency state intervention would be impractical.[37] In addition, the cooperatives are charged by the state to collect perishable goods whose collection cost is high (medical plants, secondary agricultural raw materials); goods whose collection extends over long periods of time (untanned skins, furs); and those whose local consumption is high (potatoes and such). The cooperatives collect and store all grain reserved for local consumption according to the plan set up by the federal republic authorities. This collection function is important, representing 4.7 billion rubles per year.

Sales of Agricultural Surplus in Town Markets

In addition to the collection of agricultural surpluses for the state, the cooperative also ensures the sale of these products in large cities. It fulfilled this function between 1946 and 1950, and from 1953 on.

In 1965, 15,000 commercial enterprises operating in towns had a total turnover of 1.4 billion rubles, which represents 3.5 per cent[38] of all the foodstuffs marketed in the Soviet Union. The prices in these cooperative shops are higher than the fixed prices in the state shops and lower than those in the kolkhoz free markets. The 1964 price indices were:

State shops	100
Cooperative shops	118
Kolkhoz markets	152[39]

Sale of Producers' Goods

The distribution of producers' goods to the state productive units is made through a special channel called "material and technical supply" (*materialno-tekhnicheskoe snabzhenie*). The prices of these goods are low because they do not include any purchase tax.

Up to 1958, the kolkhozy were not allowed to buy goods distributed by this network. They were supplied by the cooperative network at prices noticeably higher. For instance, they paid two and one-half times as much for tractors and fuel as the state farms. Since the transformation of the Machine and Tractor Stations (M.T.S.) into Technical Repair Stations (T.R.S.), which took place at the beginning of 1958, the delivery of spare and separate parts and some other goods has been carried out by the stations and by a new and special state depart-

[37] *Ek. gaz.*, No. 46 (1966), p. 25.

[38] A. Levin, *Ekonomicheskoe regulirovanie vnutrennego rynka* (Moscow: Ekonomika, 1967), p. 110.

[39] *Sov. potr. koop.*, No. 8 (1965), p. 7.

ment, the *Selkhoztekhnika*. The prices of these goods lie between the prices paid by the kolkhoz and those paid by the state farm. The change caused a decrease of 700 billion rubles in the turnover of the cooperatives. In 1963, the *Selkhoztekhnika* were entrusted with the supply of materials to the kolkhozy.

At present, the cooperative network sells coal, feed grains, harnesses, and work clothes to the whole rural sector, and supplies peasants with housebuilding materials and with machines, tools, fertilizers, and so forth, for farming their individual plots. However, the materials delivered to the peasants are not sufficient to meet their demand.[40]

External Commercial Exchanges

The *Tsentrosoiuz* has established commercial relations with thirty foreign cooperative organizations (in People's Democracies, Western countries, and developing countries). It imports consumer goods, construction materials, and equipment for the food industries. It exports agricultural and forest products, goods produced by *Tsentrosoiuz* plants, and goods delivered to the *Tsentrosoiuz* by the state for the internal market, but which the *Tsentrosoiuz* chooses to divert toward the export markets. These represented 52.4 per cent of the total cooperative exports in 1965.[41]

In addition, the *Tsentrosoiuz* has its own transport and construction enterprises. In fact, its economic activity, even when limited to the agricultural sector, is much greater than the normal range of activities of consumer cooperatives. They would correspond more to the normal activity of the "agricultural cooperatives."

International trade of the cooperative sector is growing rapidly and in 1965 was valued at 547 million rubles.[42]

CONCLUSION

Examination of the activities of the consumer cooperatives leads to conjecture about their economic significance and their future.

First, it is obvious that the cooperative organizations and their centralized commercial chain of distribution facilitated the process of industrialization and economic growth within the framework of the Stalinist model. The cooperative organization enabled the government to make the rural population, as a consumer group, bear a large share

---

[40] V. Tiukov, R. Lokshin, *Sovetskaia torgovlia* . . . , p. 99.
[41] *Sov. potr. koop*. No. 10 (1966), p. 16.
[42] *Ibid.*, No. 7 (1966), p. 62.

of the cost of industrialization, which was implemented by these means:
—Establishing higher prices in village shops than in city stores
—Requiring members to contribute to the cooperative's quotas and to pay entrance fees to the cooperatives
—Paying low wages to workers in the cooperatives
—Denying adequate technical equipment to the cooperative units

By giving the cooperatives a monopoly of distribution in the villages, the government was in a position to limit effectively consumption by the population.[43] This made it possible to maintain the priority of investments in industry (especially in basic industry) and to achieve a higher rate of capital accumulation. But with the end of the Stalinist period, many of the reasons that favored a separate cooperative chain have become dated:

—The rate of capital accumulation in the cooperative sector shows a continuing decline
—The special tax on rural prices has been suppressed
—The wage level of cooperative workers is equal to the wage level of workers employed in state agencies
—The commercial profit margin granted to cooperative enterprises has been increased
—The supply of goods to cooperative shops has been much improved

The rural population (to which the *Tsentrosoiuz* addresses itself) has declined and now represents only about 47 per cent of the Soviet total. If the trend continues and if Soviet society reaches the same social and professional structure possessed by Western countries, a special network of distribution in rural areas need no longer exist.

In a normal cooperative movement, the members profit by cooperative rebates, better service, and participation in an economic and ideologic movement rated more highly than the general system. But in the U.S.S.R., cooperative rebates do not exist. On the contrary, the state trade network offers the cities better prices and goods than the cooperative network does the rural areas. We may ask, therefore, why a separate cooperative chain should be maintained. When Professor G. Lasserre visited the Soviet Union, this eminent French authority on

---

[43] Supply of the means of production for agriculture was not sufficient (consciously limited) and the prices paid by cooperatives were as much as two to five times higher than those paid by state production organizations for the same means of production. M. Terentiev, "Price Fixation," *Voprosy ekonomiki*, No. 3 (1958), p. 60; L. Zlomanov, "Experience of Tractor Workers Group," *ibid.*, pp. 68, 72; D. Pavlov, *40 let sovetskoi torgovli* (Moscow: Gostorgizdat, 1958), p. 38.

cooperatives asked twenty Soviet cooperative managers and "activists" the above question, but he got no clear answer.[44]

We can also observe an increasingly important change in the origin of the funds that are used by the cooperatives and the manner in which they finance their activity. The property shares of the individual members, which represented approximately two thirds of the proper funds of the movement in 1940, and more than half in 1950, amounted in 1966 to between 6 and 8.6 per cent, according to the sources consulted.[45] This new situation will not, apparently, be reversed. We cannot expect any noticeable increase in membership shares in the future; the average of the normal statutory quotas actually paid is only a little more than 16 rubles,[46] already very high compared with the income of the rural population. Nor can we expect an increase in the number of cooperative members, since it now includes 74 per cent of the adults in rural areas.[47]

The financing of trade activities in the cooperatives is achieved (in a proportion of 90 per cent in the wholesale trade sector and of 85 per cent in the retail trade sector) by the means of Gosbank (state bank) credits. The remainder, 10 or 15 per cent, is furnished by the cooperatives themselves. The result is a state of overdependence on the central authorities, as can be seen from the fact that, even in state trade, only half of current purchasing of goods is financed by means of external credits.[48] However, the directives of the Twenty-Third Party Congress decreed, for the 1966–70 period, that cooperative rural trade should increase more than state trade. But the cooperatives do not have the necessary means at their disposal for reaching such a target. However, the rural trade network is often helped by the kolkhozy and sovkhozy, which build new shops, catering establishments, bakeries, or service centers with their own funds,[49] and help finance the building of hospitals

[44] G. Lasserre, "Visite aux coopératives de consommation de l'U.R.S.S." in: H. Chambre, G. Lasserre, and H. Wronski, *La Coopération de consommation en U.R.S.S.* (Paris: Cujas, 1969), p. 119.

[45] H. Wronski, "Les coopératives de consommation en U.R.S.S.," *Archives Internationales de Sociologie de la Coopération*, No. 19 (1966), p. 133; *Ek. gaz.*, No. 46 (1966), p. 24; N. Kolesov, *Obschestvennaia sobstvennost na sredstva proizvodstva* (Leningrad: University of Leningrad, 1967), p. 124.

[46] H. Wronski, "Les coopératives de consommation en U.R.S.S." (Paris: Cujas, 1969), p. 60.

[47] G. Błank, "Consumer cooperatives," *Rewolucja październikowa a rozwój spółdzielczości w krajach socjalistycznych* (Warsaw: CRS, 1967), II, 75.

[48] V. Buzyrev (ed.), *Denezhnoe obrashchenie i kredyt v S.S.S.R.* (Moscow: Vysshia shkola, 1965), p. 286.

[49] *Sov. potr. koop.*, No. 5 (1966), p. 3; *ibid.*, No. 7 (1966), p. 58.

and schools. In 1966, kolkhozy and sovkhozy built 1,298 new shops in the R.S.F.S.R. and 1,379 new stores in the Ukraine.[50]

Soviet writers favor the evolution of the cooperative movement in the U.S.S.R., pretending that this way of financing allows a more efficient use of economic means and gives the cooperatives some features of the superior type of ownership, i.e., the state-owned unit.[51]

As a matter of fact, the cooperative sector apparently can adapt itself more easily to the changing trade situation than can the state sector.[52] From this standpoint it can also be useful for testing economic reform plans that might be applied later to the entire trade system. This effort to reform the system is aimed at improving the adaptability of production to the consumer's need and at making the enterprise a basic, relatively autonomous, unit of the economy. In that way the cooperatives would respond better to the consumers' needs than a state body with its bureaucratic methods. The latter is unable to adapt itself to consumers' expectations in a monopolistic situation without competition, that factor being especially favorable for "trained incapacity," as Wilbert E. Moore has stated.

This presentation of the structure and of the activities of the cooperative channel of distribution shows a striking analogy between collective farms and consumer cooperatives. Actually, the peasant is supplied as a consumer by the latter and as a producer by the collective farm. The consumer cooperative, however, goes beyond the kolkhoz framework and links the kolkhoz peasants, the sovkhoz workers, and all rural consumers.

[50] For instance, during the 1950–65 period, 72 per cent of schools in rural areas were by kolkhozy and peasants, whereas only 28 per cent were built from public funds (B. Struzek, "The role of the rural cooperative," *Rewolucja październikowa a rozwój spoldzielczości* . . . , I, 180; J. Gasiorek [ed.], *Centrosojuz w 50-leciu Z.S.R.R.* [The Tsentrosoiuz during the last 50 years of the U.S.S.R.] [Warsaw: C.R.S., 1967], p. 88).

[51] M. Bagachevski, *op. cit.*, p. 202; V. Buzyrev (ed.), *Denezhnoe obrashchenie* . . . , p. 290; N. Kolesov, *Obschestvennaia sobstvennost* . . . , p. 124.

[52] H. Cholaj, "Economic socialist models," *Rewolucja październikowa* . . . , I, 68; E. Garbacik, *Wybrane zagadnienia ekonomiki handlu* (Krakow: P.T.E., 1967), 18.

NANCY NIMITZ*

Comment

Dr. Wronski has given us a useful survey of the development of Soviet consumer cooperatives and their present range of activities. His main aim is to explain the seemingly anomalous survival of a rural cooperative trade network separate from the state-owned system that serves the cities. He concludes that the explanation has varied from one period to another. In the years before collectivization, when consumer cooperatives served both urban and rural areas, their distinctive rural function was to accustom the peasant to joint enterprises, and thus prepare him for cooperative production. In 1935 (after collectivization was substantially accomplished), the state took over most urban trade, but retained cooperatives in the countryside because a separate distribution network made it easier to discriminate against the peasant consumer. Today, when discrimination is no longer sought, cooperatives persist because they are, potentially at least, more efficient (more autonomous, hence more able to respond to local needs) than the bureaucratic state system.

My reservations mainly concern the nature and significance of discrimination against the peasant consumer in the period from the 1930's to the mid-1960's. I think Dr. Wronski may overestimate the importance of savings extracted from the rural population via cooperative membership fees and higher rural prices.

Let us begin with prices. Unfortunately, evidence bearing on the prewar period is far from clear, so that even the direction of any urban-rural price differential, let alone its size, remains in doubt.[1] We do know that higher rural prices were introduced in 1942, but not for all products. At the end of 1947, when rationing was abolished, the price

---

* Any views expressed in this paper are those of the author. They should not be interpreted as reflecting the views of the RAND Corporation or the official opinion or policy of any of its governmental or private research sponsors.

differential was 13.5 per cent; from 1950 to 1959 it was 7 per cent. These percentages refer not to all rural prices, but only to those goods where a price difference existed; such goods reportedly accounted for 40 per cent of cooperative turnover in the late 1950's. Hence the rural price level as a whole was not 7 per cent above the urban level, but 2.8 per cent $(0.40 \times 107 + 0.60 \times 100)$. Some, if not all, of this difference is warranted by higher distribution costs in rural areas. All of it was apparently wiped out by price reductions that went into effect between January 1, 1960, and January 1, 1966, with aggregate savings to rural consumers of about 700 million rubles a year.[2]

Turning now to membership fees (*paevye vznosy*): Dr. Wronski notes that the share contribution currently required for membership is a little less than twenty rubles. Elsewhere the normal requirement has been described as equal to one week's wages.[3] This is certainly not a trivial sum, but the burden should be judged in the light of several facts. First, the share may be paid in installments over a two-year period.[4] Second, it is reportedly refunded to members who leave the cooperative.[5] Third, though most cooperative profits are plowed back into the business, members may receive a minute annual dividend on their investment; the average per individual shareholder in 1964 seems to have been about twenty kopecks,[6] or something like 1 to 2 per cent of the value of

[1] Annual data for 18 products, 1928—1932 (A. Malafeev, *Istoriia tsenoobrazovaniia v SSSR, 1917–1963 gg.* [Moscow: Mysl, 1964], pp. 164–65) show considerably higher rural prices for almost all products in all years; however, the source explains that the urban and rural prices are not comparable, since they do not refer to the same regions. A Gosplan statement cited in Janet Chapman, *Real Wages in Soviet Russia Since 1928* (Cambridge, Mass.: Harvard University Press, 1963), p. 358, implies that rural prices in 1928 were about 25 per cent below urban prices.

[2] Chapman, *Real Wages . . .* , pp. 361–62; V. Kornienko, "V chem sushchnost vyravnivaniia roznichnykh tsen dlia goroda i sela," *Politicheskoe samoobrazovanie*, No. 1, 1966, pp. 84–86. The figure reported for savings from the 1960–66 price cuts is consistent with the statement that rural prices as a whole were only about 3 per cent above urban prices in the late 1950s.

[3] *Ezhegodnik Bolshoi sovetskoi entsiklopedii, 1965* (Moscow: Sovetskaia entsiklopediia, 1965), pp. 81–82.

[4] *Ibid.*

[5] *Bolshaia sovetskaia entsiklopediia* (2nd ed.; Moscow: Bolshaia sovestkaia entsiklopediia, 1955), XXXI, 544, 548. The claim is supported by the fact that fees paid by new members over the years 1959–65 totalled 235 million rubles (*Ezhegodnik Bolshoi sovetskoi entsiklopedii, 1966* [Moscow: Sovetskaia entsiklopediia, 1966], p. 86), while the net increase in the shares fund (*paevoi fond*) between January 1, 1959 and January 1, 1966 was only 162 million (E. Fonarev, *Raspredelenie i ispolzovanie pribyli potrebitelskoi kooperatsii* [Moscow: Finansy, 1966], p. 69; N. Sychev, ed., *Finansy predpriiatii i otraslei narodnogo khoziaistva* [Moscow: Finansy, 1967], p. 376).

[6] Dividends distributed to individual shareholders totalled 9.9 million rubles (Fonarev, *Raspredelenie . . .* , p. 60). Number of shareholders from Table 1.

TABLE 1

MEMBERSHIP IN CONSUMER COOPERATIVES COMPARED
WITH RURAL POPULATION, 1951–1965

	Members	Rural Population[a]	Members as Per cent of Rural Population
	(In Millions)		
	(1)	(2)	(3)
1951 (Jan. 1)	32.4	108.6	30
1956 (Jan. 1)	33.3	109.7	30
1958 (Jan. 1)	34.0	109.3	31
1959	ca. 40	108.8	37
1962 (July 1)	44.2	108.0	41
1964	51 to 52	107.9	47 to 48
1965	53 to 55	107.6	49 to 51

[a] January 1 estimate, except 1959 (January 15 census).

Sources: Col. 1 1951, 1956: Ia. Pavlov, ed., *40 let sovetskoi torgovli* (Moscow: Gostorgizdat, 1957), p. 102.

1958: *Ezhegodnik Bolshoi sovetskoi entsiklopedii, 1959* (Moscow: Sovetskaia entsiklopediia, 1959), p. 60.

1959: B. Gogol, *Ekonomika sovetskoi torgovli* (Moscow: Gostorgizdat, 1960), p. 28.

1962: *Ezhegodnik . . . 1963* (Moscow: Sovetskaia entsiklopediia, 1963), p. 80.

1964: E. Fonarev, *Raspredelenie i ispolzovanie pribyli potrebitelskoi kooperatsii* (Moscow: Finansy, 1966), p. 4; *Ezhegodnik . . . 1965*, p. 81.

1965: *Ezhegodnik . . . 1966*, p. 85; N. Sychev, ed., *Finansy predpriiatii i otraslei narodnogo khoziaistva* (Moscow: Finansy, 1967), p. 376.

Col. 2 All years: *Narodnoe khoziaistvo SSSR v 1965 g.* (Moscow: Statistika, 1966), p. 7.

the investment share. Finally, membership has not been required (at least until the late 1950's) in order to buy goods in cooperative stores, which are supposed to serve the entire population in their areas. It is true that members and their families get preferential access to scarce goods and services, and in the country many goods and all services have been in short supply. Still, the preference is not supposed to extend to the basic necessities.[7] Comparison of the trends in cooperative membership and in rural population suggests to me that a sizable fraction of the rural population has, until recently, used cooperative stores without joining them as members (Table 1). Incidentally, it would be nice to know why the ratio of members to total rural population rose so rapidly between 1958 and 1965—from 31 to 50 per cent. Does this reflect an increase in the proportion of urban members?[8] Or the increasing appeal of benefits available only to members? Or administrative pressure to join?

[7] Ia. Pavlov, ed., *40 let sovetskoi torgovli* (Moscow: Gostorgizdat, 1957), pp. 94–95.

[8] Sales in urban areas (small towns and workers' settlements) accounted for 29.2 per cent of total cooperative turnover in 1958 and 32.7 per cent in 1964 (G. Dikhtiar, *Sovetskaia torgovlia v period razvernutogo stroitelstva kommunizma* [Moscow: Nauka, 1965], p. 366).

In all years rural consumers have gone to the cities for a significant share of their total purchases: 34 per cent in 1936 (according to household budget sample data), about 23 per cent in 1937, and something under 20 per cent in recent times.[9] Many such junkets to town have been dual-purpose—to sell produce at the higher collective farm market prices prevailing in cities, as well as to buy in better-stocked city stores. It is clear, however, that many items could not be purchased in the country at any price, and that this was because a disproportionate share of goods was deliberately allocated to urban trade.[10] It is this form of discrimination that I suspect to be the most galling to the rural consumer: not the fact that he helps, by his investment share, to finance the construction of cooperative stores, or that he has had to pay somewhat more, but that he has been offered in his own stores such a paltry assortment of goods. *Basic* goods.

At present one third of the rural population still has to bake its own bread. This is an improvement over 1958, when the proportion was closer to two thirds, but it still represents an enormous amount of household labor.[11] Only about one fifth of rural stores have any form of refrigeration, hence any real capability of stocking meat, milk, eggs, and perishable fruits and vegetables.[12] The man who lives in the country is virtually forced to have a private plot, whether he enjoys hand weeding and hand milking and toting the manure from here to there or not. The older generation of farmers may be content with this, but not some of the younger ones, nor most nonfarm rural people, nor the urban professionals—doctors, teachers, and so on—that the authorities obviously want to attract to rural regions in greater numbers.

So there is a lot of room for improvement, and we will hope that cooperatives indeed prove more energetic than the bureaucratic state network in seeking to serve their customers. My guess is that the rural buyer would even accept higher prices and increased membership fees if these accelerated investment in such literally bread-and-butter objects as bakeries and refrigerators.

[9] G. Dikhtiar, *Sovetskaia torgovlia v period postroeniia sotsializma* (Moscow: Akademiia nauk, 1961), p. 405; Kornienko, "V chem sushchnost . . ."

[10] V. Tiukov and R. Lokshin, *Sovetskaia torgovlia v period perekhoda k kommunizmu* (Moscow: Ekonomika, 1964), pp. 54–55.

[11] *Potrebitelskaia kooperatsiia*, No. 3, 1966, pp. 28–33.

[12] V. Morozov, *Trudoden, dengi i torgovlia na sele* (Moscow: Ekonomika, 1965), p. 244; M. Denisov in *Izvestiia*, August 25, 1967.

JERZY F. KARCZ

Certain Aspects
of New Economic Systems
in Bulgaria and Czechoslovakia*

Efforts to improve the performance of socialist agricultural systems
through the greater use of market-type (as opposed to command-style)
policy instruments antedate the introduction of the "new economic
systems." Beginning with 1953, trends in agricultural policies in the
Soviet Union as well as in the other East European countries provide
ample evidence to this effect, even though the efforts were not always
consistent and the results often disappointing. The introduction of the
new economic systems, which may be dated from 1965,[1] only intensified
the need for a broader, more encompassing change in policies and
planning procedures relating to agriculture. One such reform is now
taking place in Czechoslovakia under the name of the "improved system
of planning and management of agriculture."[2] Similar policies have

* The financial assistance of the Inter-University Committee on Travel Grants,
Indiana University, and of the Project for Comparative Study of Communist Societies, University of California, Berkeley, is gratefully acknowledged. It is also a
pleasure to express gratitude to the respective Institutes of Economics of the Bulgarian
and the Czechoslovak Academies of Sciences for the hospitable welcome extended
to the writer (and his family) in 1966/67. Only a general expression of thanks can be
made to economists in both countries (particularly those connected with the Research
Institutes of Agricultural Economics and the Research Institute of Finance in Prague)
who gave so generously of their time: they are by far too numerous to be mentioned
by name. I am also grateful to Professor A. Korbonski of the University of California
at Los Angeles for a number of pertinent comments.

[1] Cf. Gregory Grossman, "Economic Reforms: A Balance Sheet," *Problems of Communism*, XV, No. 6 (Nov.–Dec., 1966), 43.

[2] Later referred to as "new system" only. The official title reflects the fact that
maximization of gross income (under given constraints) was a characteristic of the
collective farm sector at an earlier time.

been introduced in Bulgaria and in other countries of the socialist camp, though in many instances they have not been as systematized formally as in Czechoslovakia.

This paper is essentially an exercise in selected topics of economics of decompression of the agricultural system of a Soviet-type command economy. The latter is defined broadly as that economic system which prevailed in the U.S.S.R. until 1953 and spread to the rest of Eastern Europe in the aftermath of World War II. I concentrate primarily on two key problems: planning practices and price (as well as tax) policies. No effort is made to describe the new systems in their entirety.[3] While the examples are drawn from Czechoslovak and Bulgarian experience, the fact that the problems are bloc-wide influenced their selection. The pitfalls of comparative analysis are many, and special efforts were made to avoid aspects that result from a specific experience of a given country.[4]

The emphasis is placed on problems connected with the substitution of market-type policy tools for the directives and commands. This in no way reflects a failure to recognize the very substantial progress that has been made in the direction of greater economic rationality, but rather the conviction that the process of decompression faces many formidable difficulties.

PLANNING METHODS AND DECISION MAKING AT THE FARM

A knowledgeable Polish economist recently stated that effective economic planning disappeared from socialist agriculture after 1928–29.[5] This conclusion, fully supported by recent Czechoslovak analysis and some Bulgarian practices, is based on the following argument:

At the national level, agricultural planning practices concentrated on the satisfaction of the state demand for farm products. The size of this demand was a function of the high rate of growth of the national products (and its industrial component), of an equally high income elasticity of demand for food, and of the urgent needs for foreign

[3] I also neglect problems arising from maximization of gross income rather than profit. The reader may wish to consult the writings of Benjamin Ward and Evsey Domar in this context.

[4] In many respects, Czechoslovakia and Bulgaria represent the limits of performance and characteristics in the socialist bloc of Eastern Europe. Czechoslovak farm output is only slightly higher than it was before World War II; Bulgarian output has nearly doubled. The positions are reversed (or nearly so) when we consider the level of industrial development.

[5] This is the gist (though not the formulation) of Czeslaw Bobrowski in "Granice i warunki planowania w rolnictwie," *Zagadnienia ekonomiki rolnej*, No. 2 (1965), p. 3.

exchange. On the other hand, input requirements of the agricultural sector (including at times the labor input) were satisfied only to the extent allowed by planned output targets for industry, the production capacity of the industrial sector, and by the desire to economize on foreign exchange.

As is true of all brief generalizations, this is an oversimplification.[6] But the fact remains that the ensuing limitations on the production capacity of the agricultural sector were largely (if not completely) ignored in the formulation of output, investment, and marketing plans at all planning levels. The resulting discrepancy between plan targets and the ability to fulfill them put a premium on short-run performance to the detriment of long-run trends in factor productivity.[7]

One consequence of this phenomenon was the proliferation of detailed targets dealing with output, structure of sowings, size of herds, and the like. These targets were formulated by what we shall call "above-enterprise agencies" of various kinds.[8] While the phenomenon originated in the U.S.S.R., it spread rapidly to other socialist countries in the early postwar period.

The shortcomings of this system of "planning from above" were eventually recognized, and various efforts have been made since 1955 to reduce the number of planned goals brought down to the farm level. A major change involved the abandonment of output or area targets and their replacement by marketing targets (or sales quotas in terms of volume). The ostensible purpose of these reforms was to alleviate the problems caused by lack of detailed knowledge of local conditions at the level of the above-enterprise agency and to increase the autonomy and (hopefully) the efficiency of farm management.

The resulting process of partial decompression was by no means uniform, and substantial differences still exist within Eastern Europe

[6] For example, we neglect problems illustrated by Ryszard Manteuffel's apt expression: "I do not know why we accepted the principle that agriculture *must* purchase everything (useful as well as inappropriate items) produced by 'industries serving agriculture' or—as those outside of agriculture like to put it—by industries 'helping agriculture (?).'" See his contribution to the discussion in *ibid.*, No. 5 (1966), p. 212.

[7] Cf. the calculations of Gregor Lazarčík, "The Performance of Czechoslovak Agriculture since World War II," *Soviet and East European Agriculture*, ed. Jerzy F. Karcz (Berkeley and Los Angeles: University of California Press, 1967), p. 396.

[8] The term "above-enterprise agency" is used here in the generic sense. It may refer to a production administration, or to the agricultural division of a national council, to an inspectorate of procurements or even to the local branch of the State Bank.

(including the U.S.S.R.) in the degree of farm autonomy in decision making and production planning. In some countries the matter is still not fully resolved. Thus, the most radical advocates of agricultural reform in the Soviet Union suggest that farms ought to be able to determine freely their own production structures and to offer marketing bids to state procurement agencies. Under this variant, marketing would be based on short-term as well as long-term contracts with procurement as well as with supply organizations. This is the cornerstone of the Czechoslovak improved model of planning and management, with the proviso that five-year state plans would affect farm decisions by price, tax, and credit policies within the framework of a long-range perspective plan for the development of agriculture.[9]

One of the crucial questions within this framework is that of factors affecting decision making at the farm level. It follows from the definition of decompression that command and directives are to yield to the economic impact of prices, taxes, interest rates, and credit availability (at the given rate of interest). For various reasons, a socialist farm was much more affected by outside interference than a firm in industry was.[10] As we shall see, the degree of farm autonomy in decision making is closely related to the choice of particular planning instruments and to the existing organizational structures.

Other limitations, of a more constitutional nature, are embodied in model collective farm charters or basic laws on income distribution at the farm. A good example is that of compulsory allocation of a given percentage of gross cash receipts to indivisible (or investment) funds. Gross cash receipts are a particularly inappropriate measure of the farm's ability to invest, and actions based on these provisions often had paradoxical results. Investment activity of rich farms was at times restricted, while weak farms were forced to accumulate at the expense of private consumption of their members.[11] In recent years, much of this legislation gave way to pressing economic forces. Bulgarian collectives enjoy a considerable autonomy in income distribution or internal

[9] Cf. Josef Krilek *et al.*, *Plánování rozvoje zemědělství ve zdokonalené soustavě řízení* (Prague, 1966), pp. 27–36.

[10] Nancy Nimitz, "The Lean Years," *Problems of Communism*, XIV, No. 3 (May-June, 1965), 21–22.

[11] Josef Nikl, "Dále zdokonalovat systém hodnotových ukazatelů družstevní zemědělské výroby," *Politiká ekonomie*, No. 6 (1963), pp. 457–58. In a group of farms operating in best natural conditions, allocations to the indivisible fund in 1961 came to about 25 per cent of net income (after payment to labor). For farms located in the worst natural conditions, the corresponding percentage was 51 (while labor remuneration came only to one third of that in the first group of farms).

organization. Beginning with 1965, Czechoslovak authorities dis-
continued the compulsory allocation of 13 per cent of gross cash
receipts to indivisible funds (the name itself is no longer used), but
official guidelines still specify that investment should grow faster than
the personal income of the members.[12]

The experience of the period 1958–63 suggests that these regulations
were honored mainly in their breach. Such violations were to be expected: they were also eminently sensible. Since heterogeneity of local
conditions is the rule in Eastern Europe, any attempt to force the hand
of management is likely to result in the perfection of techniques for the
avoidance of blanket rules. But rule avoidance or evasion only per-
petuates a special credibility gap, and farms and farmers may tend to
avoid sensible as well as nonsensical regulations. Yet it is the other side
of the coin that is potentially more dangerous for the implementation
of new economic systems. For while it is a truism to say that the behavior of socialist administrators toward subordinate farms was never
based on implicit faith in the honesty, sense of responsibility, and good
professional judgment of farm managers, this lack of faith tends to be
strengthened by the avoidance by farm managers of rules and regulations, no matter how nonsensical the rules may be.

We now turn to the impact of different kinds of planning targets on
the farm unit. If we are concerned with decision making at the farm
level, there are few important differences between the impact of output
(or area) targets and that of volume sales quotas. On all farms I visited
(and most of these were better than average), it quickly became
apparent that, given proper rotations, the allocation of five or six sale
quotas for the main product groups could *and* did determine the structure of sown areas to the extent of 90 per cent or more.[13] Since the
remaining acreage is likely to be under crops that tend to be retained
in the production structure regardless of the method employed in
planning, the impact of this kind of change in targeting practices is
small. The chief benefit arises from the disappearance of "loss leaders":
even here the elimination is more likely to occur if a close substitute
can be found within the same product group (such as clover for al-

[12] Josef Nikl, Stanislav Řádek, Jiří Šilar, and Vladimír Vydra, *Problémy vývoje a
plánovitého řízení reprodukce v JZD* (Prague, 1966), p. 124, note 21.

[13] This occurred in cases where grain procurements came to about half of total
output, and where virtually all meat and milk production was sold to the state. I
assume that the actual level of distributions (in kind) to members would have occurred under any system of planning. Different combinations of these assumptions
(with varying numerical values) would yield approximately the same results.

falfa). We should bear in mind that once the structure of output is determined, little latitude will be left in the planning of investments.

It could be argued that further gains would follow from the reduction in the number of physical (volume) sale quotas. This is probably true, but only beyond a certain point. This, I believe, may be reached when a single farm receives no more than one or two such indicators, and when this target does not include a combination of grains and meat.[14] Even this conclusion should be qualified by a usual *ceteris paribus* assumption (regarding the absence of more subtle forms of interference).

Bulgarian farms are still faced with physical sale targets for (at most) six products: grains, rice, beans, tomatoes, sunflower seeds, and all meat. (The decision to continue the use of such targets was reached after the evaluation of an experiment in which value of sales quotas— later referred to as value quotas—were used in four out of thirty regions.) In addition, Bulgarian farms also receive ceilings on capital investment and on acreage diverted to orchards, vineyards, and the like.[15] Beginning with 1967, physical sale quotas may be imposed on Czechoslovak farms only in exceptional circumstances, and only within the framework of "compulsory targeting." At the moment, the latter applies only to grains, and even here the target is imposed on the above-enterprise agency and not on individual farms.[16]

There must have been quite a few exceptional cases in 1967: as far as I know, allocation of grain quotas to farms was not altogether uncommon. This phenomenon raises a number of interesting questions about the mechanism of quota distribution by above-enterprise agencies. Before we proceed further, however, a few words are in order on the result of the Bulgarian experiment with the value of marketing targets conducted in 1964 and 1965 in four regions with very different production structures. A comprehensive analysis of this experiment has not yet been published in accessible sources, and my account is necessarily based on scattered and indirect evidence. It is known, however, that the results were mixed. The most positive feature was perhaps the least

---

[14] This is believed to be a contradiction in terms by Dimo Vladov, "Osnovni problemi v oblastta na selskoto stopanstvo," *Novo vreme*, No. 1 (1966), p. 29. On the other hand, procurements of products that are ultimately resold to farm members is believed to make little sense. Cf. Vasil Mishev, "Novata sistema na planirane i rukovodstvo i izkupuvaneto na selskostopanskata produktsiia," *Planovo stopanstvo i statistika*, No. 3 (1966), p. 47.

[15] *Naruchnik na agitatora*, No. 6 (1965), p. 16.

[16] *Věstník Ministerstva Zemědělství a Lesního Hospodářství*, XIII, No. 36 (Sept. 24, 1966), p. 214.

interesting from the narrow standpoint of effectiveness of various types of plan targets, but far more important in the context of general approach to agricultural planning. Farms continued to sell and a return to subsistence agriculture did not materialize.

But a reduction in sugar-beet sales did take place in the highly productive Plovdiv region (vegetables), and it was necessary to supply local mills from a rather distant source (interestingly enough, the center responded by raising the prices of beets). Apparently the reduction was caused in part by the divergence of beets to feeding uses and in part by local labor shortages. In major grain-producing areas there were apparently some problems with sales of animal products and with attempts to raise farm incomes by increasing acreage under vineyards.

Such tendencies alone could justify the continued reliance on volume (rather than value) quotas. They also explain the appearance of investment or planting ceilings. But the problem is more complex. Given the continued pressure for a high volume of marketings of *all* products, the impact of a high-value quota in certain areas does not differ greatly from that of, say, four or five physical quotas for the major products. The reason will be found in the structure of relative prices. Those of early vegetables, tobacco, and the like are so high that a farm faced with a high-value quota is still handicapped. There may be no alternative crop that could compensate for a decline in the value of sales resulting from a decrease in tobacco or vegetable acreage. Annual fluctuations of weather, which may be very sharp, only reinforce the existing limitations. By contrast, the impact of value quotas in grain (or mixed farming) areas will ordinarily be quite different. Some Bulgarian economists are quite concerned about such differential impacts resulting from the use of value quotas.[17]

THE DISTRIBUTION OF MARKETING QUOTAS
AND ABOVE-ENTERPRISE AGENCIES

Distribution of marketing quotas (whether of the obligatory or the indicative variety[18]) by above-enterprise agencies is a bloc-wide phenomenon that is insufficiently reflected in our research. This is in part because it involves practices of a government agency. Systematic treatment of a "theory of above-enterprise agencies" is still in its infancy. Such an agency is financed by the state or the local budget and it bears no direct financial responsibility for the results of its decisions. In

[17] E.g., Vladov, "Osnovni problemi . . . ," pp. 28–29.
[18] The distinction is mainly legalistic.

the very nature of the case, these decisions exert a considerable impact on production planning, production functions, investment decisions, and the performance of individual farms.

Partly for this reason, I tried to obtain as much information as possible on the mechanics and economics of quota distribution. Direct evidence was supplied in visits to a Czechoslovak production administration and to an agricultural sector of a Bulgarian regional council. Indirect evidence came from interviews with farm officials and agricultural economists. Questions addressed to the officials at the above-enterprise agency produced essentially this reply: "We know our farms, their capabilities, their weaknesses, and their perspective development plans. Quotas are distributed accordingly. On balance we have no special problems." Further prodding as to the leverage employed when a farm is clearly unable to meet the first approximation of the delivery quota and the fulfillment of the *regional* quota is in danger was answered by statements such as: "We get on the telephone and find someone who can make up the shortfall."

Now, there would be nothing wrong with this procedure at the regional (as well as the national[19]) level, provided that genuine marketing surpluses did exist. In fact, regional quotas would not be endangered as long as the farmer's market was limited or restricted to sales of less-important products: the government would be the only potential sales outlet for disposable outputs.[20] But genuine marketable surpluses (over and above the initial quota) do not arise often in the case of grains, feed crops, and the major foods. In all socialist countries, feed balances are maintained as such only at the expense of low productivity of herds. This alone makes it virtually impossible to predict the exact long-run impact of additional, forced marketings at a given time (the impact of unknown developments a year or two hence is equally important).[21] In practice, there is no way to compute the long-run marginal cost associated with quota shifts. This applies at the regional as well as the national scale.

For that reason alone, it would be impossible to solve the problem by comparing the marginal social cost with the corresponding marginal social benefit. Insofar as the fulfillment of the regional sales quota is

---

[19] In Bulgaria, the tendency is now to shift the burden of adjustment to national authorities (and thus to other regions). The extent to which this happens is very difficult to ascertain.

[20] This is roughly the case in both Czechoslovakia and Bulgaria.

[21] Particularly because a farm is a multiproduct firm.

concerned, the very concept of marginal social benefit is fuzzy and ambiguous.[22]

It is not likely that such sophisticated calculations enter into the mechanics of quota distribution. There is, however, a good deal of evidence that suggests that we can generalize (at least to some extent) about the behavioral pattern of above-enterprise agencies. As budget organizations, they do not maximize profits, but they do maximize a utility function, and it is not too difficult to specify most of the variables that enter into it.[23] But it may be argued that the St. Petersburg paradox continues to operate: the marginal utility of a gain (happy superiors, a medal, a promotion) will be smaller than the marginal disutility of a comparable loss (unhappy superiors, a reprimand, a dismissal). The upshot is that Berliner's safety factor is converted into a "reinsurance factor" through which the above-enterprise agency tries to minimize the risk of nonfulfillment of the regional quota. Farm quotas tend to be spread among a larger number of farms than would be necessary to assure the fulfillment of a regional quota under average harvest conditions. To some extent, therefore, above-enterprise agencies are biased against specialization. This bias is further strengthened by the vagaries of weather and the premium put on short-run performance by the national authorities. A number of other factors, all operating in the same direction, could also be cited. For example, if we deal with a product that is unprofitable for all farms (as was true of meat when prices failed to cover costs), equity considerations enter into the distribution of the resulting tax burden, and the entire process of quota distribution becomes very complex as well as more arbitrary.[24]

To be sure, there is some bargaining between the farm management and the above-enterprise agency in the process of quota distribution. Such bargaining has now been institutionalized in both Bulgarian and Czechoslovak practices.[25] But it is important to realize that this bargaining has taken place in a rather special environment. Although the Czechoslovak regulations now provide for full equality between parties

---

[22] Conceptually, the marginal social benefit connected with marketings is easier to discern at the national level. Here, too, the difficulties of visualizing marginal social cost in any operational sense seem formidable.

[23] The desire to enforce existing regulations, job security and advancement, protection of farms, efficient work, and a quiet life. It is not so easy to solve the problem of weighting.

[24] Another of these factors is the short tenure of office of officials employed at the above-enterprise agency.

[25] *Věstník Ministerstva Zemědělství a Lesního Hospodářství*, XIII, No. 36 (Sept. 24, 1966), p. 216 and *Naruchnik na agitatora*, No. 6 (1965), pp. 17–18.

in the preliminary bargaining,[26] farms still do not, indeed cannot, appear as equal partners. The many special powers of the agency necessarily exert considerable pressure on farm decision making.

In the recent past, above-enterprise agencies were charged with the task of reviewing and approving production, financial, and investment plans submitted by the farms. Agency decisions dealing with the implementation of output and procurement plans were binding on farms. Indeed, a delivery contract was not considered valid until after it had been approved by the above-enterprise agency.[27]

Such provisions sound harmless enough on paper, but this is not the case in practice. While reviewing investment decisions, the above-enterprise agency may object to purchases of certain machinery items or to the introduction and expansion of certain crops. The objections are usually based on the belief that a given machine cannot be used effectively or that the crop in question cannot be cultivated efficiently. They result from a firm conviction of a superior professional judgment that is expected to override the necessarily superior knowledge of local conditions by farm managers. In practice, the issues are seldom clear-cut and we are likely to deal with value judgments rather than objective scientific conclusions. For example, opinions on the relative merits or demerits of ownership versus rental of certain types of machinery are not by any means identical among farm managers (on farms of the same size and located in roughly the same natural conditions). On the other hand, the importance of special crops, such as poppy seed or strawberries in Czechoslovakia and grapes in Bulgaria, can often be decisive. In Czechoslovakia, net income from twenty acres of strawberries on a three-thousand-acre farm may well supply more than 10 per cent of its total net income (after payment to labor) or about half of the allocation to investment funds.

In practice, the powers of the above-enterprise agency are greater still. This can be illustrated by a brief listing of policy tools still available to the Czechoslovak production administration (an above-enterprise agency *par excellence*) in 1967, or after a very considerable increase in farm autonomy. Production administrations are responsible for the provision of the required volume of marketings within the region; they

---

[26] *Věstník Ministerstva Zemědělství a Lesního Hospodářství*, XIII, No. 36 (Sept. 24, 1966), p. 214.

[27] B. Prouza, V. Vydra, J. Pospíchal, J. Krilek, and D. Choma, *Základní problémy soustavy ekonomického řízení ČS zemědělství* (Prague: Materiály Ekonomického Ústavu Ceskoslovenské Akademie Věd, March, 1965), p. 42.

may also impose quotas in exceptional cases. They prepare consolidation plans for farms applying for stabilization subsidies; they approve such plans and disburse these and other subsidies. They review credit applications and cooperate with the State Bank branches in the process of credit allocation. They administer special reserve funds, a source of low-interest or interest-free loans for special purposes. They also underwrite long-term loans granted by the State Bank. They are indirectly but effectively involved in the distribution of feed grains from state resources, as well as in that of fertilizers, insecticides, and construction materials. They also grant exemptions from the existing rules of income distribution.[28]

It follows that the good will of such an agency is extremely important to the farm, and the farm management is often forced to give way on many important issues in order to get along. The process of bargaining about quotas is colored by its similarity to a card game, with the agency using a stacked deck. (The same factors blur the distinction between "obligatory" and "indicative" quotas or indicators.) The extent to which production structures are distorted is, of course, conjectural, but I find it significant that all the farms visited had plans to introduce "shortly" at least one major change in their production structure (such as abandonment of dairy operations). While my sample is necessarily small, the closer to average was the visited farm, the greater the planned changes.

The impact of such pressures on farm decision making is believed to be so strong that even "if the number of compulsory targets was reduced to one or two, and if nothing else changed in the manner of obtaining marketings, there could be no significant change in the existing practice of determining productive activity 'from above.' "[29]

Thus, the above-enterprise agency is a major bottleneck in the process of decompression and devolution of greater decision-making authority to the farm. An attempt to deal with this problem is now under way in Czechoslovakia, where production administrations are about to be replaced by regional associations of collectives, state farms, and some processing or procurement organizations. These associations, or cooperatives, are to be formed gradually and on a purely voluntary basis. They will be financed by their members and will attempt to foster vertical or horizontal integration within the framework of the agro-

---

[28] See *Věstník Ministerstva Zemědělství a Lesního Hospodářství*, XIII, No. 36 (Sept 24, 1966), 212 and *Socialistické zemědělství*, No. 7 (1967), p. 1.

[29] Prouza *et al.*, *Základní problémy* . . . , p. 24.

business complex that has just been formed in Czechoslovakia through the merger of the Ministry of Agriculture, the State Administration for Procurements and Supply, and the Ministry of Food Industry.[30] The reader familiar with Soviet developments will note certain affinities to the *raion* associations of farms, proposed by Matskevich, the U.S.S.R. Minister of Agriculture in June, 1960, or to certain proposals for the agenda of the Collective Farm Center.[31]

At this stage, one type of the above-enterprise agency is about to fade away, but some of its functions and some of its personnel are to be taken over by local national councils. Time alone will tell whether the ensuing administrative reshuffle will produce a change in attitude and behavioral pattern of certain officials. After all, the above-enterprise agency is not so much an administrative unit as a state of mind.[32]

It is time to emphasize some positive elements. Beneficial results are likely to flow from certain technical improvements in agricultural planning introduced in both countries. Recent Czechoslovak and Bulgarian regulations (but especially the latter) resulted in a shift to a period of deliberation, with the result that the entire process as well as final approval of plans now takes a much shorter time. Similar benefits accrue from the practice of planning procurements for more than a single year.[33]

As noted earlier, bargaining of a kind now takes place within the framework of planning. In the long run, preliminary tenders of procurements are likely to provide some training in marketing for farm managers. They may also exert a salutary influence on the "party of the first side." Some education is better than none, even if the process of learning takes place in a less than perfect environment. Ever since 1953, the long-run trend has pointed—with much hesitation and a few reversals—in the direction of greater farm autonomy, and any experience is likely to be very valuable. Moreover, some of the more obvious sources of inefficiency are likely to disappear.

But it is still in order to point out a peculiar impact of the environment of the command economy in agriculture on the mental processes

---

[30] See insert to *Hospodářské noviny*, No. 13 (1967); the ministry of agriculture and that of food industry were also merged in Hungary, as a part of the implementation of the new system in that country. Cf. *ibid.*, No. 23 (1967), p. 12.

[31] Here, as well as elsewhere, the Czechoslovak system is by far the most elaborated one, and the envisaged changes cut deeper. But we should note that plans of Bulgarian farms are no longer approved by above-enterprise agencies.

[32] Cf. note 8.

[33] See sources cited in note 25.

of farm managers. Today's farm managers were brought up in the tough school of planning and management "from above," when the interest of the farm was clearly at variance with the interest of the society—as the latter was revealed in the famous planners' preferences. It is immaterial in this context if these preferences did in actuality reflect the "true" interest of the society; the pertinent point is that farm managers were daily faced with situations where common sense, logic, and results of more sophisticated analysis were overridden by the necessity to consider "social requirements."

The attitudes formed in these days tend to persist. Anyone who talks with socialist farm managers in countries where decompression is in progress will be struck by the frequency with which the term "social requirements" is mentioned. This may reflect only an awareness of the need for change on the part of some managers, but it is also an indication of the existing distortion of the concept of the maximand at a time when the official rules of the game prescribe maximization of gross incomes.

The chief slogan of the new economic model in Czechoslovakia reads "what is good for the society should also be good for the firm." In agriculture, we can easily reverse the sequence without—I hope— causing the furor created by Charles Wilson's famous remark in 1953 (after all, a socialist farm, no matter how large, is not a General Motors, or even a Škoda). *Ceteris paribus*,[34] the success or failure of the new system in agriculture will depend on the emergence of a type of entrepreneur-manager who will concentrate exclusively on the interests of his farm without worrying unduly about the interest of the society. Indeed, it could be argued that many of the national problems would disappear as a result of such behavior in a conducive economic environment.

MACROECONOMIC PROBLEMS OF PLANNING

We should not leave the problems of planning without a few words on practices at the national level. In the Czechoslovak system, the basis for such plans is to be formed by a document called *The Long Range Perspective*, on the basis of which five-year and annual plans will be elaborated. The new system went into effect on January 1, 1967, but the document does not yet exist. The *Perspective* is conceptually different from earlier perspective plans for the development of agriculture prepared in various East European countries for the period ending in 1980.

[34] This is clearly a rather extreme assumption, but one that is in order in this context.

Since the difficulties of preparing a highly meaningful document may not be obvious, let me illustrate the problem with two recent quotations (the fact that the second comes from an official of the Polish State Planning Commission does not, in any way, detract from its validity):[35]

> The existing results of scientific research in agriculture do not give a complete picture of the volume of currently available production capabilities, or of the reserves to be found within the agricultural sector. Furthermore, they do not even provide a guideline suggesting how the [new] production capability is to be created.
>
> Everyone agrees that the increased utilization of these inputs [fertilizers, high protein content feed, land improvements] is generally useful, but there are no data on the average impact of these inputs in average weather conditions. We do not know whether an extra kilogram of pure matter in fertilizers will yield three, or six, or even more additional grain units. [We do not know] whether one kilogram of high protein content feed will replace one and a half, or three, or five kilograms of feed grains. There are equally important differences in evaluating the expected return from land improvement.

A major Bulgarian study of regionalization and agricultural specialization was completed in 1967. In all Eastern European countries, special problems are posed by the balance of payments and the enforced separation of their economies from the main stream of (and the correctives supplied by) international trade. There is some evidence to the effect that the existing structure of Czechoslovak foreign trade in farm products is very much distorted on both sides of the ledger. Under the circumstances, the delay in the preparation of the Czechoslovak *Perspective* is fully understandable: indeed, it may turn out to have been salutary in the end.

Equally fundamental is the issue of the reestablishment of equilibrium between the demands placed on the agricultural sector and the sector's ability to meet these demands. At the beginning of this section, this disequilibrium was identified as one of the main causes (as well as consequences) of the emergence of the command economy in agriculture. Analytically, this is a single problem, but it is still useful to distinguish between two sides of the coin. Since problems on the supply side cannot be discussed fully, we merely record the view that the improvement in capacity to supply existing demand is likely to be gradual

[35] The first quotation is from Prouza *et al.*, *Základní problémy* . . . , p. 18. Zdzisław Karczewski in *Zagadnienia Ekonomiki rolnej*, No. 5 (1966), p. 224, is the source for the second.

or slow. But a reduction in the state demand for marketings is important for other reasons as well. Feed requirements for the existing herds are now supplied in both countries to the extent of some 85 per cent in terms of grain units and 70 per cent in terms of the protein content.[36]

Another situation is specific to the problem of decompression. Major decisions on decentralization, although necessarily taken at the highest level, are easily eroded from below by intermediate officials. In agriculture, this erosion is achieved not only by procrastination and resistance to change on the part of conservatives whose jobs are about to be abolished, it also occurs because of the persisting high income elasticity of demand for food and the economy's inability to provide the necessary cushion of imports. The resulting pressures on above-enterprise agencies (and ultimately on farms) provide a tailor-made environment for gradual recentralization of decision making.

No easy solutions can be envisaged. Increased food or feed imports depend not only on the performance of the industrial sector, but on the country's own import requirements. A deliberate deceleration of the rate of growth of the national product through a reduced rate of investment might conceivably do the job, but the higher growth rates are a success indicator for the new systems. An alternative approach would call for at least a temporary ceiling on disposable money incomes, but that, too, is unpalatable. Three good harvest years would be extremely helpful.

Only the general problem of the allocation of resources to agriculture will be mentioned briefly. For various reasons, the already high capital-output ratios are likely to remain high.[37] This is owing partly to the need to adjust the capital stock to forthcoming changes in production, partly to the necessary adjustment toward the level of world prices, partly to the result of a distorted structure of the capital stock, and partly (in Czechoslovakia particularly) to the need to provide better amenities in rural life to improve the quality of the labor force. Soviet examples have indicated that the strain of a new program on the budget is likely to be great. Similarly, a commitment to raise the alloca-

[36] J. Krilek, *Hlavní zásady plánovitého řízení zemědělství* (Prague, 1966), p. 11. The figures refer to 1960–64. The situation in Bulgaria is almost the same. There was some improvement in both countries in 1966.

[37] Cf. Maurice Ernst, "Postwar Economic Growth in Eastern Europe (A Comparison With Western Europe)," *New Directions in the Soviet Economy*, Joint Economic Committee, Congress of the United States (Washington, D.C., 1966), Part IV, pp. 889–95.

tion of resources to agriculture by about 1.5 billion crowns annually has already been given by the Czechoslovak establishment.[38]

All this may not be enough. It is significant that every major Soviet economist already has in his drawer a calculation of agriculture's contribution to the national product, and that all these calculations indicate far greater shares than those produced by official statistical agencies. A similar calculation has recently been published in Czechoslovakia.[39] There is more to these calculations than simple intellectual curiosity. All are designed as instruments of lobbying for a greater shift of resources to agriculture.

PRICES AND TRANSFER PAYMENTS

As of February, 1967, Bulgarian prices of major products were still of the traditional variety, and a comprehensive price reform seems a year or more away.[40] On the other hand, major reforms were introduced in Czechoslovakia with the new system. It is for that reason that the discussion (including the necessary historical digression) is based primarily on Czechoslovak materials. Here, as elsewhere, however, the applicability of my comments is much wider.

Following the Soviet example, both countries adopted the Soviet price and procurement system, including the feature of double—or triple—prices for identical farm products.[41]

Compulsory delivery prices were set at very low levels for any one or a combination of the following reasons: (1) to force individual peasants into collectives; (2) to assist the state—in conjunction with delivery

[38] This reflects, in part, the unsatisfactory trends in agriculture's terms of trade after the reform of wholesale prices in industry. See below, p. 00.

[39] Josef Nikl, "K podílu zemědělství na tvorbě a na prvotním a druhotním rozdělování národního důchodu," *Politická ekonomie*, No. 7 (1966), pp. 545–54. For 1962, the official figure on agriculture's share in the formation of national product is 11.2 per cent. Nikl shows a figure of about 25 per cent (his various variants yield a range of 21.7 to 26.6 per cent). We cannot comment on the merits of the calculation, but see also the comment by Jiří Šilar in *Statistika*, No. 7 (1966), pp. 314–22 and Nikl's reply in *ibid.*, No. 3 (1967), pp. 115–17.

[40] In the main, these are prices introduced in 1962. Some provisions for flexibility have already been introduced. Trends in Bulgarian farm prices were particularly unfavorable between 1950–52 and 1952–55 (average), when prices of wheat, corn, sunflower, and milk declined. Cf. V. Mishev, "Za materialnata zainteresovanost v TKZS," *Ikonomicheski Misul*, No. 4 (1965), p. 4.

[41] The entire Soviet procurement model (including MTS payments in kind and the milling tax in kind) was introduced in Czechoslovakia in 1953 (or at the time when the U.S.S.R. abolished the milling tax). MTS payments in Czechoslovakia were insignificant. Cf. Vladimir Vydra, *Úloha vykupu v ekonomickém svazku dělnické třídy a rolnictva* (Prague, 1963), pp. 58–75.

quotas—in the extraction of differential rent through the price mechanism; and (3) to implement the extraction of forced savings from the agricultural sector for the purpose of financing nationwide accumulation, general administrative expenditures, and social consumption. Higher purchase prices were also introduced to induce a greater flow of marketings and as a tool for influencing the formation of farm incomes.

Among the shortcomings of the system of multiple prices were: the necessity to maintain an extensive apparatus of administrative control; a perverse relationship of trends in prices to those products marketed in quantity; the incentive to cut costs on better farms was considerably reduced, while manpower was diverted to more rewarding activities on the household plot.

Because the level of Soviet farm prices from 1928 through the early fifties was exceedingly low, a number of finer, though no less relevant, shortcomings was somewhat obscured. Among these was the impact of the double-price system on opportunities for rational specialization.

This impact was adverse. Compulsory delivery norms were set at a high level in those areas where the production of a product would normally tend to concentrate. In other areas, the quotas were much lower. It was then to the advantage of a farm located in a traditional wheat or rye area to reduce wheat or rye acreage and to shift to the production of a second-best substitute. The delivery norms for this crop would be lower, and the average realized price much higher (since the bulk of sales occurred at high purchase prices).[42] Specialization was also affected adversely by shifts of land to technical crops and by the distribution of quotas in accordance with the "reinsurance principle" referred to earlier. Some of these tendencies were particularly strong outside of the Soviet Union, since delivery quotas for Eastern European collectives were initially set at a low level (in order to provide a further incentive to join). But similar tendencies developed in the Soviet Union after the delivery quotas were reduced in 1953.

It is largely for these reasons that rye and oats tended to disappear from their traditional areas in Slovakian mountain areas, where the production of pork and wheat became profitable in spite of high production costs.[43] To the extent that the resulting shifts in the location of

[42] Vydra, *Úloha vykupu* . . . , pp. 121–22.

[43] *Ibid.* The problem was aggravated by the assignment of quotas for unsuitable products to many areas. For an example of the consequences (sugar beets and vegetables in mountain areas) see *Nová mysl* (Prague), No. 6 (1956), p. 74.

a farming activity were the result of the desire to extract differential rent, the outcome was clearly at variance with the intent of the policy. Of itself, rational specialization tends to reduce problems caused by the emergence of high rents, since high-cost products tend to disappear from the production structure of farms located in areas with less favorable conditions. Irrational specialization, of course, only intensifies the issue.

When the time came to revise the structure of procurement prices in Czechoslovakia in 1959, the need to force individual peasants into collectives had clearly diminished. But the other two factors that influenced the low level of procurement prices continued to operate.[44] As was the case in the U.S.S.R. in 1958, a system of one price for a given product was introduced in January, 1960. The resulting changes in the structure of relative prices were influenced heavily by a financial constraint for the total value of procurements in terms of new prices: this was to equal the earlier sum of expenditures on procurements *and* a large part of subsidies paid to the agricultural sector. The level of prices as such did increase, but there was no net shift of resources to agriculture.[45]

By this time some cost studies had been completed, and it became quite clear that the margin by which prices failed to cover costs was particularly high in the livestock sector. This, together with the financial constraint just referred to, made it advisable to provide a greater increase in prices in the livestock sector than in crop production. The tendency was further reinforced by factors working on the demand side: the income elasticity of demand for meat and milk was very high.[46] The upshot was that 1960 prices of animal products rose more than prices of crops in relation to 1959 as well as to 1937 and to 1955.[47] In addition, it seemed preferable to treat hog prices preferentially, since

[44] Insufficient information on agriculture's share in the formation and distribution of national product apparently influenced the decisions undertaken at the time. Cf. Josef Nikl, "Ještě k podílu zemědělství na tvorbě a rozdělování narodního důchodu," *Statistika*, No. 3 (1967), p. 117.

[45] Nikl *et al.*, *Problémy vývoje* . . . , pp. 114–15, note 18.

[46] It comes to 0.85 for Czechoslovakia. In Poland it is about 0.7 (W. Herer in *Zagadnienia Ekonomiki rolnej*, No. 5 [1966], p. 215).

[47] Ústřední Úřad Státní Kontroly a Statistiky, *Statistická ročenka Československé Socialisticke Republiky 1962* (Prague, 1962), p. 384. The whole episode illustrates the pitfalls of (i) the imposition of total financial constraints on the value of procurements without setting adequate directives for the structure of relative prices, and (ii) economic analysis that (as was often the case in the U.S.S.R.) emphasizes the "merits" of compensating farms for total costs incurred in the production of the entire product mix.

the short production cycle offered better opportunities for a faster growth in meat supplies.

The 1960 prices were thus construed from the socialist principle of price formation on the basis of production cost (plus an arbitrary profit margin).[48] In Czechoslovakia, the relevant cost of production was defined as the average cost in the main producing areas, but in the case of meat and milk, the new prices failed to cover actual costs.[49]

The cost of production principle in price formation is widely known (and accepted) in Eastern Europe. Equally well known is the fact that such costs do not include an explicit rental or capital charge. The net impact of the absence of the price of land is quite considerable and is, of course, reflected to a greater extent in the prices of crops than in those of animal products. As a result, the former tend to be under-valued in relation to the latter. The undervaluation is likely to be par-ticularly serious in the case of grain, where the desire to extract forced savings and differential rent applies with particular strength (direct collection of both would be easier and seemingly more equitable).[50]

A similar phenomenon may be observed in most Eastern European countries, albeit in different degrees. The underlying factors tend to be the same. The obsession with profitability computed against costs of production has been clearly visible in the literature: it goes a long way toward an explanation of various failures. In general, advocates of rent extraction through prices (which is a corollary of this principle) still outnumber those searching for other solutions of the problem of differ-ential rent. This is no longer the case in Czechoslovakia, where many research economists recognize the advantage of partial retention of rent with the producers.[51]

It is no accident that all countries also have to deal with the "grain problem." For the absence of the price of land and prices of the "cost of production" type explain much of the tendency to reduce grain

---

[48] Cf. Morris Bornstein, "Soviet Price Theory and Policy," *New Directions in the Soviet Economy*, Joint Economic Committee, Congress of the United States (Washing-ton, D.C.: Government Printing Office, 1966), pp. 71–72.

[49] In 1960–63, average prices covered costs of production (in the main producing areas) to the extent of 86 per cent for cattle, 84 per cent for milk and 120 per cent for hogs. These are Czechoslovak data about to be published.

[50] This observation, I believe, applied throughout the bloc.

[51] Cf. Silar in Nikl *et al.*, *Problémy vývoje* . . . , p. 70. This is not the question of allowing the retention of the so-called rent II as opposed to rent I. Just when these attitudes will be reflected in teaching is another point. In Bulgaria, all but one of the interviewed economists still felt that prices should be used to extract rent and that zonal prices were preferable for that reason (among others).

acreage in spite of the fact that handsome "profits" (computed against costs) are often realized.[52] This tendency is strengthened by the shift of better grain land to the production of technical crops. However, some problems also arise in connection with the disposition of grain that is produced. Given the relatively high coefficient of extraction of rent and forced savings embodied in grain prices, farms tried to avoid the resulting diversion of profits to the treasury by distributing profits to members as payment in kind; such grain is largely used as feed. These efforts, of course, provided additional impetus for various kinds of administrative interference with decision making at the farm level.

This is not all. As long as grain prices covered costs (and this was true on many weaker farms as well as on good grain land), it might be advantageous to divert grain to feed uses for other reasons, too. For example, gains could arise from inefficient conversion of profitable grain into unprofitable meat (in spite of the outright loss). High quotas for meat or milk provide only part of the answer. It would be possible to avoid the diversion of rent through grain prices (since rent is diverted only to the extent that grain is sold, and no rent would be diverted in sales of meat at a loss). Moreover, the entire margin over production costs of grain could be shifted to members (as the labor-cost component of total livestock costs) without incurring the deduction of a certain percentage of gross cash receipts into indivisible funds. Allocations to funds were released from bank accounts only to the extent that investment goods were available. *Desired* investment goods were not always available. What was supplied through the mechanism of material supply often reduced the effectiveness of the acquired capital to a considerable extent, either because of poor quality or because the necessary complementary items were lacking. At the limit, the productivity of some items acquired in "tied sales" was zero. More generally, the marginal productivity of capital was in many instances lower than the rate of time preference of farm managers, let alone that of farm members.

No rules were violated as long as this procedure was followed.[53]

---

[52] The argument in this and the next paragraph is made somewhat differently by Jan Bača, "O ceně půdy za socializmu," *Politická ekonomie*, No. 8 (1966), pp. 678–79. The tendency referred to was block-wide until just recently.

[53] Except the general guideline about the faster growth of investment rather than consumption funds in the collective farm sector. We should also add that "frozen" indivisible funds (which could not be used for useful purposes by the owner) often provided the source of bank credit for loans to weaker farms. The reaction of the richer farms bears on the issue of attempting to lift the agricultural sector by its own bootstraps through intrasectoral transfers.

The issue cuts deeper still, since it also affected the relative values of grains and feed crops. As long as grain is undervalued (but must be produced), feed crops appear a good deal less desirable than they really might be. This could be true even though the yields of other crops are low as a result of the neglect suffered during the rapid industrialization drive, when virtually exclusive attention was given to final products. It might even pay to feed purchased and imported grain, when the latter must be made available at subsidized prices.[54] This is another reason for the disappearance of much cattle from the Carpathian slopes and the emergence of brand-new pigpens, the occupants of which do very well on a diet of high-cost feed, often paid for in scarce foreign exchange, and necessarily transported over considerable distances.

Such practices put additional pressures on the already stretched balance of payments, and they reduce the economy's ability to acquire reserves. They also diminish the volume of imports for the modernization of the industrial sector. On the other hand, any attempts to reduce the volume of grain imports strengthen the discrepancy between the demands for a greater volume of domestic marketings and the capability of agriculture to meet such demands. At this point, problems posed by unsatisfactory principles of price formation converge with those originating in the planning sector.[55]

The absence of the price of land also affects its use in still other ways. Land tends to be shifted out of agriculture in an extremely indiscriminate manner: the best example is still provided by Poland, where the entire industrial complex of Nowa Huta near Cracow was built on land formerly used to supply (among other things) export-quality onions.[56] In addition, there is a tendency to postpone or to forego needed land improvements.

Another consequence of the adopted principle of price formation in agriculture is the introduction of unnecessary complications and arbitrary decisions into the process of price setting. All other things being equal, such prices neglect the difference in the length of the production cycle. For example, the margin of profit (on costs) in beef production must be higher than in pork production to make both pro-

---

[54] I do not refer to official exchange rates but rather to exchange rates resulting in actual trade.

[55] See the discussion on pp. 23–24.

[56] Land transferred to nonagricultural uses no longer comes free of charge in either Czechoslovakia or Bulgaria. But the structure of compensation rates is very crude indeed.

ducts equally profitable. Thus, the scope for errors and omissions in price setting is considerably increased.

The 1966–67 price reform: Obviously, it is not easy to lift the dead hand of the past. After the reform (base) farm prices are still set according to the "cost of production" principle, whereas that of the so-called "two-channel prices" was applied in the industrial sector. Although the latter calculation was based on extensive computer analysis,[57] farm prices were adjusted in a much more pragmatic manner by a process known as *guesstimate*. There was some improvement, however. Grain prices rose considerably, but it was still necessary to raise the prices in the animal sector, which continues to enjoy a preferential treatment.

The absence of an explicit capital charge in the collective farm sector is also felt. In the state farm sector, machinery used to be available free of charge with all the resulting consequences. Collectives did have to pay for the acquired machinery, but some items were made available at subsidized prices. In consequence, there is a tendency to accumulate excessive amounts of machinery on better farms. The introduction of explicit capital charges raises a number of tricky legal problems, but it could be argued that its imposition would be highly beneficial for the creation of a capital market (the absence of which will only be noticed at a later stage of operation of the new system as a whole[58]).

Although the suggestions for marginal cost pricing were not lacking,[59] they ultimately foundered on the rock of the existing level of retail prices. As is true of many compromise solutions, the present—and highly imaginative—system of Czechoslovak farm prices is almost unbelievably complex. The entire gamut of prices and transfers consists of: (1) the base prices; (2) differential payments; (3) state premiums; (4) premiums of procurement organizations; (5) stabilization subsidies; (6) other subsidies; and (7) the agricultural tax.[60]

Some of the characteristics of base prices have already been discussed. As will be seen, it is the structure of the base prices that is to perform what the textbooks call the "allocative function of prices," urging the producers to curtail the production of one product and increase that of another. They are to remain stable for a fairly long period (about five years). Free prices exist for some types of vegetables and fruit, as

[57] About 25 million prices were computed.

[58] This applies to agriculture as well as to other sectors.

[59] More accurately for pricing at average cost in marginal areas.

[60] Josef Krilek *et al.*, *Ceny a odvody ve zdokonalené soustavě plánovitého řízení zemědělství* (Prague, 1966). The source does not reflect the change in the nature of state premiums (see n. 63, following).

well as for a certain number of decidedly minor crops—herbs, mush-rooms, and the like.[61]

Differential payments are constructed as an instrument of compensation for farms located in different natural conditions. For this purpose each farm was assigned to one of 144 natural-condition units. These were ultimately aggregated into 40 groups: a differential rate of payment exists in each. The payments are expressed as percentages of the total value of all sales (and *not* sales of an individual product) to centralized state resources, provided that the sale takes place within the framework of the delivery contract.[62]

State premiums are now paid for increase in *total* marketings to centralized state funds for a certain number of products. The purpose is to stimulate in the East German fashion a greater volume of marketings. The present rate of these premiums comes to 50 per cent.[63]

Premiums of procurement organizations are intended to improve the relations between customers and suppliers by influencing the quality of output, timing of deliveries, and (within limits) the location of a given farm activity (e.g., dairy farming).

Stabilization subsidies are an instrument of general state aid "of the last resort." They must be applied for to, and are approved by, the above-enterprise agency. They will be granted for a number of years within the framework of an approved consolidation plan. Funds are also issued as a certain percentage of the *total* value of sales of *all* products to centralized resources.[64]

Other subsidies will be issued for a host of purposes, including greater specialization, elimination of tuberculosis and brucellosis, rural construction, solution of labor force problems, introduction of modern technology, and the like.

The agricultural tax is imposed in two different forms. First, there is the fixed rate, which amounts to a land tax. For this purpose, tax rates are fixed according to a slightly different grouping of the natural condition units (44 rather than 40). They vary from 0 to 930 crowns per

---

[61] Including millet and straws. Cf. *Věstník Ministerstva Zemědělství a Lesního Hospodárství*, XIII, No. 17 (May 6, 1966), 111. See also *Ekonomika zemědělství*, No. 3 (1967), pp. 81 ff. for a detailed explanation of rules applicable at the end of March, 1967.

[62] Differential payments are made to 2,490 collectives (including 1,420 in Slovakia). The total number is in the neighborhood of 6,400. Out of 360 state farms, only 18 do *not* receive these payments.

[63] *Vestník Ministerstva Zemědělství a Lesního Hospodařství*, XIV, No. 8 (March 3, 1967), 59–62. A directive element crept in at the last moment: the premiums are "as a rule" for the variable (fluctuating) fund of labor remuneration.

[64] *Ibid.*, XIV, No. 2–3 (Jan. 27, 1967), 16–18.

hectare (the top limit amounts to 9 per cent of the value of final output, or to 13 per cent of the average gross income of the best group of farms in the country).[65] The remaining part of the agricultural tax is an income tax. The tax base here is the gross income per worker, reduced by the allocations to investment and a certain amount of remuneration for labor.[66]

Considering the Czechoslovak edifice as a whole, one is simultaneously struck and comforted by the firm desire to avoid the pitfalls of zonal prices for individual products. [67]It is for that reason that (with the single exception of milk) no premiums or subsidies are meant to alter the structure of base prices. The introduction of the land tax is also a landmark in Eastern Europe. On the other hand, there are some features that may be criticized legitimately.

On paper, base prices are designed to cover 78 per cent of the total payments to the agricultural sector—the remainder is to come through the other components of the system. But the figure quoted is a country-wide average for all groups of farms. In the state farm sector, afflicted by many problems, the proportion of the base price in total remuneration is likely to be much smaller (perhaps as low as 65 per cent on the average—on individual farms, it is likely to be smaller still).[68] Hence, it is in order to ask whether the impact of this package of incentives will meet expectations. In particular, will the structure of base prices be considered as the decisive factor for on-farm decisions concerning changes in the production structure? At the moment, a guarded optimism prevails among the professionals, but the acid test is still in the future. In the meantime, some equally guarded predictions can be made.

Prices that do not clear the market can hardly be expected to act effectively as signals for the allocation of resources to various uses.[69] In

[65] *Sbírka zákonů Československé Socialistické Republiky*, No. 47 (1966), pp. 593–98.

[66] *Ibid.*, p. 595. Also deducted are certain insurance payments and the land tax.

[67] In addition to deficiencies characterizing double prices, zonal prices (a) strengthen the monopoly position of local procurement points; (b) tend to encourage sales to other buyers; (c) make it more difficult to increase the number of uncontrolled free prices; (d) are extremely difficult to calculate in practice. Virtually any attempt to observe differences in natural conditions is likely to fail, since it will be difficult to avoid the inclusion of actual performance among the criteria chosen. Cf. Ján Bača and Jiří Šilar, "K otázkám nové soustavy řízení v zemědělství," *Zemědělská ekonomie* (1966), p. 304.

[68] The figure is a guess based on the article of František Crkva, "Financování státních statků ve zdokonalené soustavě řízení zemědělství," *Finance a úvěr*, No. 7 (1966), pp. 390–99.

[69] I think it is fair to say that this fact is not recognized sufficiently in any of the new systems.

particular instances, it is easy to foresee a gray market of sorts resulting from the low level of base prices. Thus, Farm A (with no differential payments) is likely to be approached as a potential source of feed by a neighboring Farm B (which does receive these payments). This particular market will clear but at a price exceeding the official base price, since Farm A will obviously try to share in the additional profits of Farm B. Such phenomena are likely to be viewed as "speculation" by above-enterprise agencies and may lead to a new wave of administrative interference. Yet they only reflect the behavior of rational men responding to what is now known as an "economic" (as opposed to "command") incentive. It also remains to be seen whether practices of this sort will foster rational specialization.

To put it differently, the level of base prices seems low and that of differential premiums too high. In a sense, this is only a reflection of the adoption principle of price formation. In this connection, the suspicion remains that the traditional approach to agriculture as a convenient source of forced savings has not been entirely abandoned. Prices are still used as an instrument of extraction of differential rent.[70]

The level of base prices is too low for yet another reason. The increases of 1966–67 were based on an expected rise of 19 per cent in the level of industrial wholesale prices. In fact, industrial wholesale prices rose about 30 per cent; this represents an increase in input prices that is about one-fifth greater than initially envisaged.[71]

Other doubts are raised by the decision to apply state premiums to increases in the volume of marketings. As originally conceived, these premiums were designed as a flexible instrument of price policy, which could allow for short-term changes resulting from shifting market conditions at home or abroad. The basic criticism is that the "social requirement" of a high volume of marketings—already excessive in many instances—is further accentuated. Once again, this may lead to greater stress on short- as opposed to long-run performance and delay the necessary shifts in the production structure.

The land tax is still an inadequate substitute for land prices. At the

[70] See note 51.

[71] *Zemědělské noviny*, April 11, 1967. Purchases of machinery dropped (*ibid.*, March 23, 1967). By June, 1967, the decline was described as clearly visible, inventories were said to have accumulated and the gross income of machinery producers was suffering in consequence. The branch administration (an above-enterprise agency in industry) prepared a proposal for a price cut for 58 types of machines (*ibid.*, June 14, 1967).

moment, its application is causing some problems in the state farm sector—but this was only to be expected. There is also some dissatisfaction with the structure of rates. On the other hand, the income tax contains a built-in incentive *not* to economize on labor use. In the particular conditions of Czechoslovakia, this is not likely to be a serious problem on the national scale. At the local level, there is a difference: manpower problems are much less serious on farms where the level of pay (and hence also income tax liability) are higher than average.[72]

A more general comment is also in order. The so-called economic instruments of policy are being introduced for two reasons. The first is their greater effectiveness, the second their greater flexibility. With respect to the latter feature, problems are likely to arise in connection with delivery contracts that now form the basis of "commercial" relations between enterprises. The contracts are, in a sense, a substitute for the old-fashioned plan targets and supply orders: both were meant to eliminate the "chaos" of the market. The market is now coming back, and it is for that reason that I think it advisable to introduce some flexibility clauses into delivery contracts. For as we have found out in connection with wage contracts in the context of cost-push inflation, a contract tends to stabilize the existing situation. In the case discussed here, the necessary adjustments are likely to be delayed.[73]

CONCLUSION

Our discussion centered on two important and related aspects of the new systems, and many relevant problems were left aside. Among these are: manpower, investment decisions at the national level, financing of investments, size of farms, and the relation between various branches of the economy. But enough has been said to indicate that decompression in Eastern European agriculture will not be accomplished overnight.

This conclusion is supported by a host of other considerations, including balance of payments problems, the lack of reserves, the fear of inflation, and so forth. But is it not true that all the important changes in systems and attitudes can only be accomplished over a longer period? Anyone familiar with the problems of attempting to date the onset of the Industrial Revolution, or a "take-off," or the precise time when

[72] As was to be expected. Even here, however, there are some problems in connection with the age structure and recruitment of younger and better trained workers.

[73] Given the very peculiar seller's market in agriculture (almost every ounce will find a buyer, but one still has to sell more than one would like to), there may also be some tendency to preserve the existing distortions in agriculture.

French entrepreneurial attitudes were modernized, is likely to answer in the affirmative.

Many of the shortcomings discussed here are likely to become quite important at a later stage. As and when decompression to the levels presently envisaged takes place, the need for regulating agricultural activity—in the Occidental manner—will be felt more acutely than it is now.[74] At present, the dismantling of command takes precedence over anything else. But this is one more reason for great flexibility and, indeed, pragmatism in economic policy. Under no circumstances should any of the present new systems be advertised as the final—worse yet, an optimal—solution to present farm or general economic problems.

[74] Studies of agricultural policy in the West are now under way.

CARL ZOERB

Comment

A working sojourn in the East European countries by an experienced observer provides an opportunity to appraise the changing contours of agricultural policy in an area of the Communist world where shadows more often obscure than illuminate the directional furrows of change. Professor Karcz has done a pathfinding job in his paper on the dynamics of decompression of the agricultural sector of a command-type economic system.

The imperative need to improve the performance of socialized agricultural systems was recognized before the present intensive phase of restructuring that began in 1963 when East Germany started its reforms. By comparison, and in line with the Communist priority scale, industrial reforms have accelerated more rapidly than their agrarian counterparts. Yet the scope of current agrarian reforms has transcended all previous reorganizations since the socialization of agriculture in the East European countries, Poland excepted.

Professor Karcz brings up to date the swiftly moving pattern of change, using examples drawn from Czechoslovak and Bulgarian experiences. It should not go unnoticed that the source of the most challenging reforms comes precisely from these two countries: one dominantly industrialized, the other rural. Moreover, Czechoslovakia and Bulgaria have one characteristic in common: the highest degree of socialized agriculture in the COMECON bloc, with fully 80 per cent of the total farm output produced in the public sector, compared to 66 per cent for the Soviet Union. This development may not be prerequisite for the degree of innovation in policy but it does suggest obliquely that a near saturation of the socialized sector in an economy of shortages may bring about a recognition of the need for change in structure. It may be only at this point that a centrally directed agricultural system will develop a willingness to experiment in an effort to equate supply with demand.

Karcz rightly calls the Czechoslovak model the most elaborate and remarks that the envisaged changes cut deeper than any of the previous patterns of reorganization. As he was primarily concerned with planning practices and price as criteria in the decompression processes of the two countries, our approach will be along these lines but focused on still another revision of the Czechoslovak model, on what appears as the most sweeping reorganization of a socialized agricultural system. As this second innovation received only passing mention by Karcz, our effort shall be devoted to an appraisal of the programed Czechoslovak model.

In a fifteen-page supplement to the official Czechoslovak agricultural daily, a Kafkaesque document of alternating turgidity and light, the entire order of the Czechoslovak agricultural and food industries has been recast by decree and the innovations are to be introduced gradually.[1] Three central ministries—agriculture, food, and procurement —were promptly amalgamated into a single Ministry of Agriculture and Food by party decree. While such an integration is an innovation in itself, it is the amalgamation of all agricultural agencies at the district level that represents the most striking change in the Czechoslovak model. Instead of being organized exclusively horizontally, the district agricultural association is to be integrated both vertically and horizontally, including as members the state and collective farms, the MTS, the procurement and supply agencies, the several agricultural interenterprise organizations, farm construction and service firms, some food-processing enterprises, and other establishments of a local nature engaged in food and agricultural endeavors. The decree spells out the scope of the new organs that will replace the district production boards:

> The district agricultural association is a *khozraschet* supraenterprise organ of the member enterprises and, jointly with the latter, it is responsible for the development of agricultural production.

THE DISTRICT AGRICULTURAL ASSOCIATION

The general meeting of managers of member enterprises is the supreme authority of the district agricultural association. It elects its officers, organizes planning and staff departments, and is represented

[1] *The System of Management of the Agricultural and Food Sectors,* special supplement, *Zemedelske Noviny,* March 19, 1967, pp. 2–17. The document is the source of most of the material presented.

on the boards of the regional agricultural and food agencies. In planning, it is to project long and intermediate plans with the cooperation of the member enterprises and help arbitrate conflicts between the two plans. Whether this function extends to adjudication between farms over procurement plans is not specified, but then "the structure, scope, methods, and style of work shall not be determined by a pattern uniformly set for the whole state." The DAA may also act as a sales agent for its members, creator of new enterprises, distributor of surpluses, allocator of grants and credits, organizer or supervisor of productive and advisory services, including legal protection to its members, trainer of cadres, cooperator with the lower levels of state administration concerned with improving the conditions and welfare of the constituents of its members, and it may "supervise and check on the activity of its own institutions and of its other member enterprises." To finance its activities, the DAA is authorized to secure funds from earnings of its member enterprises, fees for services and specialized activities, grants and subsidies from the state, membership contributions, shares from various funds of its members. As a *khozraschet* agency, however, an unusual concept for a supraenterprise organ, it will be subject to economic accounting, and expected to operate without undue subsidy.[2]

It is apparent that the DAA has a dichotomous role and some of its duties are clearly contradictory. In one way it is the representation of the operating enterprises in the district of both farms and food processors, and, at the same time, a "recognized partner of the central sphere of management." Thus while it represents the aims and aspirations of its members externally, yet it is part of the central power structure at the district level. Equally difficult to fulfill is the dictum that it represents the conflicting interests of its members: the collective farm, the state farm, the procurement and supply agencies, the farm construction organs, and other "economic independent enterprises." It would be a formidable achievement to organize rationally such an infrastructure into a cooperative, productive mechanism for a supraenterprise agency facing in two directions.

PRICES AND PLANNING

A revised order of prices is to be put into effect in early 1970. The prices are to cover "socially necessary labor," a concept used to describe

[2] Of 108 agricultural districts in Czechoslovakia, the average DAA would comprise the following enterprises: sixty-five collective farms, three to four state farms, one MTS, one procurement agency, an undetermined number of food processors, and farm construction organs.

the "normal" cost basis for determining prices. Adjustments toward flexibility to account for shifting supply and demand conditions will be a new factor in selling prices, the special supplement emphasizes. However, prices are to be kept as stable as possible "for a given period of time" in which prices will move only within limits determined in advance. This, it is argued, is to cement the "mutuality of interest between consumer and producer." At the same time, it is contended, the relationships of purchase prices, wholesale prices, and retail prices and their mutual influence constitute a serious problem that must be settled. A reexamination of the turnover tax in pricing and of direct tax-intervention policy needs to be considered. One of the few basic principles that has been accepted is that prices must be uniform for all types of farm enterprises, including the development of a uniform basis for granting subsidies. The aim of the Czechoslovak planners is to establish a "socialist market," free of spontaneous market forces. By this is meant a market where economic forces will be allowed to exert their influence on prices, subject to central intervention as needed to redirect market movements. This intervention in the agricultural and food sectors includes the use of foreign trade as an aid to influence domestic market behavior.

Central planning at intermediate and perspective levels will feature the Czechoslovak model. It will be done in cooperation with the branch industries and the district agricultural associations beginning in 1970. The long-term plans are to provide indicative targets and an analysis of the economic outlook by sectors and to define the economic investments consistent with the objectives. A departure from past planning is that the setting of targets will be based on a consideration of the natural conditions and possibilities rather than the old parceling out of targets by sectors and their subdivisions with a minimum analysis of the resources at hand. Consultations between the center and the lower organs will replace review. The central organs are not to interfere in the operations of the farming units, and the ministry will "notify," not "assign," the enterprise its tasks. Some direction from the center is to be permitted, but this is to be limited to the backward farms. Perhaps it would be more realistic to admit that the central authorities hope they will not have to intervene. In procurement planning, earlier measures to streamline the collection processes led to a perpetuation of the monopoly power of the purchasing agencies, organized vertically with an autonomous management. With the incorporation of the purchasing and supply agencies into the DAA, the effectiveness of their monopoly power may be partially broken. The farms will no longer have to deal with a separate ministerial agency. Although only one purchasing agency will exist in a district, and the farm may not go out of the district to seek an alternative buyer, purchasing activities are to be supervised by the DAA. The new model, unfortunately, disappoints those farmers and officials who had visualized effective marketing alternatives for the collective farms. As Karcz sagely laments, and where the new Czechoslovak system sheds no light, there is still no systematic theory of the above-enterprise agency and the art of quota distribution.

On balance, the Czechoslovak reform system suffers from overorganization at the district level. It undeniably represents a partial decompression of a rigid agricultural system through its vertical and horizontal lines of integration, all centered at a district agency that shapes up more like a cooperative parent agency (the DAA) than the ominous structure of an above-enterprise agency. The fear that the granting of greater freedom to enterprises will create chaos unless directly controlled seems to pervade much of the organization. The route toward market socialism, planning without theory, is a long and tortuous one and, as Karcz warns, the ship of socialist agriculture faces some heavy seas. Yet it is under weigh, and if the lessons of four decades of collectivization project any developments, it is that the current innovation will not be the final model for a socialized agricultural system. Some component other than the use of indirect economic instruments of control and a new organizational structure is needed. We hope Karcz will be the guide on another voyage.

KONRAD MERKEL

The Agrarian Problem
in Divided Germany

The theme of our conference suggests that we give special study to divided Germany, because the two systems of agriculture that constitute the subject of our discussions here stand side by side. For this reason, Germany has often been considered ideal for the study of Communist and non-Communist agricultural policies under the conditions of a mature economy. This view rests upon the important argument that here—unlike anywhere else—a common initial position with the same historic background and essentially identical parts is to be found, permitting a precise comparison for judging and evaluating the two systems.

Divided Germany affords relatively favorable conditions for a comparative analysis of the real situation, but there are also substantial limitations. After the war the rebuilding of the economy in the two parts of Germany was carried out according to basically different concepts. This was mainly the result of the adoption of socialism in East Germany. No other sector of the economy has been as much affected through the process of socialization in East Germany as agriculture, where not only ownership and farm size but also the system of production have undergone a fundamental change. However, the years since the war have been long enough to repair the destruction and, after many trials and errors, to consolidate somewhat the new system. Continuing industrialization in both East and West Germany hampers any confirmation of the relative superiority of either of the differing agricultural systems. This is so because agriculture is faced with the need for continuing adaptation, which, however, proceeds in the two Germanies in diverging directions.

East German agriculture has not achieved its goal of establishing well-organized, specialized, large-scale socialistic enterprises: apart from problems of planning and guidance, there remain a great number of problems of a technical nature to be solved. On the other hand, West Germany is confronted with structural problems in the form of a high number of small holdings, whose capacity of production (in spite of very intensive methods) does not supply sufficient family income. In addition, the agriculture of West Germany suffers from overmechanization in certain areas of production. Regardless of the relatively high amount of manpower in agriculture, there are many farms where an economically unjustified high amount of capital has been invested in machinery.

Both parts of Germany, therefore, have their specific and unsolved agrarian problems; their agricultural economies are still fluid. Consequently, it is difficult to make comparisons, even considering the relatively favorable circumstances afforded by a divided country. Moreover, it is very difficult to make unbiased comparisons that clearly reveal the extent to which agricultural development reflects respective agricultural policies. This applies both in economic and social as well as in quantitative and qualitative respects.

Considering its relevance in terms of economic criteria, the evidence afforded by such a comparison is limited, even within the German area. One must take these limitations into account, in order to avoid mis-evaluations.

Difficulties in comparison arise principally from the fact that the economic conditions for agricultural development have been different since the division of the country. These differing conditions are almost impossible to evaluate and weigh, especially those concerning the employment of factors of production and their combinations. Not less difficult to evaluate is the importance of the wide variation in the availability of capital at the starting point and during the whole period of comparison.

The disparity began immediately after the Second World War. On one side, West Germany received Marshall Plan economic aid. On the other side, the Eastern part suffered an immense loss of economic assets through industrial dismantling, war-reparation payments, and discriminating trade relations with the occupation power. In addition, war casualties hurt the Eastern German farms much more than those of the Western part, so there was at this point a great difference in the initial capital fund for over-all economic development.

In the ensuing years, another factor influenced the economic framework to the disadvantage of Eastern Germany: the exodus of a productive labor force from East to West Germany. Even if the migration was forced to come to an end by the erection of the Wall in 1961, its economic disadvantage has been of great continuing importance, since the shortage of labor in East Germany was not mitigated by the importation of guest workers. The immigration of a productive labor force meant a considerable gain in assets for the economy of the Federal Republic of Germany (F.R.G.).

I hold up these points only as examples of the difficulties of trying to determine the specific effects of the two agricultural systems of divided Germany and of making a judgment of their relative values. Because of the complexity of the forces that influence agricultural output, it is also not possible to determine exactly the influence of economic systems on the efficiency of agricultural production. A comparison of the results in agriculture can merely show the momentary level reached by the respective economies. The interpretation and evaluation of the data, therefore, must take all these imponderables into consideration.

It is known that such investigations as this are impeded by the lack of an absolute standard for the evaluation of total agricultural productivity. Differences in the data systems preclude satisfactory correlation. Thus it seems to be more practical to evaluate the amount of output in terms of the patterns of development. Such quantitative comparisons have a disadvantage since they fail to indicate the profitability and the quality of production. They do give, however, ample information about the productivity, which, of course, depends on the comparability of the statistics involved.

At this point I must mention a statistical-methodological difficulty that is important for empirical analysis.[1] The limitations of space do not allow me to go deeper into this problem, yet I want at least to draw attention to this principal, and generally important, problem.

Methodological differences in the practice of agricultural statistics, as seen in the two parts of Germany, allow certain generalizations to be made: statistics of Communist countries are based upon concepts and principles that differ from those of non-Communist countries. Moreover, the data are not only the results of statistical gathering but they also are the by-products of planning. Comparable difficulties in the field of agricultural statistics, especially those based on differing definitions and methods of statistical survey, lead inevitably to deviations in

[1] See Konrad Merkel, *Agrarproduktion im zwischenvolkswirtschaftlichen Vergleich— Auswertungsprobleme der Statistik am Beispiel des geteilten Deutschland—*, (Berlin, 1963).

the accuracy of some statistics. As a rule, inconsistencies in the statistics of agricultural production and foodstuff consumption can be traced to the different definitions of gross and net amounts, which in the official Communist statistics are not always clearly distinguished.

For example: In the computation of grain output in East Germany, only the loss that occurs through the process of harvesting is taken into account and deducted from the natural growth. On the other hand, in the statistics of the F.R.G., an additional allowance is made for losses at the barn and losses due to moisture content, amounting to over 14 per cent. A further example: The calculation of food consumption in East Germany is based on the total amount, without regard to the losses that occur in transportation to the consumer, while transportation loss is taken into account in West Germany. Thus the final data represent gross amount in one case and net amount in the other. To bring about comparability, one must reduce the East German figures by at least 10 per cent to allow for these discrepancies.

Our objective evaluation of agricultural economic evidence from Eastern Europe is further impeded by their publication of statistical results without documentation. Despite the relatively well-developed statistical census machinery that exists in East Germany, the agricultural statistical publications lack the depth and completeness of accompanying facts and, as a result, also lack the extent and integrity of the statistical documents of the F.R.G. They are especially inadequate with respect to aggregate data on agricultural production and food supply, and basic economic facts can only be computed with the help of supplementary calculations. This problem, of course, weakens the accuracy of our estimates.

Having made these remarks, I proceed to a comparison of the agrarian conditions and results in East and West Germany by employing decisive and safe criteria. For a presentation of this sort, it is advisable to begin with a substantiated picture of agricultural development. Tables 1 and 2 show the average progress in vegetable and animal production.

To summarize agricultural products and to express the total result with one figure, the West German statistics employ the term "grain equivalent" as a volume unit. This is a more suitable characterization of the total agricultural product than an evaluation in terms of money. Such characterization permits the development of indices and makes a clear presentation of the developmental picture.

Depending on whether the quantitative calculation of agricultural

TABLE 1

GROWTH OF THE CROP YIELD IN DIVIDED GERMANY[a]

1935/38, 1960–1967

(In Hundred Kilograms per Hectare)

Crops	Region[b]	1935/38[c]	1960	1961	1962	1963	1964	1965	1966	1967
Cereals	EG	23.9	27.5	21.7	26.4	24.7	27.0	29.2	26.1	31.8
	WG	22.4	31.7	25.3	31.1	31.3	33.1	28.2	30.0	36.3
Legumes	EG	18.5	12.4	13.4	14.8	11.6	14.6	17.3	14.1	19.4
	WG	17.2	20.2	18.9	21.2	22.7	20.6	23.0	23.2	26.8
Oilseeds	EG	19.1	14.4	13.5	14.4	11.2	14.3	18.4	17.7	22.5
	WG	16.7	21.5	20.5	24.1	21.1	21.6	20.0	20.9	25.6
Potatoes	EG	194.3	192.4	123.7	179.0	172.6	172.8	177.2	184.8	205.0
	WG	185.0	235.8	220.4	260.6	279.0	242.2	231.1	257.3	301.2
Sugar beets	EG	301.2	287.6	213.8	213.8	266.0	261.3	263.1	313.5	332.6
	WG[d]	317.3	451.0	370.4	323.9	426.4	409.3	357.8	432.6	469.6
Forage; root crops	EG	449.2	533.6	402.2	436.5	508.9	479.7	491.0	591.1	623.5
	WG	421.4	540.3	488.6	437.9	538.8	481.8	461.4	559.3	622.9
Clover and alfalfa hay	EG	55.5[e]	63.9	66.4	55.5	63.1	52.1	67.7	68.3	67.0
	WG	63.7[e]	72.8	75.4	64.3	73.0	61.5	74.1	77.3	78.8
Meadow hay	EG	42.9	43.9	46.5	36.4	43.3	35.0	41.9	45.0	45.2
	WG	48.2	58.9	62.9	55.5	60.7	53.7	63.4	66.4	67.7

a Owing to differences in methods of statistical survey and in content of terms, figures in East German data are higher and not fairly comparable to West German data.

b EG—East Germany; WG—West Germany.

c Prewar figures of cereals and potatoes indicate gross yield.

d Yield per hectare according to the calculations of the BML.

e Including grass clover.

Sources: *Statistisches Jahrbuch der DDR, 1967; Statistisches Jahrbuch üb ELuF d. BRD, 1966.*

TABLE 2
RISE IN SELECTED AREAS OF PRODUCTION
1935/38, 1964—1966

	Region[a]	1935/38	1964	1965	1966
Average milk yield per cow	EG	2,580	2,719[b]	2,982[b]	3,090[b]
(in kilograms)	WG	2,480	3,572	3,642	3,649
Average butterfat of cow's milk	EG	3.26	3.50[b]	3.50[b]	3.50[b]
(per cent)	WG	3.40	3.79	3.74	3.72
Average butterfat yield by cow	EG	84	95	104	108
(in kilograms)	WG	84	135	136	136
Average egg yield per hen	EG	105	139	143	145
	WG	105	188	196	202
Average live-weights for slaughter (in kilograms)					
Beef (excepting calves)	EG	474	333	353	372
	WG	480	491	502	504
Calves	EG	74	64	62	76
	WG	84	91	105	105
Hogs	EG	122	120	123	118
	WG	118	114	112	111
Per cent of average hog population	EG	93.5	90.3	95.8	98.4
slaughtered annually.	WG	98.0	133.9	142.3	141.4

[a] EG—East Germany; WG—West Germany; EG since 1964 includes East Berlin; WG since 1964 includes Saarland and West Berlin.
[b] The EG statistics of milk production show the production, not in natural fat content, but convert all production to 3.5 per cent fat content. The effective average fat content is not shown, but it will be somewhat less than 3.5 per cent.
Sources: Statistisches Jahrbuch der DDR, 1967; Statistische Praxis, No. 9, 1967; Stat. Monatsberichte d. BML, 1964–1967; Bericht des BML über "Legeleistung der Hennen und Eiererzeugung 1966."

TABLE 3

The Quantitative Development of Agricultural Production in Divided Germany

1957–1965

(Index 1935/38 = 100)

	1957	1958	1959	1960	1961	1962	1963	1964	1965
1. Gross acreage output									
German Democratic Republic	95	98	86	107	82	91	93	93	102
Federal Republic of Germany	114	120	107	129	115	119	128	120	115
2. Foodstuff production									
German Democratic Republic	100	108	105	112	103	95	107	109	117
Federal Republic of Germany	130	138	137	150	146	152	160	163	157
3. Net foodstuff production									
German Democratic Republic	89	97	94	98	92	82	97	98	107
Federal Republic of Germany	125	133	127	145	134	141	150	148	135

Source: German Democratic Republic: My calculation, employing certain data given in the statistical year books of the Deutsche Demokratische Republik, 1958 to 1966.

Federal Republic of Germany: *Statistisches Jahrbuch über Ernährung, Landwirtschaft und Forsten der Bundesrepublik Deutschland 1963 to 1966/67.*

production includes total output in the sum of primary plant products or all foodstuff products of plant and animal origin, West German statistics differentiate between the gross acreage output and gross foodstuff output. The net foodstuff output is foodstuff output minus those animal products that can be traced back to imported fodder.

Whichever stage of production is taken for comparison, the results of development of the two parts of Germany in the last nine years show the lack of efficiency in East Germany (Table 3). This is a substantial difference of standard in favor of the F.R.G., not only in the relative rise in production compared to the prewar level, but also in growth rate. The gross acreage output of East Germany reached the prewar level for the first time in 1960 and then again in 1965, while in the Federal Republic this level was already exceeded in 1950. East Germany succeeded for the first time in 1965 in bringing the net foodstuff output to the prewar standard; the Federal Republic had already surpassed it by 1950.

The difference in success is even more impressive when we consider foodstuff production. Compared to the average of 1935–38, the average increase in the years from 1963 to 1965 was 60 per cent in the Federal Republic and only 11 per cent in East Germany. The increase was, therefore, more than five times higher in the Western than in the Eastern sector.

TABLE 4
THE RELATIVE YEARLY GROWTH OF THE VOLUME OF
AGRICULTURAL OUTPUT IN DIVIDED GERMANY
1957 TO 1965
(In Per Cent[a])

	German Democratic Republic	Federal Republic of Germany
Gross acreage output	0.19	0.47
Foodstuff output	0.93	2.55
Net foodstuff output	1.12	1.57

[a] Computed with the linear trend equation $(y=a+bx)$.
Source: Same as Table 3.

In East Germany, despite the essentially low level of output, the yearly average rate of growth of agricultural production has been far lower than that of the Federal Republic of Germany (Table 4). The yearly average growth rate of foodstuffs amounts to 0.93 in East Germany and to 2.55 per cent in the F.R.G. Hence the growth rate of West Germany is two and one-half times as much as that of East Germany.

It must be emphasized that the statistical data represent unadjusted calculations on which the official data of both parts of Germany are based. When the differences in the accuracy of the basic figures are considered, the results of East Germany must be even lower. Such adjustments are intentionally neglected, because even without them the data provided are convincing enough to make an objective judgment. Certainly the effect of the very complex differences in the conditions of production are conclusive. To compute the effects of systems, it is necessary to examine the development and the situation of agriculture within their respective economic conditions.

The two systems are alike in their endeavor to bring the agrarian sector to the highest possible productivity and efficiency. Each aims not only to bring a maximum satisfaction of the needs of the population in foodstuffs at low costs, but also to reach a reasonable income for persons employed in agriculture and to maintain the value of invested capital.

An expanding economy is subject to inherent laws and that is the main reason why the Communist countries do not stick to the inflexible plan model; plans for and attempts at reform of a more or less important extent are being carried on. The present situation in East Germany is similar to that which has existed in the Soviet Union and which brought about much intensive discussion within Soviet society. It has brought about the same soul searching in East Germany. The years following 1961 brought for East Germany a decrease in the growth rate of the over-all economy and induced serious pressures; hence, from 1963 until 1965, East Germany led the Eastern bloc in experiments designed to reform its economy.

As a matter of fact, the introduction of the "new economic system" in the summer of 1963 was the first instance within the Eastern bloc, apart from Yugoslavia, of an implementation of reforms and reorganization.[2] In the meantime, the reform movement has spread over other Communist countries, and East Germany has lost its leading position to Czechoslovakia, which is now being succeeded by Hungary. In general, there are today remarkable differences in the economic and planning systems of the various countries in the Eastern bloc. The differences are tending to be greater, and can at this point be seen clearly.

Generally, it is possible to categorize the countries in the Eastern bloc according to their attitudes toward reform of the economic system: a reforming group, a group that remains intractable until now, and

[2] Karl C. Thalheim, *Die Wirtschaft der Sowjetzone in Krise und Umbau*, Vol. I, der Schriftenreihe Wirtschaft und Gesellschaft in Mitteldeutschland, herausgegeben vom Forschungsbeirat für Fragen der Wiedervereinigung Deutschlands beim Bundesminister für gesamtdeutsche Fragen (Berlin, 1964).

between these extremes, a hesitating group.[3] The first group—the reforming countries—includes Yugoslavia, Czechoslovakia, and Hungary. On the other hand, Rumania, a strongly Communist country that seeks, in its relations to COMECON and in its external trade, a great deal of autonomy, has been astonishingly very unwilling to reform and sticks to the earlier system of central administration. To the middle group, which hesitates to undertake sweeping reforms, belong the Soviet Union, Poland, and, especially, East Germany.

Let us try to characterize briefly these differences in attitudes toward reforms in the economic system. The fundamental question of concern to Communist regimes pertains to the political-ideological limits and freedom of maneuver within a centrally controlled system.

Supporters of the path favoring the existing system feel that it is enough to improve planning technique by adopting modern technology, through the application of econometric methods and the employment of computers. By doing so they believe it is perhaps possible to solve some of the problems of the centrally administered economy that have remained unsolved till now; however, the actual problems accruing from the economic dynamics remain.

On the other hand, the supporters of progressive reform are inclined to choose those concepts of capitalist economy that seem useful for state-planned economy. Though they stick firmly to the principle of social ownership of capital goods, they want to allow competition among firms and grant a greater freedom in planning. Furthermore, there is a movement towards the decentralization of pricing, rendering prices more flexible. In Czechoslovakia and Hungary today the distinction between the planning of the economic process and economic policy is far more pronounced than in the past, when—as in the other Eastern bloc countries—both were centrally directed.

Apparently East Germany hesitates to give up central planning of economic processes. With the "new economic system," it tries to modify the old system by installing certain components of free enterprise to attain a better accomplishment of the plan. Today, an attempt is being made to induce a "plan-conforming" attitude by allowing material advantages, the "economic lever," rather than imposing changes by decree. The new system, however, still contains a great deal of admin-

[3] See Gleitze, Thalheim, Hensel, Meimberg, *Der Osten auf dem Weg zur Marktwirtschaft?*, Vol. VI, der Schriftenreihe Wirtschaft und Gesellschaft in Mitteldeutschland, herausgegeben vom Forschungsbeirat für Fragen der Wiedervereinigung Deutschlands beim Bundesminister für gesamtdeutsche Fragen (Berlin, 1967).

istration associated with the planning doctrine and the issuing of distinct instructions. Only the measures applied to it are changed: what is useful for the society must also bring advantages to each enterprise and to each working person.[4]

In this new system, profit plays a large role as an economic lever, serving as an encouragement to the enterprises to take over more plan duties. A portion of the income, the premium, depends on the level of profit, so that each working person may have an interest in the profit of his enterprise. Furthermore, the profit should be divided among all agents involved in the planned production. The profit is thus a means of fulfilling the plan but it is not the target and motive of economic activity. The prices of capital goods and salaries, as well as the products to be marketed, are dictated. Therefore, profit can be raised only by rational operation, exploitation of reserves, and the highest possible employment of all productive forces. Since profit is an index of the performance of the enterprise within the plan structure, narrow limits are set for its effectiveness.

Even if one admits universal economic concepts, different economic prerequisites in agriculture can lead to, or even result in, varied measures and conclusions. For example, in some branches of East German production and consumption of agricultural goods, shortages prevail. This applies also to the COMECON in general. Shortages are seriously felt since the lack of foreign currency impedes import of agricultural commodities. Because of these reasons the maximization of agricultural production is still one of the main targets of central planning. In the F.R.G., on the other hand, and in the European Common Market in general, overproduction is a problem in some sectors of agriculture and export is necessary. Moreover, certain agrarian products must be imported in the interest of the export of industrial goods. Therefore, the target of the agricultural policy of West Germany is the rationalization of production and the raising of labor productivity in order to achieve income parity between agriculture and the other sectors of the economy, rather than the raising of agricultural production.

The differences in regard to price relationships and to the level of technical progress, especially in supplying agriculture with some important capital goods, cause different agricultural economic measures in East and West. The response of agriculture to the economic conditions

---

[4] See Klemens Pleyer, "Rechtsfragen der überbetrieblichen Zusammenarbeit im Neuen ökonomischen System der SBZ," *Die Aktiengesellschaft*, Zeitschrift für das gesamte Aktienwesen, Nos. 7, 8, 9 (Hamburg, 1966).

is also different for the very reason that in West Germany almost all farms are family owned, whereas in East Germany, through the process of collectivization, about 400,000 individually owned farms have been transformed into 15,000 agricultural production cooperatives (LPG). The approximately 6,100 LPG's of Type III,[5] as well as the 660 nationally owned estates (VEG), which comprise about two thirds of the agricultural area of East Germany, are large farms with a wage system.

In family-owned farms, where the farmer operates on his own accounting, the endeavor is to maximize income of his family, which necessarily leads to the maximization of the total effort of the farm. On the other hand, in enterprises with a wage system, the workers strive for the highest possible wage. Therefore, the employer requires some other economic levers to promote material interest.

The targets of agricultural policies and the performance of agrarian production are thus fundamentally different. The goal of the centrally administered economy of East Germany is to attain the highest possible rational production in the interest of the state. The income level of the employed person has to be just enough to satisfy personal needs. In the West the maximization of income is the guiding principle for agricultural production. In West Germany, as in other Western countries, the formation of private capital is fostered by the state, but it is largely prevented in the Communist states, except for savings for personal needs.

The revolution of the agrarian structure through collectivization in East Germany stands in radical contrast to the development in West Germany and other Western countries. In the West we see a decrease in the number of farms since the war, because the owners of small farms with insufficient acreage, especially part-time farms, have ceased to exist. The acreage has been leased or sold. Accordingly, the remaining farms have become somewhat larger by buying or leasing abandoned farm lands. New large-scale farms, however, are not established. On the contrary, through the postwar land reform, large-scale private farms were divided and used to enlarge peasant farms or to create new small holdings. State domains have also been used for settlement. Therefore, even if a reduction in the number of farms and an enlargement of the small farms have taken place (and this process is still going on), it has not led to a fundamental change in the size of West German farm units.

---

[5] According to the degree of socialization of acreage and of capital goods and also according to the distribution of the income, three types of agricultural cooperatives are differentiated in East Germany. Explanation of the types shown in Table 5.

West German agriculture is still composed of numerous family-sized farms (Table 5). An increase of their number has occurred principally because hired labor has become uneconomical or unnecessary. Today, only 6 per cent of the agricultural labor force are wage earners.

TABLE 5
SHIFT OF FARM STRUCTURE IN DIVIDED GERMANY
1939 AND 1966

Farm Type and Size	Per Cent of Total Agricultural Area		Average Agricultural Area of Each Farm in Hectares	
	1939	1966	1939	1966
Federal Republic of Germany				
All farms	100	100	7.0	9.1
By size (in hectares)				
0.5– 2	5	3	1.1	1.1
2 – 5	14	8	3.3	3.3
5 – 10	21	16	7.1	7.3
10 – 20	25	32	13.8	14.2
20 – 50	24	30	28.9	28.4
50 –100	6	7	68.7	64.5
More than 100	5	4	190.0	167.9
German Democratic Republic				
All farms	100	100	11.2	202.7
By type:				
LPG[a], Type I,II	–	27	–	203.9
LPG, Type III	–	59	–	627.2
GPG	–	1	–	44.8
VEG	–	7	–	645.8
Others	–	6	–	30.0

[a] LPG=Agricultural Production Cooperative
GPG=Gardener's Production Cooperative
VEG=People-owned Estates
Type of LPG: I. The farmer brought in arable land only.
                II. Farmer brought in, additionally, traction power machinery and implements.
                III. Farmer gave entire farm to cooperative for collective management. No more than 0.5 hectare and limited livestock remained for individual management by each household.

Sources: *Statistisches Handbuch über Landwirtschaft und Ernährung der Bundesrepublik Deutschland, 1956; Bericht der Bundesregierung über die Lage der Landwirtschaft, 1967* (Grüner Bericht, 1967); *Statistisches Jahrbuch der Deutschen Demokratischen Republik, 1957 und 1967.*

Because there is a divergence in land tenure in the two Germanies, we can compare the farm structure to determine if the large-scale farm is preferable to the small one. The question that arises is whether it is economically justifiable for West Germany to reject a concentration of production in large-scale farms, when expansion and concentration of enterprises is succeeding in industry and commerce. There are, of course, many advantages in large agricultural enterprises, but I shall mention only the main ones.

1. Compared with the small family farm, a large farm has undoubtedly a greater organization and production buoyancy in adaptability to local differences. Since the farm organization can be adjusted exclusively to its natural and production conditions, the size of the available farm land is not the criterion of paramount importance for decision. On the other hand, the organization and the performance of production of family-sized farms must be adjusted to the labor potential of the family, which makes the size of the available farm land very important. The necessity of adjusting to the size of acreage is rightly considered by the Communists as a very important disadvantage of small-scale farms.

2. In the economy of an industrialized nation, large enterprises favor labor-saving production sectors where the labor productivity is high. Family-sized farms depend on the actual labor force, the earned income per hour is low, and the total earned income of the farm family depends on the size of the farm. Technical progress and over-all economic growth lead to higher productivity and enforce a continuous expansion of production capacity. Thereby, the size of the family-operated farm attains a dynamic character. To raise the level of income of the family farm necessitates an enlargement of the farm, whereas large-scale farms must be concerned principally with achieving a minimum labor force.

3. An operation on large areas and with large numbers of livestock achieves a decreasing trend in costs. Accordingly, the organizational and technical facilities of large farms achieve a high labor productivity not possible on many small farms.

4. The modern market requires the supply of a large quantity of products of uniformly good quality. It is obvious that such requirements can more easily be fulfilled by a large enterprise than by a great number of small farms with limited production volumes. The response of production to market requirements can be achieved only on a limited scale by small farms, and only through cooperation.

5. A special advantage of the socialist-style large agricultural enterprise may lie in the amazingly low number of farm units. There are in East Germany about 16,000 LPG and VEG, compared to 500,000 active farm units in West Germany. Since the capability of a farm manager is of great importance for farm outcome, one must assume that it is easier to achieve good management of the small number of large-sized enterprises in East Germany than in the many scattered family-sized farms of the F.R.G. It is also an advantage that in East Germany the farm management is not bound to a nonalterable, specific person,

but to one who can be selected according to capability and efficiency.

These are some of the reasons that large-sized enterprises are advantageous in both the economic and technical aspects in agriculture. There are, however, very important reasons that motivate the West to reject the concentration of production in large farm units. The Communists overestimate the economic advantage of large-sized farm units and large numbers of livestock when they shift more and more to the over-dimensional sizes of LPG and VEG, because the economic advantage of size shows a decreasing trend past a certain minimum size of farm and number of livestock. Further enlargement does not effect a decrease of costs, but rather can cause an increasing cost trend owing to the intrafarm working processes over greater distances.

At present a comparison of the results of an average farm unit in the two parts of Germany cannot afford full evidence of the social and economic prospects of the two types, independent small-scale or social-ist large-scale farms. This is due not only to the fact that East German documents remain insufficient but also because the development there is still unclear and its unsatisfactory performance may be attributable to defective technical equipment and ineffective farm management. In addition, new farming systems are emerging in West Germany that reflect the varying economic conditions, but they are being carried through by only a few progressive farms.

By comparing the available data pertaining to well-managed socialist large-scale farms in East Germany with the results of independent farms in West Germany, it is evident that the socialist type of farming is more effective in respect to labor productivity and earned income. In rationally organized and well-run large peasant farms in West Germany, operated with family labor and with an area of thirty to eighty hectares, gross income (earned income plus net return) of 1,000 to 12,000 DM per hectares can be achieved. It means an income of 30,000 to 80,000 DM per family, according to the farm size. On the other hand, the income of members of well-run LPG amounts at most to 10,000 to 12,000 DM East.[6] It must, however, be noted that people in East Germany limit the income of the members of an efficiently operating LPG by applying a great portion of the surplus to the various reserves.

---

[6] See Tümmler, Merkel, Blohm, *Die Agrarpolitik in Mitteldeutschland und ihre Auswirkung auf Produktion und Verbrauch landwirtschaftlicher Erzeugnisse*, Vol. III, der Schriftenreihe Wirtschaft und Gesellschaft in Mitteldeutschland, herausgegeben vom Forschungsbeirat für Fragen der Wiedervereinigung Deutschlands beim Bundes-minister für gesamtdeutsche Fragen (Berlin: Duncker & Humblot, 1969).

High income on the part of wage and salary earners may induce the tendency to form private capital, undesirable under the Communist system (apart from normal saving) but fostered in the non-Communist one.

It is because of the relative advantages of peasant farming compared to privately owned, cooperative, or state-owned, large-scale farming systems that West German agriculture (connected to the free market thanks to the efficiency of family-run farms) rejects the concentration of production in large-sized farm units and confines itself to cooperative measures. Let me mention a few points:

1. The wage demand on peasant farms does not mean a steady burden of fixed charges. The payroll of large-scale farming can severely disturb the liquidity.

2. A rational assignment of labor by adapting to the steadily changing manpower requirement is difficult to achieve on wage-labor based, large-scale farms because of the standardization of work hours. Since most of the work on a farm is dependent on seasonal and daily weather conditions, adaptation of labor assignments to the requirements is the most important prerequisite for a rational operation. In this respect, family farming is clearly to be preferred.

3. Members of the farmer's family, who run the farm on their own account, have a strong interest in their work because their income depends on the return from their labor. Such an interest cannot be expected from wage laborers. For efficiency, wages, and premiums cannot have the same effect in agriculture (where working conditions change very often) as they do in industry, where the conditions are more favorable and the working hours are steady. Furthermore, calculation and control of man hours in the cooperatives require extensive administrative machinery. The cost of this burdens the members of the cooperatives and the mechanics of administration draw the working force away from production.

When followers of the socialist farm system believe that in the future private initiative, which according to market-economy concepts is the most important determinant of economic development, can be over-compensated with a "socialist consciousness" of the people, they must make concessions to the material concern of the persons employed in agriculture, as the "new economic system" shows. The compulsory collectivization of farms in East Germany, a territory whose economic level is near that of Western Europe, shows clearly that economic reasons cannot always be brought up for the implementation of Communist maxims.

Besides this, more difficulties arise in the central administrative farm organization than in the other sectors of the economy. The special dependence of agricultural production on nature and the close interrelation of the various sectors of production do not permit realistic production programs to be set by central offices. According to East German reports, adherence to the principles of central planning has a cost disproportion that occurs not only between the various sectors of the economy but also between the different sections of agriculture.

Although planning has become somewhat more efficient through the new economic system, there has not been any fundamental change. Even if the production progress in East Germany, marked since 1964, continues and diminishes the gap between it and the West German level, on the basis of the progress of agriculture in the two parts of Germany it does not seem feasible that the Communist thesis of catching up with, or even surpassing, Western efficiency may find a realistic expression in the foreseeable future.

EBERHARD SCHINKE

Comment

The pattern of farming is changing today in both East and West Germany. In the Soviet-occupied zone of the East, agriculture has been completely socialized since 1960. Although the transformation into collective and state farms has been carried out superficially, satisfactory development of well-organized, specialized, large-scale farms has not been realized. Many problems of planning and management have remained unsolved; the shortcomings in some of the means of production delay the process of modernization. The former small farm structure makes itself conspicuous when, for example, in the newly constructed collective farm the necessary modern buildings are lacking and livestock are still scattered in numerous small, old barns.

In the agriculture of the Federal Republic or West Germany, on the other hand, the problems are primarily of a structural nature. Despite a rapid decrease in the number of small farms since 1950, in 1966, 27 per cent of all farms averaged less than ten hectares of agricultural area, and one third were between ten and twenty hectares, as seen in Table 3 of Professor Merkel's paper. Furthermore, unlike East Germany, West German agriculture has an oversupply of some machinery. Whereas East German collective and state farms have an average of one tractor to forty-eight hectares of farm land and one combine to over 200 hectares of grain, in West Germany there is one tractor to less than ten hectares, one combine to about thirty-five hectares of grain, one milking aggregate to about thirteen cows. Much capital has been fixed in poorly used funds, despite the fact that there are too many people working in agriculture. Although about 10 per cent of the West German labor force is still employed in this sector, it supplied less than 4.5 per cent of the gross national product. Thus, a great number of small farms cannot offer an income sufficient for a family nor match the earnings of nonagricultural workers. The finding of a solution to these problems has a high degree of priority, especially with regard to the Common Market, which is now practically completed in the field of agriculture. The traditional European family farm system is in a state of revolution, and East Germany as well as the western part have a long way to go in order to reach the goals set by their respective agrarian policies.

Under these circumstances, statistical data on agriculture in the two parts of Germany cannot give a reliable basis for comparing the effectiveness of their differing systems of farming. Such a comparison would also be difficult when maximum production is still the principal goal in East Germany, and the West German farmer is attempting to maximize his profit under a condition of overproduction. Professor Merkel's estimation that a definite, qualitative assessment of the economic successes of the two farming systems discussed here cannot yet be given should be underlined.

West Germany's agriculture has now become an integrated part of the Common Market, but in Eastern Europe the frontiers between the members of the COMECON are still closed, the exchange of agricultural products is limited, and national self-sufficiency in as many agricultural products as possible is still a goal of the East European governments, not to mention that of East Germany. International specialization of farm production is practically negligible; even the collaboration that exists in COMECON in supplying agricultural machinery, feed, and other means of production is on a very low level.[1] Contrary to the far-reaching influences of the EEC on the agriculture of West Germany, the economic community of the COMECON has not become an important factor in East Germany's agriculture.

Professor Merkel gives as exact a picture as possible of the present situation in East Germany's agriculture. Regarding the confrontation of the Eastern socialized, large-scale farm and the Western small-size family farm, however, I don't wholly agree with his emphasis. There is no doubt that the differences in farm size are considerable and significant. A study by East German experts, cited by the party leader Walter Ulbricht in a speech on problems of the New Economic System in agriculture, shows 300 to 450 hectares as optimal units in grain production, 80 to 120 hectares in sugar beets, 100 to 150 hectares in potatoes. For optimal sizes in livestock production, the same study indicates herds of 80–90 cows, at least 1,000 pigs, at least 3,000 hens.[2]

[1] See G. Jaehne, *Landwirtschaft und landwirtschaftliche Zusammenarbeit im Rat für Gegenseitige Wirtschaftshilfe—Comecon* (Wiesbaden: Harrassowitz, 1968).

[2] W. Ulbricht, "Die Anwendung des Neuen Ökonomischen Systems der Planung

The same production-unit sizes in livestock breeding are suggested therefore as optimal by Eastern as well as by Western economists; on the other hand, for crop production, the units in the East are much larger and, according to West European and American studies, secure no more profit nor even lower production cost than the smaller Western units. But the second goal of farm economy in the East, the minimizing of cost, serves as the principal criterion in establishing optimal farm sizes, and also forces the assumption of the maximal use of the biggest possible machinery. We must take into account the fact that the supposition is made—we can see this from the norm tables—that all these machines are used during the whole of the sowing or harvesting period, independent of any of the many difficulties to which machinery and agriculture are prone, and independent of the fall weather.

If we go from these theoretical capacities to pragmatically possible ones (of the same machinery), and make allowance for such other economic criteria as managerial ability of farmers and transportation cost, we arrive at recommended optimal sizes on the same level as those recommended by Western economists. Thus if we look not only at the size of farms in East and West Germany, but also at optimal volumes of individual production processes, we find few fundamental differences. It is true that in West Germany there are not many farms with such a big volume of production, but concentration and specialization of production in agriculture must also be taken into account. Since West Germany's agriculture is principally in small farms, farmers use various forms of cooperation, from the traditional cooperatives for credit, supply, and marketing, to the more recent cooperation in production. Here the individual farmer enters into a partnership with colleagues, specializing in only a relatively small part of his former production spectrum, and giving up some managerial functions to his partners, to other cooperatives, or to other connected enterprises. Such methods— used also in other West European countries—often achieve the same scope in production processes as that possible in a collective or state farm in the East. As a rule, however, new, large-scale enterprises do not come out of these Western cooperatives: individual farming is continued, and the owners of independent farms participate in cooperatives for their own profit. These cooperatives do not have a collective

und Leitung in unserer sozialistischen Landwirtschaft in den Jahren 1964–1965," *Die perspektivischen Aufgaben unserer sozialistischen Landwirtschaft* (Berlin: Dietz, 1964), pp. 27–28.

character, but an individual one, i.e., the principal goal is to help the individual farmer manage his farm and increase his income.

This distinction between cooperatives in East and West Germany is founded on a general difference between the Eastern and Western economic systems, i.e., the source of decision making. In reference to this, East Germany provides a good example of a centrally planned agriculture, and it will be very interesting to compare it with the situation in other East European countries, as shown in the paper of Professor Karcz.

OTTO SCHILLER

The Agrarian Question: Communist Experience and Its Implication for Developing Countries

INTRODUCTION

To divide the world into Communist and non-Communist countries does not entirely correspond to today's complex situation. There is a growing differentiation in some essential elements in the political and economic order of Communist states and it seems to be doubtful whether the general term "non-Communist countries" is really justified. The usual distinction between industrial countries and developing countries makes it clear that we are not dealing with a world divided into two parts, but with one divided into three parts, each of them differentiated to a high degree: the Communist countries on the one hand and the highly developed industrial countries on the other hand are faced with the vast number of developing countries that have been called the "Third World" or, to use the French term, *Tiers Monde*.

Looking at the "Third World" more closely, one can make a distinction between states whose regimes are moving toward some kind of socialism and strive for its realization, and other countries that—be they under a monarchical, a republican, or any other form of government— are not oriented toward socialism. The question is whether those developing countries that strive toward socialism in their economic policy are not closer to the Communist bloc, which officially calls itself the *socialist bloc*, than to the Western world. It is true, however, that in many developing countries the political order is not stabilized, so that the aims of economic policy may change, as has become clear from the examples of Indonesia, Ceylon, and Ghana.

These general observations have to be made before the question may be raised as to how far, in dealing with the agrarian question in developing countries, any lesson can be drawn from the experience of the Communist countries. This question is of special interest when we examine those countries that hope to implement socialist principles, such as Burma, Syria, Egypt, Kenya, and Tanzania. In such countries the socialist outlook undoubtedly plays a certain role in the handling of the agrarian question.

For developing countries generally, but especially those oriented toward socialist principles, six aspects of the experience of Communist countries are likely to be of particular interest:

The supply of rural manpower for the process of industrialization.

The contribution of agriculture to initial capital formation.

The transition from individual to collective farming.

The experience of state farms.

The experience of machine tractor stations (MTS).

The development of forms intermediary between individual and collective farming.

THE SUPPLY OF RURAL MANPOWER
FOR THE PROCESS OF INDUSTRIALIZATION

It is the aim of all developing countries to activate the process of industrialization, because only in this way can modern economic progress be achieved. The process of industrialization is necessarily linked with far-reaching demographic changes, as manpower must be shifted from agriculture to the industrial field. The most impressive example of this process of demographic change is the Soviet Union. In 1929, when with the First Five-Year Plan a systematic process of industrialization was started, the agricultural population was about 80 per cent of the total population.[1] It had decreased to less than 32 per cent in 1966.[2]

The view is often expressed that industrialization in the Soviet Union could progress so rapidly only because the collectivization of agriculture was started at the same time. With the replacement of the small-scale

---

[1] *Narodnoe khoziaistvo SSSR v 1962 g.* (Moscow, 1962), p. 7 (hereafter cited as *Narkhoz-*). This figure relates to rural population, which at that time was nearly equivalent to agricultural population. In 1967 rural population comprised 45 per cent of the total population—a much higher percentage than that of the agricultural population *SSSR v tsifrakh v 1966 g.* [Moscow, 1967], p. 7 [hereafter cited as *SSSR v tsifrakh-* 1966]).

[2] This figure relates to the working population in agriculture and forestry. See *Narkhoz- 1965*, p. 555.

peasant farm by the large-scale collective farm and by the use of machinery, manpower urgently needed for the process of industrialization was released. Some authors go so far as to state that in the Soviet Union the decision to collectivize was based not only on ideological grounds, but on the recognition that collectivization was necessary if rapid industrialization was to be achieved. Similar arguments can be heard today in India, where advocates of cooperative farming, i.e., of joint use of land, claim that only in this way can the necessary manpower be released from rural areas for a rapid process of industrialization.

The greater part of the arguments raised in this connection are, however, not valid. We know from the experience of the Western European countries that the mechanization of agriculture does not require large-scale farms. With the technological and organizational means available today, i.e., with machines adjusted to the needs of small-scale farms and with interfarm cooperation, a high degree of mechanization in agricultural production on medium- and small-scale farms can be achieved. Moreover, we know from the experience of the Western industrial countries, including the United States, that a rapid process of industrialization is possible without fundamental changes in the prevalence of the preconditions are different from those that prevailed in the Soviet Union at that time.

It has to be remembered, however, that in the initial stage of industrialization in the Soviet Union, the living and working conditions in the industrial plants were very poor. It may be that without additional pressure there would not have been sufficient rural manpower willing to give up a modest but traditional way of life in the rural hut for the primitive life in the barracks of a new industrial area. Such necessary additional pressure could be imposed better in a collective system of agriculture than in an agricultural system characterized by small holdings. But this argument is not true for other countries where the prevalence of the preconditions are different from those that prevailed in the Soviet Union at that time.

THE CONTRIBUTION OF AGRICULTURE TO INITIAL CAPITAL FORMATION

This is a basic problem that must be solved in developing countries. Somehow the initial capital formation has to be achieved in order to overcome stagnation in the agrarian sector and to start the process of economic growth. As we are concerned with countries in which more than 50 or 60 per cent of the population is occupied in agriculture, the agricultural population must participate to a large degree in the process of initial capital formation. For capital formation, saving is a necessary prerequisite; saving means restriction of consumption. The big, and almost insoluble, problem with which the developing countries are faced is how to restrict consumption in favor of capital formation with a population already living on a very low level of consumption.

It seems as if a solution to this problem has been found in the Communist states, perhaps by methods that cannot be copied in the developing countries. The question therefore is how, in the Soviet Union, which represents the most impressive example in this connection, the participation of the agricultural population in the initial capital formation could be achieved to such a remarkable extent.

Before the beginning of compulsory collectivization in 1929, the standard of living of the Soviet rural population was very low, but it still was considerably higher than, for instance, that of the Indian rural population of today. It probably would not have been possible in the Soviet Union to effect a restriction of consumption without the imposition of collective farming.

In 1929 Soviet agriculture consisted of about twenty-six million individual peasant farms.[3] After the completion of compulsory collectivization in 1933 there were approximately a quarter of a million collective farms in existence.[4] It is possible to decree delivery quotas and low compulsory prices for millions of individual farms; it was tried by the *prodrasvyorstka* (a compulsory delivery quota for agricultural products) during the time of War Communism.[5] According to the experience of that time, however, in such a situation the peasants may restrict their production to cover only their own requirements. Thus measures of pressure and terror may result in a decrease instead of an increase in deliveries.

In the Soviet Union the kolkhoz system has proved adequate as a means of placing the whole agricultural sector under government control, without the managerial risk that the government would have to take in complete socialization, i.e., the transfer of the agrarian sector into government management. In a collectivized agriculture, high delivery quotas linked with extraordinarily low producer prices could be effected with some success, while a similar result could not have been

---

[3] *Statisticheskii spravochnik za 1928 g.* (Moscow, 1929), p. 82.

[4] *Selskoe khoziaistvo SSSR, Ezhegodnik 1935* (Moscow, 1936), p. 12.

[5] Schiller, Otto, "Der neue Kurs der sowjetischen Agrarpolitik," *Osteuropa*, No. 3 (1953), p. 403–12.

achieved if the twenty-six million individual farms had remained in existence. With this method, the standard of living of the agricultural population could be kept at a very low level over a long period, until the change of course of agrarian policy after the death of Stalin in 1953. As a result of the compulsory restriction of consumption, a considerable contribution to the initial capital formation by the agricultural population was achieved. So far the argument seems to be justified: that in the Soviet Union the collectivization of agriculture was a precondition for the enforced rapid pace of industrialization.

However, it would be wrong to assume that developing countries could follow the example of the Soviet Union with regard to compulsory restriction of consumption of the agricultural population and their contribution to initial capital formation. The rigorous methods of compulsory deliveries of agricultural products applied in the Soviet Union until 1953 could not be practiced under any other political order. Moreover, the standard of living in most of the developing countries is so low that a restriction of consumption could be considered only if paralleled by a gradual rise in agricultural production. Therefore, the changeover to collective farming would make sense in a developing country only if it leads to an increase in yields. Such increase, however, depends on various other factors and does not automatically follow the conversion from individual to collective farming.

THE CHANGE FROM INDIVIDUAL TO COLLECTIVE FARMING

The experience gained in the Soviet Union in the change from individual to collective farming can be of importance in its economic as well as in its sociopsychological aspects to those developing countries that regard collective farming as one of the possible solutions to the agrarian question. As far as the economic aspect is concerned, an adequate yardstick for an appraisal of the economic results of the change to collective farming in the Soviet Union is needed. More than the figures of Soviet statistics show that the achievements of Soviet agriculture are unsatisfactory. There are the critical remarks of Soviet leaders, for instance, those by Khrushchev in speeches that were published in seven volumes shortly before his fall,[6] and by Brezhnev at the Twenty-Third Party Congress.[7]

Although the supply of foodstuffs has been relatively satisfactory in

[6] N. S. Khrushchev, *Stroitelstvo kommunizma i razvite selskogo khoziaistva v SSSR* (Moscow, Vol. I–III, 1962; Vol. IV–VII, 1963).

[7] L. I. Brezhnev, *Otchetnyi doklad komiteta KPSS XXIII siezdu kommunisticheskoi partii sovetskogo soiuza* (Moscow, 1966), pp. 63–65.

the Soviet Union in 1967, owing to the good harvest of 1966, the importation of 3.1 million tons of grain (and flour) in 1963, about 7.3 million in 1964, and about 6.4 million in 1965[8] clearly show that no satisfactory solution of the agrarian question has yet been found. The question is, however, how far these unsatisfactory achievements of Soviet agriculture are due to general shortcomings of the socioeconomic order in that country—shortcomings that also appear in the industrial sector—or whether they are specific shortcomings of collective farming. Consequently it is necessary to compare the achievements of collective farming with those of other forms of farm management used in the Soviet Union.

There are not sufficient data available in Soviet statistics for a comparison between the kolkhoz and the sovkhoz sectors. It must be taken into account that with the new land campaign emphasizing the sovkhoz form, there are even more sovkhozy than before in areas where owing to natural conditions the level of yields per acre is lower than in other areas of the Soviet Union. A fair comparison between the yields in kolkhozy and sovkhozy can be made only for specific geographical regions with somewhat uniform natural conditions, and Soviet statistics do not contain sufficient data for such a comparison. My own personal experience and observation have led me to believe that, as a rule, the level of yields of the sovkhozy has been somewhat higher than that of the neighboring kolkhozy until now. The ability of the farm manager of course plays an important role in this connection. In both cases we are dealing with large-scale farms, but the management of a sovkhoz seems to be less complicated and provides a better chance of success for an efficient manager than does a kolkhoz. It appeared to me, during the years I spent as an agronomist on Soviet sovkhozy before the war, that it was an easier and more attractive managerial task to be the director of a sovkhoz than to be the chairman of the managerial committee of a kolkhoz.

It is of special interest to compare the yields of collective farms with those of the private sector, which still exists today in the Soviet Union in the form of the small subsidiary holdings of the kolkhoz farmers and some other groups. This comparison is quite favorable to the private sector. Since grain, except for some maize, is not usually grown on the private plots, and since vegetable production as a whole cannot be compared on a yield-per-hectare basis, a comparison is possible only in the production of potatoes. More than half of their total production

[8] *Narkhoz-1965*, pp. 671–72.

falls in the private sector. In Soviet statistics, figures are given for the total number of hectares of potatoes, the number of hectares in the kolkhoz and sovkhoz sectors, the total production of potatoes, and the output of the "socialized sector." These figures indicate that on an average, in 1963–65, the yields per hectare in the private sector were 120 quintals as compared with 77 quintals in the socialized sector.[9]

The higher level of yields in the private sector is obvious to a visitor to a Soviet village, when he compares the crops in the private plots and in the kolkhoz fields. It must be taken into account, however, that nearly all of the manure obtained in private animal husbandry is used on the private plots, while only the manure from the collective livestock is used on the kolkhoz fields, resulting in much less fertilization of the kolkhoz fields.

While the private plots of kolkhoz peasants, workers, and employees comprise only about 3 per cent of the total cultivated area, the share of the private sector in the production of five important agricultural products is from 40 to 70 per cent: 40 per cent of the meat; 39 per cent of the milk; 66 per cent of the eggs; 64 per cent of the potatoes; and 43 per cent of all vegetables (figures for 1966).[10] However, this amazing efficiency is due not only to higher yields in the private sector, but also to the fact that a certain amount of fodder for individually owned livestock is taken from the kolkhozy or from other sources outside of the private sector.

THE EXPERIENCE OF COMMUNIST COUNTRIES
IN THE MANAGEMENT OF STATE FARMS

It is characteristic of the agrarian structure of all Communist countries that in addition to the sector of peasantry that, with the exception of Poland and Yugoslavia, is collectivized, a relatively small sector of state farming exists. Until the beginning of the fifties, in the Soviet Union, the share of the state sector in the total farm land amounted to about 10 per cent, which is the approximate share of the state sector for other Communist countries (Rumania 20.0 per cent [1965], Poland 13.3 per cent [1965], Hungary 14.3 per cent [1965], Eastern Germany [agricultural land] 6.4 per cent [1964]).[11] In 1966 state farms comprised

[9] *Narkhoz-1963*, pp. 251, 253; *Narkhoz-1964*, pp. 291, 293 and *Narkhoz-1965*, pp. 262–63, 284, 291.

[10] *SSSR v tsifrakh—1966*, p. 91.

[11] *Narkhoz-1965*, p. 288; *Anuarul Statistic al Republicii Socialiste Romania 1966*, p. 240; *Rocznik statystyczny* 1966 (Warsaw, 1966), p. 299; *Statisztikai Evkonyv* 1965, p. 142, and *Statistisches Jahrbuch der DDR 1965* (Berlin, 1965), p. 259.

47 per cent of the cultivated area of the Soviet Union. During the ten years prior to 1966, the share of the state sector in the total agricultural production continuously increased, although not in all branches of production equally. In the production of meat, it is 30 per cent; of milk, 26 per cent; of eggs, 20 per cent; of potatoes, 15 per cent; and of sugar beets, 9 per cent.[12]

State farms on which the work is done by hired labor exist in various countries of the world, as, for instance, in the Federal Republic of Germany, where "state domains" are managed by administrators or given on lease to a qualified agricultural entrepreneur. However, the conditions under which the manager of a farm has to operate in a Communist country are different from those in a Western country. In addition, state domains that also serve as experimental and demonstration farms—for example, the experimental farm at Beltsville near Washington, D.C.—are in a different position than sovkhozy, which are not an exceptional but an essential element of the agrarian structure.

Therefore, responsible men dealing with the agrarian question in a developing country should appraise what has been learned in Communist countries in the management of state farms. In this connection, figures given for the average productivity of labor in the sovkhozy as compared with the productivity of farm labor in the United States are of interest. An investigation by Eisendrath shows that in comparison to labor on the sovkhozy, the productivity per work hour in agriculture in the United States is approximately four times higher.[13] These are comparable figures, while the comparison often drawn between the productivity of labor on Soviet kolkhozy and farm enterprises in the United States seems out of place because of the entirely different demographic situations.

THE EXPERIENCE OF THE MACHINE TRACTOR STATIONS

In the kolkhoz sector of the Soviet Union, the MTS played an important role from the beginning of mass collectivization in 1929 until the MTS were dissolved in 1958. But the common use of machinery had developed on a cooperative basis in the precollectivization period, beginning in 1921–22.[14] The number of cooperatives increased essen-

---

[12] *SSSR v tsifrakh-1966*, p. 91.

[13] Ernst Eisendrath, "Die landwirtschaftliche Produktion der USA, der UdSSR und der Bundesrepublik—Ein internationaler Vergleich," Deutsches Institut für Wirtschaftsforschung, Sonderhefte, N.F. Nr. 61 (Berlin: Duncker & Humblot, 1962), p. 40.

[14] V. P. Danilov, in Akademia Nauk SSSR, Institut Istorii, *Sozdanie materialno-*

tially from 1926 to 1929. Their members were largely poor peasants who were not in a position to buy tools or machinery individually, so cooperatives generally had only primitive tools and only a few machines.

Apart from cooperatives for the use of machinery in the precollectivization period, other forms of common use of machinery existed as well, as, for instance, the tractor gangs *(traktornye otryady)* that were organized in the cotton regions of Central Asia and worked for the members of cotton cooperatives. In 1928, such tractor gangs carried out farming operations for approximately 30,000 peasants organized in 113 cotton cooperatives, with a total area of about 29,000 hectares.[15]

The establishment of MTS started with a station for the hire of machinery that was organized at the end of the twenties on a sovkhoz farm near Odessa for the requirements of the neighboring farms.[16] This station, which served as a model for the establishment of the MTS, worked with good success on a contract basis similar to that of the machinery cooperatives. But in this case, the peasants making use of the machinery had to pool their land. A peasant who cancelled his membership, however, could get other land as compensation.

In the collectivization period, the supply of machinery for agriculture was not made directly to the kolkhoz farms but was concentrated in the state-owned MTS. The argument for their establishment was the possibility of a more rational use of machinery. This argument was justified, especially in the initial stage of collectivization, when the supply of machinery was still very scarce.

But from the beginning, other aspects of agrarian policy also played an important role in the establishment of the MTS. The kolkhoz farms, not owning their own machinery, were technically and economically dependent upon the MTS to which they were affiliated. In this way the inclusion of the kolkhoz farms in the system of state planning and state control was facilitated. The MTS, in addition to their technical and economic functions, had to fulfill certain political tasks with regard to the kolkhoz farms affiliated with them, so political departments became a part of their organization. There were also financial advantages for the state in the MTS, since the kolkhoz farms had to pay for their ser-

---

tekhnicheskikh predposylok kollektivizatsii selskogo khoziaistva v SSSR (Moscow: Akademia Nauk SSSR, 1967), pp. 196–98.

[15] Danilov, *Sozdanie . . .* , pp. 344–45.

[16] Danilov, *Sozdanie . . .* , pp. 346–49.

vices with part of their production. In those days this procedure worked as additional taxation imposed on the kolkhoz peasants.[17]

Until some years ago, machine and tractor stations were an essential element of the agrarian structure in Communist countries. When the Soviet Union started to dissolve the MTS or to reduce them to central repair workshops in 1958, most of the other Communist countries followed suit. Similar establishments exist in such non-Communist countries as Sweden, indicating that the functioning of central machine stations for agricultural purposes is not dependent on a particular agrarian system. Such central machine stations may be established in some developing countries (as in India) independently of basic decisions on the agrarian question. Certainly some lessons can be drawn from the experience in Communist countries with this type of establishment and with the cooperative use of machinery in the Soviet Union before collectivization.

THE DEVELOPMENT OF INTERMEDIARY FORMS

In some developing countries today, forms intermediate between collective and individual farming play a certain role and it can be assumed that in the future their importance will increase. Intermediary forms of this kind also exist or have existed in the Communist countries. Four examples follow:

1. The TOZY, cooperative societies for joint use of land, played a certain role in the first stage of collectivization. They differed from the kolkhoz, which after a short transitional period was made the only valid form, insofar as only the land was cultivated jointly, while the agricultural means of production—draft animals and other livestock, and the tools and implements—continued to be used individually. In 1929 the TOZY had pooled 74 per cent of their sown area, 23.1 per cent of the draft animals, and only 2.3 per cent of their productive animals.[18] In many cases in the TOZY the individual rights to land were maintained in such a way that after joint plowing and sowing operations the boundaries of the parcels were reestablished, and individual harvesting was permitted.

However, the TOZY were regarded as transitional establishments from the very beginning. Therefore, no efforts were made to stabilize and develop them further as alternatives to the kolkhoz. They were, instead, used only to reduce the psychological resistance of the peasants

---

[17] Otto Schiller, *Das Agrarsystem der Sowjetunion* (Tübingen, 1960), pp. 27–28.
[18] *Kolkhozy v 1929 g., Itogi obsledovaniia kolkhozov* (Moscow, 1931), p. 156.

against the change to collective farming. As a result there are no scientific studies available that deal in detail with the character and the experience of this intermediary form of farm management.

2. There is a form of enterprise analogous to the TOZY in Communist Eastern Germany, the Agricultural Production Cooperative Type I or LPG Type I.[19] The LPG Type III corresponds approximately to the Soviet kolkhoz, having almost identical bylaws. In the LPG Type I, however, only the cropland is used jointly. The use of the other land, like pastures, meadows, and garden land, and above all animal husbandry, is left to the individual farmers, who also own and control the means of production.

At the time when compulsory collectivization had to be quickly accomplished, this intermediary form was widely used because it made the change to collective farming easier for the farmers. Recently, however, a gradual transformation of the LPG Type I into the final form, LPG Type III, was carried through,[20] making it clear that the intermediary form is not regarded as an alternative to collective farming, but rather as a temporary institution to facilitate the change from individual to collective farming. Therefore, those developing countries that are considering the establishment of similar intermediary forms can learn little from the experience in farm management of the TOZY and the LPG Type I.

3. A special kind of intermediary form is the "agrarian circle," which plays an important role in Polish agriculture.[21] Since the agrarian structure in Poland is still characterized by individual peasant farming, at the present stage these circles should not be regarded as a transitional form toward collective farming, but as an organizational form that will open the small individual holdings to modern technology and make them more efficient. Since many developing countries are faced with similar tasks, the experience of the Polish agrarian circles should be instructive and of value to some of them.

4. As a subunit of the production brigade the *zvenos*, or work links, have played a certain role in the initial stage of collective farming in the Soviet Union. For various reasons, however, the adoption of this form has at times been restricted to special crops. Recent emphasis on the

[19] Matthias Kramer *et al.*, *Die Landwirtschaft in der Sowjetischen Besatzungszone*, Bonner Berichte aus Mittel-und Ostdeutschland, Bd. I (Deutscher Bundesverlag Bonn, 1957), pp. 47–51.

[20] *Statistisches Jahrbuch der DDR 1965* (Berlin, 1965), p. 261.

[21] Tomasz Wybraniec, "Peasant Farming in Poland: Performance and Prospects," paper presented at Conference on Soviet and Peasant Affairs, August, 1967.

work links in the Soviet Union indicates that they deserve attention. The current question there, which has been described by Roy D. Laird,[22] is how to bring the incentive of personal interest to bear on the members of brigades working on the large-scale collective farms. Although theoretically the remuneration for the work on the collective farm is based on the principle of efficiency, a leveling effect—in view of the large gangs —is inevitable. To increase efficiency, some kolkhozy and sovkhozy had experimented with subdividing the brigades into small mechanized work links of only four to six workers. They were allocated a sector of work for which they were responsible, and they had a share of the produce. But these were special cases. At the moment, the subsections —gangs or links—are still units of an essential size. It is reported, for instance, that in the sovkhoz farms of the "new lands" region, gangs with five to ten tractors are assigned an area of more than 1,000 hectares —sometimes exceeding 2,000 hectares—for the time of crop rotation.[23] But even the smaller units, the links (or the *zveno*), usually work with two to four tractors with an area of about 100 hectares.[24] But a change appears to be taking place: some oversized farms are now being reduced in size and in some cases subsections may even become independent farming units.

The discussions going on in the Soviet Union on the importance of the work links and the attempts to take advantage of land use in small groups by subdividing large-scale farms could be instructive for the handling of the agrarian question in developing countries. Communist specialists are inclined to overestimate the advantages of economies of scale, so that it is significant that the advantages of decentralization are under discussion as well. It seems to have been realized that the smaller operational unit may sometimes be superior to the bigger— or oversized—one and that use should be made of the personal interest incentive, often induced if the work is done by relatively autonomous small units.

For the first time in Soviet technical literature the question of the optimum size of large-scale farms is also being dealt with in a somewhat objective way. It is admitted that in the Soviet Union some sovkhozy and kolkhozy are overly large and that a reduction of their size could

[22] R. D. Laird, "The New Zveno Controversy; Forerunner of Fundamental Change?," *Osteuropa-Wirtschaft*, No. 4 (Dec., 1966), pp. 254–61.

[23] A. Cheshkov, "Opyt raboty mekhanizirovanykh otriadov na tselinnykh zemliakh," *Ekonomika selskogo khoziaistva*, No. 8 (1964).

[24] M. Janiushkin and M. Kliuev, "Organizatsiia truda v kolkhozakh i sovkhozakh Severnogo Kavkasa," *Ekonomika selskogo khoziaistva*, No. 1 (Jan., 1965).

be considered. For example, A. Rumanzeva writes that "at present there are many oversized kolkhozy which are difficult to manage" and that "the large enterprise is not always superior to the small one, but only if it does not exceed a certain limit. Therefore it is not an absolute superiority." Consequently "often the large enterprises, if compared with small ones, are less effective."[25]

The experience of the Communist countries in agrarian problems is not described in the technical literature of these countries in a form that would be helpful to an objective orientation of specialists of developing countries. However, as a result of visits of delegations and official representatives of the developing countries to Communist countries, and because a large number of students of developing countries are trained in the universities and colleges of the bloc, Communist ideas and conceptions concerning the agrarian question have some influence. In addition, the developmental aid of Communist countries plays an important role in those countries on which it is concentrated.

To this point, no efforts seem to have been made by the Communist countries to propagate collective farming or to grant developmental aid for experiments with collective farming in the traditional sector of agriculture. It may be that there is a realization that measures toward collectivization would meet great psychological resistance in the traditional sector of agriculture in developing countries everywhere, and that developmental aid granted for such experiments could have undesirable political effects. This may be one of the reasons why, in the developmental aid of Communist countries, the kolkhoz model has not played any role while the sovkhoz model has been adopted here and there.

There are several examples in developing countries of the establishment of state farms with developmental aid from the Communist bloc. One of them is the mechanized large-scale farm in the Indian state of Rajastan, which was established ten years ago with Soviet developmental aid. Other examples are the state farms established in the region of Djalalabad in Afghanistan on newly reclaimed land, and state management of farms formerly belonging to foreigners, which was supported by Soviet technical aid in Ghana at the time of the Nkhruma regime. In Algeria, farms formerly belonging to foreigners were taken over by the state and self-administration of the workers was introduced in these

---

[25] A. Rumanzeva, "Optimalnye razmery kolkhozov," *Ekonomika selskogo khoziaistva*, No. 5 (May, 1965).

enterprises, which makes them similar to the Yugoslavian state farms with their coadministration of workers.[26]

So far in the developing countries—except for India—the model of collective farming is applied almost exclusively in the modern sector of agriculture, i.e., in the former private large-scale farms (sporadic examples in Kenya) or in new settlements, but not in the traditional sector of the old settlements. I do not know of any case in which such experiments with collective farming have been carried out with the technical aid of Communist countries in a developing country. However, Israel has given developmental aid in this field to Burma.

As far as the development of ideas and measures of agrarian policy in the last few years are concerned, one can possibly draw the conclusion that in the years to come what Tunisia calls the "socialist sector of agriculture" may increase in some developing countries. This is the sector that is characterized not by individual peasant farms but by state farms and agricultural-production cooperatives or other forms of joint farming, like those of the Gezira scheme in the Sudan. Consequently it is important to analyze objectively and without ideological prejudice the experience gained in the Communist countries in collective and intermediary forms of farming, so that the experience can be of use to developing countries. Undoubtedly, much work has still to be done in this field.

---

[26] Jürgen von Muralt, "Die Selbstverwaltung in der algerischen Landwirtschaft," *Zeitschrift für ausländische Landwirtschaft*, V, No. 3 (Aug., 1966), 231–42.

HARRY E. WALTERS

Comment

Professor Schiller's excellent paper focuses upon the real point of our efforts: what the experience of other countries—both Communist and non-Communist—implies for the solution to the "agrarian question" in countries now embarking on the development process.

I was pleased that he stressed at the outset that neither the Communist nor the developing countries represent homogeneous groups. The lack of homogeneity among Communist countries is not so much a new political phenomenon as a recent realization of fundamental differences in the political, social, historical, and economic make-up of these countries that have always existed.

In agriculture this is especially important. Countries differ in their natural endowment and in their economic possibilities. In attempting to apply universally the model of the command economy to Eastern Europe and the Soviet collectivization model to Eastern European agriculture, it very quickly became apparent that these models were not universally applicable. Much of the groping of Eastern Europe today for new "systems" and new approaches in agriculture is the result of attempting to find a way out of this unfortunate and unnecessary exercise in duplication of the Soviet model. It would be sad indeed if developing countries did not recognize this lesson so painfully learned in Eastern Europe.

Certainly there can be no argument with Professor Schiller that collectivization is not needed to move labor from the farm sector to the urban and industrial sectors. I would argue that during the development process, industry does not need nor can it employ very much of the total labor force. It needs skills and habits of work appropriate to industry, not just labor. In developing countries today there is, for the most part, a surplus of labor. The cities are crowded, wages are low, and housing is in short supply. Industry is unable to place these people, nor is it able to pay them high wages. The Marxian precondition of an "army of the unemployed" already exists. Moreover, industry has greater drawing power than is usually acknowledged: There are few places in the world where industry has not been able to draw workers to the towns and cities faster than they could be assimilated. If anything, the problem is that people move out of the rural sector too fast. In 1930 Russia did have a vast oversupply of labor in rural areas, but judging by the discussion at the March, 1965, Plenum, the U.S.S.R. faced serious difficulties because of too-rapid flow of labor out of agriculture.

If I understand Professor Schiller correctly when he states " . . . we know from the experience of the Western industrial countries, including the United States, that a rapid process of industrialization is possible without fundamental changes in the agrarian structure, by a natural flow of surplus manpower from the agricultural to the industrial sector," I would agree, but this statement needs some qualification. The favorable situation in the United States of abundant land, scarce labor, large inflows of immigrants, and few landownership entanglements is not likely to be duplicated in most developing countries. In Western Europe most of the industrial countries did have "fundamental changes in the agrarian structure" in the form of enclosure movements, land-reform programs, and other similar developments. I strongly suspect that something of this sort will be necessary in those developing countries where landownership is entangled and exceedingly unequally distributed. This is, of course, a far cry from collectivization, and it is not to move labor so much as to improve the possibilities for a better balance of men and land in agriculture.

Professor Schiller made another important point concerning the contribution of agriculture to the initial capital formation for industrial development. The problems of capital formation in developing countries are indeed difficult, but not as dismal as one often hears. Even in a very low-level, subsistence economy there is room for some savings, if there is some clear expectation that these savings can have some purpose that will benefit the one who saves. The basic Soviet model presupposed that agriculture was a "fixed resource," a pie which could be eaten, but not expanded. The U.S.S.R. and Eastern Europe extracted a surplus from that pie only at the expense of crippling it seriously, and that source of surplus proved not to be as important in the long run as other sources. Worse still, Communist countries have found that a crippled agriculture eventually proved to be a brake on their development and it is now necessary to plow back into agriculture the investment, inputs, and incentives it has so sorely lacked. The unfortunate aspect of this is that the damage has been done and correcting a crippled agriculture is quite difficult.

It seems clear that the development experience of all countries, both non-Communist and Communist, indicates that in the short- and the long-run, improvements in agricultural productivity and efficiency are necessarily hand-in-hand with industrial development. In this way the contribution of agriculture can expand. It was clearly a serious mistake on the part of Stalin and those who emulated him to think that industrialization is synonymous with economic development. But many other students of development have made the same mistake.

It should not be forgotten that this was clearly understood by Stalin's defeated opponents in the late twenties. Thus, there could just as well have been a much different Soviet model than the one that actually emerged under Stalin.

I take Professor Schiller's main point in the latter part of his paper to be that the form and the organization of farming are quite different things. There are many forms of organization, as he points out, that could have been used with possibly more success than collective or state farms. What matters is whether the farm organization is designed to be efficient and productive and maximize the returns of the farm and farm worker. If all decisions are made with this end in view, then the incentive structure, management, use of inputs, and structure and marketing of output can be expected to be quite different than has ever been the case on a Soviet state or collective farm.

Soviet farms—and I would argue that this is true of state as well as collective farms—have never had these as their dominant objectives. Initially, extraction of a surplus, control over the rural population, and prescribed crop structures and farm practices dominated over efficiency and productivity. The first two may have dwindled considerably in the past decade, but the latter two are still very evident, and efficiency and productivity, not to mention maximizing the returns to the farm, are not yet dominant despite all the talk and new programs.

Thus, we should not be as concerned with the particular farm organization, be it family, corporate, or cooperative farm, as with the motivations, objectives, and content of that farm, and we should, as Professor Schiller suggests in his final paragraph, analyze these various farm organizations objectively and without ideological prejudice.

I should like to add here a few remarks that seem relevant to a discussion of "the agrarian question." It has been repeatedly pointed out that "the agrarian question" is not simply an economic question, yet we have often resorted to measuring the efficacy of a country's solution to "the agrarian question" in terms of improving the efficiency or productivity of agricultural output. But this is only a small part of "the agrarian question" and I suspect less difficult to solve than the political, social, and psychological problems that are also involved.

The experience of Western countries has generally shown that "the agrarian question" is something that all countries have faced. It may change over time and vary in intensity, but it is there, nevertheless. In these countries the political power of the agricultural sector has usually resulted in a variety of measures—extension services, protective tariffs, price and income support measures, and rural assistance—being adopted by the governments of these countries to ease "the agrarian problem" as seen from the vantage point of the agricultural sector. In contrast to Communist experience, the rural sector has been more often assisted than exploited.

With respect to the Communist experience this has certain implications. First, it suggests that the agricultural sector does possess and maintain a strong hold on the direction of events during the whole period of industrial development, which was clearly a major concern of Communist leadership during the days before collectivization. Secondly, it suggests that the speed of industrial development concentrates the intensity of "the agrarian question." In the Soviet case it forces upon the farm unit, especially the collectives, a variety of social functions that have nothing to do with productivity: unemployment compensation, old age, retirement "assistance," and others. In other words, the collective farm has to absorb those individuals who are less adaptable to, or less needed in, the rapidly changing society. Any careful economic study of the efficiency of the collective farm must acknowledge these burdens, whether this was the intention of the designers of these farms or not.

The third point is simply that from the point of view of the Stalin regime, "the agrarian question" was neither the welfare of the farmers nor agricultural productivity. Clearly, the objective that motivated Stalin was to achieve industrial and presumably military power both inside and outside the U.S.S.R., and a considerable measure of success was achieved by his procedure. I am not a political scientist, but it would seem that the most important problem facing those truly concerned with "the agrarian question" is whether a balanced policy with respect to agricultural and industrial development, one that takes agri-

cultural productivity and the welfare and desires of the rural population into consideration, will appeal to those men who in fact take power
and push a country forward into the process of economic development.

Technical Transformation
of Agriculture in Communist China

INTRODUCTION

A socialist system of management and an intensive program for technological improvement are considered by the Chinese Communist regime as two essentials for its agricultural development. These are generally referred to as the "socialist transformation" and "technical transformation" of agriculture. According to Mao Tse-tung's proposal, the socialist transformation of agriculture should play a more important role than the technical transformation during the First (1953–57) and the Second (1958–62) Five-Year Plans, and the two should proceed at the same pace during the Third Five-Year Plan. Mao estimated that while the socialist transformation would reach its final stage at the end of the Third Five-Year Plan, it would take four or five five-year plans, or from twenty to twenty-five years, to complete the technical transformation.[1]

At the beginning of the socialist transformation of agriculture, land was redistributed and farms were reorganized according to the "land reform" program. Under a law promulgated in June, 1950, some 700 million *mou* (47 million hectares) of land and large numbers of draft animals, farm tools, and other property were redistributed to farmers.[2] Later, farms were further reorganized with an increasing degree of cooperativization: first into the mutual-aid teams, then into the lower

[1] Hsiung Fu, *Chieh-shao mao chu-hsi kuan-yü nung-yeh ho-tso-hua wen-t'i ti pao-kao* (Introducing Chairman Mao's Report on the Questions of Agricultural Cooperativization) (Peking: Popular Publications Press, 1956), p. 5.

[2] Liao Lu-yen, "A Great Victory in the Land Reform Movement During the Past Three Years," in *San-nien-lai hsin-chung-kuo ching-chi ti ch'eng-chiu* (New China's Economic Accomplishments in the Past Three Years), ed. Committee for the Promotion of China's Trade (Peking: People's Press, 1952), pp. 111–18.

agricultural producers' cooperatives and then into the advanced agricultural producers' cooperatives. Finally, when the "Leap Forward" campaign was launched in 1958, farms in Communist China were placed under the management of the communes. By the end of September that year, 121,936,350 rural households, or 98.2 per cent, had been organized into 26,425 communes.[3]

The socialist transformation of agriculture is now considered to have been completed, and the main attention is being given to its technical transformation.[4] During the "economic recovery period" (1949–52), programs and measures adopted for the technical improvement of agricultural production were mostly piecemeal and of regional or local nature. It was not until the National Program for Agricultural Development, 1956–67, that a comprehensive and nationwide plan was mapped out.[5]

The program was described in its preamble as "a program of endeavor to develop agricultural productivity in our country and raise the living standard of the peasants and of the people as a whole during the period from the First Five-Year Plan to the Third."[6] Besides providing for various measures of improved farming technique, it also set the targets of agricultural production for the period of 1956–67 as follows:

1. During the twelve years beginning in 1956, in areas north of the Yellow River, the Ch'inling Mountains, the Pailung River, and the Yellow River in Tsinghai Province, the average annual yield of grain should be raised from the 1955 figure of 150 to 400 *chin* per *mou* (from 1.12 to 3.00 metric tons per hectare). In areas south of the Yellow River

[3] *T'ung-chi kung-tso* (Statistical Work), Peking, No. 20, 1958, p. 23.

[4] "Actively and Systematically Bring About the Technical Transformation of Our Country's Agriculture," *Jen-min jih-pao* (People's Daily) (*JMJP*), Peking, Nov. 9, 1962, p. 1, editorial.

[5] "Resolution of the Second Session of the Second National People's Congress of the Chinese People's Republic on Striving to Fulfill the National Program for Agricultural Development Ahead of Schedule," *JMJP*, Apr. 12, 1960, p. 1. This program of forty articles was first adopted in a draft form in January, 1956, by the Political Bureau of the Central Committee of the Chinese Communist Party. It was amended slightly at the Third Plenary Session of the Eighth Central Committee of the Chinese Communist Party in September, 1957, and again at the Second Session of the Eighth National Congress of the Chinese Communist Party on May 23, 1958. The program in its present form was approved at the Second Session of the Second National People's Congress of the Chinese People's Republic on April 10, 1960.

[6] *National Programme for Agricultural Development, 1956–1967* (Peking: Foreign Languages Press, 1960), p. 3. This official English translation will be used throughout the present paper.

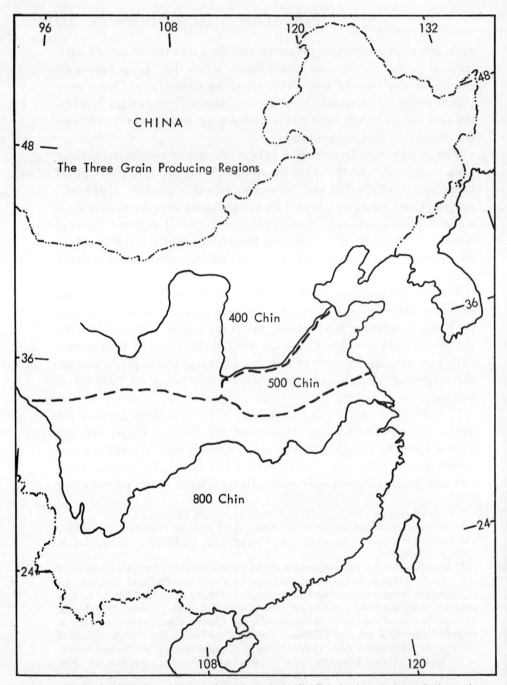

Fig. 1. The broken lines show the approximate boundaries dividing the three grain-producing regions, as specified in the National Program for Agricultural Development, 1956–1967 (article 2). The three regions are commonly referred to by the Chinese Communist authorities as the "400-*chin* region," the "500-*chin* region," and the "800-*chin* region;" that is, regions producing 400, 500, and 800 *chin* per *mou*, respectively. Natural conditions of the regions are described in *Hsin-hua pan-yueh-k'an* (New China Semi-Monthly), No. 2, 1958, p. 94.

and north of the Huai River, the yield should be raised from the 1955 figure of 208 to 500 *chin* per *mou* (from 1.55 to 3.73 metric tons per hectare). In areas south of the Huai River, the Ch'inling Mountains, and the Pailung River, it should be increased from the 1955 figure of 400 to 800 *chin* per *mou* (from 3.00 to 6.00 metric tons per hectare).

2. In the same twelve years, the average annual yield of ginned cotton should be raised from the 1955 figure of 35 *chin* per *mou* to 40, 60, 80 or 100 *chin* per *mou* (0.30, 0.45, 0.60, or 0.75 metric tons per hectare), depending on local conditions.

3. While giving priority to increasing grain production, various localities were expected to exert efforts to develop a diversified agriculture to meet the state production targets for textile raw materials, oil-bearing crops, sugar cane, sugar beet, tea, cured tobacco, fruits, vegetables, medicinal herbs, tropical and subtropical crops, and other economic crops.[7]

The approximate boundaries of the three regions, commonly referred to by the Chinese Communist authorities as the "400-*chin* region," the "500-*chin* region," and the "800-*chin* region," are shown in the accompanying map. Both the boundaries of these regions and their respective grain-production targets appear to have been set arbitrarily, although their natural conditions are apparently different.[8]

Because of its broad coverage, it is possible to discuss here only very briefly some of the more important measures for the technical transformation of agriculture, as provided for in the National Program for Agricultural Development, 1956–67.

WATER CONSERVATION

In view of the poorly distributed rainfall through the seasons and the frequent occurrence of floods and droughts, water is regarded as the life line of China's agriculture. Approximately one fourth of the cultivated land in Mainland China is subject to floods and waterlogging. Since 1949, considerable flood-control work has been carried out or planned for all the major rivers, especially the Yellow, the Huai, and the Hai rivers, which are the most treacherous. It appears, from the number of serious floods reported in recent years, that the harnessing of these rivers has not fared as well as expected.

[7] *Ibid.*, pp. 8–9.

[8] *Hsin-hua pan-yüeh-k'an* (New China Semi-Monthly), Peking, No. 2, 1958, p. 94; Li Hsü-tan, "The Meaning of Using the Pailung River for Demarcating China's Agricultural Regions," *Ti-li chih-shih* (Geographical Knowledge), Peking, No. 3, 1956, pp. 108–10.

According to an official account, the total area equipped with irrigation facilities in China was increased from 16.3 per cent of the total cultivated area in 1949 to more than 60 per cent in 1959. This would mean that China had more than one third of the world's total irrigated area and that it had become one of the most developed countries in water conservation. It was admitted, however, that irrigation could only be carried out "in a normal manner" on less than one third of the cultivated land equipped with irrigation facilities, because many projects were not well constructed and had very low resistance to drought.[9]

In addition to the many projects of various sizes that have been completed or planned, a number of ambitious programs to improve water supply for agricultural use were mapped out, especially during the Great Leap Forward. One proposed program was to transfer southern waters to the north, to balance the geographical inequity of the distribution of water. The basins of the Yellow, the Huai, and the Hai rivers have an inadequate supply for irrigation purposes, while water is so abundant in the south that there is more than enough to supply the cultivated land and develop the wasteland of the entire area. A preliminary plan to draw the water of the upper reaches of the Yangtze to the Yellow River through a series of canals and channels was prepared, but no further action has been taken, apparently because of the tremendous amount of funds, materials, and labor necessary.[10]

Another program frequently discussed was the exploitation of ground water for irrigation.[11] Although many areas in North and Northwest China are subject to frequent threat of drought because of little precipitation and lack of surface water, some are well endowed with deposits of ground water. In considering this program, the possibility of excessive salt in the water was apparently not taken into consideration, and in Hopei Province, as more wells were dug, less and less underground water was obtainable from each well. Like the program to draw water from the south to the north, the plan for increasing the use of ground water reached only a preliminary stage because of financial and technical difficulties.

[9] Ho Chi-feng, "Glorious Achievements of Water Conservation in Rural China in the Past Ten Years," *Shui-li shui-tien chien-she* (Water Conservation and Hydroelectric Construction), Peking, No. 18, 1959, pp. 13–17.

[10] "Certain Questions Concerning the Future Development of China's Water Conservation Work" (a statement by the leader of the Soviet Water Conservation Team at the National Conference on the Hydroelectrics, held in Tientsin in January, 1959), *Shui-li shui-tien chien-she*, No. 6, 1959, pp. 36–42.

[11] Ho Ch'ang-kung, "Investigate Ground Water Resources; Aid Agricultural Production," *Hung-ch'i* (Red Flag), Peking, Nos. 9/10, 1961, pp. 42–47.

One highly publicized project was the construction of a canal network in 1958 and 1959 on some 40,000,000 *mou* (2,680,000 hectares) of cultivated land north of the Huai River in Anhwei Province. The "canalization" project was carried out as a result of the extraordinary floods in 1950, 1952, and 1956, and the equally disastrous drought in 1957 in that area. The project consisted of the construction of nine canals and nearly 130,000 ditches of varying size, and was scheduled to be completed at the end of 1959. The "canalization" was expected to improve the irrigation of some 42,700,000 *mou* of cultivated land in the area, prevent floods and droughts, and provide facilities for navigation and for raising fish and aquatic plants.[12]

Eight other provinces (Hopei, Honan, Shantung, Shansi, Shensi, Liaoning, Kirin, and Heilungkiang) and the Autonomous Region of Inner Mongolia were reported to have also mapped out similar plans for an area of 366,000,000 *mou*, to be completed by the end of 1959.[13] In the latter part of 1959, 70 million people were reported to be working on the project.[14] No details of the progress have been revealed, but "canalization" apparently did not avert the serious floods and droughts in these provinces in 1960.[15] In fact, the project has resulted in salinization and alkalization of land in many areas, because of improper construction and inadequate drainage systems.[16]

In general, the water-conservation program in Communist China has been handicapped by the shortage of steel, cement, timber, and other necessary materials, as well as by lack of equipment, particularly irrigation machines and pumps. This situation, together with the lack of coordination, improper planning and execution of programs, and the withdrawal of Soviet aid, has slowed down many water-conservation plans and projects. It appears quite certain that "ordinary floods and droughts" could not be eliminated within twelve years, or by the end of 1967, as expected in the National Program for Agricultural Development.

FERTILIZATION

For centuries, China has struggled to maintain a moderate level of

[12] Chang Tso-yin, "Canalization of Huaipei," *Chung-kuo nung-pao* (Chinese Agricultural Bulletin), Peking, No. 15, 1958, pp. 3–6.

[13] "Canalization—A Measure for Water Conservation on the Plains," *Chung-kuo nung-pao*, No. 15, 1958, p. 2, editorial.

[14] *JMJP*, Sept. 28, 1959, p. 9; *JMJP*, Dec. 30, 1959, p. 1, editorial.

[15] *JMJP*, Dec. 29, 1960, p. 1.

[16] *JMJP*, Nov. 8, 1961, p. 2.

soil fertility through the use of human and animal wastes, but cropping and heavy erosion have resulted in continuing depletion. To rebuild the soil, large quantities of chemical fertilizers are required in addition to native fertilizers. The programs of multiple cropping, close planting, and deep plowing adopted in recent years have further necessitated heavy applications of fertilizers to keep land productivity at a higher level.

The Communist government has placed equal emphasis on the production of chemical and organic fertilizers, but the latter group remains the principal source of soil fertilization.[17] Hog raising has been encouraged as an important source of manure supply as well as for the production of meat, bristles, and hides. The planting of green-manure crops has been encouraged, not only for fertilizer but also as a measure for water and soil conservation and as feed for livestock. Other sources of organic fertilizers include night soil and wastes from food processing and other industries.[18]

Prior to the Communist regime, ammonium sulphate was the only chemical fertilizer produced in China, with the highest annual output estimated at 227,000 tons.[19] In 1962, thirteen varieties of chemical fertilizers were reported to have been produced.[20] But in 1959, chemical fertilizer was one of a few key industries that fell far short of the production goal for the final year (1962) of the Second Five-Year Plan. The 1959 output of 1,333,000 tons of chemical fertilizers represented only 19 to 27 per cent of the goal for 1962, which was between five and seven million tons. Fifteen million tons was the target set for 1967 in the National Program for Agricultural Development.[21]

Besides many modern fertilizer plants of various sizes, numerous small fertilizer plants have been built in the communes, mostly during the Leap Forward. These native-method fertilizer plants vary widely in size, ranging from little shacks with two or three workers and a few vats to plants capable of producing annually as much as 8,000 tons of liquid ammonia each.

[17] *National Programme for Agricultural Development, 1956–1967*, p. 12.

[18] *JMJP* commentator, "Develop Cultivation of Green Manure to Increase Soil Fertility," *JMJP*, June 5, 1965, p. 2; T'u Feng, "Make Full Use of Fertilizer Resources and Increase Accumulation of Organic Fertilizers," *Hung-ch'i*, Nos. 9/10, 1961, pp. 53–57.

[19] State Statistical Bureau, *Wei-ta ti shih-nien* (Ten Great Years) (Peking: Foreign Languages Press, 1960), p. 92.

[20] Min Chih, "China's Achievements in Building Up Her Chemical Industry," *Shih-shih shou-ts'e* (Current Events Handbook), Peking, No. 7, 1963.

[21] *JMJP*, Jan. 23, 1960, p. 1.

How much fertilizer these small plants have produced is not known, but it is possible that their production constituted an important portion of the total annual chemical fertilizer production during the Leap Forward years. In any case, most of the fertilizers produced by these plants were of low grade, being only one tenth to one twentieth as effective as those produced in modern chemical fertilizer plants, according to a survey made in 1958 in Hopei, Kiangsu, Anhwei, and several other provinces.[22] Because their efficiency was low, many of these small, native-method plants have been expanded and modernized in recent years.

Shortages of equipment, building materials, and raw materials have plagued the production of chemical fertilizers. During the First Five-Year Plan, the larger plants were outfitted with imported equipment, but in more recent years equipment of Chinese manufacture has been increasingly used.[23] The supply of steel, cement, and timber is far below actual need. And of the many phosphorous mines discovered in the past decade, too few of the deposits are of quality adequate to make the manufacture of phosphate fertilizers economically feasible.[24]

Even if chemical fertilizers could be provided in sufficient quantities, efficient use requires technical knowledge that is not yet common in the communes. It has been suggested that specialized teams should be entrusted with the handling of chemical fertilizers, indicating that even the most fundamental forms of organization are still wanting. The use of phosphate fertilizer, particularly, has presented difficulties.[25]

Finally, inadequate storage and transportation facilities have resulted in heavy damages and losses. The condition of some warehouses is so poor that chemical fertilizers are moistened and decompose, and the inefficient inland-river transport and loading techniques have added to the destruction.[26]

Even though data for recent years are not available, it seems hardly

[22] *K'o-hsüeh t'ung-pao* (Scientia), Peking, No. 21, 1958, pp. 656–57.

[23] *Hsin-hua pan-yüeh-k'an*, No. 4, 1958, pp. 97–98; *New China News Agency (NCNA)*, Peking, Feb. 13, 1963; "Chemical Fertilizer Industry Energetically Supports Agriculture," *Ta-kung pao* (The Impartial Daily), Hong Kong, Oct. 1, 1962, p. 15; *JMJP*, Dec. 10, 1962, p. 2; June 11, 1963, p. 1.

[24] Li Ch'ing-kuei, "An Examination of the Problem of Phosphate Fertilizer in China from the Viewpoint of Soil Fertility, Properties of Phosphorus Deposits and Agricultural Conditions," *K'o-hsüeh t'ung-pao*, No. 24, 1959, pp. 820–23.

[25] Chang K'ai-yen, "A Discussion of Certain Questions on the Promotion and Use of Phosphate Fertilizer," *JMJP*, Nov. 15, 1962, p. 5.

[26] Chin Yen, "Pay Attention to Reduce the Damages and Losses of Chemical Fertilizers," *Nan-fang jih-pao* (South China Daily), Canton, Mar. 20, 1963, p. 2.

possible that the annual production of chemical fertilizers would reach the fifteen-million-ton goal for 1967. With the constant shortage of manpower for hog raising and manure collecting, it also is highly doubtful that the supply of organic fertilizers would increase sufficiently to meet the minimum need. To make up deficiencies, Communist China will have to continue to import chemical fertilizers in considerable quantities for many more years.

SOIL CONSERVATION

Of the some 14,400 million *mou* (960 million hectares) of China's total land area, only about 1,650 million *mou*, or 11.5 per cent of the total, is cultivated. According to a Communist estimate, about 600 million *mou*, or more than one third, of the cultivated land are of low productivity with saline, alkaline, acidic, sandy, swampy, or eroded soils.[27] The improvement and conservation of soil thus commands great importance in the country's agricultural development. Efforts have been made by the Communist regime both to make better use of the existing farm land and to reclaim wasteland.

At the end of 1959, more than one half of the 600 million *mou* of land of low fertility was reported to have been improved by means of terracing and other methods of soil conservation.[28] Another account revealed that in 1959, of the more than 700 million *mou* of lowland subject to waterlogging, and other low-yielding land of various types, "initial improvement" had been effected on 64 per cent, 450 million *mou*.[29]

China's forested area covers 1,134 million *mou*, or less than 8 per cent of the total land area, as compared with 39.4 per cent in the Soviet Union, 32.8 per cent in the United States, 68.7 per cent in Japan, and 55.6 per cent in Taiwan. For controlling erosion, floods, and droughts, as well as for relieving the timber shortage and preventing the silting of rivers and reservoirs, several projects to reconstitute and improve natural forests and to create new forests were included in the First Five-Year Plan. These projects were expanded in 1956 into a twelve-year (1953–65) program "to make China a green country." The program envisaged the afforestation of 1,364 million *mou* in twelve years. The new forests, together with the 1,134 million *mou* of natural forests,

---

[27] Liao Lu-yen, "Ten Years of Glorious Accomplishments on the Agricultural Front," *Nung-yeh k'o-hsüeh t'ung-hsün* (Agricultural Science Bulletin), Peking, No. 19, 1959, pp. 652–58.

[28] *Ibid.*

[29] T'an Chen-lin, "Strive for the Fulfillment, Ahead of Schedule, of the National Program for Agricultural Development," *JMJP*, April 9, 1960, p. 1.

would make up a forest domain of 2,498 million *mou* by 1965; and the proportion of forested land in China would then rise to 17 per cent.[30]

Up to the end of 1958, more than 490 million *mou* of land were reported to have been afforested. It was admitted, however, that a number of shortcomings and problems existed in the afforestation program, including the low quality of the work as a whole, the low rate of forest regeneration that had been unable to match the rate of felling, and the serious destruction of forests caused by fire, improper lumbering, and other factors.[31]

Use of the Existing Farmland

Although the annual average multiple cropping index for China as a whole was reported to have risen from 130.9 in 1952 to 145.0 in 1958, the higher figure was still lower than the index given in J. Lossing Buck's study of 16,786 farms in twenty-two provinces for the period of 1929–33, which was 149.0.[32] Although Buck's index might have been somewhat lower if all of Mainland China had been included in the study, the figures given by the Chinese Communists do not indicate much success in their efforts to raise the multiple-cropping index.

In an attempt to increase agricultural production, crop-rotation systems have been changed in some areas without consideration of local conditions. In many cases, the changes have produced unfavorable results, and the deterioration of the soil as a result of overexploitation has frequently been reported. In the greater part of the Yellow River Valley, for instance, the system of three crops in two years was traditional. During the Great Leap Forward, this system was changed to that of two crops in one year. Localities where improving conditions of soil fertility, water conservation, and manpower prevail have benefited from the change, but it has produced undesirable effects on agricultural production in other areas.[33] An effort to extend the area devoted to the

[30] Jean Messines, "Forest Rehabilitation and Soil Conservation in China," *Unasylva* (Rome: Food and Agriculture Organization of the United Nations, 1958), XII, No. 3, 103–20. Percentages of forested land are based on the acreages given in *Production Yearbook, 1965* (Rome: Food and Agriculture Organization of the United Nations, 1966), XIX, 3–6.

[31] "Celebrating Our Country's Ten Great Years," *Chung-kuo lin-yeh* (Chinese Forestry), No. 19, 1959, pp. 2–5, editorial; Ministry of Forestry, "Summing Up Forestation Work in the Past Thirteen Years," *Chung-kuo lin-yeh*, No. 5, 1963, pp. 1–5.

[32] *Wei-ta ti shih-nien* (Ten Great Years), p. 113; J. Lossing Buck, *Land Utilization in China* (Chicago: University of Chicago Press, 1937), p. 274.

[33] Kao Hui-min, "China's Crop Rotation Systems," *Hung-ch'i*, No. 24, 1961, pp. 18–24.

production of two rice crops a year in the basins of the Yangtze River in recent years has also been unsuccessful. Low yields and uncertain harvests continue to exist for the late crop in many localities because of the inadequate water supply and fertilization, as well as the shortage of late-crop varieties of high productivity and quality.[34]

Deep plowing, like close planting, has been adopted as a guiding principle for plant cultivation. In a 1958 directive, it was instructed that all land that could be deeply plowed should be deeply plowed once every three years. It was estimated that more than 800 million *mou* of land had been deeply plowed by the end of 1958. Deep plowing is believed by the Communist authorities to have improved the quality of the soil, prevented plants from bending and being uprooted, promoted microbiological activities, and aided in the prevention of certain kinds of plant diseases and pests.[35] Some Chinese scientists, however, maintain that deep plowing, like close planting, has its limitations and can contribute to agricultural production only under certain circumstances.[36]

Perhaps encouraged by the achievements of intensive cultivation on some of the experimental farms and by the generally good harvest of 1958, the communes were urged in that year to "sow a smaller acreage, realize a higher yield, and reap a greater harvest." Under the "three-three system," the communes were asked to divide the existing farm land into three parts: one third for growing principal crops, one third to lie fallow or for growing fodder crops and green manure, and one third to be dug into reservoirs or used for growing trees and ornamental plants. It was hoped that a greater agricultural production with less labor, capital, and land would be accomplished.[37]

Several months after the adoption of the resolution, it was realized that though the unsparing use of manpower and materials had resulted in a greater summer harvest in some areas in 1959, the gain could not make up for the loss resulting from the reduced acreage for principal crops. A policy to the opposite extreme was adopted immediately and the communes were urged to sow every inch of land available.[38]

[34] Pai Szu-chiu, "How to Produce Two Abundant Crops in a Two-Crop Rice Culture Program?" *Chung-kuo nung-pao tseng-k'an* (Supplement to the Chinese Agriculture Bulletin), Peking, No. 2, 1958, pp. 1–3, 6.

[35] Land Utilization Bureau of the Ministry of Agriculture, "Great Achievements of Soil Work in China," *Chung-kuo nung-pao*, Peking, No. 11, 1959, pp. 12–15.

[36] "Problems Concerning the Rational Close Planting and Deep Plowing of Wheat," *K'o-hsüeh t'ung-pao*, No. 22, 1959, pp. 745–48.

[37] "Resolution on Certain Questions Concerning the People's Communes," *Hsin-hua pan-yüeh-k'an*, No. 24, 1958, pp. 3–11.

[38] *JMJP*, June 11, 1959, p. 1, editorial.

Reclamation of Virgin Land

China has some 1,500 million *mou* (100 million hectares) of virgin soil, of which about 500 million *mou* could be cultivated at a comparatively low capital cost, according to a Communist estimate. During the eleven-year period from 1949 to 1960, 70 million *mou* or less than 5 per cent of the estimated total area of virgin land were reported to have been reclaimed.[39]

An important portion of the reclaimed land has been desert. Estimating the total area of China's deserts at approximately 1,500 million *mou*, or nearly equivalent to the total area of the existing cultivated land, authorities expressed the belief that nearly 300 million *mou* of desert land could be improved to grow some plants or be developed into livestock bases. While making many claims, the government has admitted that desert transformation remains a long and arduous task and that many problems are yet to be solved.[40]

Mountainous or hilly areas occupy roughly 80 per cent of China's total land area. As a part of the regime's intensified efforts to increase agricultural production, party cadres and masses were sent to the mountainous areas in increasing numbers, particularly during the Leap Forward. They participated in producing grain, fruits, livestock, and timber, in building roads, and in developing small industries. In southern China, the cultivation of fruit trees on hilly land has been especially encouraged in order to save as much flat land as possible for planting grain and cotton.[41] Despite the reported progress, the surge into the mountainous areas was performed with little enthusiasm by the cadres and the peasants.[42]

The question of whether China's arable land could be extended by reclaiming virgin land has been discussed frequently. Huang Ping-wei, Director of the Research Institute of Geography, Chinese Academy of Sciences, maintained that most of this land would be hilly and mountainous and wind would carry the soil away, and that there would be too much salt in the soil.[43] Other scientists express the opinion that,

[39] *Kuang-ming jih-pao*, Oct. 9, 1961, p. 4.

[40] Li Ch'iao, "China's Deserts," *K'o-hsüeh ta-chung* (Popular Science), Peking, No. on 6, 1963, pp. 6–8.

[41] Li Lai-jung and others, *Nan-fang ti kuo-shu shang-shan* (Cultivating Fruit Trees Hilly Land in South China) (Peking: Science Press, 1956), pp. 1–120.

[42] *Jen-min shou-ts'e* (People's Handbook), Peking, 1958, pp. 528–32.

[43] Huang Ping-wei, "Several Problems that Should Be Considered in Expanding the Acreage of Cultivated Land," *JMJP*, May 5, 1961, p. 7.

owing to the shortage of machinery, reclamation of virgin land on a large scale is not possible.[44]

The zeal to exploit virgin land has produced unfavorable results. The dams at the two sides of the Grand Canal have been destroyed in many places because trees have been cut down for planting of wheat. The cultivation of steep land in many areas has caused soil erosion.[45] Many reclamation projects have been carried out without coordination with water and soil conservation work, and as a result, forest land and grass-land have been destroyed.[46]

AGRICULTURAL MECHANIZATION

During the First Five-Year Plan, many innovations in farm imple-ments were developed as a first step toward semimechanization. This was followed by a combination of gradual agricultural mechanization with the use of native tools and implements under the "walking on two legs" policy. It was hoped during the Leap Forward to accomplish more than half the task of agricultural mechanization in seven years, and to complete it in ten years.[47]

By the end of 1960, 5 per cent of the farm land of the country was cultivated with machines, although the target for that year was 6.9 per cent.[48] Toward the end of 1962, the area farmed by tractors accounted for less than 10 per cent of the cultivated land. In that year, 100,000 tractors were reported to be in operation. Although this was more than 100 times the number of tractors in operation in 1949, it was acknowl-edged that at least 1,000,000 tractors were needed for the estimated 1,600 million *mou* of cultivated land in China.[49]

Of the 45,330 tractors in operation in 1958, only 957, or a little over 2 per cent, were produced in China. Production figures for more recent years are not available, although it is claimed that the country now is manufacturing many types of tractors, despite the shortage of raw materials, particularly steel. Since the beginning of the "industrial aid to agriculture" campaign in 1960, the few centers of the steel in-dustry have been experimenting with new products suitable for agri-

[44] *Kuang-ming jih-pao*, Oct. 9, 1961, p. 4.

[45] *JMJP*, Nov. 13, 1961, p. 2; Mar. 23, 1962, p. 2.

[46] Chao Ming-fu, "Water and Soil Conservation Along the Middle Reaches of the Yellow River," *JMJP*, Nov. 14, 1963, p. 2.

[47] Ch'en Cheng-jen, "Speed Up Technical Transformation of Agriculture," *Hung-ch'i*, No. 4, 1960, pp. 4–10.

[48] *JMJP*, April, 1960, p. 3; Oct. 28, 1960, p. 4.

[49] *JMJP*, Nov. 9, 1962, pp. 1–2, editorial.

cultural machinery, but the amount is not commensurate with the needs of the country. Certain types of steel products and essential parts of agricultural machinery cannot be produced in China and therefore have to be imported.[50]

Aside from the lagging production, other serious problems have handicapped the mechanization of agriculture. Tractors were first managed by state-operated tractor stations, but since 1958 many of them have been turned over to the communes. The depreciation rate and maintenance costs have been high, partly because of "the lack of the sense of political responsibility to take good care of tractors on the part of drivers." In 1961, about 20 per cent of tractors and 20 to 30 per cent of irrigation machines needed repair, yet there were no repair networks nor sufficient spare parts. Many tractors were without farm tools suitable for machines, and irrigation and drainage machines were without pipes and pumps. Moreover, operators and maintenance personnel of tractors and other farm machines generally had undergone only a short period of technical training.[51]

Adding to the difficulties is the fact that much farm land, even after collectivization, is not suitable for mechanized farming. In many land units there are abandoned wells, ditches, or boundary stones. On others, irrigation canals divide the land into such small areas that mechanization is virtually impossible. Finally, some of the roads, bridges, and tunnels between the farms are not wide or strong enough for large farm machines, making travel time consuming and difficult.[52]

The problems of agricultural mechanization were thoroughly discussed at the Tenth Plenary Session of the Eighth Central Committee of the Chinese Communist Party, held in November, 1962. Those at the meeting realized that the "arduous and complicated" task of mechanization of agriculture would require a period of twenty to twenty-five years, rather than ten years as originally planned, and that semi-mechanized and improved tools would remain in a very important position for a long time to come.[53]

Special mention should be made of electrification, frequently publicized as an important measure to transform the country's agriculture. At the end of 1958, there were only 4,878 rural hydroelectric power

[50] *JMJP*, Jan. 7, 1962, p. 1.

[51] Chao Hsüeh, "Current Problems in Agricultural Mechanization," *Ta-kung pao*, Peking, May 15, 1961, p. 3.

[52] *JMJP*, Dec. 8, 1962, p. 2.

[53] "Actively and Systematically Bring About the Technical Transformation of Our Country's Agriculture," *JMJP*, Nov. 9, 1962, p. 1, editorial.

plants in Mainland China with a total capacity of 151,826 kilowatts, or an average of 31 kilowatts.[54] Most of these plants were built in 1958. Like the numerous native fertilizer plants and primitive blast furnaces for steel production constructed during the Great Leap Forward, many of these small hydroelectric plants were ineffective.[55] Only a small number of larger hydroelectric plants were constructed in connection with multiple-purpose projects pertaining to flood control, and water supply for industrial, domestic, and agricultural use. These plants, in general, are considerably more efficient than the small ones.[56] The development of rural hydroelectric plants is handicapped by the shortage of technical personnel and equipment, by the high cost of construction, and by a lack of over-all planning and accurate data for planning. Surveys of hydraulic resources have been conducted only in some isolated regions.

Up to the end of 1958, only 2,112 thermal electric power plants had been constructed, owing largely to the necessity of importing the more complicated equipment and the shortage of fuels, which are also in great demand by other industries.

Use of electricity is severely curtailed in agricultural areas of China because shortages of metals and cement have slowed the development of power transmission lines. Electric-power networks of 35-, 10-, 6.6-, and 3.3-kilovolt transmission lines are the most common ones, but even these networks are rather scarce.[57]

In 1963, there still was no supply of electricity in half of the country's rural areas.[58] Electric power in rural China is used primarily for the processing of agricultural products, especially rice husking and flour grinding, for the preparation of fertilizers and animal feed, and for illumination. Its use for irrigation is not widespread. By the end of 1961, the total area of land irrigated by use of electricity amounted to approximately 10,000,000 *mou*, or about 1 per cent of the total area irrigated by all means.[59] Owing to continued financial and technical difficulties,

---

[54] One may realize how small this average capacity is by comparing it with the 500,000-kilowatt hydroelectric generators that the Soviet Union offered to sell to the United States in March, 1967, for the expansion of power capacity of the Grand Coulee Dam in the state of Washington, as reported in *The New York Times*, April 2, 1967, p. 17.

[55] *JMJP*, Jan. 26, 1960, p. 7.

[56] *Shui-li fa-tien* (Hydroelectrics), Peking, No. 12, 1958, p. 54.

[57] B. Bannikov, "Rural Electrification in the Chinese People's Republic," *Tekhnika v selskom khozyaistve*, No. 2, 1960, pp. 88–92; translated in *JPRS*: 4529 (Washington, D.C.: Joint Publications Research Service, April 12, 1961).

[58] Hsü Shou-p'o, "About Rural Electrification," *K'o-hsüeh ta-chung*, No. 5, 1963, pp. 8–9.

[59] B. Bannikov, "Rural Electrification in the Chinese People's Republic."

it is clear that rural electrification in China has not improved substantially in recent years.

SEED IMPROVEMENT

With the wide variation in natural conditions over its vast territory, China has a great wealth of plant materials, but since it depends so much upon its rice and wheat for food and cotton for clothing, most attention has been given to the improvement of these crops. Rice breeding, particularly, was one of the fields in which considerable progress had been made prior to the Communist period.

The total area sown to better seeds for the principal crops increased from 126.7 million *mou* in 1952 to 1,800 million *mou* in 1959, or from 6.2 per cent to 80.0 per cent of the total area sown, according to government sources.[60] However, in 1959, Liu Ting-an, Director of the Seed Administration, Ministry of Agriculture, acknowledged that the development had been too hasty and much confusion had resulted from a lack of healthy systems of breeding, multiplication, and inspection.[61]

An acute shortage of seeds was admitted in a general statement at the beginning of 1961, when the situation became very serious. An editorial in the *People's Daily* revealed that the shortage of seed was not confined to regions that had suffered natural disasters. In Hopei, Shansi, Kirin, Hupeh, Hunan, Ninghsia, and other provinces, much of the high quality seed that was propagated a few years before had been spoiled by heat, insects, or dampness in the granaries and could not be used for sowing. In some areas, the value of seeds of high quality had been lost because they were sown together with other types of seeds. When natural calamities had affected the fields, seeds of lower quality were used in resowing. In other areas, care was not used in the selection of seeds at the time of harvest.[62]

During the Leap Forward, party cadres in many localities urged or ordered the communes to discard inferior seed in favor of improved seed, although the latter was not available in sufficient quantities. This zeal to introduce and popularize new varieties of crops, in many cases

[60] Liu Ting-an, "Great Achievements of Seed Improvement Work in China in the Past Decade," *Chung-kuo nung-pao*, No. 15, 1959, pp. 22–23, 27; T'an Chen-lin, "Strive for the Fulfillment, Ahead of Schedule, of the National Program for Agricultural Development," *JMJP*, April 7, 1960, p. 1.

[61] Liu Ting-an, "Great Achievements of Seed Improvement Work . . . ."

[62] *JMJP*, Jan. 17, 1961, p. 1, editorial: *JMJP*, Nov. 11, 1961, p. 2; Dec. 3, 1961, p. 2; Nov. 25, 1961, p. 1; Jan. 27, 1962, p. 1; Mar. 15, 1962, p. 2; June 3, 1962, p. 1; Sun Chia-tseng, "Let Good Strains Permanently Preserve Their Youth," *K'o-hsüeh ta-chung*, No. 4, 1964, pp. 121–22.

totally ignoring local conditions, had worsened the seed situation and had drawn many criticisms.[63]

In an article in *Kuang-ming jih-pao*, Ts'ai Hsü and Chang Shu-ch'in of the Peking University of Agriculture suggested that attention should not be confined to popularizing a few newly developed varieties of seed and that numerous kinds of "farm household seed" (also known as "local seed") should be used according to the geographical and climatic conditions and cultivation systems of localities. A newly developed strain may increase production in certain areas, but farm household seed was developed by peasants to meet certain local requirements and should therefore be included as part of the seed used. Such seed is especially important in the provinces or regions where a great variety of conditions exists.[64]

At the inaugural meeting of the Chinese Society of Crops, held in Changsha, Hunan, on December 20–28, 1961, it was almost unanimously agreed that, in the future, development of new seed should be carried out with consideration of the standard of production over wide areas, and should be adapted to a variety of regions. This means that it is as important to develop seed for production over a wide area as to produce special high-quality seed.[65]

PLANT PROTECTION

The National Program for Agricultural Development called for the general elimination by the end of 1967 of those insect pests and plant diseases most harmful to crops.[66] Included in the list were locusts, rice borers, cotton aphids, wheat smut, and army worms.

Native agricultural drugs made of various plants and minerals available locally are widely used in Communist China for the control of plant diseases and insect pests. They have several advantages over chemical pesticides: China has abundant resources of plants and other materials for making these drugs; production is simple and the cost is lower; and many of the drugs can be applied widely and safely to a great variety of crops. On the other hand, the supply of some materials for making drugs is seasonal and limited to certain localities, and more

---

[63] Lu Li, "Guidance of Agricultural Production Should be Started from Practicality," *JMJP*, Nov. 12, 1960, p. 7.

[64] Ts'ai Hsü and Chang Shu-ch'in, "Functions of the Farm Household Seeds in the Current Agricultural Production," *Kuang-ming jih-pao*, July 30, 1962, p. 1.

[65] *Kuang-ming jih-pao*, Jan. 3, 1962, p. 1.

[66] *National Programme for Agricultural Development, 1956–1967*, pp. 15–16.

labor is needed in their production and application than is required for chemical pesticides.

In 1958, 80 per cent of the pesticides used were native agricultural drugs, while only 20 per cent were made of chemicals. Although more than thirty kinds of chemical pesticides were reportedly produced in 1964,[67] their quality was not satisfactory. Some pesticides were not processed in accordance with specifications; there was no strict inspection; and instructions were not adequate for the protection of users of highly poisonous materials.[68] Even if production methods are improved, native drugs will probably continue to be in greater use for some time because such chemicals as mercury, copper, and benzene are badly needed in other industries.[69]

Many types of equipment for applying pesticides are reported to have been developed, but the sprayers, dusters, and other appliances produced are generally of low quality and efficiency and are prone to break down, especially since most peasants have very little knowledge of using, maintaining, and repairing them.[70] The use of airplanes for applying pesticides has reached only an experimental stage, because of its high cost.[71]

Although progress has been made in the development of prognostic, warning, and quarantine services, serious outbreaks of plant diseases and insect pests have been reported in recent years.

CLOSE PLANTING AND FIELD MANAGEMENT

Close planting was emphasized during the Great Leap Forward as one of the guiding principles for plant cultivation.[72] In 1958, from 20 to 30 *chin* of wheat seed were sown to one *mou* (from 0.15 to 0.22 metric tons of seed per hectare) in many areas, and the resulting harvest was reported to be from 400 to 600 *chin* per *mou*. This compares with yields of 200 to 300 *chin* per *mou* at the normal density of sowing of 6 to 15 *chin* per *mou*. For rice, a target was from 35,000 to 40,000 clusters per

[67] *NCNA*, Peking, July 19, 1965.

[68] Shen Ch'i-i, "The Role of Plant Protection in Insuring the Increase of Agricultural Production," *Hung-ch'i*, No. 22, 1962, pp. 33–41.

[69] Lu Yu-lan, "Ten Big Advantages in Popularizing Native Agricultural Drugs," *K'un-ch'ung chih-shih* (Knowledge of Insects), Peking, V, No. 1, 1959, 5–6; P'ei Li-sheng, "Comments Concerning the Energetic Development of Scientific Research on Native Agricultural Drugs," *ibid.*, pp. 49–53.

[70] Shen Ch'i-i, "The Role of Plant Protection . . . , pp. 33–41.

[71] Yang Hsien-tung, "Strive for Great Success on the Front of Plant Protection," *Chung-kuo nung-pao*, Peking, No. 6, 1963, pp. 1–4.

[72] *National Programme for Agricultural Development, 1956–1967*, p. 14.

mou (from 525,000 to 600,000 clusters per hectare) and from 350,000 to 400,000 seedlings per *mou*.[73]

Apparently because of the failure to increase agricultural production by close planting, a series of articles on this problem was published in the leading newspapers and scientific journals in 1959–61. While some writers still placed an emphasis on close planting as a means to increase agricultural production, many scientists, citing the results of some experiments on rice, wheat, cotton, corn, and other principal crops, warned that it should be practiced only to a limited degree according to certain circumstances.

In the past few years, the word "rational" has been emphasized in discussing the problems of close planting. In proclaiming the accomplishments in this field since the Great Leap Forward, however, Vice-Premier T'an Chen-lin merely stated: "Rational close planting has been widely popularized. Too-close planting and too-sparse planting are both on the wane, and the laws of rational close planting are being grasped by more and more people."[74]

Field management refers particularly to the special care and detailed handling required to make farms "look like gardens." It means the management from the time of sowing or planting to the time of harvest, including transplanting, pruning, intertillage, weed control, protection of seedlings, as well as timely application of water and fertilizers. It also includes measures to prevent crop damage by frost, bitter cold, and strong wind. The purpose of field management is "to adjust the physiological activities of crops during various stages of their growth."[75] The communes have been repeatedly asked to give 30 per cent of their efforts to sowing and 70 per cent to field management. Very little, however, has been said about the success of this program.

CONCLUSION

It is clear that the Chinese Communist regime has made some progress in carrying out the technical measures required in the National Program for Agricultural Development, but the accomplishments in general have been far behind the targets. This is true in practically all

---

[73] "What Are the Key Factors in the Realization of a Continued Leap Forward in Agriculture This Year?" *Ch'iu-shih* (Seeking the Facts), Hangchou, No. 3, 1960, pp. 1–13.

[74] T'an Chen-lin, "Strive for the Fulfillment . . ." (note 29).

[75] Research Institute of Crop Breeding and Cultivation, the Chinese Academy of Agricultural Science, "Field Management," *Hsin-hua pan-yüeh-k'an*, Peking, No. 12, 1959, pp. 129–30.

the technical phases of the program, including the production of fertilizers and tractors, and construction of water- and soil-conservation projects, the improvement of seed, and the control of plant diseases and insect pests. What is even more significant is that, qualitatively, the measures taken by the Chinese Communist regime have been far below the minimum standards that are required to improve agricultural production, as evidenced by the low efficiency of most of the irrigation projects and the inferior quality of fertilizers, pesticides, and farm machinery.

As pointed out at the beginning of this paper, the National Program for Agricultural Development, 1956–67, besides providing for various measures to improve farming technique, also called for the average of annual yield of grains to reach 400, 500, or 800 *chin* per *mou* and that of ginned cotton to reach 40, 60, 80, or 100 *chin* per *mou*, depending on local conditions, within the twelve years beginning in 1956. To what extent have these targets been fulfilled? In 1959, a total of 504, or 28 per cent, of the 1,786 grain-growing *hsien* (counties) in the country fulfilled or surpassed the target of 400, 500, or 800 *chin* per *mou* on 286,-770,000 *mou*, or 24 per cent, of a total of 1,200 million *mou*. In the same year, 204, or 20 per cent, of the 1,027 cotton-growing *hsien* fulfilled or surpassed the target of 60, 80, or 100 *chin* of ginned cotton per *mou* on 36,484,000 *mou*, or 42 per cent of a total of 85 million *mou* of land "from which cotton was actually harvested."[76] Data are not available to indicate the extent to which the targets for grain and cotton yields have been fulfilled since 1959. In view of the unsatisfactory progress in carrying out technical programs and the fact that these goals are, as a whole, unrealistically high, it is very doubtful that their fulfillment could have been attained according to schedule.

Even so, the Second National People's Congress, at its second session on April 10, 1960, adopted a resolution calling upon the people to exert concerted efforts in the struggle for realizing the National Program for Agricultural Development, 1956–67, two or three years ahead of schedule.[77] This was based on the claims that agricultural production in 1958 and 1959 registered a "big leap forward," with an increase of 35 to 46 per cent in grain production and an increase of 28 and 47 per cent in cotton production over 1957, and the assumption that a continuation

---

[76] T'an Chen-lin, "Strive for the Fulfillment . . . ." No data were revealed for the cotton fields which yielded less than 60 *chin* per *mou*, "because many localities kept no statistics on whether the cotton yield was above or below 40 *chin* per *mou*."

[77] *JMJP*, April 11, 1960, p. 1.

of the efforts to bring the advantages of the three red banners (the general line, the leap forward, and the communes) into full play would further accelerate the implementation of the program. These optimistic illusions continued until the end of 1960, when the disastrous crop failures of 1959 and 1960 were revealed. Natural calamities were blamed as the sole cause of the failures.

There is, however, massive evidence that the failure of agriculture in recent years, particularly from 1959 to 1961, was at least partly man made. Improper planning and execution of programs and projects have resulted in technical blunders. Ironically, despite the fact that the "walking on two legs" policy calls for a combination of indigenous and foreign methods, the Chinese Communists have both mocked at scientific principles as "old superstitions" and neglected contemptuously the age-old cultivation traditions of the Chinese peasants. The digging of innumerable canals in the canalization program in 1959 and 1960 without a scientific blueprint has not improved the irrigation situation, but has caused salinization and alkalization of land in many areas. The adoption of the "smaller acreage, higher yield, and greater harvest" system in 1958 and the sudden shift to the "larger acreage and greater harvest" system in 1959 both resulted in a loss in grain production. Both the arbitrary changes in crop-rotation systems in some areas without consideration of local conditions and the peremptory order for deep plowing and close planting on all farm land have led to the decline in the productivity of the soil. Also, the indiscriminate popularization of high-yield varieties of crops, meanwhile discarding the low-yield but indispensable varieties, has aggravated the shortage of seeds.

Apart from the improper planning and execution, there are other causes for failure to fulfill the targets required for the technical transformation of Chinese agriculture. A serious difficulty is the shortage of trained personnel on all levels. For carrying out various agricultural programs and plans, the government has established many institutions of research, education, and extension. As a focal point for the development of agricultural research, the Chinese Academy of Agricultural Science was founded in Peking in 1957 by the Ministry of Agriculture. The academy has established several regional branches, more than twenty specialized research institutes, and a number of experimental farms, demonstration farms, rural research bases, and agricultural extension stations. Most provinces and some large municipalities, *hsien*, and communes also have set up their own institutions or stations for agricultural research and extension.

Large numbers of agricultural workers at senior, intermediate, and junior levels are reported to have been trained. By 1964, there were more than thirty agricultural universities or colleges, but the equipment as well as the faculty among these institutions vary widely. From 1949 to 1965 a total of 119,500 students graduated from the agricultural universities or colleges, according to an official account.[78]

At the intermediate level, many secondary technical schools offer short courses in different subjects, including agriculture. Since early 1958, however, more than 200,000 agricultural middle schools have been established as the most important institutions for training intermediate technical personnel in agriculture. The academic standards of these schools, as well as their accommodations and facilities, are generally low, and have degenerated since the adoption of the part-farming and part-study system in 1964. This system was in pursuance of the party policy that education must serve proletarian politics and be linked with productive labor.

Despite numerous claims to accomplishments in agricultural education, research, and extension, Communist China is still confronted with an acute shortage of personnel needed for the technical transformation of agriculture. Even so, much of the thin stock of agricultural scientists has been misused. Before the three consecutive years (1959–61) of bad harvest, agricultural scientists and other "high-grade intellectuals" were alternately oppressed and caressed. They were classified according to their attitude toward Communism rather than by their achievements. "Agricultural geniuses," such as Ch'en Yung-k'ang, a rice farmer of Kiangsu Province, were discovered among peasants. Suggestions by scientists were generally ignored.

In recent years, the government's attitude toward scientists has changed. The disastrous agricultural failure and the absence of Russian specialists have necessitated a conciliation with China's own experts. In a directive of the Tenth Plenary Session of the Eighth Central Committee of the Chinese Communist Party, released on September 28, 1962, the government was urged to strengthen scientific and technological research, particularly that in agriculture; to subject personnel to vigorous training; and to promote cooperation with the intellectuals so that they may fully play their role as they should.[79] Shortly after

[78] Chiang I-cheng, "Positively and Steadily Push Forward the Revolution of Agricultural Education; Render Still Better Services to Socialist Agriculture," *Kuangming jih-pao*, Aug. 19, 1965, p. 2.

[79] *JMJP*, Sept. 29, 1962, p. 1.

this, in October, 1962, a conference to study measures for strengthening research work in agricultural science and for training more young agricultural scientists and technicians was called in Peking, jointly by the State Scientific and Technological Commission and the Ministry of Agriculture.[80]

Today, scientists are reinstated in their jobs. The political indoctrination still goes on, but the atmosphere of political pressure is less oppressive. The scientists are more outspoken, saying things that they dared not have said when the pressure of the Great Leap Forward was upon them. But it would appear that as long as the political indoctrination of the scientists and the arbitrary interference by the cadres exist, even in a lesser degree, the progress of the technical transformation of agriculture will be handicapped. From many warnings and criticisms published in the Chinese newspapers in recent years, one can see that the blunders of ignorant cadre leaders have not ceased.

The second difficulty in carrying out the program of technical transformation of Chinese agriculture is the deficiency of funds for capital construction investment. In its efforts to industrialize the country, the Communist regime has placed high priority on the development of heavy industry. The distribution of basic-construction investment among various major sectors of the national economy in the First Five-Year Plan period was as follows: for heavy industry, 49 per cent; for light industry, 7 per cent; for agriculture, 8.2 per cent; for transportation and communications, 18.7 per cent; and for other (trade, banking, storage, culture, education, public health, public utilities, and so on), 17.1 per cent. Thus, the investment for heavy industry was six times as much as that for agriculture; and of the total investment for industry, 87.4 per cent was allocated to heavy industry, and 12.6 per cent to light industry.[81]

When the recommendations on the Second Five-Year Plan (1958–62) were adopted at the Eighth Plenary Session of the Chinese Communist Party in September, 1956, heavy industry again received top priority. In comparison with the First Five-Year Plan, the total amount of basic investment during the second five years was expected to double, with the share for industry (heavy and light) increasing from 56.0 per cent to about 60 per cent, and that for agriculture from 8.2 per cent to 10 per cent.[82]

[80] *JMJP*, Oct. 11, 1962, p. 1.
[81] *Jen-min shou-ts'e*, 1956, pp. 17–18; *Hsin-hua pan-yüeh-k'an*, No. 8, 1959, p. 48.
[82] *Jen-min shou ts'e*, 1957, pp. 58–64.

Although exact data are not available, there are indications that the shortage of funds for capital-construction investment for agriculture has continued despite the adoption of the policy in 1960 of "developing agriculture as the foundation of the national economy." It was reported in 1961 that 41 per cent of capital-construction investment allowed to the Chinese chemical industry was allocated for the production of chemical fertilizers, a higher proportion than in any previous year. Although the actual amount of funds allocated was not revealed, it is questionable whether this percentage could have been attained, because in recent years Communist China also has given more attention to pesticides, plastics, textiles, rubber goods, and other industries, many of which require the use of chemicals.[83]

Another difficulty in the technical transformation of Chinese agriculture is the shortage of certain necessary materials and equipment such as rolled steel, copper, cement, and lumber. The production of chemical fertilizers has been handicapped by the weak deposits of phosphate and potash; that of chemical pesticides has been impeded by the shortage of such materials as mercury, copper, and benzene.

The sharply declining supply of Russian equipment and materials, together with the departure of Soviet experts, has affected a number of important agricultural construction plans. In recent years, increasing numbers of projects have been designed and constructed by Chinese engineers with Chinese-produced equipment and materials, such as the first-stage installation of the Wu Ching nitrogenous fertilizer plant in Shanghai, completed in 1963. However, the absence of Russian aid has created a serious handicap.

Despite the program of intensive industrial aid to agriculture carried out since 1960 as the most important measure to implement the policy of "developing agriculture as the foundation of the national economy," industry apparently has not been able to provide adequate amounts of steel, copper, cement, timber, benzene, and other materials that are badly needed in many fields. To increase the supply of these materials for the modernization of agriculture means that with its already heavy tasks, industry would have to shoulder an extra burden.[84]

These are among the principal problems that the Chinese Communist regime has been facing in carrying out its program for the technical transformation of agriculture. Since the three consecutive years (1959–

[83] *NCNA*, Nanking, Aug. 27, 1961.
[84] Leslie T. C. Kuo, "Industrial Aid to Agriculture in Communist China," *International Development Review*, IX, No. 2 (June, 1967), 6–10, 29.

61) of crop failure, the government has taken many remedial measures. Some improvement has been made, but there seems to be a long way to go. It is generally believed that even with more favorable weather and economic conditions, as well as with some relaxation of the organization framework of communes, no substantial increase of agricultural production in Mainland China should be expected until the planning and execution of the program for technical transformation of agriculture have been sufficiently improved.

J. LOSSING BUCK

Comment

Dr. Kuo's paper is the first study, among many on Communist China, devoted primarily to the conditions preventing the achievement of the accomplishments intended or claimed by the Communists. He is to be congratulated on his analysis.

The term "technical transformation of agriculture" implies a much greater change under the Communists than has been practical, or even possible. After all, Chinese farmers over the centuries had developed the art of farming to a very high degree, including the extensive development of irrigation, terracing of land, and considerable land reclamation. This was truly "transformation" over a long period of time. Without question, irrigation and reclamation through the use of modern methods could still be extended but could not equal past accomplishment. Therefore, although the term "transformation of agriculture" has been used by many Chinese commentators on the Mainland, the term "technological improvements" would appear to be more appropriate.

Many of the quotations from Communist sources throughout the manuscript indicate the magnitude of the plans for technological improvement. Other quotations are chiefly exaggerated claims of accomplishment. In most cases, Dr. Kuo has indicated reasons why the goals, or even the claimed results, were not achieved. Quotations of Communists' claims of achievement have little real value unless an assessment is made of the probable degree of reliability.

An example of misleading Communist statistics is found in the section on water conservation, concerning irrigation. It reads ". . . irrigation facilities in China were increased from 16.3 per cent of the total cultivated area in 1949 to more than 60 per cent in 1959." The area irrigated indicates an impossible increase from 16 million hectares in 1949 to 66.7 million hectares in 1958. Three additional Communist

sources and two pre-Communist sources indicate the degree of inaccuracy of the above data.[1] One source gives 20.8 million hectares in
1949 and 38.3 million in 1957. Another indicates 26 million hectares
irrigated in 1949 and 37.6 million in 1956. A third source records 25.7
million of hectares in rice in 1949 and 32.7 million in 1958. Since nearly
all rice is irrigated, the 25.7 million in rice in 1949 leads to the conclusion that the 16 million for 1949 is a gross understatement. The 32.7
million in rice in 1958 points to the 66.7 million hectares stated as irrigated in 1958 as an immense exaggeration.

As to pre-Communist sources, the *Statistical Monthly*, January–
February, 1932, of the Legislative Yuan, Nanking, indicates 24.8
million hectares irrigated when the total cultivated land figure is
corrected, as compared with the quoted Communist figure of 16
million hectares for 1949. The *Land Utilization in China* survey revealed
45.8 per cent of the crop area (cultivated area) as irrigated, 1929–33,
for twenty-two provinces. When other areas of Mainland China are
included, the percentage irrigated may be estimated at 39.4 per cent,
or 40.3 million hectares of cultivated land for Mainland China. Apparently the Communist claim of 66.7 million hectares irrigated in
1958 was caused by a mistaken interpretation of the following quotation
from the periodical *Chinese Youth*: "Of the cultivated area of the country,
one-third has good irrigation facilities and adequate water supply;
one-third has no facilities or very poor facilities." This quotation is an
ambiguous statement because the last phrase does not include all
nonirrigated but cultivated land, nor does it indicate the proportion
with very poor facilities. Apparently the claim of 66.7 million hectares
irrigated in 1958 was obtained by adding the two one-thirds to obtain
the amount irrigated. Thus, two thirds of the claimed cultivated area
of 107.8 million hectares in rice in 1958 gives a clue to the exaggerated
claim of 66.7 million hectares in 1958 as irrigated. Even Chou En-lai
quoted this amount as evidence of the great progress in irrigation
development.

The Russian water expert, Krylov, estimated China's irrigated area
in 1957 to be 39.8 million hectares, or 35.6 per cent of the cultivated
area of 111.8 million hectares claimed in 1957. His estimate is slightly
above the Communist figure of 38.3 million hectares for 1957.

[1] John Lossing Buck, Owen L. Dawson, and Yuan-li Wu, *Food and Agriculture in
Communist China* (New York: Frederick A. Praeger, Inc., 1966). For a full analysis on
irrigation, see Dawson's chapter on Irrigation Development, particularly Tables 1
and 2, pp. 153, 156, and 157.

Dr. Kuo's discussion of chemical fertilizers emphasizes the difference between amount available and the quantity actually reaching the farmer in good condition and properly applied to crops. Therefore, the amount of fertilizer that was available to crops is unknown.

Although agricultural mechanization is included in the National Program for Agricultural Development, 1956–67, and is discussed by Dr. Kuo, apparently little, if any, practical attention was given during the first half of the period to implements and hand tools, or animal power, without which no amount of improved seeds, irrigation, or chemical fertilizers would prove advantageous. In fact, there are reports of improper care of both tools and work animals.

The second paragraph of Dr. Kuo's conclusion, concerning the number of *hsien* fulfilling or surpassing the targets for food grains of 3000, 7750, and 6000 kilograms per hectare requires further explanation. The *Land Utilization in China* survey reveals a wide variation in yields. Several of the 167 localities had yields of food grains during 1929–33 that equalled or surpassed the above targets. Therefore, by the selection of those *hsien* with favorable soil and water supply and with good traditional farm practices, numerous *hsien* could be found meeting the targets without adoption of new practices.

The statistics on agricultural institutions and personnel were also misleading because a significant number of agricultural institutions in research, education, and extension were functioning before 1949. For instance, there were twenty-five National Colleges of Agriculture and nine agricultural schools. By 1949, 6,000 students had been graduated.[2]

In regard to Dr. Kuo's basic conclusion, I am in agreement that "no substantial increase of agricultural production in Mainland China should be expected" until there is much greater progress in the adoption of improved farming practices. Such progress is only possible with (1) adequate technical training of sufficient personnel at all levels, (2) reliable scientific research, (3) certified multiplication of improved seed adapted to each of various localities, (4) efficient farm management of all factors of production at the primary unit of farm organization, and (5) absence of interference of unwise directives from higher echelons of authority.

[2] T. H. Shen, *Agricultural Resources of China* (Ithaca, N.Y.: Cornell University Press, 1951), 407 pp.

WERNER KLATT

Comment

Dr. Kuo gives a professional account of the main ingredients of China's planned transformation from traditional to modern agriculture with which one can agree in all essentials, but a few observations may be in order.

1. It is a measure of the degree of misjudgment and mismanagement that in 1967, the last year of the twelve-year national program for agricultural development, the grain harvest was supposed to be about 450 million tons. It was probably about 40 per cent of that amount.

2. One of the reasons for the miscalculations lies in the summation in the effects of eight measures that complement each other and don't accumulate. The success of one factor depends on the application—at the right time in the right quantity to the right crop—of the other factors. It is a mistake, for instance, to take the increase in the use of fertilizers as a measure of the rate of growth in current expenditure, let alone of likely output performance. If mishandled, the use of fertilizer could have a negative effect. This could be observed in Russia. It can still be observed in India. Similarly, the wrong type of tractor may cause damage rather than lead to land improvement.

3. The faulty nature of the agricultural plan is demonstrated also by the fact that planning was done entirely in physical terms. No consideration was given to the cost and price structure, past or present, domestic or foreign. This kind of planning is by now sufficiently discredited to require no more comment.

We may well ask: Where do we go from here? Can we project the results of our analyses for the period of the first plan or the defunct program for agricultural development into the future? In the case of the Soviet Union, enough is known about food and farming during the last fifteen years or so to permit fairly firm forecasts. This cannot be said of the Chinese situation during the last ten years. Any projection, however tentative, has therefore to be undertaken within the wider framework of the whole economy. I have attempted this in a paper prepared for Professor De Jouvenel's *Analyse et Prévision* and presented at the Orientalist Congress at Ann Arbor. I am inclined to think that in 1965 China's farm production had merely recovered to the position of 1957. Allowing for increase in population, the food intake declined in spite of a regular import of five and one-half to six million tons of grain, equal to almost nine million tons of paddy produced domestically. Whereas the rate of growth in farming was zero between 1957 and 1965, my estimate of industrial growth is higher than that given by Professor Liu in the congressional hearings.

As for the future, I regard as possible an annual average increase in farm output of 2 per cent during the period of the current five-year plan, provided that the issues brought into the open by the Proletarian Cultural Revolution are settled in the near future. This rate of growth would imply a continued import of grains, but the possibility of self-sufficiency in this sphere by 1970 should not be ruled out. No substantial improvement in the volume or composition of the average diet is expected.

ANTHONY M. TANG*

Input–Output Relations
in the Agriculture of Communist China,
1952–1965

INTRODUCTION

Investigation of input-output relations in a growth context is useful in that it serves to document empirically the sources of output growth and their separate contributions. In cases where the output statistics are generally taken to be suspect, as is true with the Communist Chinese official agricultural data, input series estimated independently of output can throw critical light on official production claims as well as the explanations offered for untoward production changes. In this paper we shall consider separately the first plan period for which the statistical foundation is relatively firm and the longer time span from 1952 to 1965, which contains the post-1958 information blackout period. For the 1952–57 period our analysis draws freely on a larger study completed in 1965.[1] Our chief concern will be to identify the sources of

* The author was Visiting Professor of Economics in 1967 at the Chinese University of Hong Kong and wishes to acknowledge the support of the Committee on the Economy of China, Social Science Research Council, for the basic work done earlier on the role of agriculture in the economic development of Communist China. Much of the argument and research methodology employed in this paper draws on insights developed in the earlier work. New research on the post-1958 period was made possible by a grant from Vanderbilt University. The writer also wishes to acknowledge the cooperation of the Chinese University of Hong Kong and the assistance of the staff of the Economic Research Center. In particular he is indebted to Miss Maria Wong and Mr. Anthony Chan for clerical assistance and to Mr. Yang Nam for research assistance.

[1] Anthony M. Tang, "Policy and Performance in Agriculture," in *Economic Trends in Communist China*, eds. A. Eckstein, W. Galenson, and T. C. Liu (Chicago: Aldine Publishing Co., 1967).

growth tapped by Peking and to explain the *raison d'être* for the celebrated Great Leap Forward. In turning to the longer period we shall consider the following questions: (1) Did the Great Leap Forward constitute a temporary break from a longer trend or did it leave behind more lasting effects, resulting in a permanent lowering of the agricultural productivity trend? (2) To what extent may the Chinese agricultural (hence, also industrialization) problems be reasonably attributed to the organizational dimension that bears heavily on incentive and efficiency and that constitutes a principal instrument in Chinese agricultural policy making? (3) How does the content of the agricultural policies and action programs for the post-Leap years compare with the policies of the first plan years in terms of orientation toward modernization versus "traditional progression" as alternative ways of realizing increased production? (4) In the latter connection, insofar as informed (but impressionistic) opinions may differ, based as they are upon incomplete information, what light does statistical analysis of the "complete" input-output data throw on the critical question?

With modernization holding the key to economic growth (most particularly, agricultural growth) not only in Communist China but elsewhere, it is clear that without some knowledge of the extent and results of agricultural modernization it would be difficult to make meaningful speculations either about current problems in Peking or the prospects Peking faces. Utilizing the data for the longer time interval, from 1952 to 1965, we also plan to relate the input-output estimates to crop weather, both as a method of cross-check for internal consistency and as a way of gauging credibility of official claims. Embarrassing production shortfalls have been attributed to the natural element by Peking, especially in connection with the 1959–61 period.

More generally, for the purposes of this conference, we hope to develop in this paper insights into the specific factors underlying Chinese Communist policy failure in agriculture. Before turning to this central task it would be well to try to outline the nature of Peking's failure. Western observers tend to point to the Great Leap with its constituent rural communalization program as the factor responsible for having brought China's agricultural (and industrialization) program to a resounding crash, when in fact the problems facing the Chinese planners were far more deep-seated. It was the mounting agricultural crisis during the first plan period that forced Peking to make a hard policy decision in 1957–58 in a new direction. The party opted for the Great Leap Forward and the communes. To suggest that the failure of the agricultural program is to be traced to the 1952–57 period may well come as a surprise to some Sinologists. After all, this is the period, according to the official statistics, that witnessed an agricultural growth of almost 5 per cent a year. Even when severely discounted by some Western analysts, the increase in food (grain) production is still conceded to have been sufficient to match a population growth placed at 2 to 2.5 per cent per year during 1952–57. (It is a matter of record that many developing nations have not done nearly as well.) The latter rate of food-production increase was arrived at by Liu and Yeh in their monumental study of Mainland China's economy.[2] Consistent with their agricultural estimates is the over-all annual growth for the economy of 6 per cent, as compared with the official 9 per cent.

Professor Liu has found it tempting to argue that the switch to the Great Leap was motivated by Peking's recognition that the realized growth had been 6 instead of 9 per cent and its dissatisfaction with that figure. The argument is, however, vulnerable. In the first instance, it is problematical whether the party leadership would in fact hold in low regard the 6 per cent rate—a rate that doubles the real output approximately every twelve years and is matched by only a handful of contemporary nations. As our subsequent analysis shows, it is more plausible to hold that the Leap movement was launched not because the realized rate was considered low but because the maintenance of it was threatened by an agriculture that was on the verge of exhausting its traditional sources of growth.

In a larger sense, the appraisal of agricultural policy and performance should begin with a perspective understanding of what the Chinese Communist Party (CCP) is trying to achieve in terms of its primary long-term goal. The model that best reflects the CCP value hierarchy and development strategy is that of the Stalinist type, and, hence, the development of the modern heavy industrial sector may be taken as the desired goal of the CCP. This is the sector whose absolute size determines the political and military power posture of a country and whose growth would serve to legitimize, though ex post facto, a socialist revolution that should have been dismissed as premature by any good Marxist. Maximization for one sector of an economy is subject to certain constraints. In the literature dealing with the Stalinist-type growth model, the effective constraint is taken to be associated with the capacity of the capital-goods sector. For more liberal growth settings, it is

    [2] T. C. Liu and K. C. Yeh, *The Economy of the Chinese Mainland* (Princeton: Princeton University Press, 1965), pp. 26 ff.

traced to savings limitation. However, as shown in our larger study[3] (on which the present paper draws), even in Stalinist settings that can be succinctly characterized as pursuing "maximum speed selective growth," the effective constraint need not lie with the capacity limitations of the capital-goods sector but may well be traced to agriculture. Where the effective constraint actually lies is a purely empirical question whose answer would depend on the temporal and spatial settings under investigation. In the context of the Stalinist model, the role of agriculture is clear—to free industrialization from agricultural constraint. It is in this light that the worth of an agricultural policy must be assessed: if industrialization continues to be limited by agriculture, the underlying agricultural policy cannot be said to be successful. It is well to note at this point that the success or failure of a policy cannot be gauged directly from its effect on agricultural production.

A comparison of the experience of the Soviet Union and Communist China shows that during their respective first five-year plan periods, there was a great difference in the development of agricultural production in the two countries. Soviet output fell dramatically; China's rose steadily. Yet, as shown in our earlier study, success belonged to the Soviet policy makers, not to their Chinese counterparts. The methodology we employed in that study generates a series of testable hypotheses bearing on agricultural performance as seen from the standpoint of Stalinist industrialization requirements. Subsequent testing shows that —starting from a common vantage point on the eve of their respective first plans, when both countries' cherished industrialization programs were badly restrained by the agricultural sector—the Soviet Union soon succeeded in freeing industrialization from agriculture's restrictive influence, while China's agricultural bottlenecks remained effective during the entire plan period. Furthermore, agriculture's restrictive hold on industrialization progressively tightened in China.

The apparent paradox lies in the vast initial differences in the agricultural posture of the two countries and the consequent divergences in the content and implications of their agricultural policies. Soviet per capita food availability in 1928 was more than twice that of China in 1952, so the Soviet problem was one of marketing, not of production. The collectivization program that followed was thus extraction oriented. In terms of the internal logic of the Stalinist model and the economic realities of the time, the alleged positive effect of collective farming on production (via the Marxist association of efficiency with

[3] Tang, "Policy and Performance," Parts I and II.

sheer size) could not have been more than a rationalization by Stalin to silence the opposition: the fact is that Stalin would have gone ahead with it even if he had foreseen the 25 per cent drop in production brought about by collectivization. Peking, on the other hand, found it necessary to adopt a program for agriculture that was both extractive and developmental. A measure of the inherent conflict in the latter program can be readily appreciated from the decided antidevelopmental effect of the extraction procedure that Peking was compelled to employ. In tax-equivalent terms, the Chinese extractions are tantamount to confiscatory taxation on output in excess of some fixed minimum that Peking allowed for farm retention. In contrast, Moscow's equally strong extractive urge led only to extractions that were relatively invariant with output. That the former contains strong disincentive effect on production and the latter implies a relatively neutral consequence is clear without elaboration.[4]

The preceding paragraphs argue that under the analytical framework considered appropriate for Communist China, the agricultural policy employed cannot be said to have been successful, in broad terms, even before the Great Leap. Indeed, the Leap is best understood as but one notable part of an unbroken chain of events going back to the first plan period. In a very general way, these are the difficulties inherent in a Stalinist development strategy when applied to and embraced by a country with initial conditions similar to those of Communist China in 1952. The specific agricultural programs employed, the sources of growth tapped, and the concrete implementation problems encountered by Peking are yet to be explored. Also pending is the task of providing suggestive evidence that agriculture's hold on industrialization had tightened during 1952–57. To these matters we now turn our attention.

THE INPUT, OUTPUT, AND PRODUCTIVITY INDEXES

Table 1 presents input series for labor, land, livestock, and the principal current production expenses during 1952–65. As the notes appended to the table show, some series are in physical terms, others are in values, and still others are in index number form. Some are compiled directly or indirectly from official sources while others are our own estimates. The detailed inputs are then grouped under four headings— labor, land, capital, and current inputs—and converted into index numbers. The manner in which various capital and current items are

[4] For an elaboration of the points in this section, see *ibid.*

aggregated is explained in Table 3. The method employed is that of weighted quantity relatives.

TABLE 1

AGRICULTURAL INPUTS, COMMUNIST CHINA

1952–1965

Year	Labor[a] (In Million Workers)	Sown Land[b] (In Million *Mou*)	Livestock[c] (In Billion 1952 Yuan)	Seed[d] (In Billion 1952 Yuan)	Chemical Fertilizer[e] (In Thousand Metric Tons)	Tradi- tional Fertilizer[f]	Insecticide[g] (In Thousand Metric Tons)	Feed[h] (In Billion 1952 Yuan)
1952	238	2,119	10.9	1.151	318	100%	15	1.10
1953	241	2,161	11.6	1.173	571	104	19	1.17
1954	245	2,219	12.3	1.205	883	108	41	1.25
1955	250	2,266	11.9	1.230	1,222	107	67	1.20
1956	255	2,388	11.8	1.297	1,602	108	159	1.19
1957	260	2,359	11.8	1.281	2,087	109	149	1.19
1958	264	2,344	12.0	1.278	2,533	111	313	1.21
1959	268	2,274	10.0	1.232	2,992	102	149	1.01
1960	272	2,204	8.2	1.197	2,853	95	149	0.83
1961	276	2,133	9.1	1.163	2,901	100	149	0.91
1962	280	2,185	9.9	1.197	3,328	104	149	1.00
1963	284	2,237	10.8	1.232	4,077	109	149	1.09
1964	289	2,288	11.7	1.266	5,377	114	149	1.18
1965	293	2,340	12.5	1.312	6,676	119	149	1.26

a For 1952–57, the figures are based on estimated agricultural population adjusted downward for nonagricultural subsidiary work and for persons not in labor force (those under 12 and over 65 years of age). For estimation procedure, see Tang, "Policy and Performance in Agriculture," *Economic Trends in Communist China*, eds. A. Eckstein, W. Galenson, and T. C. Liu (Chicago: Aldine Publishing Co., 1968), Table 3. For 1958–65 we assume an annual rate of increase of 1.5 per cent. The assumption abstracts from labor policy changes with their impact on rural-urban distribution as well as on labor use within the rural sector. Methodologically, these influences that bear on agricultural production are to be reflected in the computed productivity index.

b Data for 1952–58 from *Ten Great Years* (Peking: Foreign Languages Press, 1960), p. 128 (hereafter cited as *TGY*). The 1961 and 1965 sown area estimates are from E. F. Jones, "The Emerging Pattern of China's Economic Revolution," in *An Economic Profile of Mainland China*, Joint Economic Committee (Washington, D.C.: U.S. Government Printing Office, 1967), p. 94. Data for other years are obtained by linear interpolation.

c All midyear inventory values. For 1952–57, data are from T. C. Liu and K. C. Yeh, *The Economy of the Chinese Mainland* (Princeton: Princeton University Press, 1965), p. 406. For 1958 we assume no change from the 1957 per capita value. For 1965 we assume recovery of the 1957 per capita value with respect to small animals (pigs, poultry); for large animals, however, recovery of the 1957 total numbers only is assumed. The assumption seems plausible in light of the rapid recovery of the private sector where small animals are raised and of the general recognition of the slower recovery of large animal numbers, which include draft animals. The 1965 value shown in the table is the simple average of the 1957 and the same value adjusted upward for population growth. Roughly speaking, the years of 1957 and 1961 were similar in terms of their position (in livestock numbers) relative to years preceding and following. This is speculative. In the absence of a better alternative, we assume that a three-way relationship held stable in the two years: between exports and total production of livestock, between total production and inventories (properly lagged), and between exports and inventories. Fixed proportionality between exports and inventories (lagged one year) enables us to estimate the 1960 livestock numbers from the export data for 1957 and 1961 (obtained from *Hong Kong Trade Statistics*, Government of Hong Kong) and the available inventory figure for 1956. The 1960 value of livestock numbers is so estimated. For other years, estimates are made by linear interpolation.

d Assumed to change at the same rate with the sown acreage, implying constant application per unit area. Seed cost per unit area is obtained from Liu and Yeh, *Economy* . . . , pp. 400 and 412, where the 1954 unit cost is taken to apply to all years.

e For 1952–58 from *TGY*, p. 171; for other years from M. R. Larsen, "China's Agriculture under Communism," in *An Economic Profile of Mainland China*, p. 246. The former data refer to amount "supplied," the latter to quantities "available." To minimize the year-to-year discrepancies between consumption and available supply arising from inventory changes, we have applied three-year moving averages to the supply data to arrive at consumption estimates in the table.

f Traditional fertilizer (night soil and manure, chiefly) is assumed to change at a rate equal to the average rate of population growth and livestock number increment. Earlier calculations were based on population growth only. We owe the improvement to the discussant of the paper, Dr. Werner Klatt. Only the index is shown in the table. However, the values can be easily calculated on the basis of the assigned value weights for the 1952 base year of 2.98 for traditional fertilizer to 1 for chemical fertilizer, as shown in Table 3.

g For 1952–58 from *TGY*, p. 171. The 1958 official figure, however, is clearly excessive, more than tripling the consumption in a single year. We take the simple average of the official figures for 1957 and 1958. For years after 1958 we assume no change from the 1957 consumption. The assumption is arbitrary. However, adoption of such alternatives as proportionate increases with chemical fertilizer consumption since 1957 or constant per unit area application does not change the essential conclusions drawn from this study.

h For 1952–57 from Liu and Yeh, *Economy* . . . , p. 418. For other years, we assume a constant relationship between feed and livestock numbers. The relationship is taken from the 1952–57 average. The procedure allows us to estimate feed consumption from the livestock numbers already estimated.

The summation of the four components into a single aggregate input index is accomplished by means of the weights presented in Table 2. These weights are, in the main, in line with Buck's prewar estimates as well as with Liu and Yeh's summary of several sets of Communist data. They also appear to be quite plausible in relation to the factor weights of a number of selected countries, as shown in Table 2. Gaps do exist at this and the lower levels of aggregation. These gaps are filled by plausible assumptions. The procedures are, of course, more or less arbitrary. However, as is well known (especially to the Sinologist), where there are missing weights for some series it is better to assign reasonable, though arbitrary, weights than to discard the series. This follows because to discard is to assign zero weights. Therefore, we shall make no apologies for our procedures, which are clearly stated in the tables for the reader to assess.

As is now widely recognized, the aggregate input index so constructed is really the output index that would have been obtained in the absence of "technical change." As such, it implies a particular underlying aggregate production function, together with assumptions about factor markets. When used in conjunction with the *observed* output index to

TABLE 2

RELATIVE INPUT WEIGHTS OF SELECTED COUNTRIES AND
COMMUNIST CHINA

Country, Year	Relative Input Weights*			
	Labor	Land	Capital	Current Inputs
Taiwan, 1952–56[a]	.45	.25	.11	.19
Japan, 1933–37[b]	.52	.26	.08	.14
India, 1945–48[c]	.34	.25	.30	.11
Panajachel, 1936[c]	.84	.10	.02	.04
U.S.A., 1949[d]	.33	.19	.48	d
Communist China, 1952–57[e]	.55	.25	.09	.11

* Weights based on factor income shares or value of service flows. International data not strictly comparable.

[a] From Yhi-min Ho, *Agricultural Development of Taiwan, 1903–60* (Nashville: Vanderbilt University Press, 1966), p. 63.

[b] From Anthony M. Tang, "Research and Education in Japanese Agricultural Development, 1880–1938," *The Economic Studies Quarterly* (Riron Keizai Gaku) (May, 1963), p. 93 (in English).

[c] From T. W. Schultz, *Transforming Traditional Agriculture* (New Haven: Yale University Press, 1964), pp. 99–100. India's data pertain to Punjab. Panajachel portrays a primitive agricultural setting among Guatemala's Indians. Professor Schultz, who gave generously of his time to make detailed comments on an earlier draft of this work, called my attention to Tara Shukla's all-India data in her recent book, *Capital Formation in Indian Agriculture*. Although Shukla does not show the weight for current inputs, her input weights—0.30 for labor, 0.27 for land, and 0.43 for capital—are, on the whole, close to the figures for Punjab shown in the table.

[d] From Zvi Griliches, "Sources of Measured Productivity Growth," *Journal of Political Economy* (Aug., 1963), p. 336. Classification does not permit separation into our capital and current inputs categories.

[e] J. L. Buck in his monumental studies of prewar Chinese agriculture (*Chinese Farm Economy* [Chicago: University of Chicago Press, 1930], pp. 86–87) shows data that suggest the following weights: labor, 49 per cent; current inputs, 11 per cent; others, 40 per cent. The current inputs weight from Buck's farm survey of the 1920's appears to be still current in the light of Liu and Yeh's cost estimates (*Economy of the Chinese Mainland*, p. 139): 11 per cent of gross plant output value and 10 per cent of animal product value for 1952–57. The increased labor share over Buck's is deemed plausible in view of Communist China's labor mobilization policy. The land and capital shares, though arbitrarily divided, also appear reasonable in relation to other national statistics; most relevant, those of Taiwan and Japan. The weight for capital is taken to reflect not only the return to livestock investment but also the cost of feed. Current inputs, then, consist of seeds, fertilizers (chemical and traditional), insecticides, and other expenses. The weights adopted in the table for China are also almost identical with the ones employed by Dwight Perkins in his *Agricultural Development in China, 1368–1968* (Chicago: Aldine Publishing Co., 1969), p. 82.

yield measured productivity changes, it also assumes a particular form of technical change. Here again, we shall make no apologies, even though such assumptions are highly restrictive. The aggregation procedure and the index number construction are no doubt open to challenge. Following Solow, we make no attempt "to justify what follows by calling on fancy theorems on aggregation and index numbers. Either this kind of aggregate economics appeals or it doesn't."[5]

With the obvious exception of current inputs, the other resources are measured in stocks rather than in flows. Thus, insofar as the rate of utilization of the stocks changes over time, these changes would be reflected in disparate growths between the output and the input in-indexes. That is to say, they constitute one of the sources of "productivity growth."

1952—1957
THE FIRST FIVE-YEAR PLAN PERIOD

As an accident, our current-inputs index turns out to be nearly identical to the Communist index of "means of production supplied to agriculture." The behavior of certain components of the latter index is revealing. From 1952 to 1957 Peking mounted countless crash programs, many designed to elevate the technical base of agriculture. These generated a large body of impressive statistics. As an example, the number of the new two-wheeled, double-bladed plows supplied reached 1,086,000 units in a single year (1956), only to drop unaccountably to a trickle the next year (95,000 units). It was eventually revealed that the new plow had proved to be too heavy to be usable in paddy fields.

The widespread character of this Communist ineptitude is clearly visible elsewhere. In terms of the official statistics, irrigated area rose by 218 million *mou* (approximately 36 million acres), or 68 per cent, during 1952–57. The percentage of area sown to "improved" seeds jumped from 5 per cent in 1952 to 63 per cent in 1957 for rice; from 5 to 69 per cent for wheat; from 5 to 43 per cent for coarse grains; from zero to 57 per cent for potatoes; from 50 to 94 per cent for cotton; and from 2 to 48 per cent for oil-bearing crops. For all field crops the improvement was from 5 to 55 per cent.[6] The year 1956 was hectic, with all-out campaigns in all these regards. Without necessarily taking these statistics seriously, what must be abundantly clear is that agricultural policy in China had indeed been development-oriented but that the party had gone about it in a typical Communist fashion.

Without adequate regional experimentation and without the aid of price signals to ensure the right kind of response to the right extent, the

[5] R. M. Solow, "Technical Change and the Aggregate Production Function," *Review of Economics and Statistics*, XXXIV (August, 1957), 312–20.

[6] Unless otherwise noted, all official Communist statistics are from *Ten Great Years* (Peking: Foreign Languages Press, 1960). The volume contains tabulations of the statistics as compiled by the State Statistical Bureau.

party can only resort to central directives. These directives have no built-in signal to indicate how far one should go, and to make sure that it will not be disregarded, each directive is duly marked "first priority." Campaigns via mass media follow. Little wonder then that the cadres should toss aside what would appear to be secondary considerations—output, costs, "profits," and so on—and concentrate on maximizing the object of the new directive. In Communist China, rare is the day when there is not a momentous campaign of some kind in force. Under these circumstances, it is not surprising to find that even the official output index is completely out of line with the claimed technological triumphs and the reported formation of new as well as traditional forms of capital. Taking the ratio of the official output index to the input index to form a productivity index, we find that at best there had been no productivity change during 1952–57. If our "adjusted" output index is used, the productivity index falls by 6 to 7 per cent (Table 3).

TABLE 3
AGGREGATE INPUT INDEX, OUTPUT INDEX, AND PRODUCTIVITY INDEX
COMMUNIST CHINA, 1952–1965

Year	Labor[a]	Land in Sown Acreage[b]	Capital[c]	Current Inputs[d]	Aggregate Input Index[e]	Output Index[f]	Productivity Index[g]
1952	100%	100%	100%	100%	100%	100%	100%
1953	101.3	102	107	114	103.4	101.5	98.2
1954	102.9	105	113	142	108.6	103.3	95.1
1955	105.0	107	109	170	113.0	109.5	96.9
1956	107.1	113	108	241	123.4	113.2	91.7
1957	109.3	111	108	253	125.4	117.2	93.5
1958	111.0	111	110	367	139.1	133.8	96.2
1959	112.7	107	92	284	128.3	111.4	86.8
1960	114.4	104	75	275	125.9	104.9	83.3
1961	116.0	101	83	277	127.0	111.4	87.7
1962	117.7	103	91	296	131.2	118.0	89.9
1963	119.5	106	99	328	137.2	121.3	88.4
1964	121.3	108	107	380	145.1	127.9	88.1
1965	123.1	111	115	433	153.4	131.2	85.5

[a] Calculated from Table 1 (column 1).

[b] Calculated from Table 1 (column 2).

[c] Calculated from Table 1 (columns 3,8). Index is based on livestock and feed series. Machinery as reported in *TGY* (p. 171) was negligible in value throughout the first plan period. Fragmentary reports for the information blackout period show that farm machinery in use remained insignificant in numbers. *Hung-ch'i* (Red Flag) (Nov. 4, 1960, pp. 4–10) reported 95,000 tractors of 10 h.p. each and 3 million h.p. total of mechanical equipment engaged in irrigation and drainage work. For 1965, *Jen-min jih-pao* (People's Daily) (April 13, 1966) showed 135,000 tractors of 15 h.p. each in use. Even if we consider these magnitudes as indicative of the amount of machinery engaged in current agricultural production, the total value involved would hardly amount to 1 per cent of the livestock value. Farm implements are assumed to have grown in value in line with livestock.

[d] The index is composite. The seed, chemical fertilizer, traditional fertilizer, and insecticide

series (Table 1) are first converted into index numbers. The latter are summed by means of the following value weights taken from Liu and Yeh (*Economy* . . . , p. 414): 4.4 for seeds, 5.0 for all fertilizers, and 0.9 for insecticides and other miscellaneous items. Converting into relative weights as used in our calculations we obtain: 42.7 per cent, 12.2 per cent, 36.4 per cent, and 8.7 per cent for seeds, chemical and traditional fertilizers, and insecticides (and miscellaneous), respectively. The allocation of the weights between chemical and traditional fertilizers is arbitrary but considered plausible. It may be noted in passing that the above index for current inputs turns out to be very close to the Communist series on "means of production supplied to agriculture" (*TGY*, p. 170) that shows an index of 231 per cent for 1957 (1952 = 100).

e Aggregation (arithmetic) of the four major input components is based on the weights presented in Table 2.

f The output index for 1952–57 is the "adjusted" series presented elsewhere in a larger study on Chinese agriculture (Tang, "Policy and Performance . . . ,"). The adjustment applied to the Communist gross value output series is to correct for the underreporting (or underrecovery) in the early 1950's. For 1958–65 we estimate, as explained below, the total output from Dawson's grain-output series shown in Table 4. In that table, we present the grain-production estimates of several well-known observers of the Chinese agricultural scene as well as the "official" series. The "official" figures come from scattered sources, including Viscount Montgomery's account of Mao's estimate of the 1960 production as given him in an interview. The two "Leap" years (1958 and 1959) aside, no glaring discrepancies are apparent between the "official" and the independently estimated series. Similarly, the latter series are in fairly close agreement with one another. We opted for the Dawson series both because of its length and because it produces higher rates of growth for the period since 1957 (a benchmark year for which the official figure is accepted by all). The sense of our procedure is to adopt data series and assumptions that cast relatively favorable light on Communist performance without exceeding the bounds of what is plausible. This applies to the estimation of both our output and input series. In this manner, we hope to generate conclusions and insights, useful to a perspective understanding of the economy of the Chinese mainland under communism, which would then hold with even greater force under less favorable assumptions.

The official statistics for 1952–57 show a very close correspondence between the grain and the total output series. The difference between the two indexes for any given year is usually one or two percentage points. Although during the critical years of 1959–61, when subsistence of the population became the overriding concern and where preoccupation with food grain production might have come at some expense to livestock and other farm production, there is reason to believe that the 1952–57 relationship generally held during 1958–65. For the post-Leap years, it is generally agreed that while the production of "economic" crops lagged in recovery behind grain production, the production of the private sector (pigs, chickens, vegetables, and so forth), once restored, surged ahead at a faster pace than grain production (a special concern of the collectives). In these terms, we estimate the total output series for 1958–65 from Dawson's grain output series. In doing so we assume that the annual rate of change in grain output applies to total output. For the benchmark year of 1957, the official grain output index (1952 = 100) stands at 119.8 per cent and the total output index at 121.3 per cent (after a downward correction of 3.4 per cent for known inaccuracy in reported hog production). With the proportion between these two indexes assumed to hold for all years, the total output index for the post-1957 is easily estimated from the available grain output series.

g The index is obtained by dividing the output index by the input index.

It is probably fair to say that during the first plan period the mainstay of Peking's agricultural development program had to do with labor mobilization for Nurksian capital formation but also, to a lesser extent, for current production. The use of other resources, too, was intensified. Thus, the actual decline in resource productivity had been greater than portrayed by our index. A 10 per cent rise in the intensity of labor use (via double cropping, for instance) in current production would have meant an increase of 6 percentage points in the aggregate input index and a further fall of 4 percentage points in the productivity index during 1952–57. The measured falls in the productivity index suggests that Peking was confronted with increasing costs in generating incremental output and agricultural surpluses needed for its forced industrialization program. In the following section we hope to add a further dimension to the argument that the Great Leap was mounted, not because Peking considered the realized industrial growth during 1952–57 as unsatisfactory, but because the maintenance of that rate of industrialization was threatened by an agriculture on the verge of exhausting the traditional sources of growth.

Let us begin with the Communist value output statistics without adjustment of any kind. By means of the procedure outlined in the notes to Table 3, the official increase of 25 per cent in total output obtained between 1952 and 1957 can be broken down as follows: Increases in labor force have contributed 5 per cent (or, more correctly, percentage points) of the output increment of 25 per cent, land has contributed 3 per cent, capital, 2 per cent, current inputs, 16 per cent, and productivity change, a detraction of 1 per cent. In Communist gross value terms, the output increment came to 12.1 billion yuan (in constant 1952 prices) with contributions of 2.42 billion from labor, 1.45 from land, 0.97 from capital, 7.74 from current inputs, and a minus of 0.48 from productivity change.

With the separate contributions of the individual growth factors thus estimated, we now turn to an attempt to gauge the profitability of the most important component of Peking's program to develop agriculture, i.e., labor mobilization for capital construction. Hopefully, such an appraisal may shed light on the nature and magnitude of China's agricultural problem and help lay the groundwork for a better understanding of the great policy changes that followed the first plan period and for a more realistic appraisal of future prospects. To this end, a rate of return is calculated on mass labor capital projects. Here, we take 31.6 billion yuan for the 1952 value added by agriculture instead of the Communist gross value (48.39 billon). The contribution (in value added) from sown acreage increment during 1952–57 comes to 0.937 billion yuan[7] or 0.432 billon after replacement allowance (at 5 per cent

---

[7] The figure of 31.6 billion yuan is from Liu and Yeh, *Economy . . .* , p. 213. This is close to A. Eckstein's estimate of about 31 billion in *The National Income of Communist*

of the cost as calculated below) to put the return on a perpetual basis. The historical costs of agricultural "capital construction" within and without the state plan, together with projects undertaken by work brigades and the military as well as nonstate budgeted works by cooperatives, are loosely aggregated by means of the data assembled by Liu and Yeh in their study.

It is assumed here that the output effect of water-conservation projects, reclamation works, and other "capital construction" in agriculture is reflected through the increased acreage and its more intensive use (i.e., jointly via the incremental sown acreage). Fixed investment within the state plan totaled 3.5 billion yuan and, outside the plan, 0.6 billion during the five-year period of 1953 to 1957. Investment by work brigades in conservation projects amounted to 2.3 billion or, say, 3.0 billion including work by the military.[8] Similar investment having an effect on acreage and land use by cooperatives or by the peasant is not known. As Liu and Yeh put it, it is doubtful that the expected investment of six billion yuan from this source as envisioned by the first plan had been realized. Let us put this down at four billion. In principle, one should cumulate these costs at some compound interest rate and deduct from the sum net gains already realized during 1953–56, also cumulated at some compound interest rate. The difference between the two provides the relevant capital cost as of 1957, against which a rate of return may then be computed. These procedures are not followed in our calculations because of data limitations. However, since cost compounding and subtraction of net realized returns are offsetting, the error incurred by our omission is probably small. In these terms, then, the total historical costs of the projects (during 1953–57) having effect on acreage and land use come to 10.1 billion yuan in 1952 prices. Against this cost, relevant to 1957, the net return in 1957 of 0.432 billion (in 1952 prices), as calculated above, yields a rate of return of 4.3 per cent per year.

If we consider the probable underreporting (or underrecovery) of the output in 1952 and use our "adjusted" production instead (see Table 3 above), total annual net returns fall from 0.432 to 0.326 billion yuan. And the rate of return drops from 4.3 to 3.3 per cent. To some,

---

China, 1952 (Glencoe, Ill.: The Free Press, 1961), p. 35. The figure of 0.937 billion is obtained by multiplying 1.45 (the incremental land contribution in gross output value terms) by the ratio of 31.6 to 48.39, i.e., the ratio of value added to gross output value, and further multiplying by the productivity index of 0.99. The latter index is obtained when the official total output figures (instead of the "adjusted") are used.

[8] From Liu and Yeh, *Economy* . . . , pp. 74, 171. For planned construction, see also *First Five-Year Plan* (Peking: Foreign Languages Press, 1956), pp. 21–33.

the 3.3 rate may still appear to be on the high side, since the prevalence of earthwork constructions in Chinese agricultural capital projects may well make the replacement rate of 5 per cent an understatement. Further, it might be recalled that the ancient business of extending the farm acreage had already been pushed so far afield that long ago Chinese poets were moved to write: "Cultivation culminates unto hill-top; this is but a manifestation of poverty." It is also doubtful that our rough estimate adequately reflects such items as labor cost of work brigades.[9] At any rate, taking the 3.3 per cent rate as a plausible magnitude, it is well to recognize that this is the average rate realized on all the projects undertaken between 1952 and 1957. At the margin relevant to 1957, the rate may well be close to zero.

What seems clear is that Communist China employed massive resources within the confines of the traditional production possibilities. By 1957, the country appeared to be fully caught up in the inexorable law of diminishing returns. It stood at a critical crossroads with the traditional sources of agricultural growth near exhaustion and the industrialization program threatened with severe dislocations. It was necessary for the party to find a way out of the impasse. That Peking decided on the Great Leap is now history.

However tentative, the above calculations seem to support the conclusion that the mass labor projects—on which Peking relied so heavily and to which it pointed as a great Socialist triumph—turned out to be very unrewarding indeed. Their miserable rate of returns stands in sharp contrast with the returns that have accrued to true agricultural modernization programs elsewhere. Studies of Japan and Taiwan suggest "internal" rates of social returns in the order of 30–35 per cent per year on the rewarding consequence of basic rural education, agricultural research, development, and extension.[10] Research on United States agriculture produces similarly exciting results.[11]

Communist China's productivity decrement in agriculture, too, is

[9] On the other side of the ledger, it is possible that the calculated returns do not fully capture all the benefits accruing to mass labor projects whose costs are included in the total. It may be added that since 1952 and 1957 are both relatively normal crop years (see Fig. I), the calculated returns are not affected by the choice of the years.

[10] See, for example, Anthony M. Tang, "Research and Education in Japanese Agricultural Development," *The Quarterly Economic Studies* (Japan, Part I, Feb. 1963, and Part II, May, 1963), pp. 27–41, 91–99; and Yhi-min Ho, *Agricultural Development of Taiwan, 1903–60* (Nashville: Vanderbilt University Press, 1966).

[11] See, for example, T. W. Schultz's studies, too numerous to permit a comprehensive listing here. Also, Zvi Griliches, "Research Costs and Social Returns: Hybrid Corn and Related Innovations," *Journal of Political Economy* (Oct., 1958), pp. 419–31.

an exception on the contemporary scene. Even Soviet agriculture, during much of the postwar period, had enjoyed substantial productivity gains.[12] The Chinese record is all the more noteworthy because the agricultural sector contained initially what appeared to be substantial slacks in resource use. The slacks are traceable to, among other things, the country's age-old tenure system, small operating units, and fragmented landholdings. These slacks were presumably taken up by the sequence of land redistribution and "cooperative" farming. Other things being equal, this should have given rise to productivity gains. The computed productivity declines, therefore, attest to the overriding negative pulls at work. Here, the disincentive effect of Peking's agricultural policy, alluded to earlier, and the law of diminishing returns brought into operation by the vigorous exertion at the traditional margins are no doubt the critical dimensions.

1952—1965

THE EXTENDED PERIOD

It seems clear from the Chinese experience during 1952–57 that in order to have a growth agriculture it is necessary to break out of the confines of the traditional production possibilities. To do this, however, it is equally necessary to bring industrial resources to bear on the modernization task so as to "articulate" the product of agricultural research and human investment. For far too long, Peking had shown an unmistakable aversion toward the process of "intersectoral transformation," preferring to generate agricultural growth by mobilizing the "cheap" resources. By that process we mean, in our context, one in which industry releases its resources to agriculture under the proviso that these resources, via their impact on output, enable agriculture to release resources to industry in quantities that more than compensate for the initial transfer—with all transfers reduced to comparable terms relevant to industrialization. Thus, if industrialization is constrained by agriculture (as it was in China), its pace would be quickened through intersectoral transformation, so long as, say, a motorized pump, when transferred to agriculture, boosts farm output sufficiently to allow the state to get back enough farm resources (labor, food, raw materials, and exportables) to produce (or to acquire via trade) more than one pump.

The Great Leap constituted a deliberate attempt to ignore such

[12] See, for example, D. Gale Johnson, "Agricultural Production," in *Economic Trends in the Soviet Union*, eds. A Bergson and S. Kuznets (Cambridge, Mass.: Harvard University Press, 1963).

intersectoral transformation processes. In the Leap, Peking thought it had found a cheaper alternative. The idea was to develop a rural industrialization program using indigenous resources, making no demands on the industrial sector, to produce the machinery and materials needed by agriculture for "modernization." The resulting fiasco is now a matter of record. To what extent Peking is still trying to live down the consequences or whether the economy had been permanently impaired are two of the questions that we hope to explore in this section. A related question is whether there is any empirical evidence to suggest a possible reversal in policy concerning the issue of modernization versus "traditional progression." Two other issues are of interest. Inasmuch as Peking has found it convenient to blame the weather for embarrassing drops in production, what do our input-output relations tell us about the credibility of such claims? As practitioners of psychology, the Communist leaders, in their resolution to carry out the socialist transformation, thought it efficient to take one big step forward followed

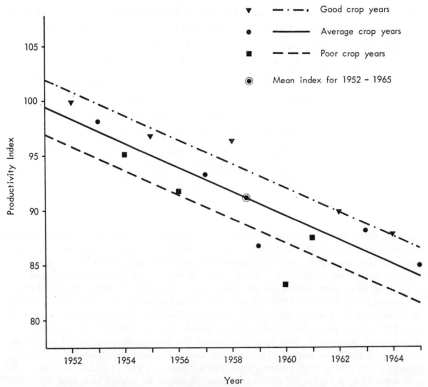

Fig. 1.   Analysis of covariance regression. *Source*: Column 7, Table 3.

by a small step or two backward. Were such vacillations accompanied by production changes such as Peking might have expected?

In Figure 1 we present the graphic equivalent of covariance regression analysis. The time series analyzed refers to the productivity index taken from Table 3. The index compares the total resource productivity of a given year against that of the base year, 1952, and sums up the collective influence on output of all the real factors other than the four categories of inputs explicitly recognized in the aggregate production function. Weather is one such real factor. Had covariance analysis been employed, weather would have entered into the calculations as a dummy variable. Its computed value would have told us how much higher the productivity trend line for good crop years is in relation to the trend line for average crop years. Similarly, the dummy for poor crop weather would have told us, when stated in different words, by how many percentage points the productivity index for a poor crop year is expected (on the average) to fall below that for an average year. The standard procedure involving dummy variables requires the assumption that, in a time series context, their influences are independent of the passage of time. That is to say, the fitted trend lines are parallel by assumption.

The graphic procedure is not subject to such inflexibilities. The three trend lines in Figure 1 are fitted by visual inspection. It so happens that the best fitting lines are all parallel to one another and also symmetrical about the average weather line.[13] This is a finding of some significance since it affords us the basis for suggesting that during the entire period from 1952 to 1965 there had been no observable technical progress or modernization in the agriculture of Mainland China. This follows because modern agricultural technology, among its other attributes, makes farm production less subject to weather, and the three trend lines

---

[13] The visual best fitting lines have been checked against the least-squares lines fitted separately to each of the three sets of data by weather classification. The technical difficulty concerning the least-squares procedure is that there are not enough observations in each weather class to make the fit statistically meaningful. Thus, there are only four observations on poor crop weather years. Nonetheless, the check result is most reassuring. The least-squares regression coefficients agree almost perfectly with those measured from the visual lines. The over-all trend (for all observations combined) fitted by least-squares also coincides, even more perfectly, with the visual line for the average crop years. This suggests that the period under investigation, 1952–65, is not unbalanced with a preponderance of either too many good years or too many poor years. This reassures us that the fitted trends are not biased by the selection of the time period. The over-all trend (by least-squares) has a midyear intercept that falls exactly on the visual average line (see Fig. I) and a slope of −1.03 as compared with −1.0 for the visual lines. It might be added here that the visual lines were drawn freehand first and then checked against the least-squares line.

would have shown convergence had substantive modernization taken place in Chinese agriculture.[14]

Before turning to the other questions raised on the preceding page, let us note that both for the 1952–57 period and for the longer period, to 1965, the configuration of the observations does not conflict with the known weather conditions. For the shorter period, if either a least-squares line or a visual trend is fitted to the data, it can be easily seen that all good years have productivity indexes lying above the line, the average years on the line, and the bad years below it. For the longer period, a look at Figure 1 shows that all annual observations cluster closely around their respective trend lines fitted according to weather class. Only one observation, that for 1959 (an average year), crosses the adjacent trend line (for poor years). That it should do so is not surprising once we recall that it was the year whose chaotic events forced Peking to abandon the Great Leap program. The cross-check is reassuring, suggesting no internal inconsistency between our estimated inputs and output and the known crop weather conditions, notwithstanding the fact that enormous information gaps had to be filled by more or less arbitrary assumptions in the estimation procedures.

It is clear from Figure 1 that there is no break in the productivity trend lines. This suggests that the disruptive effects of the Great Leap had been temporary and that in the post-Leap years, beginning as early as 1961, agriculture had rather quickly resumed the level of performance expected on the basis of harvest condition and the temporal position on the productivity trend. Long-term impairment of agricultural performance arising out of the Leap experience would have lowered the productivity trend lines. This finding is, however, less than reassuring to Peking.

First, it applies to productivity only, and the behavior of the input and output indexes in post-Leap years is not reassuring. Second, as shown above, there is no evidence to suggest effective modernization programs at work in the post-Leap years. Third, the real factors giving rise to productivity declines during 1952–57 have continued to operate in the more recent years. There is nothing in the data to suggest a

[14] The conclusion is reinforced if we express the constant vertical distances between the three trend lines as relatives (per cent as opposed to percentage points) of the productivity index trend value for the average crop years. Since the trend values are declining over time, the fixed percentage points would translate into increasing relative distances. That is to say, in relative terms the three trend lines are diverging over time. The divergence suggests increasing scarcity of resource reserves with which to combat adverse weather through reseeding, replanting, and so forth.

possible leveling off in the rate of fall in the immediate future. This rate has been one percentage point a year in the productivity index. Needless to say, increasing costs are not conducive to growth.

From Figure 1 we can also gauge the influence of weather on productivity. The distance between the trend lines shows that the influence of weather has been quite modest. The average difference in productivity is only 2.5 percentage points between a good and an average crop year (or between a poor and an average year). Between a good and a poor year the difference amounts to 5 percentage points. These are small magnitudes by international standards and indicative of China's sheer size and climatic diversity. In addition, we have to consider the scatter around each productivity trend. The deviations arise in part because our weather index is insensitive to differences among years belonging to the same weather class and in part because of the operation of other real factors (e.g., disorganization during the Leap period). The narrow scatter around each line, however, suggests that the "residual" weather effect and the strength of other real factors have been minor. This appears to hold even between two extreme years such as 1958 and 1960—the former a year of high productivity and total output, the latter low in both regards. Of the estimated decline in output of about 22 per cent (Table 3), roughly half is attributable to falls in the level of inputs and in trend productivity. Of the remainder, a little less than half represents the *expected* influence of weather, with the unknown factors (probably associated with general economic disorganization) accounting for the rest, as represented by the sum of the deviations from the respective trend lines for 1958 and 1960.

The final question listed earlier is less easy to answer. The narrow scatter in Figure 1 suggests that the production effects that Peking hoped to realize through its expedient policy of growth via socialist transformation (characterized as it was by the psychological component of "one big step forward, two small steps backward") have been rather limited. The policy bears an unmistakable imprint of Mao, a revolutionary par excellence with little appreciation for the evolutionary nature of nation building. In his headlong approach he has been prone to dismiss the thought that the task of nation building might require respect for the laws of nature and economics and recognition of the value of material incentive. The inference about the limited production response is, however, subject to an important qualification since the narrow scatter around the productivity trend lines need not preclude the possibility that the Maoist policy might have resulted in a massive

TABLE 4

AGRICULTURAL PRODUCTION, COMMUNIST CHINA 1952—1967

| | Grain in Million Metric Tons (Including Potatoes Converted at 4-1 Ratio) | | | | | | | Other Crops | |
	Weather	"Official"	O.L. Dawson[a]	R.F. Emory[b]	F.E.E.R.[c]	John Wenmohs[d]	M.R. Larsen[e]	Average of D-E-W-L	"Economic" Crops[b]	Cotton[b]
Pre-1949 Peak			170							
1949	Poor		150							
1953–56 Average				172		172				
1952	Good	154.4	170							1.6
1953	Average	156.9	166							1.9
1954	Poor	160.4	170							1.8
1955	Good	174.8	185							1.4
1956	Poor	182.5	180							0.9
1957	Average	185.0	185	185					18.3	0.9
1958	Good	250.0	204	193.5	193			199	20.2	1.0
1959	Average	270.0	170	167.7	167			169	19.0	1.2
1960	Poor	150.0	160	159.5	160			160	15.5	1.3
1961	Poor	162.0	170	166.6	166			168	13.2	n.a.
1962	Good	174.0	180	178.3	178	180		179	12.9	n.a.
1963	Average	183.0	185	179.1	179	178		181	13.5	
1964	Good	200.0	194	182.7	182	190	180	187	14.2	
1965	Average	200.0	200	179.9	180	185	178	185	14.2	
1966	Poor	n.a.	n.a.	n.a.	175	178	180		n.a.	
1967	Good	n.a.	n.a.	n.a.	n.a.	187	190		n.a.	

[a] As compiled by E. F. Jones in "The Emerging Pattern of China's Economic Revolution," in *An Economic Profile of Mainland China*, Joint Economic Committee (Washington, D.C.: U.S. Government Printing Office, 1967) p. 93.

[b] From R. F. Emory, "Recent Economic Developments in Communist China," *Asian Survey*, VI (June, 1966), 6, 303–9. Economic crops include cotton, soybeans, peanuts, cottonseed, rapeseed, sesame. Quantity in millions of metric tons (MMT).

[c] From the *Far Eastern Economic Review Yearbook*, 1964, 1966, and 1967, Hong Kong.

[d] From John Wenmohs, "Agriculture in Mainland China, 1967," *Current Scene* (Hong Kong), Dec. 15, 1967.

[e] From "A Look at Mainland China's Agriculture, 1965–66," *Foreign Agriculture*, Foreign Agriculture Service (Washington, D.C.: U.S. Dept. of Agriculture, Aug. 8, 1966). Larsen's 1966–67 figures appear in *Review of 1967 and Outlook for 1968: The Far Eastern and Oceania Agricultural Situations*, Economic Research Service (Washington, D.C.: U.S. Department of Agriculture, April 25, 1968), p. 12.

injection of additional inputs. The possibility is a real one considering the fact that resource mobilization had been the dominant feature of that policy and that the Chinese rate of increase in the aggregate agricultural input index is probably unmatched by other nations, either historically or contemporarily. Japan's index, for example, rose by about 0.5 per cent per year (compound rate) over a sixty-year span from 1880 to 1940.[15] In contrast, the annual rate of increase for Communist China stood at 4 per cent during 1952–65 (Table 3).

About all that one can say is that, given such massive input increment, the output results (with an average annual growth of a little over 2 per cent during 1952–65 and virtually no growth since 1957–58) have been disappointing and that Peking is still a long way from solving the intractable agricultural problem. True, it had begun to show a stronger disposition toward investing scarce resources in support of agricultural production. Its substantial outlays on chemical fertilizers through expansion of domestic production facilities and larger importations are a case in point. But chemical fertilizers alone cannot carry the load. Jung-chao Liu's analysis, moreover, made it clear that the double squeeze applied by Peking in the form of artificially high relative fertilizer-grain prices and the added leverage via its proportional agricultural tax on gross output, has already pushed the collective farms (under existing fertilizer inputs) to the point where, even at the current modest rate of application, they are doing not much better than breaking even.[16] A profitable play to Peking, no doubt, but its limits are already in sight. Without the vital contributions from agricultural research and information programs, it is idle to think that with the Chinese rate of fertilizer application amounting to less than one-fortieth of the Japanese rate, Peking has far to go. Under existing practices, the Chinese yield will reach zero long before the Japanese rate of application is even approached, unless new complementary inputs (e.g. education and new seed varieties and practices) are introduced. Under the traumas of the Great Leap and now the Great Proletarian Cultural Revolution, the Chinese Communist system of education has long lost much of its former substance. So, no doubt, has the agricultural research and extension system, which had little substance even during the more normal first five-year plan period. If the cracks are still less than visible on the Chinese economic scene, the full measure of the damaging consequences

---

[15] See Tang, "Research and Education," pp. 91–92.
[16] Jung-chao Liu, "Fertilizer Application in Communist China," *The China Quarterly* (Oct.–Dec., 1965), pp. 28–51.

of the topsy-turvy world that the Maoists have contrived for themselves may yet be felt in the years to come.

WERNER KLATT

Comment

I am in agreement with Professor Tang when he says that a correct assessment of input/output relations on Mainland China for the period of the First Five-Year Plan is invaluable in laying the groundwork for any realistic appraisal of future prospects, during the Second Five-Year Plan and beyond. One can also agree with Professor Tang that the aggregate input index serves as a certain check on official output statistics: output equals input plus technical change. This presupposes that one can be fairly certain of the "residual," i.e., the technical change and its effect on production and productivity. Any error in calculating the original relationship is bound to affect one's conclusions.

Errors should therefore be avoided at all cost. Even if they are seemingly insignificant during the period under review, they may have far-reaching consequences at times when the input or output mix—or both—are composed differently from the composition during the base period.

The fact that Professor Tang's input index is, as he says, nearly identical to the official index of means of production supplied to agriculture does not necessarily make it suspect, but it calls for caution. While the technique employed in calculating farm input is unimpeachable, the weights chosen may well be questioned:

1. Traditional fertilizer (farm manure) should be measured by its output, which is dependent on the number of livestock rather than the extent of the acreage sown, i.e., in 1957 at index 108 instead of 111.

2. In weighting the component parts, the share of labor (55 per cent) seems unduly high and that of current inputs (11 per cent) unduly low. I should prefer labor at 50 per cent, current input, 15 per cent.

3. The cultivated acreage is needed for estimating sown acreage, but it is of no significance for estimating the aggregate input index. Capital is represented *inter alia* by livestock (and buildings for which no data

are available), but feedstuffs have no place here since they comprise part of the current input. I calculate the capital index in 1957 at 108 instead of 120.

4. If feed is included in current input and if it is given its proper weight, the aggregate index of current input for 1957 comes down from 249 to 182—a substantial cut. I suggest as weights: seeds, 30; manure, 30; feed, 30; fertilizers, 5; other items, 5.

5. In calculating the aggregate input index, I suggest as weights: labor, 50; land, 25; capital, 10; current input, 15. I arrive at the following indices in 1957: labor, 109; land, 111; capital, 108; current input, 182; total, 120.

Although the difference between Professor Tang's figures and mine is small, it is significant enough to be considered since it affects both the conclusions of his paper and forecasts for the future. Professor Tang's output index (adjusted) shows 117 for 1957. I estimate 120, again a small difference with significant consequences. If input and output in 1957 had in fact been 20 per cent over 1952, there would have been no effect of technological change and no change in over-all productivity. If the index of labor increased to 109, productivity per man rose by 10 per cent. If sown acreage increased to 111, yields increased by 11 per cent. The improvement seems to be due entirely to increases in current input. Over a short period of five years this seems reasonable. Improvements in infrastructure and human skill take longer to make themselves felt. I conclude that Professor Tang's adjusted output index is not necessarily a firm and final estimate. My reservation would apply even more with regard to his input index, on which my doubts mainly rest.

It is true that annual variations in yields and harvests are small in large countries. The effect of the weather is therefore negligible except in extreme circumstances, e.g., in 1958 (favorable), or when the human factor is detrimentally affected, e.g., during the Great Leap Forward. I agree with Professor Tang that at that time the law of diminishing returns brought into operation by the vigorous exertion at the traditional margins was a decisive factor. It was a major mistake on the part of the Communist leaders to assume a labor surplus, not realizing that it existed side by side—in time and space—with labor shortages during the harvest. Without "intersectoral transfer" there was no prospect of a breakout from the traditional pattern. The comparison with the U.S.S.R. that Professor Tang attempts should be approached with great caution. The Soviet Union was the fifth largest industrial country in the world in 1927. Before the First World War, Russia had a grain surplus of ten million tons, and even after the war her livestock industry served as a reserve of raw product (grain) that is not available in the case of China.

I have some reservations when I see that the disaster following the Great Leap Forward is explained exclusively by the exhaustion of traditional sources of growth in agriculture. Other factors extraneous to farming have to be considered, e.g., Russia's unwillingness, following the revolt of 1956 in Eastern Europe, to bail out China during the period of her ambitious second plan. Had long-term aid been available, industry *and* agriculture could have made headway. This is an important aspect to be borne in mind when the prospects of the coming decade are considered.

LAWRENCE J. LAU

Peasant Consumption, Saving, and Investment in Mainland China*

THE SIGNIFICANCE OF PEASANT CONSUMPTION,

SAVING, AND INVESTMENT

Peasant consumption is an important indicator of the level of welfare achieved by the agricultural population. In addition, the peasant demand for consumption is intimately connected with the quantity of labor services that the peasant is willing to supply at any given wage rate or marginal compensation to labor (generally equated with the marginal productivity of labor).[1] If leisure is not an inferior good, the question of consumption versus leisure is extremely crucial. The appropriate agricultural development policy must be formulated with respect to the preference for consumption goods versus leisure of the peasants in the relevant range of values. Saving is generally regarded as a residual from income after consumption has been deducted. This is only a partial view: saving must be considered as the present value of future consumption, discounted according to the subjective time preference of the peasants. In the purely noncommercial context, saving must be equal to investment. However, in the real world, where there exists some degree of commercialization in both the product and the factor markets, saving may not necessarily equal investment because of the

* Financial support from the Agricultural Development Council, the East Asian Studies Committee of Stanford University, and the Institute of International Studies, University of Calfornia, Berkeley, is gratefully acknowledged. The author is indebted to Professors John G. Gurley, Shigeru Ishikawa, Dale W. Jorgenson, Augustine Tan, and Yuan-li Wu for helpful comments. All remaining errors are of course the author's sole responsibility.

[1] For a more detailed analysis of the interrelations between consumption and leisure see the forthcoming study by Dale W. Jorgenson *et al.*, *Resource Allocation in Agricultural Development.*

lack of financial intermediaries. Yet investment is always effectively constrained by the available supply of saving in the absence of financial intermediaries: it can never be larger than the total volume of saving.

Peasant consumption, saving, and investment also affect the rate of industrialization, where industrialization is understood to be the gradual transfer of productive resources from the agricultural (or traditional) to the manufacturing (or modern) sector, and hence the over-all rate of growth. This has been demonstrated repeatedly in models of development of dual economies: notable examples are the models of W. A. Lewis and Ranis and Fei, and the neoclassical model of Jorgenson.[2]

No attempt will be made to discuss these theoretical models in any detail. However, it suffices to say that the level of peasant consumption influences the availability of the agricultural surplus. And it is this surplus that enables the agricultural sector to release both labor and raw materials for the continual expansion of the manufacturing sector. Moreover, the level of saving in the traditional sector also determines the available supply of resources that may be tapped for investment purposes in the manufacturing sector. In this respect, then, investment opportunities in the agricultural and the manufacturing sector are mutually competitive.

The importance of the emergence of an agricultural surplus (defined as the difference between production and consumption in the traditional sector) cannot be overemphasized. Professor Simon Kuznets wrote that "an agricultural revolution—a marked rise in productivity per worker in agriculture—is a precondition of the industrial revolution in any part of the world."[3] William H. Nicholls also expressed similar sentiments in his very elegant presentation: "Until underdeveloped countries succeed in achieving and sustaining (either through domestic production or imports) a reliable food surplus, they have not fulfilled the fundamental precondition for economic development."[4] And Professor Dale W. Jorgenson stated unequivocally that "for sustained growth an agricultural surplus must come into existence and persist."[5] All these

[2] W. Arthur Lewis, "Economic Development with Unlimited Supplies of Labor," *The Manchester School of Economics and Social Studies*, XXII, No. 2 (May, 1954), 130–91; John C. H. Fei and Gustav Ranis, *Development of the Labor Surplus Economy* (Homewood, Ill.: Richard D. Irwin, Inc., 1964); Dale W. Jorgenson, "The Development of a Dual Economy," *The Economic Journal*, LXXI, No. 2 (June, 1961), 309–34.

[3] Simon Kuznets, *Six Lectures on Economic Growth* (Glencoe, Ill.: The Free Press, 1959), pp. 59–60.

[4] William H. Nicholls, "The Place of Agriculture in Economic Development," in Carl K. Eicher and Lawrence W. Witt, eds., *Agriculture in Economic Development* (New York: McGraw Hill, 1964), p. 40.

[5] Jorgenson, "The Development of a Dual Economy," pp. 333–34.

comments serve to demonstrate the relevancy of the problems of peasant consumption, saving, and investment in the process of industrialization. One must qualify these statements to the extent that food may be imported in large quantities. However, at present, imports must be discounted as a major source of food for most developing countries.

Mainland China is certainly one of the countries that may be classified as a dualistic economy. The success or failure of its present industrialization programs depend to a considerable extent on the agricultural sector: on the availability of the agricultural surplus and rural saving. Professor Anthony Tang has made an excellent study of the relationship between the rate of growth in the industrial sector and the rate of growth of the agricultural surplus.[6] The author has also analyzed the problem from a different angle.[7] In the present paper there will be no attempt to relate the macroeconomic phenomena in the two sectors. Rather, a study will be made of the preference function of the peasants and some conclusions will be drawn as to the proper policies for promoting greater output, saving, and investment, and greater agricultural surplus.[8]

Work versus Leisure

Our first concern is the peasant preference pattern with respect to the marginal compensation of work and leisure. It is assumed that each peasant household maximizes its utility, which is a function of both consumption and leisure, subject to its income constraint. Basically, the indifference surface will yield a supply curve for labor hours that is positively sloping at low levels of marginal compensation for work (wage). However, it is possible that at high levels of wages, the number of hours offered for employment may diminish with an increasing wage rate. The demand for income is derived from the peasant demand for consumption goods, both self-produced and purchased. The relevant wage rate must then be the real wage rate adjusted for the prices of the goods in the consumption bundle. Thus, any given change in the prices of outputs, inputs, or consumption goods and tax rates will change the

[6] Anthony M. Tang, "Policy and Performance in Agriculture," in Alexander Eckstein, Walter Galenson and Ta-chung Liu, eds., *Economic Trends in Communist China* (Chicago: Aldine Publishing Co., 1968), pp. 459–508.

[7] Lawrence J. Lau, "Agricultural Surplus and Capital Formation: The Experience of Communist China," unpublished paper presented at the meeting of the Association of Asian Studies on the Pacific Coast, San Francisco, June, 1966.

[8] Only a partial analysis is made for each facet of the problem with some attempt to relate them to one another.

marginal compensation for work. Whether this will have a positive or a negative effect on the utilization of labor services by the peasant household depends on the shape of the supply curve of labor.

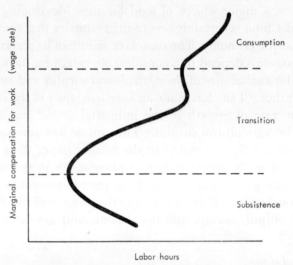

Fig. 1. A hypothetical labor supply curve.

In Figure 1 a hypothetical labor-supply curve is presented. Three ranges, each with a different response pattern, may be distinguished, namely: subsistence, transition, and consumption. In the first range, income is so low that leisure is in all probability an inferior good. Hence, the number of hours worked responds very sharply to any addition to the marginal compensation for work. However, at still lower incomes it is possible to observe the "backward-bending" phenomenon.[9] In the transitional range, the basic needs of the peasants are more or less satisfied and leisure has a positive utility. Moreover, preferences of the peasants in this range are usually restricted to the traditional consumption goods, and once this traditional pattern of consumption is achieved, there may be little incentive to increase labor efforts and hence total income. A slight positive effect may be observed for an increase in the marginal compensation for work, but on the whole the response will not be marked. There may even be a slight decrease in the work effort offered if the aspiration is low. In the third, the consumption range, the peasants are sufficiently rich to be aware of the new consumption possibilities introduced from the manufacturing

[9] Professor Anthony Tang suggested this possibility.

sector, and utility of income is high relatively to leisure. Hence their response to change in the wage rate is highly elastic unless their income is so high that the law of diminishing marginal utility of consumption steps in and at that point the response of labor to wage rate may become zero or even negative. There are probably households in all three ranges in Mainland China, but the important thing is to find out which one of the three ranges is the most representative of national behavior as a whole.

Consumption versus Saving

The choice between consumption and saving is also the choice between present and future consumption. In particular, if present consumption is strongly preferred by the peasants, no manipulations of the interest rate are likely to result in a significantly higher level of saving. Relating to the three ranges previously described, one may generalize to say that in the subsistence range, present consumption will be highly preferred to consumption in the future but in the transition and the consumption ranges, future consumption may have a higher marginal utility relative to present consumption.

Consumption of Self-Produced and Purchased Goods

Both the choice between consumption and saving and the choice between consumption of the peasants' own products and purchased goods affect the availability of the agricultural surplus. If, for instance, self-produced goods are highly preferred to those purchased, then a decrease in the price of manufactured consumption goods is not likely to bring about an increase in the marketed share of the agricultural output. One can draw examples *ad infinitum*, but the basic point is that a knowledge of the properties of the demand functions for consumption and leisure, at least in the region of values that are operationally significant, is essential to any policy maker dealing with price, tax, tenancy, and other related problems. Other things being equal, consumption of self-produced goods will be preferred to purchased consumption in the subsistence and transition ranges to a greater extent than in the consumption range.

Financial versus Real Investment

Finally, out of the total pool of saving, the peasants generally have a choice of either making physical additions or improvements of the capital stock on the farm, or buying such financial assets as savings deposit certificates, land deeds, or precious metals, or repaying debt. The choice obviously depends on the marginal productivity of capital on the farm as well as the yield of financial assets. However, it also depends on the income-leisure preference of the peasants. Other things being equal, if leisure is preferred to consumption in the relevant range of the indifference surface, it is conceivable that more saving will be held in the form of financial investments. While it is true that in a consolidated balance sheet of both the agricultural and manufacturing sectors, the distinction between financial investment and real investment vanishes as the rural saving is reinvested in the manufacturing sector (in a closed economy), this distinction may be important in the analysis of the rate of growth of investment in the agricultural sector.

THE EFFECTS OF ALTERNATIVE DISTRIBUTION
AND ORGANIZATION SCHEMES

Assuming that the peasant households do behave in an utility-maximizing manner, some implications may be derived as to the possible effect of institutional changes on total output (income), leisure, consumption, saving, and investment, and hence the agricultural surplus as well. Only three institutional schemes will be analyzed: the treatment is necessarily brief because of space limitations.

Cooperatives

Cooperatives are characterized by a sharing of the total output amongst their member peasant households, with or without an adequate compensation for such nonlabor means of production as land. In the Chinese experience two types of cooperatives, the elementary and the advanced agricultural producers' cooperatives, have been in existence, with the former disbursing the total product according to the quantity of labor services and the quantity of means of production owned, and the latter disbursing the total product on the basis of labor alone. Basically, the idea is to reward each peasant household according to its contribution to production.

The theory of the cooperative (or collective) has been discussed by many authors, notably Benjamin Ward and Evsey Domar.[10] Here we

---

[10] Benjamin M. Ward, "The Firm in Illyria: A Study of Market Syndicalism," *The American Economic Review*, XLVIII, No. 4 (Sept., 1958), 566–89; Evsey D. Domar, "The Soviet Collective Farm as a Producer Cooperative," *The American Economic Review*, LVI, No. 4 (Sept., 1966), 734–57. See also Walter Y. Oi and Elizabeth M. Clayton, "A Peasant's View of a Soviet Collective Farm," *The American Economic Review*, LVIII, No. 1 (March, 1968), 37–59.

would examine only the more important problems concerning the incentive structure. First of all, it is assumed that there exist no economies of scale, to keep matters simple. However, it is plain that the conclusions do not depend on the total absence of scale effects as long as they are sufficiently small. Let us assume that in the beginning there is a large number of independent peasant households, each producing and consuming entirely on its own. One wishes to investigate the effect on total output and the level of consumption as the different peasant households are formed into an elementary agricultural producers' cooperative, assuming that the relevant factor prices are the same as the ones prevailing before the organization of the cooperative. This is a game situation in which the sum need not be zero. Various possibilities exist. First of all, the peasant households can behave just as if nothing has happened; they will work the same number of hours, use the same amount of fertilizers, and so on. This is the familiar joint-product solution in the theory of oligopoly and results in the same level of output and consumption if there exist no economies or diseconomies of scale. Alternatively, because of the distribution system of the elementary agricultural producers' cooperatives (in which taxes and mandatory state purchases of output must precede the distribution of rental payments to the private means of production, which in turn precedes the distribution of wage payments according to the actual quantity of work performed), there might be a tendency for the private owners of the means of production to work less than before, since labor at that point becomes the residual claimant to total output. In addition, each household's share of capital earnings becomes a function of not only its own labor inputs, but also a function of the total labor applied by all the households combined. Since the influence of a single peasant household is very small on the total output, there may be a tendency for the peasant household to work less. The reason is that if all *other* peasant households operate at their preorganization levels, the total output will remain virtually unchanged and so will each share of the capital distributions. The labor distribution may be relatively small, because it is the residual claimant. Thus the total income position of the peasant household will remain approximately the same while its input of labor is decreased. On the other hand, the members of each household may take great pride in the cooperative and—in the true spirit of a cooperative—work hard for others with less thought of themselves. Whether this is in fact the case is of course an empirical question. The mandatory purchases and taxes in kind may have the direct effect of curtailing the peasant's consumption of self-produced agricultural products. But again, a game situation may develop, as not every single peasant household is required to sell a certain percentage to the state purchasing agent: Only the percentage of output to be sold from each cooperative is stipulated. Thus, it is conceivable that each supposes that everyone else behaves in the preorganization manner. He then would be able to minimize his contribution to the total quantity of compulsory purchase without changing the aggregate ratio significantly. However, if this attitude is prevalent in both production and consumption, then a solution more frequently known as the Cournot solution is operative, with the net result that total output, total input of labor, and total agricultural surplus will decrease from the preorganization levels.

On the other hand, investment is definitely encouraged by the distribution system, as each additional unit of privately owned capital is rewarded at a fixed rate before any distribution due to labor services is undertaken. Thus one would expect the saving rate to be higher than before the organization of the cooperative.

The change from the elementary agricultural producers' cooperatives to the advanced agricultural producers' cooperatives brings about an entirely new situation.[11] In the advanced cooperatives, payment is made for labor only, with the total output being distributed according to the labor services performed by each household. There is no private ownership of factors of production other than labor. The effect on personal savings is very clear: there will be no incentive to save. The effect on public or communal saving is more difficult to gauge and depends to a large extent on the degree of control that the members of the cooperative maintain over the actual operations of the cooperative. The principal determinant of the level of individual household labor services is the distribution of the capital assets before organization. If there was a perfectly even distribution before the organization of the cooperative then there would be no effect on the total level of labor services applied on the cooperative farms. However, the assumption of a perfectly even distribution of capital assets is highly unrealistic. In practice, the distribution is likely to be concentrated in the high-income groups. To the peasants in the low-income group, the increase in income due to organization into cooperatives may not call forth a significant amount of addi-

---

[11] The question of private plots is temporarily neglected. For an excellent analysis of the private sector in collectivized Chinese agriculture, see Kenneth R. Walker, *Planning in Chinese Agriculture: Socialization and the Private Sector, 1956–1962* (London: Frank Cass and Co., Ltd., 1965).

tional effort if they operate in the income-inelastic portion of the labor-supply curve (either the "backward-bending" portion of subsistence or the transition). To the peasants in the high-income group, there is a drastic reduction in the level of income, although there is a corresponding increase in the compensation per unit of labor services performed. Consequently, they will increase their offer of labor services. Thus, to the extent that the higher income group is significant, a cooperative will bring about an increased intensity in the application of labor inputs. However, if there exists only a very small high-income group, there will be little net effect on total labor input and total production. On the other hand, if most of the households own no assets and operate in the positively sloping portion of the supply curve (at subsistence level), such an organization will definitely increase the intensity of labor utilization.

One must modify the above observations if household interactions are to be taken into account. The rule, "To each according to his labor," clearly penalizes those peasant households whose dependency ratio is high. Consequently, these households may supply a disproportionate quantity of labor services in order to secure a minimum per capita income. It may be advantageous for the other households to restrict their offer of labor services and benefit from the efforts of the former households. Finally, in any such cooperative setting involving n units, the outcome is in general indeterminate. A more rigorous analysis employing game theoretic methods will be necessary to explore fully the various possibilities.

Communes

Communes are much larger than the cooperatives and differ from the advanced agricultural producers' cooperatives principally in that a percentage of the total output is distributed to each member of the commune whatever his contributions to the total labor efforts of the commune have been. These free distibutions accounted for about 50 per cent of the total income of each Chinese commune in 1958. Thus, in a sense, a peasant household is in the peculiar position of being its own "share-crop landlord." Consider the hypothetical situation of the commune with a peasant household that elects not to work at all. Assuming that everyone else works at the same rate as before, he is assured of his share of the 50 per cent free distribution. If the other families work harder, his share increases correspondingly. Thus, in general, the peasants will be less responsive to the different incentives used to promote and encourage greater production. If every one of the households in the commune tries to maximize its utility, which is a function of both income and leisure, with the expectation that the others will remain working at the former levels, a solution similar to that of the Cournot solution in oligopoly theory may be obtained and total output may even be decreased.

Finally, a word needs to be said about the distribution rule, "To each according to his need." This amounts in practice to an egalitarian distribution of income. This situation is most susceptible to the Cournot solution with the net result that no labor services may be forthcoming from the peasant households. The effects of certain nonmonetary incentives, such as fame and power, and such policies as exhortation and mass education, may certainly alter the conclusion in the short run but will not be analyzed in this paper.

Share Cropping

Share cropping generally reduces the peasant responsiveness to such external incentives as price and wage changes. Under a share-crop system, the total output and the total labor efforts expended in production may be relatively stable, without regard to prices and wages. As price increases, the benefits to the peasant households are reduced by the percentage that accrues to the landlords. As price decreases, a fixed percentage of the losses are absorbed by the landlords. Other things being equal, the share cropper expends less labor efforts on his farm than an owner-cultivator with comparable factor endowments. The former tends to equate the marginal productivity of labor reduced by the percentage at which he shares his output with the landlord with his own marginal utility of leisure. Assuming a declining marginal utility of leisure, then, the share croppers consume more leisure than owner-cultivators.

THE EMPIRICAL DATA

The empirical data are compiled from different sources and are of varying quality. The results must be considered preliminary and suggestive rather than conclusive.

Income versus Leisure

The peasants may substitute work for leisure, or vice versa, depending on the marginal rate of substitution of income for leisure, provided that some kind of subsistence minimum income has been achieved. However, for the choice to be real, it is necessary that the marginal productivity of labor in agriculture be positive. Otherwise, an increased consumption of leisure does not lead to a decrease in income and there is no real trade off. On the whole, the available empirical evidence does not favor the doctrine of an absolute zero marginal productivity of labor in Mainland Chinese agriculture. Referring to 1925, Professor J. L. Buck writes "the greater the amount of work accomplished the greater the profits."[12] The data pertaining to the labor requirements in seventeen localities in China in 1924–25 also indicate that there is a substantial deficit of labor at the peak seasons.[13] In his subsequent study, Professor Buck remarks:

Information on shortage of labor for farm operations was obtained from 260 localities, nearly two-thirds of which reported insufficient labor at harvesting time, over one-fourth too little labor at planting time, and one-eighth a shortage for irrigation.[14]

Dr. T. H. Shen reports a national shortage of agricultural workers averaging four million workers per year from 1940 to 1946.[15] Information is relatively scarce for the Communist period. However, according to calculations made by Professor Shigeru Ishikawa in 1952, the average labor productivity in agriculture came to 160 yuan in 1952 prices, significantly higher than that in construction, which was only 115 yuan.[16] Acute shortages of labor in certain seasons, ranging from 110 to 400 per cent of the available supply, are also well documented in a study made by the Ministry of Agriculture of Communist China in 1956.[17] Other things being equal, one may assume that an increased application of labor may bring about an increase in the total output.

[12] John Lossing Buck, *Chinese Farm Economy* (Chicago: University of Chicago Press, 1930), p. 119. See also Pan A. Yotopoulos, "The Elusive Test of Disguised Unemployment: Buck's Data," *The Indian Journal of Economics*, XLII, No. 164 (July, 1961), 27–35.

[13] See Chiang Hsieh, "Underemployment in Asia: I. Nature and Extent," *The International Labour Review*, LXV, No. 6 (June, 1952), 703–25; "Underemployment in Asia: II. Its Relation to Investment Policy," *The International Labour Review*, LXVI, No. 1 (July, 1952), 30–39.

[14] John Lossing Buck, *Land Utilization in China* (Chicago: University of Chicago Press, 1937), p. 299.

[15] T. H. Shen, *Agricultural Resources of China* (Ithaca: Cornell University Press, 1951), pp. 372–73, Appendix Table I.

[16] Shigeru Ishikawa, "Long-Term Projections of Mainland China's Economy: 1957–1982," *Economic Bulletin for Asia and the Far East* (Bangkok), XVI, No. 2 (Sept., 1965), 33, Table 10.

[17] Ministry of Agriculture, Bureau of Mechanization, *Chung-kuo nung-yeh chi-hsieh-hua ti hwen-ti* (Problems of Agricultural Mechanization in China) (Paoting, 1958).

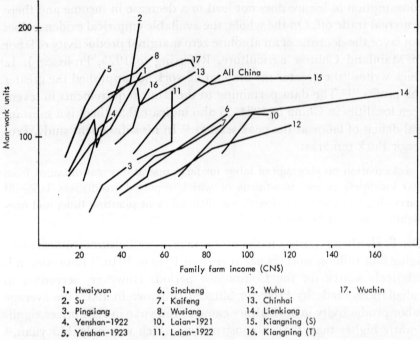

Fig. 2. Relation between man-work units per man-equivalent and family farm earnings per adult male unit. *Source*: J. L. Buck, *Chinese Farm Economy*, Appendix I, pp. 431–48. Wherever possible, family earnings are adjusted to exclude income from other than farm sources.

1. Hwaiyuan	6. Sincheng	12. Wuhu	17. Wuchin
2. Su	7. Kaifeng	13. Chinhai	
3. Pingsiang	8. Wusiang	14. Lienkiang	
4. Yenshan–1922	10. Laian–1921	15. Kiangning (S)	
5. Yenshan–1923	11. Laian–1922	16. Kiangning (T)	

Man-work units per man-equivalent is defined by Buck in his *Chinese Farm Economy* as the number of ten-hour workdays per adult male full-time agricultural worker in the peasant household. For the seventeen localities in North and East Central China in 1921–25, man-work units per man-equivalent show a uniform correlation with the physical size of the farm without a single exception.[18] That less leisure is taken on the larger farms may be explained from the marginal productivity consider-ations: The larger farms, because of their larger area, have a larger marginal productivity of labor, and consequently, more labor per man is applied.

This does not rule out the possibility that the family members may elect to work less as income or wealth increases. As the ratio of family labor to hired labor declines with increasing farm size, it is evident that the peasants have a preference for leisure as income rises. Moreover, the increases in application of labor per man-equivalent with increasing

[18] Buck, *Chinese Farm Economy*, pp. 127–29, Table 19.

farm size tends to decrease and stabilize after a certain point of magnitude.

In Figure 2, the number of man-work units per man-equivalent is plotted against the family farm earnings per adult male unit. Family farm earnings are the net income, both cash and noncash, obtained by the family from farm sources, after deducting all expenses except the imputed value of own-family labor. Thus, family earnings per adult male unit is the compensation that each family member receives for his participation in the farm work. In equilibrium, the marginal disutility of labor (or utility of leisure) is equated to family farm earnings per adult male unit, which may be considered as the imputed wage rate of the individual's labor.

From Figure 2 it is apparent that, on the whole, man-work units per man-equivalent is positively related to family farm earnings per adult male unit. It is also clear that there is no uniform slope, and that although man-work units per man-equivalent rises with the marginal compensation, the evidence is strong that at high levels of income the intensity of work tends to be stabilized. At low levels of income, the preference for income is very high and a slight increase in the marginal compensation to effort is sufficient to cause a large increase in the application of labor, although there are instances of negative correlation. This corresponds to subsistence. On the high end of the per capita farm-earnings scale, however, the intensity of work responds only weakly if at all to increase in the marginal rate of compensation. This corresponds to either the transition or the consumption range.

The man-work units per man-equivalent is plotted against the real family earnings per adult male unit in kilograms of grain-equivalent for the seventeen localities in China in Figure 3. The shape of the best fitting curve appears to be consistent with our hypothetical labor-supply curve. Admittedly, there is a large element of speculation involved as the number of data points is small, hence additional evidence must be sought.

In the *Land Utilization* study (Figs. 4, 5, 6), which covers the period 1929–33, the work done is expressed as the number of man-equivalent, that is, work equivalent to an adult male worker working on the farm for one whole year. This definition is not rigorous enough but is sufficient for the present purpose. By looking at the man-equivalent per farm, one observes that it increases monotonically with farm size in all eight agricultural regions of China without exception.[19] On the other hand,

[19] Buck, *Land Utilization in China.*

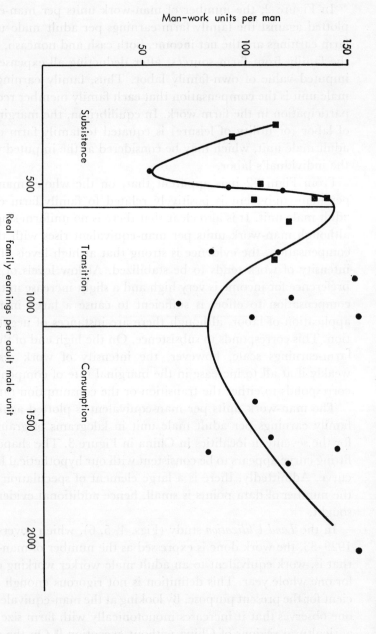

Man-work units per man

Real family earnings per adult male unit
(Kilograms of grain-equivalent)

Subsistence   Transition   Consumption

Fig. 3. Relation between man-work units per man-equivalent and real family earnings per adult male unit. *Source:* John Lossing Buck, *Chinese Farm Economy* (Chicago: University of Chicago Press, 1930), p. 127, Table 18; Appendix I, pp. 431–48. Percentage of crop hectare area, *ibid.*, pp. 184–85, Table 3; yield per hectare, *ibid.*, pp. 203–4, Table 13; price, *ibid.*, p. 214, Table 18. See Fig. IV and John Lossing Buck, *Land Utilization in China* (Chicago: University of Chicago Press, 1937), p. 299, Table 11. Production per capita is adjusted to include nonfarm income as well. Production expenditures have been neglected because of the lack of data.

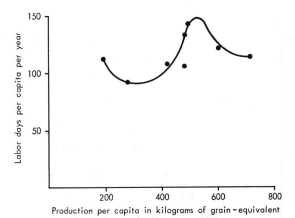

Fig. 4.   Relation between work done in man-equivalent
per capita and production per capita. *Source*: John Lossing
Buck, *Land Utilization in China* (Chicago: University of
Chicago Press, 1937), p. 275, Table 11; p. 278, Table 14;
p. 286, Table 19. Labor days per capita is obtained by
multiplying the man-equivalent per capita with 365 days.

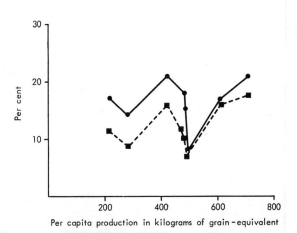

Percentage of farms having hired labor

Percentage of work performed by hired labor

Fig. 5.   Relation between production per capita and (1)
percentage of farms having hired labor, (2) percentage of
work performed by hired labor. *Source*: John Lossing Buck,
Land Utilization in China (Chicago: University of Chicago
Press, 1937), p. 286, Table 19; p. 291, Table 3; p. 293,
Table 4; p. 297, Table 9; p. 290, Table 2.

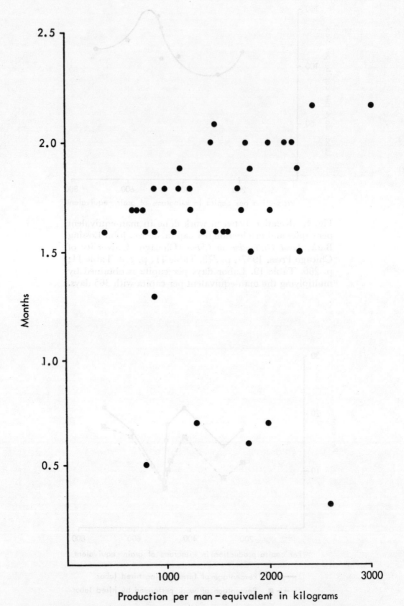

Fig. 6. Scatter diagram of the number of idle months per able-bodied man versus the production per man-equivalent in kilograms of grain-equivalent. *Source*: John Lossing Buck, *Land Utilization in China* (Chicago: University of Chicago Press, 1937), p. 283, Table 18 and p. 295, Table 7.

crop acre per man-equivalent also shows a similar increase with size.[20] Output on the large farms, at least, appears not to have been maximized, and there exists some trade off between work and income (and hence leisure and income).

Looking at the relation between work done in man-equivalent per capita and production per capita in kilograms in Figure 4, one observes an initially rising and then falling relation. This is consistent with the observation based on the 1921–25 data. Figure 3 reveals the rapid rise in work effort in response to an increase in the real family earnings per adult male unit. Figure 4 shows a similar rapid rise at or near 450 kilograms per capita. Considering that per capita production is, in general, smaller than per adult male unit production and that the real family earnings per adult male unit used in Figure 3 also include some nonfarm earnings, it is plausible to assume that the two figures reflect the same basic income-leisure characteristics.

The percentage of farms having hired labor and the percentage of farm work performed by hired labor may also be related to production per capita. The two curves run very closely together, as shown in Figure 5, and one needs to discuss only one of them. Once more, the region between 450 and 500 kilograms per capita appears to be rather critical. Between 300 and 450 kilograms per capita, the percentage of income from nonfarm sources is approximately constant while there is a rapid rise in the use of hired labor. This confirms the hypothesis that this is a region of low and negative supply elasticity of own labor. However, in the critical region of 450–500 kilograms, there is a rapid fall in the use of hired labor, a fall that is far more precipitous than the fall in the percentage of income derived from nonfarm sources. This shows that at this level of compensation, the supply elasticity of own labor is both high and positive. Income is preferred to leisure and there is a large-scale substitution of the farmer's own labor for hired labor. Beyond 500 kilograms, the ratio of hired labor rises again, reflecting the declining labor-supply curve portion in Figures 3 and 4 corresponding to the transition range.

Figure 6 shows the number of idle months per able-bodied man as a function of the production per man-equivalent. There is a wide scatter of points but there appears to be a positive correlation between the number of idle months per able-bodied man and production per man-equivalent, i.e., more leisure is taken as the marginal rate of compensa-

[20] *Ibid.*, p. 275, Table 11. The data in the Statistical Volume have not been analyzed.

tion rises. Of course, the observation must be qualified as the wide climatic variations over the eight agricultural regions in China may preclude the possibility of gainful employment in certain months of the year in one or more of the regions. Nevertheless, it is fruitful to note that if it were true that the Chinese peasants are indifferent to the level of work per person, the number of idle months per able-bodied man should be independent of the level of productivity of labor. Thus, leisure is shown to have a definite positive marginal utility to the Chinese peasant at some income levels that are achievable by a significant percentage of the peasants.

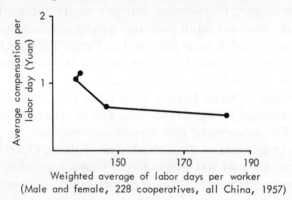

Weighted average of labor days per worker
(Male and female, 228 cooperatives, all China, 1957)

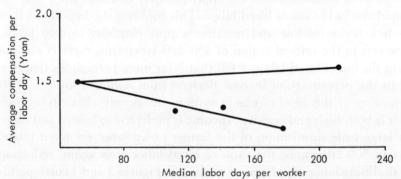

Median labor days per worker
(118 advanced cooperatives, Chiahsing special district, Chekiang Province, 1956)

Fig. 7.   Relation between average annual labor days per worker and compensation per labor day. (a) Weighted average of labor days per worker (male and female, 228 cooperatives, all China, 1957). *Source: Tung-chi yen-chiu* (Statistical Research), No. 8 (Aug., 1958), pp. 8 ff. (b) Median labor days per worker (118 advanced cooperatives, Chiahsing Special District, Chekiang Province, 1956). *Source: Hsin chien-she* (New Construction), No. 7 (July, 1957), p. 5.

Now the question arises as to whether the basic income-leisure characteristics of the Chinese peasant have been altered by the socialist transformation of the Communist regime. On this score, the data are very scarce and scattered, but there are isolated examples that may be used as partial evidence. In a survey of 228 agricultural producers' cooperatives in all 24 provinces and autonomous regions of China in 1957, it was found that as the average compensation per labor day increases, the total quantity of labor days per man-equivalent first declines and then increases (Fig. 7a).[21] A similar relation was observed in a 1956 survey of 118 advanced agricultural producers' cooperatives in the Chiahsing Special District in the province of Chekiang (Fig. 7b).[22] The same "backward-bending" phenomenon was also found in a survey of 271 households of Yenhai hsien in the province of Chekiang

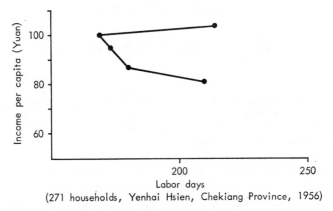

(271 households, Yenhai Hsien, Chekiang Province, 1956)

Fig. 8. Relation between labor days per man-equivalent and the average income per capita. Data for 271 households in Yenhai *hsien*, Chekiang, 1956. *Source: Hsin chien-she* (New Construction), No. 7 (July, 1957), p. 5.

in 1956 (Fig. 8).[23] In order to obtain some idea of the real magnitude of the income per capita, reference may be made to the cost of living of Chinese peasants in 1956 of 53.63 yuan per person per year computed by Professor Kenneth Walker.[24] Hence, it does appear that most of Mainland China may still be in the subsistence range. The important consideration here, from a policy formulation point of view, is this: which segment of the labor-supply curve is more significant (and representative) of the national behavior as a whole? As a rough indicator,

[21] *T'ung-chi yen-chiu* (Statistical Research), No. 8 (Aug., 1958), pp. 8 ff.
[22] *Hsin chien-she* (New Construction), No. 7 (July, 1957), p. 5.
[23] *Ibid.*
[24] Walker, *Planning in Chinese Agriculture.*

in the Chiahsing Special District the number of cooperatives operating in the negatively sloping region is 93, whereas the number in the positively sloping region is only 25.[25] For Yenhai hsien, out of a total of 271 households, 84 households operate in the positively sloping region, whereas 187 households operate in the negatively sloping region.[26] The presumption is therefore strong that on balance the aggregate of the cooperatives behaves as if the total labor-supply curve is downward sloping.[27]

In this connection, one should also note a comparative survey of elementary and advanced agricultural producers 'cooperatives in Chiahsing Special District in the province of Chekiang in 1956.[28] There are 121 advanced and 236 elementary cooperatives in the survey. The comparative group statistics are presented in Table 1.

TABLE 1
SELECTED DATA ON LABOR INPUT, PRODUCTIVITY, AND
INCOMES BY TYPE OF COOPERATIVE

	Elementary	Advanced
Labor days per man-equivalent	131.0	142
Production per man-equivalent	274.0 yuan	300.0 yuan
Compensation per labor day	1.08	1.30
Actual farm income per household	289.30	331.70

Source: *Hsin chien-she* (New Construction), No. 7 (July, 1957), p. 2.

Care must be exercised in interpreting the increase in labor day per man-equivalent from the elementary to the advanced cooperatives as a response to the increase in compensation per labor day. Some basic change in the distribution system has occurred between the elementary and the advanced cooperatives. In the first place, because the factor rental payments are abolished under the advanced cooperatives, the compensation per labor day increases, other things being equal. This might, assuming that the previous analysis of the shape of the labor-

[25] *Hsin chien-she*, No. 7 (July, 1957), pp. 4–5.

[26] *Ibid.*

[27] The national survey of 228 agricultural producers' cooperatives in 1957 also indicates that the per capita net disposable incomes for the four main regions of Mainland China are as follows:

Northwest and Inner Mongolia	67 yuan
Northeast (Manchuria)	55 yuan
Central Plains	46 yuan
South	46 yuan

Considering that the cost of living of a Chinese peasant has been computed to be 53.63 yuan, it appears obvious that the majority of the peasants must be in the subsistence range.

[28] *Hsin chien-she*, No. 7 (July, 1957), p. 2.

supply function is correct, lead to a decrease in the number of labor days per man-equivalent. On the other hand, because of the abolition of factor rental payments, the peasants previously receiving a factor payment now face a reduction in their income, which in return increases their marginal utility of income relative to leisure. There is thus a tendency to work more than before to compensate partially for the loss of income. The 8 per cent increase in the number of labor days per man-equivalent in going from the elementary to the advanced cooperatives is probably due to the asset-income effect. And because this effect seems to dominate, it is conjectured that the minimum free consumption provided by the communes probably leads to a decrease in the number of labor days per man-equivalent through the influence of the inverse-asset effect.

The results of a survey conducted of Yenhai hsien in the province of Chekiang in 1956 indicated that the degree of labor utilization in the advanced agricultural producers cooperatives, measured by the number of labor days per adult male laborer, was 50 per cent higher than when the peasants were still independent freeholders, 24.5 per cent higher than that in the period of mutual-aid teams, and only 9.8 per cent higher than in the period of elementary cooperatives.[29] The increase from the elementary to advanced cooperatives has already been explained. The increase from the mutual-aid teams to the elementary cooperatives is not so significant as the increase from independent freeholders to mutual-aid teams. The former may be explained primarily on the basis of the existence of economies of scale and the economies of consolidation of fragmented plots that raise the marginal productivity of labor relative to the pre-existing wage rate, assuming that the distribution of income is constant. In effect, the distribution of income is not constant and the high-income group is continuously disappearing. Thus, something similar to the asset effect described earlier may also have contributed to the increase in labor intensity. It is significant to note that the further institutional organization was not particularly successful in eliciting additional labor effort in comparison to the transformation from freeholders to mutual-aid teams.

Another aspect of the income-leisure problem is the total output response to changes in prices. A very simple hypothesis may be tested: If the peasants do respond to relative prices, there will be a tendency for them to plant the crops that yield the highest return for their land. Waiving the difficulties of cost and return comparisons aside, if one

[29] *Ibid.*

ranks the crops in each locality according to its percentage of the total acreage and lists alongside the expected returns (gross) per acre, an excellent correspondence is found.[30] The results are shown in Table 2.

TABLE 2
RELATION BETWEEN CROP AREA AND EXPECTED RETURN PER HECTARE

Locality	Crop	Per cent of Crop Area	Expected Return
Hwaiyuan	Wheat	32.0	19.54 CN$
	Kaoliang	13.5	18.66
Su	Wheat	21.0	39.82
	Kaoliang	11.1	36.44
	Barley	10.3	27.94
Pingsiang	Wheat	24.3	134.9
	Kaoliang	17.0	33.2
Yenshan-1922	Wheat	35.9	73.84
	Kaoliang	19.8	28.49
Yenshan-1923	Wheat	38.9	5.51
	Kaoliang	19.7	19.49
Wusiang	Millet	33.2	70.01
	Wheat	23.9	55.26
Wutai	Oats	23.9	54.15
	Millet	18.0	50.09
	Kaoliang	17.1	63.15
Laian-1921	Rice	52.7	160.06
	Wheat	12.5	73.08
Laian-1922	Rice	41.6	80.69
	Wheat	37.8	51.12

Source: John Lossing Buck, *Chinese Farm Economy* (Chicago: The University of Chicago Press, 1930).

Column (3) pp. 184–85, Table 3. Only those crops which occupy more than 10 per cent and are in the same season are considered.

Column (4). Expected Return is approximated by actual returns per hectare, calculated by multiplying the yield per hectare and the price. For yield, pp. 203–4, Table 13. For price, p. 214, Table 18.

There are other instances of adjustments to external conditions, for example:

. . . during the drought years before 1932 farmers themselves undertook to dig canals for irrigation. After 1932 prices of agricultural products decreased

[30] Buck, *Chinese Farm Economy*, pp. 228–29, Table 1; pp. 232–33, Table 2. There are two exceptions which may require some explanation. There was a bad harvest in Yenshan in 1923, which resulted in a yield of wheat far below that normally expected. The reversed positions of oats and kaoliang in the case of Wutai is probably due to differences in the cost side of the production although abnormal prices may also have caused the same effect. The following labor requirements per hectare oɪ grown crop are given:

	Man-work Units	Animal-work Units
Oats	69.28	14.50
Kaoliang	77.33	27.39

though the taxation of irrigated land had increased, resulting in the abandonment of irrigated land.[31]

Moreover, the size of the family also adjusts to the size of the farm. The large family system permits considerable elasticity in size in relation to the given resources. The average increase in family size, given an increase of ten local *mou* in farm area, is 0.86 adult male unit.[32]

Thus far, the discussion has been centered on farm employment and farm income. There is, of course, a significant proportion of income derived from nonfarm sources. Depending on the locality, the percentage of income from nonfarm sources may be as high as 25 per cent. According to the 1921–25 survey, "nearly one-third are from money sent by members of the family working elsewhere, one-fifth from trading, one-eighth from renting of land, and one-tenth from professional work."[33] The peasants on the smaller farms would be expected to derive a higher percentage of their income from supplementary sources because of their low farm income. Indeed, it is observed that twice as many operators in the small-farm group as those in the large-farm group have supplementary income.[34]

No significant relation is found between the percentage of income from nonfarm sources as plotted against the real family earnings per adult male unit from farm sources. This is to be expected, as the quantity of supplementary income may be unrelated to the quantity of nonfarm labor services. However, if the percentage of income from nonfarm *labor* sources is plotted against the real family earnings per adult male unit, an inverted U-shape is observed, confirming our previous statements on the income-leisure preference in that range of real income.

Moreover, for the period 1929–33, the percentages of net income from nonfarm sources are, in ascending order of farm size, respectively, 21, 14, 11, 10, and 9.[35] Thus, the farms appear to have operated in the "backward-bending" portion of the labor-supply curve. Considering that the sample households generally have a lower income than the earlier study, one may add a hypothetical downward-sloping section to the left-hand end of the curve in Figure 9.

Figure 10 refers to an income study of 228 collectives in 24 provinces of China in 1956–57.[36] Both the percentage and the absolute quantity

[31] Buck, *Land Utilization in China*, p. 51.
[32] Buck, *Chinese Farm Economy*, pp. 334–45.
[33] *Ibid.*, p. 99.
[34] *Ibid.*, p. 116.
[35] Buck, *Land Utilization in China*, p. 279, Table 16.
[36] *T'ung-chi yen-chiu*, No. 8 (Aug., 1958), pp. 8ff.

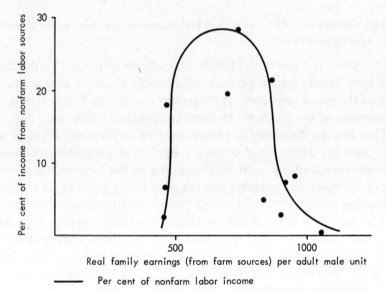

Fig. 9. Relation between per cent income from nonfarm labor sources and real family earnings (from farm sources) per adult male unit.

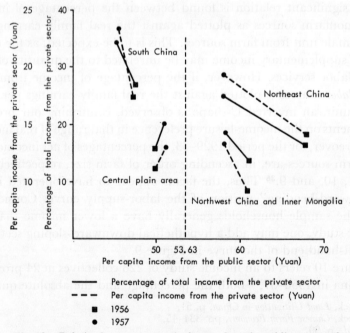

Fig. 10. Relation between per capita income from the public sector and per capita income from the private sector (and its percentage of the total), 1956–1957. *Source*: Kenneth R. Walker, *Planning in Chinese Agriculture: Socialisation and the Private Sector* (London: Frank Cass & Co., 1965) p. 34, Table 5.

of supplementary income tend to fall with increasing per capita income. It should be noted that circumstances in 1957 were far more favorable to private sector activities because considerable dislocations and un-settlements were caused by the rapid socialization drives during 1956. Thus, corresponding to the same income per capita and the same income-leisure preference, one expects a higher percentage of supplementary income in 1956 than is actually observed when it is compared with 1957. If one adjusts the figures for the Central Plain region in this manner, it is conceivable that a downward-sloping curve may be obtained for this region. At any rate, a rather straightforward interpretation of the graph is that more peasant households are operating on the downward-sloping portion of the subsistence labor-supply curve than the upward-sloping portion of the transition range. Hence, in the aggregate, they behave as if the whole group operates on the downward-sloping portion. It is also significant that the slopes of the lines are noticeably different for different sides of the dotted line. The line represents the annual cost of living of a Chinese peasant as computed by Dr. Kenneth Walker.[37] The slopes are gentler on the higher income side of the line. There are two factors contributing to this phenomenon. First of all, as income rises, more peasant households operate on the rising portion of the labor-supply curve and other things being equal, the downward-sloping curve will be less steep. Secondly, as the level of income becomes higher relative to the subsistence income, the demand for income is not as great because of the diminishing marginal utility of money. The cost of living is a good indicator of the subsistence income. Therefore, even without the peasants' class-distribution effect, one expects that the nearer the subsistence line, the steeper the slope.

Consumption versus Saving

Per capita real consumption is plotted against real income in Figure 11. One observes that at low levels of income, consumption is almost equal to income and in some cases may even exceed it. Probably there is not a constant saving rate throughout the whole range of incomes, as it is also evident that at high incomes (over 1,000 kilograms per capita) a saving rate of 30 per cent appears to fit the data quite well.

Thus, short of coercion, exhortation, and taxation, it is unlikely that a 30 per cent saving rate may be voluntarily achieved at the existing levels of income. In fact, in an income and expenditure survey of peasant households in 1954, it was found that of an average disposable income

[37] Walker, *Planning in Chinese Agriculture*, pp. 38–39.

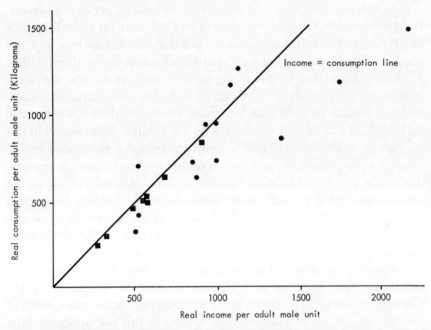

Fig. 11.   Real income per adult male unit and real consumption per adult male unit (17 localities, 1921–1925) and real income per capita and real consumption per capita (8 regions, 1929–1933). *Source*: John Lossing Buck, *Chinese Farm Economy* (Chicago: University of Chicago Press, 1930), Appendix I, pp. 431–48; p. 385, Table 2. 1. Per capita production, *ibid.*, p. 286, Table 19. Per cent of net income from nonfarm sources, *ibid.*, p. 297, Table 9. 2. Value of savings per farm, *ibid.*, p. 467, Table 21. 1929–33 data in squares (■).

per household of 692.9 yuan, only 25.2 yuan are saved, resulting in an average saving rate of only 3.65 per cent, very close to the 1929–33 figure.[38] According to a survey of nineteen agricultural producers' cooperatives in eight provinces in 1957, the average rate of public accumulation had risen to 7.95 per cent from 3.59 per cent in 1956.[39] The approximate constancy of the saving rate is also consistent with the fact that the marginal utility of consumption does not decrease very fast in the relevant range of income per capita. In 1956, in Chekiang, the suggested rate of public or communal accumulation was only 5 per cent and the cadres were cautioned not to be overzealous in trying to raise the rate of public accumulation. However, the rate of taxation was 12.7 per cent, the contribution to the public reserves was 8 per cent and that to the welfare fund 2 per cent, resulting in a net withdrawal rate of

[38] *T'ung-chi kung-tso* (Statistical Work), No. 19 (Oct., 1957), pp. 31 ff.
[39] *T'ung-chi yen-chiu*, No. 4 (April, 1958), p. 24. The eight provinces are Chekiang, Kiangsu, Anhwei, Hunan, Honan, Shansi, Hopei, and Liaoning.

31.35 per cent, including both private and public savings.[40] Total accumulation, including state taxes, public reserves, public welfare fund, cooperative public accumulation, and private household accumulation, amounted to 31.2 per cent of the net output for a commune in Fukien.[41] These high rates of withdrawal would not be possible were it not for the centralized organization of the cooperatives. The desire for greater saving, as Dr. Yuan-li Wu so aptly points out, is one of the main reasons for the conversion from collectives to communes.[42] As one example, one commune experienced the almost miraculous increase in saving of 23.1 times the figure achieved when the constituent collectives were still in separate existence. The following data are illuminating:[43]

	1957	1958
Net income after taxes	2,083,000 yuan	8,334,000 yuan
Communal accumulation	234,000	5,409,000
Saving rate	11 per cent	65 per cent

In another commune the rate of public accumulation out of net income in 1957 was 7.8 per cent, whereas the planned target rate was 31.1 per cent for 1958.[44] The saving rate is impossible without government control of the disposition of income.

Finally, a word needs to be said about the actual saving and investment made with the free labor mobilized by the communes. In general, this uncompensated contribution of labor on the part of the commune members amounts to approximately 10 per cent of their total labor services offered.[45] This should be considered as part of the involuntary saving of the peasants.

Consumption and Marketed Agricultural Surplus

The empirical Engel's law states that as real income increases, the proportion of expenditures for food will decrease. However, this holds true only when income is sufficiently high. In Figure 12, the per cent consumption supplied by the farm and the per cent consumption of

[40] *Hsin chien-she*, No. 7 (July, 1957), p. 3.

[41] *T'ung-chi yen-chiu*, No. 7 (July, 1958), pp. 13 ff.

[42] For instance, see Yuan-li Wu, "The Economics of Mainland China's Agriculture: Some Aspects of Measurement, Interpretation and Evaluation," in John Lossing Buck, Owen L. Dawson, and Yuan-li Wu, *Food and Agriculture in Communist China* (New York: Frederick A. Praeger, 1966), pp. 73–100.

[43] *T'ung-chi kung-tso*, No. 21 (Nov., 1958), pp. 67 ff.

[44] *T'ung-chi yen-chiu*, No. 6 (June, 1958), p. 29.

[45] *Hsin chien-she*, No. 7 (July, 1957), p. 5.

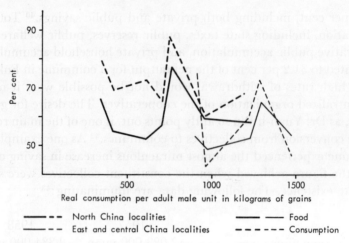

Fig. 12. Per cent consumption supplied from farm and per cent consumption of food versus real value of consumption per adult male unit (17 localities, 1921–1925). *Source*: John Lossing Buck, *Chinese Farm Economy* (Chicago: University of Chicago Press, 1930), p. 385, Table 2; p. 386, Table 3; p. 393, Table 7. The real values are obtained by deflating the money values of each locality by the respective average price per kilogram of grains of each locality. The derivation of price indices outlined in appendix.

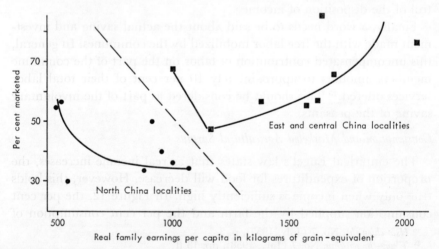

Fig. 13. Relation between real family earnings per adult male unit and the marketed ratio of farm products. *Source*: John Lossing Buck, *Chinese Farm Economy* (Chicago: University of Chicago Press, 1930), Appendix I, pp. 431–48. The marketed ratio is found in *ibid.*, p. 199, Table 10.

food are both plotted against real consumption per adult male unit for the seventeen localities in 1921–25. Both percentages almost always move in the same direction for each region. Moreover, it is clear that Engel's law does not hold in this range of real income, as both the North China and the East Central China curves show similar double-peaked characteristics. Figure 13 shows the marketed ratio versus real family earnings per adult male unit. It is apparent that there exists an initially decreasing and then increasing relationship between the marketed ratio and the real family earnings per capita.

It turns out that there exists a simple, unified interpretation of the figures. In the subsistence range, labor supply first falls and then may rise very rapidly with any increase in the marginal compensation. Consumption of one's own products as a per cent of total is also high initially because food is the most important component of subsistence consumption, especially when income is low. Saving is low or negligible. The marketed ratio is very high as the demand for cash income is equally pressing: There are the fixed obligations of cash rent, and such basic necessities as coal and salt must be purchased. As income gradually improves, the proportion of food consumption becomes stable, once a certain standard is reached. The marketed ratio declines as there exists no strong demand for cash income in this range of income. As income increases further, the marginal utility of leisure becomes relatively high and there may even be a decrease in the labor supply as well as an increase in the percentage of hired labor. Marginal utility of cash income further diminishes and the share of purchased goods and services in total consumption increases as a result. Then we come to what may be called the "Engel range" of incomes: In this range, the ratio of food

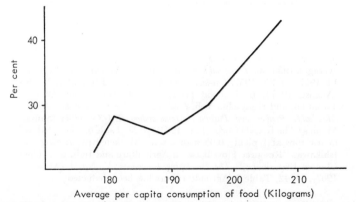

Fig. 14. Relation between the marketed ratio and average per capita consumption of food (kilograms of grain-equivalent), 1954. *Source:* *T'ung-chi kung-tso* (Statistical Work), No. 19 (Oct., 1957).

consumption to total consumption is continually declining. The demand for income is once more dominant as the manufactured consumer goods stimulate further interest in consumption. The marketed ratio rises sharply as the result of a declining demand for food and an increasing demand for cash income. Because of its low income, North China in 1921–25 operated primarily in the region of decreasing marketed ratio. It is speculated that if this particular preference structure is prevalent, any increase in the per capita real income of the peasants in China will not result in an increase in the marketed ratio.

So much for the historical record. Let us turn to examine the limited information that we have of Mainland China. Professor Shigeru Ishikawa has provided an excellent analysis of the effects of the redistribution of income on consumption as a result of land reform, and hence the marketed ratio.[46] One would add only the observation that the same data used by Professor Ishikawa support the hypothesis of a double-peaked relation between the marketed ratio and the per capita consumption of food[47] (see Fig. 14). Since per capita consumption is closely

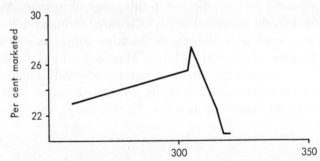

Fig. 15. Relation between per capita production of food grains and the marketed ratio of food grains. *Source*: Rural population: Annual averages, 1950–56, *T'ung-chi kung-tso* (Statistical Work), No. 11 (June 14, 1957), p. 25; 1957, *Chi-hua ching-chi* (Planned Economy), No. 8 (August, 1957), p. 7. Food production: Ta-chung Liu, Chong Twammo, and Kung-chia Yeh, *Production of Food Crops on the Chinese Mainland: Prewar and Postwar, Memorandum RM-3569-PR*; (Santa Monica: The RAND Corp., Jan., 1964), p. 27, Table 6, converted to metric tons at 1 picul=0.05 metric tons. Marketed ratio: Shigeru Ishikawa, "Resource Flow Between Agriculture and Industry: The Chinese Experience," *The Developing Economies*, V, No. 1 (March, 1967), 41–42, Table 8. Agricultural tax has been deducted.

[46] Shigeru Ishikawa, "Resource Flow between Agriculture and Industry—The Chinese Experience," *The Developing Economies*, V, No. 1 (March, 1967).
[47] *T'ung-chi kung-tso*, No. 19 (Oct., 1957).

related to per capita income, one may extrapolate to the existence of a double-peaked relation between the marketed ratio and the real income per capita. In fact, Professor Ishikawa also observes that "the income elasticity of the average farm household is extremely high because the present levels of consumption of food grains in the farm household are extremely low and because the distribution of income is being equalized."[48]

The time-series data are more difficult to interpret because of the institutional changes and of noncomparability resulting from differences in definitions. However, Figure 15 appears to confirm the characteristic of the marketed ratio-income relation in the subsistence range. A report from Communist China indicates that there is even an absolute decline in the total quantity available for the urban population with a rise in per capita production for the period 1953–57. This is all quite consistent with our previous interpretation of peasant behavior.

Saving and Investment

Very little information is available on the level of investment in either prewar or postwar China. A very crude index of gross private agricultural investment has been constructed for each locality by adding together the noncash net increase of capital, the expenditures on buildings and repairs, tools and repairs, and livestock purchases for the seventeen localities in China in 1921–25. The results are presented in Figure 16. It is observed that at low levels of real saving, real saving is very sensitive to changes in the rate of return. Investment is effectively constrained by the level of real saving. As the level of real saving becomes higher, saving is no longer very much influenced by the rate of return. However, investment is still very closely related to the rate of return: the higher the rate of return, the higher the investment. In any case, it appears that there exists a saving as well as an investment response to the rate of return in agriculture. It is also observed that owner-operated farms show a higher increase in capital than the part-owner and tenant farms. The reason is probably that, given a share contract, the potential benefits accrue only to the operator in the case of owner-operated farms, whereas otherwise potential gains must be shared with landlords. Hence, owner-operators will be more responsive to changes in the marginal rate of return (provided they are not operating in the region of low marginal utility of leisure relative to income).

[48] Ishikawa, "Resource Flow . . . ," p. 30.

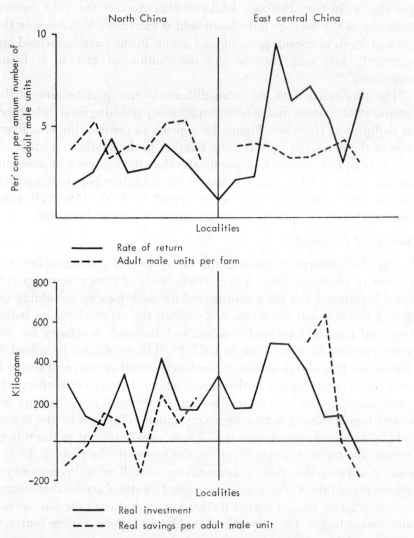

Fig. 16. Peasant savings, investment and the rate of return. *Source*: Consumption: John Lossing Buck, *Chinese Farm Economy* (Chicago: University of Chicago Press, 1930), p. 385, Table 2. Savings: The difference between real family earnings and real consumption per adult male unit. Investment: The sum of increase of capital, *ibid.*, p. 65, Table 23, buildings and their repairs, tools and their repairs and livestock purchased minus the decrease of capital, *ibid.*, p. 75, Table 31. Rate of return: *Ibid.*, Appendix I, pp. 431–48. The deflator used is the price index constructed for each locality.

CONCLUSION

On the basis of the data just explored, a few tentative conclusions may be drawn. First, it appears that there has been no observable change in the basic structural characteristics up to 1957. Second, most of the Chinese peasants are probably operating in the subsistence range, which may exhibit among other things a "backward-bending" supply curve of labor. Hence a free distribution scheme such as that practiced in the communes in 1958 may have a detrimental effect on the quantity of total labor services forthcoming. This probably provides a partial explanation for the failure of the communes in 1958. Third, it appears that most of the Chinese peasants also operate in the region of declining marketed ratio with increasing income. Thus, any marginal increase in per capita real income (or production) is unlikely to result in a significant increase in the total quantity marketed by the peasants. Fourth, the voluntary saving rate at the existing income levels is insufficient to supply all the saving demands of the Communist planners. Nevertheless, it is also obvious that the saving rate rises with income. Finally, with respect to agricultural investment, it appears that the peasants are rather responsive to the magnitude of expected rewards, and if the fruits of investment are withheld from the peasants, there may not be a strong incentive to invest.

JERZY F. KARCZ

Comment

Professor Lau is to be highly commended for approaching his subject matter with the aid of the apparatus of economic theory. This is certainly the best way to reduce the wide range of uncertainty that prevails in the discussion of collectivization. I believe that further research along these lines will ultimately lead to better understanding of the impact of collectivization as regards the efficient use of agricultural resources (including labor) on the total economy of a country in the process of development as well as solely on its agricultural sector. But the use of the powerful tools of economic theory often raises questions about the appropriateness of some assumptions. Since authors of conference papers cannot, because of space limitations, answer all such queries, it is the natural task of discussants to explore in some detail the nature of the underlying assumptions.

"Nothing is more difficult to speculate about than the shape of the supply function for labor . . ."[1] Hence, it will be in order to focus our attention first on Professor Lau's Figure 1. I am uneasy about the treatment of subsistence as a range (hereafter referred to as an area, rather than a range). If we define labor hours placed on the X axis of Figure 1 in terms of some uniform quality—and this is clearly the case in the transition and the consumption areas—then it would have been preferable to define subsistence as a level on the income axis—or a point on the supply curve. Parenthetically, I am perfectly willing to concede the existence of a certain penumbra about the physiological level of subsistence defined as a minimum caloric intake that enables the individual to put forth a certain, defined amount of effort over a relevant period of time.[2] By definition then, hours supplied below that level would de-

---

[1] Richard Moorsteen and Raymond P. Powell, *The Soviet Capital Stock, 1928–1962* (Homewood, Ill.: Richard D. Irwin, Inc., 1966), p. 303.

[2] As a consequence, the supply curve of labor below the subsistence level would

cline as the real wage (or income) is reduced further. In terms of "sixty-minute" hours of uneven quality there would be no difficulty with the explanation of the backward-bending supply curve in the subsistence area of Figure 1. It takes time to starve and any attempt to prolong the agony can easily be understood in terms of a high elasticity of expectations: We work longer hours at lower real wages because something better might happen tomorrow. The backward bend, though, may only operate as a "slide," while movement in the upward direction may still proceed toward the northeast. In any case, though, this explanation involves a problem in the conservation of (human) capital: For this purpose another diagram might be more appropriate.

Figure 1, however, also raises a number of other important questions that must be explored further before we can proceed in what is obviously a very promising direction. These questions arise primarily in relation to the very inelastic or even backward-bending portion of the supply curve for labor within Dr. Lau's transition range.

The inelasticity of labor supply (or its negative slope) in the transition range is explained partly in terms of higher positive utility of leisure but also by the persistence of the traditional consumption patterns (p. 308). I take it that the meaning of the latter is fairly broad: it may refer to the failure of the peasants to realize that some consumption goods (of the modern as opposed to the traditional variety) are available. But it may also mean that some of these goods fail to enter into the peasant preference function because of certain institutional or environmental factors, which are generally assumed away in the first step of economic theorizing under the heading of imperfections. Thus, it is of no use to know, if there is no electricity in the village, that electric washing machines exist and can be purchased. If so, the peasant indifference surface (for this village) cannot include any washing machines though it might conceivably include moving to a locality where there is electricity or gas (but other imperfections may arise at this juncture). Similarly, the effectiveness of cameras as a possible component of the real wage may be greatly reduced if the film must be developed some forty miles away (it may be eliminated altogether if film is not supplied, or if the laboratory refuses to accept mail orders for development and printing). Similar problems may arise in connection with the supply of complementary services (such as repair) or goods (such as spare parts).

At the limit then—and this may occur fairly frequently in some areas

---

tend to become horizontal and move toward the origin. The precise shape depends upon the time period to which the "labor hours" refer.

of some countries at some periods of time—the additional real wage that must now equal the higher marginal utility of leisure may consist exclusively of additional farm products, which would be forthcoming from a greater supply of household labor in agricultural activities. At the margin, however, the utility associated with these products might conceivably be zero (if not negative as a result of storage problems). In other words, self-produced farm products would become inferior goods as far as the household's demand function is concerned. If so, one wonders whether it is then proper to speak of an *increased* real wage within this particular range of the transition area of Figure 1. It is not difficult to think up a hypothetical parallel: What if I am offered a number of nonconvertible lei that I must pick up in Bucharest in return for some effort on my part, but I am unable to get a Rumanian visa and there is no way at all to transfer the lei to friends or relatives in Rumania? Would it be proper to speak of an inelastic supply of my effort until I found some way (at a cost to me) to get around the regulations? Obviously not, since any analysis of the supply of effort is usually associated with the notion of real wages consisting of goods and services of some positive marginal utility. Thus, the inelasticity of the supply of effort in this range may reflect nothing but the fact that the relevant real wage (or real income) fails to rise at all.[3]

It may be objected at this stage that while relaxing the tacitly made assumptions on which Professor Lau's Figure 1 is based, I have in turn built some highly restrictive assumptions of my own into the model. Formally this is true, though I would claim that my assumptions are not less realistic than his. But what of the opportunity to produce for sale on the market (however defined)?

I do not believe that my major conclusion, with respect to the ambiguity of the concept of the *increasing* real wage within the relevant range of the diagram, would be altered significantly though the analysis becomes a good deal more complex. First, marketing costs per unit of product might be rather high, especially for those peasants who are located away from urban centers, especially when draft animals are scarce and public transport is either nonexistent or very expensive. Second, even those peasants who do not suffer from the handicap of location are well

[3] After reading a part of the manuscript, my colleague, Llad Phillips, suggested that a similar analysis was once made by Lloyd H. Fisher in *The Harvest Labor Market in California* (Cambridge, Mass.: Harvard University Press, 1953). As it turns out, Fisher's analysis (which was in turn preceded by that of Clark Kerr) is more closely related to my analysis of shifts of the household labor between activities (Fisher, *The Harvest Labor Market . . .* , pp. 16–19).

aware of the seasonal price fluctuations, of the seasonal nature of much of the agricultural supply, and of the inverse relationships between price and the increase in supply when the latter is not offset by rising demand on the part of the urban dweller or the state—a situation that fits well into the picture of prewar China or some of the other socialist countries prior to the implementation of forced industrialization. This factor alone explains the lower elasticity of the supply of effort in the relevant range of the transition area. If we combine it with any of the other factors discussed previously (while granting that they operate with reduced strength) the total impact may well be the same as that we arrived at originally.

But this is not all, for we also encounter some ambiguity in the concept of supplied labor hours, especially in relation to the peasant household. Clearly, Professor Lau and most of us have tacitly assumed that the labor hours plotted on the X axis of his Figure 1 refer to labor hours supplied to the agricultural sector of the household's activity. The full implications of this assumption are worth a brief discussion.

Thus, it is conceivable that the peasant who enters into the inelastic or backward-bending portion of the supply curve for labor in the transition area is also confronted with alternative demands for his labor that have little or nothing to do with farming as such. Handicrafts are an obvious case in point, as is any employment opportunity outside of agriculture proper or, for that matter, outside of one's own farm. We should also recall that capital goods used in traditional (and Dr. Lau's transition) agriculture "are largely produced with family labor."[4] To the extent that we consider these factors, *increased total* real income may well call forth an *increased* supply of *total* labor effort, accompanied by a *reduced* or *constant* supply of labor hours devoted directly to farming on the household's own land. Part-time farming would still continue because of the uncertain demand for products of handicrafts or because of the uncertainty associated with the particular type of nonfarm employment.

Once again, it will probably be argued that my set of assumptions is rather unrealistic, since there are not *that* many outside employment opportunities to begin with. But here too, further reflection indicates that my major conclusion—effort is redirected away from farming as

[4] Cf. Marton Paglin, "Reply," *American Economic Review*, LVII, No. 1 (March, 1967), 207. Paglin also makes the very telling point that "the opportunity cost of a considerable portion of labor inputs used on the family farm may be near zero." *Ibid.*, p. 202.

such to other activities—need not be affected significantly.

Theoretically, the concept of real income includes psychic income, or income derived from ornamental handicraft production for one's own use (witness the beautiful window frames in Russian peasant huts), or a cleaner farm yard, a more elaborate garden, better care of animals, repairs of some implements, and the like. Thus, it is not necessary that preference for leisure should overcome disutility of all labor. All that is necessary is that the utility derived from some of these pursuits be greater at the margin than that derived from self-produced farm products that—as we have shown—may well have become inferior goods in terms of the household's demand function. The household may then shift a part of its labor supply to activities that are no longer directly connected with farming.

The case for this interpretation is further strengthened on one particular—but very plausible—definition of the peasant household. At some low level of total real income, *all* members of the household will be involved in farming to a greater or lesser extent. As real income rises, some labor hours of some members of the household—wife, children, and *babushka*—will be shifted to household duties, education, child care, and the like. This may be possible because of greater productivity of the male head of household (under some institutional arrangements total factor productivity is the relevant variable). Marketing, too, is a time-consuming activity, and I am reminded[5] that this is particularly true of barter. Alternatively, one might think of a temporal shift in the allocation of household labor to nonfarming activities. Instead of telescoping them all into the off-season period, some of these activities may now be more efficiently performed during the season (or partly during the season). In this fashion, a greater real income from agriculture might well call forth a reduced supply of effort to farming, though an increased supply of effort to all household economic activities. We should also keep in mind that the situation is complicated further once we introduce a collectivized agriculture that does allow for the existence of private plots and the necessary distinction between the supply of effort into the (i) socialized and (ii) the private sectors of activity.

Let me summarize. I do not wish to deny the existence of observed backward-sloping supply curves for labor in agriculture (in fact, I can cite a Soviet example[6]), but I do suggest that in many important and frequently encountered instances we merely see its image in a distorting

[5] By my assistant, Mr. Bastiaan Schouten.
[6] P. A. Malinovskii, "Deiatelnost partiinykh organizatsii po vospitaniiu kolkhoz-

mirror. For example, I see no easy way to correct the readily available statistical data on labor inputs for differences in the quality of supplied effort (say, in terms of ergs per hour). Another correction that is difficult to make is the one for shifts of total household labor in and out of its various activities, some of which are not directly relevant to farming. But even if we cannot correct adequately for the distortions of the data we should be aware of the introduced biases. These would exist even if my assumptions were somewhat relaxed. In other words, my conclusions would hold true even if none of the restrictive assumptions was strictly adhered to, since the conclusions clearly depend upon the joint impact of several of the discussed factors, each of which may operate with a reduced strength.

Reflections such as these suggest the possibility of forcing the peasant household to supply more effort to farming while its real income is reduced. This would be true of those households that find themselves just above the observed "slide" of the backward-bending supply function for labor in the transition area. The increase in agricultural labor would, of course, occur at the expense of other activities (which are of little if any consequence to the planners). This might well have been the Soviet case, and there is some evidence that may not be inconsistent with the hypothesis that, on the average, Soviet households may well have been located at a point well above the beginning of the backward-bending slide around 1929–30.[7] The decline in output that did occur could then be explained in part by the decline of the labor input assisted, perhaps, by the emergence of the Cournot solution, and also by the great turmoil of violence and uncertainty introduced by the implementation of collectivization. For a country where the average household finds itself on the elastic portion of the positively sloped supply curve for labor in the transition area, the consequences might well be different and less in harmony with the aims of central planners (who might be ignorant of

nogo krestianstva v dukhe kommunisticheskogo otnosheniia k trudu (1958–1960)," in Akademiia Obshchestvennykh Nauk, Kafedra istorii, *KPSS—organizator borby za krutoi podem selskogo khoziaistva* (Moscow, 1960), p. 265.

[7] See the data on the agricultural labor force in terms of 1937 man-years (adjusted for changes in hours—though not in their quality) in Moorsteen and Powell, *The Soviet Capital Stock*, p. 648. The agricultural labor force declines by 21 per cent between 1928 and 1932 and then increases again to a level above that of 1928. Virtually the same results are obtained from the data of Nancy Nimitz, *Farm Employment in the Soviet Union, 1928–1963*, RM-4623-PR (Santa Monica, Calif.: The RAND Corporation, 1965), p. 7. On trends in farm incomes see *ibid.*, pp. 90–95 and Jerzy F. Karcz, "Soviet Agriculture: A Balance Sheet," *Studies of the Soviet Union*, VI, No. 4 (1967), 108–45.

the shape of the curve in the relevant range, and who might also have to face the unpleasant consequences of the Cournot solution). This might well have been the Chinese case. But as Dr. Lau reminds us, households within each of his three ranges exist in real life in any country and it might perhaps be in order to recognize explicitly this great variation in incomes as well as motivation, to forego analysis at highly aggregated levels, and to frame policy measures aimed at something more operational than "the average peasant."

It is in this context that it might be profitable to cite the measures that one Soviet collective farm used in the early sixties to eliminate its own backward-sloping portion of the supply for labor. It built a restaurant, a communal bath house, a laundry, bakery, introduced sewers and running water, constructed a theater and a sanatorium. Another instance of attempts to introduce other goods into the operationally relevant portion of the household preference curve was observed in Bulgaria, where the only item on display in the window of a small rural retail store was a washing machine.[8]

I wish to stress emphatically that this is *not* an argument to turn—in 1928–30—the then-existing Soviet village into a carbon copy of present-day American suburbia. But here, as elsewhere, *natura non facit saltum* and even then we faced a continuum of changing peasant wants. Bicycles, rubber tires for carts, better kerosene lamps, crystal radio sets, and watches might well have done the job. Such a policy of expanding gradually the relevant portion of peasant preference functions is in fact complementary to a more appropriate price policy (which may be accompanied by taxes). For the subsistence peasant, as well as one in the process of transition, is still a part-time farmer or Jack of all trades. And part-time farmers are notoriously less responsive to the incentives of farm prices and under less pressure to embody such technological change as may be forthcoming. (This, of course, is *the* economic argument of employers who object to moonlighting.)

Some other points in Dr. Lau's paper will only be discussed briefly. First, let me note a certain asymmetry in the treatment of decisions to consume or save, or choices between work and leisure as they apply to uncollectivized peasants and to collectives (of various degrees of sophistication). Once the latter are introduced, most of the decisions relevant to savings are taken out of the hands of individual households— they are performed by the collective and by the state. On the other

---

[8] Malinovskii, "Deiatelnost partiinykh organizatsii . . . ," p. 265, and a visit to Obedinene near Vel. Turnovo, 1966.

hand, the existence of the more or less free labor market implies that choices between work and leisure are still decided primarily by the household (subject to all kinds of constraints introduced by communalized savings). What I am really driving at is the proposition that it is impossible to view the responses of the head of the collectivized household, deprived to a very considerable extent of freedom to save and to act as an entrepreneur as he sees fit, in terms appropriate to the individual peasant who is not subject to such constraints. What we obviously need is analysis of the behavior of the collectivized household *and* that of the collective farm (at various levels of its institutional framework). Professor Lau does take us a good part of the way with respect to the former, but I suspect that we cannot get very far unless we also look simultaneously at the latter and—as Dr. Wädekin's latest book makes clear—at the interdependence between the two sectors.[9]

An example of the difficulties encountered in this kind of partial analysis is afforded by the conclusion reached by Professor Lau that "the saving rate [will be] higher than before [collectivization of a certain kind]" (p. 312). This assumes (i) that capital is rewarded at constant rates akin to interest on bonds, which do not vary with contributions to state procurement or taxation and (ii) that there is an opportunity for the peasant to increase his capital contribution over time. Both are matters of fact that may apply to certain situations but are irrelevant for many others. In addition, central planners are not necessarily interested in raising the rate of saving but rather the absolute volume of saving (including the communalized saving referred to above). If incomes decline, as they are likely to do, the rate of private saving may rise, but the volume of private saving may decline (obviously, the total volume of all saving may still rise).

Finally, a brief comment on the likelihood of the Cournot solution. I would expect that it would tend to prevail more generally than Dr. Lau suggests. If the number of households in the collectivized unit is large, every household might act on the assumption that no other household would reduce its labor supply—and the total labor supply will decline and so will output and income short of investment or expansion of sowings or increased use of current inputs. If the collectives are small, then every peasant will have an opportunity to observe his neighbor and act accordingly. The result is still the same: If one household reduces its labor input, so will the others.

[9] Karl E. Wädekin, *Privatproduzenten in der sowjetischen Landwirtschaft* (Cologne: Bundesinstitut für Ostwissenschaftliche und Internationale Studien, 1967), chap. v.

SHIGERU ISHIKAWA

Changes in the Structure
of Agricultural Production
in Mainland China*

INTRODUCTION

This paper deals with some of the basic changes in the structure of agricultural production in Mainland China during the past eighteen years. It aims at exploring and evaluating the technical and economic policies of the Chinese government for meeting the requirement of increased agricultural output. The structure of production is defined here as comprising the relation between inputs and outputs and the underlying technological, land, and capital base.

The basic hypotheses upon which this discussion is predicated are three:

1. China's agriculture was, until recently, at a highly advanced stage within the framework of "traditional agriculture," i.e., all the components of the production structure were combined in such a way as to attain balance at a very high output level under the constraint of re-

* This paper constitutes the second major part of the paper originally presented, entitled "Factors Affecting China's Agriculture in the Coming Decade." The first part, which dealt with the consumption structure of major agricultural products, is omitted because of the limitations of space. This omission affects the discussion presented here in at least the following sense: In some parts of the discussion, I have used Chinese official figures for production and for cultivated and cropped areas, as well as the relevant estimated figures for 1965 by Edwin Jones (in *An Economic Profile of Mainland China*, Vol. I [Washington D.C.: U.S. Government Printing Office, 1967]). Examination of the official production figures made in this omitted part indicated that, contrary to the critiques made against them, they are fairly plausible. The writer is prepared to send a copy of the original paper to those readers who are interested in the complete presentation.

sources supplied from within the farm sector. Hence, any attempt to increase output by altering some components was likely to disrupt the balance and lead to a decrease in output unless agriculture was supported by resources from the modern nonfarm sector.

2. The agricultural disaster occurring between 1960 and 1963 is explainable by the disruption of the balance relation within traditional agriculture, and was caused by an attempt on the part of the government to increase output while relying almost exclusively on traditional resources.

3. The disrupted balance relation has been now almost restored with the aid of some nonfarm resources, while at the same time a technical foundation is gradually being established for the modernization of China's agriculture. This is assumed possible if the government is prepared to supply agriculture with substantial and increasing inputs of nonfarm origin.

Included in this study of changes will be those that have occurred in the cultivated land and cropping systems, in irrigation and other water-conservancy facilities, and in the type and application of fertilizers. Each of these is the most important component of the technological, capital, and current input structures, respectively. Some of the other major input items, like human labor, animal and mechanical traction power, and varieties of seeds, will be dealt with only briefly.

CULTIVATED LAND AND CROPPING SYSTEMS

Throughout the past ten or more years, improvement of the existing cropping system seems to have been considered by the Chinese government as the final task of technological reform—final in the sense that the technical progress achieved in the various aspects of agricultural production could bring about the highest level of output if they were synthesized in the form of an improved cropping system. This approach is understandable in view of the following two facts: (1) the cultivated area is extremely limited and while the technical possibility of expanding it is by no means exhausted, under the present condition of scarce capital resources, substantial land reclamation seems to be economically prohibited.[1] (2) Of various measures for increasing the productivity of

[1] Between 1952 and 1957, the increase in the cultivated area was only four million hectares, less than 4 per cent of the total cultivated area. Yet of these four million hectares, more than two million are officially confirmed as the cultivated land that was not registered before agricultural cooperativization, but was still recorded in official statistics as that added by new land reclamation. Hiao Yü, "Reclaim Waste Land, and Expand Cultivated Land," *Chih-hua ching-chi* (Planned Economy), No. 2,

the existing cultivated land, improvement of the cropping system seems likely to be the most effective and economical, since it is a device to utilize an otherwise unused portion of "flow resources" (nature's benefit) to the maximum extent conceivable.

However, in order for the theoretical possibility of improved cropping to be realized, some other conditions must be met. First, a larger application of current and capital input must be accompanied by an intensification of the existing cropping system. The productivity effect of additional inputs will be relatively greater with intensification than if they were employed without a change in cropping practices. Second, intensive cropping needs a technical knowledge of its own. Essentially, this knowledge requires a recognition of the optimal combination of improved technical methods to be applied to various phases of agricultural production. It seems that the drastic changes in the agricultural situation that have occurred in China during the past ten years can be accounted for by an increased need of other resources to support a modification of the cropping system.

The multiple-cropping index and the yields of major crops are two related macroscopic indicators of changes in the cropping system. First, on the national level, relevant statistical figures for the three benchmark years—1952, 1957, and 1965—which are compiled both from official statistics and Edwin Jones' estimates, enable us to make the following three observations: (1) The Chinese figures for multiple-cropping index and per hectare yields of various crops are all significantly higher than those in other developing countries in Asia, with the exception of Korea and Taiwan.[2] While India's multiple-cropping index was 111.1 in 1950/51, and 115.1 in 1962/63, in China it was 130.9, 140.6, and 143.1 in 1952, 1957, and 1965, respectively. The yield of rice in India is roughly half that in China. (2) While no drastic change

1958, p. 22. The nearly three-million hectare decrease between 1957 and 1965 is reported to have been caused by salinization of existing cultivated land and the excessive removal of land for irrigation schemes (Edwin Jones, "The Emerging Pattern of China's Economic Revolution" in *An Economic Profile of Mainland China* [Washington, D.C.: U.S. Government Printing Office, 1967] pp. 82–83). On the other hand, we have not a few reports indicating that surveys of and prospecting for cultivable waste land have been going on extensively, and by 1957 a potential of about one-third of the existing cultivated area had been discovered. The major limiting factor for extensive land reclamation is the extremely high cost compared to the cost of improving existing cultivated land. For a systematic discussion of this point, see Shigeru Ishikawa, *Economic Development in Asian Perspective* (Tokyo: Kinokuniya Bookstore Co., 1967) pp. 65–69.

[2] *Ibid.*, pp. 70, 213–14.

was seen between these years regarding the composition of the total cropland, the largest increase in crops and, hence, the largest contribution to the increase in the multiple-cropping index is found to have been achieved by grains, especially paddy rice. (3) Between 1952 and 1957, per hectare yields of most crops indicated substantial annual fluctuations, although a trend of modest increase was seen in grain crops while a decreasing trend was often found in soybean and technical crops. Between 1957 and 1965, per hectare yields of paddy rice and some technical crops showed significant increases, but for other crops the yields declined.

Since China is a vast country with wide regional variations in natural conditions, a simple investigation of national average figures may obscure the real dynamism in operation in the Chinese economy. This applies to the present case also. Table 1 presents data pertaining to large regional variations in the multiple-cropping index and changes in the index between 1952 and 1957. In general, the index is significantly larger in the rice region south of a line connecting the Hwai River and the Ch'in-ling Mountains (this line runs through the Central region referred to in Table 1), and smaller in the wheat region north of it.[3] Even within each region, the variation in the multiple-cropping index seems to have a correlation with the variation in the amount of rainfall. Moreover, the table shows that the increase in the multiple-cropping index between 1952 and 1957 was much larger in the rice than in the wheat region. Especially remarkable in this regard was the Southern region. Using the cultivated area in Column 3 as the weight of each region, it was found that, of the total increase in multiple-cropping

---

[3] Since a similar regional variation exists in India, a significant difference in the national average multiple-cropping index between India and China might seem to be caused by the difference in the regional composition of cultivated areas in both countries. However, as is seen from the following figures for 1962–63 on the multiple-cropping index (derived by "net sown area" divided by "total cropped area" in the Indian definition) by major states in both the wheat and the rice regions, this is not the case.

Wheat regions:	Punjab	132
	Maharashtra	104
Rice regions:	Andhra Pradesh	110
	Madras	120
	West Bengal	117
National average		115

(Source: Government of India, Ministry of Food and Agriculture, *Indian Agriculture in Brief*, 7th ed. [New Delhi, 1965])

Irrigation facilities were developed in Punjab when it was still under British rule; it possesses the most highly developed agriculture in India.

TABLE 1

RATIO OF UTILIZATION OF CULTIVATED AREA BY REGION*

(1) Region	Definition to Region	(2) Multiple Cropping Index in Ku's Data[a]			Regions Defined by Provinces	(3) Cultivated Area in 1954[b]	
		1952	1957			Million Hectares	Per Cent
Southernmost	South of Wu Ling Mountains	167.2	186.8		Fukien, Kwangtung	5.3	4.8
Southern	Between Wu Ling Mountains and Yangtze River	147.2	171.1		Chekiang, Kiangsi, Hunan, Kweichow, Kwangsi, Yunnan	15.9	14.4
Central	Between Yangtze and Yellow Rivers—Ch'in-ling Mountains—Pailung Kiang	149.4	154.2		Kiangsu, Anhwei, Honan, Shangtung, Hupeh, Szechwan, Tsinghai	43.1	39.1
Northern	Between Central area and Great Wall	109.2	113.5		Hopei, Shansi, Shensi, Kansu	22.8	20.7
Northernmost	North to Great Wall	—	—		Northeast, Inner Mongolia, Sinkiang	23.0	20.9
Total country		130.9	139.5			110.1	100.0

* Although common names for the regions are shown in column 1, the actual area covered differs between columns 2 and 3. However, a crude correspondence between these two can be seen by deriving average of multiple cropping indexes of the shown regions by using the percentage figures in column 3 as weight, and checking the result with the multiple-cropping index for the whole country in column 2. In this regard, the multiple-cropping index for the Northeast is taken as 99 per cent, which is derived from the data in Sun Ching-chih (ed.), *Tung-pei ti-chü ching-chi ti-li* (Economic Geography of the Northeast) (Peking: Science Publication Co., 1959).

[a] Ku Ta-ch'uan, "The Problem of Expanding the Double-Cropping Area," *Chung-kuo nung-pao* (Chinese Agricultural Bulletin), No. 24, 1957, pp. 4–5.

[b] Shih, Ching-t'ang et al. (eds.), *Chung-kuo nung-yeh ho-tso hua yün-tung shih-liao* (Compendium of Source Materials Concerning Cooperative Agriculture Movement in China) (Peking: Sheng-huo tu-shu hsin-chih san-lien shu-tien, 1957, 1959), II, 998.

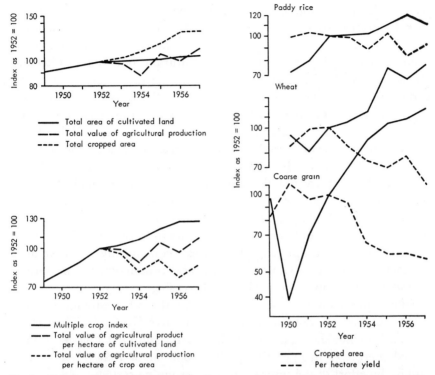

Fig. 1. Relation between the change in the cropped area and that in per hectare yield: Hunan Province between 1949 and 1957. *Source*: The original figures are from Hunan Agricultural College, *Hunan nung-yeh* (Peking: Higher Education Publication Co., 1959). For background information, refer to the text.

index during the same period, 73 per cent is accounted for by that in the Southernmost, Southern, and Central regions, while 40 per cent is accounted for by the Southern region alone. It appears that the long-standing trend of the rice region to be dynamic and the wheat region to be static remains in operation, at least in the domain of agricultural production.

An evaluation of the increase in the multiple-cropping index should be accompanied by some understanding of the yields in the rice region, especially the South. Fortunately, fairly detailed data are available regarding agricultural production both over a period of time and by crops in Hunan Province, in the central part of the South. In terms of land under double cropping of rice, the most dynamic crop in present-day China, Hunan in 1957 had 26 per cent of the total (3.1 million hectares) double-cropped land of the seven provinces along the Yangtze

Valley.[4] Double cropping of rice expanded quite rapidly in this province. Figure 1 is drawn from the above data. With regard to changes of the variables shown in the chart over a period of time, caution must be exercised concerning the decline in agricultural production in 1954 and 1956, because of a Yangtze River flood disaster in the former year and of damage by drought in the latter. Even with this reservation, however, we can observe from the chart that with the rapid increase in cropped area (the multiple-cropping index was 141 in 1952 and 177 in 1957), output per hectare of *cropped* area showed a sharply declining trend in terms of either total value of agricultural production, wheat yield, or coarse grain yield. Even in the paddy crop, which accounted for 30 per cent of the total increase in the cropped area between 1952 and 1957, the per hectare yield appears to have somewhat declined. Against these over-all trends, the only factor that appears to have made the attempt to increase the multiple-cropping index economically meaningful is the fact that the total value of agricultural production per hectare of *cultivated* area seems to be somewhat increasing.

Since similar data are not available for the other provinces of the rice region, we are not sure how representative Hunan is. The case of Hunan Province shows, however, that during the First Five-Year Plan period there was in operation at least one factor that threatened to nullify the effort of the improvement in cropping system.

In contrast to the provinces in the rice region, those in the wheat region appear to have been characterized by a relative constancy in the multiple-cropping index and modest increasing trends in yields per hectare of major crops during the First Five-Year Plan. While the data are by no means sufficient, this observation is derived from statistics for coarse grains and wheat in the provinces of the Northeast and the North China Plains.[5] From these statistics, it is clear that in the North China Plain the cropped area under wheat increased, although slowly, and the area under coarse grains correspondingly decreased. However, this change was said to have been caused by the increase in autumn rainfall

[4] Derived from the figures shown in *Hunan nung-yeh* (Hunan Agriculture) and Investigation Team on Double Cropping of Rice, Chinese Agricultural Academy, "Report on Doubly Cropped Rice in the Yangtze Basin," in Chinese Agricultural Academy (ed.), *Tao-tso k'o-hüeh lun-wen-hsüan-chi* (Selected Articles on Rice-Cultivation Science) (Peking: Agricultural Publishing Co., 1959), pp. 116–35.

[5] See Ma Ch'üeh-weng, "Prospects for the Coarse Grain Production in Our Country," *Chung-kuo nung-pao* (Chinese Agricultural Bulletin), Peking, No. 15, 1957, pp. 12–15 and Shen Yü-ch'ing, "Preliminary Treatise on the Position of Wheat in the Food Grain Production and its Prospects," *ibid.*, No. 12, 1957, pp. 16–17.

during that period, a cyclic phenomenon that seems not to have occurred since then. In any case, this did not affect the multiple-cropping index significantly.

With regard to the period between 1957 and 1965, we have not yet sufficient data to observe statistically the regional trends in the multiple-cropping index.

Turning next to the problem of the cropping systems that lie at the basis of the increase in the multiple-cropping index, it seems in order to note the following two points: First, that the cropping systems that exist, or did exist prior to recent attempts at their alteration, were in most cases highly advanced ones within the framework of traditional agriculture. Technically, they were skillful adaptations to the natural conditions in each locality. Economically, they represented methods for deriving the most stable and the largest outputs possible under the constraints of these natural conditions and such local resources as water, fertilizer, and human and animal labor. These resources are fully utilized, although in the case of human and animal labor, only during the busiest season. Thus, under these cropping systems, a kind of long-term balance between outputs and inputs appears to have been maintained. Any attempt to change these established cropping systems has meant a threat to the existing output level.[6]

In the rice region along the Yangtze Basin, there are intensive agricultural systems involving double and multiple cropping, such as combined crops of rice (the first crop) and wheat (the second crop), two crops of rice with one of oil-seed crops, beans, sweet potatoes, or others (these require a semiannual alternating of wet and dry conditions in the same field), and although the total area involved was small, a double cropping of rice through a continuous crop or interplanting. In the North China Plain, where natural conditions are especially severe mainly because of the unstable Yellow River[7] and the concentration of the meager rainfall in the summer season, a system of three crops every two years is used. Kaoliang is the main (summer) crop. Due to the shortage of water, the winter crop of wheat can be planted only once every two or three years. Dry-farming techniques developed by the local farm-

[6] For a concise description of the various cropping systems throughout China, see T. H. Shen, *Agricultural Resources of China* (Ithaca, N.Y.: Cornell University Press, 1951), pp. 144–51.

[7] A concise description is given in the United Nations publication, *Method and Problems of Flood Control in Asia and the Far East* (*Flood Control Series, No. 2* [Bangkok, 1951]), p. 22.

ers for conserving moisture for the wheat crop *(Pao-shang keng-tso)* seem to be the culmination of the traditional method.[8]

However, the second point is no less important than the first. This is the fact that the existing systems have evolved from changes in the past. These changes had been brought about both by the necessity arising from the population increase and the introduction of new technology. Professor Ping-ting Ho indicated that there have been two agricultural revolutions in southern China since the tenth century: the first was initiated by the introduction in the early eleventh century of a drought-resisting and early-maturing variety of rice *(champa)* from Indochina; and the second by the introduction since the sixteenth century of higher yielding and drought-resisting crops of American origin, such as corn, sweet potatoes, and peanuts.[9] The present cropping systems in southern China were established on the basis of the disruption of the older systems that evolved from these two agricultural revolutions. One implication of all this is that, even though the existing system may appear to have achieved a nearly perfect balance, and any alteration could be only at the sacrifice of the existing level of output, additional requirements could be met if they were balanced by the necessary technical and economic conditions.

Comprehensive and systematic data concerning the recent attempts to alter the existing cropping system are yet to be collected. It is certain, however, that these attempts are centered on the expansion of rice cropping in the rice regions. In the official literature, the direction for the reform of the existing cropping systems in the southern region was indicated as early as 1954. The change was to be the conversion from a single to a double crop of rice, from interplanting to continuous cropping (in the case of double cropping of rice), and from *indica* to *japonica* varieties.[10] Concrete shape seems to have been given to this direction at the National Conference on Wet Paddy Production Techniques held in September, 1955. The conference also presented a long-range target for the expansion of the paddy, which is given in Table 2 along with more

[8] Chang Lan-sheng, *Hua-pei kan-lao-ti sheng-yin ho fang-fa* (Causes of Drought and Waterlogging in North China and the Preventive Measures) (Peking: Chinese Youth Publication Co., 1964), pp. 31–34.

[9] Ping-ting Ho, *Studies on the Population of China, 1368–1953* (Cambridge: Harvard University Press, 1959), chap. viii.

[10] Ministry of Agriculture, General Bureau of Agricultural Production, "Preliminary Opinions Concerning the Conversions from a Single Crop of Rice to a Double Crop of Rice, from Interplanting to Continuous Crops and from *Indica* Varieties to *Japonica* in the Southern Wet Paddy Region," *Chung-kuo nung-pao*, No. 21, 1954, pp. 18–19.

detailed regional figures for 1956 for comparison. Clearly, the primary emphasis was placed on the expansion of paddy land in both regions of the Center and the North.[11]

The expansion in the Central region was to be brought about, first by an increase in the area under double cropping of rice and, second by the conversion of upland field into wet paddy field. The program for the double cropping of rice was started in 1956 over an area of 2.33 million hectares. However, after the first year, there were many instances of a decline in total crop output in the Central region, according to official journals.[12] In 1957, the crop area of double cropping was evidently reduced, although it was later increased. Sufficient data have not been available until recently regarding double cropping since then. A report published in 1964 concerning the districts around the Tung-t'ing Lake suggests the changes that occurred during this period. According to the report, the proportion of the area in rice was about 30 per cent in 1955; it was expanded to, and maintained at, the 70 per cent level during the years 1956–60; in 1961, "readjustment" began, and by 1963 it decreased to about 40 per cent.[13] In the last several years, this proportion seems to be again increasing, though with a tempo much more modest than in the second half of the 1950's.[14]

The questions to be clarified are: (1) How was the double cropping of rice brought into existing cropping system? (2) What were some of

[11] As for the southernmost region, double cropping of rice had already been prevalent before 1967. Thus, in Kwangtung the area under double cropping of rice was reported as more than two million hectares in 1953, roughly 75 per cent of the total wet paddy field (Tien Hua-nung, "A Treatise on the Increase in the Multiple Cropping Area of Agricultural Products," *Chung-kuo nung-pao*, No. 20, 1954, p. 25); for 1957 it was 2.5 million hectares, 76.8 per cent of the total area of paddy fields (Sung Ching-chih [ed.], *Hua-nan ti-ch'ü ching-chi ti-li* [Economic Geography of South China Region] [Peking: Science Publication Co., 1959], p. 22). The priority seems to be on the improvement of the quality of existing irrigation facilities. Regarding this, see T'ao Chu, "People's Commune in Advance," *Hung-chi* (Red Flag), Peking, No. 6, 1964.

[12] See articles in *Chung-kuo nung-pao*, Nos. 10, 13, 20 and *Jen-min jih-pao* (People's Daily), Peking, Oct. 12, 1956 (hereafter cited as *JMJP*).

[13] Government of I-yang Chuan-ch'ü, Hunan Province, "Changes and Development of Cropping System in the Paddy Field in Hu-ch'ü," *Chung-kuo nung-pao*, No. 8, 1964, pp. 27–30.

[14] There are many fragmental reports supporting this conjecture. The main one, however, is a report in *JMJP* on Dec. 28, 1966, announcing the largest food grain production since the "liberation" in 1966. Among the main factors for this achievement was cited the increasing tempo of the reform of cultivation methods, centering around the double cropping of rice in the southern region, and around "interplanting of various kinds" in the northern region.

the causes of the difficulties encountered between 1956 and 1960, and of the retreat in 1961? (3) What are the prospects for its renewed expansion? From scattered data, the following answers can be constructed.

1. On the basis of an extensive survey of rice cultivation along the Yangtze Basin in 1957,[15] it appears that double cropping, in the early stage of its introduction, included not only the fields originally under two crops of rice and either wheat or technical crops, and those under three crops of rice, late autumn and winter crops, but also the fields under one crop a year—those fields presumably where winter fallowing practiced for conserving water. Usually, the double cropping of rice in these fields was combined with a winter crop such as green manure, oilseed, or early maturing barley, selected on a rotation basis. Rotation systems of a much wider cycle were also introduced, such as six crops every two years, including single or double crops of rice. Whatever the program, the alternation of the same field between wet and dry conditions seems to have been required.

There are no comprehensive data pertaining to output. According to annual yields in Hunan Province between 1950 and 1957 for both single- and double-crop rice, the yield per hectare of paddy is roughly 50 per cent greater in the latter than in the former.[16] In an article dealing with the over-all situation of double cropping along the Yangtze Basin, the difference was said to vary between 20 per cent and 50 per cent.[17] The problem raised here is that the total output of a new cropping system should be sufficiently larger, in either caloric or utility value, than the total output in the original cropping system to com-

---

[15] This part is taken from Investigation Team on Double Cropping of Rice, Chinese Agricultural Academy, "Report on Doubly Cropped Rice . . . ," pp. 132–33. Many reports are available concerning the patterns in particular districts. See articles indicated in notes 16 and 17 for examples.

[16] *Hunan nung-yeh*, p. 150. The annual performances shown are as follows (*chin* per *mou* as unit):

	(1) Yield of double crops of rice per hectare of paddy field	(2) Yield of single crop of rice per hectare of paddy field	(3) $\frac{(1)-(2)}{(2)}$
1952	617	383	.61
1953	588	385	.53
1955	593	408	.45
1956	527	365	.46
1957	582	373	.56

[17] Lo Chao-hsün, "Basic Experience of Cropping System in Paddy Field in Hunan," *Chung-kuo nung-pao*, No. 11, 1963.

pensate for the extra cost of input incurred, including the imputed part. Especially important is that the additional labor return accrued from this difference be enough to satisfy the individual farmer. Although there are not sufficient data for an empirical check on this problem, our conjecture is that even though a 50 per cent difference in increased yield might be enough to compensate the farmer for his added labor, a 20 per cent difference would certainly not have satisfied him.

2. Essentially there are three areas of difficulty in the new system: technical, economic, and organizational. The technical difficulty is associated with the adaptation of double cropping to climate, topography, soils, and other natural conditions. The most critical climatic condition pertains to the number of days per year in which paddy crops can physiologically be grown. In the Central region, this varies between less than 210 days in the northernmost districts to 230–250 days in the southernmost. On the other hand, the minimum number of days required for cultivating two crops of rice is ordinarily 220 days. In view of the fact that new, earlier maturing varieties have not yet successfully been introduced, two crops of rice were unsuccessful or unstable in some (mostly northern) districts.[18] The economic difficulties of double cropping arise from the bottlenecks likely to develop in the utilization of the required resources. In the new system, the employment of the principal resources—human and animal labor in the new peak seasons, water, and fertilizer—increased substantially.[19] The organizational problem was closely related to the increase in the human labor requirement in busy seasons. When the output level and, with it, the income level of the member farmers of the production team or brigade in the People's Commune decreased in relation to the amount of labor supplied by them, they tended to refuse to abide by such a production program. This was especially true when the threat of harvest fluctuation increased. Given such behavior on the part of the member farmers, effective confronta-

[18] A most useful summary of the climatic problems regarding double cropping of rice is found in Jao Hsing, "Several Climatic Problems Regarding the Expansion of Double Cropping of Rice along the Yangtze Basin," *JMJP*, April 5, 1964.

[19] For a comprehensive analysis of these conditions, see Lo Chao-hsüan, "Basic Experience of Cropping System . . . ," Government of I-yang Chuan-ch'ü, "Changes and Development . . . ," and Ma Chien-yu, "Double Cropping of Rice is a One Further Step of Technical Revolution," *Chung-kuo nung-yeh k'o-hsüeh* (Chinese Agricultural Science), No. 6, 1965. Regarding the bottlenecks in human and animal labor that emerged due to the introduction of double cropping of rice, a western study gave a good account. See Kenneth Walker, "Organization for Agricultural Production in China," a paper presented at Conference on Economic Trends in Communist China, Oct., 1965.

tion of the new problems was largely dependent on strong organizational solidarity and the implementation of collective decision making.[20]

3. Prospects for the future may be drawn from studies of these difficulties. In summary, a fair degree of technical knowledge regarding the double cropping of rice seems to have been accumulated in each locality where the practice has been found possible. According to Japanese experience, at least ten years seem to be required for breeding and popularizing a new variety of seed successfully. Nearly ten years of experimentation, filled with trial and error, have now elapsed since double cropping was begun in the Yangtze Basin. Economic factors seem to depend mainly on the inflow of extra-agricultural inputs, which we shall examine subsequently. More critical seems to be the organizational factor.[21] While discussion about this point is somewhat beyond the scope of this study, we are sure that, as the extra-agricultural inputs are increased in the farm sector, the conflict existing between collective decision making and individual behavior will become correspondingly eased.

With regard to the changes in the cropping systems in the wheat region, the following two points are pertinent: The first concerns the attempt to increase the paddy area in the wheat region, which was pointed out in connection with Table 2. In contrast to southern China, where the program for the expansion of paddy rice formulated at the National Conference on Wet Paddy Production Techniques was inaugurated in 1956, in northern China it was started in 1958 with an area as large as 3.33 million hectares as the year's target. While the technical details of this effort are yet to be clarified, it seems that a single crop of spring rice was to be introduced in the Northeast, Inner Mongolia, and Sinkiang, and in all of the other northern regions two crops of rice and wheat were programmed. The patterns of expanding rice differed greatly, depending upon the region, although in the North

[20] This reasoning immediately suggests that the sudden decline in the proportion of paddy fields under double cropping of rice in 1961 was caused by the organizational factor, since 1961 was a year in which the government officially admitted the failure of the Big Leap Forward and the decision-making unit of the people's commune was transferred to the production brigade.

[21] It is suggested in Government of I-yang Chuan-ch'ü, *ibid.* (as in note 13) that the proportion of paddy field under double cropping of rice in 1963, which decreased to 40 per cent in Hu-ch'ü in Hunan, was below the technical and economic potentialities of this district. It can be increased under present conditions to as much as 50 per cent and, with the improvement of various production conditions, even more. The difference between the 40 per cent and 50 per cent seems to be accounted for by the organizational factor.

TABLE 2

A PRELIMINARY TARGET FOR 1967 OF PADDY-CROPPED AREA SET AT THE 1956
NATIONAL CONFERENCE ON WET PADDY PRODUCTION TECHNIQUES

		1952[a]		1967 (target)[a]	
		Cultivated Area	Cropped Area	Cultivated Area	Cropped Area
			(In Million Hectares)		
South:	Kwangtung, Kwangsi, Yunnan, Kweichow, Fukien	7.4	--	9.7~10.5	over 14.0
Central:	Kiangsu, Chekiang, Anhwei, Kiangsi, Hupeh, Hunan, Szechwan, Shanghai	15.6	--	21.0~21.1	28.0
North:	Liaoning, Kirin, Heilung-kiang, Hopei, Shansi, Shensi, Kansu, Shangtung, Honan, Inner Mongolia, Sinkiang, Peking, Tientsin	1.1	--	7.1~ 7.4	7.3
	Total country	25.1	28.3	37.3~40.0	over 49.3

		1956[b]	
		Cropped Area (In Million Hectares)	Output (In Million Metric Tons)
South:	Southern double-cropping rice region	9.0	18.5
	Southwest high-plateau rice region	2.0	7.3
Central:	Central single and double-cropping rice region	21.0	54.8
	North single-crop rice region	0.5	1.1
North:	Northeast early maturing rice region	0.9	1.9
	Northwest dry rice region	0.1	0.3
	Total country	33.3	82.5

[a]From Ministry of Agriculture, "General Conclusion of the National Conference on Wet Paddy Production Techniques," *Chung-kuo nung-pao*, No. 11, 1956, pp. 10–11. [b]From Ting Ying (ed.), *Chung-kuo shi-tao tsai-p'ei-hsüeh* (Peking: Agricultural Publishing House, 1961), pp. 172–79. The classification of the rice regions is not made according to the administrative demarcation, hence it does not correspond to that in the left column. Original figures shown in the source are percentages of national total occupied by each region. The figures shown in this table are derived by multiplying the national total figures for 1956 and these percentage figures. Since original percentage figures add up to over 100, the sum of the figures for respective regions also exceeds the national total.

China Plain the reclamation of low and waterlogged land seems to have been the principal means,[22] and it appears to have ended in failure.[23] While the reasons for this failure are still unclear, they are apparently related to the inability of farmers to quickly accommodate themselves to a new method, and to the omnipresent problem of water shortage. Although there is evidence that the effort was renewed in scattered localities,[24] the over-all situation after 1958 remains to be explored.

The second point concerns the development of the practice of interplanting in upland areas, which was said by an important official report to be the main contribution to the increase in food-grain output in 1966.[25] Scattered evidence indicates that, with the improvement of irrigation and the use of fertilizer, an annual two-crop system in upland areas is increasing, and interplanting is being required to convert the lower yielding varieties to higher yielding ones.[26] This certainly indicates a promising direction, but it is not known how widespread these cases are.

IRRIGATION AND WATER CONSERVATION

Before going into a detailed examination of irrigation and water-conservation facilities, some comments are in order regarding their function in the total production structure.

There are many types of basic investments in land: those for flood control, antiwaterlogging, irrigation, and drainage. The need for each category of investment is determined in part by the particular stage of agricultural development that is being dealt with. Usually, the need begins with flood control, goes on to irrigation, and then to irrigation

[22] "Comrade Liu Jui-lun's Remarks at the Conference for Accelerating the Increase in Production of Wet Paddy in the North," *Chung-kuo nung-pao*, No. 10, 1958, p. 3 and *JMJP*, March 8, 1958.

[23] In *JMJP*, May 24, 1958, the area under paddy in the North was cited as 1.17 million hectares in 1952, 2.0 million hectares in 1957, and 5.33 million hectares in 1958. However, in *JMJP*, Oct. 31, 1958, it was indicated that the area under paddy in 1959 in the North was 2.0 million hectares, the same level as in 1957.

[24] An important case of the renewed attempt is seen for Lin-i District in Shantung (*JMJP*, Mar. 14, 1965, and Chou Chieh, "Introducing Readjustment of Paddy Field in the Lin-i New Paddy Area," *Chung-kuo nung-yeh k'o-hsüeh*, No. 6, 1965, pp. 16–18). However, it should be stressed that the big fluctuation in the area of paddy land was in marginal areas; there is seen a slow but steady increase in paddy in northern China, especially in the northeast, as irrigation projects progress.

[25] See note 14.

[26] *E.g.*, Chang Chung-hsin, "General Conclusion of the Experience of People in T'ang-shang County on the Early Maturing and Increase in Production by Interplanting of Corn in the Wheat Field," *Chung-kuo nung-yeh k'o-hsüeh*, No. 2, 1965, pp. 15–17.

cum drainage. However, agricultural success is also determined by the climatic, topographic, and other natural conditions peculiar to each locality. Second, basic investments may play at least three different roles in a program of increasing agricultural output: (1) Eliminating harvest fluctuations due to insufficient rainfall, flooding, or waterlogging. In this case, output increases simply as an effect of the basic investment. (2) Increasing the rate of utilization of the existing cultivated land. (3) Creating a technical condition for making possible the introduction of improved varieties of seeds, an increased application of fertilizer, and the use of better methods of cultivation. In a relatively advanced stage of agricultural development, the basic investment tends to play roles (2) and (3) in combination. In fact, it was implied earlier that because of this combined role, the basic investment became a necessary precondition for the improvement of the cropping system. In the estimation of the agricultural production function, basic investment is found to be an important shift variable, also because of this combined role. Finally, the basic investment may be made through various alternative patterns of projects—either traditional or modern in the technical method, minor or major in scale, and community based or government undertaken in kind of project owner. The range of basic investment in which one pattern of projects cannot substitute for the others seems smaller than was usually thought in the earlier stages of development.[27]

Thus, an evaluation of basic investments must be made from a multidimensional viewpoint. Our study, however, is necessarily preliminary. First, some statistical data for the period of the First Five-Year Plan are available for deriving a rough idea about the relative importance of various basic investments. These data have been compiled from a few related figures concerning the amount of state capital-construction investment in water conservation, and have been published on a previous occasion.[28] According to those, about 50 per cent of the total amount allotted in the First Five-Year Plan was spent for flood control, 20 per cent for irrigation, and another 20 per cent for the prevention and amelioration of waterlogging. These percentages are biased toward flood control and antiwaterlogging, and the proportion of irrigation seems to be too small, especially in view of the stage of agricultural

[27] For a more detailed study of the nature of basic investment in Asian countries, see Ishikawa, *Economic Development . . .* , secs. 2 and 3 of chap. ii.

[28] Shigeru Ishikawa, *National Income and Capital Formation in Mainland China—An Examination of Official Statistics* (Tokyo: The Institute for Asian Economic Affairs, 1965), p. 163.

development attained in China. Comparable Indian figures may be cited: in the First to the Third Five-Year-Plan period, the actual or planned proportion of total government-development outlay (fixed capital investment *plus* some current expenditures) in water conservation that was spent for irrigation was between 91 and 96 per cent.[29] This contrast is explainable by the difference in the topographic, hydrologic, and soil conditions between the two countries.

In China, gigantic rivers like the Yellow, the Yangtze, the Hwai, and the Pearl with their vast plains make a wide area of agricultural land susceptible to flooding. In the case of the Hwai, the Yellow, and other rivers in the North China Plain, silting has made them shallow and has even built up the level of the river bed to a higher elevation than the nearby plain, creating a serious flooding and waterlogging problem in the rainy season.[30] Centering around the Yellow-Hwai-Yangtze Plain, the area that in normal years is susceptible to flood damage is said to extend to 6.67 million hectares.[31] Because of these special natural conditions, the Chinese regime has been, and will probably continue to be, required to divert a major portion of its agricultural investment to flood control and antiwaterlogging measures.[32] During the First Five-Year Plan, this requirement was especially pressing, perhaps due to the neglect in repairing and maintenance for long years in the past. Beginning with the winter of 1957, however, irrigation seems to have received increasing attention, with the exception of the years from 1960 to the end of 1962, although most of the irrigation projects were of a local, community-based nature.

Second, we must make some evaluation of the existing water-conservation facilities in terms of the three roles listed above. Flood control is evidently confined to establishing stability, and the existing facilities seem to have attained a fairly high standard, at least with respect to a few of the big rivers.[33] Antiwaterlogging should also attempt to achieve

[29] Ishikawa, *Economic Development* . . . , pp. 126–27.

[30] Ch'en Lien, "Place the Anti-Waterlogging in a Principal Position in Agricultural Condition," *Chi-hua ching-chi* (Planned Economy), Peking, No. 1, 1958, p. 16.

[31] *Ibid*. and Ho Chi-feng, "Exert Great Effort in Developing Anti-Waterlogging Work in Order to Attain Great Leap Forward in Agricultural Production," *Chung-kuo shui-li* (Chinese Water Conservation), No. 2, 1958, p. 1.

[32] A somewhat similar situation exists in Japan, where state expenditure for flood control has continuously occupied a relatively important position since the early Meiji era. See Ishikawa, *Economic Development* . . . , p. 128.

[33] As a result of the emphasis on flood control during the First Five-Year Plan period, it was said in an official article that (1) major dikes along the Yangtze River were now able to control the flood water as high as that of the 1954 flood disaster;

TABLE 3

SOME INDICATORS OF IRRIGATION AND ELIMINATION OF WATERLOGGING

	1952	1957	1963
Total area under irrigation (in million hectares)	21.3[a]	34.7[a]	(69.0)[b]
Percentage of total cultivated area[c]	*19.8*	*31.1*	*(64.3)*
Total area effectively irrigated (in million hectares)	--	23.1[d]	36.3[e]
Percentage of total cultivated area[c]	--	*20.6*	*33.3*
Accumulated area where waterlogging of a more than once-for-five-year probability has been eliminated (million hectares)	--	1.5[f]	--
Total horsepower of mechanical and electric irrigation and drainage equipment in agricultural use (thousand horsepower)		560.[g]	7,300.[h]

[a]State Statistics Bureau, *Wei-ta ti shih-nien* (Ten Great Years) (Peking, 1958), p. 115. The figures are interpreted to be included in this category, because of the correspondence to the more precisely defined figure shown in the source in Note c.

[b]This is the figure for 1959 reported in *Chi-hua yü t'ung-chi* (Planning and Statistics), No. 1, 1960, p. 1.

[c]Calculated by dividing the figure by the total number of hectares under cultivation.

[d]Taken from Ho Chi-feng, "General Conclusions of the 1957 National Conference on Water Conservancy of Agricultural Land," *Chung-kuo shui-li* (Chinese Irrigation), No. 8, 1957. It indicates that, of the existing irrigated area of 34.7 million hectares, 28.8 per cent is estimated to be inadequate in antidrought capacity and 48 per cent to be either unworkable because of bad construction, or is irrelevant because of statistical duplication. Regarding the meaning of "inadequate in antidrought capacity," see the description in the text.

[e]Derived from the statement in *JMJP* editorial, Nov. 30, 1963, that effectively irrigated area in China comprises only about one third of the existing national cultivated land. The meaning of "effectively irrigated area" is implicit in a statement immediately following the above: "according to the responsible government agencies, in irrigation districts with designated capacity of more than one hundred thousand *mou* (6,600 hectares), the area of land which has effective operation is only 60 per cent of the designated area. The remaining 40 per cent has not been able to work well, because of either of the following reasons: the lack or incompletion of attached subproject, the lack of the levelling of irrigable field, etc. . . ."

[f]Taken from Ho Chi-feng, "General Conclusions . . ." This area is defined as one whose standard of anti-waterlogging capacity is beyond the once-for-five year probability.

[g]*JMJP*, Jan. 14, 1961.

[h]*JMJP*, March 24, 1965. The figure is for the end of 1964.

stability: to eliminate the decrease in agricultural production due to the waterlogging damage, which amounts annually to as much as five to ten million tons of food grains.[34] When works for this purpose take the form of the construction of a new type of field with special drainage facilities (*Kou-hsü ch'i-tien, Kou-hsü tai-tien,* or *Kou-hsü wei-tien*) or of the construction of storage dams,[35] the second and third roles are combined

(2) as for the Hwai River, the middle and lower streams could now control flooding with a once-in-50 year frequency, and the upper streams the flooding with frequency between once-in-10-years and once-in-20-years; and (3) the Yellow River could now control the flooding with a once-in-100-year frequency (Ch'en Lien, "Place the Anti-Waterlogging in a Principal Position . . .").

[34] *Ibid.*

[35] *Ibid.*, and Ministry of Agriculture, *Nung-t'ien shui-li* (Agricultural Water Power) (Peking: Agricultural Publication Co., 1962), pp. 86–91.

with it. No comprehensive information, however, is available for assessing the over-all performance in these three roles. As is shown in Table 3, Part II, by 1957 1.5 million hectares of cultivated area had been converted to land that waterlogged no more frequently than once every five years. This is a modest result compared to the 6.7 million hectares normally damaged each year, although 3.1 million hectares more have been converted so that they withstand the waterlogging that occurs with the frequency of once in three to five years.[36] As far as accomplishment after 1957, we may derive only an inkling from the official statements regarding over-all water-conservation projects.

Irrigation facilities evidently cover all three roles: stabilization, increased utilization, and the creation of technical conditions for improved farming methods. In the sense that the second and the third roles are consequentially fulfilled by irrigation, irrigation is the most critical of all water-conservation projects. What were the roles, then, which Chinese irrigation facilities in these years did play? First, let us look at Table 3, Part I, which is a compilation of some of the global data showing the progress of the irrigation works in 1952, 1957, and 1963. The definition of irrigated area is, as noted by Owen Dawson, not necessarily clear-cut,[37] and the ratio of total cultivated area irrigated is useful only as a crude indicator of the popularization of irrigation. More meaningful is the ratio of total cultivated area to the area that is irrigated and has an adequate antidrought capability. "Adequate" seems synonymous to what is referred to in the official documents as "the level of assuring a normal or stabilized crop" *(ta-tao pao-shou-ti)*.[38] Adequate irrigation may be defined also in terms of a certain required amount of water, which must vary depending upon regions and crops. In the southern rice region, this amount varies between 2200 and 4500 cubic meters

[36] Ho Chi-feng, "Exert Great Effort. . . ."

[37] Owen L. Dawson, "Irrigation Developments under the Communist Regime," in John Lossing Buck, Owen L. Dawson, and Yuan-li Wu, *Food and Agriculture in Communist China* (Palo Alto, Calif.: Stanford University Press, 1966), pp. 149–68. In this article, Dawson examined critically the Chinese statistics regarding irrigated areas. Especially important is his criticism of the definition of the irrigated field; his second criticism is that the paddy under double cropping of rice was counted twice, and the third, that the official definition of irrigated land area is sometimes equal to the sum of the total paddy field area and the irrigated upland field. Although it is possible to identify the literature from which these calculations are made, the officially published SSB statistics do not seem to follow these methods; they appear to be similar to the more common definition in present-day Asian countries. The figures shown in Table 3 are of this kind.

[38] Ho Chi-feng, "General Conclusions of the 1957 National Conference on Water Conservancy of Agricultural Land," *Chung-kuo shui-li*, No. 8, 1957.

per hectare, adequate to supply water for the thirty or sixty rainless days. In the north, winter wheat requires 2250 to 3000 cubic meters, and cotton about 1500 cubic meters.[39] While the requirement of water certainly increases with the improvement of the cropping system (where it has been converted from single to double cropping of rice, twice as much),[40] presumably *ta-tao pao-shou-ti* denotes the requirement of the original cropping system. The figures shown in Table 3 seem to correspond to this concept.

With this methodological knowledge in mind, comparison with equivalent figures from the countries in South and Southeast Asia[41] indicates that the figures on the ratios of irrigation shown for 1957 in Table 3 are fairly large as a national average. Even the figures for 1963 show a considerable improvement, although the drastic but ill-planned attempt to increase irrigated land in the years of the "Great Leap Forward" seems to have devastated some part of the cultivated land. To derive some idea about figures for the present, which are yet unpublished, it is necessary to make some evaluation of the extensive water-conservation works renewed toward the end of 1963. In summary, the work done between the winter of 1963 and the spring of 1964 was largely concerned with the completion of the unfinished works subsidiary to existing medium-scale and major irrigation projects. Since the winter of 1964, the emphasis has been transferred to numerous minor irrigation (and antiwaterlogging) projects undertaken by the suborgans of the People's Communes. Also, since 1964, with the introduction of mechanical and electrical irrigation and drainage equipment, state projects of a completely new pattern have begun to spread. In some priority regions, this equipment has been introduced even in the local projects undertaken by the People's Communes. Table 3 indicates this increase of equipment. From these events, we presume that the ratio of effective irrigation must have increased significantly since then.[42]

In terms of the three roles of irrigation, our evaluation is necessarily preliminary and imprecise. This is especially so because our study has not yet progressed to the point of being able to examine the problems

[39] *Nung-t'ien shui-li*, p. 27.

[40] *Shui-tao tsai-pei hsüeh* (Study on Rice Cultivation), p. 417.

[41] Ishikawa, *Economic Development* . . . , secs. 1 and 2, chap. ii.

[42] Considering only the area under mechanical and electric irrigation, the area of assured irrigated water is calculated to amount to more than ten million hectares. This calculation is made by assuming that two hectares of land can be irrigated for each horsepower; of the 7.3 million horsepower available, one half is used for irrigation purposes.

by regions. It may be said, however, that the stage in which stabilization is the major concern has been drawing to a close in many parts of China, and the imminent task now is the fulfillment of the second and the third roles, increasing the utilization of land and creating a condition conducive to the introduction of improved farming techniques. In some districts, especially where electric and mechanical equipment for irrigation have been introduced, these roles seem to have been fulfilled also. Since 1965, the official literature has spoken about the districts where "the problem of water conservation has been almost solved" *(Shui-li chi-pen kuo-kuan)*.[43] In the light of these developments in basic investments, the changes in the existing cropping system seem to have been attempted in 1956–60 without the required groundwork in irrigation and drainage. By 1965, it appeared that this foundation was being gradually created and, accordingly, the more pressing bottlenecks to increased production were fertilizer and other current inputs.[44]

Finally, since our studies on the patterns of the basic investment in China have been published elsewhere,[45] only a few observations are necessary here. An overwhelming proportion of the irrigated area of China relies upon minor, traditional irrigation facilities constructed by local communities. These are largely small wells, ponds, tanks, small irrigation channels diverting water from streams, simple equipment for lifting water, and so forth. In 1957, the proportion of these minor facilities was said to have been 80 per cent of the total facilities in irrigated areas. The present situation seems much the same. In 1964, the proportion of traditional facilities was reported as 64 per cent in Hunan and 86 per cent in Fukien.[46] The limitations of traditional techniques

[43] E.g., Work Team of the Central South Office of the Central Committee, CCP, "Where Does Revolutionary Spirit Direct?" *Hsin-hua yüeh-pao* (New China Monthly), No. 9, 1965, pp. 79–81.

[44] Regarding the output-increasing effects of irrigation, various yardsticks seem to have been used during the First Five-Year Plan period. A typical one is: by converting the unirrigated upland field to irrigated upland field, a 50 per cent increase in output is generally obtainable and by converting upland field to wet-paddy field, a 100 per cent increase is obtainable, without taking into account the additional benefit accruing from the conversion of this wet-paddy field from one crop of rice to double cropping. These percentages are inclusive of the benefit accruing from other measures for increasing production. Lo Wen and Shang-kuan Chang-chun, "Problems of the Development of Irrigation in Agricultural Land," *Chi-hua ching-chi*, No. 10, 1957, pp. 15–17.

[45] Ishikawa, *Economic Development . . .* , pp. 131–53.

[46] Regarding the overwhelming weight of the minor projects in the total increase in the irrigated areas during the First Five-Year Plan period, see Ishikawa, *National Income . . .* , p. 167; for comparable figures in India, see Ishikawa, *Economic Development . . .* , p. 150.

and local resources often produce facilities with inferior technical qualities, and antidrought capacities are often less than the level of *ta-tao pao-shou-ti*.[47] In addition, the agricultural land under minor irrigation is topographically limited. However, there is a crucially important aspect in minor irrigation—the area where it does exist is commonly the area where the advanced types of traditional agriculture are found. The peasants' effort to introduce and develop small-scale irrigation is everywhere associated with their effort to improve the methods of production in various other aspects, but assessed against the experience of Japan and other Asian countries, in the areas where minor irrigation was previously not practiced, local people are very slow in responding to the possibility of introducing better farming techniques made possible by major irrigation projects. Therefore, small-scale irrigation is likely to be a sound technological foundation for a progression to modern agriculture.

Major projects, and those projects using mechanical and electrical equipment for irrigation and drainage, have been undertaken in the area where minor projects are topographically difficult to expand. Technical qualities of the facilities are sufficiently high to make the improvement of the existing cropping system and other related technical progress possible. The remaining problem is that of resource availability. This seems to be especially true in projects using mechanical and electrical equipment, probably accounting for the fact that these projects have been undertaken so far on a very discriminative and selective basis: only in the major bases of supply of marketable food grains. These include the Yangtze River Delta, the T'ai Lake area, the Hangchou-Chiahsing district, the Tung-t'ing Lake region, the west Szechwan Plain, and the Pearl River Delta.[48]

FERTILIZERS

Since fertilizers are typical current inputs, analysis of their use is relatively straightforward. Estimates of the application of fertilizer and manure for 1957 and 1965 are shown in Table 4. As the figures show, there was a markedly greater proportion of farm-supplied fertilizers in

[47] Such as in the case of the minor irrigation facilities in the vast hillock region in the central part of Anhwei Province, where the major source of irrigation water is small tanks and the greater number of these tanks had an antidrought capacity of only twenty to thirty days. Wang Ju-hsiang, "Problems of Cropping Systems and Crop Rotation in the Kiang-hwai Hillock District," *Chung-kuo nung-pao*, No. 9, 1964, pp. 37–41.

[48] *JMJP*, Sept. 26, 1964.

TABLE 4
ESTIMATES OF THE APPLICATION OF FERTILIZERS AND MANURES

	Gross Weight (In Million Metric Tons)	Fertilizer Ingredient (In Thousand Tons)				Per Cent
		N	P_2O_5	K_2O	Total	
1957						
1. Animal excreta						
Cattle, horses	481	2,170	790	1,960	4,920	38
Pigs	224	1,030	690	1,430	3,150	24
2. Night soil	183	1,098	366	549	2,013	16
Urban	18	108	36	54	198	2
Rural	165	990	330	495	1,815	14
3. Green manure	30	122	30	122	274	2
4. Oil cakes	5	350	65	110	525	4
5. Compost, plant residues	81	324	162	324	810	6
6. River and pond mud	144	360	180	217	757	6
7. Other organic fertilizer	8	32	16	32	80	1
8. Chemical fertilizers						
Nitrogenous	1.6	322	-	-	322	2
Phosphatic	.3	-	62	-	62	.5
9. TOTAL		5,808	2,361	4,744	12,913	100
10. Per hectare of cultivated area (kilograms)		52	21	42	115	
11. Per hectare of cropped area (kilograms)		37	15	30	82	
1965						
1. Animal excreta						
Cattle, horses	285	1,280	485	1,170	2,935	20
Pigs	353	1,650	1,090	2,260	5,000	34
2. Night soil	202	1,212	404	606	2,222	15
Urban	22	132	44	66	242	2
Rural	180	1,080	360	540	1,980	13
3. Green manure	66	259	66	259	584	4
4. Oil cakes	4	262	49	79	390	3
5. Compost, plant residues	81	324	162	324	810	5
6. River and pond mud	144	360	180	217	757	5
7. Other organic fertilizer	8	32	16	32	80	0.5
8. Chemical fertilizers						
Nitrogenous		1,275			1,275	9
Phosphatic			617		617	4
Potassic				30	30	0.5
9. TOTAL		6,654	3,069	4,977	14,800	100
10. Per hectare of cultivated area (kilograms)		61	28	46	135	
11. Per hectare of cropped area (kilograms)		43	20	32	95	

Sources and notes:

1957. Since my own work for the estimation of the fertilizer and manure input has been under way, I present here a very crude estimate in a very tentative way. Essentially, lines 1 through 4 and line 8 are my own estimate; lines 5, 6, and 7 are taken from Owen L. Dawson, "Fertilizer Supply and Food Requirements," in J. L. Buck, O. L. Dawson, and Y-L Wu, *Food and Agriculture in Communist China* (Palo Alto, Calif.: Stanford University Press, 1960) [1], pp. 138–40, which shows a first attempt to evaluate China's consumption of farmyard manures. The basic reference materials of my estimates are: Institute for Research on Soil and Fertilizer, Chinese Agricultural Academy, *Chung-kuo fei-liao kai-lun* (General Treatise on Fertilizer in China) (Shanghai Science and Techniques Publishing Co., 1962) [2]; Hupei Editorial Team of Teaching Materials in Commercial Middle School on Agricultural Production Means, *Hua-hsüeh fei-liao shang-ping hsüh* (Study on the Chemical Fertilizer Merchandise) (Peking: Chinese Finance and Economic Publishing Co., 1963) [3]; a fertilizer ingredient table published in *Chung-kuo nung-pao* (Chinese Agricultural Bulletin), No. 7, 1959, p. 36 [4] and in *JMJP*, Nov. 18, 1957 [5].

Line 1: Estimation of gross weight is made on the basis of (a) per unit of animal excreta per annum multiplied by (b), the number of animals multiplied by (c), the percentage of total animal excreta actually in use. (a) is taken from [2], pp. 58–59 (pig: 2 metric tons; cattle: 9 metric tons; horse: 5 metric tons). I have not taken the excreta of sheep into account. Presumably, a considerable part of it is produced on the pastures and hence not used for crops. (b) is taken, in the case of large animals (including mules and donkeys), as the number at midyear of 1957, which is derived from the same source used in Table 2 by averaging the year-end figures of 1956 and 1957. In the case of pigs, for the reasons stated (in regard to feeding and the tendency of a change in the number during the year), I take their number as the midyear figure multiplied by 1.4. (c) is assumed as 0.7, which is the number used by [1]. Fertilizer ingredient is taken from [2], p. 57. Regarding the resulting figures, there are not sufficient data for cross-checking. The problem is complicated, at least in one aspect, by the fact that animal excreta is supplied in the form of stable manures and compost combined with grasses, plant residues, and even earth. However, regarding the chemical components of pig refuse, which seems to be a source of dispute, it may be mentioned that there are many reports indicating that the yardstick used here is not out of line. One example: an important survey on pig-raising in one of the model production brigades in Szechwan (*JMJP*, April 17, 1965 [6]) reported that, according to the experience of the past several years, a pig produces eighty to one hundred buckets of excreta per year, each bucket being equivalent roughly to 0.5 kilograms of ammonia sulphate. This is fairly similar to the figure used in this estimate; furthermore, see the comments on Line 1 for the 1965 portion of this table.

Line 2: The estimation of gross weight is made on the basis of (a), per capita supply of night soil multiplied by (b), the number of residents multiplied by (c), percentage of night soil actually in use, in urban and rural areas, respectively. For the urban area, useful information is provided by the Ministry of Agriculture, "The State of Utilization of Night Soils, Rubbish, and Other Miscellaneous Manures in Various Urban Districts and Our Opinion Regarding It," *Chung-kuo nung-pao*, No. 7, 1956 [7]. In this source, (a) is given as 500 kilograms per annum. (c) varies among districts, depending on whether they are big or small, near the agricultural area or from it, and on past practices of utilization. The national average is estimated at 0.4. (b) is taken from *T'ung-chi kung-tso* (Statistical Work), No. 11, 1957. Reference [7] also indicates other sources of manures that are available in the urban area: rubbish usable for manure, 150 kilograms per capita per annum; mud in ditches, 5 kilograms per capita per annum; other miscellaneous sources, such as refuse of factories and food-processing works, 5.5 kilograms per capita per annum. However, I simply ignored taking these into account. In rural areas, modifications of the above figures are made for (b) and (c). As for (c), 60 per cent is taken, which is equal to Dawson's. Fertilizer ingredients are taken from [4]. The resultant figure can be cross-checked by at least one independent source of information: Government of India, Ministry of Food and Agriculture, *Report of the Indian Delegation to China on Agricultural Planning and Techniques*, July–Aug., 1956 [8], pp. 146 ff. It is said that the total amount of night soil available per year was around 200 million metric tons. This figure is larger than the above estimate, but one main reason accounting for the difference seems to lie in the higher availability coefficient assumed in [8].

Line 3: The estimation is made on the basis of (a), cropped area of green manures multiplied by (b), per unit area yield of green manures multiplied by (c), the proportion of total green manure output used for fertilizing multiplied by (d), the fertilizer ingredients. (a) and (b): Ministry of Agriculture, Department of Soil and Fertilizer, "Performance of the Work Relating to Fertilizer in Our Country for the Past Ten Years," *Chung-kuo nung-pao*, No. 17 1959 [9], p. 25, shows that

	Total cropped area under green manure crop	Per *mou* yield of green manures
1952	34,460 thousand *mou*	650 *chin*
1957	51,300 "	1,500 "
1958	63,000 "	2,500 "

I have taken these figures for 1957. Some problems remain. Of the total cropped area under green manure crops, which is shown here, most were used for spring or summer crops of the following year. In 1958, the cropped area for winter green manure crops was 59,780 thousand *mou*, according to Hsin-i Chang, "Go One Step Further in Developing the Production of Green Manure in the Southern Regions in Our Country," *Hung-ch'i* (Red Flag), No. 18, 1962 [10]. Relating it to the above figure on total cropped area, the proportion of winter crops amounts to 95 per cent. However, I assumed that the difference of the cropped area of winter green manure crops between 1956 and 1957 was insignificant. Next, the yield per *mou* in 1957 (11.2 metric tons per hectare) appeared to be much smaller than 14.6 metric tons per hectare, which is shown in source [7] as the probable yield for 1955. In regard to (c), the factor to be taken into consideration is only the alternative use for feed. Since there are no available data for estimating this proportion, I have used 0.8, which is assumed by Dawson. (d) is taken from [2], [5], and Liu Pai-t'ao, "Preliminary Studies on a Few Problems Concerning Cropping Systems," *Ching-chi yen-chiu* (Economic Studies), No. 4, 1963 [11]. The last source indicates the highest ingredient coefficients. The adopted one is the lowest.

Line 4: In source [8], it was stated that the use of oil cake in 1955 was 4.5 million tons, among which soybeans occupied the major part. As is shown in source [2], p. 142, there are many kinds of oil cakes, and their use is not confined to fertilizers. I have taken, however, the ratio of this figure (4.5 million tons) to the sum of the outputs of soybeans and other oilseeds in 1955 (34.6 per cent) to be applicable to 1957 also. Fertilizer ingredient coefficients have been taken from [2].

Lines 5–7: Taken from Dawson's estimates in [1]. The difference of the quantities in use between 1956 and 1957 is simply ignored.

Line 8: Derived by the total quantity of consumption, shown in Reiitsu Kojima, "China's Chemical Industry," in Ishikawa (ed.), *Chūgoku keizai no chōki tembō*, II (Long-term Projection of China's Economy, Vol. II), Institute of Asian Economic Affairs, 1962, [12], p. 282, divided by (b), the ratios of composition of total quantity of consumption planned for 1957, shown in Wang Hsin-fu and Lan Chien-hsiao, "Energetically Develop the Chemical Fertilizer Industry," *Chi-hua ching-chi*, No. 10, 1957 [13]. The coefficients of fertilizer ingredient is also given in the source.

1965. The basic method used is the same as that used for 1957. Only the changes in the numbers of livestock, residents, and outputs are taken into consideration, with various coefficients assumed to be constant, unless otherwise noted. The figures in Lines 5, 6, and 7 are held as they were in 1957.

Line 1: The number of cattle and horses is taken from E. F. Jones, "The Emerging Pattern of China's Economic Revolution," *An Economic Profile of Mainland China* I (Washington, D.C.: U.S. Government Printing Office, 1956), 82. The number of pigs is taken from *JMJP*, July 10, 1965, where it was also reported, in connection with a national conference on the work of livestock-raising, that the total fertilizer effect of pig excreta in 1964 was in terms of the total sum of the ingredients of N, P_2O_5 and K_2O equivalent to 20 million metric tons of chemical fertilizer. This is comparatively close to the figure shown in the table.

Line 2: The same coefficients of per capita supply of night soil, fertilizer ingredients, and the utilization are assumed. Midyear population figure is taken from "Data from Typical Survey of Distribution of Revenue in 228 Agricultural Production Cooperatives, 1957," *T'ung-chi yen-chiu* (Statistical Studies), No. 8, 1958.

Line 3: Total cropped area of green manures in 1964 is reported in *JMJP*, June 5, 1965, to have increased to 1.37 times the 1952 figure. From this and the information given in Line 3 of 1957, it can be estimated at 81.60 million *mou* (5.4 million hectares). Per hectare yield of green manure is taken as having increased to 15 metric tons.

Line 4: The same coefficient of 34.6 per cent as in 1955 (oil cakes used as manure divided by the output of soybean, groundnuts, rapeseed, and sesame seed) is applied to the 1965 production shown in Table 1. 377 million metric tons is derived.

Lines 5–7: The same quantities as in 1957 are assumed.
Line 8: Entirely dependent upon an estimate of the British Sulphur Corporation Ltd., as translated by the Association for Export Promotion of Chemical Fertilizer in Japan.

both years. One implication apparent in the table is that any analysis of the fertilizer problem in China is not very meaningful without taking into consideration this intra-agricultural fertilizer resource. In this regard, I would like to thank Dr. Dawson, who made the first attempt to estimate the quantity of home-prepared fertilizer, and whose estimates are utilized in part in this compilation.[49] The estimates are necessarily rough, and those for the years prior to 1957 have not yet been done. In appraising these estimates it should be recognized that the rates of utilization of the components of each type of fertilizer are not taken into account. The utilization rate of organic fertilizer is generally much lower than that of inorganic fertilizer, although the former has its own merit in improving the physical structure of soil. Utilization rate is also higher in irrigated than in dry fields, and higher in the southern than in the northern region.[50]

It should be noted that in 1957 the total quantity of fertilizer applied per hectare of cultivated land was very large in comparison to the developing countries in South and Southeast Asia. The sum of fertilizer ingredients for N, P_2O_5, and K_2O applied per hectare of cultivated land in China was 115 kilograms, as Table 4 indicates, whereas in India it was estimated for 1958–59[51] to be between nearly zero and 13 kilograms, depending upon the states. It is interesting that in this regard a recent estimate on the application of fertilizer and manure in Japan in the early Meiji era was, on a comparable basis, 108 kilograms, or close to the 1957 figure for China.[52] Independent data that can be used for

[49] Owen L. Dawson, "Fertilizer Supply and Food Requirements," in Buck, Dawson, and Wu, *Food and Agriculture* . . . , pp. 101–48. Estimates by Dawson for 1956 and the writer for 1957 differ considerably; Dawson's estimates are 37.5 per cent lower. The causes are manifold. The main one, however, seems to be that Dawson's various coefficients are taken mainly from the prewar studies, whereas the present writer's are taken mainly from the official sources.

[50] The rates seem to differ further depending upon crops. In the case of wheat cultivation, the rate of chemical fertilizer utilization is 70 to 80 per cent, that of oil cakes and human night soil 50 to 60 per cent, and stable manures and compost 30 to 40 per cent, according to a datum indicated in Chin Shan-pao (ed.), *Hsiao-mai tsai-pei-hsüeh* (Treatise on Wheat Cultivation in China) (Peking: Agricultural Publication Co., 1960), p. 251. See *Shiu-tao tsai-pei-hsüeh*, pp. 374, 390.

[51] Mainly based on figures that appeared in The Fertilizer Association of India, *Fertilizer Statistics, 1960*; see Ishikawa, *Economic Development* . . . , pp. 190–91.

[52] Total supply of fertilizer ingredient is taken from Yujiro Hayami, "Hiryō Tokaryō no Suikei (Estimates of the Applicatoin of Fertilizer and Manure)—1883–

cross-checking are not available, except for the estimates made by agricultural experts for Hunan Province. In comparable terms, the application they reported was 70 kilograms in 1952 and 169 kilograms in 1957. Considering that the multiple-cropping index is larger in Hunan than the national average, these two sets of figures do not seem to be inconsistent.[53]

1941, 1951–1959," *Nōgyō Sōgō Kenkyū* (Synthetic Research of Agriculture), Vol. XVII, No. 1, Jan., 1953; Cultivated area from M. Umemura *et al.*, *Agriculture and Forestry*, Vol. IX of *Estimates of Long-term Economic Statistics of Japan Since 1968*, ed. by Ohkawa, Shinohara, and Umemura (Tokyo: Tōyō Keizai Shinposha, 1966). The figures by fertilizer components for 1883 as well as 1937 are (in kilograms per hectare of cultivated area):

		N	P_2O_5	K_2O	Total
1883	Total	48	21	39	108
1937	Total	110	69	73	252
	(chemical fertilizer)	37	39	17	93

[53] This is the estimate of the quantity of fertilizer and manure applied to cultivated land in Hunan Province, which appeared in Hunan Agricultural College, *Hunan nung-yeh*, pp. 120–24. The details are shown as follows:

		Total quantity applied (metric tons)	Fertilizer ingredient (kilograms)		
			N	P_2O_5	K_2O
A. *Purchased fertilizer*					
(1) 1952					
1. Aggregate					
	Oil cakes	20,947	909,091	289,066	291,161
	Chemical fertilizer	2,589	538,470		
	Bone	3,671	128,485	825,975	—
	Lime	78,685	—	—	—
	Total	—	1,576,046	1,115,041	291,161
2. Per hectare of cultivated area			0.43	0.30	0.09
(2) 1957					
1. Aggregate					
	Oil cakes	66,352	2,879,677	915,658	922,293
	Ammonia sulphate	37,514	7,802,891	—	—
	Other chemical fertilizer	14,292	—	1,286	3,425
	Bone	4,992	174,722	1,123,211	—
	Lime	506,930	—	—	—
	Total	—	10,857,290	2,040,155	925,718
2. Per hectare of cultivated area			3.1	0.53	0.24
B. Green manure					
(1) 1952					
1. Aggregate		3,500,000	21,000,000	5,250,000	42,000,000
2. Per hectare			5.7	1.4	11.4

The kind of fertilizer used is also important. Of the total applied, organic fertilizer, mostly of domestic origin, amounts to 97.5 per cent. Animal excreta and human night soil comprised 78 per cent; the rest consists largely of plant residue, by-products of the processing of agricultural products, and, in the case of green manure, the product itself. This implies that the supply of fertilizer is related to the structure of the agriculture. Within the structure, livestock occupies a crucial position.

The next question concerns the balance between supply and demand. Since data on the demand are limited, it is difficult to determine precisely the balance relation between the two. The following points, however, should be mentioned in this regard: (1) The cultivated land area on which no fertilizer was applied was exceptional in 1957.[54] (2) The quantities of fertilizer applied were reported as amounting from two to three hundred kilograms for a single crop of paddy and less than one hundred kilograms for wheat, in terms of the total sum of fertilizer ingredients. When the improved cropping system was introduced, a substantial quantity of additional fertilizer was required. In the case of the conversion of single to double cropping of rice, 60 to 100 per cent more fertilizer was reported to be required,[55] and in the conversion from *indica* to *japonica* varieties, about 100 per cent more was required.[56] (3) Under the original cropping system, the requirement of fertilizer and its supply appeared to have maintained a balance at a certain output level. When changes in the cropping system were attempted with the given condition of supply, the total output tended to decrease. Cases

(2)	1957				
1.	Aggregate	11,000,000	66,000,000	16,500,000	132,000,000
2.	Per hectare		14.6	4.3	34.4
C. Farmyard manure (Per hectare of cultivated area)					
	1952	3,600	16	11	24
	1957	8,850	40	22	59
D. Total fertilizer and manure (Per hectare of cultivated area)					
	1952		22	13	35
	1957		58	27	84

[54] According to Ministry of Agriculture, Bureau of Soil and Fertilizer, "Ten Years' Performance of Fertilizer Work in Our Country," *Chung-kuo nung-pao*, No. 17, 1959, p. 25, the ratio of total cultivated area under manuring was 60 per cent in 1952 and 80 per cent in 1957.

[55] This coefficient is taken from Government of I-yang Chuan-ch'ü, Hunan Province (see note 13).

[56] *Shui-tao tsai-pei-hsüeh*, p. 370.

of such a balance relation of fertilizing under traditional agriculture were frequently publicized in the professional articles between 1963 and 1965.[57] From these, it seems broadly correct to consider that the total requirement of fertilizer in 1957 was well over the supply.

Turning next to the figure for 1965, Table 4 suggests that considerable changes were brought about in the composition of the fertilizer supply. First, the supply of animal excreta from large (draft) animals showed a decrease as large as 40 per cent of the 1957 supply, and 15 per cent of the 1957 total supply of fertilizer. This was due to the serious decrease in the number of draft animals during the agricultural depression, and since the figures used for present purposes were estimated, the above calculations are subject to error. Second, the supply of excreta from hogs showed enough of an increase to nearly make up for the decrease in the supply from draft animals. Third, the supply of chemical fertilizer increased significantly, amounting now to 14 per cent of the total. Green manure was also increasing, although the relative weight was not yet large. As a result, the total supply of fertilizer ingredients in 1965 had increased by 15 per cent over the supply in 1957.

We have not yet assembled sufficient information to make an over-all judgment on the demand in 1965, but we can surmise by circumstantial evidence that it is steadily increasing. However, one thing to be noted in this connection is the progress of research in various agricultural regions on fertilizer requirements for various crops under the varying conditions of soil, water, and fertilizing methods. Presumably, as a result, yardsticks for measuring the output response to fertilizer appear to have become more detailed and precise, and more sophisticated fertilizer response curves seem also to have been constructed, although in most of these cases fertilizer application is expressed in terms of various farmyard products; hence the figures used are not very precise.[58] On the basis of data now becoming available, and perhaps because of the

[57] One of the remarkable examples was Yang Ch'un-feng, "A Few Problems Concerning the Crop Rotation System in Kwangchung Region," *Chung-kuo nung-pao*, No. 4, 1963, pp. 9–13. In the previously cited article by Government of I-yang Chuan-ch'ü, an interesting story is found in the fact that the same manuring balance limits the possibility of expanding the area under double cropping of rice to 50 per cent of total paddy field.

[58] Institute of Soil and Fertilizer, Chinese Agricultural Academy, *Chung-kuo fei-liao kai-lun* (General Treatise on Fertilizer in China); *Shui-tao tsai-pei-hsüeh and Hsiao-mei tsai-liao-hsüeh*. It is shown in *ibid.*, p. 253, that in the provinces of Hopei and Chekiang the norms of fertilizer and manure application for different output level of wheat were prepared.

increasing availability of fertilizer, suggestions of even optimum application have begun to appear in professional journals.[59]

Viewed in terms of the entire input structure, the most significant points in the fertilizer situation in 1965 seem to be the following: (1) For the first time in history, China's agriculture has begun to rely upon a significant extra-agricultural supply of fertilizer. (2) Two underlying factors are conceivable: One is a short-term factor caused by a decrease in the number of livestock, and the other by a long-term factor brought about by required changes in the cropping systems. Of these two, the more immediate factor is probably the first; for a few years during the agricultural depression, an increased supply of chemical fertilizer might have been necessary to make up for the shortages in the supply of manure. However, by 1965 chemical fertilizers had become an additional source of input, and will continue to be used. (3) The reason for this conjecture lies in the following: A phenomenal increase in the number of hogs in the past few years was regarded in a sense as a short-term phenomenon. The rate of increase for hogs will not continue to be as high as it was during these years, especially if the number of large animals is restored to the prior peak level and continues to increase. Essentially, the rate of increase in the total number of livestock, and with it, the rate of increase in the supply of animal excreta, tend to be limited to a level lower than the rate of increase in crop production, under the given allocation coefficient of food grain to animal feed, and the given supply of uncultivated grasses. Hence, in the long run, a substantial increase in agricultural output will require an increasing quantity of fertilizer beyond what traditional agriculture can afford to supply by itself.

TENTATIVE FINDINGS

An examination of the changes in China's agriculture should include at least brief comments on the remaining major inputs: human labor, animal and mechanical drafting power, and varieties of seed.

[59] Ta'ai Hsü, "A Few Problems Concerning the Increase in Wheat Production in Suburban District of Peking," *Chung-kuo nung-pao*, No. 9, 1964, pp. 9–14. Meanwhile, an interesting study aimed at deriving an over-all output response to fertilizer in China appeared in Jung-chao Liu, "Fertilizer Supply and Grain Production in Communist China," *Journal of Farm Economics*, Vol. XLVII, No. 4 (Nov., 1965) (almost the same content is reproduced in the article in *The China Quarterly*, Oct.–Dec., 1965). Although this may be an important first step for making an estimate of the fertilizer requirement in coming years, as suggested from the description in the text, much more detailed studies about the response coefficients seem to be needed for deriving even a simple yardstick.

The nature of the problem that was encountered during the period under study concerning human labor and animal traction power was similar, in a sense, to the problem of manure and fertilizer. Starting from a low level of balance between demand and supply, these two current inputs underwent, after 1965, a severe shortage of supply, at first in the area along the Yangtze Basin. This was mainly due to the premature attempt to alter the existing cropping system, especially in the adoption of the double cropping of rice. In 1965, a new situation had begun to emerge: a considerable measure of mechanical and electric power was being introduced into agriculture in the form of tractors and other machines for agricultural operation, irrigation and drainage, and transportation; in addition, there was an increased use of petroleum and electricity. The increased use of extra-agricultural inputs was in response to changes allied to the changes that altered the supply and use of fertilizer—the decline in the number of draft animals and the increasing demand for labor and power arising with the use of new cultivation methods. Contrary to the situation with fertilizers, however, mechanical power does not seem to have reached the stage of compensating for the depleted animal power. Yet the prospects are for an increasing reliance on extra-agricultural sources of the energy for operations.

The pure-line selection of varieties of seeds seems to have been accomplished during the First Five-Year-Plan, and the present program is concerned with the interlocal dissemination of better seeds or making provision for research for breeding new seed. The problem of seed variety is closely interrelated with the changes in the cropping system, and the central concern seems not so much with the higher yielding varieties as with those better suited for special cropping systems, for example, rice varieties with a shorter growing period for use as the first crop in the double cropping of rice. Under the present situation, the latter tends to be a more efficient way of increasing output.

Our study seems to substantiate the working hypotheses presented earlier. The production structure of China's agriculture may be summarized in a description of its broad features in the three bench-mark years. In 1952, various components of the production structure were in a balanced state within the tradition pattern, the technical methods developed within that pattern were of a high standard, and the productivity was much higher than agricultural methods used in the developing countries in South and Southeast Asia.

In 1957, attempts at altering the traditional cropping system seem to have already disrupted the existing balance. The disruption was accelerated by the decrease in the number of both draft and meat animals. Most of the intra-agricultural resources upon which China's agricultural output still relied were in short supply and a threat of decreasing return was felt. These tendencies continued until 1959, and the outcome was an agricultural disaster. In 1965, two major changes in the input structure were seen: (1) After about ten years of trial and error, a technical foundation seems to have been almost accomplished upon which alteration of the cropping system can be made feasible. The remaining problems will be the availability of additional current inputs required for it. (2) For the first time in China's agricultural history, a considerable amount of nonagricultural input has begun to be brought to it: chemical fertilizer; mechanical draft power; mechanical and electrical equipment for irrigation and drainage; and electricity and petroleum. At first, most of this new input was used to make up for the decline in supply of fertilizer and animal labor, brought about by the decrease in the livestock during the agricultural depression. Gradually, however, they are becoming an additional source of the agricultural input that was required in conjunction with the adoption of new, improved, cropping systems.

ERNST HAGEMANN

Comment

Professor Ishikawa's comprehensive survey has provided us with a rigorous and provocative analysis. The paper brings together much useful information on the beginning changes in the traditional agrarian sector. Since I agree with him on many issues, my comments are mainly supplementary in nature.

Ishikawa's major thesis is that in the past ten years a process of change has been at work in the rural economy of China, characterized by an increasing stream of nonfarm resources, and that this process will be the technological basis for the modernization of Chinese agriculture. In support of this basic hypothesis he does not offer a cost structure or input-output analysis; instead the author amasses a quantity of data that he considers to be characteristic of the change in the production structure.

The static image of a state of "balance" corresponds to the traditional Chinese agricultural structure in which change occurred only gradually and rapid increases in production within the traditional framework were nearly impossible. However, the current production structure can hardly be defined as one of "balance" in this sense; on the contrary, one has the impression that the Chinese are trying to make use of a chain of disequilibria to accelerate their economic growth.

More important than the image itself is the implicit consequence of this way of presenting the data for Ishikawa's interpretation of the crisis in the years from 1960 to 1962. The crisis is made to appear as the result of a disturbance of this balance, that is (to follow the author's definitions), of a too-rapid change in the cropping system. Yet during the past twenty years the accelerated change in the cropping system and the complete change in the production relationships have broken through the traditional framework of the agricultural economy. Both measures created significant disequilibria in the production structure.

Both the land reform and the first years of step-by-step collectivization drew largely on traditional forms of mutual cooperation, and these initial phases of reorganization were still able to mobilize achievement potential; they showed little influence on the production. A different situation was revealed in the crisis after 1959, which had to take on these dimensions because the attempt was evidently made to substitute the new organizational form, the people's commune, for resources that the planners did not want to make available in the form of capital. The people's communes in their original form were not capable of compensating through mere organizational changes for the disequilibria in the production structure, and they multiplied the new problems by making management more difficult. Since the peasant of the commune was degraded to a simple farmworker, the individual work incentive was reduced to his insignificant share in the achievements of a group that was often too large for him to oversee.

The failure of this organizational experiment demonstrated that a rapid change in the cropping system is not possible without an increased input of nonfarm resources. For this reason the improvements in the organizational structure of the people's communes after 1959 are by themselves no guarantee of an increase in production. On the other hand, it seems to me to be equally unjustified to expect that an increase in nonagricultural input alone "will ease the conflict between collective decision making and individual behavior." It is probable, on the contrary, that progressive technological modernization will rather tend to aggravate this conflict. Although I would avoid giving undue importance to the traditional incentive of private landownership, it seems certain that the income and price trends will be deciding factors for individual incentive in the future as well.

The above-mentioned changes in the cropping system through nonfarm resources serve primarily as substitution for land. The empirical results of this intensification correspond on the theoretical plane, for example, to the second phase of agrarian development as analyzed by Mellor. In the immediate future there will be relatively little substitution of capital (mechanization) for labor, although in the past years a considerable number of agricultural machines have been tested and are being produced serially. The only instance in which substitution of capital for labor has already taken on significant dimensions is in the mechanized pumping of water by electrical or other means. The home production and the import of pumps are on such a high level that as of 1967 approximately fifteen million horsepower have been installed.

However, aside from this, it is to be expected that the labor expenditure will have to increase still further in order to carry through additional fertilization, plant care, and irrigation. With increasing yields per acre, the labor productivity, as in the past, will scarcely increase.

In the long run the most considerable influence toward a change in the production structure is to be expected from the extensive education campaigns in the Chinese agricultural economy. This is true of the general education programs, as well as of the specialized agricultural training that is given principally in the half-work, half-study schools. While the direct impact on production is difficult to measure, there is no doubt that education, as an inducing and accommodating agent for change, plays a deciding role in promoting agricultural development. The collective organizational form in China facilitates, on the one hand, the spread of technical knowledge, but at the same time it multiplies errors and mistaken decisions rapidly.

If I have confirmed that a trend towards increased input of nonfarm resources exists, there remains the problem of evaluating the data that were selected for this analysis. Chinese as well as Soviet publications regularly bring critical reports of waste, bad management, mistaken use of resources, and other uneconomic behavior. In an economic system that has to do without the self-regulating influence of the market, criticism has a central function. A further factor is given by the educational pretensions of a socialist system, which require the repetition of certain criticisms. But even with due consideration of these factors, a cautious estimate of the rate of diffusion of new knowledge and new technology is called for. Thus we can assume that the Chinese will continue on the path of trial and error, and they may well experience some new setbacks. Chinese agriculture is by no means proof against the effects of floods and droughts. The trend towards increasing nonagricultural input will help the agricultural economy surmount these crises more easily and will lead to a slow increase in yield per acre.

S. C. HSIEH*

Taiwan's Model of Agricultural Progress

POTENTIALS OF SMALL FAMILY FARMS
AND THEIR IMPLICATIONS FOR
OTHER DEVELOPING ASIAN COUNTRIES

INTRODUCTION

That the agricultural sector occupies the predominant role in most
developing Asian countries is evident. Whatever yardstick we may
apply, whether it be the number of people the sector employs, the
amount of income originating in it, the amount of basic food it supplies,
the size of its dependent population, its potential domestic market, or
its export earnings, agriculture clearly occupies a position of prime importance and will continue to do so for a considerable time to come.
While agriculture contributes only 30 to 50 per cent of the national income of the developing countries, it provides 50 to 85 per cent of their
employment and, for twelve out of the seventeen developing countries
in Asia,[1] 50 to 95 per cent of their export proceeds.

One of the targets for the United Nations Development Decade of the
1960's is a doubling of the rate of increase in food production. Because
of the high rate of population growth, this represents a very modest

* Although I formerly served as Chief Economist and Secretary-General of the
Sino-American Joint Commission on Rural Reconstruction in Taiwan and was
Visiting Professor of Agricultural Economics under Ford Foundation-sponsored UP–
Cornell Graduate Education Program at the College of Agriculture of the University
of the Philippines, the views expressed in this paper are purely personal observations,
and do not represent any official policy or program implications of either the JCRR
or the University of the Philippines.
[1] The five countries excluded are: India, Iran, Republic of Korea, Laos, and
Hong Kong. See United Nations ECAFE Report, *Economic Survey of Asia and the
Far East* (Bangkok, 1964), pp. 13, 70.

goal for most of the developing countries in Asia if nutritional standards are to be raised at all. Recent rates of increase in food production in most countries have fallen below the average for the 1950's and, in some countries such as India, actual declines have made the problem of how to increase food production, or even to maintain the past rates of increase, one of the most pressing problems currently confronting the Asian countries. The Philippines, Indonesia, South Vietnam, Ceylon, and many others are now each facing the same problem of rice production and import. The Asian region as a whole, which was a net exporter of food before the Second World War, has become increasingly a net importer of foodstuffs.

The need for accelerating agricultural growth, particularly food production, is obvious if a number of problems are to be resolved:

1. The satisfaction of the requirements and the improvement of the nutrition of an increasing population.

2. The improvement of agricultural products in foreign trade to help solve the problem of international payment deficits.

3. The provision of adequate industrial raw materials at reasonable prices and high quality for industrialization.

4. The expansion of a market for domestic industries through increased purchasing power of farmers.

5. The development of a highly productive agriculture as a condition for general economic growth of an agricultural country.

The real challenge is that all the Asian countries must accelerate agricultural development and increase agricultural production. The question facing us now is how it can be done.

TAIWAN'S EXPERIENCE IN AGRICULTURAL DEVELOPMENT

Taiwan's economic progress in the last one and one-half decades is quite remarkable: National income measured in real terms has increased at a yearly rate of 7.7 per cent since 1952, and per capita income has increased at a rate of 4.3 per cent. These high growth rates have been achieved despite rapid population growth, limited natural resources, and heavy defense expenditures. Taiwan's exports of goods and services increased from about U.S. $120 million in 1952 to over U.S. $500 million in 1966. The structure of the economy has been in transition, changing from one with an agricultural base to one with an agroindustrial base. By 1966, the agricultural population had declined to 45 per cent of the total population and the agricultural contribution to the national income to around 26 per cent. The export of agricultural and processed agricultural products declined to about 60 per cent of what it was in 1952. Per capita incomes, which have reached a level of a little under U.S. $200 a year, probably do not fully reflect the economic welfare of the population of Taiwan. Most people consume nutritionally adequate diets with an intake of about 2400 calories and enjoy good health facilities; life expectancy at birth is sixty-six years as compared with seventy in the United States. Approximately 97 per cent of the school-age children attend school; 75 per cent of the total population is literate.

Since the decade between 1910 and 1920, economic development in Taiwan has depended heavily upon improvement in agricultural productivity. Although it has only 0.07 hectare of cultivated land per capita as opposed to almost 0.90 hectare in the United States, crop production per hectare has been raised to a very high level, and the value of crop production per hectare now averages about six times that of the United States.

The development of agriculture in Taiwan may be considered in four distinct phases. The first phase covers the period from 1910 to 1939, and represents an initial and continued development under colonial status. The second phase, extending from 1940 to 1945 and embracing the wartime years, was characterized by a downward trend in agricultural

TABLE 1
GROWTH RATES OF AGRICULTURAL OUTPUT IN TAIWAN
1910–1960

		Average Annual Growth Rate	
State of Development	Period	Agricultural Output Per cent	Population Per cent
Initial agricultural development (Japanese colonial rule)	1910–20	1.66	1.31
Continued development of agriculture (Japanese colonial rule)	1920–39	4.19	2.40
Agricultural development under the impact of World War II	1939–45	12.32	0.46
Recovery and rehabilitation	1945–52	12.93	4.93
Development after rehabilitation	1952–60	3.98	3.61
Average (prewar period)	1910–39	3.31	2.02
Average (postwar period)	1945–60	8.06	4.17
Average (over-all)	1910–60	2.67	2.40

Source: S. C. Hsieh and T. H. Lee, *Agricultural Development and Its Contributions to Economic Growth in Taiwan* ("Economic Digest Series," No. 17 [Taipei: JCRR, April, 1966]).

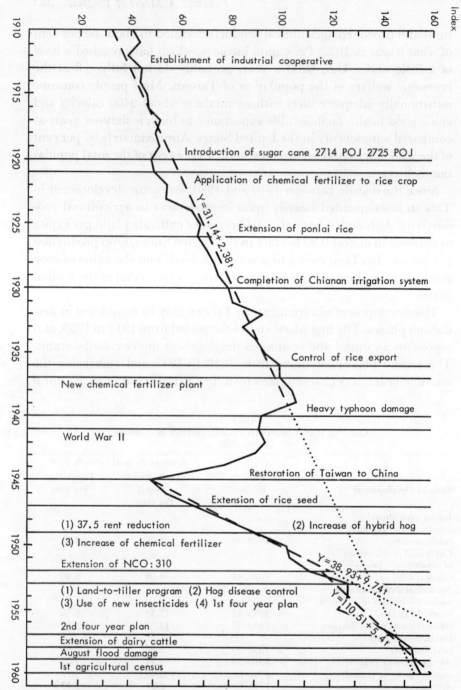

Fig. 1. Index of Aggregate Agricultural Output in Taiwan (Base Period: 1935–37). *Source*: S. C. Hsieh and T. H. Lee: *Agricultural Development and Its Contributions to Economic Growth in Taiwan,* "Economic Digest Series No. 17" (Taipei: JCRR, April, 1966) Taiwan, China.

output. The third phase covers the period from 1946 to 1952, and represents recovery and rehabilitation after the war. The greatest concern in the fourth phase, since 1952, has been the further development of agricultural resources and technology. The average annual growth rate of agricultural output in the prewar period, 1910–39, was 3.31 per cent, while that in the postwar period, 1945–60, has been 8.06 per cent. For about half a century, Taiwan has enjoyed a comparatively high growth rate in agriculture (see Table and Fig. 1)

Agricultural development in Taiwan has proceeded under certain unique situations. There has been practically no increase of cultivated land since 1950. The size of farm is very small, averaging a little more than 1.0 hectare, equivalent to or even smaller than farms in most other developing Asian countries. As a result, intensive use of the land has been implemented through multiple cropping and relay planting. The dominant pattern of crop production comprises a rice culture similar to other Asian countries, but the index of multiple cropping is about 190, the highest in Asia. Factors contributing to this high index are its tropical and subtropical climates that allow the growth of crops all year round, and the extensive development of controlled irrigation, with about two thirds of the cultivated land under irrigation. Most advanced countries with highly developed agriculture are located in temperate zone areas; extensive knowledge, therefore, about the development of tropical agriculture is still lacking, so Taiwan has proceeded on largely unproven hypotheses. About 80,000 metric tons of chemical fertilizers are used annually on about 880,000 hectares of cultivated land; this indicates a heavy application of chemical fertilizers over and above the use of farm-produced organic fertilizers. Population growth is about 3 per cent per year; the farm family averages about seven persons, with an average of three workers per farm. This, again, is similar to other Asian countries, with the exception of Japan. Few advanced countries have had so high a population growth during the period of their agricultural development.

About 95 per cent of the farmers in Taiwan are organized into township farmers' associations with multiple facilities for agricultural extension education, credit and loans, marketing, supplies, and other economic services. Irrigation associations are also organized by the farmers for maintenance and repair of irrigation systems, water management and distribution, and collection of water fees. More than three fourths of the aggregate value of agricultural production goes to commercial sales, either for the domestic market or for export. This high degree of commercialization in agriculture was achieved in the context of the small-sized family farm with intensive cultivation and a high level of technology. Furthermore, rapid agricultural growth in Taiwan has been achieved through the interaction of active government roles such as agricultural planning, development of infrastructure and export promotion, and through free enterprise in agriculture, such as decision making in farm enterprises, pricing, and marketing.

After World War II, there were four major problems facing the government and agricultural planners in Taiwan: First, the pressing problem of food supply, mainly rice, to meet the rapid population increase that resulted from high population growth rate and immigration from the mainland. Second, the rural unrest, which was the result of an irrational tenure system and the social, political, and economic instability that marked the transfer of the central government to Taiwan in 1949. Third, the serious deficit in international payments owing to a low export capacity and a high import demand. Fourth, the inflationary pressure that resulted from the government budget deficit, a high price level, the shortage of commodity supply, and the low level of both industrial and agricultural output. These are much the same problems that have been facing the majority of Asia's developing countries in the past twenty years.

Taiwan took major measures to meet these problems. Government agencies have played an active role in helping irrigation and farmers' associations in the rehabilitation and repair of irrigation facilities and in the restoration of warehouses and other adjuncts to marketing. A rice-production program has put emphasis on food output and on the import, as well as on domestic production, of fertilizers. Agricultural research and district crop-improvement stations have been improved and strengthened. A three-step land-reform program, including rental reduction, sales of public land, and a land-to-the-tiller program, was undertaken, beginning in 1949 and completed in 1952. Farmers' associations were reorganized to put the management in the hands of real farmers. Programs for the promotion of agricultural exports and of substitutes for industrial imports were also implemented. Monetary reform was carried out in 1949 to meet the pressure of inflation.

In the actual development and performance of Taiwan's agricultural program, there was an increase of output per hectare, as seen in the index from 1952 to 1964, where the rice yield rose to 3,853 kilograms in 1964 from 2,621 kilograms in 1952. Other products—sweet potato, wheat, soybean, tobacco, pineapple, and so on—have had an increase in aggregate yield by 50 per cent. The increase in actual production of such major crops as rice, sugar cane, bananas, and pineapples were quite remarkable. Hog production and fishery output were increased by 100 per cent and 150 per cent, respectively. Diversification in agricultural production was achieved.

Land reform brought favorable changes in the ownership of farm land. Tenant farmers were reduced in number from 39 per cent of the total farm families in 1949 to 15 per cent in 1960. Agricultural exports increased as a result of export promotion and diversification. Reorganized farmers' associations provided better services and facilities like credit, extension services, storage, fertilizer distribution, product marketing, and so on, to the farmer members. There has been improvement of irrigation and flood-control facilities, an increase in the supply and application of chemical fertilizer, in the granting of agricultural loans, and in the production of major processed food items for export.

All these expanded agricultural and industrial outputs, plus increased exports and imports, have checked the inflationary pressure in the economy, as indicated by the stable general wholesale price index and the decline of the black market rate of American dollars to approximately the official exchange rate. Through favorable agricultural development, increased productivity and output, plus industrial output and export expansion, the four basic economic problems have been solved successfully, providing a favorable condition for general economic growth. The United States' economic aid to the Republic of China, which has averaged about U.S. $80–100 million annually, was terminated in July, 1965. Since then, Taiwan's economy continues its trend of growth at an average rate of 7 to 8 per cent a year, and has been able to obtain capital from conventional foreign and domestic markets.

REASONS UNDERLYING TAIWAN'S PROGRESS

Taiwan's agricultural development from 1950 to 1964 can be attributed to several factors. The government has given strong support for agricultural development through three consecutive agricultural four-year development plans. Flood control and irrigation facilities are sufficiently developed to transform an agricultural production that was wholly at the mercy of climate and other natural conditions to a relatively man-controlled stability. Farmers have learned to develop managerial skills and are acquiring the ability to adopt intensive methods of cultivation and improved technologies in actual production on their farms. They have learned to have confidence in investing in fertilizer, other capital inputs and labor in production, and in accepting improved varieties and practices.

Although farms in Taiwan are very small, they enjoy large-farm advantages in the adoption of divisible inputs such as fertilizer and insecticides, and of such divisible technologies as improved varieties, intercropping, relay planting, and close spacing. On the other hand, Taiwan's farmers have adopted to a great extent the capital- and land-saving, but labor-using, technologies that provide more opportunity for family labor employment and require fewer scarce resources for increasing production. The practices of intensive multiple cropping, even of mushroom growing, and yield-increasing technologies are of this nature. The rational land-tenure system made possible by the successful completion of the three-step land-reform program, together with flood control and irrigation facilities, have provided an effective basic economic incentive to the cultivators to adopt new ideas for increased production. The existence of effective grass-roots institutions and organizations (local government, farmers' associations, irrigation associations, rural health stations) and the extension education system supported by convenient rural communications have facilitated the dissemination of the technical information and farm supplies needed for production increase.

Taiwan's agricultural production is carried out on the basis of international market competition, and prices received by the farmers for their products (possibly excepting sugar) are generally based upon the export or international prices obtainable. The government and public agencies do not give any significant financial or subsidy support to agricultural prices such as has been done in the United States, Japan, and West Germany. Government supports to agriculture are in terms of planning activities, research and extension, market promotion and development, trade regulation and negotiation, and aid to irrigation and other infrastructural development. Farmers receive fair shares of the export prices through the farmers' associations or marketing cooperatives, and the participation and regulation of government trade promotion and regulatory agencies. Taiwan's small-sized agriculture is operating on an international basis with an efficiency level quite comparable to other agricultural economies.

Agriculture has a further aid in a strong local governmental set-up with taxing power to obtain local revenue for the development and support of technical staff who are familiar with the local situation. Farmers have their own organizations to express their views on their own problems, government policy, and programs related to them. Farmers acting through their organizations can deal with the government more effectively and strongly than as individuals. Agricultural programs can be developed and carried out on a two-way flow basis.

The top and senior technicians in agricultural fields in Taiwan are comparatively few in number, even when compared with some other countries in Asia. Fortunately, Taiwan is equipped with an adequate number of middle-level and township-level agricultural technicians and workers, most of whom are agricultural college and vocational school graduates stationed at the rural areas and who work closely with the cultivators.

Another important contributing factor to Taiwan's agricultural success has been the United States' technical and economic assistance through the Sino-American Joint Commission on Rural Reconstruction. The role played by JCRR has been that of a catalyst. By providing technical and financial assistance, JCRR has been able to stimulate interest and improvement in agricultural development policies and implementation, to motivate projects difficult to activate, and to generate a spirit of self help among the local people and agencies. JCRR's experts, both Chinese and American, have been working with the local agencies for project identification and development and field implementation. These experts not only advise, they also work in the fields. In the past fifteen years of its operation in Taiwan, JCRR has spent about U.S. $135 million for a total of about six thousand work projects carried out by local sponsoring agencies on different levels.

From the standpoint of decision making in initiating developmental activities or in using inputs for agricultural production, it is necessary to recognize three levels of decision-making strategies: (1) that of government or a public agency concerning the provision of social overhead, capital investment, and infrastructure, particularly for such facilities as flood control, irrigation, feeder roads, and marketing adjuncts; (2) that of farmers and cultivators through their organizations for such programs as cooperative marketing and supplies, water distribution and management, pest control, adoption of certain technology, and so on; and (3) that of individual farmers in the use of fertilizer, insecticides and other divisible inputs, and technology. In the development of programs or activities for accelerating agricultural production, it is important to direct the action program to the point of decision making, and to have an appropriate combination of action and decision to be taken at different levels. For example, to build a reservoir to supply water for a given area, a farmers' organization presents the problem to the government or public agency in charge of water-resource development to make certain decisions before the individual farmer may make the decision to use water on crops on his farm. In Taiwan's agricultural development experience, these three levels of decision making have been recognized and implemented in a coordinated way to bring out actual development at the farm level.

POTENTIALS OF SMALL FAMILY FARMS

Taiwan's agricultural productivity growth is characterized by the economic viability and organizational strength of the small family farm system, even under heavy population pressure and very limited land resources. The average size of a farm family is about seven persons with an average of three workers per farm. In terms of economic production activities, Taiwan's small family farms are fortunately supported and assisted by (1) well-organized, multiple-purpose farmers' associations and marketing cooperatives; (2) effective extension education programs carried out jointly by the government and farmers' associations; (3) technological improvements developed and carried out by agricultural and research institutes and district improvement stations; (4) adequate procurement, supplies, and distribution of farm equipment and services through the farmers' associations and cooperatives at the local levels; (5) extensive development of controlled irrigation and water distribution and management through the district irrigation associations with government support and technical supervision, and (6) government participation in agricultural planning, project development, price negotiation and manipulation, marketing and trade arrangement and development, credit provision, and capital investment in agricultural infrastructure and other projects in cooperation with farmers' organizations. These advantages have enabled Taiwan's small family farm to be equally adaptable to modern technology and to the use of physical inputs and services. For example, through the organization of irrigation associations by farmers and with the participation of the government in planning and investment assistance in irrigation, it is possible to transform indivisible irrigation input into divisible input in terms of the use of water at the farm level. This institutional arrangement in irrigation development and water use in Taiwan is quite unique. The flow services of irrigation investment become divisible, and can be adapted to small family farms with advantage.

With a very limited land resource and small farms, intensive land use for achieving high productivity has been enforced. This has required (1) the adoption and application of divisible technologies and factor inputs, (2) farm-enterprise adjustment and multicrop combinations, (3) the substitution of capital and labor for land as a land-saving technique in farm operation, and (4) the joint operation for some farming activities under individual farm-management units. All these supporting services and operational technologies have contributed to making Taiwan's small family farm economically and structurally viable and able to attain a development and productivity sufficient to meet international competition.

There are certain disadvantages in the operation of small farms. The volume may be too small for either the marketing of farm products or the purchase of farm supplies. There is difficulty in the adoption of indivisible technology and capital inputs like farm machinery and irrigation facilities, and there is less access to modern technical knowledge and information. In addition, some social and political backwardness, coupled with an uneconomic scale of operation, may serve as deterrents in the operation of a small family farm. The need for group action and improved organization and extension services is, therefore, quite important. Taiwan's experience in agricultural development has indicated that all these problems and disadvantages may be solved by certain measures, enabling small farms to function efficiently and productively.

The general concurrence of subsistence farming and low productivity does not apply to Taiwan. The rate of commercialization in agricultural production was about 70 per cent in 1952 and increased to 77.5 per cent in 1964. The increasing degree of commercial operation on farms in Taiwan is indicated by the rising ratio of cash in the total farm receipts per family (about 40 per cent in 1958 to about 57 per cent in 1962), and the rising percentage of purchased farm supplies in total farm expenditure per family (about 42 per cent in 1958 to about 66 per cent in 1962). The total value of agricultural exports was increased from U.S. $114 million in 1952 to U.S. $313 million in 1964. The percentage of value of agricultural exports in the total value of agricultural production was increased from 24 per cent in 1952 to 34 per cent in 1964. Therefore, Taiwan's agriculture, although operated mainly on the basis of the small family farm, is highly commercialized.

Certain of the measures and programs already discussed help to elevate the earning capacity of these small farms. The increase of such nonland inputs as capital, labor, and management in conjunction with increasing intensity of operation; the introduction of improved cropping systems, crop diversification, and land-saving technology; the introduction of livestock on crop farms, land and irrigation improvement to increase the capacity: all have contributed to higher earnings. It is important to achieve an increase in farm output, not along the given production function curve, but through a shift upward of the production function. This requires technological innovations and management improvement.

IMPLICATIONS OF TAIWAN'S EXPERIENCE FOR
OTHER DEVELOPING COUNTRIES IN ASIA

While the majority of peripheral Asian countries have some common natural and climatic characteristics, agriculture is marked by different stages of development, particularly in terms of the existence of intrastructure. Among many other factors to be considered, the stage of agricultural development could be related to the dominant input pattern influencing agricultural output expansion. The dominant input pattern in the early stage of agriculture involves flood control and irrigation. In the transitional stage, the dominant inputs are irrigation and fertilizer. In the later stage of agriculture, fertilizer and insecticides and cultural practices take precedence. In the evaluation of Taiwan's experience with the purpose of applying it to other countries, it is important to take the stage of development of the other countries into consideration.

In the Philippines, Thailand, Malaysia, and Indonesia, comparatively advanced commercial plantations coexist alongside backward subsistence agriculture. In terms of the use of capital, adoption of technology, marketing of products, use of physical inputs, levels of productivity, and the structure of organization of farm business, these two sectors differ widely. While the productivity in the subsistence-food sector, mainly devoted to rice and corn, has remained virtually stagnant for several decades in most of these countries, the cultivation and operation of some commercial plantation crops, such as rubber and sugar cane, have undergone an improvement. These two different sectors within a country's agriculture ordinarily are located in different regions and the operation and production of these crops are under quite disparate conditions. The subsistence-food crops are usually produced by small family farms, while the commercial plantation crops are operated by big companies or planters with large holdings. An interchange of technology and knowledge and a flow of capital between these two distinct sectors does not exist.

Taiwan's rapid growth in agricultural productivity, within the framework of a high population pressure and the small-scale family farm, is an experience in development that is of deep technical interest to the developing countries of Asia. The central point of interest is the adoption of capital-saving and land-saving techniques in the initial period, which in Taiwan made possible an economical use of scarce capital and land resources. The adoption of new techniques required many institutional changes to provide help for the small-scale farmers. This involved functional changes in farmers' organizations, irrigation associations, the tenure system, and the local government. All of these factors have a bearing on the need for developing and transmitting technological knowledge to the farmers and for providing incentive for improved productivity. The government's role in all of these activities is important.

While Taiwan is similar to many other Asian countries in its high population growth, small family farms, subtropical and tropical climate with monsoon rainfall, dominant rice culture and so on, there are many differences. The availability of infrastructure (particularly in terms of flood control and irrigation facilities), the existence of local institutions to bring technical information down to the farm level, the structure of the land-tenure system as an economic incentive in production, the level of the farmer's managerial skill, and crop and livestock diversification, are all more advanced in Taiwan. Therefore, measures currently in use on Taiwan are not suitable for countries at an earlier stage of development. It is rather difficult to generalize the applicability of Taiwan's experience, but it is important to note that the provision of a minimum level of infrastructure is a *prerequisite* to make effective use of other physical inputs and technology. Even with land reform as an economic incentive it is important to coordinate the operational land-reform program with the development and organizational structure of agriculture. During the early stage of development, when the infrastructure, farmers' managerial skill, and local institutions are not available or are very weak, land reform does not necessarily guarantee a favorable impact on output. Land reform will be more effective in the transitional, or later, stage of development, particularly when the farmers' managerial skill and infrastructure are already favorable. In considering the transferability of the measures used in Taiwan to other developing countries in Asia, it would be important to consider all local conditions to judge what part of Taiwan's experience could be applied.

Two concepts are useful in appraising the applicability of Taiwan's programs to other Asian countries:

1. Taiwan's achievements add up to expanding the power of society to supply its members with increasing quantities of goods and services: The growing capacity of the people to carry on an increasingly successful conquest of nature, and the transformation of physical materials and forces into an ever faster flow of goods and services.

2. This expansion centers in two fundamentally distinct components: One is technological—the increasingly productive technologies, the hardware, knowledge, and skills that increase people's capacity for manipulating physical forces and materials—transforming resources into outputs. The other is organizational—the regrouping of people under new rules and structures of mutually helpful behavior that enable them to generate and put to widespread use the increasingly productive technologies.

Taiwan has met the requirements of both technological and organizational components within the context of a population growth approximately as rapid as those of other countries in Asia, refuting the generalization that decelerating the rate of population growth is a necessary precondition for accelerating economic development in Asia. Taiwan has also met the organizational requirements of increasingly productive technologies within the framework of a farm size even smaller than that of most Asian countries, disproving the belief that wholesale reorganization of farms into substantially larger sizes is a precondition of any substantial increase in farm output.

In the process of industrialization of the developing countries, agriculture, whether on small family farms or otherwise, has to be able to contribute and to perform the following functions:

1. Provide an adequate quantity of raw materials of uniformly good quality at a competitive low cost for industrial expansion
2. Provide cheap and adequate food for the country as a whole
3. Raise the level of farm income, through the intensification and diversification of land use, high enough to provide an effective domestic market for industrial goods
4. Provide an agricultural surplus for outflow to nonfarm sectors for the country's economic development
5. Maintain a wage level in agriculture comparable to that of industry through the improvement of labor efficiency and productivity.

If a small family-farm system can achieve these objectives in the process of economic development it will have the strength for existence in modern economic society, and the challenge is how to enable it to be economically and structurally viable. Taiwan's experience has indicated that it can be and that it is possible to meet world competition within this structure. In many Asian countries, the average size of farm is larger than in Taiwan, and provided that basic conditions can be improved, it is quite possible to make three- to five-hectare farms in other Asian countries also economically viable.

Another feature of Taiwan's experience that should be taken into consideration, however, is the fact that economic development has maintained a close interrelationship between the agricultural and non-agricultural sectors. The early stage of development was absolutely based on agriculture, with food processing and the production of chemicals as the main industries. Two advantages were derived from this close interrelationship. First, capital-saving techniques led to high capital efficiency, or a low capital-output ratio. Secondly, a successful advance in agricultural exports was achieved by a low production cost.

The main secret of Taiwan's development is not merely the effective use of productive technology, but the ability of her people to develop the conditions for a mutually helpful behavior necessary to achieving that technology.

In summation, Taiwan's distinctive record has been accomplished within a framework similar to that of other countries in Asia. When viewed solely from the standpoint of technological requirements, this may suggest a ready and easy transfer of Taiwan's experience. Taiwan's record of achievement clearly would have been impossible if it were not for a stable government guided by a strong commitment to use its power to achieve technical advancement and for a people guided by a traditional obligation to be as productive as possible for the sake of improving the income and status of their families. The heritage of basic convictions in other countries might or might not be compatible with the organizational rules of interpersonal behavior required by the widespread use of the techniques used in Taiwan. It means that Taiwan's record must be assessed carefully by people of other cultures to judge which particular practices for agricultural progress, if any, can be fitted into their own heritage of belief systems.

GEORGE E. TAYLOR

Comment

The success of land reform on Taiwan is at last being brought to the attention of scholars and politicians all over the world. It is a pity that we had to wait so long, but perhaps the waiting was inevitable. There were many observers who showed little interest because they were not favorably disposed to the Republic of China. There were others who thought that land reform on Taiwan was merely a late and grudging acknowledgement of obligations that should have been assumed much earlier, especially on the mainland. This view was supported by the generally accepted myth that failure to carry out land reform on the mainland was due entirely to lack of will and that this failure was the main reason for the Communist conquest. Considerations such as these have made it difficult to dramatize, especially in the United States, an achievement that has great significance for all other countries wishing to modernize their economies. They have also obscured the contrast between the Taiwan experience and that of the Chinese mainland.

What can other developing nations learn from the Taiwan model? Certainly not that land reform is either simple in concept or easy of execution, or that it can be undertaken without reference to social structure and industrial capacity. The reasons for progress on Taiwan as stated by Dr. Hsieh underline its complexity. He brings out the extraordinary combination of government and private initiative in the growth of the economy and the basic decision to keep the small family farm as the unit of production. The reference here is to the Chinese-type family unit and should not be confused with the typical American farm family, which has been called an isolated nuclear unit. One might also add that the political stability of Taiwan during the last decade and a half has been as vital to the success of the land-reform program as the decision of the government to pursue this course in the first instance. When other countries look at the Taiwan model they always come back to this point because it is the fundamental consideration. How is it possible to make the original decision to go ahead with land reform and how can you guarantee the administrative continuity to see it through? How is this first essential ingredient supplied?

Once that decision is made, Taiwan has a great deal to offer to another developing country. We can see that it is important not to undertake more than the existing infrastructure will bear. It is clear that much was gained by government promotion of water control through construction of irrigation facilities and flood-control devices, government help in raising the level of the farmer's managerial and technological skills, and government promotion of other sectors of the economy, especially exports and industry. Taiwan was fortunate to inherit from the Japanese a reasonably good system of communications and a social and administrative infrastructure of local government, farmer's associations, irrigation associations, and rural health stations upon which to build. As Dr. Hsieh points out, Taiwan does not have as many senior agricultural technicians as some other Asian countries, but it has an adequate number of middle-level and township-level agricultural technicians and workers. Most of these are agricultural college and vocational school graduates who are stationed in the rural areas where they work closely with the cultivators. Finally, United States financial and technical assistance played an important part, especially through that imaginative device for international cooperation, the Joint Commission on Rural Reconstruction. The JCRR, says Dr. Hsieh, stimulated interest and improvement in agricultural development policies and implementation, motivated projects difficult to activate, and generated a spirit of self-help among local people and agencies. The Taiwan model demonstrates well the importance of a successful integration at three levels of decision making—that of the government, which provides the social overhead, the infrastructure and capital investment; that of the farmers through their organizations, which take care of cooperative marketing, water distribution, pest control and technological advancement; and that of individual farmers who decide on the adoption of the available divisible inputs.

What Dr. Hsieh takes for granted, that is, the decision of the government to promote land reform and economic development along these lines, is still, however, the main hurdle for other countries. For obvious reasons he cannot go into the question of how this hurdle can be overcome. Taiwan's experience can show the way once the way has been decided upon, but it is not very helpful to those in other countries who have little hope of persuading their governments to follow a similar course.

However, it is clear that where a decision is made to carry out land reform, as on the mainland, the nature of the government's objectives and techniques makes all the difference. Few Communist countries have made a success of agriculture for reasons that have been shrewdly discussed by other contributors to this volume. Communist China has had more failure than most. Taiwan has managed to solve the problem of keeping the family farm (now about 1.1 hectares) and increasing agricultural production faster than the very sizable population growth. The success of Taiwan's joint farming organizations, which permit a constructive balance between cooperation and individual initiative and responsibility, may be contrasted with the failure of Communist China's communes and cooperative farms, which are based on the disappearance of the farming family as an economic unit. Neither the importance of the role of the profit motive on Taiwan nor the disastrous consequences of lack of incentive on the mainland should be overlooked. It is not that technical and other improvements have not been made by the Communists. They have, but their benefits have been corroded by the Communist political organization.

It is clear that the great success of Taiwan, when contrasted with the mainland, lies in its demonstrated capacity to maintain the social and economic values of the small family farm while compensating, through governmental and cooperative action, for its economic weaknesses. The large farm, under Communist rule, does not turn out to be economically a more viable pattern for agriculture. It is in this area, perhaps, that the real significance of the Taiwan model lies. Hsieh has shown to other developing nations that the Communist system has nothing to offer a government that is interested in modernization of the economy along lines that benefit both government and people.

FUKUO UENO

Areal Specialization
in Japanese Peasant Farming
and Agricultural Settlement

PEASANT FARMING AND AGRICULTURAL SETTLEMENTS

From the viewpoint of land use and farming, Japanese peasant agriculture has many characteristics: the small size of farms; fragmentation of farms into many tiny holdings; and the habit of the farmers of living close together, forming an agglomerated settlement. These agricultural settlements are recognized, together with their surrounding land, as basic areal units in farming. Analysis of the functional relationship between the settlement and its farming activity is fundamental to the understanding of areal specialization in agricultural production.

Agricultural Settlements[1]

The total number of agricultural settlements in Japan was reported to be more than 150,000 in the *Interim Agricultural Census* of 1955. If classified according to the number of households, settlements with 30–49 households are the most numerous and those with 20–29 are second. If nonfarm households are included, then those with 20–49 households are the most numerous, followed by those with 50 to 99 households. The average is 64, of which 39 are farm and 25 are nonfarm households (Table 1).

[1] The term *settlement* is not used in the text in a strictly defined way. It approximates the *mura* of the feudal period and can be generally referred to as a *shuraku*. The number of households may range from a few to several hundred.

TABLE 1
AGRICULTURAL SETTLEMENTS OF JAPAN
CLASSIFIED BY THE NUMBER OF HOUSEHOLDS

Number of Farm Households	Number of Settlements	Per Cent of Total Settlements	All Households	Number of Settlements	Per Cent of Total Settlements
Less than 9	4,444	3	Less than 19	21,350	14
10– 19	29,659	20	20– 49	71,731	47
20– 29	37,839	25	50– 99	38,553	25
30– 49	46,747	31	100–149	10,565	7
50– 69	17,356	11	150→	10,232	7
70– 99	9,794	6			
100–149	4,780	3			
150→	1,812	1			
Total	152,431	100	Total	152,431	100
Average Households per Settlement	39		Average Households per Settlement	64	

Source: *Agricultural Census of Japan* (1960).

Changes in Peasant Agriculture

More important than these fairly static features of agricultural settlements is the fact that Japanese peasant agriculture is undergoing revolutionary changes through mechanization, the use of more fertilizer and other farm materials, and the introduction of new techniques in the growing of crops and in the feeding of livestock. In addition, the social and economic conditions of rural communities have had a polarizing effect on the farmers; many are turning to other means of livelihood, while those that remain in farming tend to specialize. This polarization is clearly observed in the remarkable decrease in the number of persons engaged in agriculture, the increased employment in activities other than agriculture, and the increasing number of households that are quitting farming entirely. Urbanization and the rise of the standard of living have brought greater demand for such agricultural products as vegetables, fruits, flowers, fresh milk, and dairy products. Most of these products are perishable and expensive, but increased demand for them has promoted a specialization in production on a scale larger than ever before.

The revolutionary changes in Japanese peasant farming, geographically, may be seen in the change from subsistence to cash cropping on a nationwide scale through areal specialization. Crop competition between regions is intensifying over the whole country, especially in suburban areas near the great cities where the transformation is quite rapid.

To establish regional specialization, the region itself has to be provided with certain conditions to hold or enjoy a continuing comparative advantage over other regions. One of the most important conditions is the existence of an organization of farmers belonging to one or more agricultural settlements that have come to specialize in agricultural production. Another is the improvement of farms so that they can be cultivated with machines, and modern equipment can be used to increase efficiency in farm operations.

There are some features, however, that remain little changed and yet have some significance. One is the geographical location of the settlement, and another is the quality of the region's natural environment. The settlements, especially, are recognized as a fixed factor in relation to the variables. Thus, it is meaningful to analyze the relationship between the agricultural settlements and those factors involved in the process of regional specialization.

Significant Functions of the Settlements in Farming

These settlements have evolved as areal units that perform both agricultural and social functions. Since the average settlement is comprised of thirty-nine farmers, most of them are large enough to fulfill the basic functions required of a rural community, but others remain too small to handle such projects as irrigation control and the cooperative use of some resources. The settlements originated as village communes, and their functions have changed with time. Many new functions have been introduced, depending upon the requirements of the individual community. Generally speaking, social functions continue to exist longer than the economic ones, which change more readily with the introduction of progressive or new elements. However, numerous social functions originating in the village commune have been retained.

The most important function is the cooperative administration of irrigation, reflecting the importance of paddy to almost all the agricultural settlements. Others of importance are the cooperative spraying of pesticides, cooperative marketing of products and purchasing of goods, cooperative use of pastures and meadows, cooperative use of machinery and equipment, and cooperative land improvement.

Conceptual Framework for the Average Settlement

Conceptually, the average settlement is located at the center of a settled land area, with farm roads radiating outward to the surrounding fields. As the average farm is approximately one hectare, the total area of arable land cultivated by the thirty-nine farmers is about forty hectares. Another ten hectares should be added to this average for residences and for various other purposes. There may, in addition, exist some woodland and meadowland situated farther away from the settlement, but in this paper such lands shall not be taken into account. Thus, the average areal unit is comprised of about fifty hectares of land with an agglomerate settlement at its center.

Ideally, all the arable land would be reached directly by farm roads from the settlement, with the farthest field within 400 meters. However, in reality, the distance lies within 1,000 meters and time distance to the outer fields is approximately one-half hour, either by walking or by horse cart. Since most rural settlements have developed spontaneously, however, complicated, irregular patterns of distribution exist.

HANAZONO-MURA—A CASE STUDY OF AGRICULTURAL DEVELOPMENT

The study of Hanazono-mura, a village municipality, was prepared to clarify the changes in land use and the problems of areal specialization. Using this study, the writer has tried to establish a plan for the development of regional land-use specialization. The *mura*[2] is located in the suburban dry-field area about seventy kilometers from Tokyo. It takes about three hours to transport agricultural produce to the Tokyo markets by truck.

Agricultural Problems and Development Trends

Hanazono-mura is in the process of modernizing its agriculture to adapt to new social and economic conditions. However, the area is confronted with numerous problems from the standpoint of land use and individual farming. For example, Hanazono-mura will need to alter its present use of land and rearrange its fields drastically when irrigation water is brought in with the completion of the Multiple Development Project on the Ara River. At the same time some twenty kilometers to the east of the *mura*, a new industrial area is under construction. The conditions for agricultural production that are to be developed through the land improvement project are also favorable to urban development, and for this reason the project will hardly lessen competition between agricultural and urban land use.

The study of Hanazono-mura attempts to examine the land use of both the past and the present, and to project future land use in an effort to establish a plan for a viable agricultural area. Since Hanazono-

---

[2] The *mura* is the lowest nationally official administrative unit, and is often translated as *village*.

mura has many characteristics common to most suburban agricultural regions, the results could be helpful in the regional planning of other similar areas in Japan.

Changes in Land Use
Land use for subsistence farming

In Hanazono-mura, the principal crops cultivated during the Meiji era (1868–1911) were cereals from dry-field croplands for subsistence. Mulberry bushes (for sericulture) were grown as a secondary crop. Of the cereals, barley was the most important, ranking first as a staple food crop, with rice production amounting to only one-sixth that of barley. In addition, miscellaneous crops such as beans and buckwheat were grown, among which soybeans were important. Cocoons were raised by most of the farmers, and silk textiles were spun by the farm women to supplement income.

The extensive woodland furnished fuel, and leaves were gathered to produce compost. Although the ratio of rice fields to other cropland was low, they were always developed wherever irrigation water could be made available. In the process of clearing the land, areas of alluvial soil were developed first, followed by the reclamation of black volcanic soils. Red volcanic ash soil, the poorest of the three, was left in woodland.

The allocation of cereal crops to the superior soils, mulberry fields to intermediate-grade soils, and forests to the poor soils was a rational system of land use in which cereal crops had priority. Such a division of land resources was logical under relatively simple economic conditions.

The expansion of mulberry fields

Mulberry fields increased in acreage considerably during the early period of the Showa era (from 1925 on). Extensive areas of dry-field cropland in Hanazono-mura and even woodlands were converted to mulberry production. The use of purchased fertilizer increased progressively. The area in mulberry trees attained its peak in 1929 when mulberry accounted for more than one half of the total dry-field area, or 49 per cent of the total arable land (Table 2).

Land Use After Land Reform
Reclamation of the remaining woodlands for food production

The land reform after World War II transformed the internal structure of rural communities. Almost all of the woodlands that had been retained as a source of compost material for the fields were released to

TABLE 2
HANAZONO-MURA: CHANGES IN LAND USE SINCE THE BEGINNING OF THE MEIJI ERA

	Total Hectares	Rice Fields (Hectares)	Dry Fields (Hectares)			Arable Land (Per Cent of Total Village Area)	Rice Fields (Per Cent of Total Arable Land)	Dry Fields (Per Cent of Total Arable Land)		
			Total Area	Ordinary Dry Field	Mulberry			Total	Ordinary Fields	Mulberry
1875	569.39	34.25	535.14	—	—	53.9	6.0	94.0	—	—
1929	767.1	57.4	709.7	336.5	373.2	48.4	7.5	92.5	43.9	48.6
1950	953.66	64.25	889.41	586.26	303.15	60.1	6.7	93.3	61.5	31.8
1955	1,129.20	72.93	1,056.27	—	—	71.2	6.5	93.5	—	—
1957	1,158.0	225.0	933.0	546.0	387.0	73.9	19.2	79.6	46.6	33.0
1960	1,125.4	178.2	947.2	653.5	293.9	71.0	15.8	84.2	58.1	26.1
1963	1,107.2	217.5	889.7	527.5	362.2	70.4	19.5	79.6	47.2	32.4

Sources: Agricultural Census of 1950, 1955, 1960.

small farmers to enlarge their cultivated acreage. During this period, the efforts of the farmers were directed mainly to increase their production of rice, which resulted in the establishment of the Multiple Development Project on the Ara River and the development of the *rikuden*, a type of paddy field converted from dry-field croplands. The development of *rikuden* is regarded as one aspect of farm mechanization because irrigation water for the *rikuden* is pumped, mainly from wells, by electric or combustion motors. In addition, most of the commercial farmers use hand tractors. Such developments as these have become important in the modernization of Japanese farming.

Shift to commercial farming

Following World War II, agriculture in the Hanazono area also began to shift from growing mainly cereal crops to the cultivation of various produce for the city market. The change reflected the increased demand for vegetables, flowers, fruit, fresh milk, and eggs. These products, commanding higher prices than cereals, now occupy positions of central importance in suburban agricultural areas.

The growing of vegetables and flowers has come to be called "vinyl agriculture" as the crops are grown under vinyl covering, vinyl tunnel, or vinyl matting, by which the temperature of air and soil are regulated to improve growing conditions. In addition, crops are grown in artificially heated glass and vinyl houses. Such an intensive system of cultivation requires a great deal of labor and a large amount of capital investment in equipment. Flowers grown in glass houses and strawberries raised in vinyl tunnels rank first in profit return, with cucumbers and tomatoes ranking second. These crops bring high returns per unit area of land—they are several times more profitable than rice.

Trend towards polarization

Although the farmers of the Hanazono area have begun to specialize, most of them still practice diversified farming, growing rice and raising silkworms in combination with their newer enterprises. This represents a transitional stage where the existing, and more traditional, activities and the newly introduced commercial activities are competing for capital and labor within the farming unit. One of the resulting compromises, in which summers are devoted to traditional crops and the other seasons are used for the production of vegetables and flowers, has been quite profitable. Dairying in cooperation with other enterprises is also remunerative, although it demands steady labor throughout the year.

The same may be said of the cultivation of cereal crops in combination with sericulture. The farmers, nevertheless, are trying to enlarge the area devoted to more profitable enterprises, reducing that of the less profitable.

Consequently, they have established various farming combinations based on their own individual choice and with very little reference or cooperation with each other. There is, therefore, very little order or unity in production in the Hanazono area, nor is there a common attitude toward the use of the land. But the growing need for mechanization and higher standard of technique are compelling the farmers to specialize and to focus on the production of fewer and more profitable crops. For the future, regional planning should be directed toward the organization and combination of farming units into a more rational areal or regional unit.

Analysis of the Present Status of Farming

Farms surveyed

Sixty-five farmers, representing the various types of higher level farming, were included in the farm survey (Table 3). The survey data were analyzed in order to gain an understanding of characteristics essential to the establishment of viable farms and provide a basis for areal planning.

In 1963, of about 1,100 farms in Hanazono-mura, the average cultivated area per farm was approximately one hectare, 78 per cent of which consisted of dry fields. Cereal growing and sericulture were fundamental to most farms and formed two of the farming types. The other enterprises were combined with one or both of these basic elements and formed five other types: sericulture, cereal farming, hog raising, dairy-

TABLE 3
SURVEYED FARMS CLASSIFIED BY FARMING TYPE AND
VILLAGE COMMUNITY: HANAZONO-MURA, 1963

Village Community	Number of Farms	Cereal	Dairy	Seri-culture	Hogs	Poultry	Vege-tables	Flowers and Nursery
Kitane	4	1	—	—	3	—	—	—
Nagata	11	6	—	1	2	1	—	1
Arakawa	10	1	2	1	1	1	4	—
Kuroda	6	1	1	1	3	—	—	—
Omaeda	10	—	1	3	2	—	3	1
Shimogō	6	—	1	1	—	—	—	4
Nakagō	13	—	5	1	—	7	—	—
Kamigō	5	—	—	1	—	—	4	—
Total	65	9	10	9	11	9	11	6

ing, poultry raising, vegetable farming, and flower and nursery farming. Apart from cereal farming and sericulture, which were common to
all the farms, there was some tendency toward areal specialization by
ōaza,[3] the larger subdivisions of the *mura*.

Results of survey

Farm resources. All the farms were operated on a full-time and/or commercial basis, with more than 2.5 full-time adult male workers per farm.
The agricultural labor units average 932.0 hours. In livestock, the dairy
farms have an average of 14.8 units and hog farms an average of 7.5
units (37.5 heads as calculated in terms of swine), as shown in Table 4.[4]
The total amount of property per farm is valued, on an average, at almost ¥2,000,000 (¥360=U.S. $1.00), in which the evaluation of land
and buildings is based on the evaluation standard of the municipal
fixed-property tax. For this reason, the total amount indicated is considerably lower than that of current market estimation.

Agricultural income and expenses. The gross agricultural income per farm
averages about ¥1,740,000, which is quite high and indicates the productivity of full-time farms in the suburban agricultural area (Table 5).
Examining the income by farming type, the average gross income of
dairy farmers is the highest, over ¥3,000,000, while the income from
the other types ranges from a low of around ¥950,000 for vegetable
farms to a high of about ¥2,500,000 for pig farms. These figures are for
total agricultural returns, thus income ratios from the crops and other
sources would differ between the farm types, depending on the combination each type has. The ranking, therefore, does not reflect the results
of the principal activity only but also each farmer's other sources of
income. The income from sources other than agriculture averages about
¥70,000, and is obtained in large measure from part-time jobs by the
younger household members who commute to other employment.

In evaluating agricultural expenses by farming type, it is to be noted
that (1) the amount paid for hired labor in all farming types is small
compared to the scale of farming; (2) the amount paid for purchased
feed is quite high for dairy farming; and (3) the amount paid for hired
laborers is relatively higher in the flower and nursery enterprises, as are
their general expenses (Table 6).

[3] The *ōaza* is the areal unit below the *mura* level. It had official political status during the
pre-Meiji period, but it has no legal position today. Nevertheless, it still has meaning and
significance culturally and economically.
[4] See Table 4 for definition of units.

TABLE 4
FARM RESOURCES IN HANAZONO-MURA, 1963

	Cereal	Dairy	Sericulture	Pig Feeding	Poultry	Vegetable	Flowers and Nursery	Average
Number of farms[a]	9	10	9	11	9	11	6	65 (total)
Arable land[a] (average)	21.3	15.9	16.9	17.5	12.7	12.6	17.0	16.2
Rice fields[a]								
Single crop	2.6	0.3	0.9	0.8	0.3	0.2	2.7	1.0
Double crop	0.3	0.6	1.0	0.3	1.7	1.2	—	0.8
Rikuden[a]	5.0	1.4	2.7	1.3	0.8	1.5	—	2.1
Ordinary dry field[a]	6.7	11.0	4.8	8.7	5.6	5.4	10.5	7.4
Mulberry field[a]	6.1	1.8	7.3	5.7	3.9	4.0	2.3	4.5
Mulberry estimated[a]	0.8	1.3	0.7	0.8	0.6	0.6	1.8	0.9
Nonarable land[a]	1.9	2.8	2.0	6.6	1.4	4.4	2.5	3.3
Woodland[a]	0.2	0.2	0.9	0.2	0.1	2.9	0.5	0.8
Other[a]	1.7	2.6	1.1	6.4	1.3	1.5	2.0	2.5
TOTAL LAND[a]	23.2	18.7	18.9	24.1	14.1	17.0	19.5	19.4
Family size (average)	7.3	6.4	7.0	6.4	6.4	7.5	5.3	6.7
Number in family engaged in agriculture (average)	3.1	2.5	3.4	2.8	2.9	3.3	2.7	3.0
Labor, by manpower	2.7	2.2	3.0	2.2	2.2	3.0	2.3	2.5
Number of agricultural labor units[b]	764	1,346	711	1,194	1,093	525	855	932.5
Livestock units[c]	2.3	14.8	2.0	7.5	5.0	1.2	0.7	5.7
Total property value (in thousand yen)	1,800	3,072	1,635	2,424	1,250	1,337	2,306	1,970.6

[a] In units of ten ares, which equals one-tenth of a hectare.
[b] One man working ten hours per day.
[c] Predicated from the basic standard of one head of cattle as one unit.

TABLE 5

DETAILS OF AGRICULTURAL INCOMES: HANAZONO-MURA, 1963

(In Thousand Yen)

| | Farm Type | | | | | | | |
	Cereal	Dairy	Sericulture	Pig Feeding	Poultry	Vegetables	Flowers and Nursery	Average
Number of farms	9	10	9	11	9	11	6	65 (total)
Crops sold	329.3	22.9	199.4	175.8	97.4	299.5	757.2	240.5
Animal products sold	222.2	2,665.2	233.8	1,387.9	596.2	142.3	12.5	815.8
Cocoons sold	503.4	92.3	732.7	501.1	349.8	318.8	294.0	399.7
Miscellaneous income	9.0	12.7	8.0	14.0	15.1	10.5	3.8	10.9
Increased property value	0	198.3	74.9	1,288.1	169.0	28.1	150.1	300.9
Total agricultural income	1,063.9	2,991.4	1,248.8	2,366.9	1,227.5	799.2	1,217.6	1,598.5
Products produced and used on farm	241.4	120.7	141.6	141.6	130.6	154.1	153.7	153.9
Gross agricultural income	1,305.3	3,112.1	1,390.4	2,508.5	1,358.1	953.3	1,371.3	1,752.5
Income other than agriculture	80.2	55.0	122.4	22.6	55.9	107.8	44.3	70.4

TABLE 6

DETAILS OF AGRICULTURAL EXPENSES: HANAZONO-MURA, 1963

(In Thousand Yen)

	Cereal	Dairy	Seri-culture	Pig Feeding	Poultry	Vegetable	Flowers and Nursery	Average
Number of farms	9	10	9	11	9	11	6	65 (total)
Fertilizer	89.2	33.4	39.3	53.9	30.1	52.2	43.3	49.1
Livestock purchased	50.2	415.2	14.4	360.3	47.4	2.7	8.3	141.6
Feed purchased	88.6	1,496.4	143.4	703.4	422.4	57.0	6.2	450.1
Other agricultural expenses	7.7	2.0	9.3	5.3	5.7	8.2	14.3	7.1
Wages paid	11.8	92.1	15.4	9.6	8.1	145.1	145.8	58.7
General expenses	144.8	206.9	157.6	158.6	104.1	39.6	421.0	160.5
Other miscellaneous expenses	51.4	170.4	124.9	119.0	59.0	365.8	165.1	156.1
Depreciation in property	39.4	104.5	87.7	30.0	3.8	54.0	21.0	50.4
Total agricultural expenses	483.1	2,520.9	592.0	1,440.1	680.6	724.6	825.0	1,073.4
Unpaid wages for family labor	248.0	193.2	307.5	232.9	192.2	244.5	183.0	230.9
Total farm expenses for operator	731.1	2,714.1	899.5	1,673.0	872.8	969.1	1,008.0	1,304.3
Capital interest	94.0	153.6	81.9	121.3	62.6	66.9	117.5	99.3

TABLE 7

FARMING RESULTS BY TYPE: HANAZONO-MURA, 1963

	Farm Type							
	Cereal	Dairy	Seri-culture	Pig Feeding	Poultry	Vegetable	Flowers and Nursery	Average
Number of farms	9	10	9	11	9	11	6	65 (total)
Farmer's labor return (in thousand yen)	442.3	307.1	355.3	589.7	403.2	276.1	246.0	382.7
Family labor returns per capita (in thousand yen)	274.7	229.9	231.0	338.0	285.1	215.4	197.3	256.7
Interest rate on capital (in per cent)	24.0	9.7	19.5	27.4	31.2	15.1	7.1	19.7
Family labor returns (in thousand yen)	726.2	499.5	663.0	906.4	596.0	520.8	429.0	632.8

TABLE 8

AGRICULTURAL INCOME PER UNIT OF LAND AND PER UNIT OF LABOR BASED ON THE RESULTS OF FARM SURVEY IN 1963

| | Farm Type | | | | | | | |
	Cereal	Dairy	Sericulture	Pig Feeding	Poultry	Vegetable	Flowers and Nursery	Average
Number of farms	9	10	9	11	9	11	6	65(total)
Arable land (in hectares)	21.3	15.9	16.9	17.5	12.7	12.6	17.0	16.2
Labor units in manpower	2.7	2.2	3.0	2.2	2.2	3.0	2.3	2.5
Total gross returns (in thousand yen)	1,035.3	3,112.1	1,390.4	2,468.0	1,340.1	953.3	1,371.3	1,667.2
Agricultural expenses (in per cent)	30.4	74.7	31.3	55.8	53.3	31.4	52.7	47.0
Agricultural income (in per cent)	69.6	25.3	68.7	44.2	46.7	68.6	47.3	53.0
Returns per tan[a] (in thousand yen)	61.0	19.6	82	141	106	76	81	80.9
Returns per labor unit (in thousand yen)	483	1,415	463	1,122	609	318	596	715
Agricultural income per tan (in thousand yen)	42.5	49.6	56.3	62.3	49.5	12.1	38.3	44.4
Agricultural income per labor unit (in thousand yen)	336.2	358.0	318.1	495.9	284.4	218.1	281.9	327.5
Total agricultural income (in thousand yen)	908.5	787.4	955.2	1,090.9	625.8	654.0	648.6	8,100.4(total)

a Tan is equivalent to 0.245 acres.

Farming results. Three criteria were used to examine the effectiveness of the various aspects of farm management: the farmer's total labor returns; family labor return per capita; and the interest rate on capital invested. "Farmer's labor return" assesses the farm as a small business enterprise; "family labor returns per capita" indicates the profit for small-scale farming in which the concept of the farmer as manager has not yet been clearly defined within the family; "interest rate on capital" is the profit rate on the capital, assuming that farming is done with borrowed capital. The results of these three criteria are shown in Table 7.

When the factors were rearranged into a table to study the relationship between the productivity of land and labor, the agricultural income per unit of area (*tan*) emerged as about ¥53,000 and the agricultural income per unit of labor was a little more than ¥380,000 (Table 8). However, since the data covered only one year, it would be difficult to judge which farming type is the most advantageous. Nevertheless, it should be possible to select certain farming types that have proven profitable in suburban areas like Hanazono.

FUTURE LAND USE: PLANNING AND THE AGRICULTURAL SETTLEMENTS

Land Resources and Land Improvement

Soil types and productivity

In the consideration of future land use, not only aspects of farm management, but also the land resources, should be considered. Thus, the land resources in the Hanazono area were examined and classified, according to their productivity, into three soil types.

Type "A": Alluvial clay. Originating from stream deposits and occurring extensively in the low-lying areas, the natural fertility of this soil is high and is well suited for cereal crops. During the period when the growing of cereal was of principal importance, this soil type was valued highly.

Type "B": Black volcanic ash. The black volcanic soils, rich in humus, are found in lower elevations than type "C" and are considered to be fairly high in fertility, ranking second only to type "A." Although the soil is light, its moisture retention ability is relatively good. It has been shown that by proper fertilization the soil's productivity can be greatly improved.

Type "C": Red-brown volcanic ash. This soil occurs in relatively higher areas and contains less humus than the other two; it is light and sandy.

It is susceptible to wind erosion during the dry winter seasons, and water retention is rather low. Of the three soil types, it is the poorest in natural fertility. Before the introduction of improved fertilization methods, the areas occupied by "C" soil were considered inferior land on which it was difficult to maintain productivity. They have been left in woodland in the past.

The acreage and distribution of these three types of soil are shown in Figure 1.

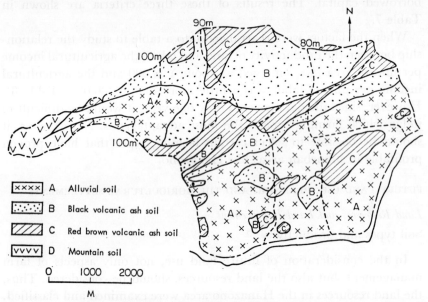

	A	Alluvial soil
	B	Black volcanic ash soil
	C	Red brown volcanic ash soil
	D	Mountain soil

Fig. 1.   Distribution of soils classified in Hanazono-mura.

Ranking of the soil types

If the farming types and technical level remain constant, an economic evaluation of the land resources can be made. Such an evaluation was attempted, based on the yield per unit area of those crops grown extensively throughout the region. Six crops were chosen for this purpose: rice, upland rice, wheat, barley, sweet potatoes, and mulberry. Their yields were classified into four grades (>80, 79–60, 59–40, and <40), according to the amount of yield per unit area (Table 9). In preparing the ratings, the yield of each crop from the best land was rated as 100.

Based on the evaluation of yields, the following crops are recommended for the three soil types: cereal crops to the "A" soil type; upland rice, sweet potatoes, and mulberry to the "B" soil type; and

TABLE 9
Productivity Rating of Principal Crops by Soil Type

Soil Type	Current Use	Rice	Upland Rice	Barley	Wheat	Sweet Potatoes	Mulberry	Remarks
A. Alluvial	1. Rice field	90		85	90			Suitable for strawberries, vegetables
	2. *Rikuden*	90	30	85	90			Drought damage to summer crops
	3. Dry field			90	90	90		
	4. Mulberry						80	Excellent for spring crops, but not fall crops
B. Black volcanic ash	1. Rice field	85		65	75			
	2. *Rikuden*	85		65	75			
	3. Dry field		80	70	75	85		Suitable for leaf and root vegetables
	4. Mulberry						80	Suitable for cutting nursery Good for fall crops
C. Red brown volcanic ash	3. Dry field		45	45	55	80		
	4. Mulberry						75	Frequent frost damage

sweet potatoes and mulberry to the "C" soil type. Actually, most crops yield poorly in "C" soil and so only those of least disadvantage can be considered. In addition to the consideration of soils, water is always an important factor.

As the number of crops were restricted to those grown in the study area, certain inherent limitations were recognized in using their ratings to establish land-use planning. Nevertheless, they are important criteria for comparing the relative productivity of various kinds of soils.

Land improvement: Soil productivity

Most of the arable land of the Hanazono area is being improved by the Multiple Project Plan. Rearrangement of the fields is transforming tiny, irregular plots into bigger, regularly shaped ones. Irrigation water will become available so that fields can be alternated between wet and dry-field cropping. These improvements will raise land productivity of the various soil types to higher levels, but the characteristics relative to each soil type will not disappear. There will still remain essential differences between volcanic-ash and alluvial soils. Therefore, there is a need for proper land-use planning so that both crops and their economic suitability may be combined most effectively in relation to the land resources.

Land-Use Planning
Division of the area

In land-use planning it is necessary to divide a given region into various areal units to achieve optimal use of the land. For this purpose, Hanazono-mura has been divided into two regions, based on the distribution of existing agricultural settlements in relation to their land resources (Fig. 2).

However, when planning for relatively small areas, the regions should be divided into still smaller areal units. Thus, the two regions of Hanazono-mura are broken down into the smaller subunits of ōaza and buraku.[5]

In regional planning, two aspects must be initially defined—first, the fixed elements, and second, the variables for the planning units. Logically, the greater the number of fixed factors, the more limited becomes the choices within the framework of the planning, as the range of alternatives is greatly reduced.

[5] A buraku is an agricultural settlement smaller than the ōaza and, like the ōaza, has no official status.

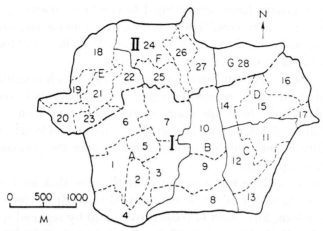

Fig. 2. Territorial boundaries of village communities (*ōaza*) and agricultural settlements (*buraku*) in Hanazono-mura; appended table shows names.

Names of Numbered Areas in Fig. 2

Region I		Region II	
Village community	Agricultural settlement	Village community	Agricultural settlement
A. Omaeda	1 Kami 2 Naka 3 Shimo 4 Nanbu 5 Shimizu 6 Hokubu 7 Nishigaito	E. Nakagō	18 Nagare 19 Kamishuku 20 Nakashuku 21 Shinden 22 Higashibayashi 23 Shimoshuku
B. Arakawa	8 Kwabata 9 Chuo 10 Tadasawa	F. Shimogō	24 Takagi 25 Saga 26 Chuo 27 Tōbu
C. Kuroda	11 Kuroda-1 12 Kuroda-2 13 Kuroda-3	G. Kitane	28 Kitane
D. Nagata	14 Kami 15 Naka 16 Shimo 17 Taki		

In Hanazono-mura, the following are important given factors: the location of the settlements, the composition of their land resources, and the convertibility of the fields between wet and dry cropping.

Location of the agricultural settlement. According to the *World Agricultural Census* of 1960, the number of *buraku* in Hanazono-mura is twenty-eight. The relationship among the farmers of each settlement is very close, and cooperative groups have been formed to conduct various agricultural activities when necessary. These *buraku*, of spontaneous, unplanned development, have existed for a long time. Therefore, the location of the settlements is recognized as a fixed factor.

Each *buraku* has about forty hectares of land, which is cultivated by about thirty to forty farmers, living in an agglomerated grouping of houses. Although there are many roads connecting each settlement center with the fields, rationalization of the road system to achieve better accessibility is being highly recommended under the proposed land-improvement program.

The *buraku* will be taken as the smallest units that have definable characteristics, which might be modernized through mechanization of farm operations, formation of cooperatives, and by regional specialization. Among the characteristics there are those that undoubtedly need to be abolished.

Then, too, the question has been raised as to whether these *buraku* are large enough and have other fundamental qualifications to provide a basis for effective planning. The general consensus is that they are not ideal for such a purpose, but because they exist in fact and their location is fixed, it would be impractical to change their sites to achieve the objective. Instead, it would be easier to achieve the desired goals by bringing about changes within the present areal structure. Regional planning for the area, therefore, is a kind of *redevelopment*, an attempt to reorganize conditions that have long existed to fit into contemporary social and economic trends. The plan does not mean to eliminate all existing factors and conditions, nor could it do so even if it were desirable.

Resources. Each *buraku* has its own distinct composition of land resources, which must be accepted as a fixed factor. The allocation of land to various uses has been done with the awareness of its particular qualities. Generally, in any given area, a similar allocation has occurred, since there were certain common requirements to be satisfied—namely, the raising of food crops for subsistence farming. However, today, when agriculture is becoming increasingly commercialized, there is need to plan for changing land use. The farmers should now select suitable crops with high market potential in planning for the optimal use of land. Then, attention should be turned to the proper scale of operation, sources of funds for development (equipment, building, livestock, and so on), and to decisions about what techniques are necessary.

Although there is an optimal use for each type of soil, optimal use of land within the settlement may vary, when considered together with other resources, both fixed and variable. Hence, it is difficult to develop an ideal use for each of the soil types at the same time. It is, then, important to determine "which land resources should take priority in use, and how to determine the order of priority."

Convertible fields. The bringing in of irrigation water to the Hanazono area as a result of the land-improvement project has greatly affected the direction of planning for the future. With water available, a four-year cycle of cropping is possible—two years in wet rice and the following two years in dry-field crops. This system would necessitate that all farmers use rice as the principal crop, combining it with other crops or enterprises.

One Settlement—One Type of Farming

Farming type

Within the settlement (*buraku*), each farmer possesses many small and separate plots of land, with varying characteristics. The crops on these plots are decided by the farmer, based on the characteristics of the soil, or their relation to his other crops. However, there has developed a tendency to use land similarly in each agricultural settlement, according to the particular attributes of the land, and the farmer has generally followed the pattern. Table 10 and Figure 3 show the acreage of the arable land; ratio of arable land by kind; number of households; and distribution limits of arable land for the agricultural settlement.

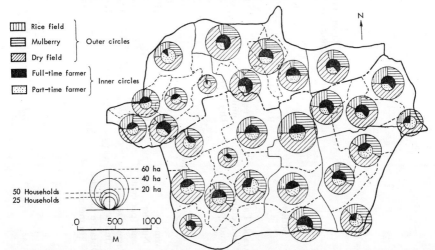

Fig. 3.   Agricultural settlements showing size, kinds of agriculture, and ratio of full-time to part-time farmers.

TABLE 10
An Example of Land Resources, Land Uses, Number of Farm Households, Farm Sizes, and Field Distance Circle by Agricultural Settlement: Omaeda Village Community

		1 Kami (%)	2 Naka (%)	3 Shimo (%)	4 Nanbu (%)	5 Shimizu (%)	6 Hokubu (%)	7 Nishigaito (%)	Total (%)
Agricultural Settlement									
Arable Land in hectares and (per cent)	Rice fields	2.93 (5.5)	2.29 (6.7)	3.22 (7.1)	1.87 (9.8)	1.80 (11.7)	1.36 (4.3)	8.71 (23.1)	22.18 (9.3)
	Tree crops (mulberry)	16.38 (30.8)	11.41 (33.2)	15.03 (32.8)	4.62 (24.2)	3.75 (24.2)	6.21 (19.5)	9.93 (26.3)	67.33 (28.4)
	Dry fields	33.90 (63.7)	20.67 (60.1)	27.43 (60.1)	12.59 (66.0)	9.82 (63.9)	24.24 (76.2)	19.11 (50.6)	147.76 (62.3)
	Total (per cent)	53.21 (100)	34.37 (100)	45.68 (100)	19.08 (100)	15.37 (100)	31.81 (100)	37.75 (100)	237.27 (100)
Farms Number and (per cent)	Total numbers	66 (100)	35 (100)	61 (100)	26 (100)	20 (100)	34 (100)	38 (100)	280 (100)
	Full time	29 (40.9)	17 (48.6)	18 (29.5)	18 (69.2)	7 (35)	8 (23.5)	19 (50)	116 (41.4)
Farm Size (in hectares)	Average size	1.0~1.5	1.0~1.5	0.7~1.0	1.0~1.5	1.0~1.5	1.0~1.5	1.0~1.5	
	Largest size	1.5~2.0	1.5~2.0	1.5~2.0	2.0~2.0	1.5~2.0	2.0~2.5	2.0~2.5	
Distance to Fields (in meters)		458	374	435	282	264	360	387	

In recent years, in the trend toward specialization, farmers have been encouraged to grow specific cash crops, mainly on the dry-field crop lands. This trend is well represented by the "pioneer" farmers. If this trend toward specialization could be focused on a particular crop or activity in each settlement, the present production regime could be replaced with a newer one.

One settlement as one farm

It is assumed that each *buraku* would be a basic economic unit for planning. It is also understood that every settlement will have the capacity in land resources to support more than ten full-time farmers. Most of the settlements have the basic elements to constitute "basic economic units," and thus farming types based on optimal use of land resources can be determined.

Each of these settlements is considered to be "one farm" in the planning for farm specialization. Once the optimal use for the land is determined, then the highest income is expected to be brought about by conversion to this use. When the plan is accepted the necessary facilities and machinery would be provided. Then it must be determined which of the available land resources is to receive first priority from the viewpoint of optimal use, then the use of other resources, of second priority, would be allocated. Accordingly, each resource would be allocated to its best use in relation to the decision for the optimal use of the land or "farm."

The decision to use the settlement (*buraku*) as a basic economic unit does away with the need for individual farm planning, as land-use planning and farm programing would be achieved simultaneously. It would be as though a large farm were divided into numerous viable units, all with the same type of farming pattern. However, the land resources, farm facilities, and the machinery would be maintained and utilized in a manner appropriate to a large farm. The difference would be that units of land, buildings, and the machinery used may be individually or cooperatively owned rather than belonging to or controlled by one individual or one concern.

Selection of farming types

As the composition of land resources by settlement becomes known, there remains the problem of determining the optimal combination of crops and/or enterprises. When considered in terms of future prospects, the promising crops and enterprises become limited in number. While care must be taken to make effective use of all natural resources and of the techniques and other abilities already possessed by the people, the greatest emphasis should be placed on the recommendations from the farm survey. Following are the three recommended combinations for the settlements of Hanazono-mura:

"A" soil. Vegetable (and small fruit) growing has been selected as the fundamental enterprise for settlements in which the "A" soil types occupies more than 70 per cent of the arable land. Suitable for intensive growing of such crops as cucumbers, tomatoes, and strawberries, "A" soil produces these crops in superior quality and yield than soil of other types. Continuous cultivation of vegetables is detrimental to the soil, however, so to avoid depletion the fields are to be converted between wet-rice and dry-field vegetable cropping. This system would enable the farmers to maintain a larger vegetable-growing area. Since this farming type would always have wet rice on half of the convertible land, rice growing would remain important.

"C" soil. Generally speaking, the "C" soil type is low in productivity, but it is comparable to other soil types if planted to mulberry. For this reason, sericulture is recommended as the most suitable enterprise for settlements where the "C" soil type occupies more than 25 per cent of the arable land. In order for mulberry fields to be advantageously established, the plots should be fairly large. As cocoons are raised only during the summer and coincide with the growing season for rice, it is recommended that some vegetables be grown during the winter season. However, in this type of farming, vegetable growing is definitely supplementary to sericulture.

"B" soil. For settlements in which the "B" soil predominates, or there is a mixture of the three soil types, dairying is recognized as the optimal land use. Intensive growing of feed crops on any type of soil seems to show little difference in productivity if the soil is adequately fertilized and well supplied with water. The main aim in growing feed crops is to strive for high yields rather than for quality, and to maintain the supply of feed evenly throughout the year. If feed crops with high yields can be grown, then the economic efficiency of land use will be raised. It would also be advantageous to maintain a superior herd of cows that respond well to the balanced feed supply in the production of milk.

The soil-type areas described here are summarized in Table 11. Those farming types selected as being the most suitable and which are relatively easily implemented for the settlement units are shown in Table 12 and Figure 4.

TABLE 11
RECOMMENDED LAND USE FOR SOIL TYPES, REGIONS I AND II

	Recommended Land Use[a]	Farm Size	
		Region I	Region II
		(in hectares)	
"A" type predominating (70%)	RV	2.0	2.0
"C" type important (25%)	RSV	2.0	2.2
"B" type predominating or 3 types are mixed ("A" 70%, "C" 25%)	RD	2.0	2.2

[a] Of possible combinations of enterprises, these three types are recommended: *RV* (rice [wet] with vegetables); *RSV* (rice with sericulture and vegetables); *RD* (rice with dairying).

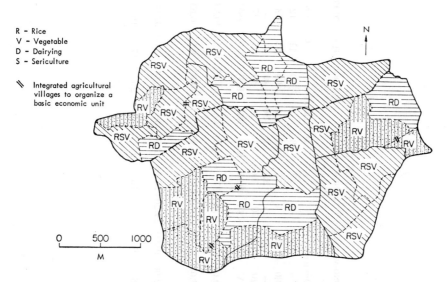

R – Rice
V – Vegetable
D – Dairying
S – Sericulture

↘ Integrated agricultural villages to organize a basic economic unit

Fig. 4. Recommended farming types, by agricultural settlement.

Size of Farm and Farm Management
Ratio of land versus labor

Once the best combination of crops and/or enterprises is determined for each agricultural settlement, establishment of viable farms would be possible. In addition, in order to achieve a certain desired agricultural income, it would be necessary to decide on the size of operation for each type of farm. It has been estimated that 2 hectares of arable land in Region I and 2.2 hectares in Region II would be necessary to achieve the stated goal. The size of operation of the individual farm unit is determined fundamentally by two factors, labor and land. For this purpose, a labor unit of 2.5 in manpower is recognized as standard for

TABLE 12

RESOURCES OF HANAZONO-MURA, BY VILLAGE COMMUNITY AND AGRICULTURAL SETTLEMENT

Region I

Village community	A Omaeda							B Arakawa			C Kuroda			D Nagata			
Agricultural settlement	1	2	3	4	5	6	7	8	9	10	11	12	13	14	15	16	17
Recommended farm type	RV	RV	RD	RV	RD	RSV	RSV	RV	RD	RSV	RSV	RSV	RSV	RSV	RV	RD	RV
Composition of land, A	70	100	65	80	50	5	15	90	50	60	73	73	80	50	80	65	80
by soil type B	10	--	35	--	40	25	35	5	30	10	--	--	--	15	10	20	--
(in per cent) C	20	--	--	20	10	70	50	5	20	30	27	27	20	35	10	15	20
Total arable area (in hectares)	53.22	34.38	45.68	19.08	15.43	31.82	37.75	50.94	39.11	61.85	42.55	40.83	54.44	45.86	44.19	37.85	20.75
Arable area for subsistence farming (in hectares)	13.22	8.38	13.68	7.08	5.43	7.62	9.15	8.94	9.11	10.85	8.55	6.83	6.44	7.86	6.19	7.85	6.75
Arable area for viable farms (in hectares)	40.00	26.00	32.00	12.00	10.00	24.20	28.60	42.00	30.00	50.00	34.00	32.00	48.00	38.00	38.00	30.00	14.00
Number of viable farms	20	16	16	6	5	11	13	21	15	25	17	16	24	19	19	15	7
Land reserved for other uses (in hectares)	10	5	5							5	5	5		5			5

Region II

Village community	E Nakagō							F Shimogō			G Kitane
Agricultural settlement	18	19	20	21	22	23	24	25	26	27	28
Composition of land, A	10	80	50	--	--	--	--	--	--	--	--
by soil type B	50	20	5	50	20	95	55	80	95	85	75
(in per cent) C	40	--	45	50	80	5	45	20	5	15	25
Recommended farm type	RSV	RV	RSV	RSV	RSV	RD	RSV	RD	RD	RD	RSV
Total arable area (in hectares)	31.92	24.91	31.22	19.09	10.62	38.00	54.26	42.65	46.24	43.19	46.50
Arable area for subsistence farming (in hectares)	7.92	4.69	7.22	5.89	4.02	9.40	10.26	9.65	6.64	7.99	9.10
Arable area for viable farms (in hectares)	24.00	20.22	24.00	13.20	6.60	28.60	44.00	33.00	39.60	35.20	37.40
Number of viable farms	11	10	12	6	3	6	20	15	18	16	17
Land reserved for other uses (in hectares)									5	5	

family farming. If the standardization of farming operation through regional specialization and the use of more efficient machinery is achieved, it is evident that the amount of land to make full use of 2.5 units of manpower must be larger than the average now shown by the farm survey.

Size of farms by type

The average size of all farms surveyed was 1.62 hectares; by farming type, the maximum average size was 2.1 hectares for cereal farming and the smallest, 1.26 hectares for growing vegetables. These differences in size occur not because the size is particularly well adapted to the type of farm, but because the size remained unchanged while the type of farming came to be differentiated. For instance, cereal farming has traditionally been associated with larger farms and that association has been maintained until today.

If we accept that the number of persons actually engaged in agriculture is decreasing at the rate of 2 to 3 per cent annually and the farm size is tending to become larger through the addition of land left idle by those who have quit farming, then the average farm size in ten years will be:

$$1.62^{ha.} \div (1-0.03)^{10} = 2.1^{ha.} \ldots \text{ if the annual rate of decrease is 3 per cent}$$

$$1.62^{ha.} \div (1-0.02)^{10} = 1.97^{ha.} \ldots \text{ if the annual rate of decrease is 2 per cent}$$

According to the agricultural census, the farms of full-time farmers in Hanazono-mura range between 1.0 and 1.5 hectares and there is a definite tendency for the farm to become larger. In fact, some farms (especially those engaged in the nursery enterprises) have already attained sizes of more than three hectares, the acreage limit set up by the Land Reform Law. At the same time, the number of farmers who have quit farming is fairly large. With this decline in the number of farmers, in the number of farm households, and the remarkable decrease in the number of full-time farmers, it is logical to assume that the farms of the remaining farmers will increase in size.

In order to quickly enlarge farm operation, it will be necessary to consolidate the presently fragmented plots into single, larger units by encouraging farmers to rearrange their fields. If mechanization of farm operations is increased, the capital structure will be improved for farm management. All these factors favor the increase in farm size of the independent farmers.

Farm size and income

If it could be assumed that the annual agricultural income would grow at the rate shown in the survey, 2.0 to 2.2 hectares of arable land should enable the farmers to obtain an income of over ¥1,000,000. However, this figure is an average for all farms and it would be more meaningful to examine income by types of farming. Nevertheless, if there is continued improvement in agricultural techniques and greater capital investment in land improvements, it is reasonable to assume that the income of the average farmer can be more than ¥1,500,000 in gross return, and more than ¥1,000,000 in agricultural income alone.

Size of farms and farming types

According to the survey, there is a difference of 10 per cent in the amount of arable land for the same farming type between Region I and II (see Fig. 2), but this no more than compensates for the difference in productivity of the soil types. The natural fertility of soils is arranged from better to poorer in the order from "A" to "B" to "C" soil types. With the additional 10 per cent of arable land in Region II, the agricultural incomes of the two regions should be about the same.

The survey data show considerable variations in size between the farming types in both regions, but these differences, as explained, are not considered to be the result of a reasonable adaptation to the respective farming types. The regional planning recommends the same acreage of arable land for all the farming types. The principal reasons for this are: Under the convertible land-use system, approximately one half of the arable land for all farming types is to be devoted to rice growing; the income of the farmers in each type of farming is to be rationalized by having a fixed ratio between land and labor power, while the ratio of capital invested will be varied according to and appropriate to the type of farming. As shown in the analysis of the farm survey data for 1963, the profit rate was as high as 19 per cent for the capital invested and, therefore, the capital needed should not be difficult to obtain.

Planning for Land Use

Land-use allocation

After the soils are evaluated as to quality, quantity, and distribution, the land would be broadly judged for allocation to its optimal use. However, some of the land is occupied by inhabitants other than the full-time farmers. Therefore, in planning for the over-all land use, lands of nonfarmers and also the land used for public facilities must be included and brought into consideration.

Farm household and urban uses

Besides arable land for the support of the farms, it is necessary to allocate some arable land for individual household use and still other land for urban uses. If all of the farmers, including those who farm only part time, maintained 0.2 hectare for growing crops for household use, the total would be about two hundred hectares, or about 20 per cent of the total arable land of Hanazono-mura. Two hundred hectares is less than the total area now farmed by the part-time farmers, so assuming they will either quit or greatly reduce their farming operations, their holdings can be reduced and part of the land allotted to full-time farmers and part reserved for future urban uses.

The land held in reserve for urban purposes will be farmed until the need for it arises, but at this point, one of the problems has been the lack of a standard to decide how much land for urban use should be set aside. The land for household use will be allocated as close to the agglomerated settlement proper as possible and, preferably, next to the homes. These fields will be small, varied in shape, and will grow a variety of household crops, including vegetables, flowers, and fruits, or perhaps may be used for nursery beds.

The land reserved for future urban needs will eventually be used mainly as housing sites, as it is expected that the number of commuters will greatly increase when the transportation system is improved, especially with the construction of a national highway through the area from south to north. It is also expected that additional industries will locate in nearby areas. Sites with poor soil will be set aside first for this purpose if other locational factors are equal.

The greatest concern in holding land for urban use and allotting it for household gardens is to avoid undesirable developments arising from an urban sprawl, which is liable to penetrate the specialized farming areas.

Land-use allocation and zoning

The number of uses to which the land will be put are many and should be clarified:

Residential land $\begin{cases} \text{Agricultural} \\ \text{Nonagricultural} \end{cases}$

Public land $\begin{cases} \text{Central area . . administrative offices, schools,} \\ \qquad\qquad\qquad\qquad \text{farmers' cooperatives, etc.} \end{cases}$

Public land	Public facilities . . . roads, irrigation canals and facilities, etc.
Reserved land	Future use for nonagricultural purposes, mainly dwellings, but at present will be used for growing crops
Land for household use (arable)	For producing vegetables, flowers, and fruits for home consumption
Farmland	Rice field (permanent) Convertible—rice and dry field Mulberry

These uses may be divided into two categories: (1) current land uses and (2) new land uses. Of those in the latter category, the most extensive allocation will be for the cultivation of crops for the market and for home use. The land reserved for urban needs will encompass a variety of designated uses which, if left to happenstance, would result in a competitive and disorganized use of land and its optimal utilization would not be realized.

The most detrimental phenomenon that would result from lack of planning would be "sprawling," where dwellings and industrial plants become mixed together without any order or control. If a zoning system that defines the use of the land can be established, a rational development can be guaranteed. It is here that the important significance of zoning lies.

The land should first be zoned into the two main uses: agricultural and urban. Then the agricultural land should be broken into several but specific subdivisions. To be economically viable, division of arable land in relatively large units is necessary not only for cultivating mulberry, but also for growing such crops as vegetables and livestock feed.

The rational establishment of specialized agricultural land use must be accompanied by investment in various kinds of equipment and facilities for specialized products so that production efficiency can be raised. That is, even though the best use for the various units of land is ascertained, if appropriate equipment and facilities for the particular crop or enterprise are not provided, its optimal use cannot be achieved. The zoning system, based upon the predetermined land-use divisions, would attempt to carry out the aims according to established priorities that would be acceptable to the majority of the people. Other uses involving fewer people would be allowed only if they do not conflict with priority decisions. In reality, if designated priorities were promoted fully, there would remain little area for other purposes. In the establishment of land-use divisions, logically, there is a very important relationship with roads, waterways, and other public facilities, for they would determine such aspects as accessibility and degree of benefit in the use of water.

If the community could realize optimum use of land through planned zoning, independent farmers could expect an increase in income. To be effective, zoning should be based on relatively long-term plans, but it should at the same time be flexible enough to accommodate changes if the necessity arises. Although investment in agricultural production can be effective for as long as ten or twenty years, zoning and land use should be re-examined toward the end of designated time periods. Long-term consideration is especially needed for tree crops, which require longer periods than others to come into production.

Relationship Between the Groups of Farming Types

The farmers in each settlement *(buraku)* could benefit from performing their specialized functions, but they could raise their functional role to higher levels by integrating and forming still larger and more prosperous agricultural regions.

In the process, relationships, both intra- and infragroup, come into existence. Relationships between groups in the same type of farming and between those of other types are different in emphasis and attitude. For example, within the farming type *RV* (rice and vegetable) the emphasis is put on the relationship between production and marketing so that a cooperative organization for marketing would be of first consideration. This organization would plan for a production area, considering demands in kind and quality of crops, amount of production, the period of marketing, and so on. In establishing such an organization, it should be clearly decided just where to put the emphasis in order to develop a production region that would be competitive with other regions producing similar crops or products.

The relationships between the heterogeneous groups are many-sided and external, and the principal aim would be to promote complementary relationships through using each other's by-products and various other resources. For example, *RV* farmers need much manure to grow vegetables, but the manure produced on their farms is usually insufficient. Such being the case, the farmers in the *RV* area could get manure from the *RD* (rice and dairy) farm region, in which there is a surplus. On the other hand, *RD* farmers could get rice straw for litter and green cut feed from the *RV* farmers. These feed crops can be grown extensively in a rotation system with vegetables, or as cover crops during periods when vegetables are not being grown.

Or in respect to labor, if the farmer of *RSV* (rice, sericulture, vegetables) could obtain his labor supply from the other groups during the short but busy work peaks, the scale of silkworm raising could be enlarged. The ideal relationship would be to balance advantageously all available resources.

Taking another example, the orderly use of irrigation and underground water is necessary, not only during rice-growing seasons, but during other seasons. If water resources were not regulated, serious competitive demands could arise, obstructing the development of a sound farming policy. To avoid this, the rationalization of demand should be determined on a mutually beneficial basis, in accordance with an agreed-upon plan. If such relationships are achieved in the use of the various resources through a sound production plan, higher levels of utilization would be possible than if each agricultural settlement planned for its development independently.

In summary, it can be said that the over-all objective is to create a highly developed and unified region to raise the level of production and to achieve higher standards of living. But at the same time it must be recognized that relationships are not static and must be adjusted periodically as situations change. The establishment of set goals, coupled with continual re-examination, is the real significance of regional planning.

GEORGE H. KAKIUCHI

Comment

Many studies have been made on the impressive post-World War II economic growth of Japan. Between 1955 and 1964, for example, the real growth in the gross national product averaged about 10 per cent per annum. (Japan is the third largest producer of steel and automobiles.) However, as might be expected, not all sectors of the economy have grown at the same pace, and agriculture has been one that has lagged. The rate of growth in agricultural production averaged only 3.9 per cent per year. One of the results has been that the average urban and farm-family incomes differ by about 30 per cent. Also, whereas the labor productivity per person in manufacturing had increased by 51 per cent between 1958 and 1963, that for agriculture had increased by only 30 per cent. It is hoped by those concerned to narrow or eliminate the differences. The problem is becoming serious as the farmers have come to have aspirations similar to those of urban dwellers, especially with the almost national exposure to television. This problem is, of course, not unique to Japan, but is, I am sure, familiar to the other countries of East Asia. It is to this topic, how the farming landscape might be changed and modernized so the aspirations of the farm families might be better achieved, that Professor Ueno's paper is addressed.

The post-World War II Land Reform had done much to provide incentives and improve rural life, making most of the former tenants into owner-cultivators. As in the years after the Meiji Restoration of 1867, there was a substantial increase in agricultural production. However, many problems still continue to frustrate the farmers. The smallness of the average farms, about 2.4 acres, did not change, nor did the law consolidate their fragmented plots, which has made mechanization and other aspects of modernization difficult to implement.

Another factor that greatly stimulated innovations in the thinking of the farmers and upon the rural landscape has been the increased demands for certain kinds of agricultural products, generally referred to as cash crops. These reflect the rise in the standard of living and demands from the expanding industries.

One of the resulting changes is what Professor Ueno has described as areal or regional specialization in cash cropping, reinforced by functional specialization in the form of agricultural cooperatives of various types. The areal specialization is the result of the rationalization of the various factors of the physical environment, location in terms of markets, regional competition, and other economic, social, and historical considerations. The role of the government in enhancing the trend must not be underestimated.

Professor Ueno has selected the settlement (*buraku*) as the basic areal unit to study and plan for this type of areal specialization. I feel that this selection is valid, not only in Japan but also in all of the non-Communist nations of East Asia, because traditionally it has been the focus of rural life. It would be at this level that changes or innovations would be accepted or rejected.

Japanese agricultural land use seems to be in another important transitional period. It is very definitely taking on aspects of commercial farming. For instance, between 1955 and 1960, the ratio of farmers engaged in commercial production to the total number of farm households rose from 28 to 41 per cent. More important as a force for innovation is the changing attitudes of the farmers, which now stress proper farm management rather than the growing of staple food crops, the traditional emphasis in subsistence or semisubsistence agriculture.

As in all nations that are modernizing successfully, there has been a conspicuous change in the types of food products consumed. If we take 1960 as 100, then the index of production of vegetables in 1965 was 114.2, 120.9 for fruits, 125.1 for industrial crops, 188.4 for dairy products, 232.3 for the number of hogs, 200.8 for egg production, and 171.1 for milk production. The production of rice has remained about the same, but that for other grains has actually declined.

Although income and productivity on the farms have been increasing through further intensification of land use, better management, and areal and functional specialization, the limitations of the small farms and fragmented plots will be harder to overcome. However, if the rural population continues to quit farming at the present rate of about 3 per cent per year, Professor Ueno indicates that the average size of farms could very well double in the next ten years. Herein lies the eventual

hope of the remaining full-time farmers to raise their living standards to
the level of the urban areas.

Professor Ueno's paper studies the various problems in the rural landscape. He has focused his attention on the basic areal unit—the settlement. His thought is that this unit should be considered one farming
unit area for planning purposes and to specialize accordingly in those
crops and/or enterprises most suited to it. This would facilitate the coordination of various phases of work, such as planting, irrigating, spraying, harvesting, and so forth. Mechanization would be easier to achieve
through cooperative buying and use. Cooperatives would be strengthened through functional specialization coincident with the crop or
enterprise, resulting in more efficient marketing systems and better
bargaining position. The rural characteristics in South Korea and
Taiwan are, I feel, similar enough to make this approach generally
applicable.

Also, planning and cooperation are becoming bywords on all levels,
which was not so in the years past. The national government is paying
more attention and giving aid in many ways—in leadership, technical,
organizational, and, very importantly, financial support to improve
the rural economy, which had been long neglected in favor of the manufacturing industries.

Professor Ueno selected Hanazono-mura, located near Tokyo, as a
case study. He takes the location of the traditional nucleated settlements, as well as the qualities of the physical environment—topography,
soils, and climate, as fixed. In this setting he considers the variables, the
various crops or enterprises in relation to market potentials. Using the
selected factors, he has set up a spatial classification system that could
be applied to all areal units to arrive at some rational use of the lands.
(Some social scientists have, in fact, suggested the establishment of a
data bank, using such small areal units but covering whole nations
and if possible the whole world, storing all possible information about
the units for retrieval.) The method and criteria used by Ueno should be
applicable to the non-Communist countries of East Asia. Statistics are
reasonably available and relatively reliable. Using the comparative
approach, a study of many representative villages and settlements under
similar and differing conditions in the various countries could reveal
very useful specifics and generalizations.

It seems from Professor Ueno's studies and from some of my own,
that Japanese agricultural land use will become increasingly more intensive and commercialized in the next few years, provided that current

incentives continue, hopefully, to improve. Enlargement of the average farm acreage to any substantial size will not occur for some years. As an alternative, cooperation among farmers to achieve both real and functional specialization in one form or another seem to be one of the possible ways to improve their livelihood. It appears that in Japan, Taiwan, and South Korea, and especially in Taiwan and Japan, that socioeconomic conditions are such that, historically speaking, rapid changes and innovations are now possible in the rural sector, and that as Professor Ueno's paper shows, evolution rather than revolution can bring about desired changes with less stress and frustrations.

KI HYUK PAK

A Comparative Study
of the Agrarian Systems
# of South and North Korea

INTRODUCTION

The purpose of this paper is to analyze and compare the agrarian systems of South and North Korea. The agricultural economy in the former is based on family farm management; that in the latter on Soviet-type collective farming.

We must admit that basic differences in the ideologies of the two regions and profound differences in the systems adopted make parallel comparison unfeasible, but despite those differences, there are some similarities in the two systems. One common feature is a shortage of food; another, the use of agriculture as a means to industrialization. As a result of economic planning in both regions, higher priority has been given to industrialization than to primary industry (agriculture), resulting in bitter experiences for both. A food shortage led to high grain prices, followed by severe inflation (at least in South Korea), which brought about unstable social and economic conditions. Recently, the tendency in both South and North Korea has been to place more emphasis on the development of agriculture and to increase agricultural productivity to cope with the ever increasing domestic food requirements.

The similarities, however, end there. In pursuit of the objective of increasing agricultural productivity, divergent paths have been taken. Not only are the fundamental philosophies of the North and the South diametrically opposite, but so also are the agricultural problems and the policies which have been adopted. The most important differences can be found in the institutional settings and the systems of economic incentives under which individual farmers must operate.

In this paper an attempt is made to analyze the farm organizations and economic incentives in the agricultural economies of the South and the North. There is a certain limitation on the study due to the lack of communication between South and North Korea. There are few North Korean statistics available, and it is extremely difficult to obtain reliable materials and accurate data. There may be errors in South Korea's economic statistics, but the government institutions do not control such data, only collect them. However, with regard to North Korea, statistical data are entirely controlled by the government body and the party. There are practically no detailed or absolute figures available from the North, and the percentage figures and materials are colored by propaganda and window dressing, which makes them dismayingly ambiguous.

GENERAL ECONOMIC STRUCTURE

Before attempting any analysis of the South and North Korean economies, one must understand the heritage of the Japanese occupation, which extended over three and one-half decades following 1910. The basic problems in Korea were inherited from Japanese colonialism, for the nation's economic structure was divided into two distinct regions. Under direct Japanese control, North Korea experienced the construction of heavy industry for the purpose of military expansion toward the north, i.e., Manchuria and China; the economy of South Korea, on the other hand, was geared to provide a food (mainly rice) supply base for Japan proper. The industrial North and the agricultural South were interdependent. The division of the country along the thirty-eighth parallel dealt a crippling blow to integration. This created the second great problem. The economic structure of Korea, i.e., industrial North vs. agricultural South, was too deeply rooted to change easily, as Table 1 shows, even after the nation was divided into two political, economic, and administrative units. Moreover, since 1945, South Korea, once preponderantly agricultural and historically a rice exporter, has had to import grains to meet her annual food requirements. This is mainly due to rapid population increase resulting from the influx of refugees from North Korea and repatriates from other parts of Asia. By the end of 1957, the population of South Korea had reached more than twenty million people, having increased by at least 1,500,000 over that of 1945 despite the evacuation of about 750,000 people in 1953.

TABLE 1
SOME INDICATORS OF THE ECONOMIES OF SOUTH AND NORTH KOREA

	South Korea			North Korea		
	1957	1962	1963	1957	1962	1963
Area (square miles)	37,959	37,959	37,959	47,097	47,097	47,097
Population (thousand persons)	22,500	26,278	27,226	10,000	11,380	11,716
Paddy fields (thousand hectares)	1,189	1,223	1,228	462	570	635
Dry fields (thousand hectares)	803	838	851	1,527	1,538	1,578
Rice (thousand metric tons)	2,361	3,015	3,758	1,593	1,900	2,050
Other grains (thousand metric tons)	707	1,064	1,207	1,677	2,500	2,300
Korean cattle (thousand head)	967	1,253	1,363	694	320	867
Marine catch (thousand metric tons)	403	450	522	564	840	640
Lumber (cubic kilometers)	365	348	473	1,000	1,581	1,670
Coal (thousand metric tons)	2,441	7,444	8,858	5,000	13,200	14,040
Iron ore (thousand metric tons)	186	471	501	1,100	3,336	3,860
Cement (thousand metric tons)	92	790	1,242	895	2,376	2,530
Electric power (million kilowatt hours)	1,323	1,978	2,209	6,900	11,445	11,766

Source: Yoon T. Kuark, "Economic Development Contrast Between South and North Korea," Patterns of Economic Development: Korea, ed. Joseph S. Chung (Detroit, Mich.: The Korea Research and Publication Inc., 1966), pp. 164–65. The rice-production figures for 1962 and 1963 for South Korea were originally 2,722 and 2,766, respectively.

Land Reform in South Korea

"Land Reform," if not a single measure, was the most popular means for the rapid and revolutionary changes in the economic, political, and social structure of Korea. There were two types of land reform, one embracing socialistic patterns, the other capitalistc.

The Republic of Korea enacted the Land Reform Law in 1950. Its purpose was set forth in Article I as follows:

... on the basis of the constitution of the Republic of Korea pertaining to farm lands to improve the living conditions of farmers, to keep the balance of, and to develop the national economy by *increasing agricultural productivity*.[1]

The maximum size of farm land was set by the law at three hectares. The terms of the Republic of Korea land-reform program were such that a tenant purchaser was sold the land at 150 per cent of the total value of one year's crop, payable at 30 per cent per year for five years. The landlords were given bonds limited in redemption in any one year to 30 per cent of the value of the crop (estimated as an average harvest) and they were allowed this 30 per cent of crops over a five-year period.

One of the basic difficulties faced in land reform in the South was the fact that it was conducted during a war period when there was extreme inflation. Expected redistribution of land was planned to affect about 40 per cent of the total arable land in South Korea, including both vested land (232,882 hectares, formerly Japanese-owned) and the area subject to tenure reform. Under the reform, however, only about 68 per cent (577,000 hectares) of the total area of distributable land (833,000 hectares) has actually been redistributed, and only about 50 per cent of the total farm households has been affected.[2]

Land Reform in North Korea

Land reform in North Korea was announced in a decree issued on March 5, 1946, approximately seven months after the beginning of the Russian occupation. The program was completed by the end of March, 1946. All land confiscated was entrusted to the North Korean People's Committee. This body was to achieve actual redistribution through village committees acting under district, county, and provincial People's Committees. The North Korean land program entailed the seizure

[1] Italics added.
[2] Ki Hyuk Pak, "Outcome of Land Reform in the Republic of Korea," *Journal of Farm Economics*, XXXVIII, No. 4 (Nov., 1956), 1015–16. For further reference, Ki Hyuk Pak and others, *A Study of Land Tenure System in Korea* (Seoul: Korea Land Economics Research Center, 1966), pp. 86–123.

of 1,000,325 hectares or 54 per cent of the total arable land in North Korea.[3]

Land reform in North Korea was effected along Communist lines, and in the process it quickly destroyed the former social classes and established a new force, a Communist army, in rural Korea. In all probability it was then the best available propaganda against the American occupation of South Korea. Since approximately 1.5 million people fled from the North to South Korea during 1946 and 1947, it would seem that the Communist land-reform plan in North Korea was not to the liking of many.

Gradually, the North Korean regime moved toward cooperative farming, partly because it had gained possession of much land, consisting of land abandoned by the refugees who had fled to the South and/or confiscated from former Japanese ownership, national traitors, Korean landlords who owned more than five hectares, absentee landlords, and religious organizations with more than five hectares. All of these lands were confiscated without compensation and were distributed without charge to landless peasants or peasants with little land; 725,524 farm households were affected.

The second step of the Communist pattern of land reform was collectivization. The Korean conflict was, however, the historic watershed for the socialization of agriculture; it helped to expedite the initial goal of a strong agricultural policy. It was timely to appeal on grounds of patriotism to the people to rehabilitate war-devastated land by expanding collective farms, establishing tractor stations, and launching irrigation projects. In fact, an early collective farm was founded by a "Frontline Cooperative Work Team" in 1951 along the war-front area of Kangwon Province, the cockpit of the Korean conflict. By the end of 1958, the whole North Korean rural community had already come into collectivization.[4]

One of the characteristics of collectivization in North Korea was the fast tempo adopted to move into the third phase (full collectivization) on the socialistic pattern.[5] This was because the need for collectivization

[3] Ryozo Kurai, "Agrarian Organization Problems in North Korea," *Current Situation of South and North Korea*, II (Tokyo: Research Department of Asahi Press, 1962), 112.

[4] *Ibid.*, p. 131.

[5] There were three types of cooperatives in North Korea until 1958, when Type I and Type II were completely transferred into Type III. Following is a summary of the characteristics of each form:

Type I: Private ownership of land, draft animals, and agricultural implements;

was not primarily to increase agricultural productivity, but to achieve socialization in the light of political reform.[6]

FARM ORGANIZATION AND FARM SIZE

In South Korea

The main feature of farm organization in South Korea is the market-oriented, family-operated unit. The family farm, being an individual proprietorship type of economic organization, is free to utilize its productive potentials: labor, land, and entrepreneurship. Decisions regarding how, how much, and what to produce are all based on the individual farmer's initiative. Living standards and production activities are closely tied in with the farmer's managerial abilities and his evaluation of what can be exchanged at the market.

Various subsidiary organizations were founded in South Korea to help accelerate the process of modernization in farming. This is in line with what Professor Wyn. F. Owen described as the process of "priming the pump."[7]

The speed of this agricultural treadmill, which a family farming system inherits along with market opportunity, quite obviously tends mainly to be conditioned by the degree to which knowledge and access to new methods and techniques are generally available to farmers.

Further, provisions are necessary to construct a framework

. . . with which increased agricultural production, on a cumulative basis, can be rendered essentially automatic and almost a direct function of public investment in agricultural research and rural education and of the adequacy of complementary rural financial institutions and farmer's financial reserves.

Two of these institutions are: National Agricultural Cooperative Federation (NACF) and Office of Rural Development (ORD).

---

individual tillage and reaping of private plots; some collective use of tools and animals and pooling of labor.

Type II: Private ownership of land; draft animals and agricultural implements may be owned privately or purchased by the cooperatives; collective use of land and pooling labor in sowing, plowing, and harvesting.

Type III: *De jure* private ownership of land but *de facto* collective ownership, as the distribution of output is based solely on labor contribution; collective use of land, operation of farm on cooperative base.

[6] Han Joo Kim, *Agriculture Collectivization Movement in North Korea* (Pyongyang: Foreign Language Publishing Co., 1958), pp. 18–22.

[7] Wyn. F. Owen, "Squeeze on Agriculture," *American Economic Review*, LVI, No. 1 (March, 1966), 53.

Supervised credit. The agricultural credit institution in South Korea today is the National Agricultural Cooperative Federation developed from the Agricultural Bank and was founded in August of 1961. NACF has devoted itself to the task of changing agriculture over to a cooperative financing system and has begun to provide loans.

Since the founding of NACF, agricultural financing has remarkably increased in volume. By the end of 1966, total credits outstanding, including all kinds of funds for farm management and other agricultural uses, amounted to 27,106 million won.[8] This is equivalent to a gain of 58.1 per cent during the past five years and to an increment of 11.6 per cent per annum. Despite this remarkable growth, there is no noticeable upward change in the share of agricultural credits out of the total credit made available to the entire economy. Thus, funds are not sufficient to meet the demand for loans by individual farmers. Although the shortage of capital funds is a general phenomenon in South Korea as a developing economy, it is even more so in South Korean agriculture. Both the limited capability of individual farmers and the availability of funds have resulted in distribution-type loans. The amount of credit is so small that it is almost in the nature of relief credit or political gifts by the governmental credit institution. In 1966, NACF credit-extension policy was somewhat changed, and now it operates on a more selective basis.

Another feature of NACF's supervised credit system lies in its collaboration with the government's "Economic Farm Unit Fostering Project" that was enforced in 1965.

From among farmers with their own plots of farm land, those who needed financial and technical aid for achieving economic self-support were selected. Of a total of 2,415,000 farm households, 761,000 households (31.5 per cent) with 0.5 hectare to less than 1.0 hectare of farm land were considered eligible.

The purpose of this project is to help develop small farmers into middle-class farmers, so that their income standards will surpass those of workers in the nonagricultural sector. A total of 10,000 farm households are to receive benefits from the "Economic Farm Unit Fostering Project." These will be selected from *up*[9] or *myon*[10] size districts. These districts are chosen at a rate of two per county. Through agreement

[8] The Bank of Korea, *Monthly Statistical Review*, XXI, No. 3 (March, 1967), 16. *Won* is standard currency in South Korea: one won is equivalent to 1/270 U.S. dollar at a floating ratio, as of June 10, 1967.

[9] *Up* is Korean for "town."

[10] *Myŏn* is a subdivision of *kun* (county).

between farmers' cooperative development workers and rural guidance workers, a total of 36 target farm households are selected from each of the districts. The following are the criteria used in the selection of the farm households:

1. Farmers with a relatively strong ambition to reach economic self-support from among farm households with five to ten *tanbo*[11] of farm land.

2. Farm households with a relatively large area of land that can be used for expansion of farm land.

3. Farm households with sufficient family labor.

Extension service. The South Korea Revolutionary Government in March, 1962, promulgated the Agricultural Development Decree with the hope of reorganizing all agricultural extension activities and organizations. Under this measure, general agricultural administration, technical guidance, and economic activities were completely differentiated, and agricultural extension in its proper sense entered a new era. Under the same decree, approximately three thousand extension workers were integrated under the agricultural extension program and various past extension plans and activities were placed under the overall control and adjustment of a single agency. The guidance bureau of the Office of Rural Development (ORD), responsible to the Minister of Agriculture and Forestry (MAF), represents a merger of the former Extension Bureau of the Institute of Agriculture and the Community Development Bureau of the MAF, and is responsible for the establishment of basic policies regarding agricultural extension and guidance activities.

The provincial officers of Rural Development, under the control of provincial governors, represent the merger of the former provincial institutes of agriculture with livestock-breeding stations, rice-breeding farms, silkworm-breeding stations, veterinary laboratories, and farmer's training facilities. As such, their offices have emerged as over-all agricultural centers in the province, responsible for agricultural progress and rural development. In each city and county, as the lowest unit of local autonomy, there is a rural guidance office to function as a local center for the development of agriculture and improvement of the farmer's living standards. There are 167 rural guidance offices at the city and *kun*[12] level, but plans are to organize two or three branch offices in each *kun*. Accordingly, there are about 450 guidance units,

[11] *Tanbo* is equal to 0.1 hectare.
[12] *Kun* is roughly equivalent to "county."

including branch officers, at the grass-roots level. These rural guidance organs at all levels and echelons are not linear in structure to the same extent as in the past, but still continue to operate as channels for technical guidance and administrative support.

Small farms. As noted above, farm management in South Korea is based on the small family farm whose economic decisions are made freely by the individual. In North, agriculture is deeply affected by the Marxist-Leninist doctrine and oriented to the large or collectivized farm, the factors of production of which are mostly owned by the government or have collective ownership under strong party leadership.

As the economy grows rapidly during the First Five-Year-Plan period (ending in 1966) in South Korea, the ceiling limit of three hectares of cropland for individual crop farms was questioned. Whether or not such a restrictive policy, adopted seventeen years ago, should be continued, is often asked.[13] The crux of the problem is, however, not the restraint of farm scale but how to improve the management aspect of the small farms so as to enable them to compete with the large farms.

An upper ceiling may not be a serious constraint in an area such as Korea where the topographic conditions of farm land make it difficult to operate more than three hectares of cropland by family labor under the given technology. It is advantageous, for example, to work shift-cultivation fields in the highlands by means of dividing them so as to conserve rain water. Farms must utilize the natural waterways and terrain in the development of farm land. Thus, the underlying economic principles upon which the limited resources are being allocated in the semisubsistence village economy are not different from what we find in the modern business sector.[14]

Most farmers are operating with less than three hectares, not because of the legal upper-ceiling limit but because of other, usually financial, restricting factors. A farm larger than three hectares requires substantial cash outlay, credit for hired labor, and other inputs. With the current technology, the abundant supply of farm labor, existing market facilities, and other economic factors now in force, the present three-hectare upper-ceiling limit would probably not impede the increase of efficiency. The most efficient farm among crop farms in South Korea today, therefore, is found to be between two to three hectares.

[13] A special study was conducted for this purpose and for other important questions in regard to land tenure policy in South Korea, 1965. Details on this problem will be seen in Pak, *A Study of Land Tenure System in Korea.*

[14] T. W. Schultz, *Transforming Traditional Agriculture* (New Haven: Yale University Press, 1964), p. 17.

While economies of scale are very difficult to attain, it is true that the sizes of farms in Korea, Japan, and Taiwan are almost identical. T. W. Schultz stated that farms in India (average farm size—2.2 hectares) are fully two and one-half times as large as they are in Japan (average farm size—0.9 hectares), yet Japanese agriculture is substantially more modern. The significant factor in farm business, therefore, is not size itself but the efficiency of farm management. This efficiency must include intensification and diversification of farm management so as to enlarge farm business and increase farm income.

In North Korea

As has been noted, the agricultural activities in North Korea are carried on either by collective or state farms. The ultimate organizational goal of Communist agricultural policy was the complete socialization of agriculture, which was achieved in 1958. By 1963, there were 3,732 collective farms, holding 1,837,000 hectares of land, and 190 state farms, of which 31 were centrally managed and the rest were provincially managed. The cultivated land under state farms amounted to approximately 130,000 hectares.[15]

The state farm is the ultimate form of socialization of North Korean agriculture. "The state farm is the agricultural homologue of the industrial enterprise, that is, a sort of state-operated factory that produces grains, milk, meat, wool, and etc."[16] The managers of state farms are appointed by the state, which owns the land, machinery, and all other means of production. The system of independent economic accounting used by industrial enterprises has also been adopted by the state farms.

It is significant to note that in the North the farm workers are mobilized by means of a "compulsory division of labor," that is, the work-brigade and work-team systems.

Work-brigade system. The work brigade constitutes the basic unit of farm labor operation in North Korean agriculture. Each agricultural cooperative must group its entire membership into work brigades, each member selected and assigned according to his ability and qualifications. Work brigades are specialized for crops, livestock, tractors, machines, and other purposes. The North Koreans claim the following advantages in employing the work-brigade, or fixed-work system:

[15] *Chosen Democratic People's Republic, National Economic Development Statistics, 1946–1963* (Tokyo: Chosen Research Center, 1965), pp. 18–19.

[16] J. S. Chung (ed.), *Patterns of Economic Development: Korea* (Detroit, Mich.: The Korea Research and Publication, Inc., 1966), p. 74.

1. The responsibilities and skills of the members can be increased when they are attached permanently to the specific brigade.

2. The efficiency of such production factors as land, equipment, and other facilities can be increased a great deal in their use, maintenance, and custody when they are fixed to a work-brigade team.

3. A maximum degree of division of labor and cooperative labor can be achieved, for the labor and its supplementary tools are jointly fixed to a work brigade.

4. The socialistic distribution can be easily and strictly implemented.

Work-team system. In each work-brigade team with the exception of the tractor brigade there are three work teams: "specialized," "mixed," and "all purpose." The activities of the specialized team are highly seasonal, covering a wider region and restricted to a specific crop or one species of livestock, while the mixed team works on two or more kinds of crops or livestock, with its regional boundary often being limited to a natural village.[17] Finally, the all-purpose team is assigned to non-specialized farming, and is often responsible for both crops and livestock.

A tractor brigade consists of several tractor companies, its size is determined by such factors as the extent of the area suitable for machine cultivation, the type of machine available, and other natural and economic factors in the location under consideration.

Large farms. Collectivized farms in North Korea are still called *cooperatives*, but in fact they differ little from the artel type of kolkhozy in the Soviet Union. Although there are no longer any individual farms, farmers are allowed to own a private plot of not more than one hectare on which vegetables, fruit, and livestock are raised for family consumption. The size of the collective farms in North Korea has been influenced by Red China's standard scale: 300 farm households in a plains area and 100 farm households in a mountainous area. The *ri*[18] was originally a unit of the cooperative, but the term was changed to encompass several villages to serve as a unit for cooperatives. The average size of the cooperatives in 1958 was 406 hectares of land with 275 farm households, in comparison to 14 hectares of land with 15 farm households in 1953, as shown in Table 2.

The efficiency of big-farm operation in North Korea is questionable for the following three reasons: first, North Korea is more mountainous

---

[17] Consisting of 20 to 60 households, a *natural* village in Korea is usually much smaller than an *administrative* village.

[18] *Ri* is "village," or roughly equivalent to a "precinct."

TABLE 2
SCALE OF GROWTH IN AGRICULTURAL COOPERATIVES, NORTH KOREA

	1953	1954	1955	1956	1957	1958 March	1958 Nov.
		(As of the end of each year)					
Average number of farm households per cooperative	15	33	42	55	64	79	275
Area of cultivation (hectares)	14	57	73	88	105	133	406

Source: Research Department of Asahi Press, *Current Situation of South and North Korea*, II (Tokyo, 1962), 131.

and the climate is more severe than in the South; second, the average farmer is lacking in revolutionary consciousness; and finally, such a latifundium is usually characterized by its low productivity. In fact, there is no evidence to prove the economies of scale in North Korea.

In South Korea there has been some experimenting with big cooperative farms; at least ten pilot projects were begun under government supervision and financing, but most of them failed, principally owing to a lack of management ability, insufficient funds, marketing, and so on. The most common farm in the South is still the family unit, which best fits the sociopolitical and economic conditions of the capitalistic system.

Kun *Cooperative Farm Management Committee (KCFMC)*. By the end of 1958, the establishment of cooperatives in agriculture and the socialization of industry in North Korea were complete. Since then, the government has envisaged continuing revolution as a far-reaching goal of Communist society. The *Kun* Cooperative Farm Management was the immediate result of such efforts. In December, 1961, the *Kun* Agricultural Farm Management Committee, being separated from the *Kun* People's Committee, was empowered to supervise and guide the cooperatives' agricultural production activities.

Although reorganization of the entire agricultural leadership was initiated by the *Kun* Cooperative Farm Management Committee, the reshuffle was toward the upper administrative levels. At the provincial level, a Farm Village Auditing Committee was organized in July, 1962, and the Central Department of Agriculture was reorganized as the National Agriculture Committee in October, 1962. Such a reorganization and the establishment of new leadership took almost a whole year.

The *Kun* CFMC Members are composed of eleven to seventeen leading workers: the Chairman, Engineering Chief (the First Vice-Chairman), the Administrative Vice-Chairman, the Vice-Chairman of

Operation, the Vice-Chairman of the *Kun* Party who is in charge of agriculture, the chairman of *Kun* People's Committee, the manager of agricultural machine-operation stations, the planning chief of management committee, and others. The first four members are most responsible for the *Kun* CFMC and are in charge of agricultural production in the *Kun*. The chairman of the committee has the authority to select members other than the first four men, but it is necessary to obtain ratification from the Provincial Farm Village Auditing Committee. The four top members and planning chief are engaged in daily routine work while the rest are not standing members. A regular committee meeting is held once a month in which all the necessary decisions regarding cooperative activities are settled.

The *Kun* CFMC sets forth monthly work directives, major work indices, work volumes, work time, and workday rates. Consequently, village life is much influenced by the *Kun* Farm Management Committee. The *Ri* People's Committee Chief became also the Chief of Cooperative Farm Management Committee in the village, but it is an entirely separate organization, consisting of a staff which differs from the people's committee.

In every *Kun* CFMC, there are ten divisions to carry out the actual details of farming. Under the direct supervision of the Engineering Chief, there are three divisions dealing with planning, technical instruction, and farm machinery. Under the Vice-Chairman of Administration, there are four divisions, dealing with labor, bookkeeping instruction, construction, and prevention of epidemics in livestock. Under the Vice-Chairman of Operation, there are three divisions—cooperative farm materials, materials for directly controlled enterprises, and transportation.

In addition to the above organization, National Service Facilities and Enterprise Stations have been placed under the immediate control of the *Kun* CFMC.

Despite this systematic and complicated farm organization, the North Korean farmer seemingly does not benefit from them. He suffers from the fundamental shortcomings of rigid system control, bureaucracy, and formalism. Kim Il-sung, premier of North Korea, himself admitted in his *Thesis on Socialization of Agricultural Problems in North Korea*[19] in 1964 that three revolutions—in technology, culture, and ideology— must be

---

[19] Il-sung Kim, *Thesis on Socialization of Agricultural Problems in North Korea* (Tokyo: The Central Standing Committee of General Federation of North Korean People in Japan, 1964), p. 5.

achieved at the same time, to wipe out the bureaucracy and formalism persisting in North Korean agricultural organizations. He emphasized especially the ideological revolution as a prerequisite to any reformation in North Korean agriculture. The troubles of North Korean agriculture, however, do not lie entirely with farm organization. One cannot overlook the effect of the incentive system, to which we turn now.

THE ECONOMIC INCENTIVE SYSTEM IN NORTH KOREA

North Korean Merit Base System

The major incentive system employed in North Korean agriculture is piece-work, which is a scheme combining surveillance with individual performance. For both control and evaluation, the system of "workday units by type of skill and labor" and "standard work amount per day" for various types of farm work is set forth. Accordingly, the actual performance of the individual worker is reckoned in the distribution of the harvest.

Workday unit system. All farm jobs are classified into several categories according to their nature—heavy or light, complicated or simple, skilled or unskilled, very important or less important. The coefficients of workday units for common farm labor are shown in Table 3.

TABLE 3
COEFFICIENCY OF WORKDAY UNIT FOR COMMON FARM LABOR, NORTH KOREA

Graded Work	Evaluated Labor Day
1	0.50
2	0.75
3	1.00
4	1.25
5	1.50
6	1.75
7	2.00

Source: Labor Party of North Korea, *Commonsense of Economics—Industry, Agriculture* (Pyongyang: Commerce, North Korea Press, 1963), Agricultural Section.

First, it should be noted that there are seven grades employed for common workers, from the first (minimum) to the seventh (maximum) grades. In each upgrading, 0.25 workday units are added. Minimum skill (the first grade) is evaluated as 0.50, which is one half of the standard. Third grade is a standard (1.00) workday. Seventh-grade labor is the most skilled, complicated, and seasonally important, and is evaluated as four times as demanding as the lowest grade labor.

For ordinary crop-farm cooperative members, only the five grades— from the first to the fifth—are used, but for the livestock-brigade mem-

TABLE 4
GRADE CLASSIFICATION BY JOB IN GENERAL FARMING, NORTH KOREA

Description	Grade
Plowing and harrowing	7
Harvesting and cutting wood	6
Transferring soil	5
Transplanting	4
Complementary land improvement	3
Roofing	2

Source: Same as Table 3.

TABLE 5
GRADE CLASSIFICATION BY JOB IN LIVESTOCK RAISING, NORTH KOREA

Description	Grade
Rabbit management	2–6
Horse management	4–6
Sericulture	2–7
Hog raising	4–7
Livestock shipping	4–7

Source: Same as Table 3.

bers, grades from the second through the seventh are applied, depending on their skills and the type of animal worked with. The details of grade classification by job in general farming and livestock are shown in Tables 4 and 5. Thus, the grade and earnings of any given worker can vary by season and by the type of job assigned, although his grade will presumably remain the same if he can stay in the same type of work. In other words, he can be underemployed, just like his counterpart in South Korean agriculture. This criticism can be also applied to co-operative managerial workers and foremen of work brigades, as shown in Table 6. Here workday units vary depending on the size of the collective and the work brigade one happens to be engaged in. Interestingly enough, the average workday units for foremen and bookkeepers are rather lower than those for common workers, reflecting a relative shortage of workhands in crop and general farming.

Standard amount of work. In addition to the workday-unit system, the North Korean regime adopted a "minimum work-amount schedule" to punish lazy workers and afford incentive to harder workers. For example, the chairman of a collective must actively participate in field work at least fifty workdays in order to earn the stipulated workday rates. His subordinate managerial staff must do a minimum of seventy workdays in field work. The standard amount of work per day for livestock workers is shown in Table 7.

TABLE 6

COEFFICIENTS OF WORKDAY UNITS FOR MANAGERIAL WORKERS
AND FOREMEN OF WORK BRIGADES, NORTH KOREA

Managerial Workers

Size of Collective (number of households)	Chairman	Vice-Chairman, Chief Clerk, Agricultural Engineer	Chief Accountant, Agricultural Technician	Statistician, Bookkeeper
200 or less	1.10	1.00	0.95	0.80–0.85
201–400	1.13	1.03	1.00	0.85–0.90
401–600	1.17	1.07	1.05	0.90–0.95
601 and above	1.22	1.12	1.10	0.95–1.10

Foremen of Work Brigades

Size of Brigade (number of workers)	
60 or less	0.65–0.70
61 to 80	0.70–0.75
81 and above	0.75–0.80

Source: Same as Table 3.

TABLE 7

STANDARD OF WORK FOR LIVESTOCK WORKERS, NORTH KOREA

	Number of Animals To Be Tended Per Day
Dairy cows	4– 5 (head)
Calves	15– 20
Hogs (breeding)	13– 14
Hogs (fattening)	30– 35
Sheep	50– 60
Chickens, ducks	300–400

Source: Same as Table 3.

The distribution of harvests is made among the members of the collectives after all such deductions as production costs, taxes in kind, education costs, contributions to welfare, fines owing for failure to meet the target output are subtracted; a bonus up to 40 per cent of the output is added if the planned output is successfully met. Every work team must keep its daily, ten-day, and monthly records and, at the same time, be an independent accounting unit, whose balance sheet is used as the yardstick for material and other pecuniary rewards granted by the party.

The individual share is carried out on the basis of the following formula:

$$Ei = H \frac{\sum\limits_{j=1} \left(R_{ij} \frac{P_{ij}}{S_{ij}} \right) D_{ij}}{\sum\limits_{i=1} \sum\limits_{i=1} \left(R_{ij} \frac{P_{ij}}{S_{ij}} \right) D_{ij}}$$

Where Ei denotes the earning of the "i"th person for the
given season

H   stands for the total net harvests for the group as a
whole,

R_{ij} denotes the workday units of the "i"th person on the
the "j"th job,

P_{ij} stands the actual performance of the "i"th person on
the "j"th job,

S_{ij} refers to the standard amount of the work of the
"i"th person falling on the "j"th job,

D_{ij} is the discount rate, ranging from 0 to 1.00, depending
on the job performed by the "i"th person on the
"j"th job.

Thus, an individual's earning is a function of not only his own job
rating and the actual amount of work he performs but also of those of
other members. The amount and quality of work performed by one's
dependents (for example, schoolboys during holidays) is credited to the
parents' income.

Under this system, neither the farmers nor the collective leaders can
foresee their individual earnings until harvest time arrives and a series
of computations have been completed. Judging from the criticisms

TABLE 8

OBSERVATION OF INDIVIDUAL WEED CONTROL, NORTH KOREA

Activity Observed	Time of Day (Hour, Minutes)	Real Time Consumed (Minutes)	Number of P'yong[a] Completed
Observation begins	7:00		
Puts tilling machine to cow	7:10	10	
Cuts weed	9:50	160	785
Rests	10:05	15	
Cuts weed	12:10	125	340
Takes off clothes	12:15	5	
Cuts weed	13: -	45	215
Lunch hour	14: -	60	
Cleans tool	14:13	13	
Cuts weed	15:45	92	485
Drinks water	15:55	10	
Rests	16:10	15	
Cuts weed	17:30	80	395
Rests	17:40	10	
Cuts weed	18:45	65	350
Cleans tool	19: -	15	
Observation ends	19: -		
Total		720	2,570

[a] P'yong is equivalent to about 6 inches.
Source: Same as Table 3.

appearing in various sources, there are a great many complaints among farmers about lower shares and unfair distribution. The Communist incentive system poses a serious problem in making advance payments and in equalizing unequal shares between localities as well as between classes. It has also had a far-reaching impact on the consumption pattern, which has encouraged the farmer to eat more of whatever he produces.

Since the inception of the Seven-Year Plan, all the peasants have been herded into Soviet-style cooperatives, working twelve to fourteen hours per day under strict supervision and the self-criticism report system. A typical illustration of surveillance over the farmer's work can be found in the sample observation record shown in Table 8. In addition, every member is expected to present himself after supper to the evening class on Communist indoctrination and self-criticism. As for the individual incentive system, various prizes are offered to those who sacrifice their labor for the cause of communism and the collectivized farm. Those who show herolike workmanship are given Chollima work-team medals, titles, special rewards, and favors. However, self-sufficiency in foodstuffs, at least by 1963, was still far from a fact.

COMPARISON OF PRODUCTION EFFICIENCY

Regardless of the type of agrarian system adopted in an economy, the basic means of pursuing agricultural development are to increase not only the absolute factors of production, but also the productivity per unit of a given factor. Hence, a comparison of the production efficiency between the two different types of farm management is attempted here.

Characteristics of Various Inputs

One of the most striking differences in farm management is to be found in the typical size of the agricultural enterprise in the two areas. One is the family-unit small farm, and the other is the village-unit large-scale farm. The latter is expansionistic in regard to its form, although there is no evidence of maximum economic size. The intensification of farm management in large-scale agricultural production has not yet been proven successful. On the other hand, the family farm of South Korea has problems peculiar to the small farm, and has been highly intensified in its management.

Table 9 shows some of the characteristics of the farm inputs in the economies of South and North Korea during the period from 1960 to 1963. The table shows that North Korea's growth rates of land, labor, fertilizer, and mechanization were all greater than those for South Korea. More fertilizers and motor tillers in absolute amounts are being used for almost the same area of cultivated land, reflecting the fact that both upland and tidal land reclamation was actively pursued. In South Korea, the major source of farm power is draft cattle; about one half of all farm households have cattle—or at least one cow. On the other hand, it is reported that in the North there were forty-eight motor tillers per collective farm by 1963. It is significant that, despite such rapid mechanization, the growth index of labor employed on collective farms in North Korea increased only 3.4 per cent between 1960 and 1963.

TABLE 9
GROWTH INDICES OF TOTAL FARM INPUTS IN
SOUTH AND NORTH KOREA, 1963

Input	South	North
	(1960 = 100)	
Cultivated Land (hectares)		
Paddies	1,238 (101.8)	583 (114.3)
Upland fields	859 (104.1)	1,413 (100.7)
Total	2,097 (102.7)	1,996 (104.3)
Labor Force (thousand persons)	4,876 (108.8)	4,951 (103.4)
Fertilizer (thousand metric tons)	347 (132.4)	599 (195.1)
Motor Tiller (fifteen horsepower each)	450 (294.1)	18,002 (144.0)

Source: South Korea: Ministry of Agriculture and Forestry (M.A.F.), *Year Book of Agriculture and Forestry Statistics (1964, 1966)*; N.A.C.F., *Agricultural Year Book* (1961, 1964).
North Korea: Chosen Union Press Co., *One Korea Year Book (1965–1966)*, and Joseph S. Chung (ed.) *Patterns of Economic Development: Korea* (Detroit, Mich.: The Korea Research and Publication, Inc., 1966).

Table 10 shows some characteristics of farm-resource uses in North and South Korea. The regions have in common a predominantly grain-oriented structure, as revealed in the land-use pattern in the table. However, the proportion of rice production to cultivated land in the South is still much higher than in the North, although the latter's expansion rate seems much faster. In 1963, there was no significant difference between the two economies in man-year labor inputs per metric ton of grain product.

Comparison of Productivity

Because of limited data, a thorough investigation of the conditions of North Korean agriculture was found impossible. A comparison of production efficiency is attempted by computing partial productivity of

TABLE 10

COMPARISON OF LAND USE AND FARM INPUTS IN SOUTH AND NORTH KOREA

| | South Korea | | North Korea | |
	1960	1963	1960	1963
Land Use				
(per cent)				
Rice	37.6	36.5	18.1	21.5
Other grains	49.5	50.5	64.3	62.0
Potatoes	3.6	4.3	4.8	3.6
Others	9.3	8.7	12.8	12.9
Total	100.0	100.0	100.0	100.0
Proportion of wet paddy				
to total (per cent)	about 50		about 20	
Labor input per metric				
ton of grain (man-year)	1.623	1.178	1.307	1.138
Fertilizer input				
(per hectare)				
Paddies	n.a.	121	248	420
Upland	n.a.	101	126	272

Source: South Korea: Ministry of Agriculture and Forestry (M.A.F.), *Year Book of Agriculture and Forestry Statistics (1964–1966)*; N.A.C.F., *Agricultural Year Book* (1961, 1964). North Korea: Chosen Union Press Co., *One Korea Year Book (1965–1966)*; Joseph S. Chung (ed.) *Patterns of Economic Development: Korea* (Detroit, Mich.: The Korea Research and Publication, Inc., 1966).

such factors as labor and land only for the aggregated economy. Such partial productivity can be interpreted as one indicator of economic efficiency-performance. As far as data are available, the base year chosen for comparison was 1957, in which North Korean agriculture was virtually (about 95.6 per cent) collectivized, and both the South and North had relatively good crops. The most recent year for which North Korean data were available was 1963. But it must be borne in mind that the summer crop (barley) of South Korea was extremely poor due to bad weather.

Productivities of land and labor are presented in Tables 11 and 12. From Table 11, one can see that, as far as rice is concerned, the recent trend in the South is outdistancing that in the North, although there are some indications that the South had been lagging behind the North in earlier years.

In terms of total grains, including[20] barley, corn, and millet, the productivity per hectare in the South is somewhat higher than in the North. It is not difficult to find the reasons for this (besides the differences arising from different systems of farm management and incentives mentioned earlier): first, the proportion of double-crop production (40.4

[20] Owing to the lack of statistical breakdowns, no weighted or itemized productivities can be derived.

TABLE 11

COMPARISON OF LAND PRODUCTIVITY, SOUTH AND NORTH KOREA

South Korea	1957	1960	1963	1964
Rice				
Yield (thousand metric tons)	2,980	2,972	3,758	3,954
Paddy area (thousand hectares)	1,103	1,121	1,155	1,195
Yield per hectare (metric tons)	2.70	2.64	2.47	3.26
Other Food Grain				
Yield (thousand metric tons)	890	1,214	594	1,397
Cultivated land (thousand hectares)	805	814	852	1,111
Yield per hectare (metric tons)	0.45	1.48	.69	1.53
Total Food Grains				
Yield (thousand metric tons)	3,870	4,175	4,353	5,357
Cultivated land (thousand hectares)	1,994	2,010	2,078	2,160
Yield per hectare (metric tons)	1.93	2.07	2.10	2.47
North Korea				
Rice				
Yield (thousand metric tons)	1,593	1,535	2,050	--
Paddy area (thousand hectares)	461	512	634	--
Yield per hectare (metric tons)	3.46	2.99	3.24	
Other Food Grains				
Yield (thousand metric tons)	1,677	2,268	3,900	
Cultivated land (thousand hectares)	1,527	1,538	931	
Yield per hectare (metric tons)	1.08	1.48	1.46	--
Total Food Grains				
Yield (thousand metric tons)	3,270	3,803	4,350	
Cultivated land (thousand hectares)	1,988	1,861	2,212	
Yield per hectare (metric tons)	1.90	2.05	1.98	--

Source: South Korea: M.A.F., *Year Book of Agriculture and Forestry Statistics* (1960, 1965, 1966).
North Korea: Derived from Joint Publications Research Service (J.P.R.S.); 901-D, 16,611, 17,890, 21,631, and *One Korea Year Book (1964)*.

per cent in 1964) is much higher than North Korea's 20.0 per cent (in 1964), due, no doubt, to the more favorable southern climate. Secondly, intensity of land utilization is believed much higher in the South than in the North; this could be due to the fact that the ratio of cultivated to total available land was considerably higher for small-scale farms than large-scale farms in North Korea. Thirdly, as previously stated, the expansion of cultivated land in North Korea must have been too aggressive to sustain the trend of land-productivity enhancement. In sum, the productivity of land between South and North is not significantly different; if any, the South reveals a slightly better performance.

TABLE 12
AGRICULTURAL LABOR PRODUCTIVITY PER CAPITA

	1957	1960	1963	1964
South Korea				
Total grains	3,870	4,175	4,353	5,357
(thousand metric tons)				
Employed in agriculture	n.a.	6,775[a]	5,129	5,255
(thousand persons)				
Yield per capita		--	0.85	1.0
(metric tons)				
North Korea				
Total grains	3,270	3,803	4,350	--
(thousand metric tons)				
Members of cooperatives	n.a.	4,790	4,951	--
(thousand persons)				
Yield per capita	0.62	0.79	0.88	--
(metric tons)				

[a]This figure is inconsistent with those in the subsequent years due to a difference in the government survey methods.

Source: South Korea: M.A.F., *Year Book of Agriculture and Forestry Statistics* (1960, 1965, 1966).
North Korea: Derived from J.P.R.S.: 901-D, 16,611, 17,890, 21,631, and *One Korea Year Book (1964)*.

The comparison of the productivity–per capita of agricultural labor[21] between South and North Korea is shown in Table 12. Productivity per capita in the South is slightly less than that in the North. It is by no means intended here to substitute this measure for the productivity of labor input proper. Certainly the entire agricultural labor force in North Korea is compulsorily active and engaged under a highly bureaucratic system, whereas in the South there are fairly large numbers of rural laborers who are underemployed. Therefore, there is sufficient reason to believe that the true productivity–per labor in the South might be higher than that in the North. In 1960, in the North a labor-to-farming mobilization was carried out under the *"Chungsan-Ri* Movement," which suggests a severe shortage of labor in the agricultural economy. Some 13,000 white-collar laborers previously engaged in administrative work on collectivized farms were forced to become agricultural laborers and average workdays were increased from 310 per annum to 345.[22] On the other hand, the average South Korean farmer's work year is estimated to be about 200 days.

[21] Once again, neither detailed data by type of crop nor more precise unit of labor input are available.

[22] P. H. M. Jones, *Far Eastern Economic Review Handbook* (Hong Kong: Far Eastern Economic Review, 1961), p. 21.

CONCLUSION

In comparing any two economic systems, the criteria employed must involve the economic choices and the alternatives that are offered to people working under the system. The South Korean farming system, based on competitive capitalism, allows maximum choice in the form of a thousand and more different commodities and services, which can be produced without coercion.

The agrarian system adopted in North Korean agriculture, based on Marxism-Leninism, is a collective and totalitarian type, in which the state owns and controls all the factors of production, inclusive of human beings. In North Korea, perhaps, "freedom" cannot be purchased by any means of payment, simply because there is no such thing. With the completion of collectivization in North Korea in 1958, there were no longer individual free farmers but, instead, landless peasants. Moreover, since the *Chungsan-Ri* Movement, the go-back-to-the-farm movement, there has been a constant struggle to strengthen the collectivized way of farming through mass ideological indoctrination. One may admit that more farm machines and chemical fertilizers were used, and extensive enlargement of farm land took place in North Korea. With all these efforts, plus strong, one-man leadership for the past decade and a half, the North Korean agriculture has not yet reached the point of self-sufficiency. In the *Thesis* of 1964, Kim Il-Sung appealed to his people to increase the production of rice so as to improve the daily diet of the people, which is evidently poor, in both quality and quantity. Although the lack of data and the limited knowledge about North Korean agriculture make a more precise comparison between the two economies unfeasible, an estimate of the productivities of land and labor reveals that agricultural productivity in North Korea is not too impressive, despite the extensive changes, mechanization, controlled farm organizations, and complicated incentive systems.

In South Korea, too, many problems are yet to be solved. The small, but free, family-farm system has a bright future. The goal of self-sufficiency is now in sight. According to the South Korean Second Five Year Plan (1967–71), it is expected that South Korea's domestic rice production will be sufficient to meet its own needs by 1971.

YOUNG C. ZEON

Comment

In view of the paucity of data on North Korea, few serious attempts have been made at comparative and analytical studies of the two agricultural systems of Korea. Thus Professor Pak's study is welcomed and his contribution will no doubt enhance our understanding of both South and North Korea.

Professor Pak maintains that the land reform in South Korea was successful in bringing about disruption of traditional socio-economic and political structures. He points out that "land reform . . . was the most popular means for the rapid and revolutionary change in the economic, political, and social structure of South Korea." It may be correct to state that the land reform in South Korea brought about the disappearance of the established master-servant relationships between landlords and tenants, and averted to a certain extent Communist agitation and penetration in South Korea, but it is a moot point whether the disruptional reforms were followed by adequate economic policies to facilitate the cultivator's entrance into a market economy. The successful agrarian reform should include three factors, the disruption of traditional social structures, the establishment of new economic structures, and the adjustment of the existing economic system.

Professor Pak maintains that under the present state of economic and technical development in Korea the family-unit small farm is better suited than the village-unit, large-scale farm adopted in North Korea. Accordingly, he implies that under the Communist system individual initiative and desire to get ahead are suppressed and suffocated. A sounder agricultural development, he feels, can be better achieved by the capitalistic system, which guarantees individual free play and encourages individual initiative. At one point, he states: "Decisions regarding how, how much, and what to produce are all based on the individual farmer's initiative." Then again in the concluding section:

In comparing any two economic systems, the criteria employed must involve the economic choices and the alternatives that are offered to people working under the system. The South Korean farming system, based on competitive capitalism, allows maximum choice in the form of a thousand and more different commodities and services, which can be produced without coercion by free individual farmers.

Theoretically, this may be true—however, the realities of South Korean agricultural conditions do not seem to confirm Professor Pak's view. According to the *Statistics Yearbook* published by the Economic Planning Board, farm households holding 0.5 hectare or less in 1960 accounted for 43.9 per cent of the total. Together with those households holding less than one hectare they constituted 73.0 per cent of the total. Under such a fragmented farm system it is almost impossible to exercise individual initiative in deciding how, how much, and what to produce and to have economic choices and alternatives. It is generally recognized that crop output yield from an area of less than 0.5 hectare is not enough to support the owners themselves. They often find themselves with an extreme shortage of food in the early spring of the year. To continue farming they are impelled to borrow money. Such loans are not always used for farming, but are spent to obtain food. Unless the South Korean farmers can free themselves from this vicious circle, the improvement of their economic condition can hardly be expected.

In regard to North Korean farm organization, Professor Pak describes the work-brigade system, the work-team system, and the *Kun* Cooperative Farm Management Committee. He then rather summarily suggests some of the causes of the inefficiency of the large farm of North Korea. He gives three primary reasons: (1) Adverse topography and climate; (2) lack of revolutionary zeal by the participating farmers; (3) lack of investment in research and education. However, these reasons are not too convincing. Can Professor Pak reasonably assert that these reasons for inefficiency are rectified or eliminated under the family system? Surely, the first reason—topography and climate—can be applied in both cases. In regard to the second, does revolutionary zeal really matter under the constant surveillance that Professor Pak so aptly describes in his paper? In the third instance, can investment in research and education be accelerated with the very limited financial resources of the submarginal family-farm unit?

In comparing production efficiency, Professor Pak supplies comparative data on farm inputs such as cultivated land, labor, fertilizer, and motor tilling in addition to figures on productivity or output. Table 9 reveals some very interesting facts: in 1963 North Korea had less cultivated land than the South by 5 per cent, and 3 per cent less labor. In this same period the North used 173 per cent more fertilizer and 4,000 per cent more motor tillers than South Korea. Despite this overwhelming use of fertilizer and motor tillers in the North, Professor Pak indicates that the over-all productivity of South Korea appears to be somewhat higher.

The main reason for this discrepancy in productivity is attributed to the difference in the intensity of land utilization in South and North Korea. Professor Pak implies in this explanation of the discrepancy that family-unit small-scale farms under the free-enterprise system can bring about better results because individual farmers have freedom to exercise individual initiative. However, as long as those tilling less than one hectare constitute 73.0 per cent of total farm households, the farmers are not likely to be able to exercise individual initiative because they will be totally occupied in the struggle for survival.

Professor Pak points out that this situation in South Korea has been alleviated by governmental programs, particularly those of the National Agricultural Cooperative Federation. Although the Federation is undoubtedly a valuable organ in helping the farmers, it should also try to instill a cooperative spirit among them. Today, this cooperative federation presents an impression to the general public of a governmental agency attempting to act as a transmission belt, rather than as a genuinely cooperative institution acting in the interests of the farmers. In order to make it more independent from government control, for instance, the cooperative should not distribute fertilizer on behalf of the government but instead should adopt a joint-purchase system. If the cooperative wishes to function as a cooperative and survive in a capitalistic society, it not only must learn to compete fairly but also must win the competition.

WERNER KLATT

Successes and Failures
of Communist Farming:
Causes and Consequences

FIFTY YEARS OF SOVIET FARMING

In October, 1967, fifty years had elapsed since the first of the two great bloodbaths of this century came to an end and the first of the two world-shaking revolutions began. It seems therefore appropriate to devote the first section of this résumé to Russia. In five decades even a regime born of the most violent convulsion may be expected to come of age. The desire to gain a state of bourgeois respectability might well appall those who experienced their revolutionary upheaval less than twenty years ago, as did China, and those who are impatiently grooming themselves for the revolutions that are yet to come, e.g., countries in Asia, Africa, and Latin America. If some feel that Soviet action is dictated nowadays by reason rather than revolutionary zeal, there will be others who cannot readily forget the price that was paid in human suffering before conditions became tolerable for many, though by no means for the majority, of the Russian people. In the anniversary celebration there were few families in Russia who did not have someone sacrificed in the name of the revolution to lament.

The year 1967 was not only the fiftieth anniversary of the Bolshevik Revolution, it was also the fortieth anniversary of the adoption by the Fifteenth Congress of the Communist Party of the Soviet Union of the resolution that set in motion the collectivization of Russia's peasant farms and completed the liquidation of the kulaks. This is described in the official party history as equivalent in its consequences to the revolution of October, 1917. In its course the villagers were classified in a manner as crude as the statistics on which it was based. The confusion and demoralization caused by collectivization reached stupendous dimensions. By 1932 the procurement of grain from the farmers was more than twice as large as in 1927, although the harvest was a good deal smaller. By 1933, half the country's livestock had disappeared. The most moving, yet the most authentic, record of this operation and the hunger and purges and deportations it brought in its wake has been preserved in the files of the headquarters of the Communist Party at Smolensk, which were captured by the invading German army and later taken to the United States.[1] It is not to be wondered at that Stalin, when questioned by Churchill about this phase of Soviet history, described it as a struggle more difficult and more dangerous than that against Nazi Germany.

In view of this historical background it was appropriate that this conference should have had Professor Nove's account of the events that led to forcible collectivization of Soviet agriculture by the "Urals-Siberian Method" and to the extortionate levies on the Russian villages that made possible "primitive socialist accumulation" and industrialization at breakneck speed. Others may have told in greater detail the story of how "somewhere along the way ten million people had 'demographically' disappeared"; Professor Nove has done a service to this conference and its participants by having retold the story at this particular moment in history. No analysis of contemporary development can be considered complete without this flashback into the grim past.

The consequences of this operation have been recounted before.[2] On the eve of the Second World War hardly any land remained in private hands. The opposition of the peasants had been broken, large-scale deportations had taken place, and irreparable damage had been done to the farming industry. Even within the framework of the collectives the peasants continued to be treated as enemies of the state rather than as vital members of a new industrial society. They had every reason to feel outcasts. Twenty-five years after collectivization, at the time of Stalin's death, farming was where it had been in the days of the tsars. Admittedly, horses had been replaced by tractor power, thus freeing a large acreage formerly under fodder crops for the production of food. But even these modest results had been achieved only at great cost in men and animals.

[1] Merle Fainsod, *Smolensk under Soviet Rule* (Cambridge: Harvard University Press, 1958).
[2] W. Klatt, "How Soviet Farming Fails," *New Society* (London), August 25, 1966.

The results were particularly disappointing in livestock farming. The number of productive livestock was one-tenth smaller than before collectivization was introduced. In the meantime, the human population had grown by almost one fifth. Milk yields and carcass weights, like grain yields, had remained unchanged. As a result, the nation's diet was smaller in volume and poorer in composition at the time of Stalin's death than it had been a quarter of a century earlier. The farming community was much worse off than it had been before collectivization began. Whereas industrial production had recovered from the devastation caused by the German invasion, the supply of farm products continued to lag behind. The cleavage created when forced industrialization and collectivization had driven the two sections of Soviet society apart in the early thirties had widened rather than narrowed.

SOVIET APPROACH TO AGRICULTURE

Throughout Soviet history, the approach to the farming industry has been marked by a much greater lack of rationality than the approach to any other sector of the Soviet economy. This lack of rationality may be explained to some extent by the very nature of agriculture, which has led to a consistently unhappy handling by the Marxist school and its followers. It would be wrong to suggest that agriculture follows patterns of behavior that are different from those observed in other spheres of human endeavor, but it has certain unique characteristics.

Farming, unlike industry, has to accept space and weather as limiting factors. In normal conditions the cost of haulage is more decisive in determining farm sizes than certain economies of scale, but in Soviet Russia the amalgamation of farms has been carried out without regard to the cost of transportation. As to the effect of weather and distance on labor, the farmhand, who ordinarily works without a roof over his head and without a superior at close quarters, operates with a measure of freedom of decision that is most unusual in the case of the industrial worker of corresponding grade. The larger the farm, the greater the need to delegate decisions to the individual. Under Communist conditions the tendency is generally to do the opposite. Also, in agriculture —unlike industry—the producer, besides being a consumer of his own product, is usually a processor of finished products also. He is therefore able to alter the pattern of production, utilization, and marketing in many ways, thus evading public controls far more effectively than the industrial producer, who rarely is a consumer of his product. Thus in agriculture, far more than in industry, a relationship of mutual trust is needed between the producer and the state. None of these characteristics of the farming industry has been taken properly into account during the last fifty years of Soviet agricultural history. It seems doubtful whether they are fully understood in Russia even today. If they were, the conclusion would be inescapable that the existing system has to be dismantled rather than amended. The political consequences of such a recognition would be momentous indeed.

In the final analysis, the misunderstandings about the role of agriculture in modern industrial society and the resulting failures of agricultural policy throughout five decades of Soviet history can be traced to a doctrinal concept that was based on a methodological error. The Marxist school and its followers have always insisted that small-scale farming, as they defined it, was economically backward, and that the peasant-cultivator was therefore bound to be tied to politically reactionary forces hostile to the industrial working class. Had they measured farm performance in the same way as production in industry, they might have discovered that farms that are small in terms of acreage can be large, modern, and progressive enterprises when considered in terms of capital input and in output per man. In other words, it is the degree of intensity that matters and not the acreage—and any economies of scale have to be seen within this context.

The interrelationship between the size of the farms, according to acreage, and the intensity of farming, in terms of input and output, has never really been understood by any of the Soviet leaders. As a result of this methodological error, they have found themselves throughout their history making enemies of the owners of large farms, antagonizing at the same time the small men in the villages. The Marxist school has never differentiated between the various forms of farm performance and has therefore never gained an understanding of the role of the intensively farming owner-occupier or tenant in a modern industrial setting. Whereas the Marxist school has supported developments in industry that are not altogether different from those in capitalist society, their agrarian concept flies in the face of all historical precedent. It is not surprising that this has created very special problems. The lack of understanding of the agrarian question arises in one of those frequently quoted statements by Lenin on the subject:

The peasant as a toiler gravitates towards socialism and prefers the dictatorship of the workers to the dictatorship of the bourgeoisie. The peasant as a seller of grain gravitates towards the bourgeoisie, to free trade, i.e., back to the "habitual" old "primordial" capitalism of former days.[3]

In fact, the peasant-cultivator does nothing of the sort. Lenin's concept of the peasant's role in Russian society was little more accurate than the romantic picture of the "naively socialist" villager that the *narodniki* had.

The Russian intellectuals, whether Social Revolutionaries or Bolsheviks, were strangely ignorant of the lives and views of four fifths of their fellow countrymen. But while the Social Revolutionaries had the utopian vision of a socialist society created on the basis of rural communes, Lenin was primarily concerned with the revolution itself, which after 1905 he saw in two stages. At the stage of the bourgeois-democratic revolution he saw the peasantry tied to the industrial proletariat. Thereafter he expected the peasants to renounce the revolution and to desert the industrial proletariat. At that stage Lenin saw the Bolsheviks dividing the farming community against itself, using the poor villagers against the rich peasants. This dual task of the proletariat was regarded by Lenin as the essence of the Bolshevik program. He never considered the possibility of a gradual continuation of the process that had set in with the Stolypin reforms. He consequently never believed in a genuine, lasting alliance of interests between the producers and consumers of the daily necessities of the nation. Thus the conflict of interests between the minority of industrial workers and the majority of villagers stood godmother to the Bolshevik Revolution of 1917. This was very nearly strangled by its own contradictions.

The contradictions exist to this day. Indeed, some of the oddities of present-day farming in Russia—such as the capital-starvation, the far-from-optimum composition of factors employed in Soviet agriculture, and the dualism of production and profit maximization—that Dr. Schinke has put before us in his paper would be inexplicable without a knowledge of the twenties and thirties.

ANOMALIES AND IRRATIONALITIES

There have been many attempts to rectify the situation and to do away with anomalies and irrationalities. In particular, the ten years of Khrushchev's rule were taken up with attempts to remedy the situation. With all his faults he was a great innovator. In spite of his involvement in Stalin's brutalities, he was willing to break with some of the practices

[3] V. T. Lenin, *Collected Works* (Moscow: State Publishing House, 1932), Vol. XXIV.

of the great tyrant. But he was a victim of his own past. He never authorized the rehabilitation of any of the revolutionary leaders of the late twenties and early thirties—nor have his successors so far done so, for that matter. In the technical and administrative field there was rarely a month in the days of Khrushchev without a major party-political gathering or a far-reaching reform. In spite of all his innovations, at the end of his reign the pattern of farming, farm productivity, and food consumption had hardly changed.[4]

The ten years of agricultural policy under Khrushchev yielded an increased, though precarious, supply of food and fodder, without approaching the ambitious targets set for 1965. The diet, still overburdened with carbohydrates and short of animal proteins, continued to lag behind that of the United States—which for ten years provided the yardstick of things supposedly within reach of the Soviet Union. The distance between the two countries was as great in output as in consumption. At the end of Khrushchev's reign the farming industry of the United States produced, with one fifth of the Soviet farm labor force on an area equal to two thirds of the Soviet sown acreage, a volume of farm products approximately three fifths larger than that of the Soviet Union. Yields of all major crops, as well as milk yields and carcass weights, were at best half as much in the Soviet Union as those attained in the United States. Productive livestock per capita of the Soviet population was only four fifths of the corresponding figure in the United States. Russia's lag was particularly great with regard to the labor requirements in agriculture. In Khrushchev's own assessment, the Soviet Union needed five to seven times as much labor in arable farming as the United States, and up to sixteen times as much in livestock farming. At the end of Khrushchev's rule the pattern of food production and consumption was still that of a backward country. Yet, in the industrial and military sphere Russia could legitimately claim to be the second most powerful nation in the world. There is no reason to think that this dichotomy will disappear as a result of the policy of consolidation, following a temporary retrenchment, on which Khrushchev's successors have embarked since 1964.

Approximately three fifths of the country's arable acreage is still in grains, and half the food intake is consumed in the form of bread, flour, and cereals. Almost half the population lives in villages, and at least a third of the labor force is employed in agriculture. Out of the season there is still much idleness in the countryside, while at the peak of the

[4] W. Klatt, "Soviet Agriculture," *Analyse et Prévision*, Vol. III, No. 6, June, 1967.

season students have to be rushed to the land—no longer virgin—to harvest its often meager grain crop. The rhythm of life in the country is still master of the capital. The patterns of food and farming resemble those of the underdeveloped parts of the world rather than those of the highly industrialized nations among which Russia now ranks—at some distance—behind the United States.

The ingredients of the farm-policy measures taken by the new leadership under Brezhnev and Kosygin are already well known and need not be recapitulated here. In brief, many of the new measures amounted to a continuation of Khrushchev's policies—by different means. Others were of an altogether different nature. The gradual introduction of a guaranteed monthly pay for members of collectives, at rates corresponding to those enforced on state farms, which was announced at the Twenty-Third Party Congress in the spring of 1966, was the most important innovation of the new leadership. If this promise is kept, it ought to remove one of the chief grievances of the collective farmers. For forty years they have not been granted any financial reward for taking the kind of risks for which farmers in the Western world feel entitled to claim a return. Nor have they been eligible for a minimum wage, as are workers on state farms and in industry. They have thus had the worst of both worlds. At long last this is to be put right—more than fifty years after the revolution.

One major promise has yet to be fulfilled. The Third Kolkhoz Congress, which is to pass a new farm charter in place of the outdated one of 1935, has still not taken place. It was first scheduled for early 1959, but it was repeatedly—and even recently—postponed for reasons not stated. As the commission charged with drafting the new agricultural model charter has not yet released its findings, the results of this conference cannot be anticipated with any degree of certainty. If the liberal critics of present farm policies were to gain ground, substantial improvements in the structure and performance of agriculture could result. If the traditionalists hold their ground—and this seems more probable in present conditions—no startling changes are likely to occur.

In the meantime the air is full of proposals from various sources as to ways and means of improving the performance of the farm industry, of increasing the standard of living of the rural community, and of integrating it with the rest of Soviet society. So far agriculture has been largely excluded from the structural changes that have been introduced, experimentally and on a limited scale, in the industrial sphere. The new leaders, like their predecessors, have yet shown no sign of wishing to interfere with the structure of the farm industry or the pattern of farm operations. This unwillingness to introduce basic changes has not prevented various authors from putting forward more or less drastic proposals, but nobody has yet succeeded in challenging effectively the basic concepts that underlie Soviet farm policy.

Russia is entering a period charged with emotion,* and an over-generous gesture could damage beyond repair the sluices of carefully controlled public opinion and private sentiment. Not only heroic achievements were remembered in October, 1967; when the flags fluttered over the platforms from which the achievements of five decades were celebrated, all too many of the demonstrating young men and women there were unable to find the graves of their fathers on which to place flowers.

For the first time in a quarter of a century the Soviet government has issued industrial wage data, without which it is difficult to estimate the portion of the industrial worker's income that is spent on food. This ratio serves as a useful rod against which to measure the likelihood of any improvement in the diet during the period under review. Approximately one half of the average industrial working family's income is spent on food.[5] This sets a rather severe limit to the prospect of a substantially improved diet at a time when the propensity to purchase industrial durables is great and the likelihood of retail prices and retail price ratios changing in favor of foodstuffs is minimal.

The latest information from Soviet sources relates to the level of consumption of certain selected foodstuffs. Per capita consumption figures are given for five foodstuffs, i.e., grains and pulses, potatoes, meat and animal fats, milk and milk products, and eggs. No information is given on the level of consumption of sugar, fish, fruit and vegetables, and vegetable fats. The items listed account only for approximately 80 per cent of the total daily food intake. As they add up to 2,400 calories and the missing items can be estimated with a reasonable degree of certainty, the total nutritive value of the Russian diet would seem to amount at present to no more than 3,000 calories. Grains and potatoes, the two main sources of carbohydrates, seem to supply three fifths of the total intake. Human requirements amount to approximately forty-five million tons, almost half of which is needed in the rural areas rather than by urban consumers. Even allowing for the additional require-

---

* The author here was referring to the 1967 celebration of the 50th Anniversary of the Bolshevik Revolution (Ed. Note).

[5] *Ibid.*

ments of industry and of the food-deficit countries of the Communist bloc, it is difficult to see for what reasons the Soviet authorities insist on an annual procurement and delivery target of over fifty-five million tons. This goal implies that all grain, including the amount consumed by the farm population, passes through state-controlled channels. This hardly seems a necessary procedure. Nor would it seem desirable in a country that is still short of country roads, storage space, and administrative skill. There is reason to suspect that at least some of the grain recorded as "procured" merely moves on paper and not in reality. Even so, the actual movements seem unnecessarily large.

In animal farming, a decline in hog numbers, both for the hog industry as a whole and in the private sector in particular, deserves to be recorded. On January 1, 1966, the hog population was registered at over eighteen million, or one-quarter larger than twelve months earlier. The members of collectives and other private hog breeders had clearly drawn their own conclusions from Brezhnev's announcements of March, 1965. Instead of taking advantage of the bonus paid for grain deliveries above the target quota, they had chosen to retain as much grain as possible. Thus in a year in which the grain harvest was low, farm retentions increased while deliveries declined sharply, thus forcing the government to augment domestic supplies through grain purchases abroad. The farmers' reaction to the price changes of 1965 was not dissimilar to that observed twelve years earlier when the increase of meat prices caused a run on the country's grain supplies and thus a shortage that led to the virgin land campaign. The decline in January, 1967, in total hog numbers, particularly in the private sector, suggests that meanwhile local authorities had persuaded farmers to accept the above-quota grain bonus to collective farms in place of the private income, earned in 1965, from turning grain into pork.

The bumper grain crop of 1966 has relieved the Soviet leaders of the need for imports, which in the two bad seasons of 1963/64 and 1965/66 cost the country a total outlay of almost two thousand million dollars in foreign exchange. Against this, the purchase—at special prices—of twenty million tons of grain over and above the obligatory delivery target probably cost the exchequer in 1966/67 over two thousand million rubles, equivalent to 2 per cent of the national budget. In an attempt to recoup some of the cost of the grain bonus, the exchequer may well urge state farms and collectives to increase their own contributions to the farm investment program. Taking the record of farm investment into account, the planned increase in gross farm output by

4 per cent during the current year seems to be the most that can be expected in normal conditions. Looking further into the future, the prospects of fulfilling the moderate farm targets of the current five-year plan by 1970 have improved as a result of the good start in the first year of the plan period. The present Soviet leadership has wisely based its plan targets in agriculture on five-year averages, but the apparent statistical manipulation in the first year of rule by the new leadership may well prove a disservice to their ultimate record of achievements in this sphere.

Present expectations are unlikely to require any drastic amendments, barring any far-reaching resolutions of the forthcoming Third Kolkhoz Congress. The plan anticipates an increase, in five years, of 25 per cent over the level achieved in the preceding five-year period. This is probably the most that can be expected. The output of the farm industry could increase by as much as 30 per cent in the case of exceptionally favorable weather, but the increase could be as little as 15 per cent in adverse circumstances.

THE EAST EUROPEAN SCENE

If an undue amount of time and space has been devoted to the Soviet scene, this seemed justified in the light of its significance for the Communist bloc as a whole, by the interest that the participants of this conference take in the record of food and farming in Russia, and by the incidence of the fiftieth anniversary of the Soviet Revolution. But there are other issues with which we have concerned ourselves. As for Eastern Europe, some countries in the area have been particularly noted for their readiness to experiment. Contrary to the Soviet Union, they still have men aware of those alternatives that were lost in Russia in the morass of collectivization and that have had to be rediscovered as if they had never been practiced anywhere in the world. Professor Karcz has covered the changes in the planning mechanism and the distortions, still in existence in spite of these changes, in prices and price relation— a subject often badly neglected by both Communist economists and their critics. In spite of a process of "partial decompression," in particular in spite of changes in both planning techniques and price fixing, in Professor Karcz's words, "the ship of socialist agriculture still faces some heavy seas." The conflict of interests between "above-enterprise agencies" and individual farm management remains strong because of the impossibility of bringing into line marginal social cost and the corresponding marginal social benefit. The absence of explicit rental and capital charges must bear part of the blame for continuous distortions in the pattern of cropping and marketing. If the implementation of farm reforms meets almost insurmountable hurdles in a country as receptive to change as Czechoslovakia, one can imagine how great they must be elsewhere in the Communist world.

FARMING IN MAINLAND CHINA

So much for the European scene. As for the Communist parts of Asia, China's agriculture has been stagnating for the last eight or nine years. A quantitative appraisal of the kind we have been able to give in the case of the Soviet Union can unfortunately not be offered, with anything like the same degree of firmness, for the mainland of China. None of the data on which an assessment of the performance of farming is normally based are available in the case of Mainland China. No absolute figures on planned and actual production of farm products have been released since 1960, and those available for 1958 and 1959 are known to be faulty in the extreme. The last reasonably reliable information thus dates back to 1957, the final year of the First Five-Year Plan. With the help of input-output tables, like those presented by Professor Tang, the official Chinese claims for the period of the first plan can be checked. Although annual variations due to changing natural conditions tend to be small in large countries, the interference by men during the periods of land reform, collectivization, the Great Leap Forward, and the Proletarian Cultural Revolution has brought a good deal of instability into China's farm production and food supply.

As Mr. Kuo's paper shows, farm input has been haphazard and amateurish, and the expectation of substantial returns from these efforts has been premature and overoptimistic. Caution is therefore required when the performance during the coming decade is under consideration, as Professor Ishikawa's contribution to the proceedings of this conference showed all too clearly. Lawrence Lau rightly points out in his historical analysis of work and leisure in Chinese village society that consumption, savings, investment, and output are interrelated aspects that deserve to be examined simultaneously. This is as true of the past record as of any projection into the future.

As for the basis on which any assessment of current and future farm performance must rest, the last reasonably reliable estimate of grain production goes back to 1957, the last year before the Great Leap Forward, when it was given officially as 185 million tons. This figure can be taken as a yardstick by which to measure all later harvests: planned, claimed, or achieved. The official record of the grain harvest of 1958—by all accounts a bumper crop—was greatly exaggerated when the statistical services lost all control to local officials and party enthusiasts. Since then no harvest estimates have been published, but at the end of 1964 Chou En-lai said that the grain crop had reached the level of "high yielding years of the past." It was probably somewhat above that of 1957, but below that of 1958, i.e., perhaps 190 million tons. The next year was less favorable and 1966 was less favorable still. The official claim of a bumper harvest in 1966 can be dismissed as unrealistic in view of prolonged droughts that hit many parts of the country "with an intensity rarely seen in history." The meteorological records compiled in Hong Kong tend to confirm this account. The grain crop of 1966 then was hardly more than 180 million tons.

Leaving the vagaries of nature aside, it is unlikely that the 1967 harvest yielded substantially more than in 1957, i.e., 185 million tons. Crops other than grain were probably not substantially better than ten years ago either—with the possible exception of vegetables, pork, and poultry, the foodstuffs produced on cultivators' private plots and marketed outside the channels under government control. This means that within ten years China's farming has made practically no progress. As the input of labor and capital on the land has probably increased by a quarter since 1957, there must have been a significant decline in the productivity of labor on the farms.

In view of this state of affairs, the question of the size of the population is of more than academic interest. A population of seven hundred million seems to me the most likely figure. Any higher estimate does not appear to tally with estimated available food supplies.[6] Allowing for seed, feed, waste, and net trade, the present supply of grain and potatoes (given in Chinese statistics in terms of grain equivalent) is unlikely to provide more than 1,650 calories per capita per day. If the nutritive value of nongrain foods is added, the total daily intake will hardly account for more than 2,100 calories. This is 5 per cent less than was available at the time of the Japanese invasion of China in 1931, as estimated by the Food and Agriculture Organization of the United Nations. Barring major changes in the natural and political climate of the country, there is no reason to expect a significant change between 1967 and 1970, the last year of the current five-year plan period. If there were small improvements in domestic supplies, imports of grain would

[6] W. Klatt, "The Economy of China," *Analyse et Prévision*, Vol. III, No. 6, June, 1967.

probably cease. While a diet of 2,100 calories is far from ample, it is sufficient to keep the population at work—provided, of course, that the distribution system continues to function normally. In the course of the Cultural Revolution it has been disrupted considerably in some of the deficit areas of the country.

It is worth remembering that in 1967 the defunct twelve-year plan for agriculture was supposed to yield an output of almost 450 million tons of grain—against a probable crop of 185 million tons. The ambitious targets of this plan were to be achieved as the result of simultaneous improvements over a wide field, resulting from the use of fertilizers and the control of irrigation water, from mechanization, land reclamation, high-quality seeds, pest controls, and from multiple cropping. The results were expected to accrue from the cumulative effect of these measures. In fact, these measures should have been treated as interdependent.

Early in 1960 Li Fu-chun, the chairman of the State Planning Commission, gave the farming industry pride of place in economic planning and in investment policy. Agriculture was to be treated as "the foundation" of the economy, and thus to rank ahead of the industrial sectors concerned with the output of both consumer and producer goods. The permission given to cultivators to engage in "side-line production" on their private plots and to sell their produce in markets free from government control has had a salutary effect on the composition of the diet, though the impact on the volume of food produced has been small.

CHINA'S UNTAPPED AGRICULTURAL RESERVES

China's agriculture has, of course, some substantial untapped reserves, but as long as fertilizer supplies are only large enough to meet part of the needs of such commercial crops as oilseeds, cotton, and tobacco, the shortages in basic foodstuffs are bound to remain. At present less than ten kilos of plant nutrients contained in commercial fertilizers are available per hectare of arable land (nine pounds per acre). In Britain more than twenty times as much commercial fertilizer is used, and in Japan it is almost forty times as much. No sizable quantities of fertilizers and other farm requisites that are essential for raising crop yields are likely to become available for grain before 1970. Present supplies are low and fertilizer plants take five years to get into production. Farm mechanization is still in its infancy. Some 100,000 tractor units (in terms of 15 h.p.) equal to 50,000 actual tractors are now available in China. This compares with ten times the number of tractors available in Britain on an acreage that is approximately one fifteenth of that in China. Mechanized irrigation facilities, though much improved since 1957, also fall far behind actual need. At present each horse power of pumping equipment has to cope with fifty acres of cultivated land.

As to the role of farming within the national economy, in spite of a shift of emphasis in favor of agriculture, the share of the farming industry in the national aggregate has probably changed relatively little. It is likely to absorb two thirds of the labor force, but to produce somewhat less than one third of the total product of the nation. The use of the gross domestic product may well have undergone some changes. It seems probable that personal consumption was curtailed during the years of the mad rush and the recovery that followed it, while the gross domestic expenditure devoted to government consumption and government-controlled communal services is likely to have increased proportionately. No more than broad outlines can be given, but these may serve to indicate certain trends that seem to have emerged from the dislocations caused in past years.

As China is—once more—in the throes of an upheaval in which, in the Chinese phrase, politics have taken command over economics, it would be presumptuous to look beyond the immediate future. If the state of affairs as it existed prior to the Proletarian Cultural Revolution could be restored speedily, a modest improvement of farm output and food consumption might be expected during the current five-year plan period. The over-all rate of growth will, of course, be affected to a considerable extent by the performance of agriculture, which has to supply not only food and agricultural raw materials for the rural and urban population, but also the financial means of "primitive accumulation" without which industrialization cannot proceed. For the time being, nature rather than man determines the level of farm production. Few farm requisites that are capable of overcoming the effects of natural hazards and of increasing the yields of the main crops are likely to become available before 1970. Thus the growth rate of the farming industry may not exceed that of the population; it may even lag behind it. In these circumstances gross domestic product and expenditure are unlikely to rise by more than one third during the period of the current plan, or by an average of 5 1/2 to 6 per cent per annum. This would correspond to the rate of performance attained during the first plan.

All this presupposes a speedy return to stability in domestic and foreign relations, an unlikely prospect at present. If the conditions of life and work remain disrupted for a year or more—as they were during and after the Great Leap Forward—the consequences might even be more serious than they were then. In that case, not only might China's industry lose the momentum regained recently, but the population might suffer even more serious hardships than those of eight years ago. It might even have to go to war. Periods of stagnation and retreat under conditions of internal and external warfare have not been unknown in the fifty years of Communist history. If it were to be China's fate to experience what Russia had to endure in the years from 1928 to 1944, the increase of the population might provide the only growth rate of the nation, and even that might disappear.

COMPARING COMMUNIST AND NON-COMMUNIST FARMING

Originally we had hoped to gain, from a comparison of comparable Communist and non-Communist farm entities, a yardstick with which to measure the degree of success or failure of Communist farm policies, as well as their causes and consequences. To some extent the congressional reports on the economy of the Soviet Union have provided this. But the expansion planned for this conference, of the comparisons between the Soviet Union and the United States, as given in several volumes of the congressional reports, and between East and West European farming, as contained in the paper by Maurice Ernst (Part IV of Congressional Report for 1966) has not materialized.

In his paper on the agrarian problem in a divided Germany, Professor Merkel has wisely drawn attention to the difficulties that are encountered in any comparison between entities that by their very nature may not lend themselves to such a treatment. Ki Hyuk Pak has similarly stressed the difficulties inherent in any such comparison. The comparison between North and South Korea might well yield different results, if figures for the net farm product rather than that of the gross product were used.

It remains for me to say a few words about the Communist pattern of agriculture and farm policy as a model for developing, preindustrial societies. Professor Schiller has rightly drawn attention to the fact that the distinction between Communist and non-Communist forms of farming amounts to an oversimplification. Following this argument, one may go so far as to say that there is not only a third, underdeveloped world, but that in fact the Communist as well as the non-Communist worlds harbor both highly industrialized societies, in which agriculture has lost much of its former significance, and developing, preindustrial societies, in which farming dominates all else and urban life is determined by the seasonal rhythm of the villages. In this respect, as in others, the agricultural economy of Russia had better be compared with that of the United States, and that of Eastern Europe with the corresponding conditions in Western Europe. Against this, China's agricultural scene is much closer to that of other preindustrial countries in Asia than to any of the Communist-controlled areas in Europe. As several contributors to this conference have suggested, the temptation is great to consider the experiences of Japan and Taiwan rather than those of Mainland China as suitable elsewhere in Asia.

It would be presumptuous to try and generalize in the concluding remarks of this conference about the applicability of the Communist pattern of agriculture and farm policy to areas outside the Communist political orbit. The papers by Professor Merkel and Dr. Hsieh are not encouraging in this respect. At the same time I seem to have detected a certain indecision in some of the discussions. A clear definition of the functions of agriculture in modern society and a recognition of the existence of different stages of agricultural development, as they were discussed in the first session of this conference, are bound to lead to a less charitable interpretation of apparent advantages within the Communist pattern than were implied in some of the papers under discussion. In particular, no ambiguity should be allowed to remain after this conference about the significance of different farm sizes at different stages of agricultural development. As Professor Schiller has pointed out, the advantages of economies of scale are less significant in agriculture than the Communist concept tries to make us believe.

FURTHER RESEARCH

With this remark, we return to where we began during the first session of this conference, at which its purpose was mapped out by Professor Wittfogel in his introductory exposition on the comparative approach to Communist and non-Communist agrarian systems. As long ago as 1930, Wittfogel presented to the University of Frankfurt a doctor's thesis of nearly two hundred pages under the title "The Economic Significance of China's Agricultural and Industrial Productive Forces." Since then he has spent the best part of a lifetime on further studies of the "productive advantages of China's hydraulic agriculture and the bureaucratic despotism inherent in the agrohydraulic system." His book, *Oriental Despotism*,[7] published ten years ago, will have been

[7] Karl A. Wittfogel, *Oriental Despotism: A Comparative Study of Total Power* (New Haven and London: Yale University Press, 1963).

read by all those interested in the topics discussed at this conference.

It seems appropriate to recapitulate some of the essentials that emerged from the discussion of Professor Wittfogel's paper and without which comparative studies of various agrarian systems cannot succeed. First of all, without a thorough knowledge of the chief characteristics of farming, major errors such as those committed by Marxist as well as by Populist theoreticians will recur. To be unable to distinguish one end of a cow from the other is a weakness of our professional background that had better be eliminated instead of being perpetuated. Secondly, an understanding of Communist agriculture and farm policy requires a thorough study of the writings of the Marxist school—from Marx to Mao. Without this grounding it is impossible to grasp the doctrinal dilemma from which Communist regimes have been unable—and are likely to remain unable—to extricate themselves. Lastly, the validity of the Communist agrarian concept and the degree of success and failure of Communist farm policy can best be tested by way of a comparative approach to Communist and non-Communist systems. A broad area of research into this specific aspect of our sphere of interest lies wide open.

This conference has pointed to a number of subjects that warrant further examination. As I see it, there are: First: general comparative studies of farm systems in the Soviet Union and the United States; in Mainland China and India; and in Mainland China and Japan. Secondly: specific studies of farm management; cost and return; output and input (in particular food, feed, and plant nutrient balances) —in Communist and non-Communist countries. Lastly: case studies of agrarian microorganisms somewhat akin to such studies of individual farming communities as those undertaken by Martin C. Yang and Jan Myrdal in Chinese villages, and by S. C. Dube and Oscar Lewis in Indian villages. Dr. Ueno of Tokyo University has presented a paper of this kind to this conference. Though we are near the end of our conference, we are still a long way away from the end of the road of our researches.

Index

Abramov, F., 83
Achilles' heel of Soviet agriculture, 4, 24–25, 62
Afghanistan, state farm in, 243
Agrarian Question, The (Die Agrarfrage), 16, 17, 28, 29
Agrarian systems: Communist and non-Communist, 3–35; North and South Korea compared, 436–58. *See* Agriculture; Adam Smith; *Aziatchina;* Land reform; Oriental despotism
Agricultural producers' cooperatives (China) 37, 38, 39, 43, 98, 251, 310–13
Agricultural production cooperatives. *See* East Germany, Agriculture
Agriculture: labor intensive, 5; labor extensive, 5; hydraulic, 7–9, 35–36, 38–41, 45–47; nature of, 12–16, 65–67; contribution to initial capital formation, 233–34
Algeria, and nationalization of farms, 243–44
Anhwei: canal network, 255; fertilizer production, 257
Anti-Dühring, 15
Armenia, collectivization, 87
Artel. *See* Soviet Union, Collective farms
Association for the joint cultivation of the land. *See* TOZ
Australia, 6
Azerbaidzhan S.S.R., sovkhozy, 124–25, 129
Aziatchina, 20

Babeuf, F., 57
Baltic Republics: agricultural areas, 113; energy available, 113; labor force, 113; natural pasture, 113; sovkhozy, 113, 115; tilled land, 113; rural households, 129
Bauer, Otto, 67
Belorussia: collectivization, 89, 99; agricultural area, 113, 115, 135; energy available, 113, 115, 135; labor force, 113, 135, 136; natural pasture, 113; sovkhozy, 113, 116, 117, 120; tilled land, 113; livestock, 115, 135; sown area, 115, 135; kolkhozy, 135
Bolshevik Revolution, 9, 63, 462
Bolsheviks, 20, 35
Brezhnev, L. I., 167, 235 467, 470
Brigades (Russia), 32, 49, 50
Buck, J. Lossing: on Communist Chinese statistics, 41; multiple cropping index for China, 259; single aggregate input index for China, 286; on labor shortages, 315
Bukharin, Nikolai, 72, 74–76

Bulgaria: new economic policies, 178–80; planning methods, 179–81, 182, 189–91; collective farm autonomy, 181; decision making, 181, 182, 188; income distribution, 181–82; quotas, 183–86, 188; above-enterprise agencies, 185–89; technical improvements, 189; agricultural specialization, 191; price and procurement system, 193–99
Burma, 232, 244

Canada, agricultural productivity, 4, 59
Capital investment: state agriculture, 143; collective agriculture, 143
Central Asia: collectivization, 87, 91; agricultural area, 113, 114, 133; energy available, 113, 114, 133; labor force, 113, 133, 136; natural pasture, 113; sovkhozy, 113, 115, 116; tilled land, 113; sown area, 114, 133; livestock, 114, 133; households, 129; tractor gangs, 239
Central Black Earth: collectivization, 82, 91; agricultural areas, 113; energy available, 113; labor force, 113; natural pasture, 113; sovkhozy, 113; tilled land, 113
Central Committee Plenum, Russia; April, 1928, 74; July, 1928, 75; November, 1928, 75; April, 1929, 76; March, 1965, 246
Central union of consumer cooperatives (*Tsentrosoiuz*), 168
Ceylon, 231, 382
China, People's Republic of: Great Leap Forward, 46–49, 66, 251, 254, 256, 259, 265, 267, 268, 272, 281, 282, 284, 291, 293, 294, 297, 300, 303, 304, 358 n., 472, 476; Great Retreat, 49–51; collectivization, 98; land reform law, 250; First Five-Year Plan, 250, 251, 257, 262, 272, 283, 288–94, 302, 352, 361, 362, 376, 472; Second Five-Year Plan, 250, 251, 256; Third Five-Year Plan, 250–51, 272, 362; economic recovery of, 251; National Program for Agricultural Development, 1956–67, 251, 253, 256, 268–69, 277; production of chemical fertilizer, 256–58, 273, 300; Second National People's Congress, 269; State Scientific and Technological Commission, 272; population growth, 282, 473; economic growth, 282, 378; mentioned, 98, 99
—Agriculture: Stalin's influence on, 36; decision to collectivize, 37–38; expansion

479

of irrigation, 38–40, 41–42, 45–47, 254–55, 275–76; plant protection, 40, 266– 67; sown areas, 40; output, 41, 42, 282, 283–88, 300, 346, 352, 353, 356, 360; labor shortage, 44, 45, 47, 53–54, 315; communes, 47–50, 313–14, 365, 379; crisis in, 48, 270, 347, 355, 377–79; private plots, 49, 52; size of units, 50–52; productivity, 53, 259–60, 268, 298, 299, 303, 319, 320, 324, 326, 380; peasant response to changes, 56; Mao's projected transformation, 250–53, 298; grain regions, 251–53; socialization, 251; yields, 251–53, 260, 268, 269, 348–52, 356; water conservation, 253–55, 275–76, 352, 360, 362, 363, 364, 366; fertilizer use, 255–58, 277, 278, 300, 347, 367–77, 474; changes in cropping techniques, 258, 260, 267–68, 347–48, 353–58, 373; cultivated area, 258, 347, 350, 351, 352, 359; soil conservation, 258–59; reclamation of virgin land, 261–62; mechanization, 262–65, 277, 379, 474–75; seed improvement, 265–66, 288; field management, 267–68; progress of transformation, 268–74, 278–79; education, 270–72, 300; investment, 272; shortage of funds for, 272–73; rice cultivation, 276, 349–60, 365, 373, 376, 383; production, 277, 278–79, 282, 299, 346, 351, 353, 472, 475; traditional practices, 277, 346, 366, 367, 376; output statistics, 280–83, 302, 472–73; input-output indexes, 284–89; productivity indexes, 284, 289, 297; aggregate input index, 289–91, 303; and industry, 294–95, 307, 475; work vs. leisure, 307–9, 339–40, 344–45; schemes of organization, 310–14; consumption vs. saving, 329–31; marketed surplus, 331–35; per capita food consumption, 332–33, 338–39, 473–74; multiple-cropping index, 348, 352, 353; increase in cropped area, 352; wheat cultivation, 352, 353; revolutions in, 354

—Collectivized farms: measures to increase productivity, 40, 300; statistical standards concerning, 41; producers' cooperatives, 43, 50, 251, 312, 324, 325, 330; size, by households, 43–44, 48, 50–52, 251; labor shortage, 44–47, 52, 53, 66; private plots, 44, 47, 49, 52; exports, 53; imports, 54–55; industrialization, 55, 304; household and worker incomes, 312–18, 322, 324, 327, 328, 329–32, 342–43

China (Pre-Communist), 8, 9, 28, 34, 35, 66; fertilizers, 256; irrigation, 276; expenditures, 335

Chinese Academy of Agricultural Science, 270

Chinese Academy of Sciences, 261

Chinese Communist Party, 263, 271–72, 282

Chinese Communists, 35–54 *passim*

Chinese Society of Crops, 266

Chou En-lai, 54, 475

Churchill, Winston, 93

Civil war (Russia), 61

Collective farms. *See* China, People's Republic of, collectivized farms; Soviet Union, collective farms

Collectivization. *See* China, People's Republic of; Soviet Union, collectivization

COMECON, 205, 219, 220, 228

Communes: Russia, 21, 22, 82, 86, 163; China, 47, 48, 49, 50, 251, 260, 281, 365, 379. *See* China, People's Republic of; Soviet Union

Communist China and Soviet Union compared, 283

Communist Manifesto, 10, 12, 48

Consumer cooperatives. *See* Soviet Union

Consumption of energy: sovkhozy, 143; kolkhozy, 143–44

Conversion of collectives to state farms (*sovkhozizatsiia*), 32. *See also* Sovkhozizatsiia

Corn program (Soviet Union), 150

Cournot solution, 312, 314, 343, 344, 345

Czechoslovakia: new economic policies, 178–80, 218, 219; planning methods, 178–81, 182, 189–90, 206, 207–8; decision making, 181, 182, 188; income distribution, 181–82; discontinuation of compulsory allocation to indivisible funds, 182; quotas, 183–86; above-enterprise agencies, 185–89, 206–9; regional associations, 188; state bank, 188; *The Long Range Perspective*, 190; price and procurement system, 193–99, 207–8

Das Kapital, 11, 13, 14, 15, 31

David, Eduard, 16, 16 n., 67

Democratic Republic of Germany. *See* East Germany

Denmark, 29, 66

"Dizzy with Success," 22, 88

Don, 93

Dube, S. C., 478

Eastern Europe, 5, 6, 65, 179, 196, 201, 205, 477

East Germany (Democratic Republic of Germany): industrialization, 210; loss of assets, 211–12; decrease in growth rate, 218; economic reform, 218–21, 228, 230; and COMECON, 220; mentioned, 56, 200

—Agriculture: socialization, 210–11; standards of production, 212; grain output, 213; vegetable output, 213–14; forage and feed output, 213–14; crop yields, 214; rise in productivity, 215, 216, 217; agricultural production cooperatives (LPG), 221, 240; collectivization, 221; farm size, 221–22, 223–24, 229; state sector, 237

Egypt, 5, 232
Eighth National Congress (CCP), 39
Emancipation (Russia), 9
Engels, F. 10–12, 15–16, 19, 67
England, 4, 14
Environmentalism, 6
Ernst, Maurice, 476
Europe, 5, 15, 16
European Common Market, 220, 228
Expansion of sovkhoz sector. *See Sovkhozizatsiia*

Famine: Russia, 96, 100, 103; China, 48
Farm size: Japan, 8, 34, 67, 399, 401, 432, 433–34; Denmark, 29; West Germany, 29, 221–22, 227, 229; United States, 30; China, 43–44, 50–52, 251; East Germany, 227, 228; North Korea, 441–45, 459–60; South Korea, 445–49, 460; Soviet Union, 465. *See also* Soviet Union
Federal Republic of Germany. *See* West Germany
Fertilizers: China, 54, 255–273 *passim*, 367–77, 474; Soviet Union, 144, 147; India, 371; Japan, 371, 400, 474; South Asia, 371; Southeast Asia, 371; Taiwan, 385, 387, 389
Fifteenth Party Congress (1927), 69–70, 462
Five-Year Plan. *See* China, People's Republic of; Soviet Union; Korean agrarian systems compared
Food consumption: Russia, 93–96, 469; East Germany, 213; West Germany, 213; China, 332–33, 338–39, 473–74
Food prices (Russia), 77, 78
Fourier, Charles, 10–11
Fourteenth Party Congress, 104
Fukien, 366

Georgia, 87
German Social Democrats, 57
Germany. *See* East Germany; West Germany
Ghana, 231, 243
Gigantism, 33, 51
Gosbank, 172
Gotha Program, 57
Grain exports: China, 53; Russia, 53, 96
Grain imports: China, 53, 54–55; Russia, 236, 470

Grain procurement prices, 70, 71, 77, 79
Grain procurements: Russia, 71, 90–96 *passim*, 100, 463; China, 99, 100
Greece, 5, 10, 16, 27

Hanazono-mura. *See* Japan, Hanazono-mura case study
Heavy industry (China), 54
Hegel, G., 31
Heilungkiang, canals in, 255
Higbee, Edward, 30
Hoarding. *See* Soviet Union, collectivization
Holland, 66
Honan, 47, 255
Hopei: salinity of water, 254; canal construction, 255; fertilizer production, 257; seed improvement, 265
Huang Ping-wei, 261
Hunan, 265, 266, 351–52, 356, 366, 372
Hungary, 281, 237
Hupeh, 265
Hydraulic agriculture, 7. *See also* Oriental despotism

Iakovlev, I. A., 81, 82
India: mechanized large-scale farm, 243; inputs relative to Chinese inputs, 287; mentioned, 5, 233, 240, 278, 348, 371, 382, 445
Indochina, 354
Indonesia, 231, 382, 392
Inner Mongolia, canal construction, 255
Irrigation: China, 34, 39, 40, 45, 46, 253, 254, 275–77, 288, 347, 360, 362–64, 366, 475; Taiwan, 385, 387–89
Israel, and aid to Burma, 244

Japan: productivity of agricultural labor, 4, 62; hydroagriculture, 8, 9, 367, 401; size of farms, 8, 34, 67, 399, 401, 432, 433–34; fertilizer use, 371, 400, 474; agricultural settlements, 399–401; agricultural changes and specialization, 400, 402, 416, 432–33; Ara River Multiple Development Project, 402, 405, 416; land-use changes, 403–6, 433; land reform, 403, 426, 432; land use planning, 427–30, 434; mentioned, 6, 31, 33, 41, 59, 68, 287, 293, 385, 388, 445, 477, 478
—Hanazono-Mura case study: location, 402; farm classification, 406, 426–27, 430–31; resources, 408, 418, 424–25; incomes, 409; expenses, 410; results of specialization, 411; per unit income, 412; type and distribution of soils, 413–14, 421–23; productivity of soils, 415, 416; area studied, by settlement, 417, 419, 420; ratio of land vs labor, 423, 426–27

Kaganovich, L., 79, 95, 96
Kalinin, M., 83
Kaliningrad *Oblast*: agricultural area, 113; energy available, 113; labor force, 113; natural pasture, 113; sovkhozy, 113; tilled land, 113
Kaminsky, G., 82
Kautsky, Karl, 15, 16–17, 28–29, 61, 67
Kazakhstan: collectivization, 87, 89, 91; agricultural areas, 113, 114, 132; energy available, 113, 114, 132; labor force, 113, 132; natural pasture, 113; sovkhozy, 113, 115–16, 118; tilled land, 113; sown area, 114, 132; livestock units, 114, 132; farm households, 129
Kenya, 232, 244
Khrushchev, Nikita, 22, 32, 59, 66, 92, 112, 118, 119, 120, 122, 123, 124, 136, 137, 150, 235, 466, 467
Kiangsu fertilizer production, 257
Kim Il-sung, 448
Kirin canals, 255
Kolkhozniki, 25, 42, 133, 163
Kolkhoz-sovkhoz yields compared, 236–37
Kolkhoztsentr (collective-farm center), 81, 82, 88
Kolkhozy. *See* Soviet Union
Korean agrarian systems compared: common features, 436; Japanese influence, 437; economic structures, 437, 438; land reform, South, 439, 459; land reform, North, 439–41; emigration to South, 440; farm organization and size, South, 441–45, 459–60; agricultural credit, 442; first Five-Year Plans, 444; farm organization and size, North, 445–49, 460; cooperatives, 447; merit system, 449–53; productivity, 453–57, 460–61, 476; Seven-Year Plan, North, 453
Krasnodar *Krai*: fertilizers, 151; structure of expenditures, 151
Kronstadt uprising, 61
Kulak(s), 70, 72–73, 75, 78–81, 83–87, 90, 92, 99–100, 462. *See also* Soviet Union, collectivization
Kun Cooperative Farm Management Committee, 447–460 *passim*
Kwangtung, 52

Labor productivity· and farm size, 13–18; under socialism, 24–25; in collectives, 25–26, 33, 45–52, 56–57; in slave societies, 27–28; on family farms, 29, 33; of hired hands, 29–31; on state farms, 32; countries compared, 59–60, 62. *See also* China, People's Republic of; East Germany; West Germany; Japan; Korean agrarian

systems compared; Soviet Union; Taiwan
Labor shortage: Russia, 42. *See also* China, People's Republic of; East Germany
Land consolidation (Russia), 104
Land reform. *See* China, People's Republic of; Japan; Korean agrarian systems compared; Taiwan; Soviet Union
Land Utilization in China survey, 276–77, 317–20
Large-scale farming, 9, 12–18, 21, 29, 32, 223, 228, 233, 446
Left opposition, 77
Left Socialist Revolutionists, 18, 20, 21. *See also* Social Revolutionaries
Lenin, V. I., 15, 16, 17–23, 34, 36, 58, 61, 78, 159, 162
Lewis, Oscar, 478
Liaoning, canals in, 255
Li Fu-chun, 474
Lithuania, labor force of, 136. *See* Baltic Republics
Liu, Ta-chung, 41, 42, 282, 286, 292
Livestock (Russia): losses, 90–91, 93, 96; units, 109–11, 114–15, 129, 130–31, 132, 133, 134, 135; in sovkhozy, 119–20, 121, 124, 125, 127; decline in numbers, 148–49, 463, 464; fodder production, 149, 467

Machine Tractor Stations, 23, 64, 100, 139, 169, 232, 238
Malaysia, 392
Mao Tse-tung, 9, 22, 34, 37, 39, 44, 45, 46, 48, 66, 250, 478
Marshall Plan, 211
Marx, Karl, 10–34 *passim*, 56, 57, 59, 61, 62, 66, 67
—*Communist Manifesto*, 10, 12; *Das Kapital*, 11, 13 n., 14–15; *Theorien über den Mehrwert*, 12, 13 n.; *The German Ideology*, 57
Marxism, 14–34 *passim*, 57, 61–64, 65–68, 464–65
Marxism-Leninism, 10, 19, 64, 458
Meiji era, 403, 407 n., 432
Mensheviks, 20, 78, 160
Middle peasants, 73, 99, 100
Mikoyan, A., 22, 42, 73
Military-feudal exploitation. *See* Bukharin, N.
Mill, John Stuart, 14, 59
Moldavia: kolkhozy, 112–13; agricultural areas, 113; energy available, 113; labor force, 113, 136; natural pasture, 113; sovkhozy, 113, 115; tilled land, 113
Molotov, V., 79, 82
Moscow *Oblast*, 140–41, 155
Moscow province, 89
Multiple cropping: China, 40, 259, 348–49,

352–54, 356, 373, 378–79, 385, 388; Japan, 67; Taiwan, 67, 348, 351; Korea, 348; India, 348
Muscovite Russia, 9, 63
Mutual-aid associations, 37
Mutual-aid teams, 51, 250
Myrdal, Jan, 478

Narkomzem (People's Commissariat of Agriculture), 81
National Agricultural Cooperative Federation (South Korea), 441, 442, 461
National Conference on Wet Paddy Production Techniques, 354, 358
New Economic Policy, 21, 24, 25, 56, 58, 61, 70, 73, 78, 79, 83
Nicholas I, 63
Ninghsia, seed improvement, 265
Non-Black-Earth region, 129
North Caucasus: collectivization, 71, 82, 89, 94–95; grain procurements, 100; brigades, 140
North China Plain, 352, 353, 359, 360
North Korea, 33. *See also* Korean agrarian systems compared
North Vietnam, 33, 56

Odessa, state farm in, 239
Office of Rural Development (South Korea), 441, 442
Oriental despotism, 7 n., 8–10, 20–21, 58–59, 62–64, 477
Output of machinery, 145, 146

People's Republic of China. *See* China, People's Republic of
Philippines, 382, 392
Plekhanov, G. V., 58
Po I-po, 54
Poland, 58, 198, 205, 237; state sector, 237; agrarian circles, 241
Polish State Planning Commission, 191
Politburo, 74, 76, 81, 95
Preobrazhensky, E., 75
Pre-Spanish America, 6, 7
Price, R. L., 53
Provisional government (Russia), 61

Revolution from above, 76, 77
Right-wing deviation, 75–76, 83, 97
Rome, 5, 10, 16, 27
Rumania: lack of economic reform, 219; state sector, 237
Rural proletariat, 99
Russia. *See* Soviet Union
Russia, pre-emancipation, 9
Russian Soviet Federal Socialist Republic

(R.S.F.S.R.): procurement decrees, 79; agricultural areas, 113, 114, 130; energy available, 113, 114, 130; labor force, 113, 130; natural pasture, 113; sovkhozy, 113, 114, 115, 118; sown area, 114, 130; tilled land, 113; livestock units, 114, 130; production potential, 114
Rykov, Alexis, 74, 77

Schlesinger, Rudolf, 125
Serf economy, 8, 28
Shansi: canal construction, 255; seed improvement, 265
Shantung, and canal construction, 255
Shen, T. H., 315
Shensi, canal construction, 255
Sholokhov, M., 92, 93
Showa era, 403
Siberia, 71, 72, 73, 82, 86, 87, 94, 129
Sino-American Joint Commission on Rural Reconstruction. *See* Korean agrarian systems compared
Sixteenth Party Congress (1929), 76
Slave labor, 27
Small-scale farming, 8, 21, 29, 68, 221, 385, 387, 390–92, 399, 445
Smith, Adam, 4–5, 13, 13 n., 14
Smolensk archives. *See* Soviet Union, Collectivization
Socialism and Agriculture. See David, Eduard
Socialized sector. *See* Soviet Union
Social Revolutionaries, 20, 21, 160, 466
South Asia, 365
Southeast Asia, 365
South Korea. *See* Korean agrarian systems compared
South Vietnam, 382
Soviet Union: procurements, 70, 71–72, 77, 79–80, 96, 99, 100; Five-Year Plans, 76, 232; population, 96; rural trade network, 159
—Agriculture: Lenin's policies toward, 10, 17–23, 58, 61, 64, 466; Marx-Engels' influence on, 12–16, 23, 24, 64; Kautsky influence on, 16–17; producers' cooperatives, 21; private plots, 24, 62; under Stalin, 25–26, 42, 69, 247; sown areas, 30; Khrushchev's policies, 32, 66, 466–67; size of units, 51, 464–65; gross production, 108; livestock, 109, 111, 112; productivity potential, 109, 111, 114–15, 124, 130–31, 132, 133, 134, 135; soils, 112, 149; capital invested, 143, 156; traction power, 144–45, 148, 156; machinery, 145–46, 166; fertilizer use, 147, 150, 156; markets for, 161, 169; population, 171, 232; private farming, 234–35; contribution to initial

capital formation, 235, 246–47; inadequacy of, 236; cooperatives, 240–41; work links, 242; labor in, 246; in relation to industry, 247–48
—Collective farms (Kolkhozy): Lenin's attitude toward, 21–22; importance to economy, 24; output, 26, 32, 106–12; households, 43, 109, 111, 117–22, 125–26, 127, 128, 129, 130–31, 132, 133, 134, 135–36; farm size, 49–51, 243; managers of, 62, 172; recent concessions to, 64; machine tractor stations, 64, 100, 238–40; development of, 84; as distributors, 94; peasant resistance, 95; purge of leaders, 100; gross production, 108; output potential, 109, 111, 112, 114–15; intensity of cultivation, 111; conversion to sovkhozy, 112–37 *passim*; labor force, 113, 125–28, 129, 130–31, 132, 133, 134, 135, 136–37, 158; capital investment, 116, 143, 156; brigade structure, 139–40; electricity consumption, 143; and specialty crops, 148; expenditures, 151; planning, 151–53; livestock and fodder production, 149; importance to industrialization, 235; mentioned, 76, 88, 90, 91, 92, 97, 102, 161, 173
—Collectivization: early efforts, 21–23, 35, 40; reasons for, 23, 69–70, 78, 103–5; 248–49; peasant response to, 23, 25, 64; effect on export, 53; role of cooperatives, 71; response of kulaks to, 72–73; Urals-Siberian method, 73–74, 75, 79, 100, 463; party resistance to, 74–76, 79; "revolution from above," 76, 77, 98; timetable for, 82–83; dekulakization, 83–88, 99; and Smolensk archives, 85–87, 463; reversal of Stalin in, 88; households involved, 89; effect, 90–97, 100, 463–64; in 1930–34, 102; as model, 102; as facilitation of industrialization, 232–33; mentioned, 36, 42, 161
—Consumer cooperatives: scope of, 159, 164, 173, 175–76; development of, 159–62; role of in distribution of goods, 163–64, 166, 169–70; commercial activities, 167; prices, 166–67, 169–70, 174–75; profit margins, 167; direct production for, 168; as product collectors, 168–69; membership shares and fees, 172, 175; financing, 172–73; inadequacies, 175–77
—Private sector: gross production, 108; production potential, 109, 111, 132, 133, 134, 135; repression, 117–18; as labor reserve, 131, 136–37; labor force, 158; compared with collectives, 236–37
—State farms (sovkhozy): efforts to increase output, 26; decline in number, 32; virgin

land farms, 74; development, 75, 85, 112–17, 129; gross production, 108, 238; agricultural areas, 109, 111, 113, 114–15, 129, 130, 132, 133, 134, 135; energy available, 109, 111, 113, 114–15, 130, 132, 133, 134, 135; production potential, 109, 111, 114–15, 124, 130, 132, 133, 134, 135–36; sown areas, 109, 111, 114–15, 130, 132, 133, 134, 135; distribution, 112–17; expansion, 112–29, 236, 237–38; tilled land, 113, 129; natural pasture, 113; labor force, 113, 129, 130, 132, 133, 134, 135; household plots, 118; types of, 119–21; Khrushchev's views, 123; capital investment, 143, 156; consumption of electricity, 143; planning, 151–53; percentage of cultivated area, 237–38; as model for developing countries, 243–44; mentioned, 24, 76, 102
—*See also*: Bukharin, N.; Engels, F.: Kausky, K.: Khruschev, N.: Lenin, V. I.; Marx, Karl; Rykov, Alexis; Stalin, J.: Tomsky, M.: TOZ
Sovkhozizatsiia, 116–22
Stalin, Joseph, 22–60 *passim*, 63–64; 69–97 *passim*, 103, 105, 161, 235, 284, 463, 464, 466. *See also* Soviet Union, Collectivization
Stolypin Land Reform, 104
Sudan: Gezira scheme in, 244

Taiwan: economic progress, 381, 382–83; exports, 382, 385, 387, 391; agricultural output, 382–83, 387; per capita income, 382–83; population growth, 382–83, 385, 386; agricultural development, 383, 385, 387–88, 391; cultivated land, 383, 385; fertilizer use, 385, 387, 389; township farmers' associations, 385; farm size, 385, 390–92, 394, 396, 398; land tenure, 388; Joint Commission on Rural Reconstruction, 389–90, 397; as model for developing countries, 392–95, 396–98; mentioned, 4, 33, 41, 59, 67, 68, 287, 293, 348, 477
T'an Chen-lin, on close planting, 268
Tanzania, 232
Technical Repair Stations, 167, 169
Teng Tsu-hui, 38
Thaer, Albrecht, 14, 28
Thailand, 68, 392
Third Kolkhoz Congress, 468, 471
Third World, 231
Tomsky, M., 74
TOZ (TOZY), 21, 71, 76, 78, 79, 81, 86, 240–41
Traction power: Soviet Union, U.S.A. compared, 144; in Soviet Union, 145
Transcaucasia: collectivization, 91; agricultural areas, 113; energy available, 113;

labor force, 113, 136; natural pasture, 113; tilled land, 113; number of sovkhozy, 119

Trotsky, Leon, 75

Tsentrosoiuz, 168, 170, 171

Tsinghai, annual grain yield, 251

Tunisia, socialized agriculture sector, 244

Turkestan, 88

Twenty-Third Party Congress (1966), 172, 235, 468

Ukraine: collectivization, 73, 79, 82, 91, 93–96; kolkhozy, 112; agricultural areas, 113, 114, 134, 135; energy available, 113, 114, 135; labor force, 113, 134, 135, 136; natural pasture, 113; tilled area, 113; sown area, 114, 134, 135; livestock units, 113, 134, 135; sovkhozy, 115, 116; fertilizer use, 146, 147, 150, 151; structure of expenditures, 151

Ulbricht, Walter, 228

United States: productivity of farm labor, 238; inputs relative to Communist China, 287; agricultural research compared with Communist China, 293; mentioned, 4, 27, 29, 30, 59, 62, 143, 144, 233, 388

Urals, 71, 72, 73, 113

Urals-Siberian method. *See* Soviet Union, Collectivization

Urban population, China, 54

Urban-rural migration, China, 45

Uzbekistan: collectivization, 71, 87, 89; sovkhozy, 121; agricultural area, 133; energy available, 133; labor force, 133; livestock units, 133; sown area, 133

Virgin lands: Soviet Union, 15, 119, 129,

148, 236, 242; China, 261–62

Volga, 71, 73, 82

Voluntariness, principle of, 23, 75

War Communism, 21, 56, 61, 72, 234

Water conservation projects. *See* China, People's Republic of

Wealth of Nations, 4, 13

Weber, Max, 28

Western Europe, 29, 62, 477

West Germany (Federal Republic of Germany): industrialization, 210; over-mechanization of production, 211; importance of Marshall Plan, 211; assets, 212; mentioned, 4, 29, 143, 388

—Agriculture: standards of productivity, 212; grain output, 213; vegetable output, 213–14; forage and feed output, 213–14; rise in productivity, 215, 216, 217, 227; farm size, 221–22; formation of private capital, 221; implications of farm size, 224–25, 227, 229–30; labor force, 227; state farms, 238

Western Region, collectivization, 89

Wu, Y-1., 40, 41, 42

Yang, Martin C., 478

Yangtze Basin, 254, 260, 353, 356, 358, 367, 376

Yeh, Kung-chia, 41, 42, 282, 286, 292

Young, Arthur, 9, 14, 28

Yugoslavia, 58, 219, 237, 244

Zernotrest, 74

Zhdanov, A., 73

Zveno, subunit of production brigade, 241

Contributors

Karl August Wittfogel is Professor Emeritus of Chinese History, University of Washington, and Director, Chinese History Project, sponsored by the University of Washington.

R. P. Rochlin is Research Fellow, German Institute for Economic Research, Berlin.

Werner Klatt, O.B.E., is Fellow, St. Antony's College, Oxford.

Alec Nove is Professor of Economics and Director, Institute of Soviet and East European Studies, University of Glasgow.

Thomas P. Bernstein is Lecturer of Political Science, Yale University, New Haven, Conn.

George L. Yaney is Associate Professor of History, University of Maryland, College Park.

Karl-Eugen Wädekin is Dozent, Institute for Continental Agrarian and Economic Research, Justus Liebig University, Giessen, Germany.

Robert C. Stuart is Assistant Professor of Economics, Rutgers—The State University of New Jersey.

Eberhard Schinke is Scientific Assistant, Institute for Continental Agrarian and Economic Research, Justus Liebig University, Giessen, Germany.

Elizabeth Clayton is Assistant Professor of Economics, University of Missouri, St. Louis, Missouri.

Henri Wronski is Master of Research at the National Center for Scientific Research, Paris.

Nancy Nimitz is a member of the Economics Department, The RAND Corporation, Santa Monica, California.

Jerzy F. Karcz is Professor of Economics, University of California, Santa Barbara.

Carl R. Zoerb is an Economic Analyst for Communist Agriculture, Munich.

Konrad Merkel is Professor, Institute of Agrarian Politics and Agricultural Statistics, Technische Universität Berlin.

Otto Schiller is Professor of Comparative Agrarian Policy and Rural Sociology, South Asia Institute, University of Heidelberg, Germany.

Harry E. Walters is Project Leader, Communist Areas Analysis Section, Europe and Soviet Union Branch, U. S. Department of Agriculture, Washington, D. C.

Leslie T. C. Kuo is Chief, Oriental Project, National Agricultural Library, U. S. Department of Agriculture, Washington, D. C.

J. Lossing Buck is an agricultural economist, Pleasant Valley, New York.

Anthony M. Tang is Professor and Chairman of the Department of Economics, Vanderbilt University, Nashville, Tennessee.

Lawrence J. Lau is Assistant Professor of Economics, Stanford University, Palo Alto, California.

Shigeru Ishikawa is Professor, Institute of Economic Research, Hitotsubashi University, Tokyo, Japan.

Ernst Hagemann is Research Associate, East Bloc Department, German Institute for Economic Research, Berlin.

George E. Taylor is Professor of Far Eastern History and Politics in the Far Eastern and Russian Institute, University of Washington, Seattle.

S. C. Hsieh is Director, Projects Department, Asian Development Bank, Manila, Republic of the Philippines.

Fukuo Ueno is Professor of Geography, Komazawa University, Tokyo.

George H. Kakiuchi is Associate Professor of Geography, University of Washington, Seattle.

Ki Hyuk Pak is Professor of Agricultural Economics and Director, Institute of Agricultural Development, Yonsei University, Seoul, Korea.

Young C. Zeon is Assistant Professor of Law and Political Science, Ewha Woman's University, Seoul, Korea.

FAR EASTERN AND RUSSIAN INSTITUTE
PUBLICATIONS ON RUSSIA AND EASTERN EUROPE

1. Sugar, Peter F., and Ivo J. Lederer (eds.). *Nationalism in Eastern Europe.* 1969.
    478 pp., index.
2. Jackon, W. A. Douglas (ed.). *Agrarian Policies and Problems in Communist and
    Non-Communist Countries.* 1971. 485 pp., maps, figures, tables, index.

Date Due